P9-EDN-382

Ex Libris

LORD BYRON

Selected Poems and Letters

THE GOTHAM LIBRARY
OF THE NEW YORK UNIVERSITY PRESS

The Gotham Library is a series of original works and critical studies, published in paperback primarily for student use. The Gotham hard-cover edition is primarily for use by libraries and the general reader. Devoted to significant works and major authors and to literary topics of enduring importance, Gotham Library texts offer the best in literature and criticism.

LORD BYRON

Selected Poems and Letters

EDITED WITH AN INTRODUCTION AND NOTES BY

William H. Marshall

NEW YORK · NEW YORK UNIVERSITY PRESS · 1977

Library of Congress Catalog Card Number: 77-76594
ISBN: 0-8147-5417-1 cloth
0-8147-5418-X paper

Manufactured in the United States of America

CONTENTS

Letters

ACKNOWLEDGMENTS

From *Astarte, A Fragment of Truth Concerning George Gordon Byron, Sixth Lord Byron,* Recorded by his Grandson, Ralph Milbanke, Earl of Lovelace, New Edition with Many Additional Letters, Edited by Mary, Countess of Lovelace, published by Christophers Ltd., in 1921, the letter which Lord Byron wrote to Lady Byron on 14 April 1816 has been reprinted by permission of Chatto & Windus Ltd., successors to Christophers Ltd. and by permission of the Editor's Literary Estate.

From *The Life and Letters of Anne Isabella, Lady Noel Byron, From Unpublished Papers in the Possession of the Late Ralph, Earl of Lovelace,* by Ethel Colburn Mayne, published by Constable and Company Ltd., in 1929, the letter which Lord Byron wrote to the then Anne Isabella Milbanke on 23 November 1814 has been reprinted by permission of Constable and Company Ltd.

From *Lord Byron's Correspondence, Chiefly with Lady Melbourne, Mr. Hobhouse, The Hon. Douglas Kinnaird, and P. B. Shelley,* Edited by John Murray, 2 volumes, published by John Murray Ltd., in 1922, the letters which Lord Byron wrote to John Cam Hobhouse (9 December 1811, 16 May 1816), Douglas Kinnaird (26 October 1819, 13 March 1824), Lady Caroline Lamb (29 April 1813), and Lady Melbourne (13 October 1813) have been reprinted by permission of John Murray Ltd.

From the Byron Collection in Memory of Meyer Davis, Jr., the previously unpublished letter which Lord Byron wrote to Francis Hodgson on 10 October 1811 has been published by permission of the Charles Patterson Van Pelt Library, of the University of Pennsylvania, to which application should be made for permission to reprint this letter.

The text of the poems is based upon that of *The Works of Lord Byron: Poetry,* edited by Ernest Hartley Coleridge, 7 volumes, published by John Murray, 1898–1904. The Notes to the Poems result from an obvious and heavy dependence upon the notes to this edition. The letters reprinted, except those listed above, were first published in *The Works of Lord Byron: Letters and Journals,* edited by Rowland E. Prothero, 6 volumes, published by John Murray Ltd., 1898–1901, from which material quoted from Byron's letters in the Notes to the Poems has also been drawn. Leslie A. Marchand's *Byron: A Biography,*

3 volumes, published by Alfred A. Knopf, 1957, has been a principal source for information not otherwise available.

Dr. Rudolf Hirsch, Dr. William E. Miller, and Dr. Neda M. Westlake, of the Charles Patterson Van Pelt Library of the University of Pennsylvania, have offered assistance and suggestions which have significantly eased the work of preparing the book. Dr. Henry F. Thoma, of Houghton Mifflin, has cheerfully and fully dealt with each of the editorial problems with which I have presented him.

My wife, Shirley E. Marshall, has worked with me continually, often at less exciting but nevertheless necessary tasks, to make this book a reality, and to her, with gratitude, I inscribe whatever in this work may be my own.

W. H. M.

INTRODUCTION

Of the major Romantic poets, none has eluded the classifications of the historians and critics so readily as George Gordon, the sixth Lord Byron. During his own lifetime (see the Chronology for the events of his life), Byron became a legend, in whose shadow subsequent generations have found it difficult to discover the man. To Lady Caroline Lamb, Byron was from the first "mad, bad, and dangerous to know"; to Robert Southey and a large number of his countrymen, he was one of the "Satanic School" of poetry; yet, to the Countess Teresa Guiccioli, his "last attachment," as well as to a small number of close friends, Byron assumed the qualities of sainthood, which increased as the years accumulated and the focus of memory became less sharp. The day of his death was to be recalled with grief, in the England from which he had exiled himself eight years earlier as well as in the Greece which he had come to save, though not everyone who mourned was really certain why he did so. The years that followed were consumed by the anger of what has been called the Byron Controversy, fought over the causes for the breakdown of the marriage with but slight display of reason or humanity, or even of honesty, on either side. Meanwhile, the spirit distilled from the Byron legend moved as a counterforce to the starkly practical and unimaginative view of life pervading the middle-class culture that was relentlessly passing over England and America.

What one made of the spirit when he encountered it was really determined by what one was. To some it seemed to bring an opportunity to escape the stifling restrictions of Victorian Grundyism, and for this reason various selected editions of Byron's work appeared, inviting their readers to the delicacies within or, more deviously, promising that the suitable passages enclosed had been culled from more interesting ones elsewhere. To others the spirit of Byron brought the opportunity for a kind of release, the ultimate bathetic indulgence, which the conditions in life did not allow elsewhere: Christina Pontifex, in Samuel Butler's novel *Ernest Pontifex, or The Way of All Flesh,* perhaps more characteristic of her generation and class than we might first suppose, "was impressionable and could not even hear the name 'Missolonghi' without bursting into tears." And to a third group, the spirit meant an intellectual independence, not yet smothered by the growing demand for bourgeois conformity; it meant something, perhaps as yet undefined, that was strikingly modern, in its view of man's place in the universe and his efforts to understand that place. From this group have come the twentieth-century biographies of Byron, which have done much to free the man from the shadow of the legend without destroying the cultural significance of the legend itself.

The evaluation of Byron's poetry has posed problems somewhat different from those faced by the biographers. Unlike Wordsworth or Coleridge or Shelley, Byron did not write from an organized point of view. Recalling for Thomas Moore in 1818 what he had said several years before to Leigh Hunt of the "strange style" of Hunt's poem *Rimini* (1816), Byron remarked: "His answer was, that his style was a system, or *upon system*, or some such cant; and, when a man talks of system, his case is hopeless." The fact that Byron's case was never *hopeless* renders at least more *difficult* the critical appraisal of his work, which therefore must be conceived in terms of itself or of the phase of human history in which it occurred, rather than in terms of a religious or philosophic tradition or of one of the emerging intellectual movements of the nineteenth century.

The only significant religious training that Byron received, at least by the standards of the day, was the Calvinistic indoctrination that came for a short time but with great intensity during his Aberdeen years; and though this deepened his already firm awareness of human evil, he was in later years to regard the doctrine of election and reprobation with irresolvable ambivalence. Byron's education was sound, and throughout his life he read widely though eclectically. The admission which he made to Robert Charles Dallas, on 21 January 1808 (see Letters), that in certain areas he had read more than he could comprehend should not be taken literally, for Byron frequently affected a Cavalier attitude toward learning, which misled many of his contemporaries and some of ours into believing that he was unaware of the currents of thought in his own time and that his work was without intellectual substance. Such was not the case: he was indeed familiar with the thought and literature of the eighteenth and early nineteenth centuries, in which his preferences were remarkably clear and his criticisms sharp.

The single literary commitment which Byron maintained throughout his mature life was to Alexander Pope and the poetry identified with England's Augustan Age. In a letter to John Murray dated 15 September 1817, characteristically insisting upon the error in the present "revolutionary poetical system, or systems" involving most of the better-known poets (including himself), Byron recalled that he had recently reread Pope's poems next to Moore's and his own and those of certain other contemporaries, "and I was really astonished . . . and mortified at the ineffable distance in point of sense, harmony, effect, and even

Imagination, passion, and *Invention*, between the little Queen Anne's man, and us of the Lower Empire." Four years later, in his most dramatic defense of "the best of poets," Byron produced two long essays aimed at Pope's editor and perhaps his severest critic, William Lisle Bowles. Yet some distance is discernible between Byron's critical pronouncements and his poetic performance. Of the several poems which he produced in the Popean tradition, only the earliest and most ambitious, *English Bards and Scotch Reviewers*, was acclaimed by his contemporaries and has survived in the estimate of ours. But even this poem, effective though much of it is, fails in the Popean attainment, and in its failure it reveals the nature of the dilemma which was Byron's so long as he attempted to write poetry that was affirmative and conclusive in its meaning. Underlying the kind of poetry that we identify with Augustan England, particularly exemplified by Alexander Pope, is the acceptance of an ideal order which the poet ironically affirms in satire by an attack upon some form of disorder in the world around him; *English Bards and Scotch Reviewers*, though trenchant in its attack upon individual wrongs in the literary world, reveals no unifying conception, no underlying ideal that these wrongs violate, and remains therefore a work of numerous parts mechanically joined. In other words, the structural weakness of *English Bards* reflects the inability on the part of Byron, like many of his contemporaries, to make the philosophic commitment required of a real Popean. It was not enough for Byron to imitate the poetic form of a past age: he must conceive his own, drawn from numerous literary traditions but capable of fulfilling the needs of an age with its particular intellectual dimensions.

The conception was difficult. It rested in large measure upon Byron's recognizing (and thereby freeing himself from) the paradoxical position which, like many intelligent men of the post-Enlightenment period, he occupied: unable to discover an intellectual basis for absolutism, he found relativism emotionally unacceptable. The difficulties were further increased by the viewpoint with which, especially during those early years, Byron regarded his art. Though he never abandoned the image of spontaneous creation, it was made especially strong before 1816, as an expression of a generally deprecatory attitude toward his role as poet. In the beginning he was not deeply committed to the pursuit of truth through poetry, though somewhat more than his critics, then and later, taking too literally his affectation of indifference, believed. What moved Byron toward clarity of poetic vision and a sense of direction for his art did so through largely unconscious means, through the hardly articulated (if apprehended) reactions to his own poetic experiments, while his statements of position and intention continued as Popean dicta or superficial generalizations and remain for us somewhat untrustworthy glosses on the nature of his art. To a significant extent, the creative act takes place far below the level of consciousness, of one's pronounced intentions toward that act, as Coleridge clearly emphasized in his writings and Byron clearly illustrated in his.

The compositions immediately following *English Bards and Scotch Reviewers* were, for the most part, conventional, imposing no intellectual burdens upon their readers and asking no unanswerable cosmological questions. The first two cantos of *Childe Harold's Pilgrimage* were products of the first year of travel on the Continent, 1809–10, written more or less spontaneously in the places with which the speaker in the poem is concerned. The result is a type of descriptive and contemplative poem rather abundant in the late eighteenth century, when some writers, unable to affirm cosmic order but unwilling to question it, were content to sketch Nature, which might conceivably embody it. The character of Harold, strikingly isolated from those among whom he passes, imposes a degree of unity upon the scenes sketched by the narrator, but within the frame of his travels there is neither narrative tension nor dramatic irony. Harold's responses to his experiences and the scenes through which he moves remain to the end simply the narrator's.

The Tales, which we associate with Byron's Years of Fame — the fragment *The Giaour* (1813), *The Bride of Abydos* (1813), *The Corsair* (1814), *Lara* (1814), *The Siege of Corinth* (1816), and *Parisina* (1816) — were, again, conventional pieces, growing out of the late eighteenth-century interest in the Oriental and the exotic and similar to (though more successful than) many other verse narratives of the time. Though only slightly more complex than *Childe Harold* I and II, they contain significant conflict within the action, thereby allowing for greater development of the few individual characters. In the simpler Tales (which are not inferior as narrative art), such as *The Bride of Abydos* and *The Corsair,* the characters tend to assume allegorical dimensions, largely in terms of their relation to the principal themes of Love and Death. Nevertheless, in each of these early works Byron's emerging use of the principal character as a dramatic reality becomes apparent; against a background of action and conflict (between physical forces if not values), he speaks, and his words are judged apart from his intentions and within the context in which they are set. To some slight degree, dramatic irony becomes a quality of these speeches. Thus, in his narrative poems Byron approached the dramatic monologue, which he was to use successfully on a number of occasions from 1816 onward.

By his choice, unconscious though it might have been, of this as the form for some of his most significant works, Byron was able not so much to escape as to evade the paradoxical position in which he found himself. Distinguishing between writer and speaker as he had not effectively done in *Childe Harold* I and II, he attributed to his speaker-protagonists the emotional compulsion to seek resolutions which were themselves intellectually unattainable, and on the ironies implicit in their situation he constructed much of his literary art.

The third canto of *Childe Harold's Pilgrimage* and *The Prisoner of Chillon,* written and published in 1816, offer the first clear illustrations. In *Childe Harold* III, the structural center of the poem rests with the speaker, as in the earlier poem it had hovered uncertainly near the figmental Harold. In the third canto, Childe Harold becomes recognizably a vehicle through which the speaker attempts to divest himself of his own pain and alienation, an object of the speaker's projection, an *alter ego.* The speaker's failure to sustain the image of Harold, occurring toward the middle of the poem, is not a mark of the collapse of the poem (or of the poet's purpose) but an aspect of the dramatic situation in which the speaker finds himself. In *The Prisoner of Chillon,* the speaker has passed through an experience so horrible that in order to sustain the sense of the purposefulness of his life, the image of his own identity, he must in his narrative express the reorientation to which the experience has moved him. Although the reader may exercise his option to accept *what* the speaker affirms about the meaning of his experiences, the poem as a whole imposes no demand upon him to do so; by the dramatic structure he may be moved to observe *how* the speaker has reached the point of affirmation. The longest, and architectonically the central, section of the poem, the eighth of the fourteen divisions, contains the climax of the speaker's experiences as recalled, the death of his younger, and remaining, brother; the ninth section presents the emotional crisis that necessarily followed, the bottom of despair, from which the speaker emerged toward reorientation.

In each of three poems which Byron wrote between 1817 and 1819 — *The Lament of Tasso, Mazeppa,* and *The Prophecy of Dante* — the speaker has been placed by men and circumstances in a position — a madhouse, flight after defeat in battle, and exile — from which he is emotionally compelled to demonstrate the meaningfulness of the universe by arguing for the ultimate triumph of himself, or in the case of Dante, of those who will represent him, over the malign forces that have momentarily defeated him. As in *Childe Harold* III and *The Prisoner of Chillon,* the controlling viewpoint in each poem is concerned not only with the affirmation made by the speaker but with the dramatic relation between that affirmation and the universe in which the speaker exists. To varying degrees, the dominant quality of that relation is irony, resulting from the discrepancy between the inner vision and the outer reality.

Somewhat after he finished *Childe Harold* III and *The Prisoner of*

Chillon, Byron turned playwright. *Manfred,* which he wrote in late 1816 and early 1817, was the first play, to be followed by seven more, written between 1820 and 1822 and published during the last three years of his life: *Marino Faliero, Doge of Venice* (1821), *Sardanapalus* (1821), *The Two Foscari* (1821), *Cain* (1821), *Werner, or the Inheritance* (1822), *Heaven and Earth* (1823), and *The Deformed Transformed* (1824). Despite Byron's close association with the theatre, even as a member of the management of the Drury Lane during 1815, his plays are primarily works of dramatic literature rather than pieces for theatrical performance. The only exception is *Werner,* a work sustained by sweeping external action involving recognition scenes and such devices as secret passages, but lacking significant literary merit. Otherwise, the plays concern not the conflict of characters sustaining conventional theatre pieces but the alternatives between ideas, choices of action, or views of life. The subjects with which Byron worked in his dramas were those demanding the *internalization* of the dramatic conflict and were suited more readily to the dramatic monologue than to a drama to be performed in the large public theatres of the time.

Of Byron's dramas the most successful are probably the three plays included here. *Manfred* might seem to be little more than a dramatic monologue with certain objective extensions in the form of the Chamois Hunter and the Abbot, concerned with the problem of the divided sensibility: by the beginning of the play, Manfred has attained total intellectual awareness but without the capacity to make emotional affirmation, toward which he moves in the course of the action. In *Cain* the principal character intellectually passes from his own self-tutored absolutism toward Lucifer's cosmic relativism without being able to make the emotional transition demanded of him by this situation; in the end he responds to a lingering need for absolute action, a vestige of his physical being, by murdering Abel. And once more, in *Heaven and Earth,* the split sensibility is central to the meaning of the work: Japhet, the principal character, cannot emotionally reconcile himself to what must be the fate of those he loves in a universe dominated by the kind of deity of which Byron learned in his distant youth.

In one of the letters that he wrote to Lady Byron during the weeks preceding the signing of the separation, Byron remarked, "In this as in many things, one must either laugh or cry — & I prefer the former (while I can) even if it should be Sardonically." The lines probably came before blind eyes, but they remain today as one of the most significant glosses upon Byrons' view of life and his own art. Tears and laughter were for him never far apart, and in his mature years the seriousness and pathos of *The Lament of Tasso* could easily give way to the sense of the absurd that dominates *Beppo* (written later the same year, 1817) without in any way suggesting a change in the underlying world view. *Beppo,* precursor to *Don Juan,* accepts as its point of departure the ironic vision toward which the serious dramatic monologues move and exploits the literary potential that it offers. Man's universe is one in which there is no significant relation between aspiration and fulfillment, in which one strives vainly for the absolute because he cannot endure the relative, but in the end he can only laugh and tell a story which has little sequence and no point. The dramatic techniques which Byron had been learning in his monologues served him well in *Beppo,* where he carried irony to the point that the speaker even undercuts his own function and identity. The protagonist is of little importance, chosen because his name offers the convenience of rhyme and certainly secondary to the other principals in the episode. And the narrative itself is lost among multiple digressions and obscured by consciously bad rhymes, to be concluded by Beppo's own account of his adventures during his long absence from Venice —

> He was cast away
> About where Troy stood once, and nothing stands;
> Became a slave of course, and for his pay
> Had bread and bastinadoes, till some bands
> Of pirates landing in a neighbouring bay,
> He joined the rogues and prospered, and became
> A renegado of indifferent fame

— which reads like an indifferent parody of the story of survival and reorientation so familiar in Romantic literature.

Without sacrificing his lyric capacities or his ability to sustain personal sincerity when these were required, Byron had moved in several years to a literary art sufficiently complex to express his ironic vision. That he understood the reasons for the direction that his work was taking, or was even significantly aware of the direction itself, is at least doubtful. Certainly, though later critics might explain aspects of his poetry by convenient constructs, Byron himself wrote from no systematic preconceptions. That from mid-1816 onward his work reveals a complexity and dramatic sophistication not previously apparent suggests, perhaps rather obviously, that the principal causes lay in the termination of his marriage and the self-imposed exile. The impact upon his writings of the collapse of his personal life in 1816 is undeniable but immeasurable, so that conjecture becomes somewhat pointless. One circumstance of his life after 1816 stands forth, however, perhaps significantly relating to his literary development — the importance of the letters which he wrote and received.

All his life Byron was an active correspondent, and among the English poets he stands forth as one of the most successful. It is remarkable that even in the correspondence of the English years — during which he often wrote to nearby persons, in circumstances in which today one would probably use the telephone — there are comparatively few letters that are dull, that merely communicate. Even those which Byron wrote to his early literary adviser, Robert Charles Dallas, himself strikingly self-righteous and memorably uninspiring, have a touch of originality and warmth. For each of Byron's correspondents there was a particular area of discourse and, consequently, a particular Byron who wrote. In his letters to his mother he reflected the characteristic ambivalence, the suppressed agitation, and during his travels on the Continent these letters became principally travelogues, for in the objective recording of experiences and sights there can be little opportunity to quarrel. To Francis Hodgson he showed a warmth, a levity, a friendliness expressed less frequently in these early years than later, even when he was mystifying Hodgson or disputing with him on matters of religion. To Augusta he unburdened himself as he could to no one else, setting her forth as the benign foil to his irascible mother, in a role which, after the years had passed and his mother had died, would have to change. And to Lady Melbourne, wise and firm in her worldly position, he turned to make his confessions during the Years of Fame, but not without first assuming the sophisticated persona demanded of him by the society in which they both lived.

In the years of the exile, the assumption of roles became an even more important aspect of the correspondence that Byron maintained than it had been before 1816. During the English years he had had at least a recurring, if not continual, association with his correspondents, but on a number of occasions during the last eight years of his life, his own letter itself became the ultimate reality, and he constructed therein a world in which, as in the dramatic monologue, all participants derived their identity from the role that the speaker himself assumed. Though Byron, as much as any English exile, mixed with those among whom he passed, he could never become truly one of them. Beside the world of everyday life in Switzerland or Italy or finally Greece, he maintained another — and in most ways, a dearer — world, peopled with those whom he had known in the months and years before April 1816 and sustained by the pen and the long mail routes between England and Italy. Obviously, where Byron had laid down a fragment of his own life in 1816, life had gone on in more or less full fashion for John Murray and Thomas Moore and Douglas Kinnaird, and it was not emotionally necessary for them, as for Byron, to sustain a rapid interchange of letters. Byron's own letters during the last eight years were filled with plaintive cries for answers to his former letters, which, when they came, seemed always late. In his role as correspondent he was forced to impose upon the silent Murray or the tardy Hobhouse something of the identity which they too infrequently assumed for themselves; in this structuring of a microcosm, Byron took on the roles and attained the order not unlike those achieved by the speakers in his various monologues.

It is perhaps this Byron, standing alone in his letters amid the ruins of his own life as in his poems amid the ruins of man's certitude about order, who, whether crying or laughing at the human dilemma, has the greatest meaning for the twentieth century. He comes to us bearing questions which in our own time we have heard before, and he offers us ways to endure the incertitude that must follow because he will not also bring false answers.

CHRONOLOGY

1785 13 May, John ("Mad Jack") Byron (1756–91) marries Catherine Gordon (1765–1811), uniting an English family of Norman origin and a Scottish family descended from the Stuarts.

1788 22 January, George Gordon Byron is born at 16 Holles Street, London. He has a deformed right foot.

1789 Mrs. Byron takes her infant to Aberdeen, Scotland, where she hopes to live comfortably on a small annuity, all that remains of her modest fortune after the extravagance of her husband, who is with her part of the time but dies in France, where he has fled as a debtor, in 1791.

1792–98 Attends schools in Scotland.

1794 31 July, becomes heir presumptive to the Barony and the estates, with the death, at the battle of Calvi, of William John Byron (b. 1772), grandson of the fifth Lord Byron.

1798 19 May, becomes sixth Baron Byron of Rochdale, in the County of Lancaster, with the death of William, fifth Lord Byron. Arrives with his mother at Newstead Abbey, Nottingham, the principal estate, where he meets John Hanson, now his London solicitor and to be his friend in the years of his youth and maturity.

1799 Enrolls in Dr. Glennie's Academy at Dulwich. Frederick Howard, fifth Earl of Carlisle (1748–1825), appointed Byron's guardian.

1801–05 At Harrow-on-the-Hill, where he finds himself ill-prepared, both socially and academically, and makes few friends. Undergoes futile but painful treatments for his bad foot. His mother's financial situation is at best difficult.

1803 Newstead Abbey leased for five years to Lord Grey de Ruthyn. Mrs. Byron established in a house in Southwell, fourteen miles from Nottingham. Byron becomes deeply infatuated with Mary Chaworth, a distant cousin, who lives at Annesley Hall, near Newstead Abbey.

1804 Begins correspondence with his half-sister, Augusta (who marries Colonel George Leigh, in 1807). During the summer, at

Southwell, he enjoys the company of Elizabeth Pigot and her brothers.

1805 In October, enters Trinity College, Cambridge. His relationship with his emotionally unstable mother at an extremely low point.

1806 *Fugitive Pieces* privately printed but (except for four copies) subsequently destroyed, after one of Byron's friends finds one poem included objectionable. First involvement with money-lenders. In the autumn he does not return to Cambridge.

1807 *Poems on Various Occasions* privately printed, *Hours of Idleness* published. 27 June, returns to Cambridge, where he begins his close association with John Cam Hobhouse (1786–1869). Later in the year he has made friends with Francis Hodgson (1781–1852) and Scrope Berdmore Davies (1783–1852).

1808 *Poems Original and Translated* published. Robert Charles Dallas (1754–1824) becomes temporarily his literary adviser. In June, he receives M.A. from Cambridge, and in September, he returns to Newstead, after a somewhat purposeless existence in London. He works upon a satire of contemporary men of letters.

1809 *English Bards and Scotch Reviewers* published. Attains his majority and takes his seat in the House of Lords. On 14 June, he signs his will. On 2 July, he sails with Hobhouse to the Continent. In October, he is entertained by Ali Pasha.

1810 In May, he swims the Hellespont, a feat of which he is proud throughout his remaining years. During much of the year he is in Athens, though he travels to Constantinople, where in July he has an audience with the Sultan. Hobhouse returns to England.

1811 In April, he sails for England, arriving in July. The sudden death of his mother and the unexpected deaths of two of his friends of earlier years. In the late autumn, the beginning of the friendship with Douglas Kinnaird (1788–1830) and the growing literary acquaintance that includes Thomas Moore (1779–1852), Samuel Rogers (1763–1855), and Thomas Campbell (1777–1844).

1812 *Childe Harold's Pilgrimage,* Cantos I and II, published; the beginning of Byron's association with John Murray. Sudden fame and entrance into Regency society. Meeting both Caroline Lamb (1785–1828) and Anne Isabella Milbanke (1792–1860); the steadying influence of Lady Melbourne (1750?–1818), a worldly woman of great understanding. Miss Milbanke rejects his proposal of marriage.

1813 *Waltz* privately printed. *The Giaour: A Fragment of a Turkish Tale* and *The Bride of Abydos. A Turkish Tale* published by Murray. Beginning of intimate association with Augusta Leigh.

1814 *The Corsair, Ode to Napoleon Buonaparte,* and *Lara* published. Byron begins to accept money for his poetry. Active social life and preoccupation with the theatre. Still involved with Augusta Leigh, he proposes for a second time to Anne Isabella Milbanke and is accepted.

1815 2 January, marries Anne Isabella Milbanke and, after three months, settles in London, at 13 Piccadilly Terrace. Introduced to Walter Scott (1771–1832). Active in management of Drury Lane Theatre. Publication of *Hebrew Melodies.* 10 December, birth of his daughter, Augusta Ada Byron. Continuing financial difficulties.

1816 15 January, Lady Byron leaves supposedly for visit with parents, but several weeks thereafter asks for a separation. Negotiation terminating in deed of separation, signed 21 April. Liquidation of household at 13 Piccadilly Terrace. On 25 April, Byron sails from England, for what is to be the last time. At Lake Geneva he becomes friends with Percy Bysshe Shelley (1792–1822) and Mary Godwin (1797–1851), tiring of his affair with Claire Clairmont (1798–1879), Mary's stepsister. In November, after touring the Bernese Alps with Hobhouse, he settles in Venice. During the year, *The Siege of Corinth, Parisina, Childe Harold* III, and *The Prisoner of Chillon* are published.

1817 January, birth of Allegra, daughter of Byron and Claire Clairmont. Publication of *Manfred* and *The Lament of Tasso.* Sale of Newstead Abbey to Colonel Thomas Wildman.

1818 *Beppo* and *Childe Harold* IV published. Takes a three-year lease on the Palazzo Mocenigo, in Venice, and sends for Allegra. Places active management of his (improving) financial affairs in hands of Douglas Kinnaird and John Cam Hobhouse.

1819 Publication of *Mazeppa* and *Ode on Venice* in June, the first two cantos of *Don Juan* in July. Growing attachment, from April onward, to the Countess Teresa Guiccioli (1800?–73), in Venice, Ravenna, Bologna. In October, at La Mira, he gives Thomas Moore his "Memoirs," to use as he might wish after Byron's death (he consented to their destruction).

1820 At Ravenna he becomes Teresa's acknowledged *Cavalier Servente;* he is soon very friendly with her father and brother, the Counts Ruggero and Pietro Gamba, through whom he becomes somewhat active in the Carboneria.

1821 Publication of *Marino Faliero* and *The Prophecy of Dante* (as one volume), *Don Juan* III–V, and the three plays (as one volume) *Sardanapalus, The Two Foscari,* and *Cain.* Allegra placed in the convent at Bagnacavallo. In November, with Shelley's encouragement, Byron moves to Pisa, to the Palazzo Lanfranchi, where Teresa can join him; Leigh Hunt (1784–1859), radical journalist and friend of Shelley, expected in Pisa, to edit a liberal magazine, to which Byron and Shelley and he will contribute.

1822 The Pisan Circle: Byron and Teresa, Shelley and Mary, Edward (1793–1822) and Jane Williams (1798–1884), Thomas Medwin (1788–1869), Edward John Trelawny (1792–1881), and others. Yacht *Bolivar* built for Byron, sailboat *Don Juan* for Shelley. 28 January, death of Lady Noel, Byron's mother-in-law, leaves him moderately wealthy. 20 April, death of Allegra, of a fever, at the convent. 1 July, the arrival of Leigh Hunt and his family. 8 July, Shelley and Williams drowned; the disintegration of the Pisan Circle. In September, Byron and Teresa move to the Casa Saluzzo, in Albaro, overlooking Genoa. Byron much preoccupied with the idea of going to Greece. 15 October, publication of the first number of *The Liberal,* containing Byron's *The Vision of Judgment,* on which the hostile attack of conservative press centers. John Hunt, Leigh's brother, indicted as publisher of this poem.

1823 *The Age of Bronze, The Island,* and *Don Juan* VI–XIV published by John Hunt. *The Liberal* appears three more times (1 January, 26 April, and 30 July), despite Byron's declining interest and the growing indifference of the public and the press (*Heaven and Earth* in second number). Byron actively raising money for the Greeks. 13 July, with Pietro Gamba and Trelawny, Byron sails for Greece. For some weeks he remains in Cephalonia, supporting Prince Mavrocordatos' provisional government among many factions. 28 December, sails for Missolonghi.

1824 Publication of *Don Juan* XV–XVI by John Hunt. Lending large sums to the Greeks and attempting to bring peace to the factions, Byron passes many weeks amid seemingly unproductive confusion (the moral impact of his work is immeasurable, to be felt in the years that follow). 22 January, composes "On This Day I Complete My Thirty-sixth Year." 19 April, dies of a severe fever beginning some days before. His remains placed among those of his ancestors, in the church at Hucknall, near Newstead Abbey.

POEMS

LACHIN Y GAIR

1

Away, ye gay landscapes, ye gardens of roses!
In you let the minions of luxury rove;
Restore me the rocks, where the snow-flake reposes,
Though still they are sacred to freedom and love:
Yet, Caledonia, belov'd are thy mountains,
Round their white summits though elements war;
Though cataracts foam 'stead of smooth-flowing fountains,
I sigh for the valley of dark Loch na Garr.

2

Ah! there my young footsteps in infancy, wander'd:
My cap was the bonnet, my cloak was the plaid;
On chieftains, long perish'd, my memory ponder'd,
As daily I strode through the pine-cover'd glade;
I sought not my home, till the day's dying glory
Gave place to the rays of the bright polar star;
For fancy was cheer'd, by traditional story,
Disclos'd by the natives of dark Loch na Garr.

3

"Shades of the dead! have I not heard your voices
Rise on the night-rolling breath of the gale?"
Surely, the soul of the hero rejoices,
And rides on the wind, o'er his own Highland vale!
Round Loch na Garr, while the stormy mist gathers,
Winter presides in his cold icy car:
Clouds, there, encircle the forms of my Fathers;
They dwell in the tempests of dark Loch na Garr.

4

"Ill starr'd, though brave, did no visions foreboding
Tell you that fate had forsaken your cause?"
Ah! were you destined to die at Culloden,
Victory crown'd not your fall with applause:
Still were you happy, in death's earthy slumber,
You rest with your clan, in the caves of Braemar;
The Pibroch resounds, to the piper's loud number,
Your deeds, on the echoes of dark Loch na Garr.

5

Years have roll'd on, Loch na Garr, since I left you,
Years must elapse, ere I tread you again:
Nature of verdure and flowers has bereft you,
Yet still are you dearer than Albion's plain:
England! thy beauties are tame and domestic,
To one who has rov'd on the mountains afar:
Oh! for the crags that are wild and majestic,
The steep, frowning glories of dark Loch na Garr.

LINES INSCRIBED UPON A CUP FORMED FROM A SKULL

1

START not — nor deem my spirit fled:
In me behold the only skull,
From which, unlike a living head,
Whatever flows is never dull.

2

I lived, I loved, I quaff'd, like thee:
I died: let earth my bones resign;
Fill up — thou canst not injure me;
The worm hath fouler lips than thine.

3

Better to hold the sparkling grape,
Than nurse the earth-worm's slimy brood;
And circle in the goblet's shape
The drink of Gods, than reptile's food.

4

Where once my wit, perchance, hath shone,
In aid of others' let me shine;
And when, alas! our brains are gone,
What nobler substitute than wine?

5

Quaff while thou canst: another race,
When thou and thine, like me, are sped,

May rescue thee from earth's embrace,
  And rhyme and revel with the dead.

6

Why not? since through life's little day
  Our heads such sad effects produce;
Redeem'd from worms and wasting clay,
  This chance is theirs, to be of use.

WELL! THOU ART HAPPY

1

WELL! thou art happy, and I feel
  That I should thus be happy too;
For still my heart regards thy weal
  Warmly, as it was wont to do.

2

Thy husband's blest — and 'twill impart
  Some pangs to view his happier lot:
But let them pass — Oh! how my heart
  Would hate him if he loved thee not!

3

When late I saw thy favourite child,
  I thought my jealous heart would break;
But when the unconscious infant smil'd,
  I kiss'd it for its mother's sake.

4

I kiss'd it, — and repress'd my sighs
  Its father in its face to see;
But then it had its mother's eyes,
  And they were all to love and me.

5

Mary, adieu! I must away:
  While thou art blest I'll not repine;
But near thee I can never stay;
  My heart would soon again be thine.

6

I deem'd that Time, I deem'd that Pride,
Had quench'd at length my boyish flame;
Nor knew, till seated by thy side,
My heart in all, — save hope, — the same

7

Yet was I calm: I knew the time
My breast would thrill before thy look;
But now to tremble were a crime —
We met, — and not a nerve was shook.

8

I saw thee gaze upon my face,
Yet meet with no confusion there:
One only feeling couldst thou trace;
The sullen calmness of despair.

9

Away! away! my early dream
Remembrance never must awake:
Oh! where is Lethe's fabled stream?
My foolish heart be still, or break.

ENGLISH BARDS,
AND
SCOTCH REVIEWERS;

A SATIRE

"I had rather be a kitten, and cry mew!
Than one of these metre ballad-mongers."
SHAKESPEARE.

"Such shameless Bards we have; and yet 'tis true,
There are as mad, abandon'd Critics, too."
POPE.

STILL must I hear? — shall hoarse FITZGERALD bawl
His creaking couplets in a tavern hall,
And I not sing, lest, haply, Scotch Reviews
Should dub me scribbler, and denounce my *Muse*?
Prepare for rhyme — I'll publish, right or wrong:
Fools are my theme, let Satire be my song.

Oh! Nature's noblest gift — my grey goose-quill!
Slave of my thoughts, obedient to my will,
Torn from thy parent bird to form a pen,
That mighty instrument of little men!
The pen! foredoomed to aid the mental throes
Of brains that labour, big with Verse or Prose;
Though Nymphs forsake, and Critics may deride,
The Lover's solace, and the Author's pride.
What Wits! what Poets dost thou daily raise!
How frequent is thy use, how small thy praise!
Condemned at length to be forgotten quite,
With all the pages which 'twas thine to write.
But thou, at least, mine own especial pen!
Once laid aside, but now assumed again,
Our task complete, like Hamet's shall be free;
Though spurned by others, yet beloved by me:
Then let us soar to-day; no common theme,
No Eastern vision, no distempered dream
Inspires — our path, though full of thorns, is plain;
Smooth be the verse, and easy be the strain.

When Vice triumphant holds her sov'reign sway,
Obey'd by all who nought beside obey;

When Folly, frequent harbinger of crime,
Bedecks her cap with bells of every Clime;
When knaves and fools combined o'er all prevail,
And weigh their Justice in a Golden Scale;
E'en then the boldest start from public sneers,
Afraid of Shame, unknown to other fears,
More darkly sin, by Satire kept in awe,
And shrink from Ridicule, though not from Law.

Such is the force of Wit! but not belong
To me the arrows of satiric song;
The royal vices of our age demand
A keener weapon, and a mightier hand.
Still there are follies, e'en for me to chase,
And yield at least amusement in the race:
Laugh when I laugh, I seek no other fame,
The cry is up, and scribblers are my game:
Speed, Pegasus! — ye strains of great and small,
Ode! Epic! Elegy! — have at you all!
I, too, can scrawl, and once upon a time
I poured along the town a flood of rhyme,
A schoolboy freak, unworthy praise or blame;
I printed — older children do the same.
'Tis pleasant, sure, to see one's name in print;
A Book's a Book, altho' there's nothing in't.
Not that a Title's sounding charm can save
Or scrawl or scribbler from an equal grave:
This LAMB must own, since his patrician name
Failed to preserve the spurious Farce from shame.
No matter, GEORGE continues still to write,
Tho' now the name is veiled from public sight.
Moved by the great example, I pursue
The self-same road, but make my own review:
Not seek great JEFFREY'S, yet like him will be
Self-constituted Judge of Poesy.

A man must serve his time to every trade
Save Censure — Critics all are ready made.
Take hackneyed jokes from MILLER, got by rote,
With just enough of learning to misquote;
A man well skilled to find, or forge a fault;
A turn for punning — call it Attic salt;
To JEFFREY go, be silent and discreet,
His pay is just ten sterling pounds per sheet:
Fear not to lie, 'twill seem a *sharper* hit;
Shrink not from blasphemy, 'twill pass for wit;

Care not for feeling — pass your proper jest,
And stand a Critic, hated yet caress'd.

And shall we own such judgment? no — as soon
Seek roses in December — ice in June;
Hope constancy in wind, or corn in chaff,
Believe a woman or an epitaph,
Or any other thing that's false, before
You trust in Critics, who themselves are sore;
Or yield one single thought to be misled
By JEFFREY's heart, or LAMB's Bœotian head.
To these young tyrants, by themselves misplaced,
Combined usurpers on the Throne of Taste;
To these, when Authors bend in humble awe,
And hail their voice as Truth, their word as Law;
While these are Censors, 'twould be sin to spare;
While such are Critics, why should I forbear?
But yet, so near all modern worthies run,
'Tis doubtful whom to seek, or whom to shun;
Nor know we when to spare, or where to strike,
Our Bards and Censors are so much alike.

Then should you ask me, why I venture o'er
The path which POPE and GIFFORD trod before;
If not yet sickened, you can still proceed;
Go on; my rhyme will tell you as you read.
"But hold!" exclaims a friend, — "here's some neglect:
This — that — and t'other line seem incorrect."
What then? the self-same blunder Pope has got,
And careless Dryden — "Aye, but Pye has not:" —
Indeed! — 'tis granted, faith! — but what care I?
Better to err with POPE, than shine with PYE.

Time was, ere yet in these degenerate days
Ignoble themes obtained mistaken praise,
When Sense and Wit with Poesy allied,
No fabled Graces, flourished side by side,
From the same fount their inspiration drew,
And, reared by Taste, bloomed fairer as they grew.
Then, in this happy Isle, a POPE's pure strain
Sought the rapt soul to charm, nor sought in vain;
A polished nation's praise aspired to claim,
And raised the people's, as the poet's fame.
Like him great DRYDEN poured the tide of song,
In stream less smooth, indeed, yet doubly strong.
Then CONGREVE's scenes could cheer, or OTWAY's melt;

For Nature then an English audience felt —
But why these names, or greater still, retrace,
When all to feebler Bards resign their place?
Yet to such times our lingering looks are cast,
When taste and reason with those times are past.
Now look around, and turn each trifling page,
Survey the precious works that please the age;
This truth at least let Satire's self allow,
No dearth of Bards can be complained of now.
The loaded Press beneath her labour groans,
And Printers' devils shake their weary bones;
While SOUTHEY's Epics cram the creaking shelves,
And LITTLE's Lyrics shine in hot-pressed twelves.
Thus saith the *Preacher:* "Nought beneath the sun
Is new," yet still from change to change we run.
What varied wonders tempt us as they pass!
The Cow-pox, Tractors, Galvanism, and Gas,
In turns appear, to make the vulgar stare,
Till the swoln bubble bursts — and all is air!
Nor less new schools of Poetry arise,
Where dull pretenders grapple for the prize:
O'er Taste awhile these Pseudo-bards prevail;
Each country Book-club bows the knee to Baal,
And, hurling lawful Genius from the throne,
Erects a shrine and idol of its own;
Some leaden calf — but whom it matters not,
From soaring SOUTHEY, down to groveling STOTT.

Behold! in various throngs the scribbling crew,
For notice eager, pass in long review:
Each spurs his jaded Pegasus apace,
And Rhyme and Blank maintain an equal race;
Sonnets on sonnets crowd, and ode on ode;
And Tales of Terror jostle on the road;
Immeasurable measures move along;
For simpering Folly loves a varied song,
To strange, mysterious Dulness still the friend,
Admires the strain she cannot comprehend.
Thus Lays of Minstrels — may they be the last! —
On half-strung harps whine mournful to the blast.
While mountain spirits prate to river sprites,
That dames may listen to the sound at nights;
And goblin brats, of Gilpin Horner's brood
Decoy young Border-nobles through the wood,
And skip at every step, Lord knows how high,
And frighten foolish babes, the Lord knows why;
While high-born ladies in their magic cell,

Forbidding Knights to read who cannot spell,
Despatch a courier to a wizard's grave,
And fight with honest men to shield a knave.

Next view in state, proud prancing on his roan,
The golden-crested haughty Marmion,
Now forging scrolls, now foremost in the fight,
Not quite a Felon, yet but half a Knight,
The gibbet or the field prepared to grace;
A mighty mixture of the great and base.
And think'st thou, SCOTT! by vain conceit perchance,
On public taste to foist thy stale romance,
Though MURRAY with his MILLER may combine
To yield thy muse just half-a-crown per line?
No! when the sons of song descend to trade,
Their bays are sear, their former laurels fade,
Let such forego the poet's sacred name,
Who rack their brains for lucre, not for fame:
Still for stern Mammon may they toil in vain!
And sadly gaze on Gold they cannot gain!
Such be their meed, such still the just reward
Of prostituted Muse and hireling bard!
For this we spurn Apollo's venal son,
And bid a long "good night to Marmion."

These are the themes that claim our plaudits now;
These are the Bards to whom the Muse must bow;
While MILTON, DRYDEN, POPE, alike forgot,
Resign their hallowed Bays to WALTER SCOTT.

The time has been, when yet the Muse was young,
When HOMER swept the lyre, and MARO sung,
An Epic scarce ten centuries could claim,
While awe-struck nations hailed the magic name:
The work of each immortal Bard appears
The single wonder of a thousand years.
Empires have mouldered from the face of earth,
Tongues have expired with those who gave them birth,
Without the glory such a strain can give,
As even in ruin bids the language live.
Not so with us, though minor Bards, content,
On one great work a life of labour spent:
With eagle pinion soaring to the skies,
Behold the Ballad-monger SOUTHEY rise!
To him let CAMOËNS, MILTON, TASSO yield,
Whose annual strains, like armies, take the field.
First in the ranks see Joan of Arc advance,

The scourge of England and the boast of France!
Though burnt by wicked Bedford for a witch,
Behold her statue placed in Glory's niche;
Her fetters burst, and just released from prison,
A virgin Phœnix from her ashes risen.
Next see tremendous Thalaba come on,
Arabia's monstrous, wild, and wond'rous son;
Domdaniel's dread destroyer, who o'erthrew
More mad magicians than the world e'er knew.
Immortal Hero! all thy foes o'ercome,
For ever reign — the rival of Tom Thumb!
Since startled Metre fled before thy face,
Well wert thou doomed the last of all thy race!
Well might triumphant Genii bear thee hence,
Illustrious conqueror of common sense!
Now, last and greatest, Madoc spreads his sails,
Cacique in Mexico, and Prince in Wales;
Tells us strange tales, as other travellers do,
More old than Mandeville's, and not so true.
Oh, Southey! Southey! cease thy varied song!
A bard may chaunt too often and too long:
As thou art strong in verse, in mercy, spare!
A fourth, alas! were more than we could bear.
But if, in spite of all the world can say,
Thou still wilt verseward plod thy weary way;
If still in Berkeley-Ballads most uncivil,
Thou wilt devote old women to the devil,
The babe unborn thy dread intent may rue:
"God help thee," Southey, and thy readers too.

Next comes the dull disciple of thy school,
That mild apostate from poetic rule,
The simple Wordsworth, framer of a lay
As soft as evening in his favourite May,
Who warns his friend "to shake off toil and trouble,
And quit his books, for fear of growing double;"
Who, both by precept and example, shows
That prose is verse, and verse is merely prose;
Convincing all, by demonstration plain,
Poetic souls delight in prose insane;
And Christmas stories tortured into rhyme
Contain the essence of the true sublime.
Thus, when he tells the tale of Betty Foy,
The idiot mother of "an idiot Boy;"
A moon-struck, silly lad, who lost his way,
And, like his bard, confounded night with day;
So close on each pathetic part he dwells,
And each adventure so sublimely tells,

That all who view the "idiot in his glory"
Conceive the Bard the hero of the story.

Shall gentle COLERIDGE pass unnoticed here,
To turgid ode and tumid stanza dear?
Though themes of innocence amuse him best,
Yet still Obscurity's a welcome guest.
If Inspiration should her aid refuse
To him who takes a Pixy for a muse,
Yet none in lofty numbers can surpass
The bard who soars to elegize an ass:
So well the subject suits his noble mind,
He brays, the Laureate of the long-eared kind.

Oh! wonder-working LEWIS! Monk, or Bard,
Who fain would make Parnassus a church-yard!
Lo! wreaths of yew, not laurel, bind thy brow,
Thy Muse a Sprite, Apollo's sexton thou!
Whether on ancient tombs thou tak'st thy stand,
By gibb'ring spectres hailed, thy kindred band;
Or tracest chaste descriptions on thy page,
To please the females of our modest age;
All hail, M.P.! from whose infernal brain
Thin-sheeted phantoms glide, a grisly train;
At whose command "grim women" throng in crowds,
And kings of fire, of water, and of clouds,
With "small grey men," — "wild yagers," and what not,
To crown with honour thee and WALTER SCOTT:
Again, all hail! if tales like thine may please,
St. Luke alone can vanquish the disease:
Even Satan's self with thee might dread to dwell,
And in thy skull discern a deeper Hell.

Who in soft guise, surrounded by a choir
Of virgins melting, not to Vesta's fire,
With sparkling eyes, and cheek by passion flushed
Strikes his wild lyre, whilst listening dames are hushed?
'Tis LITTLE! young Catullus of his day,
As sweet, but as immoral, in his Lay!
Grieved to condemn, the Muse must still be just,
Nor spare melodious advocates of lust.
Pure is the flame which o'er her altar burns;
From grosser incense with disgust she turns
Yet kind to youth, this expiation o'er,
She bids thee "mend thy line, and sin no more."

For thee, translator of the tinsel song,
To whom such glittering ornaments belong,

Hibernian STRANGFORD! with thine eyes of blue,
And boasted locks of red or auburn hue,
Whose plaintive strain each love-sick Miss admires,
And o'er harmonious fustian half expires,
Learn, if thou canst, to yield thine author's sense,
Nor vend thy sonnets on a false pretence.
Think'st thou to gain thy verse a higher place,
By dressing Camoëns in a suit of lace?
Mend, STRANGFORD! mend thy morals and thy taste;
Be warm, but pure; be amorous, but be chaste:
Cease to deceive; thy pilfered harp restore,
Nor teach the Lusian Bard to copy MOORE.

Behold — Ye Tarts! — one moment spare the text! —
HAYLEY's last work, and worst — until his next;
Whether he spin poor couplets into plays,
Or damn the dead with purgatorial praise,
His style in youth or age is still the same,
For ever feeble and for ever tame.
Triumphant first see "Temper's Triumphs" shine!
At least I'm sure they triumphed over mine.
Of "Music's Triumphs," all who read may swear
That luckless Music never triumph'd there.

Moravians, rise! bestow some meet reward
On dull devotion — Lo! the Sabbath Bard,
Sepulchral GRAHAME, pours his notes sublime
In mangled prose, nor e'en aspires to rhyme;
Breaks into blank the Gospel of St. Luke,
And boldly pilfers from the Pentateuch;
And, undisturbed by conscientious qualms,
Perverts the Prophets, and purloins the Psalms.

Hail, Sympathy! thy soft idea brings
A thousand visions of a thousand things,
And shows, still whimpering thro' threescore of years,
The maudlin prince of mournful sonneteers.
And art thou not their prince, harmonious Bowles!
Thou first, great oracle of tender souls?
Whether thou sing'st with equal ease, and grief,
The fall of empires, or a yellow leaf;
Whether thy muse most lamentably tells
What merry sounds proceed from Oxford bells,
Or, still in bells delighting, finds a friend
In every chime that jingled from Ostend;
Ah! how much juster were thy Muse's hap,
If to thy bells thou would'st but add a cap!

Delightful BOWLES! still blessing and still blest,
All love thy strain, but children like it best.
'Tis thine, with gentle LITTLE's moral song,
To soothe the mania of the amorous throng!
With thee our nursery damsels shed their tears,
Ere Miss as yet completes her infant years:
But in her teens thy whining powers are vain;
She quits poor BOWLES for LITTLE's purer strain.
Now to soft themes thou scornest to confine
The lofty numbers of a harp like thine;
"Awake a louder and a loftier strain,"
Such as none heard before, or will again!
Where all discoveries jumbled from the flood,
Since first the leaky ark reposed in mud,
By more or less, are sung in every book,
From Captain Noah down to Captain Cook.
Nor this alone — but, pausing on the road,
The Bard sighs forth a gentle episode,
And gravely tells — attend, each beauteous Miss! —
When first Madeira trembled to a kiss.
Bowles! in thy memory let this precept dwell,
Stick to thy Sonnets, Man! — at least they sell.
But if some new-born whim, or larger bribe,
Prompt thy crude brain, and claim thee for a scribe:
If 'chance some bard, though once by dunces feared,
Now, prone in dust, can only be revered;
If Pope, whose fame and genius, from the first,
Have foiled the best of critics, needs the worst,
Do thou essay: each fault, each failing scan;
The first of poets was, alas! but man.
Rake from each ancient dunghill ev'ry pearl,
Consult Lord Fanny, and confide in CURLL;
Let all the scandals of a former age
Perch on thy pen, and flutter o'er thy page;
Affect a candour which thou canst not feel,
Clothe envy in a garb of honest zeal;
Write, as if St. John's soul could still inspire,
And do from hate what MALLET did for hire.
Oh! hadst thou lived in that congenial time,
To rave with DENNIS, and with RALPH to rhyme;
Thronged with the rest around his living head,
Not raised thy hoof against the lion dead,
A meet reward had crowned thy glorious gains,
And linked thee to the Dunciad for thy pains.

Another Epic! Who inflicts again
More books of blank upon the sons of men?

Bœotian COTTLE, rich Bristowa's boast,
Imports old stories from the Cambrian coast,
And sends his goods to market — all alive!
Lines forty thousand, Cantos twenty-five!
Fresh fish from Hippocrene! who'll buy? who'll buy?
The precious bargain's cheap — in faith, not I.
Your turtle-feeder's verse must needs be flat,
Though Bristol bloat him with the verdant fat;
If Commerce fills the purse, she clogs the brain,
And AMOS COTTLE strikes the Lyre in vain.
In him an author's luckless lot behold!
Condemned to make the books which once he sold.
Oh, AMOS COTTLE! — Phœbus! what a name
To fill the speaking-trump of future fame! —
Oh, AMOS COTTLE! for a moment think
What meagre profits spring from pen and ink!
When thus devoted to poetic dreams,
Who will peruse thy prostituted reams?
Oh! pen perverted! paper misapplied!
Had COTTLE still adorned the counter's side,
Bent o'er the desk, or, born to useful toils,
Been taught to make the paper which he soils,
Ploughed, delved, or plied the oar with lusty limb,
He had not sung of Wales, nor I of him.

As Sisyphus against the infernal steep
Rolls the huge rock whose motions ne'er may sleep,
So up thy hill, ambrosial Richmond! heaves
Dull MAURICE all his granite weight of leaves:
Smooth, solid monuments of mental pain!
The petrifactions of a plodding brain,
That, ere they reach the top, fall lumbering back again.

With broken lyre and cheek serenely pale,
Lo! sad Alcæus wanders down the vale;
Though fair they rose, and might have bloomed at last,
His hopes have perished by the northern blast:
Nipped in the bud by Caledonian gales,
His blossoms wither as the blast prevails!
O'er his lost works let *classic* SHEFFIELD weep;
May no rude hand disturb their early sleep!

Yet say! why should the Bard, at once, resign
His claim to favour from the sacred Nine?
For ever startled by the mingled howl
Of Northern Wolves, that still in darkness prowl;
A coward Brood, which mangle as they prey,

By hellish instinct, all that cross their way;
Aged or young, the living or the dead,
No mercy find — these harpies must be fed.
Why do the injured unresisting yield
The calm possession of their native field?
Why tamely thus before their fangs retreat,
Nor hunt the blood-hounds back to Arthur's Seat?

Health to immortal JEFFREY! once, in name,
England could boast a judge almost the same;
In soul so like, so merciful, yet just,
Some think that Satan has resigned his trust,
And given the Spirit to the world again,
To sentence Letters, as he sentenced men.
With hand less mighty, but with heart as black,
With voice as willing to decree the rack;
Bred in the Courts betimes, though all that law
As yet hath taught him is to find a flaw, —
Since well instructed in the patriot school
To rail at party, though a party tool —
Who knows? if chance his patrons should restore
Back to the sway they forfeited before,
His scribbling toils some recompense may meet,
And raise this Daniel to the Judgment-Seat.
Let JEFFREY's shade indulge the pious hope,
And greeting thus, present him with a rope:
"Heir to my virtues! man of equal mind!
Skilled to condemn as to traduce mankind,
This cord receive! for thee reserved with care,
To wield in judgment, and at length to wear."

Health to great JEFFREY! Heaven preserve his life,
To flourish on the fertile shores of Fife,
And guard it sacred in its future wars,
Since authors sometimes seek the field of Mars!
Can none remember that eventful day,
That ever-glorious, almost fatal fray,
When LITTLE's leadless pistol met his eye,
And Bow-street Myrmidons stood laughing by?
Oh, day disastrous! on her firm-set rock,
Dunedin's castle felt a secret shock;
Dark rolled the sympathetic waves of Forth,
Low groaned the startled whirlwinds of the north;
TWEED ruffled half his waves to form a tear,
The other half pursued his calm career,
ARTHUR's steep summit nodded to its base,
The surly Tolbooth scarcely kept her place.

The Tolbooth felt — for marble sometimes can,
On such occasions, feel as much as man —
The Tolbooth felt defrauded of his charms,
If Jeffrey died, except within her arms:
Nay last, not least, on that portentous morn,
The sixteenth story, where himself was born,
His patrimonial garret, fell to ground,
And pale Edina shuddered at the sound:
Strewed were the streets around with milk-white reams,
Flowed all the Canongate with inky streams;
This of his candour seemed the sable dew,
That of his valour showed the bloodless hue;
And all with justice deemed the two combined
The mingled emblems of his mighty mind.
But Caledonia's goddess hovered o'er
The field, and saved him from the wrath of Moore;
From either pistol snatched the vengeful lead,
And straight restored it to her favourite's head;
That head, with greater than magnetic power,
Caught it, as Danäe caught the golden shower,
And, though the thickening dross will scarce refine,
Augments its ore, and is itself a mine.
"My son," she cried, "ne'er thirst for gore again,
Resign the pistol and resume the pen;
O'er politics and poesy preside,
Boast of thy country, and Britannia's guide!
For long as Albion's heedless sons submit,
Or Scottish taste decides on English wit,
So long shall last thine unmolested reign,
Nor any dare to take thy name in vain.
Behold, a chosen band shall aid thy plan,
And own thee chieftain of the critic clan.
First in the oat-fed phalanx shall be seen
The travelled Thane, Athenian Aberdeen.
Herbert shall wield Thor's hammer, and sometimes
In gratitude, thou'lt praise his rugged rhymes.
Smug Sydney too thy bitter page shall seek,
And classic Hallam, much renowned for Greek;
Scott may perchance his name and influence lend,
And paltry Pillans shall traduce his friend;
While gay Thalia's luckless votary, Lamb,
Damned like the Devil — Devil-like will damn.
Known be thy name! unbounded be thy sway!
Thy Holland's banquets shall each toil repay!
While grateful Britain yields the praise she owes
To Holland's hirelings and to Learning's foes.
Yet mark one caution ere thy next Review

Spread its light wings of Saffron and of Blue,
Beware lest blundering BROUGHAM destroy the sale,
Turn Beef to Bannocks, Cauliflowers to Kail."
Thus having said, the kilted Goddess kist
Her son, and vanished in a Scottish mist.

Then prosper, JEFFREY! pertest of the train
Whom Scotland pampers with her fiery grain!
Whatever blessing waits a genuine Scot,
In double portion swells thy glorious lot;
For thee Edina culls her evening sweets,
And showers their odours on thy candid sheets,
Whose Hue and Fragrance to thy work adhere —
This scents its pages, and that gilds its rear.
Lo! blushing Itch, coy nymph, enamoured grown,
Forsakes the rest, and cleaves to thee alone,
And, too unjust to other Pictish men,
Enjoys thy person, and inspires thy pen!

Illustrious HOLLAND! hard would be his lot,
His hirelings mentioned, and himself forgot!
HOLLAND, with HENRY PETTY at his back,
The whipper-in and huntsman of the pack.
Blest be the banquets spread at Holland House,
Where Scotchmen feed, and Critics may carouse!
Long, long beneath that hospitable roof
Shall Grub-street dine, while duns are kept aloof.
See honest HALLAM lay aside his fork,
Resume his pen, review his Lordship's work,
And, grateful for the dainties on his plate,
Declare his landlord can at least translate!
Dunedin! view thy children with delight,
They write for food — and feed because they write:
And lest, when heated with the unusual grape,
Some glowing thoughts should to the press escape,
And tinge with red the female reader's cheek,
My lady skims the cream of each critique;
Breathes o'er the page her purity of soul,
Reforms each error, and refines the whole.

Now to the Drama turn — Oh! motley sight!
What precious scenes the wondering eyes invite:
Puns, and a Prince within a barrel pent,
And Dibdins' nonsense yield complete content.
Though now, thank Heaven! the Rosciomania's o'er.
And full-grown actors are endured once more;
Yet what avail their vain attempts to please,

While British critics suffer scenes like these;
While REYNOLDS vents his *"dammes!"* "poohs!" and "zounds!"
And common-place and common sense confounds?
While KENNEY'S "World" — ah! where is KENNEY'S wit? —
Tires the sad gallery, lulls the listless Pit;
And BEAUMONT'S pilfered Caratach affords
A tragedy complete in all but words?
Who but must mourn, while these are all the rage
The degradation of our vaunted stage?
Heavens! is all sense of shame and talent gone?
Have we no living Bard of merit? — none?
Awake, GEORGE COLMAN! CUMBERLAND, awake!
Ring the alarum bell! let folly quake!
Oh! SHERIDAN! if aught can move thy pen,
Let Comedy assume her throne again;
Abjure the mummery of German schools;
Leave new Pizarros to translating fools;
Give, as thy last memorial to the age,
One classic drama, and reform the stage.
Gods! o'er those boards shall Folly rear her head,
Where GARRICK trod, and SIDDONS lives to tread?
On those shall Farce display buffoonery's mask,
And HOOK conceal his heroes in a cask?
Shall sapient managers new scenes produce
From CHERRY, SKEFFINGTON, and Mother GOOSE?
While SHAKESPEARE, OTWAY, MASSINGER, forgot,
On stalls must moulder, or in closets rot?
Lo! with what pomp the daily prints proclaim
The rival candidates for Attic fame!
In grim array though LEWIS' spectres rise,
Still SKEFFINGTON and GOOSE divide the prize.
And sure *great* Skeffington must claim our praise,
For skirtless coats and skeletons of plays
Renowned alike; whose genius ne'er confines
Her flight to garnish Greenwood's gay designs;
Nor sleeps with "Sleeping Beauties," but anon
In five facetious acts comes thundering on.
While poor John Bull, bewildered with the scene,
Stares, wondering what the devil it can mean;
But as some hands applaud, a venal few!
Rather than sleep, why John applauds it too.

Such are we now. Ah! wherefore should we turn
To what our fathers were, unless to mourn?
Degenerate Britons! are ye dead to shame,
Or, kind to dulness, do you fear to blame?
Well may the nobles of our present race

Watch each distortion of a NALDI's face;
Well may they smile on Italy's buffoons,
And worship CATALANI's pantaloons,
Since their own Drama yields no fairer trace
Of wit than puns, of humour than grimace.

Then let Ausonia, skill'd in every art
To soften manners, but corrupt the heart,
Pour her exotic follies o'er the town,
To sanction Vice, and hunt Decorum down:
Let wedded strumpets languish o'er DESHAYES,
And bless the promise which his form displays;
While Gayton bounds before th' enraptured looks
Of hoary Marquises, and stripling Dukes:
Let high-born lechers eye the lively Presle
Twirl her light limbs, that spurn the needless veil;
Let Angiolini bare her breast of snow,
Wave the white arm, and point the pliant toe;
Collini trill her love-inspiring song,
Strain her fair neck, and charm the listening throng!
Whet not your scythe, Suppressors of our Vice!
Reforming Saints! too delicately nice!
By whose decrees, our sinful souls to save,
No Sunday tankards foam, no barbers shave;
And beer undrawn, and beards unmown, display
Your holy reverence for the Sabbath-day.

Or hail at once the patron and the pile
Of vice and folly, Greville and Argyle!
Where yon proud palace, Fashion's hallow'd fane,
Spreads wide her portals for the motley train,
Behold the new Petronius of the day,
Our arbiter of pleasure and of play!
There the hired eunuch, the Hesperian choir,
The melting lute, the soft lascivious lyre,
The song from Italy, the step from France,
The midnight orgy, and the mazy dance,
The smile of beauty, and the flush of wine,
For fops, fools, gamesters, knaves, and Lords combine:
Each to his humour — Comus all allows;
Champaign, dice, music, or your neighbour's spouse.
Talk not to us, ye starving sons of trade!
Of piteous ruin, which ourselves have made;
In Plenty's sunshine Fortune's minions bask,
Nor think of Poverty, except "en masque,"
When for the night some lately titled ass
Appears the beggar which his grandsire was,

The curtain dropped, the gay Burletta o'er,
The audience take their turn upon the floor:
Now round the room the circling dow'gers sweep,
Now in loose waltz the thin-clad daughters leap;
The first in lengthened line majestic swim,
The last display the free unfettered limb!
Those for Hibernia's lusty sons repair
With art the charms which Nature could not spare;
These after husbands wing their eager flight,
Nor leave much mystery for the nuptial night.

Oh! blest retreats of infamy and ease,
Where, all forgotten but the power to please,
Each maid may give a loose to genial thought,
Each swain may teach new systems, or be taught:
There the blithe youngster, just returned from Spain,
Cuts the light pack, or calls the rattling main;
The jovial Caster's set, and seven's the Nick,
Or — done! — a thousand on the coming trick!
If, mad with loss, existence 'gins to tire,
And all your hope or wish is to expire,
Here's POWELL's pistol ready for your life,
And, kinder still, two PAGETS for your wife:
Fit consummation of an earthly race
Begun in folly, ended in disgrace,
While none but menials o'er the bed of death,
Wash thy red wounds, or watch thy wavering breath;
Traduced by liars, and forgot by all,
The mangled victim of a drunken brawl,
To live like CLODIUS, and like FALKLAND fall.

Truth! rouse some genuine Bard, and guide his hand
To drive this pestilence from out the land.
E'en I — least thinking of a thoughtless throng,
Just skilled to know the right and choose the wrong,
Freed at that age when Reason's shield is lost,
To fight my course through Passion's countless host,
Whom every path of Pleasure's flow'ry way
Has lured in turn, and all have led astray —
E'en I must raise my voice, e'en I must feel
Such scenes, such men, destroy the public weal:
Altho' some kind, censorious friend will say,
"What art thou better, meddling fool, than they?"
And every Brother Rake will smile to see
That miracle, a Moralist in me.
No matter — when some Bard in virtue strong,
Gifford perchance, shall raise the chastening song,

Then sleep my pen for ever! and my voice
Be only heard to hail him, and rejoice,
Rejoice, and yield my feeble praise, thought I
May feel the lash that Virtue must apply.

As for the smaller fry, who swarm in shoals
From silly HAFIZ up to simple BOWLES,
Why should we call them from their dark abode,
In Broad St. Giles's or Tottenham-Road?
Or (since some men of fashion nobly dare
To scrawl in verse) from Bond-street or the Square?
If things of Ton their harmless lays indite,
Most wisely doomed to shun the public sight,
What harm? in spite of every critic elf,
Sir T. may read his stanzas to himself;
MILES ANDREWS still his strength in couplets try,
And live in prologues, though his dramas die.
Lords too are Bards: such things at times befall,
And 'tis some praise in Peers to write at all.
Yet, did or Taste or Reason sway the times,
Ah! who would take their titles with their rhymes?
ROSCOMMON! SHEFFIELD! with your spirits fled,
No future laurels deck a noble head;
No Muse will cheer, with renovating smile,
The paralytic puling of CARLISLE.
The puny schoolboy and his early lay
Men pardon, if his follies pass away;
But who forgives the Senior's ceaseless verse,
Whose hairs grow hoary as his rhymes grow worse?
What heterogeneous honours deck the Peer!
Lord, rhymester, petit-maître, pampleteer!
So dull in youth, so drivelling in his age,
His scenes alone had damned our sinking stage;
But Managers for once cried, "Hold, enough!"
Nor drugged their audience with the tragic stuff.
Yet at their judgment let his Lordship laugh,
And case his volumes in congenial calf;
Yes! doff that covering, where Morocco shines,
And hang a calf-skin on those recreant lines.

With you, ye Druids! rich in native lead,
Who daily scribble for your daily bread:
With you I war not: GIFFORD's heavy hand
Has crushed, without remorse, your numerous band.
On "All the Talents" vent your venal spleen;
Want is your plea, let Pity be your screen.
Let Monodies on Fox regale your crew,

And Melville's Mantle prove a Blanket too!
One common Lethe waits each hapless Bard,
And, peace be with you! 'tis your best reward.
Such damning fame; as Dunciads only give
Could bid your lines beyond a morning live;
But now at once your fleeting labours close,
With names of greater note in blest repose.
Far be't from me unkindly to upbraid
The lovely ROSA's prose in masquerade,
Whose strains, the faithful echoes of her mind,
Leave wondering comprehension far behind.
Though Crusca's bards no more our journals fill,
Some stragglers skirmish round the columns still;
Last of the howling host which once was Bell's,
Matilda snivels yet, and Hafiz yells;
And Merry's metaphors appear anew,
Chained to the signature of O. P. Q.

When some brisk youth, the tenant of a stall,
Employs a pen less pointed than his awl,
Leaves his snug shop, forsakes his store of shoes,
St. Crispin quits, and cobbles for the Muse,
Heavens! how the vulgar stare! how crowds applaud!
How ladies read, and Literati laud!
If chance some wicked wag should pass his jest,
'Tis sheer ill-nature — don't the world know best?
Genius must guide when wits admire the rhyme,
And CAPEL LOFFT declares 'tis quite sublime.
Hear, then, ye happy sons of needless trade!
Swains! quit the plough, resign the useless spade!
Lo! BURNS and BLOOMFIELD, nay, a greater far,
GIFFORD was born beneath an adverse star,
Forsook the labours of a servile state,
Stemmed the rude storm, and triumphed over Fate:
Then why no more? if Phœbus smiled on you,
BLOOMFIELD! why not on brother Nathan too?
Him too the Mania, not the Muse, has seized;
Not inspiration, but a mind diseased:
And now no Boor can seek his last abode,
No common be inclosed without an ode.
Oh! since increased refinement deigns to smile
On Britain's sons, and bless our genial Isle,
Let Poesy go forth, pervade the whole,
Alike the rustic, and mechanic soul!
Ye tuneful cobblers! still your notes prolong,
Compose at once a slipper and a song;
So shall the fair your handywork peruse,
Your sonnets sure shall please — perhaps your shoes.

May Moorland weavers boast Pindaric skill,
And tailors' lays be longer than their bill!
While punctual beaux reward the grateful notes,
And pay for poems — when they pay for coats.

To the famed throng now paid the tribute due,
Neglected Genius! let me turn to you.
Come forth, oh CAMPBELL! give thy talents scope;
Who dares aspire if thou must cease to hope?
And thou, melodious ROGERS! rise at last,
Recall the pleasing memory of the past;
Arise! let blest remembrance still inspire,
And strike to wonted tones thy hallowed lyre;
Restore Apollo to his vacant throne,
Assert thy country's honour and thine own.
What! must deserted Poesy still weep
Where her last hopes with pious COWPER sleep?
Unless, perchance, from his cold bier she turns,
To deck the turf that wraps her minstrel, BURNS!
No! though contempt hath marked the spurious brood,
The race who rhyme from folly, or for food,
Yet still some genuine sons 'tis hers to boast,
Who, least affecting, still affect the most:
Feel as they write, and write but as they feel —
Bear witness GIFFORD, SOTHEBY, MACNEIL.

"Why slumbers GIFFORD?" once was asked in vain;
Why slumbers GIFFORD? let us ask again.
Are there no follies for his pen to purge?
Are there no fools whose backs demand the scourge?
Are there no sins for Satire's Bard to greet?
Stalks not gigantic Vice in every street?
Shall Peers or Princes tread pollution's path,
And 'scape alike the Laws and Muse's wrath?
Nor blaze with guilty glare through future time,
Eternal beacons of consummate crime?
Arouse thee, GIFFORD! be thy promise claimed,
Make bad men better, or at least ashamed.

Unhappy WHITE! while life was in its spring,
And thy young Muse just waved her joyous wing,
The Spoiler swept that soaring Lyre away,
Which else had sounded an immortal lay.
Oh! what a noble heart was here undone,
When Science' self destroyed her favourite son!
Yes, she too much indulged thy fond pursuit,
She sowed the seeds, but Death has reaped the fruit.
'Twas thine own Genius gave the final blow,

And helped to plant the wound that laid thee low:
So the struck Eagle, stretched upon the plain,
No more through rolling clouds to soar again,
Viewed his own feather on the fatal dart,
And winged the shaft that quivered in his heart;
Keen were his pangs, but keener far to feel
He nursed the pinion which impelled the steel;
While the same plumage that had warmed his nest
Drank the last life-drop of his bleeding breast.

There be who say, in these enlightened days,
That splendid lies are all the poet's praise;
That strained Invention, ever on the wing,
Alone impels the modern Bard to sing:
'Tis true, that all who rhyme — nay, all who write,
Shrink from that fatal word to Genius — Trite;
Yet Truth sometimes will lend her noblest fires,
And decorate the verse herself inspires:
This fact in Virtue's name let CRABBE attest;
Though Nature's sternest Painter, yet the best.

And here let SHEE and Genius find a place,
Whose pen and pencil yield an equal grace;
To guide whose hand the sister Arts combine,
And trace the Poet's or the Painter's line;
Whose magic touch can bid the canvas glow,
Or pour the easy rhyme's harmonious flow;
While honours, doubly merited, attend
The Poet's rival, but the Painter's friend.

Blest is the man who dares approach the bower
Where dwelt the Muses at their natal hour;
Whose steps have pressed, whose eye has marked afar,
The clime that nursed the sons of song and war,
The scenes which Glory still must hover o'er,
Her place of birth, her own Achaian shore.
But doubly blest is he whose heart expands
With hallowed feelings for those classic lands;
Who rends the veil of ages long gone by,
And views their remnants with a poet's eye!
WRIGHT! 'twas thy happy lot at once to view
Those shores of glory, and to sing them too;
And sure no common Muse inspired thy pen
To hail the land of Gods and Godlike men.

And you, associate Bards! who snatched to light
Those gems too long withheld from modern sight;

Whose mingling taste combined to cull the wreath
While Attic flowers Aonian odours breathe,
And all their renovated fragrance flung,
To grace the beauties of your native tongue;
Now let those minds, that nobly could transfuse
The glorious Spirit of the Grecian Muse,
Though soft the echo, scorn a borrowed tone:
Resign Achaia's lyre, and strike your own.

Let these, or such as these, with just applause,
Restore the Muse's violated laws;
But not in flimsy DARWIN's pompous chime,
That mighty master of unmeaning rhyme,
Whose gilded cymbals, more adorned than clear,
The eye delighted, but fatigued the ear,
In show the simple lyre could once surpass,
But now, worn down, appear in native brass;
While all his train of hovering sylphs around
Evaporate in similes and sound:
Him let them shun, with him let tinsel die:
False glare attracts, but more offends the eye.

Yet let them not to vulgar WORDSWORTH stoop,
The meanest object of the lowly group,
Whose verse, of all but childish prattle void,
Seems blessed harmony to LAMB and LLOYD:
Let them — but hold, my Muse, nor dare to teach
A strain far, far beyond thy humble reach:
The native genius with their being given
Will point the path, and peal their notes to heaven.

And thou, too, SCOTT! resign to minstrels rude
The wilder Slogan of a Border feud:
Let others spin their meagre lines for hire;
Enough for Genius, if itself inspire!
Let SOUTHEY sing, altho' his teeming muse,
Prolific every spring, be too profuse;
Let simple WORDSWORTH chime his childish verse,
And brother COLERIDGE lull the babe at nurse;
Let Spectre-mongering LEWIS aim, at most,
To rouse the Galleries, or to raise a ghost;
Let MOORE still sigh; let STRANGFORD steal from MOORE,
And swear that CAMOËNS sang such notes of yore;
Let HAYLEY hobble on, MONTGOMERY rave,
And godly GRAHAME chant a stupid stave;
Let sonneteering BOWLES his strains refine,
And whine and whimper to the fourteenth line;

Let Stott, Carlisle, Matilda, and the rest
Of Grub Street, and of Grosvenor Place the best,
Scrawl on, 'till death release us from the strain,
Or Common Sense assert her rights again;
But Thou, with powers that mock the aid of praise,
Should'st leave to humbler Bards ignoble lays:
Thy country's voice, the voice of all the Nine,
Demand a hallowed harp — that harp is thine.
Say! will not Caledonia's annals yield
The glorious record of some nobler field,
Than the vile foray of a plundering clan,
Whose proudest deeds disgrace the name of man?
Or Marmion's acts of darkness, fitter food
For Sherwood's outlaw tales of Robin Hood?
Scotland! still proudly claim thy native Bard,
And be thy praise his first, his best reward!
Yet not with thee alone his name should live,
But own the vast renown a world can give;
Be known, perchance, when Albion is no more,
And tell the tale of what she was before;
To future times her faded fame recall,
And save her glory, though his country fall.

Yet what avails the sanguine Poet's hope,
To conquer ages, and with time to cope?
New eras spread their wings, new nations rise,
And other Victors fill th' applauding skies;
A few brief generations fleet along,
Whose sons forget the Poet and his song:
E'en now, what once-loved Minstrels scarce may claim
The transient mention of a dubious name!
When Fame's loud trump hath blown its noblest blast,
Though long the sound, the echo sleeps at last;
And glory, like the Phœnix midst her fires,
Exhales her odours, blazes, and expires.

Shall hoary Granta call her sable sons,
Expert in science, more expert at puns?
Shall these approach the Muse? ah, no! she flies,
Even from the tempting ore of Seaton's prize;
Though Printers condescend the press to soil
With rhyme by Hoare, and epic blank by Hoyle:
Not him whose page, if still upheld by whist,
Requires no sacred theme to bid us list.
Ye! who in Granta's honours would surpass,
Must mount her Pegasus, a full-grown ass;

A foal well worthy of her ancient Dam,
Whose Helicon is duller than her Cam.

There CLARKE, still striving piteously "to please,"
Forgetting doggerel leads not to degrees,
A would-be satirist, a hired Buffoon,
A monthly scribbler of some low Lampoon,
Condemned to drudge, the meanest of the mean,
And furbish falsehoods for a magazine,
Devotes to scandal his congenial mind;
Himself a living libel on mankind.

Oh! dark asylum of a Vandal race!
At once the boast of learning, and disgrace!
So lost to Phœbus, that nor Hodgson's verse
Can make thee better, nor poor Hewson's worse.
But where fair Isis rolls her purer wave,
The partial Muse delighted loves to lave;
On her green banks a greener wreath she wove,
To crown the Bards that haunt her classic grove;
Where RICHARDS wakes a genuine poet's fires,
And modern Britons glory in their Sires.

For me, who, thus unasked, have dared to tell
My country, what her sons should know too well,
Zeal for her honour bade me here engage
The host of idiots that infest her age;
No just applause her honoured name shall lose,
As first in freedom, dearest to the Muse.
Oh! would thy bards but emulate thy fame,
And rise more worthy, Albion, of thy name!
What Athens was in science, Rome in power,
What Tyre appeared in her meridian hour,
'Tis thine at once, fair Albion! to have been —
Earth's chief Dictatress, Ocean's lovely Queen:
But Rome decayed, and Athens strewed the plain,
And Tyre's proud piers lie shattered in the main;
Like these, thy strength may sink, in ruin hurled,
And Britain fall, the bulwark of the world.
But let me cease, and dread Cassandra's fate,
With warning ever scoffed at, till too late;
To themes less lofty still my lay confine,
And urge thy Bards to gain a name like thine.

Then, hapless Britain! be thy rulers blest,
The senate's oracles, the people's jest!

Still hear thy motley orators dispense
The flowers of rhetoric, though not of sense,
While CANNING's colleagues hate him for his wit,
And old dame PORTLAND fills the place of PITT.

Yet once again, adieu! ere this the sail
That wafts me hence is shivering in the gale;
And Afric's coast and Calpe's adverse height,
And Stamboul's minarets must greet my sight:
Thence shall I stray through Beauty's native clime,
Where Kaff is clad in rocks, and crowned with snows sublime.
But should I back return, no tempting press
Shall drag my Journal from the desk's recess;
Let coxcombs, printing as they come from far,
Snatch his own wreath of Ridicule from Carr;
Let ABERDEEN and ELGIN still pursue
The shade of fame through regions of Virtù;
Waste useless thousands on their Phidian freaks,
Misshapen monuments and maimed antiques;
And make their grand saloons a general mart
For all the mutilated blocks of art:
Or Dardan tours let Dilettanti tell,
I leave topography to rapid GELL;
And, quite content, no more shall interpose
To stun the public ear — at least with Prose.

Thus far I've held my undisturbed career,
Prepared for rancour, steeled 'gainst selfish fear;
This thing of rhyme I ne'er disdained to own —
Though not obtrusive, yet not quite unknown:
My voice was heard again, though not so loud,
My page, though nameless, never disavowed;
And now at once I tear the veil away: —
Cheer on the pack! the Quarry stands at bay,
Unscared by all the din of MELBOURNE house,
By LAMB's resentment, or by HOLLAND's spouse,
By JEFFREY's harmless pistol, HALLAM's rage,
Edina's brawny sons and brimstone page.
Our men in buckram shall have blows enough,
And feel they too are "penetrable stuff:"
And though I hope not hence unscathed to go,
Who conquers me shall find a stubborn foe.
The time hath been, when no harsh sound would fall
From lips that now may seem imbued with gall;
Nor fools nor follies tempt me to despise
The meanest thing that crawled beneath my eyes:
But now, so callous grown, so changed since youth,

I've learned to think, and sternly speak the truth;
Learned to deride the critic's starch decree,
And break him on the wheel he meant for me;
To spurn the rod a scribbler bids me kiss,
Nor care if courts and crowds applaud or hiss:
Nay more, though all my rival rhymesters frown,
I too can hunt a Poetaster down;
And, armed in proof, the gauntlet cast at once
To Scotch marauder, and to Southern dunce.
Thus much I've dared; if my incondite lay
Hath wronged these righteous times, let others say:
This, let the world, which knows not how to spare,
Yet rarely blames unjustly, now declare.

CHILDE HAROLD'S PILGRIMAGE

A ROMAUNT

"L'univers est une espèce de livre, dont on n'a lu que la première page quand on n'a vu que son pays. J'en ai feuilleté un assez grand nombre, que j'ai trouvé également mauvaises. Cet examen ne m'a point été infructueux. Je haissais ma patrie. Toutes les impertinences des peuples divers, parmi lesquels j'ai vécu, m'ont réconcilié avec elle. Quand je n'aurais tiré d'autre bénéfice de mes voyages que celui-là, je n'en regretterais ni les frais ni les fatigues." — *Le Cosmopolite, ou, le Citoyen du Monde,* par Fougeret de Monbron. Londres, 1753.

TO IANTHE

Not in those climes where I have late been straying,
Though Beauty long hath there been matchless deemed,
Not in those visions to the heart displaying
Forms which it sighs but to have only dreamed,
Hath aught like thee in Truth or Fancy seemed:
Nor, having seen thee, shall I vainly seek
To paint those charms which varied as they beamed —
To such as see thee not my words were weak;
To those who gaze on thee what language could they speak?

Ah! may'st thou ever be what now thou art,
Nor unbeseem the promise of thy Spring —
As fair in form, as warm yet pure in heart,
Love's image upon earth without his wing,

And guileless beyond Hope's imagining!
And surely she who now so fondly rears
Thy youth, in thee, thus hourly brightening,
Beholds the Rainbow of her future years,
Before whose heavenly hues all Sorrow disappears.

Young Peri of the West! — 'tis well for me
My years already doubly number thine;
My loveless eye unmoved may gaze on thee,
And safely view thy ripening beauties shine;
Happy, I ne'er shall see them in decline;
Happier, that, while all younger hearts shall bleed,
Mine shall escape the doom thine eyes assign
To those whose admiration shall succeed,
But mixed with pangs to Love's even loveliest hours decreed.

Oh! let that eye, which, wild as the Gazelle's,
Now brightly bold or beautifully shy,
Wins as it wanders, dazzles where it dwells,
Glance o'er this page, nor to my verse deny
That smile for which my breast might vainly sigh
Could I to thee be ever more than friend:
This much, dear Maid, accord; nor question why
To one so young my strain I would commend,
But bid me with my wreath one matchless Lily blend.

Such is thy name with this my verse entwined;
And long as kinder eyes a look shall cast
On Harold's page, Ianthe's here enshrined
Shall thus be *first* beheld, forgotten *last:*
My days once numbered — should this homage past
Attract thy fairy fingers near the Lyre
Of him who hailed thee loveliest, as thou wast —
Such is the most my Memory may desire;
Though more than Hope can claim, could Friendship less require?

CANTO THE FIRST

I

Oh, thou! in Hellas deemed of heavenly birth,
Muse! formed or fabled at the Minstrel's will!
Since shamed full oft by later lyres on earth,
Mine dares not call thee from thy sacred Hill:
Yet there I've wandered by thy vaunted rill;
Yes! sighed o'er Delphi's long deserted shrine,

Where, save that feeble fountain, all is still;
Nor mote my shell awake the weary Nine
To grace so plain a tale — this lowly lay of mine.

II

Whilome in Albion's isle there dwelt a youth,
Who ne in Virtue's ways did take delight;
But spent his days in riot most uncouth,
And vexed with mirth the drowsy ear of Night.
Ah me! in sooth he was a shameless wight,
Sore given to revel and ungoldly glee;
Few earthly things found favour in his sight
Save concubines and carnal companie,
And flaunting wassailers of high and low degree.

III

Childe Harold was he hight: — but whence his name
And lineage long, it suits me not to say;
Suffice it, that perchance they were of fame,
And had been glorious in another day:
But one sad losel soils a name for ay,
However mighty in the olden time;
Nor all that heralds rake from coffined clay,
Nor florid prose, nor honied lies of rhyme,
Can blazon evil deeds, or consecrate a crime.

IV

Childe Harold basked him in the Noontide sun,
Disporting there like any other fly;
Nor deemed before his little day was done
One blast might chill him into misery.
But long ere scarce a third of his passed by,
Worse than Adversity the Childe befell;
He felt the fulness of Satiety:
Then loathed he in his native land to dwell,
Which seemed to him more lone than Eremite's sad cell.

V

For he through Sin's long labyrinth had run,
Nor made atonement when he did amiss,
Had sighed to many though he loved but one,
And that loved one, alas! could ne'er be his.
Ah, happy she! to 'scape from him whose kiss

Had been pollution unto aught so chaste;
Who soon had left her charms for vulgar bliss,
And spoiled her goodly lands to gild his waste,
Nor calm domestic peace had ever deigned to taste.

VI

And now Childe Harold was sore sick at heart,
And from his fellow Bacchanals would flee;
'Tis said, at times the sullen tear would start,
But Pride congealed the drop within his ee:
Apart he stalked in joyless reverie,
And from his native land resolved to go,
And visit scorching climes beyond the sea;
With pleasure drugged, he almost longed for woe,
And e'en for change of scene would seek the shades below.

VII

The Childe departed from his father's hall:
It was a vast and venerable pile;
So old, it seemèd only not to fall,
Yet strength was pillared in each massy aisle.
Monastic dome! condemned to uses vile!
Where Superstition once had made her den
Now Paphian girls were known to sing and smile;
And monks might deem their time was come agen,
If ancient tales say true, nor wrong these holy men.

VIII

Yet oft-times in his maddest mirthful mood
Strange pangs would flash along Childe Harold's brow,
As if the Memory of some deadly feud
Or disappointed passion lurked below:
But this none knew, nor haply cared to know;
For his was not that open, artless soul
That feels relief by bidding sorrow flow,
Nor sought he friend to counsel or condole,
Whate'er this grief mote be, which he could not control.

IX

And none did love him! — though to hall and bower
He gathered revellers from far and near,
He knew them flatterers of the festal hour,
The heartless Parasites of present cheer.

Yea! none did love him — not his lemans dear —
But pomp and power alone are Woman's care,
And where these are light Eros finds a feere;
Maidens, like moths, are ever caught by glare,
And Mammon wins his way where Seraphs might despair.

X

Childe Harold had a mother — not forgot,
Though parting from that mother he did shun;
A sister whom he loved, but saw her not
Before his weary pilgrimage begun:
If friends he had, he bade adieu to none.
Yet deem not thence his breast a breast of steel:
Ye, who have known what 'tis to dote upon
A few dear objects, will in sadness feel
Such partings break the heart they fondly hope to heal.

XI

His house, his home, his heritage, his lands,
The laughing dames in whom he did delight,
Whose large blue eyes, fair locks, and snowy hands,
Might shake the Saintship of an Anchorite,
And long had fed his youthful appetite;
His goblets brimmed with every costly wine,
And all that mote to luxury invite,
Without a sigh he left, to cross the brine,
And traverse Paynim shores, and pass Earth's central line.

XII

The sails were filled, and fair the light winds blew,
As glad to waft him from his native home;
And fast the white rocks faded from his view,
And soon were lost in circumambient foam:
And then, it may be, of his wish to roam
Repented he, but in his bosom slept
The silent thought, nor from his lips did come
One word of wail, whilst others sate and wept,
And to the reckless gales unmanly moaning kept.

XIII

But when the Sun was sinking in the sea
He seized his harp, which he at times could string,
And strike, albeit with untaught melody,

When deemed he no strange ear was listening:
And now his fingers o'er it he did fling,
And tuned his farewell in the dim twilight;
While flew the vessel on her snowy wing,
And fleeting shores receded from his sight,
Thus to the elements he poured his last "Good Night."

CHILDE HAROLD'S GOOD NIGHT

1

"Adieu, adieu! my native shore
Fades o'er the waters blue;
The night-winds sigh, the breakers roar,
And shrieks the wild sea-mew.
Yon Sun that sets upon the sea
We follow in his flight;
Farewell awhile to him and thee,
My native Land — Good Night!

2

"A few short hours and He will rise
To give the Morrow birth;
And I shall hail the main and skies,
But not my mother Earth.
Deserted is my own good Hall,
Its hearth is desolate;
Wild weeds are gathering on the wall;
My Dog howls at the gate.

3

"Come hither, hither, my little page!
Why dost thou weep and wail?
Or dost thou dread the billow's rage,
Or tremble at the gale?
But dash the tear-drop from thine eye;
Our ship is swift and strong:
Our fleetest falcon scarce can fly
More merrily along."

4

"Let winds be shrill, let waves roll high,
I fear not wave nor wind:

Yet marvel not, Sir Childe, that I
  Am sorrowful in mind;
For I have from my father gone,
  A mother whom I love,
And have no friend, save these alone,
  But thee — and One above.

5

'My father blessed me fervently,
  Yet did not much complain;
But sorely will my mother sigh
  Till I come back again.' —
"Enough, enough, my little lad!
  Such tears become thine eye;
If I thy guileless bosom had,
  Mine own would not be dry.

6

"Come hither, hither, my staunch yeoman,
  Why dost thou look so pale?
Or dost thou dread a French foeman?
  Or shiver at the gale?" —
'Deem'st thou I tremble for my life?
  Sir Childe, I'm not so weak;
But thinking on an absent wife
  Will blanch a faithful cheek.

7

'My spouse and boys dwell near thy hall,
  Along the bordering Lake,
And when they on their father call,
  What answer shall she make?' —
"Enough, enough, my yeoman good,
  Thy grief let none gainsay;
But I, who am of lighter mood,
  Will laugh to flee away.

8

"For who would trust the seeming sighs
  Of wife or paramour?
Fresh feeres will dry the bright blue eyes
  We late saw streaming o'er.
For pleasures past I do not grieve,

Nor perils gathering near;
My greatest grief is that I leave
No thing that claims a tear.

9

"And now I'm in the world alone,
Upon the wide, wide sea:
But why should I for others groan,
When none will sigh for me?
Perchance my Dog will whine in vain,
Till fed by stranger hands;
But long ere I come back again,
He'd tear me where he stands.

10

"With thee, my bark, I'll swiftly go
Athwart the foaming brine;
Nor care what land thou bear'st me to,
So not again to mine.
Welcome, welcome, ye dark-blue waves!
And when you fail my sight,
Welcome, ye deserts, and ye caves!
My native Land — Good Night!"

XIV

On, on the vessel flies, the land is gone,
And winds are rude in Biscay's sleepless bay.
Four days are sped, but with the fifth, anon,
New shores descried make every bosom gay;
And Cintra's mountain greets them on their way,
And Tagus dashing onward to the Deep,
His fabled golden tribute bent to pay;
And soon on board the Lusian pilots leap,
And steer 'twixt fertile shores where yet few rustics reap.

XV

Oh, Christ! it is a goodly sight to see
What Heaven hath done for this delicious land!
What fruits of fragrance blush on every tree!
What goodly prospects o'er the hills expand!
But man would mar them with an impious hand:
And when the Almighty lifts his fiercest scourge
'Gainst those who most transgress his high command,

With treble vengeance will his hot shafts urge
Gaul's locust host, and earth from fellest foemen purge

XVI

What beauties doth Lisboa first unfold!
Her image floating on that noble tide,
Which poets vainly pave with sands of gold,
But now whereon a thousand keels did ride
Of mighty strength, since Albion was allied,
And to the Lusians did her aid afford:
A nation swoln with ignorance and pride,
Who lick yet loathe the hand that waves the sword
To save them from the wrath of Gaul's unsparing lord.

XVII

But whoso entereth within this town,
That, sheening far, celestial seems to be,
Disconsolate will wander up and down,
'Mid many things unsightly to strange ee;
For hut and palace show like filthily:
The dingy denizens are reared in dirt;
Ne personage of high or mean degree
Doth care for cleanness of surtout or shirt,
Though shent with Egypt's plague, unkempt, unwashed, unhurt.

XVIII

Poor, paltry slaves! yet born 'midst noblest scenes —
Why, Nature, waste thy wonders on such men?
Lo! Cintra's glorious Eden intervenes
In variegated maze of mount and glen.
Ah, me! what hand can pencil guide, or pen,
To follow half on which the eye dilates
Through views more dazzling unto mortal ken
Than those whereof such things the Bard relates,
Who to the awe-struck world unlocked Elysium's gates.

XIX

The horrid crags, by toppling convent crowned,
The cork-trees hoar that clothe the shaggy steep,
The mountain-moss by scorching skies imbrowned,
The sunken glen, whose sunless shrubs must weep,
The tender azure of the unruffled deep,
The orange tints that gild the greenest bough,

The torrents that from cliff to valley leap,
The vine on high, the willow branch below,
Mixed in one mighty scene, with varied beauty glow.

XX

Then slowly climb the many-winding way,
And frequent turn to linger as you go,
From loftier rocks new loveliness survey,
And rest ye at "Our Lady's house of Woe;"
Where frugal monks their little relics show,
And sundry legends to the stranger tell:
Here impious men have punished been, and lo!
Deep in yon cave Honorius long did dwell,
In hope to merit Heaven by making earth a Hell.

XXI

And here and there, as up the crags you spring,
Mark many rude-carved crosses near the path:
Yet deem not these Devotion's offering —
These are memorials frail of murderous wrath:
For wheresoe'er the shrieking victim hath
Pour'd forth his blood beneath the assassin's knife,
Some hand erects a cross of mouldering lath;
And grove and glen with thousand such are rife
Throughout this purple land, where Law secures not life.

XXII

On sloping mounds, or in the vale beneath,
Are domes where whilome kings did make repair;
But now the wild flowers round them only breathe:
Yet ruined Splendour still is lingering there.
And yonder towers the Prince's palace fair:
There thou too, Vathek! England's wealthiest son,
Once formed thy Paradise, as not aware
When wanton Wealth her mightiest deeds hath done,
Meek Peace voluptuous lures was ever wont to shun.

XXIII

Here didst thou dwell, here schemes of pleasure plan,
Beneath yon mountain's ever beauteous brow:
But now, as if a thing unblest by Man,
Thy fairy dwelling is as lone as Thou!
Here giant weeds a passage scarce allow

To Halls deserted, portals gaping wide:
Fresh lessons to the thinking bosom, how
Vain are the pleasaunces on earth supplied;
Swept into wrecks anon by Time's ungentle tide!

XXIV

Behold the hall where chiefs were late convened!
Oh! dome displeasing unto British eye!
With diadem hight Foolscap, lo! a Fiend,
A little Fiend that scoffs incessantly,
There sits in parchment robe arrayed, and by
His side is hung a seal and sable scroll,
Where blazoned glare names known to chivalry,
And sundry signatures adorn the roll,
Whereat the Urchin points and laughs with all his soul.

XXV

Convention is the dwarfish demon styled
That foiled the knights in Marialva's dome:
Of brains (if brains they had) he them beguiled,
And turned a nation's shallow joy to gloom.
Here Folly dashed to earth the victor's plume,
And Policy regained what arms had lost:
For chiefs like ours in vain may laurels bloom!
Woe to the conquering, not the conquered host,
Since baffled Triumph droops on Lusitania's coast.

XXVI

And ever since that martial Synod met,
Britannia sickens, Cintra! at thy name;
And folks in office at the mention fret,
And fain would blush, if blush they could, for shame.
How will Posterity the deed proclaim!
Will not our own and fellow-nations sneer,
To view these champions cheated of their fame,
By foes in fight o'erthrown, yet victors here,
Where Scorn her finger points through many a coming year?

XXVII

So deemed the Childe, as o'er the mountains he
Did take his way in solitary guise:
Sweet was the scene, yet soon he thought to flee,
More restless than the swallow in the skies:

Though here awhile he learned to moralise,
For Meditation fixed at times on him;
And conscious Reason whispered to despise
His early youth, misspent in maddest whim;
But as he gazed on truth his aching eyes grew dim.

XXVIII

To horse! to horse! he quits, for ever quits
A scene of peace, though soothing to his soul:
Again he rouses from his moping fits,
But seeks not now the harlot and the bowl.
Onward he flies, nor fixed as yet the goal
Where he shall rest him on his pilgrimage;
And o'er him many changing scenes must roll
Ere toil his thirst for travel can assuage,
Or he shall calm his breast, or learn experience sage.

XXIX

Yet Mafra shall one moment claim delay,
Where dwelt of yore the Lusians' luckless queen;
And Church and Court did mingle their array,
And Mass and revel were alternate seen;
Lordlings and freres — ill-sorted fry I ween!
But here the Babylonian Whore hath built
A dome, where flaunts she in such glorious sheen,
That men forget the blood which she hath spilt,
And bow the knee to Pomp that loves to varnish guilt.

XXX

O'er vales that teem with fruits, romantic hills,
(Oh, that such hills upheld a freeborn race!)
Whereon to gaze the eye with joyaunce fills,
Childe Harold wends through many a pleasant place.
Though sluggards deem it but a foolish chase,
And marvel men should quit their easy chair,
The toilsome way, and long, long league to trace,
Oh! there is sweetness in the mountain air,
And Life, that bloated Ease can never hope to share.

XXXI

More bleak to view the hills at length recede,
And, less luxuriant, smoother vales extend:
Immense horizon-bounded plains succeed!

Far as the eye discerns, withouten end,
Spain's realms appear whereon her shepherds tend
Flocks, whose rich fleece right well the trader knows —
Now must the Pastor's arm his *lambs* defend:
For Spain is compassed by unyielding foes,
And *all* must shield their *all*, or share Subjection's woes.

XXXII

Where Lusitania and her Sister meet,
Deem ye what bounds the rival realms divide?
Or ere the jealous Queens of Nations greet,
Doth Tayo interpose his mighty tide?
Or dark Sierras rise in craggy pride?
Or fence of art, like China's vasty wall? —
Ne barrier wall, ne river deep and wide,
Ne horrid crags, nor mountains dark and tall,
Rise like the rocks that part Hispania's land from Gaul:

XXXIII

But these between a silver streamlet glides,
And scarce a name distinguisheth the brook,
Though rival kingdoms press its verdant sides:
Here leans the idle shepherd on his crook,
And vacant on the rippling waves doth look,
That peaceful still 'twixt bitterest foemen flow;
For proud each peasant as the noblest duke:
Well doth the Spanish hind the difference know
'Twixt him and Lusian slave, the lowest of the low.

XXXIV

But ere the mingling bounds have far been passed,
Dark Guadiana rolls his power along
In sullen billows, murmuring and vast,
So noted ancient roundelays among.
Whilome upon his banks did legions throng
Of Moor and Knight, in mailéd splendour drest:
Here ceased the swift their race, here sunk the strong;
The Paynim turban and the Christian crest
Mixed on the bleeding stream, by floating hosts oppressed.

XXXV

Oh, lovely Spain! renowned, romantic Land!
Where is that standard which Pelagio bore,

When Cava's traitor-sire first called the band
That dyed thy mountain streams with Gothic gore?
Where are those bloody Banners which of yore
Waved o'er thy sons, victorious to the gale,
And drove at last the spoilers to their shore?
Red gleamed the Cross, and waned the Crescent pale,
While Afric's echoes thrilled with Moorish matrons' wail.

XXXVI

Teems not each ditty with the glorious tale?
Ah! such, alas! the hero's amplest fate!
When granite moulders and when records fail,
A peasant's plaint prolongs his dubious date.
Pride! bend thine eye from Heaven to thine estate,
See how the Mighty shrink into a song!
Can Volume, Pillar, Pile preserve thee great?
Or must thou trust Tradition's simple tongue,
When Flattery sleeps with thee, and History does thee wrong?

XXXVII

Awake, ye Sons of Spain! awake! advance!
Lo! Chivalry, your ancient Goddess, cries,
But wields not, as of old, her thirsty lance,
Nor shakes her crimson plumage in the skies:
Now on the smoke of blazing bolts she flies,
And speaks in thunder through yon engine's roar:
In every peal she calls — "Awake! arise!"
Say, is her voice more feeble than of yore,
When her war-song was heard on Andalusia's shore?

XXXVIII

Hark! — heard you not those hoofs of dreadful note?
Sounds not the clang of conflict on the heath?
Saw ye not whom the reeking sabre smote,
Nor saved your brethren ere they sank beneath
Tyrants and Tyrants' slaves? — the fires of Death,
The Bale-fires flash on high: — from rock to rock
Each volley tells that thousands cease to breathe;
Death rides upon the sulphury Siroc,
Red Battle stamps his foot, and Nations feel the shock.

XXXIX

Lo! where the Giant on the mountain stands,
His blood-red tresses deepening in the Sun,

With death-shot glowing in his fiery hands,
And eye that scorcheth all it glares upon;
Restless it rolls, now fixed, and now anon
Flashing afar, — and at his iron feet
Destruction cowers, to mark what deeds are done;
For on this morn three potent Nations meet,
To shed before his Shrine the blood he deems most sweet.

XL

By Heaven! it is a splendid sight to see
(For one who hath no friend, no brother there)
Their rival scarfs of mixed embroidery,
Their various arms that glitter in the air!
What gallant War-hounds rouse them from their lair,
And gnash their fangs, loud yelling for the prey!
All join the chase, but few the triumph share;
The Grave shall bear the chiefest prize away,
And Havoc scarce for joy can number their array.

XLI

Three hosts combine to offer sacrifice;
Three tongues prefer strange orisons on high;
Three gaudy standards flout the pale blue skies;
The shouts are France, Spain, Albion, Victory!
The Foe, the Victim, and the fond Ally
That fights for all, but ever fights in vain,
Are met — as if at home they could not die —
To feed the crow on Talavera's plain,
And fertilise the field that each pretends to gain.

XLII

There shall they rot — Ambition's honoured fools!
Yes, Honour decks the turf that wraps their clay!
Vain Sophistry! in these behold the tools,
The broken tools, that Tyrants cast away
By myriads, when they dare to pave their way
With human hearts — to what? — a dream alone.
Can Despots compass aught that hails their sway?
Or call with truth one span of earth their own,
Save that wherein at last they crumble bone by bone?

XLIII

Oh, Albuera! glorious field of grief!
As o'er thy plain the Pilgrim pricked his steed,

Who could foresee thee, in a space so brief,
A scene where mingling foes should boast and bleed!
Peace to the perished! may the warrior's meed
And tears of triumph their reward prolong!
Till others fall where other chieftains lead
Thy name shall circle round the gaping throng,
And shine in worthless lays, the theme of transient song.

XLIV

Enough of Battle's minions! let them play
Their game of lives, and barter breath for fame:
Fame that will scarce reanimate their clay,
Though thousands fall to deck some single name.
In sooth 'twere sad to thwart their noble aim
Who strike, blest hirelings! for their country's good,
And die, that living might have proved her shame;
Perished, perchance, in some domestic feud,
Or in a narrower sphere wild Rapine's path pursued.

XLV

Full swiftly Harold wends his lonely way
Where proud Sevilla triumphs unsubdued:
Yet is she free? the Spoiler's wished-for prey!
Soon, soon shall Conquest's fiery foot intrude,
Blackening her lovely domes with traces rude.
Inevitable hour! 'Gainst fate to strive
Where Desolation plants her famished brood
Is vain, or Ilion, Tyre might yet survive,
And Virtue vanquish all, and Murder cease to thrive

XLVI

But all unconscious of the coming doom,
The feast, the song, the revel here abounds;
Strange modes of merriment the hours consume,
Nor bleed these patriots with their country's wounds:
Nor here War's clarion, but Love's rebeck sounds;
Here Folly still his votaries inthralls;
And young-eyed Lewdness walks her midnight rounds:
Girt with the silent crimes of Capitals,
Still to the last kind Vice clings to the tott'ring walls.

XLVII

Not so the rustic — with his trembling mate
He lurks, nor casts his heavy eye afar,

Lest he should view his vineyard desolate,
Blasted below the dun hot breath of War.
No more beneath soft Eve's consenting star
Fandango twirls his jocund castanet:
Ah, Monarchs! could ye taste the mirth ye mar,
Not in the toils of Glory would ye fret;
The hoarse dull drum would sleep, and Man be happy yet!

XLVIII

How carols now the lusty muleteer?
Of Love, Romance, Devotion is his lay,
As whilome he was wont the leagues to cheer,
His quick bells wildly jingling on the way?
No! as he speeds, he chants "Vivā el Rey!"
And checks his song to execrate Godoy,
The royal wittol Charles, and curse the day
When first Spain's queen beheld the black-eyed boy,
And gore-faced Treason sprung from her adulterate joy.

XLIX

On yon long level plain, at distance crowned
With crags, whereon those Moorish turrets rest,
Wide-scattered hoof-marks dint the wounded ground;
And, scathed by fire, the greensward's darkened vest
Tells that the foe was Andalusia's guest:
Here was the camp, the watch-flame, and the host,
Here the bold peasant stormed the Dragon's nest;
Still does he mark it with triumphant boast,
And points to yonder cliffs, which oft were won and lost.

L

And whomsoe'er along the path you meet
Bears in his cap the badge of crimson hue,
Which tells you whom to shun and whom to greet:
Woe to the man that walks in public view
Without of loyalty this token true:
Sharp is the knife, and sudden is the stroke;
And sorely would the Gallic foeman rue,
If subtle poniards, wrapt beneath the cloke,
Could blunt the sabre's edge, or clear the cannon's smoke.

LI

At every turn Morena's dusky height
Sustains aloft the battery's iron load;

And, far as mortal eye can compass sight,
The mountain-howitzer, the broken road,
The bristling palisade, the fosse o'erflowed,
The stationed bands, the never-vacant watch,
The magazine in rocky durance stowed,
The holstered steed beneath the shed of thatch,
The ball-piled pyramid, the ever-blazing match,

LII

Portend the deeds to come: — but he whose nod
Has tumbled feebler despots from their sway,
A moment pauseth ere he lifts the rod;
A little moment deigneth to delay:
Soon will his legions sweep through these their way;
The West must own the Scourger of the world.
Ah! Spain! how sad will be thy reckoning-day,
When soars Gaul's Vulture, with his wings unfurled,
And thou shalt view thy sons in crowds to Hades hurled.

LIII

And must they fall? the young, the proud, the brave,
To swell one bloated Chief's unwholesome reign?
No step between submission and a grave?
The rise of Rapine and the fall of Spain?
And doth the Power that man adores ordain
Their doom, nor heed the suppliant's appeal?
Is all that desperate Valour acts in vain?
And Counsel sage, and patriotic Zeal —
The Veteran's skill — Youth's fire — and Manhood's heart of steel?

LIV

Is it for this the Spanish maid, aroused,
Hangs on the willow her unstrung guitar,
And, all unsexed, the Anlace hath espoused,
Sung the loud song, and dared the deed of war?
And she, whom once the semblance of a scar
Appalled, an owlet's 'larum chilled with dread,
Now views the column-scattering bay'net jar,
The falchion flash, and o'er the yet warm dead
Stalks with Minerva's step where Mars might quake to tread.

LV

Ye who shall marvel when you hear her tale,
Oh! had you known her in her softer hour,

Marked her black eye that mocks her coal-black veil,
Heard her light, lively tones in Lady's bower,
Seen her long locks that foil the painter's power,
Her fairy form, with more than female grace,
Scarce would you deem that Saragoza's tower
Beheld her smile in Danger's Gorgon face,
Thin the closed ranks, and lead in Glory's fearful chase.

LVI

Her lover sinks — she sheds no ill-timed tear;
Her Chief is slain — she fills his fatal post;
Her fellows flee — she checks their base career;
The Foe retires — she heads the sallying host:
Who can appease like her a lover's ghost?
Who can avenge so well a leader's fall?
What maid retrieve when man's flushed hope is lost?
Who hang so fiercely on the flying Gaul,
Foiled by a woman's hand, before a battered wall?

LVII

Yet are Spain's maids no race of Amazons,
But formed for all the witching arts of love:
Though thus in arms they emulate her sons,
And in the horrid phalanx dare to move,
'Tis but the tender fierceness of the dove,
Pecking the hand that hovers o'er her mate:
Remoter females, famed for sickening prate;
Her mind is nobler sure, her charms perchance as great.

LVIII

The seal Love's dimpling finger hath impressed
Denotes how soft that chin which bears his touch:
Her lips, whose kisses pout to leave their nest,
Bid man be valiant ere he merit such:
Her glance how wildly beautiful! how much
Hath Phœbus wooed in vain to spoil her cheek,
Which glows yet smoother from his amorous clutch!
Who round the North for paler dames would seek?
How poor their forms appear! how languid, wan, and weak!

LIX

Match me, ye climes! which poets love to laud;
Match me, ye harems of the land! where now
I strike my strain, far distant, to applaud

Beauties that ev'n a cynic must avow;
Match me those Houries, whom ye scarce allow
To taste the gale lest Love should ride the wind,
With Spain's dark-glancing daughters — deign to know,
There your wise Prophet's Paradise we find,
His black-eyed maids of Heaven, angelically kind.

LX

Oh, thou Parnassus! whom I now survey,
Not in the phrensy of a dreamer's eye,
Not in the fabled landscape of a lay,
But soaring snow-clad through thy native sky,
In the wild pomp of mountain-majesty!
What marvel if I thus essay to sing?
The humblest of thy pilgrims passing by
Would gladly woo thine Echoes with his string,
Though from thy heights no more one Muse will wave her wing.

LXI

Oft have I dreamed of Thee! whose glorious name
Who knows not, knows not man's divinest lore:
And now I view thee — 'tis, alas, with shame
That I in feeblest accents must adore.
When I recount thy worshippers of yore
I tremble, and can only bend the knee;
Nor raise my voice, nor vainly dare to soar,
But gaze beneath thy cloudy canopy
In silent joy to think at last I look on Thee!

LXII

Happier in this than mightiest Bards have been,
Whose Fate to distant homes confined their lot,
Shall I unmoved behold the hallowed scene,
Which others rave of, though they know it not?
Though here no more Apollo haunts his Grot,
And thou, the Muses' seat, art now their grave,
Some gentle Spirit still pervades the spot,
Sighs in the gale, keeps silence in the Cave,
And glides with glassy foot o'er yon melodious wave.

LXIII

Of thee hereafter. — Ev'n amidst my strain
I turned aside to pay my homage here;
Forgot the land, the sons, the maids of Spain;

Her fate, to every freeborn bosom dear;
And hailed thee, not perchance without a tear.
Now to my theme — but from thy holy haunt
Let me some remnant, some memorial bear;
Yield me one leaf of Daphne's deathless plant,
Nor let thy votary's hope be deemed an idle vaunt.

LXIV

But ne'er didst thou, fair Mount! when Greece was young,
See round thy giant base a brighter choir,
Nor e'er did Delphi, when her Priestess sung
The Pythian hymn with more than mortal fire,
Behold a train more fitting to inspire
The song of love, than Andalusia's maids,
Nurst in the glowing lap of soft Desire:
Ah! that to these were given such peaceful shades
As Greece can still bestow, though Glory fly her glades.

LXV

Fair is proud Seville; let her country boast
Her strength, her wealth, her site of ancient days;
But Cadiz, rising on the distant coast,
Calls forth a sweeter, though ignoble praise.
Ah, Vice! how soft are thy voluptuous ways!
While boyish blood is mantling, who can 'scape
The fascination of thy magic gaze?
A Cherub-Hydra round us dost thou gape,
And mould to every taste thy dear delusive shape.

LXVI

When Paphos fell by Time — accurséd Time!
The Queen who conquers all must yield to thee —
The Pleasures fled, but sought as warm a clime;
And Venus, constant to her native Sea,
To nought else constant, hither deigned to flee,
And fixed her shrine within these walls of white:
Though not to one dome circumscribeth She
Her worship, but, devoted to her rite,
A thousand Altars rise, for ever blazing bright.

LXVII

From morn till night, from night till startled Morn
Peeps blushing on the Revel's laughing crew,
The Song is heard, the rosy Garland worn;

Devices quaint, and Frolics ever new,
Tread on each other's kibes. A long adieu
He bids to sober joy that here sojourns:
Nought interrupts the riot, though in lieu
Of true devotion monkish incense burns,
And Love and Prayer unite, or rule the hour by turns.

LXVIII

The Sabbath comes, a day of blessed rest:
What hallows it upon this Christian shore?
Lo! it is sacred to a solemn Feast:
Hark! heard you not the forest-monarch's roar?
Crashing the lance, he snuffs the spouting gore
Of man and steed, o'erthrown beneath his horn;
The thronged arena shakes with shouts for more;
Yells the mad crowd o'er entrails freshly torn,
Nor shrinks the female eye, nor ev'n affects to mourn.

LXIX

The seventh day this — the Jubilee of man!
London! right well thou know'st the day of prayer:
Then thy spruce citizen, washed artisan,
And smug apprentice gulp their weekly air:
Thy coach of hackney, whiskey, one-horse chair,
And humblest gig through sundry suburbs whirl,
To Hampstead, Brentford, Harrow make repair;
Till the tired jade the wheel forgets to hurl,
Provoking envious gibe from each pedestrian churl.

LXX

Some o'er thy Thamis row the ribboned fair,
Others along the safer turnpike fly;
Some Richmond-hill ascend, some scud to Ware,
And many to the steep of Highgate hie.
Ask ye, Bœotian Shades! the reason why?
'Tis to the worship of the solemn Horn,
Grasped in the holy hand of Mystery,
In whose dread name both men and maids are sworn,
And consecrate the oath with draught, and dance till morn.

LXXI

All have their fooleries — not alike are thine,
Fair Cadiz, rising o'er the dark blue sea!
Soon as the Matin bell proclaimeth nine,

Thy Saint-adorers count the Rosary:
Much is the VIRGIN teased to shrive them free
(Well do I ween the only virgin there)
From crimes as numerous as her beadsmen be;
Then to the crowded circus forth they fare:
Young, old, high, low, at once the same diversion share.

LXXII

The lists are oped, the spacious area cleared,
Thousands on thousands piled are seated round;
Long ere the first loud trumpet's note is heard,
Ne vacant space for lated wight is found:
Here Dons, Grandees, but chiefly Dames abound,
Skilled in the ogle of a roguish eye,
Yet ever well inclined to heal the wound;
None through their cold disdain are doomed to die,
As moon-struck bards complain, by Love's sad archery.

LXXIII

Hushed is the din of tongues — on gallant steeds,
With milk-white crest, gold spur, and light-poised lance,
Four cavaliers prepare for venturous deeds,
And lowly-bending to the lists advance;
Rich are their scarfs, their chargers featly prance:
If in the dangerous game they shine to-day,
The crowd's loud shout and ladies' lovely glance,
Best prize of better acts! they bear away,
And all that kings or chiefs e'er gain their toils repay.

LXXIV

In costly sheen and gaudy cloak arrayed,
But all afoot, the light-limbed Matadore
Stands in the centre, eager to invade
The lord of lowing herds; but not before
The ground, with cautious tread, is traversed o'er,
Lest aught unseen should lurk to thwart his speed:
His arms a dart, he fights aloof, nor more
Can Man achieve without the friendly steed —
Alas! too oft condemned for him to bear and bleed.

LXXV

Thrice sounds the Clarion; lo! the signal falls,
The den expands, and Expectation mute
Gapes round the silent circle's peopled walls.

Bounds with one lashing spring the mighty brute,
And, wildly staring, spurns, with sounding foot,
The sand, nor blindly rushes on his foe:
Here, there, he points his threatening front, to suit
His first attack, wide-waving to and fro
His angry tail; red rolls his eye's dilated glow.

LXXVI

Sudden he stops — his eye is fixed — away —
Away, thou heedless boy! prepare the spear:
Now is thy time, to perish, or display
The skill that yet may check his mad career!
With well-timed croupe the nimble coursers veer;
On foams the Bull, but not unscathed he goes;
Streams from his flank the crimson torrent clear:
He flies, he wheels, distracted with his throes;
Dart follows dart — lance, lance — loud bellowings speak his woes.

LXXVII

Again he comes; nor dart nor lance avail,
Nor the wild plunging of the tortured horse;
Though Man and Man's avenging arms assail,
Vain are his weapons, vainer is his force.
One gallant steed is stretched a mangled corse;
Another, hideous sight! unseamed appears,
His gory chest unveils life's panting source;
Though death-struck, still his feeble frame he rears;
Staggering, but stemming all, his Lord unharmed he bears.

LXXVIII

Foiled, bleeding, breathless, furious to the last,
Full in the centre stands the Bull at bay,
Mid wounds, and clinging darts, and lances brast,
And foes disabled in the brutal fray:
And now the Matadores around him play,
Shake the red cloak, and poise the ready brand:
Once more through all he bursts his thundering way —
Vain rage! the mantle quits the conynge hand,
Wraps his fierce eye — 'tis past — he sinks upon the sand!

LXXIX

Where his vast neck just mingles with the spine,
Sheathed in his form the deadly weapon lies.
He stops — he starts — disdaining to decline:

Slowly he falls, amidst triumphant cries,
Without a groan, without a struggle dies.
The decorated car appears — on high
The corse is piled — sweet sight for vulgar eyes —
Four steeds that spurn the rein, as swift as shy,
Hurl the dark bulk along, scarce seen in dashing by.

LXXX

Such the ungentle sport that oft invites
The Spanish maid, and cheers the Spanish swain.
Nurtured in blood betimes, his heart delights
In vengeance, gloating on another's pain.
What private feuds the troubled village stain!
Though now one phalanxed host should meet the foe,
Enough, alas! in humble homes remain,
To meditate 'gainst friend the secret blow,
For some slight cause of wrath, whence Life's warm stream must flow.

LXXXI

But Jealousy has fled: his bars, his bolts,
His withered Centinel, Duenna sage!
And all whereat the generous soul revolts,
Which the stern dotard deemed he could encage,
Have passed to darkness with the vanished age.
Who late so free as Spanish girls were seen,
(Ere War uprose in his volcanic rage,)
With braided tresses bounding o'er the green,
While on the gay dance shone Night's lover-loving Queen?

LXXXII

Oh! many a time and oft, had Harold loved,
Or dreamed he loved, since Rapture is a dream;
But now his wayward bosom was unmoved,
For not yet had he drunk of Lethe's stream;
And lately had he learned with truth to deem
Love has no gift so grateful as his wings:
How fair, how young, how soft soe'er he seem,
Full from the fount of Joy's delicious springs
Some bitter o'er the flowers its bubbling venom flings.

LXXXIII

Yet to the beauteous form he was not blind,
Though now it moved him as it moves the wise;
Not that Philosophy on such a mind

E'er deigned to bend her chastely-awful eyes:
But Passion raves herself to rest, or flies;
And Vice, that digs her own voluptuous tomb,
Had buried long his hopes, no more to rise:
Pleasure's palled Victim! life-abhorring Gloom
Wrote on his faded brow curst Cain's unresting doom.

LXXXIV

Still he beheld, nor mingled with the throng;
But viewed them not with misanthropic hate:
Fain would he now have joined the dance, the song;
But who may smile that sinks beneath his fate?
Nought that he saw his sadness could abate:
Yet once he struggled 'gainst the Demon's sway,
And as in Beauty's bower he pensive sate,
Poured forth his unpremeditated lay,
To charms as fair as those that soothed his happier day.

TO INEZ

1

NAY, smile not at my sullen brow;
Alas! I cannot smile again:
Yet Heaven avert that ever thou
Shouldst weep, and haply weep in vain.

2

And dost thou ask what secret woe
I bear, corroding Joy and Youth?
And wilt thou vainly seek to know
A pang, ev'n thou must fail to soothe?

3

It is not love, it is not hate,
Nor low Ambition's honours lost,
That bids me loathe my present state,
And fly from all I prized the most:

4

It is that weariness which springs
From all I meet, or hear, or see:

To me no pleasure Beauty brings;
  Thine eyes have scarce a charm for me.

5

It is that settled, ceaseless gloom
  The fabled Hebrew Wanderer bore;
That will not look beyond the tomb,
  But cannot hope for rest before.

6

What Exile from himself can flee?
  To zones though more and more remote,
Still, still pursues, where'er I be,
  The blight of Life — the Demon Thought.

7

Yet others rapt in pleasure seem,
  And taste of all that I forsake;
Oh! may they still of transport dream,
  And ne'er — at least like me — awake!

8

Through many a clime 'tis mine to go,
  With many a retrospection curst;
And all my solace is to know,
  Whate'er betides, I've known the worst.

9

What is that worst? Nay do not ask —
  In pity from the search forbear:
Smile on — nor venture to unmask
  Man's heart, and view the Hell that's there.

LXXXV

Adieu, fair Cadiz! yea, a long adieu!
  Who may forget how well thy walls have stood?
  When all were changing thou alone wert true,
  First to be free and last to be subdued:
  And if amidst a scene, a shock so rude,
  Some native blood was seen thy streets to dye,
  A Traitor only fell beneath the feud:

Here all were noble, save Nobility;
None hugged a Conqueror's chain, save fallen Chivalry!

LXXXVI

Such be the sons of Spain, and strange her Fate!
They fight for Freedom who were never free,
A Kingless people for a nerveless state;
Her vassals combat when their Chieftains flee,
True to the veriest slaves of Treachery:
Fond of a land which gave them nought but life,
Pride points the path that leads to Liberty;
Back to the struggle, baffled in the strife,
War, war is still the cry, "War even to the knife!"

LXXXVII

Ye, who would more of Spain and Spaniards know
Go, read whate'er is writ of bloodiest strife:
Whate'er keen Vengeance urged on foreign foe
Can act, is acting there against man's life:
From flashing scimitar to secret knife,
War mouldeth there each weapon to his need —
So may he guard the sister and the wife,
So may he make each curst oppressor bleed —
So may such foes deserve the most remorseless deed!

LXXXVIII

Flows there a tear of Pity for the dead?
Look o'er the ravage of the reeking plain;
Look on the hands with female slaughter red;
Then to the dogs resign the unburied slain,
Then to the vulture let each corse remain,
Albeit unworthy of the prey-bird's maw;
Let their bleached bones, and blood's unbleaching stain,
Long mark the battle-field with hideous awe:
Thus only may our sons conceive the scenes we saw!

LXXXIX

Nor yet, alas! the dreadful work is done;
Fresh legions pour adown the Pyrenees:
It deepens still, the work is scarce begun,
Nor mortal eye the distant end foresees.
Fall'n nations gaze on Spain; if freed, she frees
More than her fell Pizarros once enchained:

Strange retribution! now Columbia's ease
Repairs the wrongs that Quito's sons sustained,
While o'er the parent clime prowls Murder unrestrained.

XC

Not all the blood at Talavera shed,
Not all the marvels of Barossa's fight,
Not Albuera lavish of the dead,
Have won for Spain her well asserted right.
When shall her Olive-Branch be free from blight?
When shall she breathe her from the blushing toil?
How many a doubtful day shall sink in night,
Ere the Frank robber turn him from his spoil,
And Freedom's stranger-tree grow native of the soil!

XCI

And thou, my friend! — since unavailing woe
Bursts from my heart, and mingles with the strain —
Had the sword laid thee with the mighty low,
Pride might forbid e'en Friendship to complain:
But thus unlaurelled to descend in vain,
By all forgotten, save the lonely breast,
And mix unbleeding with the boasted slain,
While Glory crowns so many a meaner crest!
What hadst thou done to sink so peacefully to rest?

XCII

Oh, known the earliest, and esteemed the most!
Dear to a heart where nought was left so dear!
Though to my hopeless days for ever lost,
In dreams deny me not to see thee here!
And Morn in secret shall renew the tear
Of Consciousness awaking to her woes,
And Fancy hover o'er thy bloodless bier,
Till my frail frame return to whence it rose,
And mourned and mourner lie united in repose.

XCIII

Here is one fytte of Harold's pilgrimage:
Ye who of him may further seek to know,
Shall find some tidings in a future page,
If he that rhymeth now may scribble moe.
Is this too much? stern Critic! say not so:

Patience! and ye shall hear what he beheld
In other lands, where he was doomed to go:
Lands that contain the monuments of Eld,
Ere Greece and Grecian arts by barbarous hands were quelled.

CANTO THE SECOND

I

Come, blue-eyed Maid of Heaven! — but Thou, alas!
Didst never yet one mortal song inspire —
Goddess of Wisdom! here thy temple was,
And is, despite of War and wasting fire,
And years, that bade thy worship to expire:
But worse than steel, and flame, and ages slow,
Is the dread sceptre and dominion dire
Of men who never felt the sacred glow
That thoughts of thee and thine on polished breasts bestow.

II

Ancient of days! august Athena! where,
Where are thy men of might? thy grand in soul?
Gone — glimmering through the dream of things that were:
First in the race that led to Glory's goal,
They won, and passed away — is this the whole?
A schoolboy's tale, the wonder of an hour!
The Warrior's weapon and the Sophist's stole
Are sought in vain, and o'er each mouldering tower,
Dim with the mist of years, gray flits the shade of power.

III

Son of the Morning, rise! approach you here!
Come — but molest not yon defenceless Urn:
Look on this spot — a Nation's sepulchre!
Abode of Gods, whose shrines no longer burn.
Even Gods must yield — Religions take their turn:
'Twas Jove's — 'tis Mahomet's — and other Creeds
Will rise with other years, till Man shall learn
Vainly his incense soars, his victim bleeds;
Poor child of Doubt and Death, whose hope is built on reeds.

IV

Bound to the Earth, he lifts his eye to Heaven —
Is 't not enough, Unhappy Thing! to know

Thou art? Is this a boon so kindly given,
That being, thou would'st be again, and go,
Thou know'st not, reck'st not to what region, so
On Earth no more, but mingled with the skies?
Still wilt thou dream on future Joy and Woe?
Regard and weigh yon dust before it flies:
That little urn saith more than thousand Homilies.

V

Or burst the vanished Hero's lofty mound;
Far on the solitary shore he sleeps:
He fell, and falling nations mourned around;
But now not one of saddening thousands weeps,
Nor warlike worshipper his vigil keeps
Where demi-gods appeared, as records tell.
Remove yon skull from out the scattered heaps:
Is that a Temple where a God may dwell?
Why ev'n the Worm at last disdains her shattered cell!

VI

Look on its broken arch, its ruined wall,
Its chambers desolate, and portals foul:
Yes, this was once Ambition's airy hall,
The Dome of Thought, the Palace of the Soul:
Behold through each lack-lustre, eyeless hole,
The gay recess of Wisdom and of Wit
And Passion's host, that never brooked control:
Can all Saint, Sage, or Sophist ever writ,
People this lonely tower, this tenement refit?

VII

Well didst thou speak, Athena's wisest son!
"All that we know is, nothing can be known."
Why should we shrink from what we cannot shun?
Each hath its pang, but feeble sufferers groan
With brain-born dreams of Evil all their own.
Pursue what Chance or Fate proclaimeth best;
Peace waits us on the shores of Acheron:
There no forced banquet claims the sated guest,
But Silence spreads the couch of ever welcome Rest.

VIII

Yet if, as holiest men have deemed, there be
A land of Souls beyond that sable shore,

To shame the Doctrine of the Sadducee
And Sophists, madly vain of dubious lore;
How sweet it were in concert to adore
With those who made our mortal labours light!
To hear each voice we feared to hear no more!
Behold each mighty shade revealed to sight,
The Bactrian, Samian sage, and all who taught the Right!

IX

There, Thou! — whose Love and Life together fled,
Have left me here to love and live in vain —
Twined with my heart, and can I deem thee dead
When busy Memory flashes on my brain?
Well — I will dream that we may meet again,
And woo the vision to my vacant breast:
If aught of young Remembrance then remain,
Be as it may Futurity's behest,
For me 'twere bliss enough to know thy spirit blest!

X

Here let me sit upon this massy stone,
The marble column's yet unshaken base;
Here, son of Saturn! was thy favourite throne:
Mightiest of many such! Hence let me trace
The latent grandeur of thy dwelling-place.
It may not be: nor ev'n can Fancy's eye
Restore what Time hath laboured to deface.
Yet these proud Pillars claim no passing sigh;
Unmoved the Moslem sits, the light Greek carols by.

XI

But who, of all the plunderers of yon Fane
On high — where Pallas linger'd, loth to flee
The latest relic of her ancient reign —
The last, the worst, dull spoiler, who was he?
Blush, Caledonia! such thy son could be!
England! I joy no child he was of thine:
Thy free-born men should spare what once was free;
Yet they could violate each saddening shrine,
And bear these altars o'er the long-reluctant brine.

XII

But most the modern Pict's ignoble boast,
To rive what Goth, and Turk, and Time hath spared:

Cold as the crags upon his native coast,
His mind as barren and his heart as hard,
Is he whose head conceived, whose hand prepared,
Aught to displace Athenæ's poor remains:
Her Sons too weak the sacred shrine to guard,
Yet felt some portion of their Mother's pains,
And never knew, till then, the weight of Despot's chains.

XIII

What! shall it e'er be said by British tongue,
Albion was happy in Athena's tears?
Though in thy name the slaves her bosom wrung,
Tell not the deed to blushing Europe's ears;
The Ocean Queen, the free Britannia, bears
The last poor plunder from a bleeding land:
Yes, she, whose generous aid her name endears,
Tore down those remnants with a Harpy's hand,
Which envious Eld forbore, and tyrants left to stand.

XIV

Where was thine Ægis, Pallas! that appalled
Stern Alaric and Havoc on their way?
Where Peleus' son? whom Hell in vain enthralled,
His shade from Hades upon that dread day
Bursting to light in terrible array!
What! could not Pluto spare the Chief once more,
To scare a second robber from his prey?
Idly he wandered on the Stygian shore,
Nor now preserved the walls he loved to shield before.

XV

Cold is the heart, fair Greece! that looks on Thee,
Nor feels as Lovers o'er the dust they loved;
Dull is the eye that will not weep to see
Thy walls defaced, thy mouldering shrines removed
By British hands, which it had best behoved
To guard those relics ne'er to be restored: —
Curst be the hour when from their isle they roved,
And once again thy hapless bosom gored,
And snatched thy shrinking Gods to Northern climes abhorred!

XVI

But where is Harold? shall I then forget
To urge the gloomy Wanderer o'er the wave?

Little recked he of all that Men regret;
No loved-one now in feigned lament could rave;
No friend the parting hand extended gave,
Ere the cold Stranger passed to other climes:
Hard is his heart whom charms may not enslave;
But Harold felt not as in other times,
And left without a sigh the land of War and Crimes.

XVII

He that has sailed upon the dark blue sea
Has viewed at times, I ween, a full fair sight,
When the fresh breeze is fair as breeze may be,
The white sail set, the gallant Frigate tight —
Masts, spires, and strand retiring to the right,
The glorious Main expanding o'er the bow,
The Convoy spread like wild swans in their flight,
The dullest sailer wearing bravely now —
So gaily curl the waves before each dashing prow.

XVIII

And oh, the little warlike world within!
The well-reeved guns, the netted canopy,
The hoarse command, the busy humming din,
When, at a word, the tops are manned on high:
Hark, to the Boatswain's call, the cheering cry!
While through the seaman's hand the tackle glides;
Or schoolboy Midshipman that, standing by,
Strains his shrill pipe as good or ill betides,
And well the docile crew that skilful Urchin guides.

XIX

White is the glassy deck, without a stain,
Where on the watch the staid Lieutenant walks:
Look on that part which sacred doth remain
For the lone Chieftain, who majestic stalks,
Silent and feared by all — not oft he talks
With aught beneath him, if he would preserve
That strict restraint, which broken, ever balks
Conquest and Fame: but Britons rarely swerve
From law, however stern, which tends their strength to nerve.

XX

Blow! swiftly blow, thou keel-compelling gale!
Till the broad Sun withdraws his lessening ray;

Then must the Pennant-bearer slacken sail,
That lagging barks may make their lazy way.
Ah! grievance sore, and listless dull delay,
To waste on sluggish hulks the sweetest breeze!
What leagues are lost, before the dawn of day,
Thus loitering pensive on the willing seas,
The flapping sail hauled down to halt for logs like these!

XXI

The Moon is up; by Heaven, a lovely eve!
Long streams of light o'er dancing waves expand;
Now lads on shore may sigh, and maids believe:
Such be our fate when we return to land!
Meantime some rude Arion's restless hand
Wakes the brisk harmony that sailors love;
A circle there of merry listeners stand
Or to some well-known measure featly move,
Thoughtless, as if on shore they still were free to rove.

XXII

Through Calpe's straits survey the steepy shore;
Europe and Afric on each other gaze!
Lands of the dark-eyed Maid and dusky Moor
Alike beheld beneath pale Hecate's blaze:
How softly on the Spanish shore she plays!
Disclosing rock, and slope, and forest brown,
Distinct, though darkening with her waning phase;
But Mauritania's giant-shadows frown,
From mountain-cliff to coast descending sombre down.

XXIII

'Tis night, when Meditation bids us feel
We once have loved, though Love is at an end:
The Heart, lone mourner of its baffled zeal,
Though friendless now, will dream it had a friend.
Who with the weight of years would wish to bend,
When Youth itself survives young Love and Joy?
Alas! when mingling souls forget to blend,
Death hath but little left him to destroy!
Ah! happy years! once more who would not be a boy?

XXIV

Thus bending o'er the vessel's laving side,
To gaze on Dian's wave-reflected sphere,

The Soul forgets her schemes of Hope and Pride,
And flies unconscious o'er each backward year;
None are so desolate but something dear,
Dearer than self, possesses or possessed
A thought, and claims the homage of a tear;
A flashing pang! of which the weary breast
Would still, albeit in vain, the heavy heart divest.

XXV

To sit on rocks — to muse o'er flood and fell —
To slowly trace the forest's shady scene,
Where things that own not Man's dominion dwell,
And mortal foot hath ne'er or rarely been;
To climb the trackless mountain all unseen,
With the wild flock that never needs a fold;
Alone o'er steeps and foaming falls to lean;
This is not Solitude — 'tis but to hold
Converse with Nature's charms, and view her stores unrolled.

XXVI

But midst the crowd, the hum, the shock of men,
To hear, to see, to feel, and to possess,
And roam along, the World's tired denizen,
With none who bless us, none whom we can bless;
Minions of Splendour shrinking from distress!
None that, with kindred consciousness endued,
If we were not, would seem to smile the less,
Of all that flattered — followed — sought, and sued;
This is to be alone — This, This is Solitude!

XXVII

More blest the life of godly Eremite,
Such as on lonely Athos may be seen,
Watching at eve upon the Giant Height,
Which looks o'er waves so blue, skies so serene,
That he who there at such an hour hath been
Will wistful linger on that hallowed spot;
Then slowly tear him from the 'witching scene,
Sigh forth one wish that such had been his lot,
Then turn to hate a world he had almost forgot.

XXVIII

Pass we the long unvarying course, the track
Oft trod, that never leaves a trace behind;

Pass we the calm — the gale — the change — the tack,
And each well known caprice of wave and wind;
Pass we the joys and sorrows sailors find,
Cooped in their wingéd sea-girt citadel;
The foul — the fair — the contrary — the kind —
As breezes rise and fall and billows swell,
Till on some jocund morn — lo, Land! and All is well!

XXIX

But not in silence pass Calypso's isles,
The sister tenants of the middle deep;
There for the weary still a Haven smiles,
Though the fair Goddess long hath ceased to weep,
And o'er her cliffs a fruitless watch to keep
For him who dared prefer a mortal bride:
Here, too, his boy essayed the dreadful leap
Stern Mentor urged from high to yonder tide;
While thus of both bereft, the Nymph-Queen doubly sighed.

XXX

Her reign is past, her gentle glories gone:
But trust not this; too easy Youth, beware!
A mortal Sovereign holds her dangerous throne,
And thou may'st find a new Calypso there.
Sweet Florence! could another ever share
This wayward, loveless heart, it would be thine:
But checked by every tie, I may not dare
To cast a worthless offering at thy shrine,
Nor ask so dear a breast to feel one pang for *mine*.

XXXI

Thus Harold deemed, as on that Lady's eye
He looked, and met its beam without a thought,
Save Admiration glancing harmless by:
Love kept aloof, albeit not far remote,
Who knew his Votary often lost and caught,
But knew him as his Worshipper no more,
And ne'er again the Boy his bosom sought:
Since now he vainly urged him to adore,
Well deemed the little God his ancient sway was o'er.

XXXII

Fair Florence found, in sooth with some amaze,
One who, 'twas said, still sighed to all he saw,

Withstand, unmoved, the lustre of her gaze,
Which others hailed with real or mimic awe,
Their hope, their doom, their punishment, their law;
All that gay Beauty from her bondsmen claims:
And much she marvelled that a youth so raw
Nor felt, nor feigned at least, the oft-told flames,
Which though sometimes they frown, yet rarely anger dames.

XXXIII

Little knew she that seeming marble heart,
Now masked in silence or withheld by Pride,
Was not unskilful in the spoiler's art,
And spread its snares licentious far and wide;
Nor from the base pursuit had turned aside,
As long as aught was worthy to pursue:
But Harold on such arts no more relied;
And had he doted on those eyes so blue,
Yet never would he join the lover's whining crew.

XXXIV

Not much he kens, I ween, of Woman's breast,
Who thinks that wanton thing is won by sighs;
What careth she for hearts when once possessed?
Do proper homage to thine Idol's eyes;
But not too humbly, or she will despise
Thee and thy suit, though told in moving tropes:
Disguise ev'n tenderness, if thou art wise;
Brisk Confidence still best with woman copes:
Pique her and soothe in turn — soon Passion crowns thy hopes.

XXXV

'Tis an old lesson — Time approves it true,
And those who know it best, deplore it most;
When all is won that all desire to woo,
The paltry prize is hardly worth the cost:
Youth wasted — Minds degraded — Honour lost —
These are thy fruits, successful Passion! these!
If, kindly cruel, early Hope is crost,
Still to the last it rankles, a disease,
Not to be cured when Love itself forgets to please.

XXXVI

Away! nor let me loiter in my song,
For we have many a mountain-path to tread,

And many a varied shore to sail along,
By pensive Sadness, not by Fiction, led —
Climes, fair withal as ever mortal head
Imagined in its little schemes of thought;
Or e'er in new Utopias were ared,
To teach Man what he might be, or he ought —
If that corrupted thing could ever such be taught.

XXXVII

Dear Nature is the kindest mother still!
Though always changing, in her aspect mild;
From her bare bosom let me take my fill,
Her never-weaned, though not her favoured child.
Oh! she is fairest in her features wild,
Where nothing polished dares pollute her path:
To me by day or night she ever smiled,
Though I have marked her when none other hath,
And sought her more and more, and loved her best in wrath.

XXXVIII

Land of Albania! where Iskander rose,
Theme of the young, and beacon of the wise,
And he his namesake, whose oft-baffled foes
Shrunk from his deeds of chivalrous emprize:
Land of Albania! let me bend mine eyes
On thee, thou rugged Nurse of savage men!
The Cross descends, thy Minarets arise,
And the pale Crescent sparkles in the glen,
Through many a cypress-grove within each city's ken.

XXXIX

Childe Harold sailed, and passed the barren spot,
Where sad Penelope o'erlooked the wave;
And onward viewed the mount, not yet forgot,
The Lover's refuge, and the Lesbian's grave.
Dark Sappho! could not Verse immortal save
That breast imbued with such immortal fire?
Could she not live who life eternal gave?
If life eternal may await the lyre,
That only Heaven to which Earth's children may aspire.

XL

'Twas on a Grecian autumn's gentle eve
Childe Harold hailed Leucadia's cape afar;

A spot he longed to see, nor cared to leave:
Oft did he mark the scenes of vanished war,
Actium — Lepanto — fatal Trafalgar;
Mark them unmoved, for he would not delight
(Born beneath some remote inglorious star)
In themes of bloody fray, or gallant fight,
But loathed the bravo's trade, and laughed at martial wight.

XLI

But when he saw the Evening star above
Leucadia's far-projecting rock of woe,
And hailed the last resort of fruitless love,
He felt, or deemed he felt, no common glow:
And as the stately vessel glided slow
Beneath the shadow of that ancient mount,
He watched the billows' melancholy flow,
And, sunk albeit in thought as he was wont,
More placid seemed his eye, and smooth his pallid front.

XLII

Morn dawns; and with it stern Albania's hills,
Dark Suli's rocks, and Pindus' inland peak,
Robed half in mist, bedewed with snowy rills,
Arrayed in many a dun and purple streak,
Arise; and, as the clouds along them break,
Disclose the dwelling of the mountaineer:
Here roams the wolf — the eagle whets his beak —
Birds — beasts of prey — and wilder men appear,
And gathering storms around convulse the closing year.

XLIII

Now Harold felt himself at length alone,
And bade to Christian tongues a long adieu;
Now he adventured on a shore unknown,
Which all admire, but many dread to view:
His breast was armed 'gainst fate, his wants were few;
Peril he sought not, but ne'er shrank to meet:
The scene was savage, but the scene was new;
This made the ceaseless toil of travel sweet,
Beat back keen Winter's blast, and welcomed Summer's heat.

XLIV

Here the red Cross, for still the Cross is here,
Though sadly scoffed at by the circumcised,

Forgets that Pride to pampered priesthood dear;
Churchman and Votary alike despised.
Foul Superstition! howsoe'er disguised,
Idol — Saint — Virgin — Prophet — Crescent — Cross —
For whatsoever symbol thou art prized,
Thou sacerdotal gain, but general loss!
Who from true Worship's gold can separate thy dross?

XLV

Ambracia's gulf behold, where once was lost
A world for Woman, lovely, harmless thing!
In yonder rippling bay, their naval host
Did many a Roman chief and Asian King
To doubtful conflict, certain slaughter bring:
Look where the second Cæsar's trophies rose!
Now, like the hands that reared them, withering:
Imperial Anarchs, doubling human woes!
God! was thy globe ordained for such to win and lose?

XLVI

From the dark barriers of that rugged clime,
Ev'n to the centre of Illyria's vales,
Childe Harold passed o'er many a mount sublime,
Through lands scarce noticed in historic tales:
Yet in famed Attica such lovely dales
Are rarely seen; nor can fair Tempe boast
A charm they know not; loved Parnassus fails,
Though classic ground and consecrated most,
To match some spots that lurk within this lowering coast.

XLVII

He passed bleak Pindus, Acherusia's lake,
And left the primal city of the land,
And onwards did his further journey take
To greet Albania's Chief, whose dread command
Is lawless law; for with a bloody hand
He sways a nation, turbulent and bold:
Yet here and there some daring mountain-band
Disdain his power, and from their rocky hold
Hurl their defiance far, nor yield, unless to gold.

XLVIII

Monastic Zitza! from thy shady brow,
Thou small, but favoured spot of holy ground!

Where'er we gaze — around — above — below, —
What rainbow tints, what magic charms are found!
Rock, river, forest, mountain, all abound,
And bluest skies that harmonise the whole:
Beneath, the distant Torrent's rushing sound
Tells where the volumed Cataract doth roll
Between those hanging rocks, that shock yet please the soul.

XLIX

Amidst the grove that crowns yon tufted hill,
Which, were it not for many a mountain nigh
Rising in lofty ranks, and loftier still,
Might well itself be deemed of dignity,
The Convent's white walls glisten fair on high:
Here dwells the caloyer, nor rude is he,
Nor niggard of his cheer; the passer by
Is welcome still; nor heedless will he flee
From hence, if he delight kind Nature's sheen to see.

L

Here in the sultriest season let him rest,
Fresh is the green beneath those aged trees;
Here winds of gentlest wing will fan his breast,
From Heaven itself he may inhale the breeze:
The plain is far beneath — oh! let him seize
Pure pleasure while he can; the scorching ray
Here pierceth not, impregnate with disease:
Then let his length the loitering pilgrim lay,
And gaze, untired, the Morn — the Noon — the Eve away.

LI

Dusky and huge, enlarging on the sight,
Nature's volcanic Amphitheatre,
Chimæra's Alps extend from left to right:
Beneath, a living valley seems to stir;
Flocks play, trees wave, streams flow, the mountain-fir
Nodding above; behold black Acheron!
Once consecrated to the sepulchre.
Pluto! if this be Hell I look upon,
Close shamed Elysium's gates, my shade shall seek for none.

LII

Ne city's towers pollute the lovely view;
Unseen is Yanina, though not remote,

Veiled by the screen of hills: here men are few,
Scanty the hamlet, rare the lonely cot:
But, peering down each precipice, the goat
Browseth; and, pensive o'er his scattered flock,
The little shepherd in his white capote
Doth lean his boyish form along the rock,
Or in his cave awaits the Tempest's short-lived shock.

LIII

Oh! where, Dodona! is thine agéd Grove,
Prophetic Fount, and Oracle divine?
What valley echoed the response of Jove?
What trace remaineth of the Thunderer's shrine?
All, all forgotten — and shall Man repine
That his frail bonds to fleeting life are broke?
Cease, Fool! the fate of Gods may well be thine:
Wouldst thou survive the marble or the oak?
When nations, tongues, and worlds must sink beneath the stroke!

LIV

Epirus' bounds recede, and mountains fail;
Tired of up-gazing still, the wearied eye
Reposes gladly on as smooth a vale
As ever Spring yclad in grassy dye:
Ev'n on a plain no humble beauties lie,
Where some bold river breaks the long expanse,
And woods along the banks are waving high,
Whose shadows in the glassy waters dance,
Or with the moonbeam sleep in Midnight's solemn trance.

LV

The Sun had sunk behind vast Tomerit,
And Laos wide and fierce came roaring by;
The shades of wonted night were gathering yet,
When, down the steep banks winding warily,
Childe Harold saw, like meteors in the sky,
The glittering minarets of Tepalen,
Whose walls o'erlook the stream; and drawing nigh,
He heard the busy hum of warrior-men
Swelling the breeze that sighed along the lengthening glen.

LVI

He passed the sacred Haram's silent tower,
And underneath the wide o'erarching gate

Surveyed the dwelling of this Chief of power,
Where all around proclaimed his high estate.
Amidst no common pomp the Despot sate,
While busy preparation shook the court,
Slaves, eunuchs, soldiers, guests, and santons wait;
Within, a palace, and without, a fort:
Here men of every clime appear to make resort.

LVII

Richly caparisoned, a ready row
Of arméd horse, and many a warlike store,
Circled the wide-extending court below;
Above, strange groups adorned the corridore;
And oft-times through the area's echoing door
Some high-capped Tartar spurred his steed away:
The Turk — the Greek — the Albanian — and the Moor,
Here mingled in their many-hued array,
While the deep war-drum's sound announced the close of day.

LVIII

The wild Albanian kirtled to his knee,
With shawl-girt head and ornamented gun,
And gold-embroidered garments, fair to see;
The crimson-scarféd men of Macedon;
The Delhi with his cap of terror on,
And crooked glaive — the lively, supple Greek
And swarthy Nubia's mutilated son;
The bearded Turk that rarely deigns to speak,
Master of all around, too potent to be meek,

LIX

Are mixed conspicuous: some recline in groups,
Scanning the motley scene that varies round;
There some grave Moslem to devotion stoops,
And some that smoke, and some that play, are found;
Here the Albanian proudly treads the ground;
Half-whispering there the Greek is heard to prate;
Hark! from the Mosque the nightly solemn sound,
The Muezzin's call doth shake the minaret,
"There is no god but God! — to prayer — lo! God is great!"

LX

Just at this season Ramazani's fast
Through the long day its penance did maintain:

But when the lingering twilight hour was past,
Revel and feast assumed the rule again:
Now all was bustle, and the menial train
Prepared and spread the plenteous board within;
The vacant Gallery now seemed made in vain,
But from the chambers came the mingling din,
As page and slave anon were passing out and in.

LXI

Here woman's voice is never heard: apart,
And scarce permitted, guarded, veiled, to move,
She yields to one her person and her heart,
Tamed to her cage, nor feels a wish to rove:
For, not unhappy in her Master's love,
And joyful in a mother's gentlest cares,
Blest cares! all other feelings far above!
Herself more sweetly rears the babe she bears
Who never quits the breast — no meaner passion shares.

LXII

In marble-paved pavilion, where a spring
Of living water from the centre rose,
Whose bubbling did a genial freshness fling,
And soft voluptuous couches breathed repose,
ALI reclined, a man of war and woes:
Yet in his lineaments ye cannot trace,
While Gentleness her milder radiance throws
Along that agéd venerable face,
The deeds that lurk beneath, and stain him with disgrace.

LXIII

It is not that yon hoary lengthening beard
Ill suits the passions which belong to Youth;
Love conquers Age — so Hafiz hath averr'd,
So sings the Teian, and he sings in sooth —
But crimes that scorn the tender voice of ruth,
Beseeming all men ill, but most the man
In years, have marked him with a tiger's tooth;
Blood follows blood, and, through their mortal span,
In bloodier acts conclude those who with blood began.

LXIV

'Mid many things most new to ear and eye
The Pilgrim rested here his weary feet,

And gazed around on Moslem luxury,
Till quickly wearied with that spacious seat
Of Wealth and Wantonness, the choice retreat
Of sated Grandeur from the city's noise:
And were it humbler it in sooth were sweet;
But Peace abhorreth artificial joys,
And Pleasure, leagued with Pomp, the zest of both destroys.

LXV

Fierce are Albania's children, yet they lack
Not virtues, were those virtues more mature.
Where is the foe that ever saw their back?
Who can so well the toil of War endure?
Their native fastnesses not more secure
Than they in doubtful time of troublous need:
Their wrath how deadly! but their friendship sure,
When Gratitude or Valour bids them bleed,
Unshaken rushing on where'er their Chief may lead.

LXVI

Childe Harold saw them in their Chieftain's tower
Thronging to War in splendour and success;
And after viewed them, when, within their power,
Himself awhile the victim of distress;
That saddening hour when bad men hotlier press:
But these did shelter him beneath their roof,
When less barbarians would have cheered him less,
And fellow-countrymen have stood aloof —
In aught that tries the heart, how few withstand the proof!

LXVII

It chanced that adverse winds once drove his bark
Full on the coast of Suli's shaggy shore,
When all around was desolate and dark;
To land was perilous, to sojourn more;
Yet for awhile the mariners forbore,
Dubious to trust where Treachery might lurk:
At length they ventured forth, though doubting sore
That those who loathe alike the Frank and Turk
Might once again renew their ancient butcher-work.

LXVIII

Vain fear! the Suliotes stretched the welcome hand,
Led them o'er rocks and past the dangerous swamp,

Kinder than polished slaves though not so bland,
And piled the hearth, and wrung their garments damp,
And filled the bowl, and trimmed the cheerful lamp,
And spread their fare; though homely, all they had:
Such conduct bears Philanthropy's rare stamp:
To rest the weary and to soothe the sad,
Doth lesson happier men, and shames at least the bad.

LXIX

It came to pass, that when he did address
Himself to quit at length this mountain-land,
Combined marauders half-way barred egress,
And wasted far and near with glaive and brand;
And therefore did he take a trusty band
To traverse Acarnania's forest wide,
In war well-seasoned, and with labours tanned,
Till he did greet white Achelous' tide,
And from his further bank Ætolia's wolds espied.

LXX

Where lone Utraikey forms its circling cove,
And weary waves retire to gleam at rest,
How brown the foliage of the green hill's grove,
Nodding at midnight o'er the calm bay's breast,
As winds come lightly whispering from the West,
Kissing, not ruffling, the blue deep's serene: —
Here Harold was received a welcome guest;
Nor did he pass unmoved the gentle scene,
For many a joy could he from Night's soft presence glean.

LXXI

On the smooth shore the night-fires brightly blazed,
The feast was done, the red wine circling fast,
And he that unawares had there ygazed
With gaping wonderment had stared aghast;
For ere night's midmost, stillest hour was past,
The native revels of the troop began;
Each Palikar his sabre from him cast,
And bounding hand in hand, man linked to man,
Yelling their uncouth dirge, long daunced the kirtled clan.

LXXII

Childe Harold at a little distance stood
And viewed, but not displeased, the revelrie,

Nor hated harmless mirth, however rude:
In sooth, it was no vulgar sight to see
Their barbarous, yet their not indecent, glee;
And, as the flames along their faces gleamed,
Their gestures nimble, dark eyes flashing free,
The long wild locks that to their girdles streamed,
While thus in concert they this lay half sang, half screamed: —

1

TAMBOURGI! Tambourgi! thy 'larum afar
Gives hope to the valiant, and promise of war;
All the Sons of the mountains arise at the note,
Chimariot, Illyrian, and dark Suliote!

2

Oh! who is more brave than a dark Suliote,
In his snowy camese and his shaggy capote?
To the wolf and the vulture he leaves his wild flock,
And descends to the plain like the stream from the rock.

3

Shall the sons of Chimari, who never forgive
The fault of a friend, bid an enemy live?
Let those guns so unerring such vengeance forego?
What mark is so fair as the breast of a foe?

4

Macedonia sends forth her invincible race;
For a time they abandon the cave and the chase:
But those scarfs of blood-red shall be redder, before
The sabre is sheathed and the battle is o'er.

5

Then the Pirates of Parga that dwell by the waves,
And teach the pale Franks what it is to be slaves,
Shall leave on the beach the long galley and oar,
And track to his covert the captive on shore.

6

I ask not the pleasures that riches supply,
My sabre shall win what the feeble must buy;

Shall win the young bride with her long flowing hair,
And many a maid from her mother shall tear.

7

I love the fair face of the maid in her youth,
Her caresses shall lull me, her music shall soothe;
Let her bring from the chamber her many-toned lyre,
And sing us a song on the fall of her Sire.

8

Remember the moment when Previsa fell,
The shrieks of the conquered, the conquerors' yell;
The roofs that we fired, and the plunder we shared,
The wealthy we slaughtered, the lovely we spared.

9

I talk not of mercy, I talk not of fear;
He neither must know who would serve the Vizier:
Since the days of our Prophet the Crescent ne'er saw
A chief ever glorious like Ali Pashaw.

10

Dark Muchtar his son to the Danube is sped,
Let the yellow-haired Giaours view his horse-tail with dread;
When his Delhis come dashing in blood o'er the banks,
How few shall escape from the Muscovite ranks!

11

Selictar! unsheathe then our chief's Scimitār;
Tambourgi! thy 'larum gives promise of War.
Ye Mountains, that see us descend to the shore,
Shall view us as Victors, or view us no more!

LXXIII

Fair Greece! sad relic of departed Worth!
  Immortal, though no more; though fallen, great!
  Who now shall lead thy scattered children forth,
  And long accustomed bondage uncreate?
  Not such thy sons who whilome did await,
  The helpless warriors of a willing doom,
  In bleak Thermopylæ's sepulchral strait —

Oh! who that gallant spirit shall resume,
Leap from Eurotas' banks, and call thee from the tomb?

LXXIV

Spirit of Freedom! when on Phyle's brow
Thou sat'st with Thrasybulus and his train,
Couldst thou forebode the dismal hour which now
Dims the green beauties of thine Attic plain?
Not thirty tyrants now enforce the chain,
But every carle can lord it o'er thy land;
Nor rise thy sons, but idly rail in vain,
Trembling beneath the scourge of Turkish hand,
From birth till death enslaved; in word, in deed, unmanned.

LXXV

In all save form alone, how changed! and who
That marks the fire still sparkling in each eye,
Who but would deem their bosoms burned anew
With thy unquenchéd beam, lost Liberty!
And many dream withal the hour is nigh
That gives them back their fathers' heritage:
For foreign arms and aid they fondly sigh,
Nor solely dare encounter hostile rage,
Or tear their name defiled from Slavery's mournful page.

LXXVI

Hereditary Bondsmen! know ye not
Who would be free *themselves* must strike the blow?
By their right arms the conquest must be wrought?
Will Gaul or Muscovite redress ye? No!
True — they may lay your proud despoilers low,
But not for you will Freedom's Altars flame.
Shades of the Helots! triumph o'er your foe!
Greece! change thy lords, thy state is still the same;
Thy glorious day is o'er, but not thine years of shame.

LXXVII

The city won for Allah from the Giaour
The Giaour from Othman's race again may wrest;
And the Serai's impenetrable tower
Receive the fiery Frank, her former guest;
Or Wahab's rebel brood who dared divest
The Prophet's tomb of all its pious spoil,

May wind their path of blood along the West;
But ne'er will Freedom seek this fated soil,
But slave succeed to slave through years of endless toil.

LXXVIII

Yet mark their mirth — ere Lenten days begin,
That penance which their holy rites prepare
To shrive from Man his weight of mortal sin,
By daily abstinence and nightly prayer;
But ere his sackcloth garb Repentance wear,
Some days of joyaunce are decreed to all,
To take of pleasaunce each his secret share,
In motley robe to dance at masking ball,
And join the mimic train of merry Carnival.

LXXIX

And whose more rife with merriment than thine,
Oh Stamboul! once the Empress of their reign?
Though turbans now pollute Sophia's shrine,
And Greece her very altars eyes in vain:
(Alas! her woes will still pervade my strain!)
Gay were her minstrels once, for free her throng,
All felt the common joy they now must feign,
Nor oft I've seen such sight, nor heard such song,
As wooed the eye, and thrilled the Bosphorus along.

LXXX

Loud was the lightsome tumult on the shore,
Oft Music changed, but never ceased her tone,
And timely echoed back the measured oar,
And rippling waters made a pleasant moan:
The Queen of tides on high consenting shone,
And when a transient breeze swept o'er the wave,
'Twas, as if darting from her heavenly throne,
A brighter glance her form reflected gave,
Till sparkling billows seemed to light the banks they lave.

LXXXI

Glanced many a light Caique along the foam,
Danced on the shore the daughters of the land,
No thought had man or maid of rest or home,
While many a languid eye and thrilling hand
Exchanged the look few bosoms may withstand,

Or gently prest, returned the pressure still:
Oh Love! young Love! bound in thy rosy band,
Let sage or cynic prattle as he will,
These hours, and only these, redeem Life's years of ill!

LXXXII

But, midst the throng in merry masquerade,
Lurk there no hearts that throb with secret pain,
Even through the closest searment half betrayed?
To such the gentle murmurs of the main
Seem to re-echo all they mourn in vain;
To such the gladness of the gamesome crowd
Is source of wayward thought and stern disdain:
How do they loathe the laughter idly loud,
And long to change the robe of revel for the shroud!

LXXXIII

This must he feel, the true-born son of Greece,
If Greece one true-born patriot still can boast:
Not such as prate of War, but skulk in Peace,
The bondsman's peace, who sighs for all he lost,
Yet with smooth smile his Tyrant can accost,
And wield the slavish sickle, not the sword:
Ah! Greece! they love thee least who owe thee most —
Their birth, their blood, and that sublime record
Of hero Sires, who shame thy now degenerate horde!

LXXXIV

When riseth Lacedemon's Hardihood,
When Thebes Epaminondas rears again,
When Athens' children are with hearts endued,
When Grecian mothers shall give birth to men,
Then may'st thou be restored; but not till then.
A thousand years scarce serve to form a state;
An hour may lay it in the dust: and when
Can Man its shattered splendour renovate,
Recall its virtues back, and vanquish Time and Fate?

LXXXV

And yet how lovely in thine age of woe,
Land of lost Gods and godlike men, art thou!
Thy vales of evergreen, thy hills of snow,
Proclaim thee Nature's varied favourite now:

Thy fanes, thy temples to thy surface bow,
Commingling slowly with heroic earth,
Broke by the share of every rustic plough:
So perish monuments of mortal birth,
So perish all in turn, save well-recorded *Worth:*

LXXXVI

Save where some solitary column mourns
Above its prostrate brethren of the cave;
Save where Tritonia's airy shrine adorns
Colonna's cliff, and gleams along the wave;
Save o'er some warrior's half-forgotten grave,
Where the gray stones and unmolested grass
Ages, but not Oblivion, feebly brave;
While strangers, only, not regardless pass,
Lingering like me, perchance, to gaze, and sigh "Alas!"

LXXXVII

Yet are thy skies as blue, thy crags as wild;
Sweet are thy groves, and verdant are thy fields,
Thine olive ripe as when Minerva smiled,
And still his honied wealth Hymettus yields;
There the blithe Bee his fragrant fortress builds,
The free-born wanderer of thy mountain-air;
Apollo still thy long, long summer gilds,
Still in his beam Mendeli's marbles glare:
Art, Glory, Freedom fail, but Nature still is fair.

LXXXVIII

Where'er we tread 'tis haunted, holy ground;
No earth of thine is lost in vulgar mould,
But one vast realm of Wonder spreads around,
And all the Muse's tales seem truly told,
Till the sense aches with gazing to behold
The scenes our earliest dreams have dwelt upon;
Each hill and dale, each deepening glen and wold
Defies the power which crushed thy temples gone:
Age shakes Athenæ's tower, but spares gray Marathon.

LXXXIX

The Sun, the soil — but not the slave, the same; —
Unchanged in all except its foreign Lord,
Preserves alike its bounds and boundless fame

The Battle-field, where Persia's victim horde
First bowed beneath the brunt of Hellas' sword,
As on the morn to distant Glory dear,
When Marathon became a magic word;
Which uttered, to the hearer's eye appear
The camp, the host, the fight, the Conqueror's career,

XC

The flying Mede, his shaftless broken bow —
The fiery Greek, his red pursuing spear;
Mountains above — Earth's, Ocean's plain below —
Death in the front, Destruction in the rear!
Such was the scene — what now remaineth here?
What sacred Trophy marks the hallowed ground,
Recording Freedom's smile and Asia's tear?
The rifled urn, the violated mound,
The dust thy courser's hoof, rude stranger! spurns around.

XCI

Yet to the remnants of thy Splendour past
Shall pilgrims, pensive, but unwearied, throng;
Long shall the voyager, with th' Ionian blast,
Hail the bright clime of Battle and of Song:
Long shall thine annals and immortal tongue
Fill with thy fame the youth of many a shore;
Boast of the agéd! lesson of the young!
Which Sages venerate and Bards adore,
As Pallas and the Muse unveil their awful lore.

XCII

The parted bosom clings to wonted home,
If aught that's kindred cheer the welcome hearth;
He that is lonely — hither let him roam,
And gaze complacent on congenial earth.
Greece is no lightsome land of social mirth:
But he whom Sadness sootheth may abide,
And scarce regret the region of his birth,
When wandering slow by Delphi's sacred side,
Or gazing o'er the plains where Greek and Persian died.

XCIII

Let such approach this consecrated Land,
And pass in peace along the magic waste;
But spare its relics — let no busy hand

Deface the scenes, already how defaced!
Not for such purpose were these altars placed:
Revere the remnants Nations once revered:
So may our Country's name be undisgraced,
So may'st thou prosper where thy youth was reared,
By every honest joy of Love and Life endeared!

XCIV

For thee, who thus in too protracted song
Hast soothed thine Idlesse with inglorious lays,
Soon shall thy voice be lost amid the throng
Of louder Minstrels in these later days:
To such resign the strife for fading Bays —
Ill may such contest now the spirit move
Which heeds nor keen Reproach nor partial Praise,
Since cold each kinder heart that might approve —
And none are left to please when none are left to love.

XCV

Thou too art gone, thou loved and lovely one!
Whom Youth and Youth's affections bound to me;
Who did for me what none besides have done,
Nor shrank from one albeit unworthy thee.
What is my Being! thou hast ceased to be!
Nor staid to welcome here thy wanderer home,
Who mourns o'er hours which we no more shall see —
Would they had never been, or were to come!
Would he had ne'er returned to find fresh cause to roam!

XCVI

Oh! ever loving, lovely, and beloved!
How selfish Sorrow ponders on the past,
And clings to thoughts now better far removed!
But Time shall tear thy shadow from me last.
All thou couldst have of mine, stern Death! thou hast;
The Parent, Friend, and now the more than Friend:
Ne'er yet for one thine arrows flew so fast,
And grief with grief continuing still to blend,
Hath snatched the little joy that Life had yet to lend.

XCVII

Then must I plunge again into the crowd,
And follow all that Peace disdains to seek?
Where Revel calls, and Laughter, vainly loud,

False to the heart, distorts the hollow cheek,
To leave the flagging spirit doubly weak;
Still o'er the features, which perforce they cheer,
To feign the pleasure or conceal the pique:
Smiles form the channel of a future tear,
Or raise the writhing lip with ill-dissembled sneer.

XCVIII

What is the worst of woes that wait on Age?
What stamps the wrinkle deeper on the brow?
To view each loved one blotted from Life's page,
And be alone on earth, as I am now.
Before the Chastener humbly let me bow,
O'er Hearts divided and o'er Hopes destroyed:
Roll on, vain days! full reckless may ye flow,
Since Time hath reft whate'er my soul enjoyed,
And with the ills of Eld mine earlier years alloyed.

CANTO THE THIRD

"Afin que cette application vous forçât de penser à autre chose; il n'y a en vérité de remède que celui-là et le temps.

Lettre du Roi de Prusse à D'Alembert, Sept. 7, 1776.

I

Is thy face like thy mother's, my fair child!
Ada! sole daughter of my house and heart?
When last I saw thy young blue eyes they smiled,
And then we parted, — not as now we part,
But with a hope. —
Awaking with a start,
The waters heave around me; and on high
The winds lift up their voices: I depart,
Whither I know not; but the hour's gone by,
When Albion's lessening shores could grieve or glad mine eye.

II

Once more upon the waters! yet once more!
And the waves bound beneath me as a steed
That knows his rider. Welcome to their roar!
Swift be their guidance, wheresoe'er it lead!
Though the strained mast should quiver as a reed,
And the rent canvass fluttering strew the gale,

Still must I on; for I am as a weed,
Flung from the rock, on Ocean's foam, to sail
Where'er the surge may sweep, the tempest's breath prevail.

III

In my youth's summer I did sing of One,
The wandering outlaw of his own dark mind;
Again I seize the theme, then but begun,
And bear it with me, as the rushing wind
Bears the cloud onwards: in that Tale I find
The furrows of long thought, and dried-up tears,
Which, ebbing, leave a sterile track behind,
O'er which all heavily the journeying years
Plod the last sands of life, — where not a flower appears.

IV

Since my young days of passion — joy, or pain —
Perchance my heart and harp have lost a string —
And both may jar: it may be, that in vain
I would essay as I have sung to sing:
Yet, though a dreary strain, to this I cling;
So that it wean me from the weary dream
Of selfish grief or gladness — so it fling
Forgetfulness around me — it shall seem
To me, though to none else, a not ungrateful theme.

V

He, who grown agèd in this world of woe,
In deeds, not years, piercing the depths of life,
So that no wonder waits him — nor below
Can Love or Sorrow, Fame, Ambition, Strife,
Cut to his heart again with the keen knife
Of silent, sharp endurance — he can tell
Why Thought seeks refuge in lone caves, yet rife
With airy images, and shapes which dwell
Still unimpaired, though old, in the Soul's haunted cell.

VI

'Tis to create, and in creating live
A being more intense that we endow
With form our fancy, gaining as we give
The life we image, even as I do now —
What am I? Nothing: but not so art thou,

Soul of my thought! with whom I traverse earth,
Invisible but gazing, as I glow
Mixed with thy spirit, blended with thy birth,
And feeling still with thee in my crushed feelings' dearth.

VII

Yet must I think less wildly: — I *have* thought
Too long and darkly, till my brain became,
In its own eddy boiling and o'erwrought,
A whirling gulf of phantasy and flame:
And thus, untaught in youth my heart to tame,
My springs of life were poisoned. 'Tis too late:
Yet am I changed; though still enough the same
In strength to bear what Time can not abate,
And feed on bitter fruits without accusing Fate.

VIII

Something too much of this: — but now 'tis past,
And the spell closes with its silent seal —
Long absent Harold re-appears at last;
He of the breast which fain no more would feel,
Wrung with the wounds which kill not, but ne'er heal;
Yet Time, who changes all, had altered him
In soul and aspect as in age: years steal
Fire from the mind as vigour from the limb;
And Life's enchanted cup but sparkles near the brim.

IX

His had been quaffed too quickly, and he found
The dregs were wormwood; but he filled again,
And from a purer fount, on holier ground,
And deemed its spring perpetual — but in vain!
Still round him clung invisibly a chain
Which galled for ever, fettering though unseen,
And heavy though it clanked not; worn with pain,
Which pined although it spoke not, and grew keen,
Entering with every step he took through many a scene.

X

Secure in guarded coldness, he had mixed
Again in fancied safety with his kind,
And deemed his spirit now so firmly fixed
And sheathed with an invulnerable mind,

That, if no joy, no sorrow lurked behind;
And he, as one, might 'midst the many stand
Unheeded, searching through the crowd to find
Fit speculation — such as in strange land
He found in wonder-works of God and Nature's hand.

XI

But who can view the ripened rose, nor seek
To wear it? who can curiously behold
The smoothness and the sheen of Beauty's cheek,
Nor feel the heart can never all grow old?
Who can contemplate Fame through clouds unfold
The star which rises o'er her steep, nor climb?
Harold, once more within the vortex, rolled
On with the giddy circle, chasing Time,
Yet with a nobler aim than in his Youth's fond prime.

XII

But soon he knew himself the most unfit
Of men to herd with Man, with whom he held
Little in common; untaught to submit
His thoughts to others, though his soul was quelled
In youth by his own thoughts; still uncompelled,
He would not yield dominion of his mind
To Spirits against whom his own rebelled,
Proud though in desolation — which could find
A life within itself, to breathe without mankind.

XIII

Where rose the mountains, there to him were friends;
Where rolled the ocean, thereon was his home;
Where a blue sky, and glowing clime, extends,
He had the passion and the power to roam;
The desert, forest, cavern, breaker's foam,
Were unto him companionship; they spake
A mutual language, clearer than the tome
Of his land's tongue, which he would oft forsake
For Nature's pages glassed by sunbeams on the lake.

XIV

Like the Chaldean, he could watch the stars,
Till he had peopled them with beings bright
As their own beams; and earth, and earth-born jars,

And human frailties, were forgotten quite:
Could he have kept his spirit to that flight
He had been happy; but this clay will sink
Its spark immortal, envying it the light
To which it mounts, as if to break the link
That keeps us from yon heaven which woos us to its brink.

XV

But in Man's dwellings he became a thing
Restless and worn, and stern and wearisome,
Drooped as a wild-born falcon with clipt wing,
To whom the boundless air alone were home:
Then came his fit again, which to o'ercome,
As eagerly the barred-up bird will beat
His breast and beak against his wiry dome
Till the blood tinge his plumage — so the heat
Of his impeded Soul would through his bosom eat.

XVI

Self-exiled Harold wanders forth again,
With nought of Hope left — but with less of gloom;
The very knowledge that he lived in vain,
That all was over on this side the tomb,
Had made Despair a smilingness assume,
Which, though 'twere wild, — as on the plundered wreck
When mariners would madly meet their doom
With draughts intemperate on the sinking deck, —
Did yet inspire a cheer, which he forbore to check.

XVII

Stop! — for thy tread is on an Empire's dust!
An Earthquake's spoil is sepulchred below!
Is the spot marked with no colossal bust?
Nor column trophied for triumphal show?
None; but *the moral's truth* tells simpler so. —
As the ground was before, thus let it be; —
How that red rain hath made the harvest grow!
And is this all the world has gained by thee,
Thou first and last of Fields! king-making Victory?

XVIII

And Harold stands upon this place of skulls,
The grave of France, the deadly Waterloo!
How in an hour the Power which gave annuls

Its gifts, transferring fame as fleeting too! —
In "pride of place" here last the Eagle flew,
Then tore with bloody talon the rent plain,
Pierced by the shaft of banded nations through;
Ambition's life and labours all were vain —
He wears the shattered links of the World's broken chain.

XIX

Fit retribution! Gaul may champ the bit
And foam in fetters; — but is Earth more free?
Did nations combat to make *One* submit?
Or league to teach all Kings true Sovereignty?
What! shall reviving Thraldom again be
The patched-up Idol of enlightened days?
Shall we, who struck the Lion down, shall we
Pay the Wolf homage? proffering lowly gaze
And servile knees to Thrones? No! *prove* before ye praise!

XX

If not, o'er one fallen Despot boast no more!
In vain fair cheeks were furrowed with hot tears
For Europe's flowers long rooted up before
The trampler of her vineyards; in vain, years
Of death, depopulation, bondage, fears,
Have all been borne, and broken by the accord
Of roused-up millions: all that most endears
Glory, is when the myrtle wreathes a Sword,
Such as Harmodius drew on Athens' tyrant Lord.

XXI

There was a sound of revelry by night,
And Belgium's Capital had gathered then
Her Beauty and her Chivalry — and bright
The lamps shone o'er fair women and brave men;
A thousand hearts beat happily; and when
Music arose with its voluptuous swell,
Soft eyes looked love to eyes which spake again,
And all went merry as a marriage bell;
But hush! hark! a deep sound strikes like a rising knell!

XXII

Did ye not hear it? — No — 'twas but the Wind,
Or the car rattling o'er the stony street;
On with the dance! let joy be unconfined;

No sleep till morn, when Youth and Pleasure meet
To chase the glowing Hours with flying feet —
But hark! — that heavy sound breaks in once more,
As if the clouds its echo would repeat;
And nearer — clearer — deadlier than before!
Arm! Arm! it is — it is — the cannon's opening roar!

XXIII

Within a windowed niche of that high hall
Sate Brunswick's fated Chieftain; he did hear
That sound the first amidst the festival,
And caught its tone with Death's prophetic ear;
And when they smiled because he deemed it near,
His heart more truly knew that peal too well
Which stretched his father on a bloody bier,
And roused the vengeance blood alone could quell;
He rushed into the field, and, foremost fighting, fell.

XXIV

Ah! then and there was hurrying to and fro —
And gathering tears, and tremblings of distress,
And cheeks all pale, which but an hour ago
Blushed at the praise of their own loveliness —
And there were sudden partings, such as press
The life from out young hearts, and choking sighs
Which ne'er might be repeated; who could guess
If ever more should meet those mutual eyes,
Since upon night so sweet such awful morn could rise!

XXV

And there was mounting in hot haste — the steed,
The mustering squadron, and the clattering car,
Went pouring forward with impetuous speed,
And swiftly forming in the ranks of war —
And the deep thunder peal on peal afar;
And near, the beat of the alarming drum
Roused up the soldier ere the Morning Star;
While thronged the citizens with terror dumb,
Or whispering, with white lips — "The foe! They come! they come!"

XXVI

And wild and high the "Cameron's Gathering" rose!
The war-note of Lochiel, which Albyn's hills
Have heard, and heard, too, have her Saxon foes: —

How in the noon of night that pibroch thrills,
Savage and shrill! But with the breath which fills
Their mountain-pipe, so fill the mountaineers
With the fierce native daring which instils
The stirring memory of a thousand years,
And Evan's — Donald's fame rings in each clansman's ears!

XXVII

And Ardennes waves above them her green leaves,
Dewy with Nature's tear-drops, as they pass —
Grieving, if aught inanimate e'er grieves,
Over the unreturning brave, — alas!
Ere evening to be trodden like the grass
Which now beneath them, but above shall grow
In its next verdure, when this fiery mass
Of living Valour, rolling on the foe
And burning with high Hope, shall moulder cold and low.

XXVIII

Last noon beheld them full of lusty life; —
Last eve in Beauty's circle proudly gay;
The Midnight brought the signal-sound of strife,
The Morn the marshalling in arms, — the Day
Battle's magnificently-stern array!
The thunder-clouds close o'er it, which when rent
The earth is covered thick with other clay
Which her own clay shall cover, heaped and pent,
Rider and horse, — friend, — foe, — in one red burial blent!

XXIX

Their praise is hymned by loftier harps than mine;
Yet one I would select from that proud throng,
Partly because they blend me with his line,
And partly that I did his Sire some wrong,
And partly that bright names will hallow song;
And his was of the bravest, and when showered
The death-bolts deadliest the thinned files along,
Even where the thickest of War's tempest lowered,
They reached no nobler breast than thine, young, gallant Howard!

XXX

There have been tears and breaking hearts for thee,
And mine were nothing, had I such to give;
But when I stood beneath the fresh green tree,

Which living waves where thou didst cease to live,
And saw around me the wide field revive
With fruits and fertile promise, and the Spring
Come forth her work of gladness to contrive,
With all her reckless birds upon the wing,
I turned from all she brought to those she could not bring.

XXXI

I turned to thee, to thousands, of whom each
And one as all a ghastly gap did make
In his own kind and kindred, whom to teach
Forgetfulness were mercy for their sake;
The Archangel's trump, not Glory's, must awake
Those whom they thirst for; though the sound of Fame
May for a moment soothe, it cannot slake
The fever of vain longing, and the name
So honoured but assumes a stronger, bitterer claim.

XXXII

They mourn, but smile at length — and, smiling, mourn:
The tree will wither long before it fall;
The hull drives on, though mast and sail be torn;
The roof-tree sinks, but moulders on the hall
In massy hoariness; the ruined wall
Stands when its wind-worn battlements are gone;
The bars survive the captive they enthral;
The day drags through though storms keep out the sun;
And thus the heart will break, yet brokenly live on:

XXXIII

Even as a broken Mirror, which the glass
In every fragment multiplies — and makes
A thousand images of one that was,
The same — and still the more, the more it breaks;
And thus the heart will do which not forsakes,
Living in shattered guise; and still, and cold,
And bloodless, with its sleepless sorrow aches,
Yet withers on till all without is old,
Showing no visible sign, for such things are untold.

XXXIV

There is a very life in our despair,
Vitality of poison, — a quick root
Which feeds these deadly branches; for it were

As nothing did we die; but Life will suit
Itself to Sorrow's most detested fruit,
Like to the apples on the Dead Sea's shore,
All ashes to the taste: Did man compute
Existence by enjoyment, and count o'er
Such hours 'gainst years of life, — say, would he name threescore?

XXXV

The Psalmist numbered out the years of man:
They are enough; and if thy tale be *true*,
Thou, who didst grudge him even that fleeting span,
More than enough, thou fatal Waterloo!
Millions of tongues record thee, and anew
Their children's lips shall echo them, and say —
"Here, where the sword united nations drew,
Our countrymen were warring on that day!"
And this is much — and all — which will not pass away.

XXXVI

There sunk the greatest, nor the worst of men,
Whose Spirit, antithetically mixed,
One moment of the mightiest, and again
On little objects with like firmness fixed;
Extreme in all things! hadst thou been betwixt,
Thy throne had still been thine, or never been;
For Daring made thy rise as fall: thou seek'st
Even now to re-assume the imperial mien,
And shake again the world, the Thunderer of the scene!

XXXVII

Conqueror and Captive of the Earth art thou!
She trembles at thee still, and thy wild name
Was ne'er more bruited in men's minds than now
That thou art nothing, save the jest of Fame,
Who wooed thee once, thy Vassal, and became
The flatterer of thy fierceness — till thou wert
A God unto thyself; nor less the same
To the astounded kingdoms all inert,
Who deemed thee for a time whate'er thou didst assert.

XXXVIII

Oh, more or less than man — in high or low —
Battling with nations, flying from the field;
Now making monarchs' necks thy footstool, now

More than thy meanest soldier taught to yield;
An Empire thou couldst crush, command, rebuild,
But govern not thy pettiest passion, nor,
However deeply in men's spirits skilled,
Look through thine own, nor curb the lust of War,
Nor learn that tempted Fate will leave the loftiest Star.

XXXIX

Yet well thy soul hath brooked the turning tide
With that untaught innate philosophy,
Which, be it Wisdom, Coldness, or deep Pride,
Is gall and wormwood to an enemy.
When the whole host of hatred stood hard by,
To watch and mock thee shrinking, thou hast smiled
With a sedate and all-enduring eye; —
When Fortune fled her spoiled and favourite child,
He stood unbowed beneath the ills upon him piled.

XL

Sager than in thy fortunes; for in them
Ambition steeled thee on too far to show
That just habitual scorn, which could contemn
Men and their thoughts; 'twas wise to feel, not so
To wear it ever on thy lip and brow,
And spurn the instruments thou wert to use
Till they were turned unto thine overthrow:
'Tis but a worthless world to win or lose;
So hath it proved to thee, and all such lot who choose.

XLI

If, like a tower upon a headlong rock,
Thou hadst been made to stand or fall alone,
Such scorn of man had helped to brave the shock;
But men's thoughts were the steps which paved thy throne,
Their admiration thy best weapon shone;
The part of Philip's son was thine, not then
(Unless aside thy Purple had been thrown)
Like stern Diogenes to mock at men —
For sceptred Cynics Earth were far too wide a den.

XLII

But Quiet to quick bosoms is a Hell,
And *there* hath been thy bane; there is a fire
And motion of the Soul which will not dwell

In its own narrow being, but aspire
Beyond the fitting medium of desire;
And, but once kindled, quenchless evermore,
Preys upon high adventure, nor can tire
Of aught but rest; a fever at the core,
Fatal to him who bears, to all who ever bore.

XLIII

This makes the madmen who have made men mad
By their contagion; Conquerors and Kings,
Founders of sects and systems, to whom add
Sophists, Bards, Statesmen, all unquiet things
Which stir too strongly the soul's secret springs,
And are themselves the fools to those they fool;
Envied, yet how unenviable! what stings
Are theirs! One breast laid open were a school
Which would unteach Mankind the lust to shine or rule:

XLIV

Their breath is agitation, and their life
A storm whereon they ride, to sink at last,
And yet so nursed and bigoted to strife,
That should their days, surviving perils past,
Melt to calm twilight, they feel overcast
With sorrow and supineness, and so die;
Even as a flame unfed, which runs to waste
With its own flickering, or a sword laid by,
Which eats into itself, and rusts ingloriously.

XLV

He who ascends to mountain-tops, shall find
The loftiest peaks most wrapt in clouds and snow;
He who surpasses or subdues mankind,
Must look down on the hate of those below.
Though high *above* the Sun of Glory glow,
And far *beneath* the Earth and Ocean spread,
Round him are icy rocks, and loudly blow
Contending tempests on his naked head,
And thus reward the toils which to those summits led.

XLVI

Away with these! true Wisdom's world will be
Within its own creation, or in thine,
Maternal Nature! for who teems like thee,

Thus on the banks of thy majestic Rhine?
There Harold gazes on a work divine,
A blending of all beauties; streams and dells,
Fruit, foliage, crag, wood, cornfield, mountain, vine,
And chiefless castles breathing stern farewells
From gray but leafy walls, where Ruin greenly dwells,

XLVII

And there they stand, as stands a lofty mind,
Worn, but unstooping to the baser crowd,
All tenantless, save to the crannying Wind,
Or holding dark communion with the Cloud
There was a day when they were young and proud;
Banners on high, and battles passed below;
But they who fought are in a bloody shroud,
And those which waved are shredless dust ere now,
And the bleak battlements shall bear no future blow.

XLVIII

Beneath these battlements, within those walls,
Power dwelt amidst her passions; in proud state
Each robber chief upheld his armèd halls,
Doing his evil will, nor less elate
Than mightier heroes of a longer date.
What want these outlaws conquerors should have
But History's purchased page to call them great?
A wider space — an ornamented grave?
Their hopes were not less warm, their souls were full as brave.

XLIX

In their baronial feuds and single fields,
What deeds of prowess unrecorded died!
And Love, which lent a blazon to their shields,
With emblems well devised by amorous pride,
Through all the mail of iron hearts would glide;
But still their flame was fierceness, and drew on
Keen contest and destruction near allied,
And many a tower for some fair mischief won,
Saw the discoloured Rhine beneath its ruin run.

L

But Thou, exulting and abounding river!
Making thy waves a blessing as they flow
Through banks whose beauty would endure for ever

Could man but leave thy bright creation so,
Nor its fair promise from the surface mow
With the sharp scythe of conflict, — then to see
Thy valley of sweet waters, were to know
Earth paved like Heaven — and to seem such to me,
Even now what wants thy stream? — that it should Lethe be.

LI

A thousand battles have assailed thy banks,
But these and half their fame have passed away,
And Slaughter heaped on high his weltering ranks:
Their very graves are gone, and what are they?
Thy tide washed down the blood of yesterday,
And all was stainless, and on thy clear stream
Glassed, with its dancing light, the sunny ray;
But o'er the blacken'd memory's blighting dream
Thy waves would vainly roll, all sweeping as they seem.

LII

Thus Harold inly said, and passed along,
Yet not insensible to all which here
Awoke the jocund birds to early song
In glens which might have made even exile dear:
Though on his brow were graven lines austere,
And tranquil sternness, which had ta'en the place
Of feelings fierier far but less severe —
Joy was not always absent from his face,
But o'er it in such scenes would steal with transient trace.

LIII

Nor was all Love shut from him, though his days
Of Passion had consumed themselves to dust.
It is in vain that we would coldly gaze
On such as smile upon us; the heart must
Leap kindly back to kindness, though Disgust
Hath weaned it from all worldlings: thus he felt,
For there was soft Remembrance, and sweet Trust
In one fond breast, to which his own would melt,
And in its tenderer hour on that his bosom dwelt.

LIV

And he had learned to love, — I know not why,
For this in such as him seems strange of mood, —
The helpless looks of blooming Infancy,

Even in its earliest nurture; what subdued,
To change like this, a mind so far imbued
With scorn of man, it little boots to know;
But thus it was; and though in solitude
Small power the nipped affections have to grow,
In him this glowed when all beside had ceased to glow.

LV

And there was one soft breast, as hath been said,
Which unto his was bound by stronger ties
Than the church links withal; and — though unwed,
That love was pure — and, far above disguise,
Had stood the test of mortal enmities
Still undivided, and cemented more
By peril, dreaded most in female eyes;
But this was firm, and from a foreign shore
Well to that heart might his these absent greetings pour!

1

The castled Crag of Drachenfels
Frowns o'er the wide and winding Rhine,
Whose breast of waters broadly swells
Between the banks which bear the vine,
And hills all rich with blossomed trees,
And fields which promise corn and wine,
And scattered cities crowning these,
Whose far white walls along them shine,
Have strewed a scene, which I should see
With double joy wert *thou* with me.

2

And peasant girls, with deep blue eyes,
And hands which offer early flowers,
Walk smiling o'er this Paradise;
Above, the frequent feudal towers
Through green leaves lift their walls of gray;
And many a rock which steeply lowers,
And noble arch in proud decay,
Look o'er this vale of vintage-bowers;
But one thing want these banks of Rhine, —
Thy gentle hand to clasp in mine!

3

I send the lilies given to me —
Though long before thy hand they touch,

I know that they must withered be,
But yet reject them not as such;
For I have cherished them as dear,
Because they yet may meet thine eye,
And guide thy soul to mine even here,
When thou behold'st them drooping nigh,
And know'st them gathered by the Rhine,
And offered from my heart to thine!

4

The river nobly foams and flows —
The charm of this enchanted ground,
And all its thousand turns disclose
Some fresher beauty varying round:
The haughtiest breast its wish might bound
Through life to dwell delighted here;
Nor could on earth a spot be found
To Nature and to me so dear —
Could thy dear eyes in following mine
Still sweeten more these banks of Rhine!

LVI

By Coblentz, on a rise of gentle ground,
There is a small and simple Pyramid,
Crowning the summit of the verdant mound;
Beneath its base are Heroes' ashes hid —
Our enemy's — but let not that forbid
Honour to Marceau! o'er whose early tomb
Tears, big tears, gushed from the rough soldier's lid,
Lamenting and yet envying such a doom,
Falling for France, whose rights he battled to resume.

LVII

Brief, brave, and glorious was his young career, —
His mourners were two hosts, his friends and foes;
And fitly may the stranger lingering here
Pray for his gallant Spirit's bright repose; —
For he was Freedom's Champion, one of those,
The few in number, who had not o'erstept
The charter to chastise which she bestows
On such as wield her weapons; he had kept
The whiteness of his soul — and thus men o'er him wept.

LVIII

Here Ehrenbreitstein, with her shattered wall
Black with the miner's blast, upon her height

Yet shows of what she was, when shell and ball
Rebounding idly on her strength did light: —
A Tower of Victory! from whence the flight
Of baffled foes was watched along the plain:
But Peace destroyed what War could never blight,
And laid those proud roofs bare to Summer's rain —
On which the iron shower for years had poured in vain.

LIX

Adieu to thee, fair Rhine! How long delighted
The stranger fain would linger on his way!
Thine is a scene alike where souls united
Or lonely Contemplation thus might stray;
And could the ceaseless vultures cease to prey
On self-condemning bosoms, it were here,
Where Nature, nor too sombre nor too gay,
Wild but not rude, awful yet not austere,
Is to the mellow Earth as Autumn to the year.

LX

Adieu to thee again! a vain adieu!
There can be no farewell to scene like thine;
The mind is coloured by thy every hue;
And if reluctantly the eyes resign
Their cherished gaze upon thee, lovely Rhine!
'Tis with the thankful glance of parting praise;
More mighty spots may rise — more glaring shine,
But none unite in one attaching maze
The brilliant, fair, and soft, — the glories of old days,

LXI

The negligently grand, the fruitful bloom
Of coming ripeness, the white city's sheen,
The rolling stream, the precipice's gloom,
The forest's growth, and Gothic walls between, —
The wild rocks shaped, as they had turrets been,
In mockery of man's art; and these withal
A race of faces happy as the scene,
Whose fertile bounties here extend to all,
Still springing o'er thy banks, though Empires near them fall.

LXII

But these recede. Above me are the Alps,
The Palaces of Nature, whose vast walls

Have pinnacled in clouds their snowy scalps,
And throned Eternity in icy halls
Of cold Sublimity, where forms and falls
The Avalanche — the thunderbolt of snow!
All that expands the spirit, yet appals,
Gather around these summits, as to show
How Earth may pierce to Heaven, yet leave vain man below.

LXIII

But ere these matchless heights I dare to scan,
There is a spot should not be passed in vain, —
Morat! the proud, the patriot field! where man
May gaze on ghastly trophies of the slain,
Nor blush for those who conquered on that plain;
Here Burgundy bequeathed his tombless host,
A bony heap, through ages to remain,
Themselves their monument; — the Stygian coast
Unsepulchred they roamed, and shrieked each wandering ghost.

LXIV

While Waterloo with Cannæ's carnage vies,
Morat and Marathon twin names shall stand;
They were true Glory's stainless victories,
Won by the unambitious heart and hand
Of a proud, brotherly, and civic band,
All unbought champions in no princely cause
Of vice-entailed Corruption; they no land
Doomed to bewail the blasphemy of laws
Making Kings' rights divine, by some Draconic clause.

LXV

By a lone wall a lonelier column rears
A gray and grief-worn aspect of old days;
'Tis the last remnant of the wreck of years,
And looks as with the wild-bewildered gaze
Of one to stone converted by amaze,
Yet still with consciousness; and there it stands
Making a marvel that it not decays,
When the coeval pride of human hands,
Levelled Aventicum, hath strewed her subject lands.

LXVI

And there — oh! sweet and sacred be the name! —
Julia — the daughter — the devoted — gave

Her youth to Heaven; her heart, beneath a claim
Nearest to Heaven's, broke o'er a father's grave.
Justice is sworn 'gainst tears, and hers would crave
The life she lived in — but the Judge was just —
And then she died on him she could not save.
Their tomb was simple, and without a bust,
And held within their urn one mind — one heart — one dust.

LXVII

But these are deeds which should not pass away,
And names that must not wither, though the Earth
Forgets her empires with a just decay,
The enslavers and the enslaved — their death and birth;
The high, the mountain-majesty of Worth
Should be — and shall, survivor of its woe,
And from its immortality, look forth
In the sun's face, like yonder Alpine snow,
Imperishably pure beyond all things below.

LXVIII

Lake Leman woos me with its crystal face,
The mirror where the stars and mountains view
The stillness of their aspect in each trace
Its clear depth yields of their far height and hue:
There is too much of Man here, to look through
With a fit mind the might which I behold;
But soon in me shall Loneliness renew
Thoughts hid, but not less cherished than of old,
Ere mingling with the herd had penned me in their fold.

LXIX

To fly from, need not be to hate, mankind:
All are not fit with them to stir and toil,
Nor is it discontent to keep the mind
Deep in its fountain, lest it overboil
In the hot throng, where we become the spoil
Of our infection, till too late and long
We may deplore and struggle with the coil,
In wretched interchange of wrong for wrong
Midst a contentious world, striving where none are strong.

LXX

There, in a moment, we may plunge our years
In fatal penitence, and in the blight

Of our own Soul turn all our blood to tears,
And colour things to come with hues of Night;
The race of life becomes a hopeless flight
To those that walk in darkness: on the sea
The boldest steer but where their ports invite —
But there are wanderers o'er Eternity
Whose bark drives on and on, and anchored ne'er shall be.

LXXI

Is it not better, then, to be alone,
And love Earth only for its earthly sake?
By the blue rushing of the arrowy Rhone,
Or the pure bosom of its nursing Lake,
Which feeds it as a mother who doth make
A fair but froward infant her own care,
Kissing its cries away as these awake; —
Is it not better thus our lives to wear,
Than join the crushing crowd, doomed to inflict or bear?

LXXII

I live not in myself, but I become
Portion of that around me; and to me
High mountains are a feeling, but the hum
Of human cities torture: I can see
Nothing to loathe in Nature, save to be
A link reluctant in a fleshly chain,
Classed among creatures, when the soul can flee,
And with the sky — the peak — the heaving plain
Of Ocean, or the stars, mingle — and not in vain.

LXXIII

And thus I am absorbed, and this is life: —
I look upon the peopled desert past,
As on a place of agony and strife,
Where, for some sin, to Sorrow I was cast,
To act and suffer, but remount at last
With a fresh pinion; which I feel to spring,
Though young, yet waxing vigorous as the Blast
Which it would cope with, on delighted wing,
Spurning the clay-cold bonds which round our being cling.

LXXIV

And when, at length, the mind shall be all free
From what it hates in this degraded form,

Reft of its carnal life, save what shall be
Existent happier in the fly and worm, —
When Elements to Elements conform,
And dust is as it should be, shall I not
Feel all I see less dazzling but more warm?
The bodiless thought? the Spirit of each spot?
Of which, even now, I share at times the immortal lot?

LXXV

Are not the mountains, waves, and skies, a part
Of me and of my Soul, as I of them?
Is not the love of these deep in my heart
With a pure passion? should I not contemn
All objects, if compared with these? and stem
A tide of suffering, rather than forego
Such feelings for the hard and worldly phlegm
Of those whose eyes are only turned below,
Gazing upon the ground, with thoughts which dare not glow?

LXXVI

But this is not my theme; and I return
To that which is immediate, and require
Those who find contemplation in the urn,
To look on One, whose dust was once all fire, —
A native of the land where I respire
The clear air for a while — a passing guest,
Where he became a being, — whose desire
Was to be glorious; 'twas a foolish quest,
The which to gain and keep, he sacrificed all rest.

LXXVII

Here the self-torturing sophist, wild Rousseau,
The apostle of Affliction, he who threw
Enchantment over Passion, and from Woe
Wrung overwhelming eloquence, first drew
The breath which made him wretched; yet he knew
How to make Madness beautiful, and cast
O'er erring deeds and thoughts, a heavenly hue
Of words, like sunbeams, dazzling as they past
The eyes, which o'er them shed tears feelingly and fast.

LXXVIII

His love was Passion's essence — as a tree
On fire by lightning; with ethereal flame

Kindled he was, and blasted; for to be
Thus, and enamoured, were in him the same.
But his was not the love of living dame,
Nor of the dead who rise upon our dreams,
But of ideal Beauty, which became
In him existence, and o'erflowing teems
Along his burning page, distempered though it seems.

LXXIX

This breathed itself to life in Julie, *this*
Invested her with all that's wild and sweet;
This hallowed, too, the memorable kiss
Which every morn his fevered lip would greet,
From hers, who but with friendship his would meet;
But to that gentle touch, through brain and breast
Flashed the thrilled Spirit's love-devouring heat;
In that absorbing sigh perchance more blest
Than vulgar minds may be with all they seek possest.

LXXX

His life was one long war with self-sought foes,
Or friends by him self-banished; for his mind
Had grown Suspicion's sanctuary, and chose,
For its own cruel sacrifice, the kind,
'Gainst whom he raged with fury strange and blind.
But he was phrensied, — wherefore, who may know?
Since cause might be which Skill could never find;
But he was phrensied by disease or woe,
To that worst pitch of all, which wears a reasoning show.

LXXXI

For then he was inspired, and from him came,
As from the Pythian's mystic cave of yore,
Those oracles which set the world in flame,
Nor ceased to burn till kingdoms were no more:
Did he not this for France? which lay before
Bowed to the inborn tyranny of years?
Broken and trembling to the yoke she bore,
Till by the voice of him and his compeers,
Roused up to too much wrath which follows o'ergrown fears?

LXXXII

They made themselves a fearful monument!
The wreck of old opinions — things which grew,

Breathed from the birth of Time: the veil they rent,
And what behind it lay, all earth shall view.
But good with ill they also overthrew,
Leaving but ruins, wherewith to rebuild
Upon the same foundation, and renew
Dungeons and thrones, which the same hour refilled,
As heretofore, because Ambition was self-willed.

LXXXIII

But this will not endure, nor be endured!
Mankind have felt their strength, and made it felt.
They might have used it better, but, allured
By their new vigour, sternly have they dealt
On one another; Pity ceased to melt
With her once natural charities. But they,
Who in Oppression's darkness caved had dwelt,
They were not eagles, nourished with the day;
What marvel then, at times, if they mistook their prey?

LXXXIV

What deep wounds ever closed without a scar?
The heart's bleed longest, and but heal to wear
That which disfigures it; and they who war
With their own hopes, and have been vanquished, bear
Silence, but not submission: in his lair
Fixed Passion holds his breath, until the hour
Which shall atone for years; none need despair:
It came — it cometh — and will come, — the power
To punish or forgive — in *one* we shall be slower.

LXXXV

Clear, placid Leman! thy contrasted lake,
With the wild world I dwelt in, is a thing
Which warns me, with its stillness, to forsake
Earth's troubled waters for a purer spring.
This quiet sail is as a noiseless wing
To waft me from distraction; once I loved
Torn Ocean's roar, but thy soft murmuring
Sounds sweet as if a Sister's voice reproved,
That I with stern delights should e'er have been so moved.

LXXXVI

It is the hush of night, and all between
Thy margin and the mountains, dusk, yet clear,

Mellowed and mingling, yet distinctly seen,
Save darkened Jura, whose capt heights appear
Precipitously steep; and drawing near,
There breathes a living fragrance from the shore,
Of flowers yet fresh with childhood; on the ear
Drops the light drip of the suspended oar,
Or chirps the grasshopper one good-night carol more.

LXXXVII

He is an evening reveller, who makes
His life an infancy, and sings his fill;
At intervals, some bird from out the brakes
Starts into voice a moment, then is still.
There seems a floating whisper on the hill,
But that is fancy — for the Starlight dews
All silently their tears of Love instil,
Weeping themselves away, till they infuse
Deep into Nature's breast the spirit of her hues.

LXXXVIII

Ye Stars! which are the poetry of Heaven!
If in your bright leaves we would read the fate
Of men and empires, — 'tis to be forgiven,
That in our aspirations to be great,
Our destinies o'erleap their mortal state,
And claim a kindred with you; for ye are
A Beauty and a Mystery, and create
In us such love and reverence from afar,
That Fortune, — Fame, — Power, — Life, have named themselves a Star.

LXXXIX

All Heaven and Earth are still — though not in sleep,
But breathless, as we grow when feeling most;
And silent, as we stand in thoughts too deep: —
All Heaven and Earth are still: From the high host
Of stars, to the lulled lake and mountain-coast,
All is concentered in a life intense.
Where not a beam, nor air, nor leaf is lost,
But hath a part of Being, and a sense
Of that which is of all Creator and Defence.

XC

Then stirs the feeling infinite, so felt
In solitude, where we are *least* alone;

A truth, which through our being then doth melt,
And purifies from self: it is a tone,
The soul and source of Music, which makes known
Eternal harmony, and sheds a charm
Like to the fabled Cytherea's zone,
Binding all things with beauty; — 'twouid disarm
The spectre Death, had he substantial power to harm.

XCI

Not vainly did the early Persian make
His altar the high places, and the peak
Of earth-o'ergazing mountains, and thus take
A fit and unwalled temple, there to seek
The Spirit, in whose honour shrines are weak
Upreared of human hands. Come, and compare
Columns and idol-dwellings — Goth or Greek —
With Nature's realms of worship, earth and air —
Nor fix on fond abodes to circumscribe thy prayer!

XCII

The sky is changed! — and such a change! Oh Night,
And Storm, and Darkness, ye are wondrous strong,
Yet lovely in your strength, as is the light
Of a dark eye in Woman! Far along,
From peak to peak, the rattling crags among
Leaps the live thunder! Not from one lone cloud,
But every mountain now hath found a tongue,
And Jura answers, through her misty shroud,
Back to the joyous Alps, who call to her aloud!

XCIII

And this is in the Night: — Most glorious Night!
Thou wert not sent for slumber! let me be
A sharer in thy fierce and far delight, —
A portion of the tempest and of thee!
How the lit lake shines, a phosphoric sea,
And the big rain comes dancing to the earth!
And now again 'tis black, — and now, the glee
Of the loud hills shakes with its mountain-mirth,
As if they did rejoice o'er a young Earthquake's birth.

XCIV

Now, where the swift Rhone cleaves his way between
Heights which appear as lovers who have parted

In hate, whose mining depths so intervene,
That they can meet no more, though broken-hearted:
Though in their souls, which thus each other thwarted,
Love was the very root of the fond rage
Which blighted their life's bloom, and then departed: —
Itself expired, but leaving them an age
Of years all winters, — war within themselves to wage:

XCV

Now, where the quick Rhone thus hath cleft his way,
The mightiest of the storms hath ta'en his stand:
For here, not one, but many, make their play,
And fling their thunder-bolts from hand to hand,
Flashing and cast around: of all the band,
The brightest through these parted hills hath forked
His lightnings, — as if he did understand,
That in such gaps as Desolation worked,
There the hot shaft should blast whatever therein lurked.

XCVI

Sky — Mountains — River — Winds — Lake — Lightnings! ye!
With night, and clouds, and thunder — and a Soul
To make these felt and feeling, well may be
Things that have made me watchful; the far roll
Of your departing voices, is the knoll
Of what in me is sleepless, — if I rest.
But where of ye, O Tempests! is the goal?
Are ye like those within the human breast?
Or do ye find, at length, like eagles, some high nest?

XCVII

Could I embody and unbosom now
That which is most within me, — could I wreak
My thoughts upon expression, and thus throw
Soul — heart — mind — passions — feelings — strong or weak —
All that I would have sought, and all I seek,
Bear, know, feel — and yet breathe — into *one* word,
And that one word were Lightning, I would speak;
But as it is, I live and die unheard,
With a most voiceless thought, sheathing it as a sword.

XCVIII

The Morn is up again, the dewy Morn,
With breath all incense, and with cheek all bloom —

Laughing the clouds away with playful scorn,
And living as if earth contained no tomb, —
And glowing into day: we may resume
The march of our existence: and thus I,
Still on thy shores, fair Leman! may find room
And food for meditation, nor pass by
Much, that may give us pause, if pondered fittingly.

XCIX

Clarens! sweet Clarens birthplace of deep Love!
Thine air is the young breath of passionate Thought;
Thy trees take root in Love; the snows above,
The very Glaciers have his colours caught,
And Sun-set into rose-hues sees them wrought
By rays which sleep there lovingly: the rocks,
The permanent crags, tell here of Love, who sought
In them a refuge from the worldly shocks,
Which stir and sting the Soul with Hope that woos, then mocks.

C

Clarens! by heavenly feet thy paths are trod, —
Undying Love's, who here ascends a throne
To which the steps are mountains; where the God
Is a pervading Life and Light, — so shown
Not on those summits solely, nor alone
In the still cave and forest; o'er the flower
His eye is sparkling, and his breath hath blown,
His soft and summer breath, whose tender power
Passes the strength of storms in their most desolate hour.

CI

All things are here of *Him;* from the black pines,
Which are his shade on high, and the loud roar
Of torrents, where he listeneth, to the vines
Which slope his green path downward to the shore,
Where the bowed Waters meet him, and adore,
Kissing his feet with murmurs; and the Wood,
The covert of old trees, with trunks all hoar,
But light leaves, young as joy, stands where it stood,
Offering to him, and his, a populous solitude.

CII

A populous solitude of bees and birds,
And fairy-formed and many-coloured things,

Who worship him with notes more sweet than words,
And innocently open their glad wings,
Fearless and full of life: the gush of springs,
And fall of lofty fountains, and the bend
Of stirring branches, and the bud which brings
The swiftest thought of Beauty, here extend
Mingling — and made by Love — unto one mighty end.

CIII

He who hath loved not, here would learn that lore,
And make his heart a spirit; he who knows
That tender mystery, will love the more;
For this is Love's recess, where vain men's woes,
And the world's waste, have driven him far from those,
For 'tis his nature to advance or die;
He stands not still, but or decays, or grows
Into a boundless blessing, which may vie
With the immortal lights, in its eternity!

CIV

'Twas not for fiction chose Rousseau this spot,
Peopling it with affections; but he found
It was the scene which Passion must allot
To the Mind's purified beings; 'twas the ground
Where early Love his Psyche's zone unbound,
And hallowed it with loveliness: 'tis lone,
And wonderful, and deep, and hath a sound,
And sense, and sight of sweetness; here the Rhone
Hath spread himself a couch, the Alps have reared a throne.

CV

Lausanne! and Ferney! ye have been the abodes
Of Names which unto you bequeathed a name;
Mortals, who sought and found, by dangerous roads,
A path to perpetuity of Fame:
They were gigantic minds, and their steep aim
Was, Titan-like, on daring doubts to pile
Thoughts which should call down thunder, and the flame
Of Heaven again assailed — if Heaven, the while,
On man and man's research could deign do more than smile.

CVI

The one was fire and fickleness, a child
Most mutable in wishes, but in mind

A wit as various, — gay, grave, sage, or wild, —
Historian, bard, philosopher, combined;
He multiplied himself among mankind,
The Proteus of their talents: But his own
Breathed most in ridicule, — which, as the wind,
Blew where it listed, laying all things prone, —
Now to o'erthrow a fool, and now to shake a throne.

CVII

The other, deep and slow, exhausting thought,
And hiving wisdom with each studious year,
In meditation dwelt — with learning wrought,
And shaped his weapon with an edge severe,
Sapping a solemn creed with solemn sneer;
The lord of irony, — that master-spell,
Which stung his foes to wrath, which grew from fear
And doomed him to the zealot's ready Hell,
Which answers to all doubts so eloquently well.

CVIII

Yet, peace be with their ashes, — for by them,
If merited, the penalty is paid;
It is not ours to judge, — far less condemn;
The hour must come when such things shall be made
Known unto all, — or hope and dread allayed
By slumber, on one pillow, in the dust,
Which, thus much we are sure, must lie decayed;
And when it shall revive, as is our trust,
'Twill be to be forgiven — or suffer what is just.

CIX

But let me quit Man's works, again to read
His Maker's, spread around me, and suspend
This page, which from my reveries I feed,
Until it seems prolonging without end.
The clouds above me to the white Alps tend,
And I must pierce them, and survey whate'er
May be permitted, as my steps I bend
To their most great and growing region, where
The earth to her embrace compels the powers of air.

CX

Italia too! Italia! looking on thee,
Full flashes on the Soul the light of ages,

Since the fierce Carthaginian almost won thee,
To the last halo of the Chiefs and Sages
Who glorify thy consecrated pages;
Thou wert the throne and grave of empires; still,
The fount at which the panting Mind assuages
Her thirst of knowledge, quaffing there her fill,
Flows from the eternal source of Rome's imperial hill.

CXI

Thus far have I proceeded in a theme
Renewed with no kind auspices: — to feel
We are not what we have been, and to deem
We are not what we should be, — and to steel
The heart against itself; and to conceal,
With a proud caution, love, or hate, or aught, —
Passion or feeling, purpose, grief, or zeal, —
Which is the tyrant Spirit of our thought,
Is a stern task of soul: — No matter, — it is taught.

CXII

And for these words, thus woven into song,
It may be that they are a harmless wile, —
The colouring of the scenes which fleet along,
Which I would seize, in passing, to beguile
My breast, or that of others, for a while.
Fame is the thirst of youth, — but I am not
So young as to regard men's frown or smile,
As loss or guerdon of a glorious lot; —
I stood and stand alone, — remembered or forgot.

CXIII

I have not loved the World, nor the World me;
I have not flattered its rank breath, nor bowed
To its idolatries a patient knee,
Nor coined my cheek to smiles, — nor cried aloud
In worship of an echo: in the crowd
They could not deem me one of such — I stood
Among them, but not of them — in a shroud
Of thoughts which were not their thoughts, and still could,
Had I not filed my mind, which thus itself subdued.

CXIV

I have not loved the World, nor the World me, —
But let us part fair foes; I do believe,

Though I have found them not, that there may be
Words which are things, — hopes which will not deceive,
And Virtues which are merciful, nor weave
Snares for the failing; I would also deem
O'er others' griefs that some sincerely grieve —
That two, or one, are almost what they seem, —
That Goodness is no name — and Happiness no dream.

CXV

My daughter! with thy name this song begun!
My daughter! with thy name thus much shall end! —
I see thee not — I hear thee not — but none
Can be so wrapt in thee; Thou art the Friend
To whom the shadows of far years extend:
Albeit my brow thou never should'st behold,
My voice shall with thy future visions blend,
And reach into thy heart, — when mine is cold, —
A token and a tone, even from thy father's mould.

CXVI

To aid thy mind's developement, — to watch
Thy dawn of little joys, — to sit and see
Almost thy very growth, — to view thee catch
Knowledge of objects, — wonders yet to thee!
To hold thee lightly on a gentle knee,
And print on thy soft cheek a parent's kiss, —
This, it should seem, was not reserved for me —
Yet this was in my nature: — as it is,
I know not what is there, yet something like to this.

CXVII

Yet, though dull Hate as duty should be taught,
I know that thou wilt love me: though my name
Should be shut from thee, as a spell still fraught
With desolation, and a broken claim:
Though the grave closed between us, — 'twere the same,
I know that thou wilt love me — though to drain
My blood from out thy being were an aim,
And an attainment, — all would be in vain, —
Still thou would'st love me, still that more than life retain.

CXVIII

The child of Love! though born in bitterness,
And nurtured in Convulsion! Of thy sire

These were the elements, — and thine no less.
As yet such are around thee, — but thy fire
Shall be more tempered, and thy hope far higher!
Sweet be thy cradled slumbers! O'er the sea
And from the mountains where I now respire,
Fain would I waft such blessing upon thee,
As — with a sigh — I deem thou might'st have been to me!

CANTO THE FOURTH

"Visto ho Toscana Lombardia Romagna
Quel monte che divide, e quel che serra
Italia, e un mare e l'altro che la bagna."
Ariosto, *Satira.*

I

I STOOD in Venice, on the "Bridge of Sighs;"
A Palace and a prison on each hand:
I saw from out the wave her structures rise
As from the stroke of the Enchanter's wand:
A thousand Years their cloudy wings expand
Around me, and a dying Glory smiles
O'er the far times, when many a subject land
Looked to the wingéd Lion's marble piles,
Where Venice sate in state, throned on her hundred isles!

II

She looks a sea Cybele, fresh from Ocean,
Rising with her tiara of proud towers
At airy distance, with majestic motion,
A Ruler of the waters and their powers:
And such she was; — her daughters had their dowers
From spoils of nations, and the exhaustless East
Poured in her lap all gems in sparkling showers.
In purple was she robed, and of her feast
Monarchs partook, and deemed their dignity increased.

III

In Venice Tasso's echoes are no more,
And silent rows the songless Gondolier;
Her palaces are crumbling to the shore,
And Music meets not always now the ear:
Those days are gone — but Beauty still is here.
States fall — Arts fade — but Nature doth not die,

Nor yet forget how Venice once was dear,
The pleasant place of all festivity,
The Revel of the earth — the Masque of Italy!

IV

But unto us she hath a spell beyond
Her name in story, and her long array
Of mighty shadows, whose dim forms despond
Above the Dogeless city's vanished sway;
Ours is a trophy which will not decay
With the Rialto; Shylock and the Moor,
And Pierre, can not be swept or worn away —
The keystones of the Arch! though all were o'er,
For us repeopled were the solitary shore.

V

The Beings of the Mind are not of clay:
Essentially immortal, they create
And multiply in us a brighter ray
And more beloved existence: that which Fate
Prohibits to dull life in this our state
Of mortal bondage, by these Spirits supplied,
First exiles, then replaces what we hate;
Watering the heart whose early flowers have died,
And with a fresher growth replenishing the void.

VI

Such is the refuge of our youth and age —
The first from Hope, the last from Vacancy;
And this wan feeling peoples many a page —
And, may be, that which grows beneath mine eye:
Yet there are things whose strong reality
Outshines our fairy-land; in shape and hues
More beautiful than our fantastic sky,
And the strange constellations which the Muse
O'er her wild universe is skilful to diffuse:

VII

I saw or dreamed of such, — but let them go, —
They came like Truth — and disappeared like dreams;
And whatsoe'er they were — are now but so:
I could replace them if I would; still teems
My mind with many a form which aptly seems

Such as I sought for, and at moments found;
Let these too go — for waking Reason deems
Such over-weening phantasies unsound,
And other voices speak, and other sights surround.

VIII

I've taught me other tongues — and in strange eyes
Have made me not a stranger; to the mind
Which is itself, no changes bring surprise;
Nor is it harsh to make, nor hard to find
A country with — aye, or without mankind;
Yet was I born where men are proud to be, —
Not without cause; and should I leave behind
The inviolate Island of the sage and free,
And seek me out a home by a remoter sea,

IX

Perhaps I loved it well; and should I lay
My ashes in a soil which is not mine,
My Spirit shall resume it — if we may
Unbodied choose a sanctuary. I twine
My hopes of being remembered in my line
With my land's language: if too fond and far
These aspirations in their scope incline, —
If my Fame should be, as my fortunes are,
Of hasty growth and blight, and dull Oblivion bar

X

My name from out the temple where the dead
Are honoured by the Nations — let it be —
And light the Laurels on a loftier head!
And be the Spartan's epitaph on me —
"Sparta hath many a worthier son than he."
Meantime I seek no sympathies, nor need —
The thorns which I have reaped are of the tree
I planted, — they have torn me, — and I bleed:
I should have known what fruit would spring from such a seed.

XI

The spouseless Adriatic mourns her Lord,
And annual marriage now no more renewed —
The Bucentaur lies rotting unrestored,
Neglected garment of her widowhood!

St. Mark yet sees his Lion where he stood
Stand, but in mockery of his withered power,
Over the proud Place where an Emperor sued,
And monarchs gazed and envied in the hour
When Venice was a Queen with an unequalled dower.

XII

The Suabian sued, and now the Austrian reigns —
An Emperor tramples where an Emperor knelt;
Kingdoms are shrunk to provinces, and chains
Clank over sceptred cities; Nations melt
From Power's high pinnacle, when they have felt
The sunshine for a while, and downward go
Like Lauwine loosened from the mountain's belt;
Oh for one hour of blind old Dandolo!
Th' octogenarian chief, Byzantium's conquering foe.

XIII

Before St. Mark still glow his Steeds of brass,
Their gilded collars glittering in the sun;
But is not Doria's menace come to pass?
Are they not bridled? — Venice, lost and won,
Her thirteen hundred years of freedom done,
Sinks, like a sea-weed, unto whence she rose!
Better be whelmed beneath the waves, and shun,
Even in Destruction's depth, her foreign foes,
From whom Submission wrings an infamous repose.

XIV

In youth She was all glory, — a new Tyre, —
Her very by-word sprung from Victory,
The "Planter of the Lion," which through fire
And blood she bore o'er subject Earth and Sea;
Though making many slaves, Herself still free,
And Europe's bulwark 'gainst the Ottomite;
Witness Troy's rival, Candia! Vouch it, ye
Immortal waves that saw Lepanto's fight!
For ye are names no Time nor Tyranny can blight.

XV

Statues of glass — all shivered — the long file
Of her dead Doges are declined to dust;
But where they dwelt, the vast and sumptuous pile
Bespeaks the pageant of their splendid trust;

Their sceptre broken, and their sword in rust,
Have yielded to the stranger: empty halls,
Thin streets, and foreign aspects, such as must
Too oft remind her who and what enthrals,
Have flung a desolate cloud o'er Venice' lovely walls.

XVI

When Athens' armies fell at Syracuse,
And fettered thousands bore the yoke of war,
Redemption rose up in the Attic Muse,
Her voice their only ransom from afar:
See! as they chant the tragic hymn, the car
Of the o'ermastered Victor stops — the reins
Fall from his hands — his idle scimitar
Starts from its belt — he rends his captive's chains,
And bids him thank the Bard for Freedom and his strains.

XVII

Thus, Venice! if no stronger claim were thine,
Were all thy proud historic deeds forgot —
Thy choral memory of the Bard divine,
Thy love of Tasso, should have cut the knot
Which ties thee to thy tyrants; and thy lot
Is shameful to the nations, — most of all,
Albion! to thee: the Ocean queen should not
Abandon Ocean's children; in the fall
Of Venice think of thine, despite thy watery wall.

XVIII

I loved her from my boyhood — she to me
Was as a fairy city of the heart,
Rising like water-columns from the sea —
Of Joy the sojourn, and of Wealth the mart;
And Otway, Radcliffe, Schiller, Shakespeare's art,
Had stamped her image in me, and even so,
Although I found her thus, we did not part;
Perchance even dearer in her day of woe,
Than when she was a boast, a marvel, and a show.

XIX

I can repeople with the past — and of
The present there is still for eye and thought,
And meditation chastened down, enough;
And more, it may be, than I hoped or sought;

And of the happiest moments which were wrought
Within the web of my existence, some
From thee, fair Venice! have their colours caught:
There are some feelings Time can not benumb,
Nor Torture shake, or mine would now be cold and dumb.

XX

But from their nature will the Tannen grow
Loftiest on loftiest and least sheltered rocks,
Rooted in barrenness, where nought below
Of soil supports them 'gainst the Alpine shocks
Of eddying storms; yet springs the trunk, and mocks
The howling tempest, till its height and frame
Are worthy of the mountains from whose blocks
Of bleak, gray granite into life it came,
And grew a giant tree; — the Mind may grow the same.

XXI

Existence may be borne, and the deep root
Of life and sufferance make its firm abode
In bare and desolated bosoms: mute
The camel labours with the heaviest load,
And the wolf dies in silence — not bestowed
In vain should such example be; if they,
Things of ignoble or of savage mood,
Endure and shrink not, we of nobler clay
May temper it to bear, — it is but for a day.

XXII

All suffering doth destroy, or is destroyed,
Even by the sufferer — and, in each event,
Ends: — Some, with hope replenished and rebuoyed,
Return to whence they came — with like intent,
And weave their web again; some, bowed and bent,
Wax gray and ghastly, withering ere their time,
And perish with the reed on which they leant;
Some seek devotion — toil — war — good or crime,
According as their souls were formed to sink or climb.

XXIII

But ever and anon of griefs subdued
There comes a token like a Scorpion's sting,
Scarce seen, but with fresh bitterness imbued;

And slight withal may be the things which bring
Back on the heart the weight which it would fling
Aside for ever: it may be a sound —
A tone of music — summer's eve — or spring —
A flower — the wind — the Ocean — which shall wound,
Striking the electric chain wherewith we are darkly bound;

XXIV

And how and why we know not, nor can trace
Home to its cloud this lightning of the mind,
But feel the shock renewed, nor can efface
The blight and blackening which it leaves behind,
Which out of things familiar, undesigned,
When least we deem of such, calls up to view
The Spectres whom no exorcism can bind, —
The cold — the changed — perchance the dead, anew —
The mourned — the loved — the lost — too many! yet how few!

XXV

But my Soul wanders; I demand it back
To meditate amongst decay, and stand
A ruin amidst ruins; there to track
Fall'n states and buried greatness, o'er a land
Which *was* the mightiest in its old command,
And *is* the loveliest, and must ever be
The master-mould of Nature's heavenly hand;
Wherein were cast the heroic and the free, —
The beautiful — the brave — the Lords of earth and sea,

XXVI

The Commonwealth of Kings — the Men of Rome!
And even since, and now, fair Italy!
Thou art the Garden of the World, the Home
Of all Art yields, and Nature can decree;
Even in thy desert, what is like to thee?
Thy very weeds are beautiful — thy waste
More rich than other climes' fertility;
Thy wreck a glory — and thy ruin graced
With an immaculate charm which cannot be defaced.

XXVII

The Moon is up, and yet it is not night —
Sunset divides the sky with her — a sea

Of glory streams along the Alpine height
Of blue Friuli's mountains; Heaven is free
From clouds, but of all colours seems to be, —
Melted to one vast Iris of the West, —
Where the Day joins the past Eternity;
While, on the other hand, meek Dian's crest
Floats through the azure air — an island of the blest!

XXVIII

A single star is at her side, and reigns
With her o'er half the lovely heaven; but still
Yon sunny Sea heaves brightly, and remains
Rolled o'er the peak of the far Rhætian hill,
As Day and Night contending were, until
Nature reclaimed her order: — gently flows
The deep-dyed Brenta, where their hues instil
The odorous purple of a new-born rose,
Which streams upon her stream, and glassed within it glows,

XXIX

Filled with the face of heaven, which, from afar,
Comes down upon the waters! all its hues,
From the rich sunset to the rising star,
Their magical variety diffuse:
And now they change — a paler Shadow strews
Its mantle o'er the mountains; parting Day
Dies like the Dolphin, whom each pang imbues
With a new colour as it gasps away —
The last still loveliest, till — 'tis gone — and all is gray.

XXX

There is a tomb in Arqua; — reared in air,
Pillared in their sarcophagus, repose
The bones of Laura's lover: here repair
Many familiar with his well-sung woes,
The Pilgrims of his Genius. He arose
To raise a language, and his land reclaim
From the dull yoke of her barbaric foes:
Watering the tree which bears his Lady's name
With his melodious tears, he gave himself to Fame.

XXXI

They keep his dust in Arqua, where he died —
The mountain-village where his latter days

Went down the vale of years; and 'tis their pride —
An honest pride — and let it be their praise,
To offer to the passing stranger's gaze
His mansion and his sepulchre — both plain
And venerably simple — such as raise
A feeling more accordant with his strain
Than if a Pyramid formed his monumental fane.

XXXII

And the soft quiet hamlet where he dwelt
Is one of that complexion which seems made
For those who their mortality have felt,
And sought a refuge from their hopes decayed
In the deep umbrage of a green hill's shade,
Which shows a distant prospect far away
Of busy cities, now in vain displayed,
For they can lure no further; and the ray
Of a bright Sun can make sufficient holiday,

XXXIII

Developing the mountains, leaves, and flowers,
And shining in the brawling brook, where-by,
Clear as its current, glide the sauntering hours
With a calm languor, which, though to the eye
Idlesse it seem, hath its morality —
If from society we learn to live,
'Tis Solitude should teach us how to die;
It hath no flatterers — Vanity can give
No hollow aid; alone — man with his God must strive:

XXXIV

Or, it may be, with Demons, who impair
The strength of better thoughts, and seek their prey
In melancholy bosoms — such as were
Of moody texture from their earliest day,
And loved to dwell in darkness and dismay
Deeming themselves predestined to a doom
Which is not of the pangs that pass away;
Making the Sun like blood, the Earth a tomb,
The tomb a hell — and Hell itself a murkier gloom.

XXXV

Ferrara! in thy wide and grass-grown streets,
Whose symmetry was not for solitude,

There seems as 'twere a curse upon the Seats
Of former Sovereigns, and the antique brood
Of Este, which for many an age made good
Its strength within thy walls, and was of yore
Patron or Tyrant, as the changing mood
Of petty power impelled, of those who wore
The wreath which Dante's brow alone had worn before.

XXXVI

And Tasso is their glory and their shame —
Hark to his strain! and then survey his cell!
And see how dearly earned Torquato's fame,
And where Alfonso bade his poet dwell:
The miserable Despot could not quell
The insulted mind he sought to quench, and blend
With the surrounding maniacs, in the hell
Where he had plunged it. Glory without end
Scattered the clouds away — and on that name attend

XXXVII

The tears and praises of all time, while thine
Would rot in its oblivion — in the sink
Of worthless dust, which from thy boasted line
Is shaken into nothing — but the link
Thou formest in his fortunes bids us think
Of thy poor malice, naming thee with scorn:
Alfonso! how thy ducal pageants shrink
From thee! if in another station born,
Scarce fit to be the slave of him thou mad'st to mourn:

XXXVIII

Thou! formed to eat, and be despised, and die,
Even as the beasts that perish — save that thou
Hadst a more splendid trough and wider sty: —
He! with a glory round his furrowed brow,
Which emanated then, and dazzles now,
In face of all his foes, the Cruscan quire,
And Boileau, whose rash envy could allow
No strain which shamed his country's creaking lyre,
That whetstone of the teeth — Monotony in wire!

XXXIX

Peace to Torquato's injured shade! 'twas his
In life and death to be the mark where Wrong

Aimed with her poisoned arrows, — but to miss.
Oh, Victor unsurpassed in modern song!
Each year brings forth its millions — but how long
The tide of Generations shall roll on,
And not the whole combined and countless throng
Compose a mind like thine? though all in one
Condensed their scattered rays — they would not form a Sun.

XL

Great as thou art, yet paralleled by those,
Thy countrymen, before thee born to shine,
The Bards of Hell and Chivalry: first rose
The Tuscan Father's Comedy Divine;
Then, not unequal to the Florentine,
The southern Scott, the minstrel who called forth
A new creation with his magic line,
And, like the Ariosto of the North,
Sang Ladye-love and War, Romance and Knightly Worth.

XLI

The lightning rent from Ariosto's bust
The iron crown of laurel's mimicked leaves;
Nor was the ominous element unjust,
For the true laurel-wreath which Glory weaves
Is of the tree no bolt of thunder cleaves,
And the false semblance but disgraced his brow;
Yet still, if fondly Superstition grieves,
Know, that the lightning sanctifies below
Whate'er it strikes; — yon head is doubly sacred now.

XLII

Italia! oh, Italia! thou who hast
The fatal gift of Beauty, which became
A funeral dower of present woes and past —
On thy sweet brow is sorrow ploughed by shame,
And annals graved in characters of flame.
Oh, God! that thou wert in thy nakedness
Less lovely or more powerful, and couldst claim
Thy right, and awe the robbers back, who press
To shed thy blood, and drink the tears of thy distress;

XLIII

Then might'st thou more appal — or, less desired,
Be homely and be peaceful, undeplored

For thy destructive charms; then, still untired,
Would not be seen the armèd torrents poured
Down the deep Alps; nor would the hostile horde
Of many-nationed spoilers from the Po
Quaff blood and water; nor the stranger's sword
Be thy sad weapon of defence — and so,
Victor or vanquished, thou the slave of friend or foe.

XLIV

Wandering in youth, I traced the path of him,
The Roman friend of Rome's least-mortal mind,
The friend of Tully: as my bark did skim
The bright blue waters with a fanning wind,
Came Megara before me, and behind
Ægina lay — Piræus on the right,
And Corinth on the left; I lay reclined
Along the prow, and saw all these unite
In ruin — even as he had seen the desolate sight;

XLV

For Time hath not rebuilt them, but upreared
Barbaric dwellings on their shattered site,
Which only make more mourned and more endeared
The few last rays of their far-scattered light,
And the crushed relics of their vanished might.
The Roman saw these tombs in his own age,
These sepulchres of cities, which excite
Sad wonder, and his yet surviving page
The moral lesson bears, drawn from such pilgrimage.

XLVI

That page is now before me, and on mine
His Country's ruin added to the mass
Of perished states he mourned in their decline,
And I in desolation: all that *was*
Of then destruction *is;* and now, alas!
Rome — Rome imperial, bows her to the storm,
In the same dust and blackness, and we pass
The skeleton of her Titanic form,
Wrecks of another world, whose ashes still are warm.

XLVII

Yet, Italy! through every other land
Thy wrongs should ring — and shall — from side to side;

Mother of Arts! as once of Arms! thy hand
Was then our Guardian, and is still our Guide;
Parent of our Religion! whom the wide
Nations have knelt to for the keys of Heaven!
Europe, repentant of her parricide,
Shall yet redeem thee, and, all backward driven,
Roll the barbarian tide, and sue to be forgiven.

XLVIII

But Arno wins us to the fair white walls,
Where the Etrurian Athens claims and keeps
A softer feeling for her fairy halls:
Girt by her theatre of hills, she reaps
Her corn, and wine, and oil — and Plenty leaps
To laughing life, with her redundant Horn.
Along the banks where smiling Arno sweeps
Was modern Luxury of Commerce born,
And buried Learning rose, redeemed to a new Morn.

XLIX

There, too, the Goddess loves in stone, and fills
The air around with Beauty — we inhale
The ambrosial aspect, which, beheld, instils
Part of its immortality — the veil
Of heaven is half undrawn — within the pale
We stand, and in that form and face behold
What Mind can make, when Nature's self would fail;
And to the fond Idolaters of old
Envy the innate flash which such a Soul could mould:

L

We gaze and turn away, and know not where,
Dazzled and drunk with Beauty, till the heart
Reels with its fulness; there — for ever there —
Chained to the chariot of triumphal Art,
We stand as captives, and would not depart.
Away! — there need no words, nor terms precise,
The paltry jargon of the marble mart,
Where Pedantry gulls Folly — we have eyes:
Blood — pulse — and breast confirm the Dardan Shepherd's prize.

LI

Appear'dst thou not to Paris in this guise?
Or to more deeply blest Anchises? or,

In all thy perfect Goddess-ship, when lies
Before thee thy own vanquished Lord of War?
And gazing in thy face as toward a star,
Laid on thy lap, his eyes to thee upturn,
Feeding on thy sweet cheek! while thy lips are
With lava kisses melting while they burn,
Showered on his eyelids, brow, and mouth, as from an urn!

LII

Glowing, and circumfused in speechless love —
Their full divinity inadequate
That feeling to express, or to improve —
The Gods become as mortals — and man's fate
Has moments like their brightest; but the weight
Of earth recoils upon us; — let it go!
We can recall such visions, and create,
From what has been, or might be, things which grow
Into thy statue's form, and look like gods below.

LIII

I leave to learnèd fingers, and wise hands,
The Artist and his Ape, to teach and tell
How well his Connoisseurship understands
The graceful bend, and the voluptuous swell:
Let these describe the undescribable:
I would not their vile breath should crisp the stream
Wherein that Image shall for ever dwell —
The unruffled mirror of the loveliest dream
That ever left the sky on the deep soul to beam.

LIV

In Santa Croce's holy precincts lie
Ashes which make it holier, dust which is
Even in itself an immortality,
Though there were nothing save the past, and this,
The particle of those sublimities
Which have relapsed to chaos: — here repose
Angelo's — Alfieri's bones — and his,
The starry Galileo, with his woes;
Here Machiavelli's earth returned to whence it rose.

LV

These are four minds, which, like the elements,
Might furnish forth creation: — Italy!

Time, which hath wronged thee with ten thousand rents
Of thine imperial garment, shall deny
And hath denied, to every other sky,
Spirits which soar from ruin: — thy Decay
Is still impregnate with divinity,
Which gilds it with revivifying ray;
Such as the great of yore, Canova is to-day.

LVI

But where repose the all Etruscan three —
Dante, and Petrarch, and, scarce less than they,
The Bard of Prose, creative Spirit! he
Of the Hundred Tales of Love — where did they lay
Their bones, distinguished from our common clay
In death as life? Are they resolved to dust,
And have their Country's Marbles nought to say?
Could not her quarries furnish forth one bust?
Did they not to her breast their filial earth entrust?

LVII

Ungrateful Florence! Dante sleeps afar,
Like Scipio, buried by the upbraiding shore:
Thy factions, in their worse than civil war,
Proscribed the Bard whose name for evermore
Their children's children would in vain adore
With the remorse of ages; and the crown
Which Petrarch's laureate brow supremely wore,
Upon a far and foreign soil had grown,
His Life, his Fame, his Grave, though rifled — not thine own.

LVIII

Boccaccio to his parent earth bequeathed
His dust, — and lies it not her Great among,
With many a sweet and solemn requiem breathed
O'er him who formed the Tuscan's siren tongue?
That music in itself, whose sounds are song,
The poetry of speech? No; — even his tomb
Uptorn, must bear the hyæna bigot's wrong,
No more amidst the meaner dead find room,
Nor claim a passing sigh, because it told for *whom!*

LIX

And Santa Croce wants their mighty dust;
Yet for this want more noted, as of yore

The Cæsar's pageant, shorn of Brutus' bust,
Did but of Rome's best Son remind her more:
Happier Ravenna! on thy hoary shore,
Fortress of falling Empire! honoured sleeps
The immortal Exile; — Arqua, too, her store
Of tuneful relics proudly claims and keeps,
While Florence vainly begs her banished dead and weeps.

LX

What is her Pyramid of precious stones?
Of porphyry, jasper, agate, and all hues
Of gem and marble, to encrust the bones
Of merchant-dukes? the momentary dews
Which, sparkling to the twilight stars, infuse
Freshness in the green turf that wraps the dead,
Whose names are Mausoleums of the Muse,
Are gently prest with far more reverent tread
Than ever paced the slab which paves the princely head.

LXI

There be more things to greet the heart and eyes
In Arno's dome of Art's most princely shrine,
Where Sculpture with her rainbow Sister vies;
There be more marvels yet — but not for mine;
For I have been accustomed to entwine
My thoughts with Nature rather in the fields,
Than Art in galleries: though a work divine
Calls for my Spirit's homage, yet it yields
Less than it feels, because the weapon which it wields

LXII

Is of another temper, and I roam
By Thrasimene's lake, in the defiles
Fatal to Roman rashness, more at home;
For there the Carthaginian's warlike wiles
Come back before me, as his skill beguiles
The host between the mountains and the shore,
Where Courage falls in her despairing files,
And torrents, swoll'n to rivers with their gore,
Reek through the sultry plain, with legions scattered o'er.

LXIII

Like to a forest felled by mountain winds;
And such the storm of battle on this day,

And such the frenzy, whose convulsion blinds
To all save Carnage, that, beneath the fray,
An Earthquake reeled unheededly away!
None felt stern Nature rocking at his feet,
And yawning forth a grave for those who lay
Upon their bucklers for a winding sheet —
Such is the absorbing hate when warring nations meet!

LXIV

The Earth to them was as a rolling bark
Which bore them to Eternity — they saw
The Ocean round, but had no time to mark
The motions of their vessel; Nature's law,
In them suspended, recked not of the awe
Which reigns when mountains tremble, and the birds
Plunge in the clouds for refuge, and withdraw
From their down-toppling nests; and bellowing herds
Stumble o'er heaving plains — and Man's dread hath no words.

LXV

Far other scene is Thrasimene now;
Her lake a sheet of silver, and her plain
Rent by no ravage save the gentle plough;
Her agéd trees rise thick as once the slain
Lay where their roots are; but a brook hath ta'en —
A little rill of scanty stream and bed —
A name of blood from that day's sanguine rain;
And Sanguinetto tells ye where the dead
Made the earth wet, and turned the unwilling waters red.

LXVI

But thou, Clitumnus! in thy sweetest wave
Of the most living crystal that was e'er
The haunt of river-Nymph, to gaze and lave
Her limbs where nothing hid them, thou dost rear
Thy grassy banks whereon the milk-white steer
Grazes — the purest God of gentle waters!
And most serene of aspect, and most clear;
Surely that stream was unprofaned by slaughters —
A mirror and a bath for Beauty's youngest daughters!

LXVII

And on thy happy shore a Temple still,
Of small and delicate proportion, keeps

Upon a mild declivity of hill,
Its memory of thee; beneath it sweeps
Thy current's calmness; oft from out it leaps
The finny darter with the glittering scales,
Who dwells and revels in thy glassy deeps;
While, chance, some scattered water-lily sails
Down where the shallower wave still tells its bubbling tales.

LXVIII

Pass not unblest the Genius of the place!
If through the air a Zephyr more serene
Win to the brow, 'tis his; and if ye trace
Along his margin a more eloquent green,
If on the heart the freshness of the scene
Sprinkles its coolness, and from the dry dust
Of weary life a moment lave it clean
With Nature's baptism, — 'tis to him ye must
Pay orisons for this suspension of disgust.

LXIX

The roar of waters! — from the headlong height
Velino cleaves the wave-worn precipice;
The fall of waters! rapid as the light
The flashing mass foams shaking the abyss;
The Hell of Waters! where they howl and hiss,
And boil in endless torture; while the sweat
Of their great agony, wrung out from this
Their Phlegethon, curls round the rocks of jet
That gird the gulf around, in pitiless horror set,

LXX

And mounts in spray the skies, and thence again
Returns in an unceasing shower, which round,
With its unemptied cloud of gentle rain,
Is an eternal April to the ground,
Making it all one emerald: — how profound
The gulf! and how the Giant Element
From rock to rock leaps with delirious bound,
Crushing the cliffs, which, downward worn and rent
With his fierce footsteps, yield in chasms a fearful vent

LXXI

To the broad column which rolls on, and shows
More like the fountain of an infant sea

Torn from the womb of mountains by the throes
Of a new world, than only thus to be
Parent of rivers, which flow gushingly,
With many windings, through the vale: — Look back!
Lo! where it comes like an Eternity,
As if to sweep down all things in its track,
Charming the eye with dread, — a matchless cataract,

LXXII

Horribly beautiful! but on the verge,
From side to side, beneath the glittering morn,
An Iris sits, amidst the infernal surge,
Like Hope upon a death-bed, and, unworn
Its steady dyes, while all around is torn
By the distracted waters, bears serene
Its brilliant hues with all their beams unshorn:
Resembling, 'mid the torture of the scene,
Love watching Madness with unalterable mien.

LXXIII

Once more upon the woody Apennine —
The infant Alps, which — had I not before
Gazed on their mightier Parents, where the pine
Sits on more shaggy summits, and where roar
The thundering Lauwine — might be worshipped more;
But I have seen the soaring Jungfrau rear
Her never-trodden snow, and seen the hoar
Glaciers of bleak Mont Blanc both far and near —
And in Chimari heard the Thunder-Hills of fear,

LXXIV

Th' Acroceraunian mountains of old name;
And on Parnassus seen the Eagles fly
Like Spirits of the spot, as 'twere for fame,
For still they soared unutterably high:
I've looked on Ida with a Trojan's eye;
Athos — Olympus — Ætna — Atlas — made
These hills seem things of lesser dignity;
All, save the lone Soracte's height, displayed
Not *now* in snow, which asks the lyric Roman's aid

LXXV

For our remembrance, and from out the plain
Heaves like a long-swept wave about to break,

And on the curl hangs pausing: not in vain
May he, who will, his recollections rake,
And quote in classic raptures, and awake
The hills with Latian echoes — I abhorred
Too much, to conquer for the Poet's sake,
The drilled dull lesson, forced down word by word
In my repugnant youth, with pleasure to record

LXXVI

Aught that recalls the daily drug which turned
My sickening memory; and, though Time hath taught
My mind to meditate what then it learned,
Yet such the fixed inveteracy wrought
By the impatience of my early thought,
That, with the freshness wearing out before
My mind could relish what it might have sought,
If free to choose, I cannot now restore
Its health — but what it then detested, still abhor.

LXXVII

Then farewell, Horace — whom I hated so,
Not for thy faults, but mine: it is a curse
To understand, not feel thy lyric flow,
To comprehend, but never love thy verse;
Although no deeper Moralist rehearse
Our little life, nor Bard prescribe his art,
Nor livelier Satirist the conscience pierce,
Awakening without wounding the touched heart,
Yet fare thee well — upon Soracte's ridge we part.

LXXVIII

Oh, Rome! my Country! City of the Soul!
The orphans of the heart must turn to thee,
Lone Mother of dead Empires! and control
In their shut breasts their petty misery.
What are our woes and sufferance? Come and see
The cypress — hear the owl — and plod your way
O'er steps of broken thrones and temples — Ye!
Whose agonies are evils of a day —
A world is at our feet as fragile as our clay.

LXXIX

The Niobe of nations! there she stands,
Childless and crownless, in her voiceless woe;

An empty urn within her withered hands,
Whose holy dust was scattered long ago;
The Scipios' tomb contains no ashes now;
The very sepulchres lie tenantless
Of their heroic dwellers: dost thou flow,
Old Tiber! through a marble wilderness?
Rise, with thy yellow waves, and mantle her distress.

LXXX

The Goth, the Christian — Time — War — Flood, and Fire,
Have dealt upon the seven-hilled City's pride;
She saw her glories star by star expire,
And up the steep barbarian Monarchs ride,
Where the car climbed the Capitol; far and wide
Temple and tower went down, nor left a site:
Chaos of ruins! who shall trace the void,
O'er the dim fragments cast a lunar light,
And say, "here was, or is," where all is doubly night?

LXXXI

The double night of ages, and of her,
Night's daughter, Ignorance, hath wrapt and wrap
All round us; we but feel our way to err:
The Ocean hath his chart, the Stars their map,
And Knowledge spreads them on her ample lap;
But Rome is as the desert — where we steer
Stumbling o'er recollections; now we clap
Our hands, and cry "Eureka!" "it is clear" —
When but some false Mirage of ruin rises near.

LXXXII

Alas! the lofty city! and alas!
The trebly hundred triumphs! and the day
When Brutus made the dagger's edge surpass
The Conqueror's sword in bearing fame away!
Alas, for Tully's voice, and Virgil's lay,
And Livy's pictured page! — but these shall be
Her resurrection; all beside — decay.
Alas, for Earth, for never shall we see
That brightness in her eye she bore when Rome was free!

LXXXIII

Oh, thou, whose chariot rolled on Fortune's wheel,
Triumphant Sylla! Thou, who didst subdue

Thy country's foes ere thou wouldst pause to feel
The wrath of thy own wrongs, or reap the due
Of hoarded vengeance till thine Eagles flew
O'er prostrate Asia; — thou, who with thy frown
Annihilated senates; — Roman, too,
With all thy vices — for thou didst lay down
With an atoning smile a more than earthly crown,

LXXXIV

Thy dictatorial wreath — couldst thou divine
To what would one day dwindle that which made
Thee more than mortal? and that so supine
By aught than Romans Rome should thus be laid?
She who was named Eternal, and arrayed
Her warriors but to conquer — she who veiled
Earth with her haughty shadow, and displayed,
Until the o'er-canopied horizon failed,
Her rushing wings — Oh! she who was Almighty hailed!

LXXXV

Sylla was first of victors; but our own,
The sagest of usurpers, Cromwell! — he
Too swept off senates while he hewed the throne
Down to a block — immortal rebel! See
What crimes it costs to be a moment free,
And famous through all ages! but beneath
His fate the moral lurks of destiny;
His day of double victory and death
Beheld him win two realms, and, happier, yield his breath.

LXXXVI

The third of the same Moon whose former course
Had all but crowned him, on the selfsame day
Deposed him gently from his throne of force,
And laid him with the Earth's preceding clay.
And showed not Fortune thus how fame and sway,
And all we deem delightful, and consume
Our souls to compass through each arduous way,
Are in her eyes less happy than the tomb?
Were they but so in Man's, how different were his doom!

LXXXVII

And thou, dread Statue! yet existent in
The austerest form of naked majesty —

Thou who beheldest, 'mid the assassins' din,
At thy bathed base the bloody Cæsar lie,
Folding his robe in dying dignity —
An offering to thine altar from the Queen
Of gods and men, great Nemesis! did he die,
And thou, too, perish, Pompey? have ye been
Victors of countless kings, or puppets of a scene?

LXXXVIII

And thou, the thunder-stricken nurse of Rome!
She-wolf! whose brazen-imaged dugs impart
The milk of conquest yet within the dome
Where, as a monument of antique art,
Thou standest: — Mother of the mighty heart,
Which the great Founder sucked from thy wild teat,
Scorched by the Roman Jove's ethereal dart,
And thy limbs black with lightning — dost thou yet
Guard thine immortal cubs, nor thy fond charge forget?

LXXXIX

Thou dost; — but all thy foster-babes are dead —
The men of iron; and the World hath reared
Cities from out their sepulchres: men bled
In imitation of the things they feared,
And fought and conquered, and the same course steered,
At apish distance; but as yet none have,
Nor could, the same supremacy have neared,
Save one vain Man, who is not in the grave —
But, vanquished by himself, to his own slaves a slave —

XC

The fool of false dominion — and a kind
Of bastard Cæsar, following him of old
With steps unequal; for the Roman's mind
Was modelled in a less terrestrial mould,
With passions fiercer, yet a judgment cold,
And an immortal instinct which redeemed
The frailties of a heart so soft, yet bold —
Alcides with the distaff now he seemed
At Cleopatra's feet, — and now himself he beamed,

XCI

And came — and saw — and conquered! But the man
Who would have tamed his Eagles down to flee,

Like a trained falcon, in the Gallic van,
Which he, in sooth, long led to Victory,
With a deaf heart which never seemed to be
A listener to itself, was strangely framed;
With but one weakest weakness — Vanity —
Coquettish in ambition — still he aimed —
And what? can he avouch, or answer what he claimed?

XCII

And would be all or nothing — nor could wait
For the sure grave to level him; few years
Had fixed him with the Cæsars in his fate
On whom we tread: For *this* the conqueror rears
The Arch of Triumph! and for this the tears
And blood of earth flow on as they have flowed,
An universal Deluge, which appears
Without an Ark for wretched Man's abode,
And ebbs but to reflow! — Renew thy rainbow, God!

XCIII

What from this barren being do we reap?
Our senses narrow, and our reason frail,
Life short, and truth a gem which loves the deep,
And all things weighed in Custom's falsest scale;
Opinion an Omnipotence, — whose veil
Mantles the earth with darkness, until right
And wrong are accidents, and Men grow pale
Lest their own judgments should become too bright,
And their free thoughts be crimes, and Earth have too much light.

XCIV

And thus they plod in sluggish misery,
Rotting from sire to son, and age to age,
Proud of their trampled nature, and so die,
Bequeathing their hereditary rage
To the new race of inborn slaves, who wage
War for their chains, and rather than be free,
Bleed gladiator-like, and still engage
Within the same Arena where they see
Their fellows fall before, like leaves of the same tree.

XCV

I speak not of men's creeds — they rest between
Man and his Maker — but of things allowed,

Averred, and known, and daily, hourly seen —
The yoke that is upon us doubly bowed,
And the intent of Tyranny avowed,
The edict of Earth's rulers, who are grown
The apes of him who humbled once the proud,
And shook them from their slumbers on the throne;
Too glorious, were this all his mighty arm had done.

XCVI

Can tyrants but by tyrants conquered be,
And Freedom find no Champion and no Child
Such as Columbia saw arise when she
Sprung forth a Pallas, armed and undefiled?
Or must such minds be nourished in the wild,
Deep in the unpruned forest, 'midst the roar
Of cataracts, where nursing Nature smiled
On infant Washington? Has Earth no more
Such seeds within her breast, or Europe no such shore?

XCVII

But France got drunk with blood to vomit crime;
And fatal have her Saturnalia been
To Freedom's cause, in every age and clime;
Because the deadly days which we have seen,
And vile Ambition, that built up between
Man and his hopes an adamantine wall,
And the base pageant last upon the scene,
Are grown the pretext for the eternal thrall
Which nips Life's tree, and dooms Man's worst — his second fall.

XCVIII

Yet, Freedom! yet thy banner, torn, but flying,
Streams like the thunder-storm *against* the wind;
Thy trumpet voice, though broken now and dying,
The loudest still the Tempest leaves behind;
Thy tree hath lost its blossoms, and the rind,
Chopped by the axe, looks rough and little worth,
But the sap lasts, — and still the seed we find
Sown deep, even in the bosom of the North;
So shall a better spring less bitter fruit bring forth.

XCIX

There is a stern round tower of other days,
Firm as a fortress, with its fence of stone,

Such as an army's baffled strength delays,
Standing with half its battlements alone,
And with two thousand years of ivy grown,
The garland of Eternity, where wave
The green leaves over all by Time o'erthrown; —
What was this tower of strength? within its cave
What treasure lay so locked, so hid? — A woman's grave.

C

But who was she, the Lady of the dead,
Tombed in a palace? Was she chaste and fair?
Worthy a king's — or more — a Roman's bed?
What race of Chiefs and Heroes did she bear?
What daughter of her beauties was the heir?
How lived — how loved — how died she? Was she not
So honoured — and conspicuously there,
Where meaner relics must not dare to rot,
Placed to commemorate a more than mortal lot?

CI

Was she as those who love their lords, or they
Who love the lords of others? such have been
Even in the olden time, Rome's annals say.
Was she a matron of Cornelia's mien,
Or the light air of Egypt's graceful Queen,
Profuse of joy — or 'gainst it did she war,
Inveterate in virtue? Did she lean
To the soft side of the heart, or wisely bar
Love from amongst her griefs? — for such the affections are.

CII

Perchance she died in youth — it may be, bowed
With woes far heavier than the ponderous tomb
That weighed upon her gentle dust: a cloud
Might gather o'er her beauty, and a gloom
In her dark eye, prophetic of the doom
Heaven gives its favourites — early death — yet shed
A sunset charm around her, and illume
With hectic light, the Hesperus of the dead,
Of her consuming cheek the autumnal leaf-like red.

CIII

Perchance she died in age — surviving all,
Charms — kindred — children — with the silver gray

On her long tresses, which might yet recall,
It may be, still a something of the day
When they were braided, and her proud array
And lovely form were envied, praised, and eyed
By Rome — But whither would Conjecture stray?
Thus much alone we know — Metella died,
The wealthiest Roman's wife: Behold his love or pride!

CIV

I know not why — but standing thus by thee
It seems as if I had thine inmate known,
Thou Tomb! and other days come back on me
With recollected music, though the tone
Is changed and solemn, like the cloudy groan
Of dying thunder on the distant wind;
Yet could I seat me by this ivied stone
Till I had bodied forth the heated mind
Forms from the floating wreck which Ruin leaves behind:

CV

And from the planks, far shattered o'er the rocks,
Built me a little bark of hope, once more
To battle with the Ocean and the shocks
Of the loud breakers, and the ceaseless roar
Which rushes on the solitary shore
Where all lies foundered that was ever dear:
But could I gather from the wave-worn store
Enough for my rude boat, where should I steer?
There woos no home, nor hope, nor life, save what is here.

CVI

Then let the Winds howl on! their harmony
Shall henceforth be my music, and the Night
The sound shall temper with the owlets' cry,
As I now hear them, in the fading light
Dim o'er the bird of darkness' native site,
Answering each other on the Palatine,
With their large eyes, all glistening gray and bright,
And sailing pinions. — Upon such a shrine
What are our petty griefs? — let me not number mine.

CVII

Cypress and ivy, weed and wallflower grown
Matted and massed together — hillocks heaped

On what were chambers — arch crushed, column strown
In fragments — choked up vaults, and frescos steeped
In subterranean damps, where the owl peeped,
Deeming it midnight: — Temples — Baths — or Halls?
Pronounce who can: for all that Learning reaped
From her research hath been, that these are walls —
Behold the Imperial Mount! 'tis thus the Mighty falls.

CVIII

There is the moral of all human tales;
'Tis but the same rehearsal of the past,
First Freedom, and then Glory — when that fails,
Wealth — Vice — Corruption, — Barbarism at last.
And History, with all her volumes vast,
Hath but *one* page, — 'tis better written here,
Where gorgeous Tyranny hath thus amassed
All treasures, all delights, that Eye or Ear,
Heart, Soul could seek — Tongue ask — Away with words! draw near,

CIX

Admire — exult — despise — laugh — weep, — for here
There is such matter for all feeling: — Man!
Thou pendulum betwixt a smile and tear,
Ages and Realms are crowded in this span,
This mountain, whose obliterated plan
The pyramid of Empires pinnacled,
Of Glory's gewgaws shining in the van
Till the Sun's rays with added flame were filled!
Where are its golden roofs? where those who dared to build?

CX

Tully was not so eloquent as thou,
Thou nameless column with the buried base!
What are the laurels of the Cæsar's brow?
Crown me with ivy from his dwelling-place.
Whose arch or pillar meets me in the face,
Titus or Trajan's? No — 'tis that of Time:
Triumph, arch, pillar, all he doth displace
Scoffing; and apostolic statues climb
To crush the imperial urn, whose ashes slept sublime,

CXI

Buried in air, the deep blue sky of Rome,
And looking to the stars: they had contained

A Spirit which with these would find a home,
The last of those who o'er the whole earth reigned,
The Roman Globe — for, after, none sustained,
But yielded back his conquests: — he was more
Than a mere Alexander, and, unstained
With household blood and wine, serenely wore
His sovereign virtues — still we Trajan's name adore.

CXII

Where is the rock of Triumph, the high place
Where Rome embraced her heroes? — where the steep
Tarpeian? — fittest goal of Treason's race,
The Promontory whence the Traitor's Leap
Cured all ambition? Did the conquerors heap
Their spoils here? Yes; and in yon field below,
A thousand years of silenced factions sleep —
The Forum, where the immortal accents glow,
And still the eloquent air breathes — burns with Cicero!

CXIII

The field of Freedom — Faction — Fame — and Blood:
Here a proud people's passions were exhaled,
From the first hour of Empire in the bud
To that when further worlds to conquer failed;
But long before had Freedom's face been veiled,
And Anarchy assumed her attributes;
Till every lawless soldier who assailed
Trod on the trembling Senate's slavish mutes,
Or raised the venal voice of baser prostitutes.

CXIV

Then turn we to her latest Tribune's name,
From her ten thousand tyrants turn to thee,
Redeemer of dark centuries of shame —
The friend of Petrarch — hope of Italy —
Rienzi! last of Romans! While the tree
Of Freedom's withered trunk puts forth a leaf,
Even for thy tomb a garland let it be —
The Forum's champion, and the people's chief —
Her new-born Numa thou — with reign, alas! too brief.

CXV

Egeria! sweet creation of some heart
Which found no mortal resting-place so fair

As thine ideal breast; whate'er thou art
Or wert, — a young Aurora of the air,
The nympholepsy of some fond despair —
Or — it might be — a Beauty of the earth,
Who found a more than common Votary there
Too much adoring — whatsoe'er thy birth,
Thou wert a beautiful Thought, and softly bodied forth.

CXVI

The mosses of thy Fountain still are sprinkled
With thine Elysian water-drops; the face
Of thy cave-guarded Spring, with years unwrinkled,
Reflects the meek-eyed Genius of the place,
Whose green, wild margin now no more erase
Art's works; nor must the delicate waters sleep
Prisoned in marble — bubbling from the base
Of the cleft statue, with a gentle leap
The rill runs o'er — and round, fern, flowers, and ivy, creep

CXVII

Fantastically tangled: the green hills
Are clothed with early blossoms — through the grass
The quick-eyed lizard rustles — and the bills
Of summer-birds sing welcome as ye pass;
Flowers fresh in hue, and many in their class,
Implore the pausing step, and with their dyes
Dance in the soft breeze in a fairy mass;
The sweetness of the Violet's deep blue eyes,
Kissed by the breath of heaven, seems coloured by its skies.

CXVIII

Here didst thou dwell, in this enchanted cover,
Egeria! thy all heavenly bosom beating
For the far footsteps of thy mortal lover;
The purple Midnight veiled that mystic meeting
With her most starry canopy — and seating
Thyself by thine adorer, what befel?
This cave was surely shaped out for the greeting
Of an enamoured Goddess, and the cell
Haunted by holy Love — the earliest Oracle!

CXIX

And didst thou not, thy breast to his replying,
Blend a celestial with a human heart;

And Love, which dies as it was born, in sighing,
Share with immortal transports? could thine art
Make them indeed immortal, and impart
The purity of Heaven to earthly joys,
Expel the venom and not blunt the dart —
The dull satiety which all destroys —
And root from out the soul the deadly weed which cloys?

CXX

Alas! our young affections run to waste,
Or water but the desert! whence arise
But weeds of dark luxuriance, tares of haste,
Rank at the core, though tempting to the eyes
Flowers whose wild odours breathe but agonies,
And trees whose gums are poison; such the plants
Which spring beneath her steps as Passion flies
O'er the World's wilderness, and vainly pants
For some celestial fruit forbidden to our wants.

CXXI

Oh, Love! no habitant of earth thou art —
An unseen Seraph, we believe in thee, —
A faith whose martyrs are the broken heart, —
But never yet hath seen, nor e'er shall see
The naked eye, thy form, as it should be;
The mind hath made thee, as it peopled Heaven,
Even with its own desiring phantasy,
And to a thought such shape and image given,
As haunts the unquenched soul — parched — wearied — wrung — and riven.

CXXII

Of its own beauty is the mind diseased,
And fevers into false creation: — where,
Where are the forms the sculptor's soul hath seized?
In him alone. Can Nature show so fair?
Where are the charms and virtues which we dare
Conceive in boyhood and pursue as men,
The unreached Paradise of our despair,
Which o'er-informs the pencil and the pen,
And overpowers the page where it would bloom again?

CXXIII

Who loves, raves — 'tis youth's frenzy — but the cure
Is bitterer still, as charm by charm unwinds

Which robed our idols, and we see too sure
Nor Worth nor Beauty dwells from out the mind's
Ideal shape of such; yet still it binds
The fatal spell, and still it draws us on,
Reaping the whirlwind from the oft-sown winds;
The stubborn heart, its alchemy begun,
Seems ever near the prize — wealthiest when most undone.

CXXIV

We wither from our youth, we gasp away —
Sick — sick; unfound the boon — unslaked the thirst,
Though to the last, in verge of our decay,
Some phantom lures, such as we sought at first —
But all too late, — so are we doubly curst.
Love, Fame, Ambition, Avarice — 'tis the same,
Each idle — and all ill — and none the worst —
For all are meteors with a different name,
And Death the sable smoke where vanishes the flame.

CXXV

Few — none — find what they love or could have loved,
Though accident, blind contact, and the strong
Necessity of loving, have removed
Antipathies — but to recur, ere long,
Envenomed with irrevocable wrong;
And Circumstance, that unspiritual God
And Miscreator, makes and helps along
Our coming evils with a crutch-like rod,
Whose touch turns Hope to dust, — the dust we all have trod.

CXXVI

Our life is a false nature — 'tis not in
The harmony of things, — this hard decree,
This uneradicable taint of Sin,
This boundless Upas, this all-blasting tree,
Whose root is Earth — whose leaves and branches be
The skies which rain their plagues on men like dew —
Disease, death, bondage — all the woes we see,
And worse, the woes we see not — which throb through
The immedicable soul, with heart-aches ever new.

CXXVII

Yet let us ponder boldly — 'tis a base
Abandonment of reason to resign

Our right of thought — our last and only place
Of refuge; this, at least, shall still be mine:
Though from our birth the Faculty divine
Is chained and tortured — cabined, cribbed, confined,
And bred in darkness, lest the Truth should shine
Too brightly on the unpreparéd mind,
The beam pours in — for Time and Skill will couch the blind.

CXXVIII

Arches on arches! as it were that Rome,
Collecting the chief trophies of her line,
Would build up all her triumphs in one dome,
Her Coliseum stands; the moonbeams shine
As 'twere its natural torches — for divine
Should be the light which streams here, — to illume
This long-explored but still exhaustless mine
Of Contemplation; and the azure gloom
Of an Italian night, where the deep skies assume

CXXIX

Hues which have words, and speak to ye of Heaven,
Floats o'er this vast and wondrous monument,
And shadows forth its glory. There is given
Unto the things of earth, which Time hath bent,
A Spirit's feeling, and where he hath leant
His hand, but broke his scythe, there is a power
And magic in the ruined battlement,
For which the Palace of the present hour
Must yield its pomp, and wait till Ages are its dower.

CXXX

Oh, Time! the Beautifier of the dead,
Adorner of the ruin — Comforter
And only Healer when the heart hath bled;
Time! the Corrector where our judgments err,
The test of Truth, Love — sole philosopher,
For all beside are sophists — from thy thrift,
Which never loses though it doth defer —
Time, the Avenger! unto thee I lift
My hands, and eyes, and heart, and crave of thee a gift:

CXXXI

Amidst this wreck, where thou hast made a shrine
And temple more divinely desolate —

Among thy mightier offerings here are mine,
Ruins of years — though few, yet full of fate: —
If thou hast ever seen me too elate,
Hear me not; but if calmly I have borne
Good, and reserved my pride against the hate
Which shall not whelm me, let me not have worn
This iron in my soul in vain — shall *they* not mourn?

CXXXII

And Thou, who never yet of human wrong
Left the unbalanced scale, great Nemesis!
Here, where the ancient paid thee homage long —
Thou, who didst call the Furies from the abyss,
And round Orestes bade them howl and hiss
For that unnatural retribution — just,
Had it but been from hands less near — in this
Thy former realm, I call thee from the dust!
Dost thou not hear my heart? — Awake! thou shalt, and must.

CXXXIII

It is not that I may not have incurred,
For my ancestral faults or mine, the wound
I bleed withal; and, had it been conferred
With a just weapon, it had flowed unbound;
But now my blood shall not sink in the ground —
To thee I do devote it — *Thou* shalt take
The vengeance, which shall yet be sought and found —
Which if *I* have not taken for the sake ——
But let that pass — I sleep — but Thou shalt yet awake.

CXXXIV

And if my voice break forth, 'tis not that now
I shrink from what is suffered: let him speak
Who hath beheld decline upon my brow,
Or seen my mind's convulsion leave it weak;
But in this page a record will I seek.
Not in the air shall these my words disperse,
Though I be ashes; a far hour shall wreak
The deep prophetic fulness of this verse,
And pile on human heads the mountain of my curse!

CXXXV

That curse shall be Forgiveness. — Have I not —
Hear me, my mother Earth! behold it, Heaven! —

Have I not had to wrestle with my lot?
Have I not suffered things to be forgiven?
Have I not had my brain seared, my heart riven,
Hopes sapped, name blighted, Life's life lied away?
And only not to desperation driven,
Because not altogether of such clay
As rots into the souls of those whom I survey.

CXXXVI

From mighty wrongs to petty perfidy
Have I not seen what human things could do?
From the loud roar of foaming calumny
To the small whisper of the as paltry few —
And subtler venom of the reptile crew,
The Janus glance of whose significant eye,
Learning to lie with silence, would *seem* true —
And without utterance, save the shrug or sigh,
Deal round to happy fools its speechless obloquy.

CXXXVII

But I have lived, and have not lived in vain:
My mind may lose its force, my blood its fire,
And my frame perish even in conquering pain;
But there is that within me which shall tire
Torture and Time, and breathe when I expire;
Something unearthly, which they deem not of,
Like the remembered tone of a mute lyre,
Shall on their softened spirits sink, and move
In hearts all rocky now the late remorse of Love.

CXXXVIII

The seal is set. — Now welcome, thou dread Power!
Nameless, yet thus omnipotent, which here
Walk'st in the shadow of the midnight hour
With a deep awe, yet all distinct from fear;
Thy haunts are ever where the dead walls rear
Their ivy mantles, and the solemn scene
Derives from thee a sense so deep and clear
That we become a part of what has been,
And grow upon the spot — all-seeing but unseen.

CXXXIX

And here the buzz of eager nations ran,
In murmured pity, or loud-roared applause,

As man was slaughtered by his fellow man.
And wherefore slaughtered? wherefore, but because
Such were the bloody Circus' genial laws,
And the imperial pleasure. — Wherefore not?
What matters where we fall to fill the maws
Of worms — on battle-plains or listed spot?
Both are but theatres — where the chief actors rot.

CXL

I see before me the Gladiator lie:
He leans upon his hand — his manly brow
Consents to death, but conquers agony,
And his drooped head sinks gradually low —
And through his side the last drops, ebbing slow
From the red gash, fall heavy, one by one,
Like the first of a thunder-shower; and now
The arena swims around him — he is gone,
Ere ceased the inhuman shout which hailed the wretch who won.

CXLI

He heard it, but he heeded not — his eyes
Were with his heart — and that was far away;
He recked not of the life he lost nor prize,
But where his rude hut by the Danube lay —
There were his young barbarians all at play,
There was their Dacian mother — he, their sire,
Butchered to make a Roman holiday —
All this rushed with his blood — Shall he expire
And unavenged? — Arise! ye Goths, and glut your ire!

CXLII

But here, where Murder breathed her bloody steam; —
And here, where buzzing nations choked the ways,
And roared or murmured like a mountain stream
Dashing or winding as it torrent strays;
Here, where the Roman million's blame or praise
Was Death or Life — the playthings of a crowd —
My voice sounds much — and fall the stars' faint rays
On the arena void — seats crushed — walls bowed —
And galleries, where my steps seem echoes strangely loud.

CXLIII

A Ruin — yet what Ruin! from its mass
Walls — palaces — half-cities, have been reared;

Yet oft the enormous skeleton ye pass,
And marvel where the spoil could have appeared.
Hath it indeed been plundered, or but cleared?
Alas! developed, opens the decay,
When the colossal fabric's form is neared:
It will not bear the brightness of the day,
Which streams too much on all — years — man — have reft away.

CXLIV

But when the rising moon begins to climb
Its topmost arch, and gently pauses there —
When the stars twinkle through the loops of Time,
And the low night-breeze waves along the air
The garland-forest, which the gray walls wear,
Like laurels on the bald first Cæsar's head —
When the light shines serene but doth not glare —
Then in this magic circle raise the dead; —
Heroes have trod this spot — 'tis on their dust ye tread.

CXLV

"While stands the Coliseum, Rome shall stand:
"When falls the Coliseum, Rome shall fall;
"And when Rome falls — the World." From our own land
Thus spake the pilgrims o'er this mighty wall
In Saxon times, which we are wont to call
Ancient; and these three mortal things are still
On their foundations, and unaltered all —
Rome and her Ruin past Redemption's skill —
The World — the same wide den — of thieves, or what ye will.

CXLVI

Simple, erect, severe, austere, sublime —
Shrine of all saints and temple of all Gods,
From Jove to Jesus — spared and blest by Time —
Looking tranquillity, while falls or nods
Arch — empire — each thing round thee — and Man plods
His way through thorns to ashes — glorious Dome!
Shalt thou not last? Time's scythe and Tyrants' rods
Shiver upon thee — sanctuary and home
Of Art and Piety — Pantheon! — pride of Rome!

CXLVII

Relic of nobler days, and noblest arts!
Despoiled yet perfect! with thy circle spreads

A holiness appealing to all hearts;
To Art a model — and to him who treads
Rome for the sake of ages, Glory sheds
Her light through thy sole aperture; to those
Who worship, here are altars for their beads —
And they who feel for Genius may repose
Their eyes on honoured forms, whose busts around them close.

CXLVIII

There is a dungeon, in whose dim drear light
What do I gaze on? Nothing — Look again!
Two forms are slowly shadowed on my sight —
Two insulated phantoms of the brain:
It is not so — I see them full and plain —
An old man, and a female young and fair,
Fresh as a nursing mother, in whose vein
The blood is nectar: — but what doth she there,
With her unmantled neck, and bosom white and bare?

CXLIX

Full swells the deep pure fountain of young life,
Where *on* the heart and *from* the heart we took
Our first and sweetest nurture — when the wife,
Blest into mother, in the innocent look,
Or even the piping cry of lips that brook
No pain and small suspense, a joy perceives
Man knows not — when from out its cradled nook
She sees her little bud put forth its leaves —
What may the fruit be yet? — I know not — Cain was Eve's.

CL

But here Youth offers to Old Age the food,
The milk of his own gift: it is her Sire
To whom she renders back the debt of blood
Born with her birth: — No — he shall not expire
While in those warm and lovely veins the fire
Of health and holy feeling can provide
Great Nature's Nile, whose deep stream rises higher
Than Egypt's river: — from that gentle side
Drink — drink, and live — Old Man! Heaven's realm holds no such tide.

CLI

The starry fable of the Milky Way
Has not thy story's purity; it is

A constellation of a sweeter ray,
And sacred Nature triumphs more in this
Reverse of her decree, than in the abyss
Where sparkle distant worlds: — Oh, holiest Nurse!
No drop of that clear stream its way shall miss
To thy Sire's heart, replenishing its source
With life, as our freed souls rejoin the Universe.

CLII

Turn to the Mole which Hadrian reared on high,
Imperial mimic of old Egypt's piles,
Colossal copyist of deformity —
Whose travelled phantasy from the far Nile's
Enormous model, doomed the artist's toils
To build for Giants, and for his vain earth,
His shrunken ashes, raise this Dome: How smiles
The gazer's eye with philosophic mirth,
To view the huge design which sprung from such a birth!

CLIII

But lo! the Dome — the vast and wondrous Dome,
To which Diana's marvel was a cell —
Christ's mighty shrine above His martyr's tomb!
I have beheld the Ephesian's miracle —
Its columns strew the wilderness, and dwell
The hyæna and the jackal in their shade;
I have beheld Sophia's bright roofs swell
Their glittering mass i' the Sun, and have surveyed
Its sanctuary the while the usurping Moslem prayed;

CLIV

But thou, of temples old, or altars new,
Standest alone — with nothing like to thee —
Worthiest of God, the Holy and the True!
Since Zion's desolation, when that He
Forsook his former city, what could be,
Of earthly structures, in His honour piled,
Of a sublimer aspect? Majesty —
Power — Glory — Strength — and Beauty all are aisled
In this eternal Ark of worship undefiled.

CLV

Enter: its grandeur overwhelms thee not;
And why? it is not lessened — but thy mind,

Expanded by the Genius of the spot,
Has grown colossal, and can only find
A fit abode wherein appear enshrined
Thy hopes of Immortality — and thou
Shalt one day, if found worthy, so defined
See thy God face to face, as thou dost now
His Holy of Holies — nor be blasted by his brow.

CLVI

Thou movest — but increasing with the advance,
Like climbing some great Alp, which still doth rise,
Deceived by its gigantic elegance —
Vastness which grows, but grows to harmonize —
All musical in its immensities;
Rich marbles, richer painting — shrines where flame
The lamps of gold — and haughty dome which vies
In air with Earth's chief structures, though their frame
Sits on the firm-set ground — and this the clouds must claim.

CLVII

Thou seest not all — but piecemeal thou must break,
To separate contemplation, the great whole;
And as the Ocean many bays will make
That ask the eye — so here condense thy soul
To more immediate objects, and control
Thy thoughts until thy mind hath got by heart
Its eloquent proportions, and unroll
In mighty graduations, part by part,
The Glory which at once upon thee did not dart,

CLVIII

Not by its fault — but thine: Our outward sense
Is but of gradual grasp — and as it is
That what we have of feeling most intense
Outstrips our faint expression; even so this
Outshining and o'erwhelming edifice
Fools our fond gaze, and greatest of the great
Defies at first our Nature's littleness,
Till, growing with its growth, we thus dilate
Our Spirits to the size of that they contemplate.

CLIX

Then pause, and be enlightened; there is more
In such a survey than the sating gaze

Of wonder pleased, or awe which would adore
The worship of the place, or the mere praise
Of Art and its great Masters, who could raise
What former time, nor skill, nor thought could plan:
The fountain of Sublimity displays
Its depth, and thence may draw the mind of Man
Its golden sands, and learn what great Conceptions can.

CLX

Or, turning to the Vatican, go see
Laocoön's torture dignifying pain —
A Father's love and Mortal's agony
With an Immortal's patience blending: — Vain
The struggle — vain, against the coiling strain
And gripe, and deepening of the dragon's grasp,
The Old Man's clench; the long envenomed chain
Rivets the living links, — the enormous Asp
Enforces pang on pang, and stifles gasp on gasp.

CLXI

Or view the Lord of the unerring bow,
The God of Life, and Poesy, and Light —
The Sun in human limbs arrayed, and brow
All radiant from his triumph in the fight;
The shaft hath just been shot — the arrow bright
With an Immortal's vengeance — in his eye
And nostril beautiful Disdain, and Might
And Majesty, flash their full lightnings by,
Developing in that one glance the Deity.

CLXII

But in his delicate form — a dream of Love,
Shaped by some solitary Nymph, whose breast
Longed for a deathless lover from above,
And maddened in that vision — are exprest
All that ideal Beauty ever blessed
The mind with in its most unearthly mood,
When each Conception was a heavenly Guest —
A ray of Immortality — and stood,
Starlike, around, until they gathered to a God!

CLXIII

And if it be Prometheus stole from Heaven
The fire which we endure — it was repaid

By him to whom the energy was given
Which this poetic marble hath arrayed
With an eternal Glory — which, if made
By human hands, is not of human thought —
And Time himself hath hallowed it, nor laid
One ringlet in the dust — nor hath it caught
A tinge of years, but breathes the flame with which 'twas wrought.

CLXIV

But where is he, the Pilgrim of my Song,
The Being who upheld it through the past?
Methinks he cometh late and tarries long.
He is no more — these breathings are his last —
His wanderings done — his visions ebbing fast,
And he himself as nothing: — if he was
Aught but a phantasy, and could be classed
With forms which live and suffer — let that pass —
His shadow fades away into Destruction's mass,

CLXV

Which gathers shadow — substance — life, and all
That we inherit in its mortal shroud —
And spreads the dim and universal pall
Through which all things grow phantoms; and the cloud
Between us sinks and all which ever glowed,
Till Glory's self is twilight, and displays
A melancholy halo scarce allowed
To hover on the verge of darkness — rays
Sadder than saddest night, for they distract the gaze,

CLXVI

And send us prying into the abyss,
To gather what we shall be when the frame
Shall be resolved to something less than this —
Its wretched essence; and to dream of fame,
And wipe the dust from off the idle name
We never more shall hear, — but never more,
Oh, happier thought! can we be made the same: —
It is enough in sooth that *once* we bore
These fardels of the heart — the heart whose sweat was gore.

CLXVII

Hark! forth from the abyss a voice proceeds,
A long low distant murmur of dread sound,

Such as arises when a nation bleeds
With some deep and immedicable wound; —
Through storm and darkness yawns the rending ground —
The gulf is thick with phantoms, but the Chief
Seems royal still, though with her head discrowned,
And pale, but lovely, with maternal grief —
She clasps a babe, to whom her breast yields no relief.

CLXVIII

Scion of Chiefs and Monarchs, where art thou?
Fond Hope of many nations, art thou dead?
Could not the Grave forget thee, and lay low
Some less majestic, less belovéd head?
In the sad midnight, while thy heart still bled,
The mother of a moment, o'er thy boy,
Death hushed that pang for ever: with thee fled
The present happiness and promised joy
Which filled the Imperial Isles so full it seemed to cloy.

CLXIX

Peasants bring forth in safety. — Can it be,
Oh thou that wert so happy, so adored!
Those who weep not for Kings shall weep for thee,
And Freedom's heart, grown heavy, cease to hoard
Her many griefs for ONE; for she had poured
Her orisons for thee, and o'er thy head
Beheld her Iris. — Thou, too, lonely Lord,
And desolate Consort — vainly wert thou wed!
The husband of a year! the father of the dead!

CLXX

Of sackcloth was thy wedding garment made;
Thy bridal's fruit is ashes: in the dust
The fair-haired Daughter of the Isles is laid,
The love of millions! How we did entrust
Futurity to her! and, though it must
Darken above our bones, yet fondly deemed
Our children should obey her child, and blessed
Her and her hoped-for seed, whose promise seemed
Like stars to shepherd's eyes: — 'twas but a meteor beamed.

CLXXI

Woe unto us — not her — for she sleeps well:
The fickle reek of popular breath, the tongue

Of hollow counsel, the false oracle,
Which from the birth of Monarchy hath rung
Its knell in princely ears, till the o'erstung
Nations have armed in madness — the strange fate
Which tumbles mightiest sovereigns, and hath flung
Against their blind omnipotence a weight
Within the opposing scale, which crushes soon or late, —

CLXXII

These might have been her destiny — but no —
Our hearts deny it: and so young, so fair,
Good without effort, great without a foe;
But now a Bride and Mother — and now *there!*
How many ties did that stern moment tear!
From thy Sire's to his humblest subject's breast
Is linked the electric chain of that despair,
Whose shock was as an Earthquake's, and opprest
The land which loved thee so that none could love thee best.

CLXXIII

Lo, Nemi! navelled in the woody hills
So far, that the uprooting Wind which tears
The oak from his foundation, and which spills
The Ocean o'er its boundary, and bears
Its foam against the skies, reluctant spares
The oval mirror of thy glassy lake;
And calm as cherished hate, its surface wears
A deep cold settled aspect nought can shake,
All coiled into itself and round, as sleeps the snake.

CLXXIV

And near, Albano's scarce divided waves
Shine from a sister valley; — and afar
The Tiber winds, and the broad Ocean laves
The Latian coast where sprung the Epic war,
"Arms and the Man," whose re-ascending star
Rose o'er an empire: — but beneath thy right
Tully reposed from Rome; — and where yon bar
Of girdling mountains intercepts the sight
The Sabine farm was tilled, the weary Bard's delight.

CLXXV

But I forget. — My Pilgrim's shrine is won,
And he and I must part, — so let it be, —

His task and mine alike are nearly done;
Yet once more let us look upon the Sea;
The Midland Ocean breaks on him and me,
And from the Alban Mount we now behold
Our friend of youth, that Ocean, which when we
Beheld it last by Calpe's rock unfold
Those waves, we followed on till the dark Euxine rolled

CLXXVI

Upon the blue Symplegades: long years —
Long, though not very many — since have done
Their work on both; some suffering and some tears
Have left us nearly where we had begun:
Yet not in vain our mortal race hath run —
We have had our reward — and it is here, —
That we can yet feel gladdened by the Sun,
And reap from Earth — Sea — joy almost as dear
As if there were no Man to trouble what is clear.

CLXXVII

Oh! that the Desert were my dwelling-place,
With one fair Spirit for my minister,
That I might all forget the human race,
And, hating no one, love but only her!
Ye elements! — in whose ennobling stir
I feel myself exalted — Can ye not
Accord me such a Being? Do I err
In deeming such inhabit many a spot?
Though with them to converse can rarely be our lot.

CLXXVIII

There is a pleasure in the pathless woods,
There is a rapture on the lonely shore,
There is society, where none intrudes,
By the deep Sea, and Music in its roar:
I love not Man the less, but Nature more,
From these our interviews, in which I steal
From all I may be, or have been before,
To mingle with the Universe, and feel
What I can ne'er express — yet can not all conceal.

CLXXIX

Roll on, thou deep and dark blue Ocean — roll!
Ten thousand fleets sweep over thee in vain;

Man marks the earth with ruin — his control
Stops with the shore; — upon the watery plain
The wrecks are all thy deed, nor doth remain
A shadow of man's ravage, save his own,
When, for a moment, like a drop of rain,
He sinks into thy depths with bubbling groan —
Without a grave — unknelled, uncoffined, and unknown.

CLXXX

His steps are not upon thy paths, — thy fields
Are not a spoil for him, — thou dost arise
And shake him from thee; the vile strength he wields
For Earth's destruction thou dost all despise,
Spurning him from thy bosom to the skies —
And send'st him, shivering in thy playful spray
And howling, to his Gods, where haply lies
His petty hope in some near port or bay,
And dashest him again to Earth: — there let him lay.

CLXXXI

The armaments which thunderstrike the walls
Of rock-built cities, bidding nations quake,
And Monarchs tremble in their Capitals,
The oak Leviathans, whose huge ribs make
Their clay creator the vain title take
Of Lord of thee, and Arbiter of War —
These are thy toys, and, as the snowy flake,
They melt into thy yeast of waves, which mar
Alike the Armada's pride or spoils of Trafalgar.

CLXXXII

Thy shores are empires, changed in all save thee —
Assyria — Greece — Rome — Carthage — what are they?
Thy waters washed them power while they were free,
And many a tyrant since; their shores obey
The stranger, slave, or savage; their decay
Has dried up realms to deserts: — not so thou,
Unchangeable save to thy wild waves' play,
Time writes no wrinkle on thine azure brow —
Such as Creation's dawn beheld, thou rollest now.

CLXXXIII

Thou glorious mirror, where the Almighty's form
Glasses itself in tempests; in all time,

Calm or convulsed — in breeze, or gale, or storm —
Icing the Pole, or in the torrid clime
Dark-heaving — boundless, endless, and sublime —
The image of Eternity — the throne
Of the Invisible; even from out thy slime
The monsters of the deep are made — each Zone
Obeys thee — thou goest forth, dread, fathomless, alone.

CLXXXIV

And I have loved thee, Ocean! and my joy
Of youthful sports was on thy breast to be
Borne, like thy bubbles, onward: from a boy
I wantoned with thy breakers — they to me
Were a delight; and if the freshening sea
Made them a terror — 'twas a pleasing fear,
For I was as it were a Child of thee,
And trusted to thy billows far and near,
And laid my hand upon thy mane — as I do here.

CLXXXV

My task is done — my song hath ceased — my theme
Has died into an echo; it is fit
The spell should break of this protracted dream.
The torch shall be extinguished which hath lit
My midnight lamp — and what is writ, is writ, —
Would it were worthier! but I am not now
That which I have been — and my visions flit
Less palpably before me — and the glow
Which in my Spirit dwelt is fluttering, faint, and low.

CLXXXVI

Farewell! a word that must be, and hath been —
A sound which makes us linger; — yet — farewell!
Ye! who have traced the Pilgrim to the scene
Which is his last — if in your memories dwell
A thought which once was his — if on ye swell
A single recollection — not in vain
He wore his sandal-shoon, and scallop-shell;
Farewell! with *him* alone may rest the pain,
If such there were — with *you,* the Moral of his Strain.

MAID OF ATHENS, ERE WE PART

1

Maid of Athens, ere we part,
Give, oh give me back my heart!
Or, since that has left my breast,
Keep it now, and take the rest!
Hear my vow before I go,
Ζωή μον, σᾶς ἀγαπῶ.

2

By those tresses unconfined,
Wooed by each Ægean wind;
By those lids whose jetty fringe
Kiss thy soft cheeks' blooming tinge;
By those wild eyes like the roe,
Ζωή μον, σᾶς ἀγαπῶ.

3

By that lip I long to taste;
By that zone-encircled waist;
By all the token-flowers that tell
What words can never speak so well;
By love's alternate joy and woe,
Ζωή μον, σᾶς ἀγαπῶ.

4

Maid of Athens! I am gone:
Think of me, sweet! when alone.
Though I fly to Istambol,
Athens holds my heart and soul:
Can I cease to love thee? No!
Ζωή μον, σᾶς ἀγαπῶ.

LINES TO A LADY WEEPING

Weep, daughter of a royal line,
   A Sire's disgrace, a realm's decay;
Ah! happy if each tear of thine
   Could wash a Father's fault away!

Weep — for thy tears are Virtue's tears —
  Auspicious to these suffering Isles;
And be each drop in future years
  Repaid thee by thy People's smiles!

THE BRIDE OF ABYDOS

A TURKISH TALE

"Had we never loved sae kindly,
Had we never loved sae blindly,
Never met — or never parted,
We had ne'er been broken-hearted." —

BURNS

CANTO THE FIRST

I

KNOW ye the land where the cypress and myrtle
  Are emblems of deeds that are done in their clime?
Where the rage of the vulture, the love of the turtle,
  Now melt into sorrow, now madden to crime?
Know ye the land of the cedar and vine,
Where the flowers ever blossom, the beams ever shine;
Where the light wings of Zephyr, oppressed with perfume,
Wax faint o'er the gardens of Gúl in her bloom;
Where the citron and olive are fairest of fruit,
And the voice of the nightingale never is mute;
Where the tints of the earth, and the hues of the sky,
In colour though varied, in beauty may vie,
And the purple of Ocean is deepest in dye;
Where the virgins are soft as the roses they twine,
And all, save the spirit of man, is divine —
'Tis the clime of the East — 'tis the land of the Sun —
Can he smile on such deeds as his children have done?
Oh! wild as the accents of lovers' farewell
Are the hearts which they bear, and the tales which they tell.

II

Begirt with many a gallant slave,
Apparelled as becomes the brave,
Awaiting each his Lord's behest
To guide his steps, or guard his rest,
Old Giaffir sate in his Divan:

Deep thought was in his agéd eye;
And though the face of Mussulman
Not oft betrays to standers by
The mind within, well skilled to hide
All but unconquerable pride,
His pensive cheek and pondering brow
Did more than he was wont avow.

III

"Let the chamber be cleared." — The train disappeared —
"Now call me the chief of the Haram guard" —
With Giaffir is none but his only son,
And the Nubian awaiting the sire's award.
"Haroun — when all the crowd that wait
Are passed beyond the outer gate,
(Woe to the head whose eye beheld
My child Zuleika's face unveiled!)
Hence, lead my daughter from her tower —
Her fate is fixed this very hour;
Yet not to her repeat my thought —
By me alone be duty taught!"

"Pacha! to hear is to obey." —
No more must slave to despot say —
Then to the tower had ta'en his way:
But here young Selim silence brake,
First lowly rendering reverence meet;
And downcast looked, and gently spake,
Still standing at the Pacha's feet:
For son of Moslem must expire,
Ere dare to sit before his sire!
"Father! for fear that thou shouldst chide
My sister, or her sable guide —
Know — for the fault, if fault there be,
Was mine — then fall thy frowns on me!
So lovelily the morning shone,
That — let the old and weary sleep —
I could not; and to view alone
The fairest scenes of land and deep,
With none to listen and reply
To thoughts with which my heart beat high
Were irksome — for whate'er my mood,
In sooth I love not solitude;
I on Zuleika's slumber broke,
And, as thou knowest that for me
Soon turns the Haram's grating key,

Before the guardian slaves awoke
We to the cypress groves had flown,
And made earth, main, and heaven our own!
There lingered we, beguiled too long
With Mejnoun's tale, or Sadi's song;
Till I, who heard the deep tambour
Beat thy Divan's approaching hour,
To thee, and to my duty true,
Warned by the sound, to greet thee flew:
But there Zuleika wanders yet —
Nay, Father, rage not — nor forget
That none can pierce that secret bower
But those who watch the women's tower."

IV

"Son of a slave" — the Pacha said —
"From unbelieving mother bred,
Vain were a father's hope to see
Aught that beseems a man in thee.
Thou, when thine arm should bend the bow,
  And hurl the dart, and curb the steed,
  Thou, Greek in soul if not in creed,
Must pore where babbling waters flow,
And watch unfolding roses blow.
Would that yon Orb, whose matin glow
Thy listless eyes so much admire,
Would lend thee something of his fire!
Thou, who woulds't see this battlement
By Christian cannon piecemeal rent;
Nay, tamely view old Stambol's wall
Before the dogs of Moscow fall,
Nor strike one stroke for life and death
Against the curs of Nazareth!
Go — let thy less than woman's hand
Assume the distaff — not the brand.
But, Haroun! — to my daughter speed:
And hark — of thine own head take heed —
If thus Zuleika oft takes wing —
Thou see'st yon bow — it hath a string!"

V

No sound from Selim's lip was heard,
  At least that met old Giaffir's ear,
But every frown and every word
Pierced keener than a Christian's sword.

"Son of a slave! — reproached with fear!
Those gibes had cost another dear.
Son of a slave! — and *who* my Sire?"
Thus held his thoughts their dark career;
And glances ev'n of more than ire
Flash forth, then faintly disappear.
Old Giaffir gazed upon his son
And started; for within his eye
He read how much his wrath had done;
He saw rebellion there begun:
"Come hither, boy — what, no reply?
I mark thee — and I know thee too;
But there be deeds thou dar'st not do:
But if thy beard had manlier length,
And if thy hand had skill and strength,
I'd joy to see thee break a lance,
Albeit against my own perchance."
As sneeringly these accents fell,
On Selim's eye he fiercely gazed:
That eye returned him glance for glance,
And proudly to his Sire's was raised,
Till Giaffir's quailed and shrunk askance —
And why — he felt, but durst not tell.
"Much I misdoubt this wayward boy
Will one day work me more annoy:
I never loved him from his birth,
And — but his arm is little worth,
And scarcely in the chase could cope
With timid fawn or antelope,
Far less would venture into strife
Where man contends for fame and life —
I would not trust that look or tone:
No — nor the blood so near my own.
That blood — he hath not heard — no more —
I'll watch him closer than before.
He is an Arab to my sight,
Or Christian crouching in the fight —
But hark! — I hear Zuleika's voice;
Like Houris' hymn it meets mine ear:
She is the offspring of my choice;
Oh! more than ev'n her mother dear,
With all to hope, and nought to fear —
My Peri! ever welcome here!
Sweet, as the desert fountain's wave
To lips just cooled in time to save —
Such to my longing sight art thou;
Nor can they waft to Mecca's shrine

More thanks for life, than I for thine,
  Who blest thy birth and bless thee now."

VI

Fair, as the first that fell of womankind,
  When on that dread yet lovely serpent smiling,
Whose Image then was stamped upon her mind —
  But once beguiled — and ever more beguiling;
Dazzling, as that, oh! too transcendent vision
  To Sorrow's phantom-peopled slumber given,
When heart meets heart again in dreams Elysian,
  And paints the lost on Earth revived in Heaven;
Soft, as the memory of buried love;
Pure, as the prayer which Childhood wafts above;
Was she — the daughter of that rude old Chief,
Who met the maid with tears — but not of grief.

Who hath not proved how feebly words essay
To fix one spark of Beauty's heavenly ray?
Who doth not feel, until his failing sight
Faints into dimness with its own delight,
His changing cheek, his sinking heart confess
The might — the majesty of Loveliness?
Such was Zuleika — such around her shone
The nameless charms unmarked by her alone —
The light of Love, the purity of Grace,
The mind, the Music breathing from her face,
The heart whose softness harmonized the whole,
And oh! that eye was in itself a Soul!

Her graceful arms in meekness bending
  Across her gently-budding breast;
At one kind word those arms extending
  To clasp the neck of him who blest
  His child caressing and carest,
  Zuleika came — and Giaffir felt
  His purpose half within him melt:
  Not that against her fancied weal
  His heart though stern could ever feel;
  Affection chained her to that heart;
  Ambition tore the links apart.

VII

"Zuleika! child of Gentleness!
  How dear this very day must tell,

When I forget my own distress,
   In losing what I love so well,
To bid thee with another dwell:
Another! and a braver man
Was never seen in battle's van.
We Moslem reck not much of blood:
   But yet the line of Carasman
Unchanged, unchangeable hath stood
   First of the bold Timariot bands
That won and well can keep their lands.
Enough that he who comes to woo
Is kinsman of the Bey Oglou:
His years need scarce a thought employ;
I would not have thee wed a boy.
And thou shalt have a noble dower:
And his and my united power
Will laugh to scorn the death-firman,
Which others tremble but to scan,
And teach the messenger what fate
The bearer of such boon may wait.
And now thou know'st thy father's will;
   All that thy sex hath need to know:
'Twas mine to teach obedience still —
   The way to love, thy Lord may show."

VIII

In silence bowed the virgin's head;
   And if her eye was filled with tears
That stifled feeling dare not shed,
And changed her cheek from pale to red,
   And red to pale, as through her ears
Those wingéd words like arrows sped,
   What could such be but maiden fears?
So bright the tear in Beauty's eye,
Love half regrets to kiss it dry;
So sweet the blush of Bashfulness,
Even Pity scarce can wish it less!

Whate'er it was the sire forgot:
Or if remembered, marked it not;
Thrice clapped his hands, and called his steed,
   Resigned his gem-adorned chibouque,
And mounting featly for the mead,
   With Maugrabee and Mamaluke,
   His way amid his Delis took,
To witness many an active deed

With sabre keen, or blunt jerreed.
The Kislar only and his Moors
Watch well the Haram's massy doors.

IX

His head was leant upon his hand,
His eye looked o'er the dark blue water
That swiftly glides and gently swells
Between the winding Dardanelles;
But yet he saw nor sea nor strand,
Nor even his Pacha's turbaned band
Mix in the game of mimic slaughter,
Careering cleave the folded felt
With sabre stroke right sharply dealt;
Nor marked the javelin-darting crowd,
Nor heard their Ollahs wild and loud —
He thought but of old Giaffir's daughter!

X

No word from Selim's bosom broke;
One sigh Zuleika's thought bespoke:
Still gazed he through the lattice grate,
Pale, mute, and mournfully sedate.
To him Zuleika's eye was turned,
But little from his aspect learned:
Equal her grief, yet not the same;
Her heart confessed a gentler flame:
But yet that heart, alarmed or weak,
She knew not why, forbade to speak.
Yet speak she must — but when essay?
"How strange he thus should turn away!
Not thus we e'er before have met;
Not thus shall be our parting yet."
Thrice paced she slowly through the room,
And watched his eye — it still was fixed:
She snatched the urn wherein was mixed
The Persian Atar-gul's perfume,
And sprinkled all its odours o'er
The pictured roof and marble floor:
The drops, that through his glittering vest
The playful girl's appeal addressed,
Unheeded o'er his bosom flew,
As if that breast were marble too.
"What, sullen yet? it must not be —
Oh! gentle Selim, this from thee!"

She saw in curious order set
  The fairest flowers of Eastern land —
"He loved them once; may touch them yet,
  If offered by Zuleika's hand."
The childish thought was hardly breathed
Before the rose was plucked and wreathed;
The next fond moment saw her seat
Her fairy form at Selim's feet:
"This rose to calm my brother's cares
A message from the Bulbul bears;
It says to-night he will prolong
For Selim's ear his sweetest song;
And though his note is somewhat sad,
He'll try for once a strain more glad,
With some faint hope his altered lay
May sing these gloomy thoughts away.

XI

"What! not receive my foolish flower?
  Nay then I am indeed unblest:
On me can thus thy forehead lower?
  And know'st thou not who loves thee best?
Oh, Selim dear! oh, more than dearest!
Say, is it me thou hat'st or fearest?
Come, lay thy head upon my breast,
And I will kiss thee into rest,
Since words of mine, and songs must fail,
Ev'n from my fabled nightingale.
I knew our sire at times was stern,
But this from thee had yet to learn:
Too well I know he loves thee not;
But is Zuleika's love forgot?
Ah! deem I right? the Pacha's plan —
This kinsman Bey of Carasman
Perhaps may prove some foe of thine.
If so, I swear by Mecca's shrine, —
If shrines that ne'er approach allow
To woman's step admit her vow, —
Without thy free consent — command —
The Sultan should not have my hand!
Think'st thou that I could bear to part
With thee, and learn to halve my heart?
Ah! were I severed from thy side,
Where were thy friend — and who my guide?
Years have not seen, Time shall not see,
The hour that tears my soul from thee:

Ev'n Azrael, from his deadly quiver
  When flies that shaft, and fly it must,
That parts all else, shall doom for ever
  Our hearts to undivided dust!"

XII

He lived — he breathed — he moved — he felt;
He raised the maid from where she knelt;
His trance was gone, his keen eye shone
With thoughts that long in darkness dwelt;
With thoughts that burn — in rays that melt.
As the stream late concealed
  By the fringe of its willows,
When it rushes reveal'd
  In the light of its billows;
As the bolt bursts on high
  From the black cloud that bound it,
Flashed the soul of that eye
  Through the long lashes round it.
A war-horse at the trumpet's sound,
A lion roused by heedless hound,
A tyrant waked to sudden strife
By graze of ill-directed knife,
Starts not to more convulsive life
Than he, who heard that vow, displayed,
And all, before repressed, betrayed:
"Now thou art mine, for ever mine,
With life to keep, and scarce with life resign;
Now thou art mine, that sacred oath,
Though sworn by one, hath bound us both.
Yes, fondly, wisely hast thou done;
That vow hath saved more heads than one:
But blench not thou — thy simplest tress
Claims more from me than tenderness;
I would not wrong the slenderest hair
That clusters round thy forehead fair,
For all the treasures buried far
Within the caves of Istakar.
This morning clouds upon me lowered,
Reproaches on my head were showered,
And Giaffir almost called me coward!
Now I have motive to be brave;
The son of his neglected slave,
Nay, start not, 'twas the term he gave,
May show, though little apt to vaunt,
A heart his words nor deeds can daunt.

His son, indeed! — yet, thanks to thee,
Perchance I am, at least shall be;
But let our plighted secret vow
Be only known to us as now.
I know the wretch who dares demand
From Giaffir thy reluctant hand;
More ill-got wealth, a meaner soul
Holds not a Musselim's control;
Was he not bred in Egripo?
A viler race let Israel show!
But let that pass — to none be told
Our oath; the rest shall time unfold.
To me and mine leave Osman Bey!
I've partisans for Peril's day:
Think not I am what I appear;
I've arms — and friends — and vengeance near."

XIII

"Think not thou art what thou appearest!
My Selim, thou art sadly changed:
This morn I saw thee gentlest — dearest —
But now thou'rt from thyself estranged.
My love thou surely knew'st before,
It ne'er was less — nor can be more.
To see thee — hear thee — near thee stay —
And hate the night — I know not why,
Save that we meet not but by day;
With thee to live, with thee to die,
I dare not to my hope deny:
Thy cheek — thine eyes — thy lips to kiss —
Like this — and this — no more than this;
For, Allah! sure thy lips are flame:
What fever in thy veins is flushing?
My own have nearly caught the same,
At least I feel my cheek, too, blushing.
To soothe thy sickness, watch thy health,
Partake, but never waste thy wealth,
Or stand with smiles unmurmuring by,
And lighten half thy poverty;
Do all but close thy dying eye,
For that I could not live to try;
To these alone my thoughts aspire:
More can I do? or thou require?
But, Selim, thou must answer why
We need so much of mystery?
The cause I cannot dream nor tell,

But be it, since thou say'st 'tis well;
Yet what thou mean'st by 'arms' and 'friends,'
Beyond my weaker sense extends.
I meant that Giaffir should have heard
  The very vow I plighted thee;
His wrath would not revoke my word:
  But surely he would leave me free.
  Can this fond wish seem strange in me,
To be what I have ever been?
What other hath Zuleika seen
From simple childhood's earliest hour?
  What other can she seek to see
Than thee, companion of her bower,
  The partner of her infancy?
These cherished thoughts with life begun,
  Say, why must I no more avow?
What change is wrought to make me shun
  The truth — my pride, and thine till now?
To meet the gaze of stranger's eyes
Our law — our creed — our God denies;
Nor shall one wandering thought of mine
At such, our Prophet's will, repine:
No! happier made by that decree,
He left me all in leaving thee.
Deep were my anguish, thus compelled
To wed with one I ne'er beheld:
This wherefore should I not reveal?
Why wilt thou urge me to conceal?
I know the Pacha's haughty mood
To thee hath never boded good;
And he so often storms at nought,
Allah! forbid that e'er he ought!
And why I know not, but within
My heart concealment weighs like sin.
If then such secrecy be crime,
  And such it feels while lurking here;
Oh, Selim! tell me yet in time,
  Nor leave me thus to thoughts of fear.
Ah! yonder see the Tchocadar,
My father leaves the mimic war;
I tremble now to meet his eye —
Say, Selim, canst thou tell me why?"

XIV

"Zuleika — to thy tower's retreat
Betake thee — Giaffir I can greet:

And now with him I fain must prate
Of firmans, imposts, levies, state.
There's fearful news from Danube's banks,
Our Vizier nobly thins his ranks
For which the Giaour may give him thanks!
Our Sultan hath a shorter way
Such costly triumph to repay.
But, mark me, when the twilight drum
   Hath warned the troops to food and sleep,
Unto thy cell with Selim come;
   Then softly from the Haram creep
   Where we may wander by the deep:
   Our garden battlements are steep;
Nor these will rash intruder climb
To list our words, or stint our time;
And if he doth, I want not steel
Which some have felt, and more may feel.
Then shalt thou learn of Selim more
Than thou hast heard or thought before:
Trust me, Zuleika — fear not me!
Thou know'st I hold a Haram key."

"Fear thee, my Selim! ne'er till now
Did words like this ——"
                                    "Delay not thou;
I keep the key — and Haroun's guard
Have *some*, and hope of *more* reward.
To-night, Zuleika, thou shalt hear
My tale, my purpose, and my fear:
I am not, love! what I appear."

CANTO THE SECOND

I

THE winds are high on Helle's wave,
   As on that night of stormy water
When Love, who sent, forgot to save
The young — the beautiful — the brave —
   The lonely hope of Sestos' daughter.
Oh! when alone along the sky
Her turret-torch was blazing high,
Though rising gale, and breaking foam,
And shrieking sea-birds warned him home;
And clouds aloft and tides below,
With signs and sounds, forbade to go,
He could not see, he would not hear,

Or sound or sign foreboding fear;
His eye but saw that light of Love,
The only star it hailed above;
His ear but rang with Hero's song,
"Ye waves, divide not lovers long!" —
That tale is old, but Love anew
May nerve young hearts to prove as true.

II

The winds are high and Helle's tide
  Rolls darkly heaving to the main;
And Night's descending shadows hide
  That field with blood bedewed in vain,
The desert of old Priam's pride;
  The tombs, sole relics of his reign,
All — save immortal dreams that could beguile
The blind old man of Scio's rocky isle!

III

Oh! yet — for there my steps have been;
  These feet have pressed the sacred shore,
These limbs that buoyant wave hath borne —
Minstrel! with thee to muse, to mourn,
  To trace again those fields of yore,
Believing every hillock green
  Contains no fabled hero's ashes,
And that around the undoubted scene
  Thine own "broad Hellespont" still dashes,
Be long my lot! and cold were he
Who there could gaze denying thee!

IV

The Night hath closed on Helle's stream,
  Nor yet hath risen on Ida's hill
That Moon, which shone on his high theme:
No warrior chides her peaceful beam,
  But conscious shepherds bless it still.
Their flocks are grazing on the Mound
  Of him who felt the Dardan's arrow:
That mighty heap of gathered ground
Which Ammon's son ran proudly round,
By nations raised, by monarchs crowned,
  Is now a lone and nameless barrow!
Within — thy dwelling-place how narrow!
Without — can only strangers breathe

The name of him that *was* beneath:
Dust long outlasts the storied stone;
But Thou — thy very dust is gone!

V

Late, late to-night will Dian cheer
The swain, and chase the boatmans' fear;
Till then — no beacon on the cliff
May shape the course of struggling skiff;
The scattered lights that skirt the bay,
All, one by one, have died away;
The only lamp of this lone hour
Is glimmering in Zuleika's tower.
Yes! there is light in that lone chamber,
  And o'er her silken ottoman
Are thrown the fragrant beads of amber,
  O'er which her fairy fingers ran;
Near these, with emerald rays beset,
(How could she thus that gem forget?)
Her mother's sainted amulet,
Whereon engraved the Koorsee text,
Could smooth this life, and win the next;
And by her Comboloio lies
A Koran of illumined dyes;
And many a bright emblazoned rhyme
By Persian scribes redeemed from Time;
And o'er those scrolls, not oft so mute,
Reclines her now neglected lute;
And round her lamp of fretted gold
Bloom flowers in urns of China's mould;
The richest work of Iran's loom,
And Sheeraz' tribute of perfume;
All that can eye or sense delight
  Are gathered in that gorgeous room:
  But yet it hath an air of gloom.
She, of this Peri cell the sprite,
What doth she hence, and on so rude a night?

VI

Wrapt in the darkest sable vest,
  Which none save noblest Moslem wear,
To guard from winds of Heaven the breast
  As Heaven itself to Selim dear,
With cautious steps the thicket threading,
  And starting oft, as through the glade
  The gust its hollow moanings made,

Till on the smoother pathway treading,
More free her timid bosom beat,
  The maid pursued her silent guide;
And though her terror urged retreat,
  How could she quit her Selim's side?
  How teach her tender lips to chide?

VII

They reached at length a grotto, hewn
  By nature, but enlarged by art,
Where oft her lute she wont to tune,
  And oft her Koran conned apart;
And oft in youthful reverie
She dreamed what Paradise might be:
Where Woman's parted soul shall go
Her Prophet had disdained to show;
But Selim's mansion was secure,
Nor deemed she, could he long endure
His bower in other worlds of bliss
Without *her*, most beloved in this!
Oh! who so dear with him could dwell?
What Houri soothe him half so well?

VIII

Since last she visited the spot
Some change seemed wrought within the grot:
It might be only that the night
Disguised things seen by better light:
That brazen lamp but dimly threw
A ray of no celestial hue;
But in a nook within the cell
Her eye on stranger objects fell.
There arms were piled, not such as wield
The turbaned Delis in the field;
But brands of foreign blade and hilt,
And one was red — perchance with guilt!
Ah! how without can blood be spilt?
A cup too on the board was set
That did not seem to hold sherbet.
What may this mean? she turned to see
Her Selim — "Oh! can this be he?"

IX

His robe of pride was thrown aside,
  His brow no high-crowned turban bore,

But in its stead a shawl of red,
   Wreathed lightly round, his temples wore:
That dagger, on whose hilt the gem
Were worthy of a diadem,
No longer glittered at his waist,
Where pistols unadorned were braced;
And from his belt a sabre swung,
And from his shoulder loosely hung
The cloak of white, the thin capote
That decks the wandering Candiote;
Beneath — his golden plated vest
Clung like a cuirass to his breast;
The greaves below his knee that wound
With silvery scales were sheathed and bound.
But were it not that high command
Spake in his eye, and tone, and hand,
All that a careless eye could see
In him was some young Galiongée.

X

"I said I was not what I seemed;
   And now thou see'st my words were true:
I have a tale thou hast not dreamed,
   If sooth — its truth must others rue.
My story now 'twere vain to hide,
I must not see thee Osman's bride:
But had not thine own lips declared
How much of that young heart I shared,
I could not, must not, yet have shown
The darker secret of my own.
In this I speak not now of love;
That — let Time — Truth — and Peril prove:
But first — Oh! never wed another —
Zuleika! I am not thy brother!"

XI

"Oh! not my brother! — yet unsay —
   God! am I left alone on earth
To mourn — I dare not curse — the day
   That saw my solitary birth?
Oh, thou wilt love me now no more!
   My sinking heart foreboded ill;
But know *me* all I was before,
   Thy sister — friend — Zuleika still.
Thou led'st me here perchance to kill;

If thou hast cause for vengeance, see!
My breast is offered — take thy fill!
Far better with the dead to be
Than live thus nothing now to thee:
Perhaps far worse, for now I know
Why Giaffir always seemed thy foe;
And I, alas! am Giaffir's child,
For whom thou wert contemned, reviled.
If not thy sister — would'st thou save
My life — Oh! bid me be thy slave!"

XII

"My slave, Zuleika! — nay, I'm thine:
But; gentle love, this transport calm,
Thy lot shall yet be linked with mine;
I swear it by our Prophet's shrine,
And be that thought thy sorrow's balm.
So may the Koran verse displayed
Upon its steel direct my blade,
In danger's hour to guard us both,
As I preserve that awful oath!
The name in which thy heart hath prided
Must change; but, my Zuleika, know,
That tie is widened, not divided,
Although thy Sire's my deadliest foe.
My father was to Giaffir all
That Selim late was deemed to thee;
That brother wrought a brother's fall,
But spared, at least, my infancy!
And lulled me with a vain deceit
That yet a like return may meet.
He reared me, not with tender help,
But like the nephew of a Cain;
He watched me like a lion's whelp,
That gnaws and yet may break his chain.
My father's blood in every vein
Is boiling! but for thy dear sake
No present vengeance will I take;
Though here I must no more remain.
But first, beloved Zuleika! hear
How Giaffir wrought this deed of fear.

XIII

"How first their strife to rancour grew,
If Love or Envy made them foes,

It matters little if I knew;
In fiery spirits, slights, though few
   And thoughtless, will disturb repose.
In war Abdallah's arm was strong,
Remembered yet in Bosniac song,
And Paswan's rebel hordes attest
How little love they bore such guest:
His death is all I need relate,
The stern effect of Giaffir's hate;
And how my birth disclosed to me,
Whate'er beside it makes, hath made me free.

XIV

"When Paswan, after years of strife,
At last for power, but first for life,
In Widdin's walls too proudly sate,
Our Pachas rallied round the state;
Not last nor least in high command,
Each brother led a separate band;
They gave their Horse-tails to the wind,
   And mustering in Sophia's plain
Their tents were pitched, their post assigned;
   To one, alas! assigned in vain!
What need of words? the deadly bowl,
   By Giaffir's order drugged and given,
With venom subtle as his soul,
   Dismissed Abdallah's hence to heaven.
Reclined and feverish in the bath,
He, when the hunter's sport was up,
But little deemed a brother's wrath
   To quench his thirst had such a cup:
The bowl a bribed attendant bore;
He drank one draught, nor needed more!
If thou my tale, Zuleika, doubt,
Call Haroun — he can tell it out.

XV

"The deed once done, and Paswan's feud
In part suppressed, though ne'er subdued,
   Abdallah's Pachalick was gained: —
Thou know'st not what in our Divan
Can wealth procure for worse than man —
   Abdallah's honours were obtained
By him a brother's murder stained;
'Tis true, the purchase nearly drained

His ill-got treasure, soon replaced.
Would'st question whence? Survey the waste,
And ask the squalid peasant how
His gains repay his broiling brow! —
Why me the stern Usurper spared,
Why thus with me his palace shared,
I know not. Shame — regret — remorse —
And little fear from infant's force —
Besides, adoption as a son
By him whom Heaven accorded none,
Or some unknown cabal, caprice,
Preserved me thus: — but not in peace:
He cannot curb his haughty mood,
Nor I forgive a father's blood.

XVI

"Within thy Father's house are foes;
  Not all who break his bread are true:
To these should I my birth disclose,
  His days — his very hours were few:
They only want a heart to lead,
A hand to point them to the deed.
But Haroun only knows, or knew
  This tale, whose close is almost nigh:
He in Abdallah's palace grew,
  And held that post in his Serai
  Which holds he here — he saw him die;
But what could single slavery do?
Avenge his lord? alas! too late;
Or save his son from such a fate?
He chose the last, and when elate
  With foes subdued, or friends betrayed,
Proud Giaffir in high triumph sate,
He led me helpless to his gate,
  And not in vain it seems essayed
  To save the life for which he prayed.
The knowledge of my birth secured
  From all and each, but most from me;
Thus Giaffir's safety was ensured.
  Removed he too from Roumelie
To this our Asiatic side,
Far from our seats by Danube's tide,
  With none but Haroun, who retains
Such knowledge — and that Nubian feels
  A Tyrant's secrets are but chains,
From which the captive gladly steals,

And this and more to me reveals:
Such still to guilt just Allah sends —
Slaves, tools, accomplices — no friends!

XVII

"All this, Zuleika, harshly sounds;
  But harsher still my tale must be:
Howe'er my tongue thy softness wounds,
  Yet I must prove all truth to thee.
  I saw thee start this garb to see,
Yet is it one I oft have worn,
  And long must wear: this Galiongée,
To whom thy plighted vow is sworn,
  Is leader of those pirate hordes,
  Whose laws and lives are on their swords;
To hear whose desolating tale
Would make thy waning cheek more pale:
Those arms thou see'st my band have brought,
The hands that wield are not remote;
This cup too for the rugged knaves
  Is filled — once quaffed, they ne'er repine:
Our Prophet might forgive the slaves;
  They're only infidels in wine.

XVIII

"What could I be? Proscribed at home,
And taunted to a wish to roam;
And listless left — for Giaffir's fear
Denied the courser and the spear —
Though oft — Oh, Mahomet! how oft! —
In full Divan the despot scoffed,
As if *my* weak unwilling hand
Refused the bridle or the brand:
He ever went to war alone,
And pent me here untried — unknown;
To Haroun's care with women left,
By hope unblest, of fame bereft,
While thou — whose softness long endeared,
Though it unmanned me, still had cheered —
To Brusa's walls for safety sent,
Awaited'st there the field's event.
Haroun who saw my spirit pining
  Beneath inaction's sluggish yoke,
His captive, though with dread resigning,
  My thraldom for a season broke,

On promise to return before
The day when Giaffir's charge was o'er.
'Tis vain — my tongue can not impart
My almost drunkenness of heart,
When first this liberated eye
Surveyed Earth — Ocean — Sun — and Sky —
As if my Spirit pierced them through,
And all their inmost wonders knew!
One word alone can paint to thee
That more than feeling — I was Free!
E'en for thy presence ceased to pine;
The World — nay, Heaven itself was mine!

XIX

"The shallop of a trusty Moor
Conveyed me from this idle shore;
I longed to see the isles that gem
Old Ocean's purple diadem:
I sought by turns, and saw them all;
  But when and where I joined the crew,
With whom I'm pledged to rise or fall,
  When all that we design to do
Is done, 'twill then be time more meet
To tell thee, when the tale's complete.

XX

" 'Tis true, they are a lawless brood,
But rough in form, nor mild in mood;
And every creed, and every race,
With them hath found — may find a place:
But open speech, and ready hand,
Obedience to their Chief's command;
A soul for every enterprise,
That never sees with Terror's eyes;
Friendship for each, and faith to all,
And vengeance vowed for those who fall,
Have made them fitting instruments
For more than e'en my own intents.
And some — and I have studied all
  Distinguished from the vulgar rank,
But chiefly to my council call
  The wisdom of the cautious Frank: —
And some to higher thoughts aspire.
  The last of Lambro's patriots there
  Anticipated freedom share;

And oft around the cavern fire
On visionary schemes debate,
To snatch the Rayahs from their fate.
So let them ease their hearts with prate
Of equal rights, which man ne'er knew;
I have a love for freedom too.
Aye! let me like the ocean-Patriarch roam,
Or only know on land the Tartar's home!
My tent on shore, my galley on the sea,
Are more than cities and Serais to me:
Borne by my steed, or wafted by my sail,
Across the desert, or before the gale,
Bound where thou wilt, my barb! or glide, my prow!
But be the Star that guides the wanderer, Thou!
Thou, my Zuleika, share and bless my bark;
The Dove of peace and promise to mine ark!
Or, since that hope denied in worlds of strife,
Be thou the rainbow to the storms of life!
The evening beam that smiles the clouds away,
And tints to-morrow with prophetic ray!
Blest — as the Muezzin's strain from Mecca's wall
To pilgrims pure and prostrate at his call;
Soft — as the melody of youthful days,
That steals the trembling tear of speechless praise;
Dear — as his native song to Exile's ears,
Shall sound each tone thy long-loved voice endears.
For thee in those bright isles is built a bower
Blooming as Aden in its earliest hour.
A thousand swords, with Selim's heart and hand,
Wait — wave — defend — destroy — at thy command!
Girt by my band, Zuleika at my side,
The spoil of nations shall bedeck my bride.
The Haram's languid years of listless ease
Are well resigned for cares — for joys like these:
Not blind to Fate, I see, where'er I rove,
Unnumbered perils, — but one only love!
Yet well my toils shall that fond breast repay,
Though Fortune frown, or falser friends betray.
How dear the dream in darkest hours of ill,
Should all be changed, to find thee faithful still!
Be but thy soul, like Selim's firmly shown;
To thee be Selim's tender as thine own;
To soothe each sorrow, share in each delight,
Blend every thought, do all — but disunite!
Once free, 'tis mine our horde again to guide;
Friends to each other, foes to aught beside:
Yet there we follow but the bent assigned
By fatal Nature to man's warring kind:

Mark! where his carnage and his conquests cease!
He makes a solitude, and calls it — peace!
I like the rest must use my skill or strength,
But ask no land beyond my sabre's length:
Power sways but by division — her resource
The blest alternative of fraud or force!
Ours be the last; in time Deceit may come
When cities cage us in a social home:
There ev'n thy soul might err — how oft the heart
Corruption shakes which Peril could not part!
And Woman, more than Man, when Death or Woe,
Or even Disgrace, would lay her lover low,
Sunk in the lap of Luxury will shame —
Away suspicion! — *not* Zuleika's name!
But life is hazard at the best; and here
No more remains to win, and much to fear:
Yes, fear! — the doubt, the dread of losing thee,
By Osman's power, and Giaffir's stern decree.
That dread shall vanish with the favouring gale,
Which Love to-night hath promised to my sail:
No danger daunts the pair his smile hath blest,
Their steps still roving, but their hearts at rest.
With thee all toils are sweet, each clime hath charms;
Earth — sea alike — our world within our arms!
Aye — let the loud winds whistle o'er the deck,
So that those arms cling closer round my neck:
The deepest murmur of this lip shall be,
No sigh for safety, but a prayer for thee!
The war of elements no fears impart
To Love, whose deadliest bane is human Art:
There lie the only rocks our course can check;
Here moments menace — *there* are years of wreck!
But hence ye thoughts that rise in Horror's shape!
This hour bestows, or ever bars escape.
Few words remain of mine my tale to close;
Of thine but *one* to waft us from our foes;
Yea — foes — to me will Giaffir's hate decline?
And is not Osman, who would part us, thine?

XXI

"His head and faith from doubt and death
  Returned in time my guard to save;
  Few heard, none told, that o'er the wave
From isle to isle I roved the while:
And since, though parted from my band
Too seldom now I leave the land,
No deed they've done, nor deed shall do,

Ere I have heard and doomed it too:
I form the plan — decree the spoil —
'Tis fit I oftener share the toil.
But now too long I've held thine ear;
Time presses — floats my bark — and here
We leave behind but hate and fear.
To-morrow Osman with his train
Arrives — to-night must break thy chain:
And would'st thou save that haughty Bey, —
Perchance *his* life who gave thee thine, —
With me this hour away — away!
But yet, though thou art plighted mine,
Would'st thou recall thy willing vow,
Appalled by truths imparted now,
Here rest I — not to see thee wed:
But be that peril on *my* head!"

XXII

Zuleika, mute and motionless,
Stood like that Statue of Distress,
When, her last hope for ever gone,
The Mother hardened into stone;
All in the maid that eye could see
Was but a younger Niobé.
But ere her lip, or even her eye,
Essayed to speak, or look reply,
Beneath the garden's wicket porch
Far flashed on high a blazing torch!
Another — and another — and another —
"Oh! fly — no more — yet now my more than brother!"
Far, wide, through every thicket spread
The fearful lights are gleaming red;
Nor these alone — for each right hand
Is ready with a sheathless brand.
They part — pursue — return, and wheel
With searching flambeau, shining steel;
And last of all, his sabre waving,
Stern Giaffir in his fury raving:
And now almost they touch the cave —
Oh! must that grot be Selim's grave?

XXIII

Dauntless he stood — " 'Tis come — soon past —
One kiss, Zuleika — 'tis my last:
But yet my band not far from shore
May hear this signal, see the flash;

Yet now too few — the attempt were rash:
   No matter — yet one effort more."
Forth to the cavern mouth he stept;
   His pistol's echo rang on high,
Zuleika started not, nor wept,
   Despair benumbed her breast and eye! —
"They hear me not, or if they ply
Their oars, 'tis but to see me die;
That sound hath drawn my foes more nigh.
Then forth my father's scimitar,
Thou ne'er hast seen less equal war!
Farewell, Zuleika! — Sweet! retire:
   Yet stay within — here linger safe,
   At thee his rage will only chafe.
Stir not — lest even to thee perchance
Some erring blade or ball should glance.
Fear'st thou for him? — may I expire
If in this strife I seek thy sire!
No — though by him that poison poured;
No — though again he call me coward!
But tamely shall I meet their steel?
No — as each crest save *his* may feel!"

XXIV

One bound he made, and gained the sand:
   Already at his feet hath sunk
The foremost of the prying band,
   A gasping head, a quivering trunk:
Another falls — but round him close
A swarming circle of his foes;
From right to left his path he cleft,
   And almost met the meeting wave:
His boat appears — not five oars' length —
His comrades strain with desperate strength —
   Oh! are they yet in time to save?
   His feet the foremost breakers lave;
His band are plunging in the bay,
Their sabres glitter through the spray;
Wet — wild — unwearied to the strand
They struggle — now they touch the land!
They come — 'tis but to add to slaughter —
His heart's best blood is on the water.

XXV

Escaped from shot, unharmed by steel,
Or scarcely grazed its force to feel,

Had Selim won, betrayed, beset,
To where the strand and billows met;
There as his last step left the land,
And the last death-blow dealt his hand —
Ah! wherefore did he turn to look
   For her his eye but sought in vain?
That pause, that fatal gaze he took,
   Hath doomed his death, or fixed his chain.
Sad proof, in peril and in pain,
How late will Lover's hope remain!
His back was to the dashing spray;
Behind, but close, his comrades lay,
When, at the instant, hissed the ball —
"So may the foes of Giaffir fall!"
Whose voice is heard? whose carbine rang?
Whose bullet through the night-air sang,
Too nearly, deadly aimed to err?
'Tis thine — Abdallah's Murderer!
The father slowly rued thy hate,
The son hath found a quicker fate:
Fast from his breast the blood is bubbling,
The whiteness of the sea-foam troubling —
If aught his lips essayed to groan,
The rushing billows choked the tone!

XXVI

Morn slowly rolls the clouds away;
   Few trophies of the fight are there:
The shouts that shook the midnight-bay
Are silent; but some signs of fray
   That strand of strife may bear,
And fragments of each shivered brand;
Steps stamped; and dashed into the sand
The print of many a struggling hand
   May there be marked; nor far remote
   A broken torch, an oarless boat;
And tangled on the weeds that heap
The beach where shelving to the deep
   There lies a white capote!
'Tis rent in twain — one dark-red stain
The wave yet ripples o'er in vain:
      But where is he who wore?
Ye! who would o'er his relics weep,
Go, seek them where the surges sweep
Their burthen round Sigæum's steep
      And cast on Lemnos' shore:

The sea-birds shriek above the prey,
O'er which their hungry beaks delay,
As shaken on his restless pillow,
His head heaves with the heaving billow;
That hand, whose motion is not life,
Yet feebly seems to menace strife,
Flung by the tossing tide on high,
   Then levelled with the wave —
What recks it, though that corse shall lie
   Within a living grave?
The bird that tears that prostrate form
Hath only robbed the meaner worm;
The only heart, the only eye
Had bled or wept to see him die,
Had seen those scattered limbs composed,
   And mourned above his turban-stone,
That heart hath burst — that eye was closed —
   Yea — closed before his own!

XXVII

By Helle's stream there is a voice of wail!
And Woman's eye is wet — Man's cheek is pale:
Zuleika! last of Giaffir's race,
   Thy destined lord is come too late:
He sees not — ne'er shall see thy face!
         Can he not hear
The loud Wul-wulleh warn his distant ear?
   Thy handmaids weeping at the gate,
   The Koran-chanters of the Hymn of Fate,
   The silent slaves with folded arms that wait,
Sighs in the hall, and shrieks upon the gale,
         Tell him thy tale!
Thou didst not view thy Selim fall!
   That fearful moment when he left the cave
         Thy heart grew chill:
   He was thy hope — thy joy — thy love — thine all,
   And that last thought on him thou could'st not save
            Sufficed to kill;
Burst forth in one wild cry — and all was still.
   Peace to thy broken heart — and virgin grave!
Ah! happy! but of life to lose the worst!
That grief — though deep — though fatal — was thy first!
Thrice happy! ne'er to feel nor fear the force
Of absence — shame — pride — hate — revenge — remorse!
And, oh! that pang where more than Madness lies
The Worm that will not sleep — and never dies;

Thought of the gloomy day and ghastly night,
That dreads the darkness, and yet loathes the light,
That winds around, and tears the quivering heart!
Ah! wherefore not consume it — and depart!
Woe to thee, rash and unrelenting Chief!
  Vainly thou heap'st the dust upon thy head,
  Vainly the sackcloth o'er thy limbs dost spread:
  By that same hand Abdallah — Selim bled.
Now let it tear thy beard in idle grief:
Thy pride of heart, thy bride for Osman's bed,
She, whom thy Sultan had but seen to wed,
      Thy Daughter's dead!
  Hope of thine age, thy twilight's lonely beam,
  The Star hath set that shone on Helle's stream.
What quenched its ray? — the blood that thou hast shed!
Hark! to the hurried question of Despair:
"Where is my child?" — an Echo answers — "Where?"

XXVIII

Within the place of thousand tombs
  That shine beneath, while dark above
The sad but living cypress glooms
  And withers not, though branch and leaf
Are stamped with an eternal grief,
  Like early unrequited Love,
One spot exists, which ever blooms,
  Ev'n in that deadly grove —
A single rose is shedding there
  Its lonely lustre, meek and pale:
It looks as planted by Despair —
  So white — so faint — the slightest gale
Might whirl the leaves on high;
  And yet, though storms and blight assail,
And hands more rude than wintry sky
  May wring it from the stem — in vain —
  To-morrow sees it bloom again!
The stalk some Spirit gently rears,
And waters with celestial tears;
  For well may maids of Helle deem
That this can be no earthly flower,
Which mocks the tempest's withering hour,
And buds unsheltered by a bower;
Nor droops, though Spring refuse her shower,
  Nor woos the Summer beam:
To it the livelong night there sings
  A Bird unseen — but not remote:

Invisible his airy wings,
But soft as harp that Houri strings
His long entrancing note!
It were the Bulbul; but his throat,
Though mournful, pours not such a strain:
For they who listen cannot leave
The spot, but linger there and grieve,
As if they loved in vain!
And yet so sweet the tears they shed,
'Tis sorrow so unmixed with dread,
They scarce can bear the morn to break
That melancholy spell,
And longer yet would weep and wake,
He sings so wild and well!
But when the day-blush bursts from high
Expires that magic melody.
And some have been who could believe,
(So fondly youthful dreams deceive,
Yet harsh be they that blame,)
That note so piercing and profound
Will shape and syllable its sound
Into Zuleika's name.
'Tis from her cypress summit heard,
That melts in air the liquid word:
'Tis from her lowly virgin earth
That white rose takes its tender birth.
There late was laid a marble stone;
Eve saw it placed — the Morrow gone!
It was no mortal arm that bore
That deep fixed pillar to the shore;
For there, as Helle's legends tell,
Next morn 'twas found where Selim fell;
Lashed by the tumbling tide, whose wave
Denied his bones a holier grave:
And there by night, reclined, 'tis said,
Is seen a ghastly turbaned head:
And hence extended by the billow,
'Tis named the "Pirate-phantom's pillow!"
Where first it lay that mourning flower
Hath flourished; flourisheth this hour,
Alone and dewy — coldly pure and pale;
As weeping Beauty's cheek at Sorrow's tale!

ODE TO NAPOLEON BUONAPARTE

"Expende Annibalem: — quot libras in duce summo
Invenies?" —

JUVENAL, Sat. X

"The Emperor Nepos was acknowledged by the *Senate*, by the *Italians*, and by the Provincials of *Gaul;* his moral virtues, and military talents, were loudly celebrated; and those who derived any private benefit from his government announced in prophetic strains the restoration of public felicity. . . . By this shameful abdication, he protracted his life a few years, in a very ambiguous state, between an Emperor and an Exile, till —"

Gibbon's *Decline and Fall.*

I

'Tis done — but yesterday a King!
And armed with Kings to strive —
And now thou art a nameless thing:
So abject — yet alive!
Is this the man of thousand thrones,
Who strewed our earth with hostile bones,
And can he thus survive?
Since he, miscalled the Morning Star,
Nor man nor fiend hath fallen so far.

II

Ill-minded man! why scourge thy kind
Who bowed so low the knee?
By gazing on thyself grown blind,
Thou taught'st the rest to see.
With might unquestioned, — power to save, —
Thine only gift hath been the grave
To those that worshipped thee;
Nor till thy fall could mortals guess
Ambition's less than littleness!

III

Thanks for that lesson — it will teach
To after-warriors more
Than high Philosophy can preach,
And vainly preached before.
That spell upon the minds of men

Breaks never to unite again,
  That led them to adore
Those Pagod things of sabre-sway,
With fronts of brass, and feet of clay.

IV

The triumph, and the vanity,
  The rapture of the strife —
The earthquake-voice of Victory,
  To thee the breath of life;
The sword, the sceptre, and that sway
Which man seemed made but to obey,
  Wherewith renown was rife —
All quelled! — Dark Spirit! what must be
The madness of thy memory!

V

The Desolator desolate!
  The Victor overthrown!
The Arbiter of others' fate
  A Suppliant for his own!
Is it some yet imperial hope
That with such change can calmly cope?
  Or dread of death alone?
To die a Prince — or live a slave —
Thy choice is most ignobly brave!

VI

He who of old would rend the oak,
  Dreamed not of the rebound;
Chained by the trunk he vainly broke —
  Alone — how looked he round?
Thou, in the sternness of thy strength,
An equal deed hast done at length,
  And darker fate hast found:
He fell, the forest prowlers' prey;
But thou must eat thy heart away!

VII

The Roman, when his burning heart
  Was slaked with blood of Rome,
Threw down the dagger — dared depart,
  In savage grandeur, home. —

He dared depart in utter scorn
Of men that such a yoke had borne,
   Yet left him such a doom!
His only glory was that hour
Of self-upheld abandoned power.

VIII

The Spaniard, when the lust of sway
   Had lost its quickening spell,
Cast crowns for rosaries away,
   An empire for a cell;
A strict accountant of his beads,
A subtle disputant on creeds,
   His dotage trifled well:
Yet better had he neither known
A bigot's shrine, nor despot's throne.

IX

But thou — from thy reluctant hand
   The thunderbolt is wrung —
Too late thou leav'st the high command
   To which thy weakness clung;
All Evil Spirit as thou art,
It is enough to grieve the heart
   To see thine own unstrung;
To think that God's fair world hath been
The footstool of a thing so mean;

X

And Earth hath spilt her blood for him,
   Who thus can hoard his own!
And Monarchs bowed the trembling limb,
   And thanked him for a throne!
Fair Freedom! we may hold thee dear,
When thus thy mightiest foes their fear
   In humblest guise have shown.
Oh! ne'er may tyrant leave behind
A brighter name to lure mankind!

XI

Thine evil deeds are writ in gore,
   Nor written thus in vain —
Thy triumphs tell of fame no more,
   Or deepen every stain:

If thou hadst died as Honour dies,
Some new Napoleon might arise,
  To shame the world again —
But who would soar the solar height,
To set in such a starless night?

XII

Weigh'd in the balance, hero dust
  Is vile as vulgar clay;
Thy scales, Mortality! are just
  To all that pass away:
But yet methought the living great
Some higher sparks should animate,
  To dazzle and dismay:
Nor deem'd Contempt could thus make mirth
Of these, the Conquerors of the earth.

XIII

And she, proud Austria's mournful flower,
  Thy still imperial bride;
How bears her breast the torturing hour?
  Still clings she to thy side?
Must she too bend, must she too share
Thy late repentance, long despair,
  Thou throneless Homicide?
If still she loves thee, hoard that gem, —
'Tis worth thy vanished diadem!

XIV

Then haste thee to thy sullen Isle,
  And gaze upon the sea;
That element may meet thy smile —
  It ne'er was ruled by thee!
Or trace with thine all idle hand
In loitering mood upon the sand
  That Earth is now as free!
That Corinth's pedagogue hath now
Transferred his by-word to thy brow.

XV

Thou Timour! in his captive's cage
  What thoughts will there be thine,
While brooding in thy prisoned rage?
  But one — "The world *was* mine!"

Unless, like he of Babylon,
All sense is with thy sceptre gone,
  Life will not long confine
That spirit poured so widely forth —
So long obeyed — so little worth!

XVI

Or, like the thief of fire from heaven,
  Wilt thou withstand the shock?
And share with him, the unforgiven,
  His vulture and his rock!
Foredoomed by God — by man accurst,
And that last act, though not thy worst,
  The very Fiend's arch mock;
He in his fall preserved his pride,
And, if a mortal, had as proudly died!

XVII

There was a day — there was an hour,
  While earth was Gaul's — Gaul thine —
When that immeasurable power
  Unsated to resign
Had been an act of purer fame
Than gathers round Marengo's name
  And gilded thy decline,
Through the long twilight of all time,
Despite some passing clouds of crime.

XVIII

But thou forsooth must be a King
  And don the purple vest,
As if that foolish robe could wring
  Remembrance from thy breast.
Where is that faded garment? where
The gewgaws thou wert fond to wear,
  The star, the string, the crest?
Vain froward child of Empire! say,
Are all thy playthings snatched away?

XIX

Where may the wearied eye repose
  When gazing on the Great;
Where neither guilty glory glows,
  Nor despicable state?

Yes — One — the first — the last — the best —
The Cincinnatus of the West,
  Whom Envy dared not hate,
Bequeathed the name of Washington,
To make man blush there was but one!

FROM HEBREW MELODIES

SHE WALKS IN BEAUTY

I

She walks in Beauty, like the night
  Of cloudless climes and starry skies;
And all that's best of dark and bright
  Meet in her aspect and her eyes:
Thus mellowed to that tender light
  Which Heaven to gaudy day denies.

II

One shade the more, one ray the less,
  Had half impaired the nameless grace
Which waves in every raven tress,
  Or softly lightens o'er her face;
Where thoughts serenely sweet express,
  How pure, how dear their dwelling-place.

III

And on that cheek, and o'er that brow,
  So soft, so calm, yet eloquent,
The smiles that win, the tints that glow,
  But tell of days in goodness spent,
A mind at peace with all below,
  A heart whose love is innocent!

OH! SNATCHED AWAY IN BEAUTY'S BLOOM

I

Oh! snatched away in beauty's bloom,
On thee shall press no ponderous tomb;
  But on thy turf shall roses rear
  Their leaves, the earliest of the year;
And the wild cypress wave in tender gloom:

II

And oft by yon blue gushing stream
  Shall Sorrow lean her drooping head,
And feed deep thought with many a dream,
  And lingering pause and lightly tread;
Fond wretch! as if her step disturbed the dead!

III

Away! we know that tears are vain,
  That Death nor heeds nor hears distress:
Will this unteach us to complain?
  Or make one mourner weep the less?
And thou — who tell'st me to forget,
Thy looks are wan, thine eyes are wet.

BY THE RIVERS OF BABYLON WE SAT DOWN AND WEPT

I

We sat down and wept by the waters
  Of Babel, and thought of the day
When our foe, in the hue of his slaughters,
  Made Salem's high places his prey;
And Ye, oh her desolate daughters!
  Were scattered all weeping away.

II

While sadly we gazed on the river
  Which rolled on in freedom below,
They demanded the song; but, oh never
  That triumph the Stranger shall know!
May this right hand be withered for ever,
  Ere it string our high harp for the foe!

III

On the willow that harp is suspended,
  Oh Salem! its sound should be free;
And the hour when thy glories were ended
  But left me that token of thee:
And ne'er shall its soft tones be blended
  With the voice of the Spoiler by me!

THE DESTRUCTION OF SENNACHERIB

I

THE Assyrian came down like the wolf on the fold,
And his cohorts were gleaming in purple and gold;
And the sheen of their spears was like stars on the sea,
When the blue wave rolls nightly on deep Galilee.

II

Like the leaves of the forest when Summer is green,
That host with their banners at sunset were seen:
Like the leaves of the forest when Autumn hath blown,
That host on the morrow lay withered and strown.

III

For the Angel of Death spread his wings on the blast,
And breathed in the face of the foe as he passed;
And the eyes of the sleepers waxed deadly and chill,
And their hearts but once heaved — and for ever grew still!

IV

And there lay the steed with his nostril all wide,
But through it there rolled not the breath of his pride;
And the foam of his gasping lay white on the turf,
And cold as the spray of the rock-beating surf.

V

And there lay the rider distorted and pale,
With the dew on his brow, and the rust on his mail:
And the tents were all silent — the banners alone —
The lances unlifted — the trumpet unblown.

VI

And the widows of Ashur are loud in their wail,
And the idols are broke in the temple of Baal;
And the might of the Gentile, unsmote by the sword,
Hath melted like snow in the glance of the Lord!

STANZAS FOR MUSIC

1

I SPEAK not, I trace not, I breathe not thy name,
There is grief in the sound, there is guilt in the fame:
But the tear which now burns on my cheek may impart
The deep thoughts that dwell in that silence of heart.

2

Too brief for our passion, too long for our peace,
Were those hours — can their joy or their bitterness cease?
We repent, we abjure, we will break from our chain, —
We will part, we will fly to — unite it again!

3

Oh! thine be the gladness, and mine be the guilt!
Forgive me, adored one! — forsake, if thou wilt; —
But the heart which is thine shall expire undebased
And *man* shall not break it — whatever *thou* mayst.

4

And stern to the haughty, but humble to thee,
This soul, in its bitterest blackness, shall be:
And our days seem as swift, and our moments more sweet,
With thee by my side, than with worlds at our feet.

5

One sigh of thy sorrow, one look of thy love,
Shall turn me or fix, shall reward or reprove;
And the heartless may wonder at all I resign —
Thy lip shall reply, not to them, but to *mine*.

WHEN WE TWO PARTED

1

WHEN we two parted
    In silence and tears,
Half broken-hearted

To sever for years,
Pale grew thy cheek and cold,
Colder thy kiss;
Truly that hour foretold
Sorrow to this.

2

The dew of the morning
Sunk chill on my brow —
It felt like the warning
Of what I feel now.
Thy vows are all broken,
And light is thy fame:
I hear thy name spoken,
And share in its shame.

3

They name thee before me,
A knell to mine ear;
A shudder comes o'er me —
Why wert thou so dear?
They know not I knew thee,
Who knew thee too well: —
Long, long shall I rue thee,
Too deeply to tell.

4

In secret we met —
In silence I grieve,
That thy heart could forget,
Thy spirit deceive.
If I should meet thee
After long years,
How should I greet thee? —
With silence and tears.

FARE THEE WELL

Fare thee well! and if for ever,
Still for ever, fare *thee well:*
Even though unforgiving, never
'Gainst thee shall my heart rebel.
Would that breast were bared before thee

Where thy head so oft hath lain,
While that placid sleep came o'er thee
Which thou ne'er canst know again:
Would that breast, by thee glanced over,
Every inmost thought could show!
Then thou would'st at last discover
'Twas not well to spurn it so.
Though the world for this commend thee —
Though it smile upon the blow,
Even its praises must offend thee,
Founded on another's woe:
Though my many faults defaced me,
Could no other arm be found,
Than the one which once embraced me,
To inflict a cureless wound?
Yet, oh yet, thyself deceive not —
Love may sink by slow decay,
But by sudden wrench, believe not
Hearts can thus be torn away:
Still thine own its life retaineth —
Still must mine, though bleeding, beat;
And the undying thought which paineth
Is — that we no more may meet.
These are words of deeper sorrow
Than the wail above the dead;
Both shall live — but every morrow
Wake us from a widowed bed.
And when thou would'st solace gather —
When our child's first accents flow —
Wilt thou teach her to say "Father!"
Though his care she must forego?
When her little hands shall press thee —
When her lip to thine is pressed —
Think of him whose prayer shall bless thee —
Think of him thy love *had* blessed!
Should her lineaments resemble
Those thou never more may'st see,
Then thy heart will softly tremble
With a pulse yet true to me.
All my faults perchance thou knowest —
All my madness — none can know;
All my hopes — where'er thou goest —
Wither — yet with *thee* they go.
Every feeling hath been shaken;
Pride — which not a world could bow —
Bows to thee — by thee forsaken,
Even my soul forsakes me now.

But 'tis done — all words are idle —
  Words from me are vainer still;
But the thoughts we cannot bridle
  Force their way without the will.
Fare thee well! thus disunited —
  Torn from every nearer tie —
Seared in heart — and lone — and blighted —
  More than this I scarce can die.

THE PRISONER OF CHILLON

SONNET ON CHILLON

Eternal Spirit of the chainless Mind!
  Brightest in dungeons, Liberty! thou art:
  For there thy habitation is the heart —
The heart which love of thee alone can bind;
And when thy sons to fetters are consigned —
  To fetters, and the damp vault's dayless gloom,
  Their country conquers with their martyrdom,
And Freedom's fame finds wings on every wind.
Chillon! thy prison is a holy place,
  And thy sad floor an altar — for 'twas trod,
Until his very steps have left a trace
  Worn, as if thy cold pavement were a sod,
By Bonnivard! — May none those marks efface!
  For they appeal from tyranny to God.

I

My hair is grey, but not with years,
Nor grew it white
    In a single night,
As men's have grown from sudden fears:
My limbs are bowed, though not with toil,
  But rusted with a vile repose,
For they have been a dungeon's spoil,
  And mine has been the fate of those
To whom the goodly earth and air
Are banned, and barred — forbidden fare;
But this was for my father's faith
I suffered chains and courted death;
That father perished at the stake
For tenets he would not forsake;
And for the same his lineal race
In darkness found a dwelling place;

We were seven — who now are one,
  Six in youth, and one in age,
Finished as they had begun,
  Proud of Persecution's rage;
One in fire, and two in field,
Their belief with blood have sealed,
Dying as their father died,
For the God their foes denied; —
Three were in a dungeon cast,
Of whom this wreck is left the last.

II

There are seven pillars of Gothic mould,
In Chillon's dungeons deep and old,
There are seven columns, massy and grey,
Dim with a dull imprisoned ray,
A sunbeam which hath lost its way,
And through the crevice and the cleft
Of the thick wall is fallen and left;
Creeping o'er the floor so damp,
Like a marsh's meteor lamp:
And in each pillar there is a ring,
  And in each ring there is a chain;
That iron is a cankering thing,
  For in these limbs its teeth remain,
With marks that will not wear away,
Till I have done with this new day,
Which now is painful to these eyes,
Which have not seen the sun so rise
For years — I cannot count them o'er,
I lost their long and heavy score
When my last brother drooped and died,
And I lay living by his side.

III

They chained us each to a column stone,
And we were three — yet, each alone;
We could not move a single pace,
We could not see each other's face,
But with that pale and livid light
That made us strangers in our sight:
And thus together — yet apart,
Fettered in hand, but joined in heart,
'Twas still some solace in the dearth
Of the pure elements of earth,

To hearken to each other's speech,
And each turn comforter to each
With some new hope, or legend old,
Or song heroically bold;
But even these at length grew cold.
Our voices took a dreary tone,
An echo of the dungeon stone,
A grating sound, not full and free,
As they of yore were wont to be:
It might be fancy — but to me
They never sounded like our own.

IV

I was the eldest of the three,
And to uphold and cheer the rest
I ought to do — and did my best —
And each did well in his degree.
The youngest, whom my father loved,
Because our mother's brow was given
To him, with eyes as blue as heaven —
For him my soul was sorely moved:
And truly might it be distressed
To see such bird in such a nest;
For he was beautiful as day —
(When day was beautiful to me
As to young eagles, being free) —
A polar day, which will not see
A sunset till its summer's gone,
Its sleepless summer of long light,
The snow-clad offspring of the sun:
And thus he was as pure and bright,
And in his natural spirit gay,
With tears for nought but others' ills,
And then they flowed like mountain rills,
Unless he could assuage the woe
Which he abhorred to view below.

V

The other was as pure of mind,
But formed to combat with his kind;
Strong in his frame, and of a mood
Which 'gainst the world in war had stood,
And perished in the foremost rank
With joy: — but not in chains to pine:
His spirit withered with their clank,

I saw it silently decline —
And so perchance in sooth did mine:
But yet I forced it on to cheer
Those relics of a home so dear.
He was a hunter of the hills,
Had followed there the deer and wolf;
To him this dungeon was a gulf,
And fettered feet the worst of ills.

VI

Lake Leman lies by Chillon's walls:
A thousand feet in depth below
Its massy waters meet and flow;
Thus much the fathom-line was sent
From Chillon's snow-white battlement,
Which round about the wave inthralls:
A double dungeon wall and wave
Have made — and like a living grave.
Below the surface of the lake
The dark vault lies wherein we lay:
We heard it ripple night and day;
Sounding o'er our heads it knocked;
And I have felt the winter's spray
Wash through the bars when winds were high
And wanton in the happy sky;
And then the very rock hath rocked,
And I have felt it shake, unshocked,
Because I could have smiled to see
The death that would have set me free.

VII

I said my nearer brother pined,
I said his mighty heart declined,
He loathed and put away his food;
It was not that 'twas coarse and rude,
For we were used to hunter's fare,
And for the like had little care:
The milk drawn from the mountain goat
Was changed for water from the moat,
Our bread was such as captives' tears
Have moistened many a thousand years,
Since man first pent his fellow men
Like brutes within an iron den;
But what were these to us or him?
These wasted not his heart or limb;

My brother's soul was of that mould
Which in a palace had grown cold,
Had his free breathing been denied
The range of the steep mountain's side;
But why delay the truth? — he died.
I saw, and could not hold his head,
Nor reach his dying hand — nor dead, —
Though hard I strove, but strove in vain,
To rend and gnash my bonds in twain.
He died — and they unlocked his chain,
And scooped for him a shallow grave
Even from the cold earth of our cave.
I begged them, as a boon, to lay
His corse in dust whereon the day
Might shine — it was a foolish thought,
But then within my brain it wrought,
That even in death his freeborn breast
In such a dungeon could not rest.
I might have spared my idle prayer —
They coldly laughed — and laid him there:
The flat and turfless earth above
The being we so much did love;
His empty chain above it leant,
Such Murder's fitting monument!

VIII

But he, the favourite and the flower,
Most cherished since his natal hour,
His mother's image in fair face,
The infant love of all his race,
His martyred father's dearest thought,
My latest care, for whom I sought
To hoard my life, that his might be
Less wretched now, and one day free;
He, too, who yet had held untired
A spirit natural or inspired —
He, too, was struck, and day by day
Was withered on the stalk away.
Oh, God! it is a fearful thing
To see the human soul take wing
In any shape, in any mood:
I've seen it rushing forth in blood,
I've seen it on the breaking ocean
Strive with a swoln convulsive motion,
I've seen the sick and ghastly bed
Of Sin delirious with its dread:

But these were horrors — this was woe
Unmixed with such — but sure and slow:
He faded, and so calm and meek,
So softly worn, so sweetly weak,
So tearless, yet so tender — kind,
And grieved for those he left behind;
With all the while a cheek whose bloom
Was as a mockery of the tomb,
Whose tints as gently sunk away
As a departing rainbow's ray;
An eye of most transparent light,
That almost made the dungeon bright;
And not a word of murmur — not
A groan o'er his untimely lot, —
A little talk of better days,
A little hope my own to raise,
For I was sunk in silence — lost
In this last loss, of all the most;
And then the sighs he would suppress
Of fainting Nature's feebleness,
More slowly drawn, grew less and less:
I listened, but I could not hear;
I called, for I was wild with fear;
I knew 'twas hopeless, but my dread
Would not be thus admonishéd;
I called, and thought I heard a sound —
I burst my chain with one strong bound,
And rushed to him: — I found him not,
I only stirred in this black spot,
I only lived, *I* only drew
The accursed breath of dungeon-dew;
The last, the sole, the dearest link
Between me and the eternal brink,
Which bound me to my failing race,
Was broken in this fatal place.
One on the earth, and one beneath —
My brothers — both had ceased to breathe:
I took that hand which lay so still,
Alas! my own was full as chill;
I had not strength to stir, or strive,
But felt that I was still alive —
A frantic feeling, when we know
That what we love shall ne'er be so.
        I know not why
        I could not die,
I had no earthly hope — but faith,
And that forbade a selfish death.

IX

What next befell me then and there
  I know not well — I never knew —
First came the loss of light, and air,
  And then of darkness too:
I had no thought, no feeling — none —
Among the stones I stood a stone,
And was, scarce conscious what I wist,
As shrubless crags within the mist;
For all was blank, and bleak, and grey;
It was not night — it was not day;
It was not even the dungeon-light,
So hateful to my heavy sight,
But vacancy absorbing space,
And fixedness — without a place;
There were no stars — no earth — no time —
No check — no change — no good — no crime —
But silence, and a stirless breath
Which neither was of life nor death;
A sea of stagnant idleness,
Blind, boundless, mute, and motionless!

X

A light broke in upon my brain, —
  It was the carol of a bird;
It ceased, and then it came again,
  The sweetest song ear ever heard,
And mine was thankful till my eyes
Ran over with the glad surprise,
And they that moment could not see
I was the mate of misery;
But then by dull degrees came back
My senses to their wonted track;
I saw the dungeon walls and floor
Close slowly round me as before,
I saw the glimmer of the sun
Creeping as it before had done,
But through the crevice where it came
That bird was perched, as fond and tame,
  And tamer than upon the tree;
A lovely bird, with azure wings,
And song that said a thousand things,
  And seemed to say them all for me!
I never saw its like before,
I ne'er shall see its likeness more:

It seemed like me to want a mate,
But was not half so desolate,
And it was come to love me when
None lived to love me so again,
And cheering from my dungeon's brink,
Had brought me back to feel and think.
I know not if it late were free,
  Or broke its cage to perch on mine,
But knowing well captivity,
  Sweet bird! I could not wish for thine!
Or if it were, in wingéd guise,
A visitant from Paradise;
For — Heaven forgive that thought! the while
Which made me both to weep and smile —
I sometimes deemed that it might be
My brother's soul come down to me;
But then at last away it flew,
And then 'twas mortal well I knew,
For he would never thus have flown —
And left me twice so doubly lone, —
Lone — as the corse within its shroud,
Lone — as a solitary cloud,
  A single cloud on a sunny day,
While all the rest of heaven is clear,
A frown upon the atmosphere,
That hath no business to appear
  When skies are blue, and earth is gay.

XI

A kind of change came in my fate,
My keepers grew compassionate;
I know not what had made them so,
They were inured to sights of woe,
But so it was: — my broken chain
With links unfastened did remain,
And it was liberty to stride
Along my cell from side to side,
And up and down, and then athwart,
And tread it over every part;
And round the pillars one by one,
Returning where my walk begun,
Avoiding only, as I trod,
My brothers' graves without a sod;
For if I thought with heedless tread
My step profaned their lowly bed,
My breath came gaspingly and thick,
And my crushed heart felt blind and sick.

XII

I made a footing in the wall,
It was not therefrom to escape,
For I had buried one and all,
Who loved me in a human shape;
And the whole earth would henceforth be
A wider prison unto me:
No child — no sire — no kin had I,
No partner in my misery;
I thought of this, and I was glad,
For thought of them had made me mad;
But I was curious to ascend
To my barred windows, and to bend
Once more, upon the mountains high,
The quiet of a loving eye.

XIII

I saw them — and they were the same,
They were not changed like me in frame;
I saw their thousand years of snow
On high — their wide long lake below,
And the blue Rhone in fullest flow;
I heard the torrents leap and gush
O'er channelled rock and broken bush;
I saw the white-walled distant town,
And whiter sails go skimming down;
And then there was a little isle,
Which in my very face did smile,
The only one in view;
A small green isle, it seemed no more,
Scarce broader than my dungeon floor,
But in it there were three tall trees,
And o'er it blew the mountain breeze,
And by it there were waters flowing,
And on it there were young flowers growing,
Of gentle breath and hue.
The fish swam by the castle wall,
And they seemed joyous each and all;
The eagle rode the rising blast,
Methought he never flew so fast
As then to me he seemed to fly;
And then new tears came in my eye,
And I felt troubled — and would fain
I had not left my recent chain;
And when I did descend again,
The darkness of my dim abode

Fell on me as a heavy load;
It was as is a new-dug grave,
Closing o'er one we sought to save, —
And yet my glance, too much opprest,
Had almost need of such a rest.

XIV

It might be months, or years, or days —
I kept no count, I took no note —
I had no hope my eyes to raise,
And clear them of their dreary mote;
At last men came to set me free;
I asked not why, and recked not where;
It was at length the same to me,
Fettered or fetterless to be,
I learned to love despair.
And thus when they appeared at last,
And all my bonds aside were cast,
These heavy walls to me had grown
A hermitage — and all my own!
And half I felt as they were come
To tear me from a second home:
With spiders I had friendship made,
And watched them in their sullen trade,
Had seen the mice by moonlight play,
And why should I feel less than they?
We were all inmates of one place,
And I, the monarch of each race,
Had power to kill — yet, strange to tell!
In quiet we had learned to dwell;
My very chains and I grew friends,
So much a long communion tends
To make us what we are: — even I
Regained my freedom with a sigh.

THE DREAM

I

Our life is twofold: Sleep hath its own world,
A boundary between the things misnamed
Death and existence: Sleep hath its own world,
And a wide realm of wild reality,
And dreams in their development have breath,
And tears, and tortures, and the touch of Joy;
They leave a weight upon our waking thoughts,

They take a weight from off our waking toils,
They do divide our being; they become
A portion of ourselves as of our time,
And look like heralds of Eternity;
They pass like spirits of the past, — they speak
Like Sibyls of the future; they have power —
The tyranny of pleasure and of pain;
They make us what we were not — what they will,
And shake us with the vision that's gone by,
The dread of vanished shadows — Are they so?
Is not the past all shadow? — What are they?
Creations of the mind? — The mind can make
Substance, and people planets of its own
With beings brighter than have been, and give
A breath to forms which can outlive all flesh.
I would recall a vision which I dreamed
Perchance in sleep — for in itself a thought,
A slumbering thought, is capable of years,
And curdles a long life into one hour.

II

I saw two beings in the hues of youth
Standing upon a hill, a gentle hill,
Green and of mild declivity, the last
As 'twere the cape of a long ridge of such,
Save that there was no sea to lave its base,
But a most living landscape, and the wave
Of woods and cornfields, and the abodes of men
Scattered at intervals, and wreathing smoke
Arising from such rustic roofs; — the hill
Was crowned with a peculiar diadem
Of trees, in circular array, so fixed,
Not by the sport of nature, but of man:
These two, a maiden and a youth, were there
Gazing — the one on all that was beneath
Fair as herself — but the Boy gazed on her;
And both were young, and one was beautiful:
And both were young — yet not alike in youth.
As the sweet moon on the horizon's verge,
The Maid was on the eve of Womanhood;
The Boy had fewer summers, but his heart
Had far outgrown his years, and to his eye
There was but one belovéd face on earth,
And that was shining on him: he had looked
Upon it till it could not pass away;
He had no breath, no being, but in hers;
She was his voice; he did not speak to her,

But trembled on her words; she was his sight,
For his eye followed hers, and saw with hers,
Which coloured all his objects: — he had ceased
To live within himself; she was his life,
The ocean to the river of his thoughts,
Which terminated all: upon a tone,
A touch of hers, his blood would ebb and flow,
And his cheek change tempestuously — his heart
Unknowing of its cause of agony.
But she in these fond feelings had no share:
Her sighs were not for him; to her he was
Even as a brother — but no more; 'twas much,
For brotherless she was, save in the name
Her infant friendship had bestowed on him;
Herself the solitary scion left
Of a time-honoured race. — It was a name
Which pleased him, and yet pleased him not — and why?
Time taught him a deep answer — when she loved
Another: even *now* she loved another,
And on the summit of that hill she stood
Looking afar if yet her lover's steed
Kept pace with her expectancy, and flew.

III

A change came o'er the spirit of my dream.
There was an ancient mansion, and before
Its walls there was a steed caparisoned:
Within an antique Oratory stood
The Boy of whom I spake; — he was alone,
And pale, and pacing to and fro: anon
He sate him down, and seized a pen, and traced
Words which I could not guess of; then he leaned
His bowed head on his hands, and shook as 'twere
With a convulsion — then arose again,
And with his teeth and quivering hands did tear
What he had written, but he shed no tears.
And he did calm himself, and fix his brow
Into a kind of quiet: as he paused,
The Lady of his love re-entered there;
She was serene and smiling then, and yet
She knew she was by him beloved — she knew,
For quickly comes such knowledge, that his heart
Was darkened with her shadow, and she saw
That he was wretched, but she saw not all.
He rose, and with a cold and gentle grasp
He took her hand; a moment o'er his face
A tablet of unutterable thoughts

Was traced, and then it faded, as it came;
He dropped the hand he held, and with slow steps
Retired, but not as bidding her adieu,
For they did part with mutual smiles; he passed
From out the massy gate of that old Hall,
And mounting on his steed he went his way;
And ne'er repassed that hoary threshold more.

IV

A change came o'er the spirit of my dream.
The Boy was sprung to manhood: in the wilds
Of fiery climes he made himself a home,
And his Soul drank their sunbeams: he was girt
With strange and dusky aspects; he was not
Himself like what he had been; on the sea
And on the shore he was a wanderer;
There was a mass of many images
Crowded like waves upon me, but he was
A part of all; and in the last he lay
Reposing from the noontide sultriness,
Couched among fallen columns, in the shade
Of ruined walls that had survived the names
Of those who reared them; by his sleeping side
Stood camels grazing, and some goodly steeds
Were fastened near a fountain; and a man
Clad in a flowing garb did watch the while,
While many of his tribe slumbered around:
And they were canopied by the blue sky,
So cloudless, clear, and purely beautiful,
That God alone was to be seen in Heaven.

V

A change came o'er the spirit of my dream.
The Lady of his love was wed with One
Who did not love her better: — in her home,
A thousand leagues from his, — her native home,
She dwelt, begirt with growing Infancy,
Daughters and sons of Beauty, — but behold!
Upon her face there was the tint of grief,
The settled shadow of an inward strife,
And an unquiet drooping of the eye,
As if its lid were charged with unshed tears.
What could her grief be? — she had all she loved,
And he who had so loved her was not there
To trouble with bad hopes, or evil wish,
Or ill-repressed affliction, her pure thoughts.

What could her grief be? — she had loved him not,
Nor given him cause to deem himself beloved,
Nor could he be a part of that which preyed
Upon her mind — a spectre of the past.

VI

A change came o'er the spirit of my dream.
The Wanderer was returned. — I saw him stand
Before an Altar — with a gentle bride;
Her face was fair, but was not that which made
The Starlight of his Boyhood; — as he stood
Even at the altar, o'er his brow there came
The self-same aspect, and the quivering shock
That in the antique Oratory shook
His bosom in its solitude; and then —
As in that hour — a moment o'er his face
The tablet of unutterable thoughts
Was traced, — and then it faded as it came,
And he stood calm and quiet, and he spoke
The fitting vows, but heard not his own words,
And all things reeled around him; he could see
Not that which was, nor that which should have been —
But the old mansion, and the accustomed hall,
And the remembered chambers, and the place,
The day, the hour, the sunshine, and the shade,
All things pertaining to that place and hour
And her who was his destiny, came back
And thrust themselves between him and the light:
What business had they there at such a time?

VII

A change came o'er the spirit of my dream.
The Lady of his love; — Oh! she was changed
As by the sickness of the soul; her mind
Had wandered from its dwelling, and her eyes
They had not their own lustre, but the look
Which is not of the earth; she was become
The Queen of a fantastic realm; her thoughts
Were combinations of disjointed things;
And forms, impalpable and unperceived
Of others' sight, familiar were to hers.
And this the world calls frenzy; but the wise
Have a far deeper madness — and the glance
Of melancholy is a fearful gift;
What is it but the telescope of truth?
Which strips the distance of its fantasies,

And brings life near in utter nakedness,
Making the cold reality too real!

VIII

A change came o'er the spirit of my dream.
The Wanderer was alone as heretofore,
The beings which surrounded him were gone,
Or were at war with him; he was a mark
For blight and desolation, compassed round
With Hatred and Contention; Pain was mixed
In all which was served up to him, until,
Like to the Pontic monarch of old days,
He fed on poisons, and they had no power,
But were a kind of nutriment; he lived
Through that which had been death to many men,
And made him friends of mountains: with the stars
And the quick Spirit of the Universe
He held his dialogues; and they did teach
To him the magic of their mysteries;
To him the book of Night was opened wide,
And voices from the deep abyss revealed
A marvel and a secret — Be it so.

IX

My dream was past; it had no further change.
It was of a strange order, that the doom
Of these two creatures should be thus traced out
Almost like a reality — the one
To end in madness — both in misery.

DARKNESS

I HAD a dream, which was not all a dream.
The bright sun was extinguished, and the stars
Did wander darkling in the eternal space,
Rayless, and pathless, and the icy Earth
Swung blind and blackening in the moonless air;
Morn came and went — and came, and brought no day,
And men forgot their passions in the dread
Of this their desolation; and all hearts
Were chilled into a selfish prayer for light:
And they did live by watchfires — and the thrones,
The palaces of crownéd kings — the huts,
The habitations of all things which dwell,
Were burnt for beacons; cities were consumed,

And men were gathered round their blazing homes
To look once more into each other's face;
Happy were those who dwelt within the eye
Of the volcanos, and their mountain-torch:
A fearful hope was all the World contained;
Forests were set on fire — but hour by hour
They fell and faded — and the crackling trunks
Extinguished with a crash — and all was black.
The brows of men by the despairing light
Wore an unearthly aspect, as by fits
The flashes fell upon them; some lay down
And hid their eyes and wept; and some did rest
Their chins upon their clenchéd hands, and smiled;
And others hurried to and fro, and fed
Their funeral piles with fuel, and looked up
With mad disquietude on the dull sky,
The pall of a past World; and then again
With curses cast them down upon the dust,
And gnashed their teeth and howled: the wild birds shrieked,
And, terrified, did flutter on the ground,
And flap their useless wings; the wildest brutes
Came tame and tremulous; and vipers crawled
And twined themselves among the multitude,
Hissing, but stingless — they were slain for food:
And War, which for a moment was no more,
Did glut himself again: — a meal was bought
With blood, and each sate sullenly apart
Gorging himself in gloom: no Love was left;
All earth was but one thought — and that was Death,
Immediate and inglorious; and the pang
Of famine fed upon all entrails — men
Died, and their bones were tombless as their flesh;
The meagre by the meagre were devoured,
Even dogs assailed their masters, all save one,
And he was faithful to a corse, and kept
The birds and beasts and famished men at bay,
Till hunger clung them, or the dropping dead
Lured their lank jaws; himself sought out no food,
But with a piteous and perpetual moan,
And a quick desolate cry, licking the hand
Which answered not with a caress — he died.
The crowd was famished by degrees; but two
Of an enormous city did survive,
And they were enemies: they met beside
The dying embers of an altar-place
Where had been heaped a mass of holy things
For an unholy usage; they raked up,

And shivering scraped with their cold skeleton hands
The feeble ashes, and their feeble breath
Blew for a little life, and made a flame
Which was a mockery; then they lifted up
Their eyes as it grew lighter, and beheld
Each other's aspects — saw, and shrieked, and died —
Even of their mutual hideousness they died,
Unknowing who he was upon whose brow
Famine had written Fiend. The World was void,
The populous and the powerful was a lump,
Seasonless, herbless, treeless, manless, lifeless —
A lump of death — a chaos of hard clay.
The rivers, lakes, and ocean all stood still,
And nothing stirred within their silent depths;
Ships sailorless lay rotting on the sea,
And their masts fell down piecemeal: as they dropped
They slept on the abyss without a surge —
The waves were dead; the tides were in their grave,
The Moon, their mistress, had expired before;
The winds were withered in the stagnant air,
And the clouds perished; Darkness had no need
Of aid from them — She was the Universe.

PROMETHEUS

I

TITAN! to whose immortal eyes
    The sufferings of mortality,
    Seen in their sad reality,
Were not as things that gods despise;
What was thy pity's recompense?
A silent suffering, and intense;
The rock, the vulture, and the chain,
All that the proud can feel of pain,
The agony they do not show,
The suffocating sense of woe,
    Which speaks but in its loneliness,
And then is jealous lest the sky
Should have a listener, nor will sigh
    Until its voice is echoless.

II

Titan! to thee the strife was given
    Between the suffering and the will,

Which torture where they cannot kill;
And the inexorable Heaven,
And the deaf tyranny of Fate,
The ruling principle of Hate,
Which for its pleasure doth create
The things it may annihilate,
Refused thee even the boon to die:
The wretched gift Eternity
Was thine — and thou hast borne it well.
All that the Thunderer wrung from thee
Was but the menace which flung back
On him the torments of thy rack;
The fate thou didst so well foresee,
But would not to appease him tell;
And in thy Silence was his Sentence,
And in his Soul a vain repentance,
And evil dread so ill dissembled,
That in his hand the lightnings trembled.

III

Thy Godlike crime was to be kind,
To render with thy precepts less
The sum of human wretchedness,
And strengthen Man with his own mind;
But baffled as thou wert from high,
Still in thy patient energy,
In the endurance, and repulse
Of thine impenetrable Spirit,
Which Earth and Heaven could not convulse,
A mighty lesson we inherit:
Thou art a symbol and a sign
To Mortals of their fate and force;
Like thee, Man is in part divine,
A troubled stream from a pure source;
And Man in portions can foresee
His own funereal destiny;
His wretchedness, and his resistance,
And his sad unallied existence:
To which his Spirit may oppose
Itself — an equal to all woes —
And a firm will, and a deep sense,
Which even in torture can descry
Its own concentered recompense,
Triumphant where it dares defy,
And making Death a Victory.

MONODY ON THE DEATH OF THE RIGHT HON. R. B. SHERIDAN

SPOKEN AT DRURY-LANE THEATRE, LONDON

WHEN the last sunshine of expiring Day
In Summer's twilight weeps itself away,
Who hath not felt the softness of the hour
Sink on the heart, as dew along the flower?
With a pure feeling which absorbs and awes
While Nature makes that melancholy pause —
Her breathing moment on the bridge where Time
Of light and darkness forms an arch sublime —
Who hath not shared that calm, so still and deep,
The voiceless thought which would not speak but weep,
A holy concord, and a bright regret,
A glorious sympathy with suns that set?
'Tis not harsh sorrow, but a tenderer woe,
Nameless, but dear to gentle hearts below,
Felt without bitterness — but full and clear,
A sweet dejection — a transparent tear,
Unmixed with worldly grief or selfish stain —
Shed without shame, and secret without pain.
Even as the tenderness that hour instils
When Summer's day declines along the hills,
So feels the fulness of our heart and eyes
When all of Genius which can perish dies.
A mighty Spirit is eclipsed — a Power
Hath passed from day to darkness — to whose hour
Of light no likeness is bequeathed — no name,
Focus at once of all the rays of Fame!
The flash of Wit — the bright Intelligence,
The beam of Song — the blaze of Eloquence,
Set with their Sun, but still have left behind
The enduring produce of immortal Mind;
Fruits of a genial morn, and glorious noon,
A deathless part of him who died too soon.
But small that portion of the wondrous whole,
These sparkling segments of that circling Soul,
Which all embraced, and lightened over all,
To cheer — to pierce — to please — or to appal.
From the charmed council to the festive board,
Of human feelings the unbounded lord;
In whose acclaim the loftiest voices vied,
The praised — the proud — who made his praise their pride.
When the loud cry of trampled Hindostan
Arose to Heaven in her appeal from Man,
His was the thunder — his the avenging rod,

The wrath — the delegated voice of God!
Which shook the nations through his lips, and blazed
Till vanquished senates trembled as they praised.

And here, oh! here, where yet all young and warm,
The gay creations of his spirit charm,
The matchless dialogue — the deathless wit,
Which knew not what it was to intermit;
The glowing portraits, fresh from life, that bring
Home to our hearts the truth from which they spring;
These wondrous beings of his fancy, wrought
To fulness by the fiat of his thought,
Here in their first abode you still may meet,
Bright with the hues of his Promethean heat;
A Halo of the light of other days,
Which still the splendour of its orb betrays.
But should there be to whom the fatal blight
Of failing Wisdom yields a base delight,
Men who exult when minds of heavenly tone
Jar in the music which was born their own,
Still let them pause — ah! little do they know
That what to them seemed Vice might be but Woe.
Hard is his fate on whom the public gaze
Is fixed for ever to detract or praise;
Repose denies her requiem to his name,
And Folly loves the martyrdom of Fame.
The secret Enemy whose sleepless eye
Stands sentinel — accuser — judge — and spy.
The foe, the fool, the jealous, and the vain,
The envious who but breathe in other's pain —
Behold the host! delighting to deprave,
Who track the steps of Glory to the grave,
Watch every fault that daring Genius owes
Half to the ardour which its birth bestows,
Distort the truth, accumulate the lie,
And pile the Pyramid of Calumny!
These are his portion — but if joined to these
Gaunt Poverty should league with deep Disease,
If the high Spirit must forget to soar,
And stoop to strive with Misery at the door,
To soothe Indignity — and face to face
Meet sordid Rage, and wrestle with Disgrace,
To find in Hope but the renewed caress,
The serpent-fold of further Faithlessness: —
If such may be the Ills which men assail,
What marvel if at last the mightiest fail?
Breasts to whom all the strength of feeling given
Bear hearts electric — charged with fire from Heaven,

Black with the rude collision, inly torn,
By clouds surrounded, and on whirlwinds borne,
Driven o'er the lowering atmosphere that nurst
Thoughts which have turned to thunder — scorch, and burst.

But far from us and from our mimic scene
Such things should be — if such have ever been;
Ours be the gentler wish, the kinder task,
To give the tribute Glory need not ask,
To mourn the vanished beam, and add our mite
Of praise in payment of a long delight.
Ye Orators! whom yet our councils yield,
Mourn for the veteran Hero of your field!
The worthy rival of the wondrous *Three!*
Whose words were sparks of Immortality!
Ye Bards! to whom the Drama's Muse is dear,
He was your Master — emulate him *here!*
Ye men of wit and social eloquence!
He was your brother — bear his ashes hence!
While Powers of mind almost of boundless range,
Complete in kind, as various in their change,
While Eloquence — Wit — Poesy — and Mirth,
That humbler Harmonist of care on Earth,
Survive within our souls — while lives our sense
Of pride in Merit's proud pre-eminence,
Long shall we seek his likeness — long in vain,
And turn to all of him which may remain,
Sighing that Nature formed but one such man,
And broke the die — in moulding Sheridan!

STANZAS TO AUGUSTA

I

THOUGH the day of my Destiny's over,
  And the star of my Fate hath declined,
Thy soft heart refused to discover
  The faults which so many could find;
Though thy Soul with my grief was acquainted,
  It shrunk not to share it with me,
And the Love which my Spirit hath painted
  It never hath found but in *Thee*.

II

Then when Nature around me is smiling,
  The last smile which answers to mine,
I do not believe it beguiling,

Because it reminds me of thine;
And when winds are at war with the ocean,
As the breasts I believed in with me,
If their billows excite an emotion,
It is that they bear me from *Thee*.

III

Though the rock of my last Hope is shivered,
And its fragments are sunk in the wave,
Though I feel that my soul is delivered
To Pain — it shall not be its slave.
There is many a pang to pursue me:
They may crush, but they shall not contemn;
They may torture, but shall not subdue me;
'Tis of *Thee* that I think — not of them.

IV

Though human, thou didst not deceive me,
Though woman, thou didst not forsake,
Though loved, thou forborest to grieve me,
Though slandered, thou never couldst shake;
Though trusted, thou didst not disclaim me,
Though parted, it was not to fly,
Though watchful, 'twas not to defame me,
Nor, mute, that the world might belie.

V

Yet I blame not the World, nor despise it,
Nor the war of the many with one;
If my Soul was not fitted to prize it,
'Twas folly not sooner to shun:
And if dearly that error hath cost me,
And more than I once could foresee,
I have found that, whatever it lost me,
It could not deprive me of *Thee*.

VI

From the wreck of the past, which hath perished,
Thus much I at least may recall,
It hath taught me that what I most cherished
Deserved to be dearest of all:
In the Desert a fountain is springing,
In the wide waste there still is a tree,
And a bird in the solitude singing,
Which speaks to my spirit of *Thee*.

MANFRED:

A DRAMATIC POEM

"There are more things in heaven and earth, Horatio,
Than are dreamt of in your philosophy."

Dramatis Personæ

MANFRED
CHAMOIS HUNTER
ABBOT OF ST. MAURICE
MANUEL
HERMAN

WITCH OF THE ALPS
ARIMANES
NEMESIS
THE DESTINIES
SPIRITS, ETC.

The Scene of the Drama is amongst the Higher Alps — partly in the Castle of Manfred, and partly in the Mountains.

ACT I

Scene I. — Manfred *alone. — Scene, a Gothic Gallery. — Time, Midnight.*

Manfred. The lamp must be replenished, but even then
It will not burn so long as I must watch:
My slumbers — if I slumber — are not sleep,
But a continuance of enduring thought,
Which then I can resist not: in my heart
There is a vigil, and these eyes but close
To look within; and yet I live, and bear
The aspect and the form of breathing men.
But Grief should be the Instructor of the wise;
Sorrow is Knowledge: they who know the most
Must mourn the deepest o'er the fatal truth,
The Tree of Knowledge is not that of Life.

Philosophy and science, and the springs
Of Wonder, and the wisdom of the World,
I have essayed, and in my mind there is
A power to make these subject to itself —
But they avail not: I have done men good,
And I have met with good even among men —
But this availed not: I have had my foes,
And none have baffled, many fallen before me —
But this availed not: — Good — or evil — life —
Powers, passions — all I see in other beings,
Have been to me as rain unto the sands,
Since that all-nameless hour. I have no dread,
And feel the curse to have no natural fear,
Nor fluttering throb, that beats with hopes or wishes,
Or lurking love of something on the earth.
Now to my task. —
Mysterious Agency!
Ye Spirits of the unbounded Universe!
Whom I have sought in darkness and in light —
Ye, who do compass earth about, and dwell
In subtler essence — ye, to whom the tops
Of mountains inaccessible are haunts,
And Earth's and Ocean's caves familiar things —
I call upon ye by the written charm
Which gives me power upon you — Rise! Appear!
[*A pause.*

They come not yet. — Now by the voice of him
Who is the first among you — by this sign,
Which makes you tremble — by the claims of him
Who is undying, — Rise! Appear! —— Appear!
[*A pause.*

If it be so. — Spirits of Earth and Air,
Ye shall not so elude me! By a power,
Deeper than all yet urged, a tyrant-spell,
Which had its birthplace in a star condemned,
The burning wreck of a demolished world,
A wandering hell in the eternal Space;
By the strong curse which is upon my Soul,
The thought which is within me and around me,
I do compel ye to my will. — Appear!

[*A star is seen at the darker end of the gallery: it is stationary; and a voice is heard singing.*

First Spirit

Mortal! to thy bidding bowed,
From my mansion in the cloud,

Which the breath of Twilight builds,
And the Summer's sunset gilds
With the azure and vermilion,
Which is mixed for my pavilion;
Though thy quest may be forbidden,
On a star-beam I have ridden,
To thine adjuration bowed:
Mortal — be thy wish avowed!

Voice of the SECOND SPIRIT.

Mont Blanc is the Monarch of mountains;
They crowned him long ago
On a throne of rocks, in a robe of clouds,
With a Diadem of snow.
Around his waist are forests braced,
The Avalanche in his hand;
But ere it fall, that thundering ball
Must pause for my command.
The Glacier's cold and restless mass
Moves onward day by day;
But I am he who bids it pass,
Or with its ice delay.
I am the Spirit of the place,
Could make the mountain bow
And quiver to his caverned base —
And what with me would'st *Thou?*

Voice of the THIRD SPIRIT.

In the blue depth of the waters,
Where the wave hath no strife,
Where the Wind is a stranger,
And the Sea-snake hath life,
Where the Mermaid is decking
Her green hair with shells,
Like the storm on the surface
Came the sound of thy spells;
O'er my calm Hall of Coral
The deep Echo rolled —
To the Spirit of Ocean
Thy wishes unfold!

FOURTH SPIRIT.

Where the slumbering Earthquake
Lies pillowed on fire,
And the lakes of bitumen

Rise boilingly higher;
Where the roots of the Andes
Strike deep in the earth,
As their summits to heaven
Shoot soaringly forth;
I have quitted my birthplace,
Thy bidding to bide —
Thy spell hath subdued me,
Thy will be my guide!

FIFTH SPIRIT.

I am the Rider of the wind,
The Stirrer of the storm;
The hurricane I left behind
Is yet with lightning warm;
To speed to thee, o'er shore and sea
I swept upon the blast:
The fleet I met sailed well — and yet
'Twill sink ere night be past.

SIXTH SPIRIT.

My dwelling is the shadow of the Night,
Why doth thy magic torture me with light?

SEVENTH SPIRIT.

The Star which rules thy destiny
Was ruled, ere earth began, by me:
It was a World as fresh and fair
As e'er revolved round Sun in air;
Its course was free and regular,
Space bosomed not a lovelier star.
The Hour arrived — and it became
A wandering mass of shapeless flame,
A pathless Comet, and a curse,
The menace of the Universe;
Still rolling on with innate force,
Without a sphere, without a course,
A bright deformity on high,
The monster of the upper sky!
And Thou! beneath its influence born —
Thou worm! whom I obey and scorn —
Forced by a Power (which is not thine,
And lent thee but to make thee mine)
For this brief moment to descend,

Where these weak Spirits round thee bend
And parley with a thing like thee —
What would'st thou, Child of Clay! with me?

The SEVEN SPIRITS.

Earth — ocean — air — night — mountains — winds — thy Star,
Are at thy beck and bidding, Child of Clay!
Before thee at thy quest their Spirits are —
What would'st thou with us, Son of mortals — say?
Manfred. Forgetfulness ——
First Spirit. Of what — of whom — and why?
Manfred. Of that which is within me; read it there —
Ye know it — and I cannot utter it.
Spirit. We can but give thee that which we possess:
Ask of us subjects, sovereignty, the power
O'er earth — the whole, or portion — or a sign
Which shall control the elements, whereof
We are the dominators, — each and all,
These shall be thine.
Manfred. Oblivion — self-oblivion!
Can ye not wring from out the hidden realms
Ye offer so profusely — what I ask?
Spirit. It is not in our essence, in our skill;
But — thou may'st die.
Manfred. Will Death bestow it on me?
Spirit. We are immortal, and do not forget;
We are eternal; and to us the past
Is, as the future, present. Art thou answered?
Manfred. Ye mock me — but the Power which brought ye here
Hath made you mine. Slaves, scoff not at my will!
The Mind — the Spirit — the Promethean spark,
The lightning of my being, is as bright,
Pervading, and far darting as your own,
And shall not yield to yours, though cooped in clay!
Answer, or I will teach you what I am.
Spirit. We answer — as we answered; our reply
Is even in thine own words.
Manfred. Why say ye so?
Spirit. If, as thou say'st, thine essence be as ours,
We have replied in telling thee, the thing
Mortals call death hath nought to do with us.
Manfred. I then have called ye from your realms in vain;
Ye cannot, or ye will not, aid me.
Spirit. Say —
What we possess we offer; it is thine:
Bethink ere thou dismiss us; ask again;

Kingdom, and sway, and strength, and length of days —
Manfred. Accursèd! what have I to do with days?
They are too long already. — Hence — begone!
Spirit. Yet pause: being here, our will would do thee service;
Bethink thee, is there then no other gift
Which we can make not worthless in thine eyes?
Manfred. No, none: yet stay — one moment, ere we part,
I would behold ye face to face. I hear
Your voices, sweet and melancholy sounds,
As Music on the waters; and I see
The steady aspect of a clear large Star;
But nothing more. Approach me as ye are,
Or one — or all — in your accustomed forms.
Spirit. We have no forms, beyond the elements
Of which we are the mind and principle:
But choose a form — in that we will appear.
Manfred. I have no choice; there is no form on earth
Hideous or beautiful to me. Let him,
Who is most powerful of ye, take such aspect
As unto him may seem most fitting — Come!
Seventh Spirit (*appearing in the shape of a beautiful female figure*).
Behold!
Manfred. Oh God! if it be thus, and *thou*
Art not a madness and a mockery,
I yet might be most happy. I will clasp thee,
And we again will be ——

[*The figure vanishes.*

My heart is crushed!

[Manfred *falls senseless.*

(*A voice is heard in the Incantation which follows.*)

When the Moon is on the wave,
And the glow-worm in the grass,
And the meteor on the grave,
And the wisp on the morass;
When the falling stars are shooting,
And the answered owls are hooting,
And the silent leaves are still
In the shadow of the hill,
Shall my soul be upon thine,
With a power and with a sign.

Though thy slumber may be deep,
Yet thy Spirit shall not sleep;
There are shades which will not vanish,

There are thoughts thou canst not banish;
By a Power to thee unknown,
Thou canst never be alone;
Thou art wrapt as with a shroud,
Thou art gathered in a cloud;
And for ever shalt thou dwell
In the spirit of this spell.

Though thou seest me not pass by,
Thou shalt feel me with thine eye
As a thing that, though unseen,
Must be near thee, and hath been;
And when in that secret dread
Thou hast turned around thy head,
Thou shalt marvel I am not
As thy shadow on the spot,
And the power which thou dost feel
Shall be what thou must conceal.

And a magic voice and verse
Hath baptized thee with a curse;
And a Spirit of the air
Hath begirt thee with a snare;
In the wind there is a voice
Shall forbid thee to rejoice;
And to thee shall Night deny
All the quiet of her sky;
And the day shall have a sun,
Which shall make thee wish it done.

From thy false tears I did distil
An essence which hath strength to kill;
From thy own heart I then did wring
The black blood in its blackest spring;
From thy own smile I snatched the snake,
For there it coiled as in a brake;
From thy own lip I drew the charm
Which gave all these their chiefest harm;
In proving every poison known,
I found the strongest was thine own.

By the cold breast and serpent smile,
By thy unfathomed gulfs of guile,
By that most seeming virtuous eye,
By thy shut soul's hypocrisy;
By the perfection of thine art

Which passed for human thine own heart;
By thy delight in others' pain,
And by thy brotherhood of Cain,
I call upon thee! and compel
Thyself to be thy proper Hell!

And on thy head I pour the vial
Which doth devote thee to this trial;
Nor to slumber, nor to die,
Shall be in thy destiny;
Though thy death shall still seem near
To thy wish, but as a fear;
Lo! the spell now works around thee,
And the clankless chain hath bound thee;
O'er thy heart and brain together
Hath the word been passed — now wither!

SCENE II. — *The Mountain of the Jungfrau. — Time, Morning.* — MANFRED *alone upon the cliffs.*

Manfred. The spirits I have raised abandon me,
The spells which I have studied baffle me,
The remedy I recked of tortured me;
I lean no more on superhuman aid;
It hath no power upon the past, and for
The future, till the past be gulfed in darkness,
It is not of my search. — My Mother Earth!
And thou fresh-breaking Day, and you, ye Mountains,
Why are ye beautiful? I cannot love ye.
And thou, the bright Eye of the Universe,
That openest over all, and unto all
Art a delight — thou shin'st not on my heart.
And you, ye crags, upon whose extreme edge
I stand, and on the torrent's brink beneath
Behold the tall pines dwindled as to shrubs
In dizziness of distance; when a leap,
A stir, a motion, even a breath, would bring
My breast upon its rocky bosom's bed
To rest for ever — wherefore do I pause?
I feel the impulse — yet I do not plunge;
I see the peril — yet do not recede;
And my brain reels — and yet my foot is firm:
There is a power upon me which withholds,
And makes it my fatality to live, —
If it be life to wear within myself
This barrenness of Spirit, and to be

My own Soul's sepulchre, for I have ceased
To justify my deeds unto myself —
The last infirmity of evil. Aye,
Thou winged and cloud-cleaving minister,

[*An Eagle passes.*

Whose happy flight is highest into heaven,
Well may'st thou swoop so near me — I should be
Thy prey, and gorge thine eaglets; thou art gone
Where the eye cannot follow thee; but thine
Yet pierces downward, onward, or above,
With a pervading vision. — Beautiful!
How beautiful is all this visible world!
How glorious in its action and itself!
But we, who name ourselves its sovereigns, we,
Half dust, half deity, alike unfit
To sink or soar, with our mixed essence make
A conflict of its elements, and breathe
The breath of degradation and of pride,
Contending with low wants and lofty will,
Till our Mortality predominates,
And men are — what they name not to themselves,
And trust not to each other. Hark! the note,

[*The Shepherd's pipe in the distance is heard.*

The natural music of the mountain reed —
For here the patriarchal days are not
A pastoral fable — pipes in the liberal air,
Mixed with the sweet bells of the sauntering herd;
My soul would drink those echoes. Oh, that I were
The viewless spirit of a lovely sound,
A living voice, a breathing harmony,
A bodiless enjoyment — born and dying
With the blest tone which made me!

Enter from below a CHAMOIS HUNTER.

Chamois Hunter. Even so
This way the Chamois leapt: her nimble feet
Have baffled me; my gains to-day will scarce
Repay my break-neck travail. — What is here?
Who seems not of my trade, and yet hath reached
A height which none even of our mountaineers,
Save our best hunters, may attain: his garb
Is goodly, his mien manly, and his air
Proud as a free-born peasant's, at this distance:
I will approach him nearer.

Manfred. (*not perceiving the other*). To be thus —

Grey-haired with anguish, like these blasted pines,
Wrecks of a single winter, barkless, branchless,
A blighted trunk upon a curséd root,
Which but supplies a feeling to Decay —
And to be thus, eternally but thus,
Having been otherwise! Now furrowed o'er
With wrinkles, ploughed by moments, not by years
And hours, all tortured into ages — hours
Which I outlive! — Ye toppling crags of ice!
Ye Avalanches, whom a breath draws down
In mountainous o'erwhelming, come and crush me!
I hear ye momently above, beneath,
Crash with a frequent conflict; but ye pass,
And only fall on things that still would live;
On the young flourishing forest, or the hut
And hamlet of the harmless villager.
  Chamois Hunter. The mists begin to rise from up the valley;
I'll warn him to descend, or he may chance
To lose at once his way and life together.
  Manfred. The mists boil up around the glaciers; clouds
Rise curling fast beneath me, white and sulphury,
Like foam from the roused ocean of deep Hell,
Whose every wave breaks on a living shore,
Heaped with the damned like pebbles. — I am giddy.
  Chamois Hunter. I must approach him cautiously; if near,
A sudden step will startle him, and he
Seems tottering already.
  Manfred.   Mountains have fallen,
Leaving a gap in the clouds, and with the shock
Rocking their Alpine brethren; filling up
The ripe green valleys with Destruction's splinters;
Damming the rivers with a sudden dash,
Which crushed the waters into mist, and made
Their fountains find another channel — thus,
Thus, in its old age, did Mount Rosenberg —
Why stood I not beneath it?
  Chamois Hunter.   Friend! have a care,
Your next step may be fatal! — for the love
Of Him who made you, stand not on that brink!
  Manfred. (*not hearing him*). Such would have been for me a fitting tomb;
My bones had then been quiet in their depth;
They had not then been strewn upon the rocks
For the wind's pastime — as thus — thus they shall be —
In this one plunge. — Farewell, ye opening Heavens!
Look not upon me thus reproachfully —

You were not meant for me — Earth! take these atoms!

[*As* MANFRED *is in act to spring from the cliff, the* CHAMOIS HUNTER *seizes and retains him with a sudden grasp.*

Chamois Hunter. Hold, madman! — though aweary of thy life,
Stain not our pure vales with thy guilty blood:
Away with me —— I will not quit my hold.

Manfred. I am most sick at heart — nay, grasp me not —
I am all feebleness — the mountains whirl
Spinning round me —— I grow blind —— What art thou?

Chamois Hunter. I'll answer that anon. — Away with me ——
The clouds grow thicker —— there — now lean on me —
Place your foot here — here, take this staff, and cling
A moment to that shrub — now give me your hand,
And hold fast by my girdle — softly — well —
The Chalet will be gained within an hour:
Come on, we'll quickly find a surer footing,
And something like a pathway, which the torrent
Hath washed since winter. — Come, 'tis bravely done —
You should have been a hunter. — Follow me.

[*As they descend the rocks with difficulty, the scene closes.*

ACT II

SCENE I. — *A Cottage among the Bernese Alps.* — MANFRED *and the* CHAMOIS HUNTER.

Chamois Hunter. No — no — yet pause — thou must not yet go forth:
Thy mind and body are alike unfit
To trust each other, for some hours, at least;
When thou art better, I will be thy guide —
But whither?

Manfred. It imports not: I do know
My route full well, and need no further guidance.

Chamois Hunter. Thy garb and gait bespeak thee of high lineage —
One of the many chiefs, whose castled crags
Look o'er the lower valleys — which of these
May call thee lord? I only know their portals;
My way of life leads me but rarely down
To bask by the huge hearths of those old halls,
Carousing with the vassals; but the paths,
Which step from out our mountains to their doors,
I know from childhood — which of these is thine?

Manfred. No matter.
Chamois Hunter. Well, Sir, pardon me the question,
And be of better cheer. Come, taste my wine;
'Tis of an ancient vintage; many a day
'T has thawed my veins among our glaciers, now
Let it do thus for thine — Come, pledge me fairly!
Manfred. Away, away! there's blood upon the brim!
Will it then never — never sink in the earth?
Chamois Hunter. What dost thou mean? thy senses wander from thee.
Manfred. I say 'tis blood — my blood! the pure warm stream
Which ran in the veins of my fathers, and in ours
When we were in our youth, and had one heart,
And loved each other as we should not love,
And this was shed: but still it rises up,
Colouring the clouds, that shut me out from Heaven,
Where thou art not — and I shall never be.
Chamois Hunter. Man of strange words, and some half-maddening sin,
Which makes thee people vacancy, whate'er
Thy dread and sufferance be, there's comfort yet —
The aid of holy men, and heavenly patience ——
Manfred. Patience — and patience! Hence that word was made
For brutes of burthen, not for birds of prey!
Preach it to mortals of a dust like thine, —
I am not of thine order.
Chamois Hunter. Thanks to Heaven!
I would not be of thine for the free fame
Of William Tell; but whatsoe'er thine ill,
It must be borne, and these wild starts are useless.
Manfred. Do I not bear it? — Look on me — I live.
Chamois Hunter. This is convulsion, and no healthful life.
Manfred. I tell thee, man! I have lived many years,
Many long years, but they are nothing now
To those which I must number: ages — ages —
Space and eternity — and consciousness,
With the fierce thirst of death — and still unslaked!
Chamois Hunter. Why on thy brow the seal of middle age
Hath scarce been set; I am thine elder far.
Manfred. Think'st thou existence doth depend on time?
It doth; but actions are our epochs: mine
Have made my days and nights imperishable,
Endless, and all alike, as sands on the shore,
Innumerable atoms; and one desert,
Barren and cold, on which the wild waves break,
But nothing rests, save carcasses and wrecks,

Rocks, and the salt-surf weeds of bitterness.
Chamois Hunter. Alas! he's mad — but yet I must not leave him.
Manfred. I would I were — for then the things I see
Would be but a distempered dream.
Chamois Hunter. What is it
That thou dost see, or think thou look'st upon?
Manfred. Myself, and thee — a peasant of the Alps —
Thy humble virtues, hospitable home,
And spirit patient, pious, proud, and free;
Thy self-respect, grafted on innocent thoughts;
Thy days of health, and nights of sleep; thy toils,
By danger dignified, yet guiltless; hopes
Of cheerful old age and a quiet grave,
With cross and garland over its green turf,
And thy grandchildren's love for epitaph!
This do I see — and then I look within —
It matters not — my Soul was scorched already!
Chamois Hunter. And would'st thou then exchange thy lot for mine?
Manfred. No, friend! I would not wrong thee, nor exchange
My lot with living being: I can bear —
However wretchedly, 'tis still to bear —
In life what others could not brook to dream,
But perish in their slumber.
Chamois Hunter. And with this —
This cautious feeling for another's pain
Canst thou be black with evil? — say not so.
Can one of gentle thoughts have wreaked revenge
Upon his enemies?
Manfred. Oh! no, no, no!
My injuries came down on those who loved me —
On those whom I best loved: I never quelled
An enemy, save in my just defence —
But my embrace was fatal.
Chamois Hunter. Heaven give thee rest!
And Penitence restore thee to thyself;
My prayers shall be for thee.
Manfred. I need them not,
But can endure thy pity. I depart —
'Tis time — farewell! — Here's gold, and thanks for thee —
No words — it is thy due. — Follow me not —
I know my path the mountain peril's past:
And once again I charge thee, follow not!

[*Exit* MANFRED.

SCENE II. — *A lower Valley in the Alps.* — *A Cataract.*

Enter MANFRED.

It is not noon — the Sunbow's rays still arch
The torrent with the many hues of heaven,
And roll the sheeted silver's waving column
O'er the crag's headlong perpendicular,
And fling its lines of foaming light along,
And to and fro, like the pale courser's tail,
The Giant steed, to be bestrode by Death,
As told in the Apocalypse. No eyes
But mine now drink this sight of loveliness;
I should be sole in this sweet solitude,
And with the Spirit of the place divide
The homage of these waters. — I will call her.

[MANFRED *takes some of the water into the palm of his hand and flings it into the air, muttering the adjuration. After a pause, the* WITCH OF THE ALPS *rises beneath the arch of the sunbow of the torrent.*

Beautiful Spirit! with thy hair of light,
And dazzling eyes of glory, in whose form
The charms of Earth's least mortal daughters grow
To an unearthly stature, in an essence
Of purer elements; while the hues of youth, —
Carnationed like a sleeping Infant's cheek,
Rocked by the beating of her mother's heart,
Or the rose tints, which Summer's twilight leaves
Upon the lofty Glacier's virgin snow,
The blush of earth embracing with her Heaven, —
Tinge thy celestial aspect, and make tame
The beauties of the Sunbow which bends o'er thee.
Beautiful Spirit! in thy calm clear brow,
Wherein is glassed serenity of Soul,
Which of itself shows immortality,
I read that thou wilt pardon to a Son
Of Earth, whom the abstruser powers permit
At times to commune with them — if that he
Avail him of his spells — to call thee thus,
And gaze on thee a moment.

Witch. Son of Earth!
I know thee, and the Powers which give thee power!
I know thee for a man of many thoughts,
And deeds of good and ill, extreme in both,
Fatal and fated in thy sufferings.
I have expected this — what would'st thou with me?

Manfred. To look upon thy beauty — nothing further.

The face of the earth hath maddened me, and I
Take refuge in her mysteries, and pierce
To the abodes of those who govern her —
But they can nothing aid me. I have sought
From them what they could not bestow, and now
I search no further.
Witch. What could be the quest
Which is not in the power of the most powerful,
The rulers of the invisible?
Manfred A boon; —
But why should I repeat it? 'twere in vain.
Witch. I know not that; let thy lips utter it.
Manfred. Well, though it torture me, 'tis but the same;
My pang shall find a voice. From my youth upwards
My Spirit walked not with the souls of men,
Nor looked upon the earth with human eyes;
The thirst of their ambition was not mine,
The aim of their existence was not mine;
My joys — my griefs — my passions — and my powers,
Made me a stranger; though I wore the form,
I had no sympathy with breathing flesh,
Nor midst the Creatures of Clay that girded me
Was there but One who — but of her anon.
I said with men, and with the thoughts of men,
I held but slight communion; but instead,
My joy was in the wilderness, — to breathe
The difficult air of the iced mountain's top,
Where the birds dare not build — nor insect's wing
Flit o'er the herbless granite; or to plunge
Into the torrent, and to roll along
On the swift whirl of the new-breaking wave
Of river-stream, or Ocean, in their flow.
In these my early strength exulted; or
To follow through the night the moving moon,
The stars and their development; or catch
The dazzling lightnings till my eyes grew dim;
Or to look, list'ning, on the scattered leaves,
While Autumn winds were at their evening song.
These were my pastimes, and to be alone;
For if the beings, of whom I was one, —
Hating to be so, — crossed me in my path,
I felt myself degraded back to them,
And was all clay again. And then I dived,
In my lone wanderings, to the caves of Death,
Searching its cause in its effect; and drew
From withered bones, and skulls, and heaped up dust,
Conclusions most forbidden. Then I passed

The nights of years in sciences untaught,
Save in the old-time; and with time and toil,
And terrible ordeal, and such penance
As in itself hath power upon the air,
And spirits that do compass air and earth,
Space, and the peopled Infinite, I made
Mine eyes familiar with Eternity,
Such as, before me, did the Magi, and
He who from out their fountain-dwellings raised
Eros and Anteros, at Gadara,
As I do thee; — and with my knowledge grew
The thirst of knowledge, and the power and joy
Of this most bright intelligence, until ——
  Witch. Proceed.
  Manfred. Oh! I but thus prolonged my words,
Boasting these idle attributes, because
As I approach the core of my heart's grief —
But — to my task. I have not named to thee
Father or mother, mistress, friend, or being,
With whom I wore the chain of human ties;
If I had such, they seemed not such to me —
Yet there was One ——
  Witch. Spare not thyself — proceed.
  Manfred. She was like me in lineaments — her eyes —
Her hair — her features — all, to the very tone
Even of her voice, they said were like to mine;
But softened all, and tempered into beauty:
She had the same lone thoughts and wanderings,
The quest of hidden knowledge, and a mind
To comprehend the Universe: nor these
Alone, but with them gentler powers than mine,
Pity, and smiles, and tears — which I had not;
And tenderness — but that I had for her;
Humility — and that I never had.
Her faults were mine — her virtues were her own —
I loved her, and destroyed her!
  Witch. With thy hand?
  Manfred. Not with my hand, but heart, which broke her heart;
It gazed on mine, and withered. I have shed
Blood, but not hers — and yet her blood was shed;
I saw — and could not stanch it.
  Witch. And for this —
A being of the race thou dost despise —
The order, which thine own would rise above,
Mingling with us and ours, — thou dost forego
The gifts of our great knowledge, and shrink'st back
To recreant mortality —— Away!

Manfred. Daughter of Air! I tell thee, since that hour —
But words are breath — look on me in my sleep,
Or watch my watchings — Come and sit by me!
My solitude is solitude no more,
But peopled with the Furies; — I have gnashed
My teeth in darkness till returning morn,
Then cursed myself till sunset; — I have prayed
For madness as a blessing — 'tis denied me.
I have affronted Death — but in the war
Of elements the waters shrunk from me,
And fatal things passed harmless; the cold hand
Of an all-pitiless Demon held me back,
Back by a single hair, which would not break.
In Fantasy, Imagination, all
The affluence of my soul — which one day was
A Crœsus in creation — I plunged deep,
But, like an ebbing wave, it dashed me back
Into the gulf of unfathomed thought.
I plunged amidst Mankind — Forgetfulness
I sought in all, save where 'tis to be found —
And that I have to learn — my Sciences,
My long pursued and superhuman art,
Is mortal here: I dwell in my despair —
And live — and live for ever.
Witch. It may be
That I can aid thee.
Manfred. To do this thy power
Must wake the dead, or lay me low with them.
Do so — in any shape — in any hour —
With any torture — so it be the last.
Witch. That is not in my province; but if thou
Wilt swear obedience to my will, and do
My bidding, it may help thee to thy wishes.
Manfred. I will not swear — Obey! and whom? the Spirits
Whose presence I command, and be the slave
Of those who served me — Never!
Witch. Is this all?
Hast thou no gentler answer? — Yet bethink thee,
And pause ere thou rejectest.
Manfred. I have said it.
Witch. Enough! I may retire then — say!
Manfred. Retire!
[*The* WITCH *disappears.*
Manfred. (*alone*). We are the fools of Time and Terror:
Steal on us, and steal from us; yet we live,
Loathing our life, and dreading still to die.
In all the days of this detested yoke —

This vital weight upon the struggling heart,
Which sinks with sorrow, or beats quick with pain,
Or joy that ends in agony or faintness —
In all the days of past and future — for
In life there is no present — we can number
How few — how less than few — wherein the soul
Forbears to pant for death, and yet draws back
As from a stream in winter, though the chill
Be but a moment's. I have one resource
Still in my science — I can call the dead,
And ask them what it is we dread to be:
The sternest answer can but be the Grave,
And that is nothing: if they answered not ——
The buried Prophet answered to the Hag
Of Endor; and the Spartan Monarch drew
From the Byzantine maid's unsleeping spirit
An answer and his destiny — he slew
That which he loved, unknowing what he slew,
And died unpardoned — though he called in aid
The Phyxian Jove, and in Phigalia roused
The Arcadian Evocators to compel
The indignant shadow to depose her wrath,
Or fix her term of vengeance — she replied
In words of dubious import, but fulfilled.
If I had never lived, that which I love
Had still been living; had I never loved,
That which I love would still be beautiful,
Happy and giving happiness. What is she?
What is she now? — a sufferer for my sins —
A thing I dare not think upon — or nothing.
Within few hours I shall not call in vain —
Yet in this hour I dread the thing I dare:
Until this hour I never shrunk to gaze
On spirit, good or evil — now I tremble,
And feel a strange cold thaw upon my heart.
But I can act even what I most abhor,
And champion human fears. — The night approaches.

[*Exit.*

SCENE III. — *The summit of the Jungfrau Mountain.*

Enter FIRST DESTINY.

The Moon is rising broad, and round, and bright;
And here on snows, where never human foot
Of common mortal trod, we nightly tread,
And leave no traces: o'er the savage sea,
The glassy ocean of the mountain ice,

We skim its rugged breakers, which put on
The aspect of a tumbling tempest's foam,
Frozen in a moment — a dead Whirlpool's image:
And this most steep fantastic pinnacle,
The fretwork of some earthquake — where the clouds
Pause to repose themselves in passing by —
Is sacred to our revels, or our vigils;
Here do I wait my sisters, on our way
To the Hall of Arimanes — for to-night
Is our great festival — 'tis strange they come not.

A Voice without, singing.

The Captive Usurper,
  Hurled down from the throne,
Lay buried in torpor,
  Forgotten and lone;
I broke through his slumbers,
  I shivered his chain,
I leagued him with numbers —
  He's Tyrant again!
With the blood of a million he'll answer my care,
With a Nation's destruction — his flight and despair!

Second Voice, without.

The Ship sailed on, the Ship sailed fast,
But I left not a sail, and I left not a mast;
There is not a plank of the hull or the deck,
And there is not a wretch to lament o'er his wreck;
Save one, whom I held, as he swam, by the hair,
And he was a subject well worthy my care;
A traitor on land, and a pirate at sea —
But I saved him to wreak further havoc for me!

First Destiny, *answering.*

The City lies sleeping;
  The morn, to deplore it,
May dawn on it weeping:
  Sullenly, slowly,
The black plague flew o'er it —
  Thousands lie lowly;
Tens of thousands shall perish;
  The living shall fly from
The sick they should cherish;
  But nothing can vanquish
The touch that they die from.

Sorrow and anguish,
And evil and dread,
Envelope a nation;
The blest are the dead,
Who see not the sight
Of their own desolation;
This work of a night —
This wreck of a realm — this deed of my doing —
For ages I've done, and shall still be renewing!

Enter the SECOND *and* THIRD DESTINIES.

The Three.

Our hands contain the hearts of men,
Our footsteps are their graves;
We only give to take again
The Spirits of our slaves!

First Destiny. Welcome! — Where's Nemesis?
Second Destiny. At some great work;
But what I know not, for my hands were full.
Third Destiny. Behold she cometh.

Enter NEMESIS.

First Destiny. Say, where hast thou been?
My Sisters and thyself are slow to-night.
Nemesis. I was detained repairing shattered thrones —
Marrying fools, restoring dynasties —
Avenging men upon their enemies,
And making them repent their own revenge;
Goading the wise to madness; from the dull
Shaping out oracles to rule the world
Afresh — for they were waxing out of date,
And mortals dared to ponder for themselves,
To weigh kings in the balance — and to speak
Of Freedom, the forbidden fruit. — Away!
We have outstayed the hour — mount we our clouds!

[*Exeunt.*

SCENE IV. — *The Hall of Arimanes.* — *Arimanes on his Throne, a Globe of Fire, surrounded by the Spirits.*

Hymn of the SPIRITS.

Hail to our Master! — Prince of Earth and Air!
Who walks the clouds and waters — in his hand

The sceptre of the Elements, which tear
  Themselves to chaos at his high command!
He breatheth — and a tempest shakes the sea;
  He speaketh — and the clouds reply in thunder;
He gazeth — from his glance the sunbeams flee;
  He moveth — Earthquakes rend the world asunder.
Beneath his footsteps the Volcanoes rise;
  His shadow is the Pestilence: his path
The comets herald through the crackling skies;
  And Planets turn to ashes at his wrath.
To him War offers daily sacrifice;
  To him Death pays his tribute; Life is his,
With all its Infinite of agonies —
  And his the Spirit of whatever is!

Enter the DESTINIES *and* NEMESIS.

First Destiny. Glory to Arimanes! on the earth
His power increaseth — both my sisters did
His bidding, nor did I neglect my duty!
Second Destiny. Glory to Arimanes! we who bow
The necks of men, bow down before his throne!
Third Destiny. Glory to Arimanes! we await
His nod!
Nemesis. Sovereign of Sovereigns! we are thine,
And all that liveth, more or less, is ours,
And most things wholly so; still to increase
Our power, increasing thine, demands our care,
And we are vigilant. Thy late commands
Have been fulfilled to the utmost.

Enter MANFRED

A Spirit. What is here?
A mortal! — Thou most rash and fatal wretch,
Bow down and worship!
Second Spirit. I do know the man —
A Magian of great power, and fearful skill!
Third Spirit. Bow down and worship, slave! — What, know'st thou not
Thine and our Sovereign? — Tremble, and obey!
All the Spirits. Prostrate thyself, and thy condemnéd clay,
Child of the Earth! or dread the worst.
Manfred. I know it;
And yet ye see I kneel not.
Fourth Spirit. 'Twill be taught thee.
Manfred. 'Tis taught already; — many a night of the earth,
On the bare ground, have I bowed down my face,

And strewed my head with ashes; I have known
The fulness of humiliation — for
I sunk before my vain despair, and knelt
To my own desolation.
Fifth Spirit. Dost thou dare
Refuse to Arimanes on his throne
What the whole earth accords, beholding not
The terror of his Glory? — Crouch! I say.
Manfred. Bid *him* bow down to that which is above him,
The overruling Infinite — the Maker
Who made him not for worship — let him kneel,
And we will kneel together.
The Spirits. Crush the worm!
Tear him in pieces! —
First Destiny. Hence! Avaunt! — he's mine.
Prince of the Powers invisible! This man
Is of no common order, as his port
And presence here denote: his sufferings
Have been of an immortal nature — like
Our own; his knowledge, and his powers and will,
As far as is compatible with clay,
Which clogs the ethereal essence, have been such
As clay hath seldom borne; his aspirations
Have been beyond the dwellers of the earth,
And they have only taught him what we know —
That knowledge is not happiness, and science
But an exchange of ignorance for that
Which is another kind of ignorance.
This is not all — the passions, attributes
Of Earth and Heaven, from which no power, nor being,
Nor breath from the worm upwards is exempt,
Have pierced his heart; and in their consequence
Made him a thing — which — I who pity not,
Yet pardon those who pity. He is mine —
And thine it may be; be it so, or not —
No other Spirit in this region hath
A soul like his — or power upon his soul.
Nemesis. What doth he here then?
First Destiny. Let *him* answer that.
Manfred. Ye know what I have known; and without power
I could not be amongst ye: but there are
Powers deeper still beyond — I come in quest
Of such, to answer unto what I seek.
Nemesis. What would'st thou?
Manfred. *Thou* canst not reply to me.
Call up the dead — my question is for them.
Nemesis. Great Arimanes, doth thy will avouch

The wishes of this mortal?
Arimanes. Yea.
Nemesis Whom wouldst thou
Uncharnel?
Manfred. One without a tomb — call up
Astarte.

NEMESIS.

Shadow! or Spirit!
Whatever thou art,
Which still doth inherit
The whole or a part
Of the form of thy birth,
Of the mould of thy clay,
Which returned to the earth,
Re-appear to the day!
Bear what thou borest,
The heart and the form,
And the aspect thou worest
Redeem from the worm.
Appear! — Appear! — Appear!
Who sent thee there requires thee here!

[*The Phantom of* ASTARTE *rises and stands in the midst.*

Manfred. Can this be death? there's bloom upon her cheek;
But now I see it is no living hue,
But a strange hectic — like the unnatural red
Which Autumn plants upon the perished leaf.
It is the same! Oh, God! that I should dread
To look upon the same — Astarte! — No,
I cannot speak to her — but bid her speak —
Forgive me or condemn me.

NEMESIS.

By the Power which hath broken
The grave which enthralled thee,
Speak to him who hath spoken,
Or those who have called thee!

Manfred. She is silent,
And in that silence I am more than answered.
Nemesis. My power extends no further. Prince of Air!
It rests with thee alone — command her voice.
Arimanes. Spirit — obey this sceptre!
Nemesis. Silent still!
She is not of our order, but belongs
To the other powers. Mortal! thy quest is vain,

And we are baffled also.
Manfred. Hear me, hear me —
Astarte! my belovéd! speak to me:
I have so much endured — so much endure —
Look on me! the grave hath not changed thee more
Than I am changed for thee. Thou lovedst me
Too much, as I loved thee: we were not made
To torture thus each other — though it were
The deadliest sin to love as we have loved.
Say that thou loath'st me not — that I do bear
This punishment for both — that thou wilt be
One of the blesséd — and that I shall die;
For hitherto all hateful things conspire
To bind me in existence — in a life
Which makes me shrink from Immortality —
A future like the past. I cannot rest.
I know not what I ask, nor what I seek:
I feel but what thou art, and what I am;
And I would hear yet once before I perish
The voice which was my music — Speak to me!
For I have called on thee in the still night,
Startled the slumbering birds from the hushed boughs,
And woke the mountain wolves, and made the caves
Acquainted with thy vainly echoed name,
Which answered me — many things answered me —
Spirits and men — but thou wert silent all.
Yet speak to me! I have outwatched the stars,
And gazed o'er heaven in vain in search of thee.
Speak to me! I have wandered o'er the earth,
And never found thy likeness — Speak to me!
Look on the fiends around — they feel for me:
I fear them not, and feel for thee alone.
Speak to me! though it be in wrath; — but say —
I reck not what — but let me hear thee once —
This once — once more!
Phantom of Astarte. Manfred!
Manfred. Say on, say on —
I live but in the sound — it is thy voice!
Phantom. Manfred! To-morrow ends thine earthly ills. Farewell!
Manfred. Yet one word more — am I forgiven?
Phantom. Farewell!
Manfred. Say, shall we meet again?
Phantom. Farewell!
Manfred. One word for mercy! Say thou lovest me.
Phantom. Manfred!
[*The Spirit of* ASTARTE *disappears.*
Nemesis. She's gone, and will not be recalled:

Her words will be fulfilled. Return to the earth.
A Spirit. He is convulsed — This is to be a mortal,
And seek the things beyond mortality.
Another Spirit. Yet, see, he mastereth himself, and makes
His torture tributary to his will.
Had he been one of us, he would have made
An awful Spirit.
Nemesis. Hast thou further question
Of our great Sovereign, or his worshippers?
Manfred. None.
Nemesis. Then for a time farewell.
Manfred. We meet then! Where? On the earth? —
Even as thou wilt: and for the grace accorded
I now depart a debtor. Fare ye well!

[*Exit* MANFRED.

(*Scene closes.*)

ACT III

SCENE I. — *A Hall in the Castle of Manfred.*

MANFRED *and* HERMAN.

Manfred. What is the hour?
Herman. It wants but one till sunset,
And promises a lovely twilight.
Manfred. Say,
Are all things so disposed of in the tower
As I directed?
Herman. All, my Lord, are ready:
Here is the key and casket.
Manfred. It is well:
Thou mayst retire. [*Exit* HERMAN.
Manfred. (*alone*). There is a calm upon me —
Inexplicable stillness! which till now
Did not belong to what I knew of life.
If that I did not know Philosophy
To be of all our vanities the motliest,
The merest word that ever fooled the ear
From out the schoolman's jargon, I should deem
The golden secret, the sought "Kalon," found,
And seated in my soul. It will not last,
But it is well to have known it, though but once:
It hath enlarged my thoughts with a new sense,
And I within my tablets would note down
That there is such a feeling. Who is there?

Re-enter HERMAN.

Herman. My Lord, the Abbot of St. Maurice craves
To greet your presence.

Enter the ABBOT OF ST. MAURICE.

Abbot. Peace be with Count Manfred!
Manfred. Thanks, holy father! welcome to these walls;
Thy presence honours them, and blesseth those
Who dwell within them.
Abbot. Would it were so, Count! —
But I would fain confer with thee alone.
Manfred. Herman, retire. — What would my reverend guest?
Abbot. Thus, without prelude: — Age and zeal — my office —
And good intent must plead my privilege;
Our near, though not acquainted neighbourhood,
May also be my herald. Rumours strange,
And of unholy nature, are abroad,
And busy with thy name — a noble name
For centuries: may he who bears it now
Transmit it unimpaired!
Manfred. Proceed, — I listen.
Abbot. 'Tis said thou holdest converse with the things
Which are forbidden to the search of man;
That with the dwellers of the dark abodes,
The many evil and unheavenly spirits
Which walk the valley of the Shade of Death,
Thou communest. I know that with mankind,
Thy fellows in creation, thou dost rarely
Exchange thy thoughts, and that thy solitude
Is as an Anchorite's — were it but holy.
Manfred. And what are they who do avouch these things?
Abbot. My pious brethren — the scarèd peasantry —
Even thy own vassals — who do look on thee
With most unquiet eyes. Thy life's in peril!
Manfred. Take it.
Abbot. I come to save, and not destroy:
I would not pry into thy secret soul;
But if these things be sooth, there still is time
For penitence and pity: reconcile thee
With the true church, and through the church to Heaven.
Manfred. I hear thee. This is my reply — whate'er
I may have been, or am, doth rest between
Heaven and myself — I shall not choose a mortal
To be my mediator — Have I sinned
Against your ordinances? prove and punish!

Abbot. My son! I did not speak of punishment,
But penitence and pardon; — with thyself
The choice of such remains — and for the last,
Our institutions and our strong belief
Have given me power to smooth the path from sin
To higher hope and better thoughts; the first
I leave to Heaven, — "Vengeance is mine alone!"
So saith the Lord, and with all humbleness
His servant echoes back the awful word.

Manfred. Old man! there is no power in holy men,
Nor charm in prayer, nor purifying form
Of penitence, nor outward look, nor fast,
Nor agony — nor, greater than all these,
The innate tortures of that deep Despair,
Which is Remorse without the fear of Hell,
But all in all sufficient to itself
Would make a hell of Heaven — can exorcise
From out the unbounded spirit the quick sense
Of its own sins — wrongs — sufferance — and revenge
Upon itself; there is no future pang
Can deal that justice on the self-condemned
He deals on his own soul.

Abbot. All this is well;
For this will pass away, and be succeeded
By an auspicious hope, which shall look up
With calm assurance to that blessed place,
Which all who seek may win, whatever be
Their earthly errors, so they be atoned:
And the commencement of atonement is
The sense of its necessity. Say on —
And all our church can teach thee shall be taught;
And all we can absolve thee shall be pardoned.

Manfred. When Rome's sixth Emperor was near his last,
The victim of a self-inflicted wound,
To shun the torments of a public death
From senates once his slaves, a certain soldier,
With show of loyal pity, would have stanched
The gushing throat with his officious robe;
The dying Roman thrust him back, and said —
Some empire still in his expiring glance —
"It is too late — is this fidelity?"

Abbot. And what of this?

Manfred I answer with the Roman —
"It is too late!"

Abbot. It never can be so,
To reconcile thyself with thy own soul,
And thy own soul with Heaven. Hast thou no hope?

'Tis strange — even those who do despair above,
Yet shape themselves some fantasy on earth,
To which frail twig they cling, like drowning men.
Manfred. Aye — father! I have had those early visions,
And noble aspirations in my youth,
To make my own the mind of other men,
The enlightener of nations; and to rise
I knew not whither — it might be to fall;
But fall, even as the mountain-cataract,
Which having leapt from its more dazzling height,
Even in the foaming strength of its abyss,
(Which casts up misty columns that become
Clouds raining from the re-ascended skies,)
Lies low but mighty still. — But this is past,
My thoughts mistook themselves.
Abbot. And wherefore so?
Manfred. I could not tame my nature down; for he
Must serve who fain would sway; and soothe, and sue,
And watch all time, and pry into all place,
And be a living Lie, who would become
A mighty thing amongst the mean — and such
The mass are; I disdained to mingle with
A herd, though to be leader — and of wolves.
The lion is alone, and so am I.
Abbot. And why not live and act with other men?
Manfred. Because my nature was averse from life;
And yet not cruel; for I would not make,
But find a desolation. Like the Wind,
The red-hot breath of the most lone Simoom,
Which dwells but in the desert, and sweeps o'er
The barren sands which bear no shrubs to blast,
And revels o'er their wild and arid waves,
And seeketh not, so that it is not sought,
But being met is deadly, — such hath been
The course of my existence; but there came
Things in my path which are no more.
Abbot. Alas!
I 'gin to fear that thou art past all aid
From me and from my calling; yet so young,
I still would ——
Manfred. Look on me! there is an order
Of mortals on the earth, who do become
Old in their youth, and die ere middle age,
Without the violence of warlike death;
Some perishing of pleasure — some of study —
Some worn with toil, some of mere weariness, —
Some of disease — and some insanity —

And some of withered, or of broken hearts;
For this last is a malady which slays
More than are numbered in the lists of Fate,
Taking all shapes, and bearing many names.
Look upon me! for even of all these things
Have I partaken; and of all these things,
One were enough; then wonder not that I
Am what I am, but that I ever was,
Or having been, that I am still on earth.

Abbot. Yet, hear me still ——

Manfred. Old man! I do respect
Thine order, and revere thine years; I deem
Thy purpose pious, but it is in vain:
Think me not churlish; I would spare thyself,
Far more than me, in shunning at this time
All further colloquy — and so — farewell.

[*Exit* MANFRED.

Abbot. This should have been a noble creature: he
Hath all the energy which would have made
A goodly frame of glorious elements,
Had they been wisely mingled; as it is,
It is an awful chaos — Light and Darkness —
And mind and dust — and passions and pure thoughts
Mixed, and contending without end or order, —
All dormant or destructive. He will perish —
And yet he must not — I will try once more,
For such are worth redemption; and my duty
Is to dare all things for a righteous end.
I'll follow him — but cautiously, though surely.

[*Exit* ABBOT.

SCENE II. — *Another Chamber.*

MANFRED *and* HERMAN

Herman. My lord, you bade me wait on you at sunset:
He sinks behind the mountain.

Manfred. Doth he so?
I will look on him.

[MANFRED *advances to the Window of the Hall.*

Glorious Orb! the idol
Of early nature, and the vigorous race
Of undiseased mankind, the giant sons
Of the embrace of Angels, with a sex
More beautiful than they, which did draw down
The erring Spirits who can ne'er return. —
Most glorious Orb! that wert a worship, ere

The mystery of thy making was revealed!
Thou earliest minister of the Almighty,
Which gladdened, on their mountain tops, the hearts
Of the Chaldean shepherds, till they poured
Themselves in orisons! Thou material God!
And representative of the Unknown —
Who chose thee for his shadow! Thou chief Star!
Centre of many stars! which mak'st our earth
Endurable, and temperest the hues
And hearts of all who walk within thy rays!
Sire of the seasons! Monarch of the climes,
And those who dwell in them! for near or far,
Our inborn spirits have a tint of thee
Even as our outward aspects; — thou dost rise,
And shine, and set in glory. Fare thee well!
I ne'er shall see thee more. As my first glance
Of love and wonder was for thee, then take
My latest look: thou wilt not beam on one
To whom the gifts of life and warmth have been
Of a more fatal nature. He is gone —
I follow [*Exit* MANFRED.

SCENE III. — *The Mountains — The Castle of Manfred at some distance — A Terrace before a Tower. — Time, Twilight.*

HERMAN, MANUEL, *and other dependants of* MANFRED.

Herman. 'Tis strange enough! night after night, for years,
He hath pursued long vigils in this tower,
Without a witness. I have been within it, —
So have we all been oft-times; but from it,
Or its contents, it were impossible
To draw conclusions absolute, of aught
His studies tend to. To be sure, there is
One chamber where none enter: I would give
The fee of what I have to come these three years,
To pore upon its mysteries.
Manuel. 'Twere dangerous;
Content thyself with what thou know'st already.
Herman. Ah! Manuel! thou art elderly and wise,
And couldst say much; thou hast dwelt within the castle —
How many years is't?
Manuel. Ere Count Manfred's birth,
I served his father, whom he nought resembles.
Herman. There be more sons in like predicament!
But wherein do they differ?

Manuel. I speak not
Of features or of form, but mind and habits;
Count Sigismund was proud, but gay and free, —
A warrior and a reveller; he dwelt not
With books and solitude, nor made the night
A gloomy vigil, but a festal time,
Merrier than day; he did not walk the rocks
And forests like a wolf, nor turn aside
From men and their delights.
Herman. Beshrew the hour,
But those were jocund times! I would that such
Would visit the old walls again; they look
As if they had forgotten them.
Manuel. These walls
Must change their chieftain first. Oh! I have seen
Some strange things in them, Herman.
Herman Come, be friendly;
Relate me some to while away our watch:
I've heard thee darkly speak of an event
Which happened hereabouts, by this same tower.
Manuel. That was a night indeed! I do remember
'Twas twilight, as it may be now, and such
Another evening: — yon red cloud, which rests
On Eigher's pinnacle, so rested then, —
So like that it might be the same; the wind
Was faint and gusty, and the mountain snows
Began to glitter with the climbing moon;
Count Manfred was, as now, within his tower, —
How occupied, we knew not, but with him
The sole companion of his wanderings
And watchings — her, whom of all earthly things
That lived, the only thing he seemed to love, —
As he, indeed, by blood was bound to do,
The Lady Astarte, his ——
Hush! who comes here?

Enter the Abbot.

Abbot. Where is your master?
Herman. Yonder in the tower.
Abbot. I must speak with him.
Manuel. 'Tis impossible;
He is most private, and must not be thus
Intruded on.
Abbot. Upon myself I take
The forfeit of my fault, if fault there be —
But I must see him.

Herman. Thou hast seen him once
This eve already.
Abbot. Herman! I command thee,
Knock, and apprize the Count of my approach.
Herman. We dare not.
Abbot. Then it seems I must be herald
Of my own purpose.
Manuel. Reverend father, stop —
I pray you pause.
Abbot. Why so?
Manuel. But step this way,
And I will tell you further. [*Exeunt.*

Scene IV. — *Interior of the Tower.*

Manfred *alone.*

The stars are forth, the moon above the tops
Of the snow-shining mountains. — Beautiful!
I linger yet with Nature, for the Night
Hath been to me a more familiar face
Than that of man; and in her starry shade
Of dim and solitary loveliness,
I learned the language of another world.
I do remember me, that in my youth,
When I was wandering, — upon such a night
I stood within the Coliseum's wall,
'Midst the chief relics of almighty Rome;
The trees which grew along the broken arches
Waved dark in the blue midnight, and the stars
Shone through the rents of ruin; from afar
The watch-dog bayed beyond the Tiber; and
More near from out the Cæsars' palace came
The owl's long cry, and, interruptedly,
Of distant sentinels the fitful song
Begun and died upon the gentle wind.
Some cypresses beyond the time-worn breach
Appeared to skirt the horizon, yet they stood
Within a bowshot. Where the Cæsars dwelt,
And dwell the tuneless birds of night, amidst
A grove which springs through levelled battlements,
And twines its roots with the imperial hearths,
Ivy usurps the laurel's place of growth;
But the gladiators' bloody Circus stands,
A noble wreck in ruinous perfection,
While Cæsar's chambers, and the Augustan halls,
Grovel on earth in indistinct decay. —

And thou didst shine, thou rolling Moon, upon
All this, and cast a wide and tender light,
Which softened down the hoar austerity
Of rugged desolation, and filled up,
As 'twere anew, the gaps of centuries;
Leaving that beautiful which still was so,
And making that which was not — till the place
Became religion, and the heart ran o'er
With silent worship of the Great of old, —
The dead, but sceptred, Sovereigns, who still rule
Our spirits from their urns.
'Twas such a night!
'Tis strange that I recall it at this time;
But I have found our thoughts take wildest flight
Even at the moment when they should array
Themselves in pensive order.

Enter the ABBOT.

Abbot. My good Lord!
I crave a second grace for this approach;
But yet let not my humble zeal offend
By its abruptness — all it hath of ill
Recoils on me; its good in the effect
May light upon your head — could I say *heart* —
Could I touch *that,* with words or prayers, I should
Recall a noble spirit which hath wandered,
But is not yet all lost.
Manfred. Thou know'st me not;
My days are numbered, and my deeds recorded:
Retire, or 'twill be dangerous — Away!
Abbot. Thou dost not mean to menace me?
Manfred. Not I!
I simply tell thee peril is at hand,
And would preserve thee.
Abbot. What dost thou mean?
Manfred. Look there!
What dost thou see?
Abbot. Nothing.
Manfred. Look there, I say,
And steadfastly; — now tell me what thou seest?
Abbot. That which should shake me, — but I fear it not:
I see a dusk and awful figure rise,
Like an infernal god, from out the earth;
His face wrapt in a mantle, and his form
Robed as with angry clouds: he stands between
Thyself and me — but I do fear him not.

Manfred. Thou hast no cause — he shall not harm thee — but
His sight may shock thine old limbs into palsy.
I say to thee — Retire!
Abbot. And I reply —
Never — till I have battled with this fiend: —
What doth he here?
Manfred. Why — aye — what doth he here?
I did not send for him, — he is unbidden.
Abbot. Alas! lost Mortal! what with guests like these
Hast thou to do? I tremble for thy sake:
Why doth he gaze on thee, and thou on him?
Ah! he unveils his aspect: on his brow
The thunder-scars are graven; from his eye
Glares forth the immortality of Hell —
Avaunt! —
Manfred. Pronounce — what is thy mission?
Spirit. Come!
Abbot. What art thou, unknown being? answer! — speak!
Spirit. The genius of this mortal. — Come! 'tis time.
Manfred. I am prepared for all things, but deny
The Power which summons me. Who sent thee here?
Spirit. Thou'lt know anon — Come! come!
Manfred. I have commanded
Things of an essence greater far than thine,
And striven with thy masters. Get thee hence!
Spirit. Mortal! thine hour is come — Away! I say.
Manfred. I knew, and know my hour is come, but not
To render up my soul to such as thee:
Away! I'll die as I have lived — alone.
Spirit. Then I must summon up my brethren. — Rise!
[*Other Spirits rise up.*
Abbot. Avaunt! ye evil ones! — Avaunt! I say, —
Ye have no power where Piety hath power,
And I do charge ye in the name —
Spirit. Old man!
We know ourselves, our mission, and thine order;
Waste not thy holy words on idle uses,
It were in vain: this man is forfeited.
Once more — I summon him — Away! Away!
Manfred. I do defy ye, — though I feel my soul
Is ebbing from me, yet I do defy ye;
Nor will I hence, while I have earthly breath
To breathe my scorn upon ye — earthly strength
To wrestle, though with spirits; what ye take
Shall be ta'en limb by limb.
Spirit. Reluctant mortal!
Is this the Magian who would so pervade

The world invisible, and make himself
Almost our equal? Can it be that thou
Art thus in love with life? the very life
Which made thee wretched?
Manfred. Thou false fiend, thou liest!
My life is in its last hour, — *that* I know,
Nor would redeem a moment of that hour;
I do not combat against Death, but thee
And thy surrounding angels; my past power
Was purchased by no compact with thy crew,
But by superior science — penance, daring,
And length of watching, strength of mind, and skill
In knowledge of our Fathers — when the earth
Saw men and spirits walking side by side,
And gave ye no supremacy: I stand
Upon my strength — I do defy — deny —
Spurn back, and scorn ye! —
Spirit. But thy many crimes
Have made thee ——
Manfred. What are they to such as thee?
Must crimes be punished but by other crimes,
And greater criminals? — Back to thy hell!
Thou hast no power upon me, *that* I feel;
Thou never shalt possess me, *that* I know:
What I have done is done; I bear within
A torture which could nothing gain from thine:
The Mind which is immortal makes itself
Requital for its good or evil thoughts, —
Is its own origin of ill and end —
And its own place and time: its innate sense,
When stripped of this mortality, derives
No colour from the fleeting things without,
But is absorbed in sufferance or in joy,
Born from the knowledge of its own desert.
Thou didst not tempt me, and thou couldst not tempt me;
I have not been thy dupe, nor am thy prey —
But was my own destroyer, and will be
My own hereafter. — Back, ye baffled fiends!
The hand of Death is on me — but not yours!
[*The Demons disappear.*
Abbot. Alas! how pale thou art — thy lips are white —
And thy breast heaves — and in thy gasping throat
The accents rattle: Give thy prayers to Heaven —
Pray — albeit but in thought, — but die not thus.
Manfred. 'Tis over — my dull eyes can fix thee not;
But all things swim around me, and the earth
Heaves as it were beneath me. Fare thee well —

Give me thy hand.

Abbot. Cold — cold — even to the heart —
But yet one prayer — Alas! how fares it with thee?

Manfred. Old man! 'tis not so difficult to die.

[MANFRED *expires.*

Abbot. He's gone — his soul hath ta'en its earthless flight;
Whither? I dread to think — but he is gone.

SO WE'LL GO NO MORE A-ROVING

1

So we'll go no more a-roving
So late into the night,
Though the heart be still as loving,
And the moon be still as bright.

2

For the sword outwears its sheath,
And the soul wears out the breast,
And the heart must pause to breathe,
And Love itself have rest.

3

Though the night was made for loving,
And the day returns too soon,
Yet we'll go no more a-roving
By the light of the moon.

THE LAMENT OF TASSO

I

LONG years! — It tries the thrilling frame to bear
And eagle-spirit of a Child of Song —
Long years of outrage — calumny — and wrong;
Imputed madness, prisoned solitude,
And the Mind's canker in its savage mood,
When the impatient thirst of light and air
Parches the heart; and the abhorred grate,
Marring the sunbeams with its hideous shade,
Works through the throbbing eyeball to the brain,
With a hot sense of heaviness and pain;

And bare, at once, Captivity displayed
Stands scoffing through the never-opened gate,
Which nothing through its bars admits, save day,
And tasteless food, which I have eat alone
Till its unsocial bitterness is gone;
And I can banquet like a beast of prey,
Sullen and lonely, couching in the cave
Which is my lair, and — it may be — my grave.
All this hath somewhat worn me, and may wear,
But must be borne. I stoop not to despair;
For I have battled with mine agony,
And made me wings wherewith to overfly
The narrow circus of my dungeon wall,
And freed the Holy Sepulchre from thrall;
And revelled among men and things divine,
And poured my spirit over Palestine,
In honour of the sacred war for Him,
The God who was on earth and is in Heaven,
For He has strengthened me in heart and limb.
That through this sufferance I might be forgiven,
I have employed my penance to record
How Salem's shrine was won, and how adored.

II

But this is o'er — my pleasant task is done: —
My long-sustaining Friend of many years!
If I do blot thy final page with tears,
Know, that my sorrows have wrung from me none.
But Thou, my young creation! my Soul's child!
Which ever playing round me came and smiled,
And wooed me from myself with thy sweet sight,
Thou too art gone — and so is my delight:
And therefore do I weep and inly bleed
With this last bruise upon a broken reed.
Thou too art ended — what is left me now?
For I have anguish yet to bear — and how?
I know not that — but in the innate force
Of my own spirit shall be found resource.
I have not sunk, for I had no remorse,
Nor cause for such: they called me mad — and why?
Oh Leonora! wilt not *thou* reply?
I was indeed delirious in my heart
To lift my love so lofty as thou art;
But still my frenzy was not of the mind:
I knew my fault, and feel my punishment
Not less because I suffer it unbent.

That thou wert beautiful, and I not blind,
Hath been the sin which shuts me from mankind;
But let them go, or torture as they will,
My heart can multiply thine image still;
Successful Love may sate itself away;
The wretchéd are the faithful; 't is their fate
To have all feeling, save the one, decay,
And every passion into one dilate,
As rapid rivers into Ocean pour;
But ours is fathomless, and hath no shore.

III

Above me, hark! the long and maniac cry
Of minds and bodies in captivity.
And hark! the lash and the increasing howl,
And the half-inarticulate blasphemy!
There be some here with worse than frenzy foul,
Some who do still goad on the o'er-laboured mind,
And dim the little light that's left behind
With needless torture, as their tyrant Will
Is wound up to the lust of doing ill:
With these and with their victims am I classed,
'Mid sounds and sights like these long years have passed;
'Mid sights and sounds like these my life may close:
So let it be — for then I shall repose.

IV

I have been patient, let me be so yet;
I had forgotten half I would forget,
But it revives — Oh! would it were my lot
To be forgetful as I am forgot! —
Feel I not wroth with those who bade me dwell
In this vast Lazar-house of many woes?
Where laughter is not mirth, nor thought the mind,
Nor words a language, nor ev'n men mankind;
Where cries reply to curses, shrieks to blows,
And each is tortured in his separate hell —
For we are crowded in our solitudes —
Many, but each divided by the wall,
Which echoes Madness in her babbling moods;
While all can hear, none heed his neighbour's call —
None! save that One, the veriest wretch of all,
Who was not made to be the mate of these,
Nor bound between Distraction and Disease.
Feel I not wroth with those who placed me here?

Who have debased me in the minds of men,
Debarring me the usage of my own,
Blighting my life in best of its career,
Branding my thoughts as things to shun and fear?
Would I not pay them back these pangs again,
And teach them inward Sorrow's stifled groan?
The struggle to be calm, and cold distress,
Which undermines our Stoical success?
No! — still too proud to be vindictive — I
Have pardoned Princes' insults, and would die.
Yes, Sister of my Sovereign! for thy sake
I weed all bitterness from out my breast,
It hath no business where *thou* art a guest:
Thy brother hates — but I can not detest;
Thou pitiest not — but I can not forsake.

V

Look on a love which knows not to despair,
But all unquenched is still my better part,
Dwelling deep in my shut and silent heart,
As dwells the gathered lightning in its cloud,
Encompassed with its dark and rolling shroud,
Till struck, — forth flies the all-ethereal dart!
And thus at the collision of thy name
The vivid thought still flashes through my frame,
And for a moment all things as they were
Flit by me; — they are gone — I am the same.
And yet my love without ambition grew;
I knew thy state — my station — and I knew
A Princess was no love-mate for a bard;
I told it not — I breathed it not — it was
Sufficient to itself, its own reward;
And if my eyes revealed it, they, alas!
Were punished by the silentness of thine,
And yet I did not venture to repine.
Thou wert to me a crystal-girded shrine,
Worshipped at holy distance, and around
Hallowed and meekly kissed and saintly ground;
Not for thou wert a Princess, but that Love
Had robed thee with a glory, and arrayed
Thy lineaments in beauty that dismayed —
Oh! not dismayed — but awed, like One above!
And in that sweet severity there was
A something which all softness did surpass —
I know not how — thy Genius mastered mine —
My Star stood still before thee: — if it were

Presumptuous thus to love without design,
That sad fatality hath cost me dear;
But thou art dearest still, and I should be
Fit for this cell, which wrongs me — but for *thee.*
The very love which locked me to my chain
Hath lightened half its weight; and for the rest,
Though heavy, lent me vigour to sustain,
And look to thee with undivided breast,
And foil the ingenuity of Pain.

VI

It is no marvel — from my very birth
My soul was drunk with Love, — which did pervade
And mingle with whate'er I saw on earth:
Of objects all inanimate I made
Idols, and out of wild and lonely flowers,
And rocks, whereby they grew, a Paradise,
Where I did lay me down within the shade
Of waving trees, and dreamed uncounted hours,
Though I was chid for wandering; and the Wise
Shook their white agéd heads o'er me, and said
Of such materials wretched men were made,
And such a truant boy would end in woe,
And that the only lesson was a blow; —
And then they smote me, and I did not weep,
But cursed them in my heart, and to my haunt
Returned and wept alone, and dreamed again
The visions which arise without a sleep.
And with my years my soul began to pant
With feelings of strange tumult and soft pain;
And the whole heart exhaled into One Want,
But undefined and wandering, till the day
I found the thing I sought — and that was thee;
And then I lost my being, all to be
Absorbed in thine; — the world was past away; —
Thou didst annihilate the earth to me!

VII

I loved all Solitude — but little thought
To spend I know not what of life, remote
From all communion with existence, save
The maniac and his tyrant; — had I been
Their fellow, many years ere this had seen
My mind like theirs corrupted to its grave.
But who hath seen me writhe, or heard me rave?

Perchance in such a cell we suffer more
Than the wrecked sailor on his desert shore;
The world is all before him — *mine* is *here,*
Scarce twice the space they must accord my bier.
What though *he* perish, he may lift his eye,
And with a dying glance upbraid the sky;
I will not raise my own in such reproof,
Although 'tis clouded by my dungeon roof.

VIII

Yet do I feel at times my mind decline,
But with a sense of its decay: I see
Unwonted lights along my prison shine,
And a strange Demon, who is vexing me
With pilfering pranks and petty pains, below
The feeling of the healthful and the free;
But much to One, who hath suffered so,
Sickness of heart, and narrowness of place,
And all that may be borne, or can debase.
I thought mine enemies had been but Man,
But Spirits may be leagued with them — all Earth
Abandons — Heaven forgets me; — in the dearth
Of such defence the Powers of Evil can —
It may be — tempt me further, — and prevail
Against the outworn creature they assail.
Why in this furnace is my spirit proved,
Like steel in tempering fire? because I loved?
Because I loved what not to love, and see,
Was more or less than mortal, and than me.

IX

I once was quick in feeling — that is o'er; —
My scars are callous, or I should have dashed
My brain against these bars, as the sun flashed
In mockery through them; — If I bear and bore
The much I have recounted, and the more
Which hath no words, — 't is that I would not die
And sanction with self-slaughter the dull lie
Which snared me here, and with the brand of shame
Stamp Madness deep into my memory,
And woo Compassion to a blighted name,
Sealing the sentence which my foes proclaim.
No — it shall be immortal! — and I make
A future temple of my present cell,
Which nations yet shall visit for my sake.

While thou, Ferrara! when no longer dwell
The ducal chiefs within thee, shalt fall down,
And crumbling piecemeal view thy hearthless halls,
A Poet's wreath shall be thine only crown, —
A Poet's dungeon thy most far renown,
While strangers wonder o'er thy unpeopled walls!
And thou, Leonora! — thou — who wert ashamed
That such as I could love — who blushed to hear
To less than monarchs that thou couldst be dear,
Go! tell thy brother, that my heart, untamed
By grief — years — weariness — and it may be
A taint of that he would impute to me —
From long infection of a den like this,
Where the mind rots congenial with the abyss, —
Adores thee still; — and add — that when the towers
And battlements which guard his joyous hours
Of banquet, dance, and revel, are forgot,
Or left untended in a dull repose,
This — this — shall be a consecrated spot!
But *Thou* — when all that Birth and Beauty throws
Of magic round thee is extinct — shalt have
One half the laurel which o'ershades my grave.
No power in death can tear our names apart,
As none in life could rend thee from my heart.
Yes, Leonora! it shall be our fate
To be entwined for ever — but too late!

TO THOMAS MOORE

1

My boat is on the shore,
And my bark is on the sea;
But, before I go, Tom Moore,
Here's a double health to thee!

2

Here's a sigh to those who love me,
And a smile to those who hate;
And, whatever sky's above me,
Here's a heart for every fate.

3

Though the Ocean roar around me,
Yet it still shall bear me on;

Though a desert shall surround me,
  It hath springs that may be won.

4

Were 't the last drop in the well,
  As I gasped upon the brink,
Ere my fainting spirit fell,
  'T is to thee that I would drink.

5

With that water, as this wine,
  The libation I would pour
Should be — peace with thine and mine,
  And a health to thee, Tom Moore.

BEPPO:

A VENETIAN STORY

Rosalind. Farewell, Monsieur Traveller; Look, you lisp, and wear strange suits: disable all the benefits of your own country; be out of love with your Nativity, and almost chide God for making you that countenance you are; or I will scarce think you have swam in a *Gondola.*

As You Like It, Act IV, Scene i.

Annotation of the Commentators

That is, *been at Venice,* which was much visited by the young English gentlemen of those times, and was *then* what *Paris* is *now* — the seat of all dissoluteness. — S. A.

I

'Tis known, at least it should be, that throughout
  All countries of the Catholic persuasion,
Some weeks before Shrove Tuesday comes about,
  The People take their fill of recreation,
And buy repentance, ere they grow devout,
  However high their rank, or low their station,
With fiddling, feasting, dancing, drinking, masquing,
And other things which may be had for asking.

II

The moment night with dusky mantle covers
The skies (and the more duskily the better),
The Time less liked by husbands than by lovers
Begins, and Prudery flings aside her fetter;
And Gaiety on restless tiptoe hovers,
Giggling with all the gallants who beset her;
And there are songs and quavers, roaring, humming,
Guitars, and every other sort of strumming.

III

And there are dresses splendid, but fantastical,
Masks of all times and nations, Turks and Jews,
And harlequins and clowns, with feats gymnastical,
Greeks, Romans, Yankee-doodles, and Hindoos;
All kinds of dress, except the ecclesiastical,
All people, as their fancies hit, may choose,
But no one in these parts may quiz the Clergy, —
Therefore take heed, ye Freethinkers! I charge ye.

IV

You'd better walk about begirt with briars,
Instead of coat and smallclothes, than put on
A single stitch reflecting upon friars,
Although you swore it only was in fun;
They'd haul you o'er the coals, and stir the fires
Of Phlegethon with every mother's son,
Nor say one mass to cool the cauldron's bubble
That boiled your bones, unless you paid them double.

V

But saving this, you may put on whate'er
You like by way of doublet, cape, or cloak,
Such as in Monmouth-street, or in Rag Fair,
Would rig you out in seriousness or joke;
And even in Italy such places are,
With prettier name in softer accents spoke,
For, bating Covent Garden, I can hit on
No place that's called "Piazza" in Great Britain.

VI

This feast is named the Carnival, which being
Interpreted, implies "farewell to flesh:"

So called, because the name and thing agreeing,
    Through Lent they live on fish both salt and fresh.
But why they usher Lent with so much glee in,
    Is more than I can tell, although I guess
'Tis as we take a glass with friends at parting,
In the Stage-Coach or Packet, just at starting.

VII

And thus they bid farewell to carnal dishes,
    And solid meats, and highly spiced ragouts,
To live for forty days on ill-dressed fishes,
    Because they have no sauces to their stews;
A thing which causes many "poohs" and "pishes,"
    And several oaths (which would not suit the Muse),
From travellers accustomed from a boy
To eat their salmon, at the least, with soy;

VIII

And therefore humbly I would recommend
    "The curious in fish-sauce," before they cross
The sea, to bid their cook, or wife, or friend,
    Walk or ride to the Strand, and buy in gross
(Or if set out beforehand, these may send
    By any means least liable to loss),
Ketchup, Soy, Chili-vinegar, and Harvey,
Or, by the Lord! a Lent will well nigh starve ye;

IX

That is to say, if your religion's Roman,
    And you at Rome would do as Romans do,
According to the proverb, — although no man,
    If foreign, is obliged to fast; and you,
If Protestant, or sickly, or a woman,
    Would rather dine in sin on a ragout —
Dine and be d—d! I don't mean to be coarse,
But that's the penalty, to say no worse.

X

Of all the places where the Carnival
    Was most facetious in the days of yore,
For dance, and song, and serenade, and ball,
    And Masque, and Mime, and Mystery, and more
Than I have time to tell now, or at all,
    Venice the bell from every city bore, —

And at the moment when I fix my story,
That sea-born city was in all her glory.

XI

They've pretty faces yet, those same Venetians,
   Black eyes, arched brows, and sweet expressions still;
Such as of old were copied from the Grecians,
   In ancient arts by moderns mimicked ill;
And like so many Venuses of Titian's
   (The best's at Florence — see it, if ye will,)
They look when leaning over the balcony,
Or stepped from out a picture by Giorgione,

XII

Whose tints are Truth and Beauty at their best;
   And when you to Manfrini's palace go,
That picture (howsoever fine the rest)
   Is loveliest to my mind of all the show;
It may perhaps be also to *your* zest,
   And that's the cause I rhyme upon it so:
'Tis but a portrait of his Son, and Wife,
And self; but *such* a Woman! Love in life!

XIII

Love in full life and length, not love ideal,
   No, nor ideal beauty, that fine name,
But something better still, so very real,
   That the sweet Model must have been the same;
A thing that you would purchase, beg, or steal,
   Wer't not impossible, besides a shame:
The face recalls some face, as 'twere with pain,
You once have seen, but ne'er will see again;

XIV

One of those forms which flit by us, when we
   Are young, and fix our eyes on every face;
And, oh! the Loveliness at times we see
   In momentary gliding, the soft grace,
The Youth, the Bloom, the Beauty which agree,
   In many a nameless being we retrace,
Whose course and home we knew not, nor shall know,
Like the lost Pleiad seen no more below.

XV

I said that like a picture by Giorgione
    Venetian women were, and so they *are*,
Particularly seen from a balcony,
    (For beauty's sometimes best set off afar)
And there, just like a heroine of Goldoni,
    They peep from out the blind, or o'er the bar;
And truth to say, they're mostly very pretty,
And rather like to show it, more's the pity!

XVI

For glances beget ogles, ogles sighs,
    Sighs wishes, wishes words, and words a letter,
Which flies on wings of light-heeled Mercuries,
    Who do such things because they know no better;
And then, God knows what mischief may arise,
    When Love links two young people in one fetter,
Vile assignations, and adulterous beds,
Elopements, broken vows, and hearts, and heads.

XVII

Shakespeare described the sex in Desdemona
    As very fair, but yet suspect in fame,
And to this day from Venice to Verona
    Such matters may be probably the same,
Except that since those times was never known
    Husband whom mere suspicion could inflame
To suffocate a wife no more than twenty,
Because she had a "Cavalier Servente."

XVIII

Their jealousy (if they are ever jealous)
    Is of a fair complexion altogether,
Not like that sooty devil of Othello's,
    Which smothers women in a bed of feather,
But worthier of these much more jolly fellows,
    When weary of the matrimonial tether
His head for such a wife no mortal bothers,
But takes at once another, or *another's*.

XIX

Didst ever see a Gondola? For fear
    You should not, I'll describe it you exactly:

'Tis a long covered boat that's common here,
Carved at the prow, built lightly, but compactly,
Rowed by two rowers, each call'd "Gondolier,"
It glides along the water looking blackly,
Just like a coffin clapt in a canoe,
Where none can make out what you say or do.

XX

And up and down the long canals they go,
And under the Rialto shoot along,
By night and day, all paces, swift or slow,
And round the theatres, a sable throng,
They wait in their dusk livery of woe, —
But not to them do woeful things belong,
For sometimes they contain a deal of fun,
Like mourning coaches when the funeral's done.

XXI

But to my story. — 'Twas some years ago,
It may be thirty, forty, more or less,
The Carnival was at its height, and so
Were all kinds of buffoonery and dress;
A certain lady went to see the show,
Her real name I know not, nor can guess,
And so we'll call her Laura, if you please,
Because it slips into my verse with ease.

XXII

She was not old, nor young, nor at the years
Which certain people call a "*certain age*,"
Which yet the most uncertain age appears,
Because I never heard, nor could engage
A person yet by prayers, or bribes, or tears,
To name, define by speech, or write on page,
The period meant precisely by that word, —
Which surely is exceedingly absurd.

XXIII

Laura was blooming still, had made the best
Of Time, and Time returned the compliment,
And treated her genteelly, so that, dressed,
She looked extremely well where'er she went;
A pretty woman is a welcome guest,

And Laura's brow a frown had rarely bent;
Indeed, she shone all smiles, and seemed to flatter
Mankind with her black eyes for looking at her.

XXIV

She was a married woman; 'tis convenient,
Because in Christian countries 'tis a rule
To view their little slips with eyes more lenient;
Whereas if single ladies play the fool,
(Unless within the period intervenient
A well-timed wedding makes the scandal cool)
I don't know how they ever can get over it,
Except they manage never to discover it.

XXV

Her husband sailed upon the Adriatic,
And made some voyages, too, in other seas,
And when he lay in Quarantine for pratique
(A forty days' precaution 'gainst disease),
His wife would mount, at times, her highest attic,
For thence she could discern the ship with ease:
He was a merchant trading to Aleppo,
His name Giuseppe, called more briefly, Beppo.

XXVI

He was a man as dusky as a Spaniard,
Sunburnt with travel, yet a portly figure;
Though coloured, as it were, within a tanyard,
He was a person both of sense and vigour —
A better seaman never yet did man yard;
And she, although her manners showed no rigour,
Was deemed a woman of the strictest principle,
So much as to be thought almost invincible.

XXVII

But several years elapsed since they had met;
Some people thought the ship was lost, and some
That he had somehow blundered into debt,
And did not like the thought of steering home;
And there were several offered any bet,
Or that he would, or that he would not come;
For most men (till by losing rendered sager)
Will back their own opinions with a wager.

XXVIII

'Tis said that their last parting was pathetic,
   As partings often are, or ought to be,
And their presentiment was quite prophetic,
   That they should never more each other see,
(A sort of morbid feeling, half poetic,
   Which I have known occur in two or three,)
When kneeling on the shore upon her sad knee
He left this Adriatic Ariadne.

XXIX

And Laura waited long, and wept a little,
   And thought of wearing weeds, as well she might;
She almost lost all appetite for victual,
   And could not sleep with ease alone at night;
She deemed the window-frames and shutters brittle
   Against a daring housebreaker or sprite,
And so she thought it prudent to connect her
With a vice-husband, *chiefly* to *protect her.*

XXX

She chose, (and what is there they will not choose,
   If only you will but oppose their choice?)
Till Beppo should return from his long cruise,
   And bid once more her faithful heart rejoice,
A man some women like, and yet abuse —
   A Coxcomb was he by the public voice;
A Count of wealth, they said, as well as quality,
And in his pleasures of great liberality.

XXXI

And then he was a Count, and then he knew
   Music, and dancing, fiddling, French and Tuscan;
The last not easy, be it known to you,
   For few Italians speak the right Etruscan.
He was a critic upon operas, too,
   And knew all niceties of sock and buskin;
And no Venetian audience could endure a
Song, scene, or air, when he cried "seccatura!"

XXXII

His "bravo" was decisive, for that sound
   Hushed "Academie" sighed in silent awe;

The fiddlers trembled as he looked around,
For fear of some false note's detected flaw;
The "Prima Donna's" tuneful heart would bound,
Dreading the deep damnation of his "Bah!"
Soprano, Basso, even the Contra-Alto,
Wished him five fathom under the Rialto.

XXXIII

He patronised the Improvisatori,
Nay, could himself extemporise some stanzas,
Wrote rhymes, sang songs, could also tell a story,
Sold pictures, and was skilful in the dance as
Italians can be, though in this their glory
Must surely yield the palm to that which France has;
In short, he was a perfect Cavaliero,
And to his very valet seemed a hero.

XXXIV

Then he was faithful too, as well as amorous;
So that no sort of female could complain,
Although they're now and then a little clamorous,
He never put the pretty souls in pain;
His heart was one of those which most enamour us,
Wax to receive, and marble to retain:
He was a lover of the good old school,
Who still become more constant as they cool.

XXXV

No wonder such accomplishments should turn
A female head, however sage and steady —
With scarce a hope that Beppo could return,
In law he was almost as good as dead, he
Nor sent, nor wrote, nor showed the least concern,
And she had waited several years already:
And really if a man won't let us know
That he's alive, he's *dead* — or should be so.

XXXVI

Besides, within the Alps, to every woman,
(Although, God knows, it is a grievous sin,)
'Tis, I may say, permitted to have *two* men;
I can't tell who first brought the custom in,
But "Cavalier Serventes" are quite common,
And no one notices or cares a pin;

And we may call this (not to say the worst)
A *second* marriage which corrupts the *first*.

XXXVII

The word was formerly a "Cicisbeo,"
But *that* is now grown vulgar and indecent;
The Spaniards call the person a "*Cortejo*,"
For the same mode subsists in Spain, though recent;
In short it reaches from the Po to Teio,
And may perhaps at last be o'er the sea sent:
But Heaven preserve Old England from such courses!
Or what becomes of damage and divorces?

XXXVIII

However, I still think, with all due deference
To the fair *single* part of the creation;
That married ladies should preserve the preference
In *tête à tête* or general conversation —
And this I say without peculiar reference
To England, France, or any other nation —
Because they know the world, and are at ease,
And being natural, naturally please.

XXXIX

'Tis true, your budding Miss is very charming,
But shy and awkward at first coming out,
So much alarmed, that she is quite alarming,
All Giggle, Blush; half Pertness, and half Pout;
And glancing at *Mamma*, for fear there's harm in
What you, she, it, or they, may be about:
The Nursery still lisps out in all they utter —
Besides, they always smell of bread and butter.

XL

But "Cavalier Servente" is the phrase
Used in politest circles to express
This supernumerary slave, who stays
Close to the lady as a part of dress,
Her word the only law which he obeys.
His is no sinecure, as you may guess;
Coach, servants, gondola, he goes to call,
And carries fan and tippet, gloves and shawl.

XLI

With all its sinful doings, I must say,
That Italy's a pleasant place to me,
Who love to see the Sun shine every day,
And vines (not nailed to walls) from tree to tree
Festooned, much like the back scene of a play,
Or melodrame, which people flock to see,
When the first act is ended by a dance
In vineyards copied from the South of France.

XLII

I like on Autumn evenings to ride out,
Without being forced to bid my groom be sure
My cloak is round his middle strapped about,
Because the skies are not the most secure;
I know too that, if stopped upon my route,
Where the green alleys windingly allure,
Reeling with *grapes* red wagons choke the way, —
In England 'twould be dung, dust, or a dray.

XLIII

I also like to dine on becaficas,
To see the Sun set, sure he'll rise to-morrow,
Not through a misty morning twinkling weak as
A drunken man's dead eye in maudlin sorrow,
But with all Heaven t'himself; the day will break as
Beauteous as cloudless, nor be forced to borrow
That sort of farthing candlelight which glimmers
Where reeking London's smoky cauldron simmers.

XLIV

I love the language, that soft bastard Latin,
Which melts like kisses from a female mouth,
And sounds as if it should be writ on satin,
With syllables which breathe of the sweet South,
And gentle liquids gliding all so pat in,
That not a single accent seems uncouth,
Like our harsh northern whistling, grunting guttural,
Which we're obliged to hiss, and spit, and sputter all.

XLV

I like the women too (forgive my folly!),
From the rich peasant cheek of ruddy bronze,

And large black eyes that flash on you a volley
  Of rays that say a thousand things at once,
To the high Dama's brow, more melancholy,
  But clear, and with a wild and liquid glance,
Heart on her lips, and soul within her eyes,
Soft as her clime, and sunny as her skies.

XLVI

Eve of the land which still is Paradise!
  Italian Beauty didst thou not inspire
Raphael, who died in thy embrace, and vies
  With all we know of Heaven, or can desire,
In what he hath bequeathed us? — in what guise,
  Though flashing from the fervour of the Lyre,
Would *words* describe thy past and present glow,
While yet Canova can create below?

XLVII

"England! with all thy faults I love thee still,"
  I said at Calais, and have not forgot it;
I like to speak and lucubrate my fill;
  I like the government (but that is not it);
I like the freedom of the press and quill;
  I like the Habeas Corpus (when we've got it);
I like a Parliamentary debate,
Particularly when 'tis not too late;

XLVIII

I like the taxes, when they're not too many;
  I like a seacoal fire, when not too dear;
I like a beef-steak, too, as well as any;
  Have no objection to a pot of beer;
I like the weather, — when it is not rainy,
  That is, I like two months of every year.
And so God save the Regent, Church, and King!
Which means that I like all and every thing.

XLIX

Our standing army, and disbanded seamen,
  Poor's rate, Reform, my own, the nation's debt,
Our little riots just to show we're free men,
  Our trifling bankruptcies in the Gazette,
Our cloudy climate, and our chilly women,

All these I can forgive, and those forget,
And greatly venerate our recent glories,
And wish they were not owing to the Tories.

L

But to my tale of Laura, — for I find
Digression is a sin, that by degrees
Becomes exceeding tedious to my mind,
And, therefore, may the reader too displease —
The gentle reader, who may wax unkind,
And caring little for the Author's ease,
Insist on knowing what he means — a hard
And hapless situation for a Bard.

LI

Oh! that I had the art of easy writing
What should be easy reading! could I scale
Parnassus, where the Muses sit inditing
Those pretty poems never known to fail,
How quickly would I print (the world delighting)
A Grecian, Syrian, or Assyrian tale;
And sell you, mixed with western Sentimentalism,
Some samples of the *finest Orientalism*.

LII

But I am but a nameless sort of person,
(A broken Dandy lately on my travels)
And take for rhyme, to hook my rambling verse on,
The first that Walker's Lexicon unravels,
And when I can't find that, I put a worse on,
Not caring as I ought for critics' cavils;
I've half a mind to tumble down to prose,
But verse is more in fashion — so here goes!

LIII

The Count and Laura made their new arrangement,
Which lasted, as arrangements sometimes do,
For half a dozen years without estrangement;
They had their little differences, too;
Those jealous whiffs, which never any change meant;
In such affairs there probably are few
Who have not had this pouting sort of squabble,
From sinners of high station to the rabble.

LIV

But, on the whole, they were a happy pair,
  As happy as unlawful love could make them;
The gentleman was fond, the lady fair,
  Their chains so slight, 'twas not worth while to break them:
The World beheld them with indulgent air;
  The pious only wished "the Devil take them!"
He took them not; he very often waits,
And leaves old sinners to be young ones' baits.

LV

But they were young: Oh! what without our Youth
  Would Love be! What would Youth be without Love!
Youth lends its joy, and sweetness, vigour, truth,
  Heart, soul, and all that seems as from above;
But, languishing with years, it grows uncouth —
  One of few things Experience don't improve;
Which is, perhaps, the reason why old fellows
Are always so preposterously jealous.

LVI

It was the Carnival, as I have said
  Some six and thirty stanzas back, and so
Laura the usual preparations made,
  Which you do when your mind's made up to go
To-night to Mrs. Boehm's masquerade,
  Spectator, or Partaker in the show;
The only difference known between the cases
Is — *here,* we have six weeks of "varnished faces."

LVII

Laura, when dressed, was (as I sang before)
  A pretty woman as was ever seen,
Fresh as the Angel o'er a new inn door,
  Or frontispiece of a new Magazine,
With all the fashions which the last month wore,
  Coloured, and silver paper leaved between
That and the title-page, for fear the Press
Should soil with parts of speech the parts of dress.

LVIII

They went to the Ridotto; 'tis a hall
  Where People dance, and sup, and dance again;

Its proper name, perhaps, were a masqued ball,
  But that's of no importance to my strain;
'Tis (on a smaller scale) like our Vauxhall,
  Excepting that it can't be spoit by rain;
The company is "mixed" (the phrase I quote is
As much as saying, they're below your notice);

LIX

For a "mixed company" implies that, save
  Yourself and friends, and half a hundred more,
Whom you may bow to without looking grave,
  The rest are but a vulgar set, the Bore
Of public places, where they basely brave
  The fashionable stare of twenty score
Of well-bred persons, called *"The World;"* but I,
Although I know them, really don't know why.

LX

This is the case in England; at least was
  During the dynasty of Dandies, now
Perchance succeeded by some other class
  Of imitated Imitators: — how
Irreparably soon decline, alas!
  The Demagogues of fashion: all below
Is frail; how easily the world is lost
By Love, or War, and, now and then, — by Frost!

LXI

Crushed was Napoleon by the northern Thor,
  Who knocked his army down with icy hammer,
Stopped by the *Elements* — like a Whaler — or
  A blundering novice in his new French grammar;
Good cause had he to doubt the chance of war,
  And as for Fortune — but I dare not d—n her,
Because, were I to ponder to Infinity,
The more I should believe in her Divinity.

LXII

She rules the present, past, and all to be yet,
  She gives us luck in lotteries, love, and marriage;
I cannot say that she's done much for me yet;
  Not that I mean her bounties to disparage,
We've not yet closed accounts, and we shall see yet
  How much she'll make amends for past miscarriage;

Meantime the Goddess I'll no more importune,
Unless to thank her when she's made my fortune.

LXIII

To turn, — and to return; — the Devil take it!
This story slips for ever through my fingers,
Because, just as the stanza likes to make it,
It needs must be — and so it rather lingers;
This form of verse began, I can't well break it,
But must keep time and tune like public singers;
But if I once get through my present measure,
I'll take another when I'm next at leisure.

LXIV

They went to the Ridotto ('tis a place
To which I mean to go myself to-morrow,
Just to divert my thoughts a little space
Because I'm rather hippish, and may borrow
Some spirits, guessing at what kind of face
May lurk beneath each mask; and as my sorrow
Slackens its pace sometimes, I'll make, or find,
Something shall leave it half an hour behind.)

LXV

Now Laura moves along the joyous crowd,
Smiles in her eyes, and simpers on her lips;
To some she whispers, others speaks aloud;
To some she curtsies, and to some she dips,
Complains of warmth, and this complaint avowed,
Her lover brings the lemonade, she sips;
She then surveys, condemns, but pities still
Her dearest friends for being dressed so ill.

LXVI

One has false curls, another too much paint,
A third — where did she buy that frightful turban?
A fourth's so pale she fears she's going to faint,
A fifth's look's vulgar, dowdyish, and suburban,
A sixth's white silk has got a yellow taint,
A seventh's thin muslim surely will be her bane,
And lo! an eighth appears, — "I'll see no more!"
For fear, like Banquo's kings, they reach a score.

LXVII

Meantime, while she was thus at others gazing,
  Others were levelling their looks at her;
She heard the men's half-whispered mode of praising
  And, till 'twas done, determined not to stir;
The women only thought it quite amazing
  That, at her time of life, so many were
Admirers still, — but "Men are so debased,
Those brazen Creatures always suit their taste."

LXVIII

For my part, now, I ne'er could understand
  Why naughty women — but I won't discuss
A thing which is a scandal to the land,
  I only don't see why it should be thus;
And if I were but in a gown and band,
  Just to entitle me to make a fuss,
I'd preach on this till Wilberforce and Romilly
Should quote in their next speeches from my homily.

LXIX

While Laura thus was seen, and seeing, smiling,
  Talking, she knew not why, and cared not what,
So that her female friends, with envy broiling,
  Beheld her airs, and triumph, and all that;
And well-dressed males still kept before her filing,
  And passing bowed and mingled with her chat;
More than the rest one person seemed to stare
With pertinacity that's rather rare.

LXX

He was a Turk, the colour of mahogany;
  And Laura saw him, and at first was glad,
Because the Turks so much admire philogyny,
  Although their usage of their wives is sad;
'Tis said they use no better than a dog any
  Poor woman, whom they purchase like a pad:
They have a number, though they ne'er exhibit 'em,
Four wives by law, and concubines "ad libitum."

LXXI

They lock them up, and veil, and guard them daily,
  They scarcely can behold their male relations,

So that their moments do not pass so gaily
 As is supposed the case with northern nations;
Confinement, too, must make them look quite palely;
 And as the Turks abhor long conversations,
Their days are either passed in doing nothing,
Or bathing, nursing, making love, and clothing.

LXXII

They cannot read, and so don't lisp in criticism;
 Nor write, and so they don't affect the Muse;
Were never caught in epigram or witticism,
 Have no romances, sermons, plays, reviews,—
In Harams learning soon would make a pretty schism,
 But luckily these Beauties are no "Blues;"
No bustling *Botherby* have they to show 'em
"That charming passage in the last new poem:"

LXXIII

No solemn, antique gentleman of rhyme,
 Who having angled all his life for Fame,
And getting but a nibble at a time,
 Still fussily keeps fishing on, the same
Small "Triton of the minnows," the sublime
 Of Mediocrity, the furious tame,
The Echo's echo, usher of the school
Of female wits, boy bards — in short, a fool!

LXXIV

A stalking oracle of awful phrase,
 The approving "*Good!*" (by no means GOOD in law)
Humming like flies around the newest blaze,
 The bluest of bluebottles you e'er saw,
Teasing with blame, excruciating with praise,
 Gorging the little fame he gets all raw,
Translating tongues he knows not even by letter,
And sweating plays so middling, bad were better.

LXXV

One hates an author that's *all author* — fellows
 In foolscap uniforms turned up with ink,
So very anxious, clever, fine, and jealous,
 One don't know what to say to them, or think,
Unless to puff them with a pair of bellows;

Of Coxcombry's worst coxcombs e'en the pink
Are preferable to these shreds of paper,
These unquenched snuffings of the midnight taper.

LXXVI

Of these same we see several, and of others,
Men of the world, who know the World like Men,
Scott, Rogers, Moore, and all the better brothers,
Who think of something else besides the pen;
But for the children of the "Mighty Mother's,"
The would-be wits, and can't-be gentlemen,
I leave them to their daily "tea is ready,"
Smug coterie, and literary lady.

LXXVII

The poor dear Mussul*women* whom I mention
Have none of these instructive pleasant people,
And *one* would seem to them a new invention,
Unknown as bells within a Turkish steeple;
I think 'twould almost be worth while to pension
(Though best-sown projects very often reap ill)
A missionary author — just to preach
Our Christian usage of the parts of speech.

LXXVIII

No Chemistry for them unfolds her gases,
No Metaphysics are let loose in lectures,
No Circulating Library amasses
Religious novels, moral tales, and strictures
Upon the living manners, as they pass us;
No Exhibition glares with annual pictures;
They stare not on the stars from out their attics,
Nor deal (thank God for that!) in Mathematics.

LXXIX

Why I thank God for that is not great matter,
I have my reasons, you no doubt suppose,
And as, perhaps, they would not highly flatter,
I'll keep them for my life (to come) in prose;
I fear I have a little turn for Satire,
And yet methinks the older that one grows
Inclines us more to laugh than scold, though Laughter
Leaves us so doubly serious shortly after.

LXXX

Oh, Mirth and Innocence! Oh, Milk and Water!
  Ye happy mixtures of more happy days!
In these sad centuries of sin and slaughter,
  Abominable Man no more allays
His thirst with such pure beverage. No matter,
  I love you both, and both shall have my praise:
Oh, for old Saturn's reign of sugar-candy! —
Meantime I drink to your return in brandy.

LXXXI

Our Laura's Turk still kept his eyes upon her,
  Less in the Mussulman than Christian way,
Which seems to say, "Madam, I do you honour,
  And while I please to stare, you'll please to stay."
Could staring win a woman, this had won her,
  But Laura could not thus be led astray;
She had stood fire too long and well, to boggle
Even at this Stranger's most outlandish ogle.

LXXXII

The morning now was on the point of breaking,
  A turn of time at which I would advise
Ladies who have been dancing, or partaking
  In any other kind of exercise,
To make their preparations for forsaking
  The ball-room ere the Sun begins to rise,
Because when once the lamps and candles fail,
His blushes make them look a little pale.

LXXXIII

I've seen some balls and revels in my time,
  And stayed them over for some silly reason,
And then I looked (I hope it was no crime)
  To see what lady best stood out the season;
And though I've seen some thousands in their prime
  Lovely and pleasing, and who still may please on,
I never saw but one (the stars withdrawn)
Whose bloom could after dancing dare the Dawn.

LXXXIV

The name of this Aurora I'll not mention,
  Although I might, for she was nought to me

More than that patent work of God's invention,
  A charming woman, whom we like to see;
But writing names would merit reprehension,
  Yet if you like to find out this fair *She*,
At the next London or Parisian ball
You still may mark her cheek, out-blooming all.

LXXXV

Laura, who knew it would not do at all
  To meet the daylight after seven hours' sitting
Among three thousand people at a ball,
  To make her curtsey thought it right and fitting;
The Count was at her elbow with her shawl,
  And they the room were on the point of quitting,
When lo! those curséd Gondoliers had got
Just in the very place where they *should not*.

LXXXVI

In this they're like our coachmen, and the cause
  Is much the same — the crowd, and pulling, hauling,
With blasphemies enough to break their jaws,
  They make a never intermitted bawling.
At home, our Bow-street gem'men keep the laws,
  And here a sentry stands within your calling;
But for all that, there is a deal of swearing,
And nauseous words past mentioning or bearing.

LXXXVII

The Count and Laura found their boat at last,
  And homeward floated o'er the silent tide,
Discussing all the dances gone and past;
  The dancers and their dresses, too, beside;
Some little scandals eke; but all aghast
  (As to their palace-stairs the rowers glide)
Sate Laura by the side of her adorer,
When lo! the Mussulman was there before her!

LXXXVIII

"Sir," said the Count, with brow exceeding grave,
  "Your unexpected presence here will make
It necessary for myself to crave
  Its import? But perhaps 'tis a mistake;
I hope it is so; and, at once to waive
  All compliment, I hope so for *your* sake;

You understand my meaning, or you *shall.*"
"Sir," (quoth the Turk) " 'tis no mistake at all:

LXXXIX

"That Lady is *my wife!*" Much wonder paints
  The lady's changing cheek, as well it might;
But where an Englishwoman sometimes faints,
  Italian females don't do so outright;
They only call a little on their Saints,
  And then come to themselves, almost, or quite;
Which saves much hartshorn, salts, and sprinkling faces,
And cutting stays, as usual in such cases.

XC

She said, — what could she say? Why, not a word;
  But the Count courteously invited in
The Stranger, much appeased by what he heard:
  "Such things, perhaps, we'd best discuss within,"
Said he; "don't let us make ourselves absurd
  In public, by a scene, nor raise a din,
For then the chief and only satisfaction
Will be much quizzing on the whole transaction."

XCI

They entered, and for Coffee called — it came,
  A beverage for Turks and Christians both,
Although the way they make it's not the same.
  Now Laura, much recovered, or less loth
To speak, cries "Beppo! what's your pagan name?
  Bless me! your beard is of amazing growth!
And how came you to keep away so long?
Are you not sensible 'twas very wrong?

XCII

"And are you *really, truly,* now a Turk?
  With any other women did you wive?
Is't true they use their fingers for a fork?
  Well, that's the prettiest Shawl — as I'm alive!
You'll give it me? They say you eat no pork.
  And how so many years did you contrive
To — Bless me! did I ever? No, I never
Saw a man grown so yellow! How's your liver?

XCIII

"Beppo! that beard of yours becomes you not;
It shall be shaved before you're a day older:
Why do you wear it? Oh! I had forgot —
Pray don't you think the weather here is colder?
How do I look? You shan't stir from this spot
In that queer dress, for fear that some beholder
Should find you out, and make the story known.
How short your hair is! Lord! how grey it's grown!"

XCIV

What answer Beppo made to these demands
Is more than I know. He was cast away
About where Troy stood once, and nothing stands;
Became a slave of course, and for his pay
Had bread and bastinadoes, till some bands
Of pirates landing in a neighbouring bay,
He joined the rogues and prospered, and became
A renegado of indifferent fame.

XCV

But he grew rich, and with his riches grew so
Keen the desire to see his home again,
He thought himself in duty bound to do so,
And not be always thieving on the main;
Lonely he felt, at times, as Robin Crusoe,
And so he hired a vessel come from Spain,
Bound for Corfu: she was a fine polacca,
Manned with twelve hands, and laden with tobacco.

XCVI

Himself, and much (heaven knows how gotten!) cash,
He then embarked, with risk of life and limb,
And got clear off, although the attempt was rash;
He said that *Providence* protected him —
For my part, I say nothing — lest we clash
In our opinions: — well — the ship was trim,
Set sail, and kept her reckoning fairly on,
Except three days of calm when off Cape Bonn.

XCVII

They reached the Island, he transferred his lading,
And self and live stock to another bottom,

And passed for a true Turkey-merchant, trading
  With goods of various names — but I've forgot 'em.
However, he got off by this evading,
  Or else the people would perhaps have shot him;
And thus at Venice landed to reclaim
His wife, religion, house, and Christian name.

XCVIII

His wife received, the Patriarch re-baptised him,
  (He made the Church a present, by the way;)
He then threw off the garments which disguised him,
  And borrowed the Count's smallclothes for a day:
His friends the more for his long absence prized him,
  Finding he'd wherewithal to make them gay,
With dinners, where he oft became the laugh of them,
For stories — but *I* don't believe the half of them.

XCIX

Whate'er his youth had suffered, his old age
  With wealth and talking made him some amends;
Though Laura sometimes put him in a rage,
  I've heard the Count and he were always friends.
My pen is at the bottom of a page,
  Which being finished, here the story ends:
'Tis to be wished it had been sooner done,
But stories somehow lengthen when begun.

MAZEPPA

I

'Twas after dread Pultowa's day,
  When Fortune left the royal Swede —
Around a slaughtered army lay,
  No more to combat and to bleed.
The power and glory of the war,
  Faithless as their vain votaries, men,
Had passed to the triumphant Czar,
  And Moscow's walls were safe again —
Until a day more dark and drear,
And a more memorable year,
Should give to slaughter and to shame
A mightier host and haughtier name;
A greater wreck, a deeper fall,
A shock to one — a thunderbolt to all.

II

Such was the hazard of the die;
The wounded Charles was taught to fly
By day and night through field and flood,
Stained with his own and subjects' blood;
For thousands fell that flight to aid:
And not a voice was heard to upbraid
Ambition in his humbled hour,
When Truth had nought to dread from Power.
His horse was slain, and Gieta gave
His own — and died the Russians' slave.
This, too, sinks after many a league
Of well-sustained, but vain fatigue;
And in the depth of forests darkling,
The watch-fires in the distance sparkling —
The beacons of surrounding foes —
A King must lay his limbs at length.
Are these the laurels and repose
For which the nations strain their strength?
They laid him by a savage tree,
In outworn Nature's agony;
His wounds were stiff, his limbs were stark;
The heavy hour was chill and dark;
The fever in his blood forbade
A transient slumber's fitful aid:
And thus it was; but yet through all,
Kinglike the monarch bore his fall,
And made, in this extreme of ill,
His pangs the vassals of his will:
All silent and subdued were they,
As once the nations round him lay.

III

A band of chiefs! — alas! how few,
Since but the fleeting of a day
Had thinned it; but this wreck was true
And chivalrous: upon the clay
Each sate him down, all sad and mute,
Beside his monarch and his steed;
For danger levels man and brute,
And all are fellows in their need.
Among the rest, Mazeppa made
His pillow in an old oak's shade —
Himself as rough, and scarce less old,
The Ukraine's Hetman, calm and bold;
But first, outspent with this long course,

The Cossack prince rubbed down his horse,
And made for him a leafy bed,
  And smoothed his fetlocks and his mane,
  And slacked his girth, and stripped his rein,
And joyed to see how well he fed;
For until now he had the dread
His wearied courser might refuse
To browse beneath the midnight dews:
But he was hardy as his lord,
And little cared for bed and board;
But spirited and docile too,
Whate'er was to be done, would do.
Shaggy and swift, and strong of limb,
All Tartar-like he carried him;
Obeyed his voice, and came to call,
And knew him in the midst of all:
Though thousands were around, — and Night,
Without a star, pursued her flight, —
That steed from sunset until dawn
His chief would follow like a fawn.

IV

This done, Mazeppa spread his cloak,
And laid his lance beneath his oak,
Felt if his arms in order good
The long day's march had well withstood —
If still the powder filled the pan,
  And flints unloosened kept their lock —
His sabre's hilt and scabbard felt,
And whether they had chafed his belt;
And next the venerable man,
From out his havresack and can,
  Prepared and spread his slender stock;
And to the Monarch and his men
The whole or portion offered then
With far less of inquietude
Than courtiers at a banquet would.
And Charles of this his slender share
With smiles partook a moment there,
To force of cheer a greater show,
And seem above both wounds and woe; —
And then he said — "Of all our band,
Though firm of heart and strong of hand,
In skirmish, march, or forage, none
Can less have said or more have done
Than thee, Mazeppa! On the earth

So fit a pair had never birth,
Since Alexander's days till now,
As thy Bucephalus and thou:
All Scythia's fame to thine should yield
For pricking on o'er flood and field."
Mazeppa answered — "Ill betide
The school wherein I learned to ride!"
Quoth Charles — "Old Hetman, wherefore so,
Since thou hast learned the art so well?"
Mazeppa said — " 'Twere long to tell;
And we have many a league to go,
With every now and then a blow,
And ten to one at least the foe,
Before our steeds may graze at ease,
Beyond the swift Borysthenes:
And, Sire, your limbs have need of rest,
And I will be the sentinel
Of this your troop." — "But I request,"
Said Sweden's monarch, "thou wilt tell
This tale of thine, and I may reap,
Perchance, from this the boon of sleep;
For at this moment from my eyes
The hope of present slumber flies."

"Well, Sire, with such a hope, I'll track
My seventy years of memory back:
I think 'twas in my twentieth spring, —
Aye 'twas, — when Casimir was king —
John Casimir, — I was his page
Six summers, in my earlier age:
A learnéd monarch, faith! was he,
And most unlike your Majesty;
He made no wars, and did not gain
New realms to lose them back again;
And (save debates in Warsaw's diet)
He reigned in most unseemly quiet;
Not that he had no cares to vex;
He loved the Muses and the Sex;
And sometimes these so froward are,
They made him wish himself at war;
But soon his wrath being o'er, he took
Another mistress — or new book:
And then he gave prodigious fêtes —
All Warsaw gathered round his gates
To gaze upon his splendid court,
And dames, and chiefs, of princely port.
He was the Polish Solomon.

So sung his poets, all but one,
Who, being unpensioned, made a satire,
And boasted that he could not flatter.
It was a court of jousts and mimes,
Where every courtier tried at rhymes;
Even I for once produced some verses,
And signed my odes 'Despairing Thyrsis.'
There was a certain Palatine,
   A Count of far and high descent,
Rich as a salt or silver mine;
And he was proud, ye may divine,
   As if from Heaven he had been sent;
He had such wealth in blood and ore
   As few could match beneath the throne;
And he would gaze upon his store,
And o'er his pedigree would pore,
Until by some confusion led,
Which almost looked like want of head,
   He thought their merits were his own.
His wife was not of this opinion;
   His junior she by thirty years,
Grew daily tired of his dominion;
   And, after wishes, hopes, and fears,
   To Virtue a few farewell tears,
A restless dream or two — some glances
At Warsaw's youth — some songs, and dances,
Awaited but the usual chances,
Those happy accidents which render
The coldest dames so very tender,
To deck her Count with titles given,
'Tis said, as passports into Heaven;
But, strange to say, they rarely boast
Of these, who have deserved them most.

v

"I was a goodly stripling then;
   At seventy years I so may say,
That there were few, or boys or men,
   Who, in my dawning time of day,
Of vassal or of knight's degree,
Could vie in vanities with me;
For I had strength — youth — gaiety,
A port, not like to this ye see,
But smooth, as all is rugged now;
   For Time, and Care, and War, have ploughed
My very soul from out my brow;

And thus I should be disavowed
By all my kind and kin, could they
Compare my day and yesterday;
This change was wrought, too, long ere age
Had ta'en my features for his page:
With years, ye know, have not declined
My strength — my courage — or my mind,
Or at this hour I should not be
Telling old tales beneath a tree,
With starless skies my canopy.
But let me on: Theresa's form —
Methinks it glides before me now,
Between me and yon chestnut's bough,
The memory is so quick and warm;
And yet I find no words to tell
The shape of her I loved so well:
She had the Asiatic eye,
Such as our Turkish neighbourhood
Hath mingled with our Polish blood,
Dark as above us is the sky;
But through it stole a tender light,
Like the first moonrise of midnight;
Large, dark, and swimming in the stream,
Which seemed to melt to its own beam;
All love, half languor, and half fire,
Like saints that at the stake expire,
And lift their raptured looks on high,
As though it were a joy to die.
A brow like a midsummer lake,
Transparent with the sun therein,
When waves no murmur dare to make,
And heaven beholds her face within.
A cheek and lip — but why proceed?
I loved her then, I love her still;
And such as I am, love indeed
In fierce extremes — in good and ill.
But still we love even in our rage,
And haunted to our very age
With the vain shadow of the past, —
As is Mazeppa to the last.

VI

"We met — we gazed — I saw, and sighed;
She did not speak, and yet replied;
There are ten thousand tones and signs
We hear and see, but none defines —

Involuntary sparks of thought,
Which strike from out the heart o'erwrought,
And form a strange intelligence,
Alike mysterious and intense,
Which link the burning chain that binds,
Without their will, young hearts and minds;
Conveying, as the electric wire,
We know not how, the absorbing fire.
I saw, and sighed — in silence wept,
And still reluctant distance kept,
Until I was made known to her,
And we might then and there confer
Without suspicion — then, even then,
  I longed, and was resolved to speak;
But on my lips they died again,
  The accents tremulous and weak,
Until one hour. — There is a game,
  A frivolous and foolish play,
  Wherewith we while away the day;
It is — I have forgot the name —
And we to this, it seems, were set,
By some strange chance, which I forget:
I recked not if I won or lost,
  It was enough for me to be
  So near to hear, and oh! to see
The being whom I loved the most.
I watched her as a sentinel,
(May ours this dark night watch as well!)
  Until I saw, and thus it was,
That she was pensive, nor perceived
Her occupation, nor was grieved
Nor glad to lose or gain; but still
Played on for hours, as if her will
Yet bound her to the place, though not
That hers might be the winning lot.
  Then through my brain the thought did pass,
Even as a flash of lightning there,
That there was something in her air
Which would not doom me to despair;
And on the thought my words broke forth,
  All incoherent as they were;
Their eloquence was little worth,
But yet she listened — 'tis enough —
  Who listens once will listen twice;
  Her heart, be sure, is not of ice —
And one refusal no rebuff.

VII

"I loved, and was beloved again —
They tell me, Sire, you never knew
Those gentle frailties; if 'tis true,
I shorten all my joy or pain;
To you 'twould seem absurd as vain;
But all men are not born to reign,
Or o'er their passions, or as you
Thus o'er themselves and nations too.
I am — or rather *was* — a Prince,
A chief of thousands, and could lead
Them on where each would foremost bleed;
But could not o'er myself evince
The like control — But to resume:
I loved, and was beloved again;
In sooth, it is a happy doom,
But yet where happiest ends in pain. —
We met in secret, and the hour
Which led me to that lady's bower
Was fiery Expectation's dower.
My days and nights were nothing — all
Except that hour which doth recall,
In the long lapse from youth to age,
No other like itself: I'd give
The Ukraine back again to live
It o'er once more, and be a page,
The happy page, who was the lord
Of one soft heart, and his own sword,
And had no other gem nor wealth,
Save Nature's gift of Youth and Health.
We met in secret — doubly sweet,
Some say, they find it so to meet;
I know not that — I would have given
My life but to have called her mine
In the full view of Earth and Heaven;
For I did oft and long repine
That we could only meet by stealth.

VIII

"For lovers there are many eyes,
And such there were on us; the Devil
On such occasions should be civil —
The Devil! — I'm loth to do him wrong,
It might be some untoward saint,
Who would not be at rest too long,

But to his pious bile gave vent —
But one fair night, some lurking spies
Surprised and seized us both.
The Count was something more than wroth —
I was unarmed; but if in steel,
All cap-à-pie from head to heel,
What 'gainst their numbers could I do?
'Twas near his castle, far away
From city or from succour near,
And almost on the break of day;
I did not think to see another,
My moments seemed reduced to few;
And with one prayer to Mary Mother,
And, it may be, a saint or two,
As I resigned me to my fate,
They led me to the castle gate:
Theresa's doom I never knew,
Our lot was henceforth separate.
An angry man, ye may opine,
Was he, the proud Count Palatine;
And he had reason good to be,
But he was most enraged lest such
An accident should chance to touch
Upon his future pedigree;
Nor less amazed, that such a blot
His noble 'scutcheon should have got,
While he was highest of his line;
Because unto himself he seemed
The first of men, nor less he deemed
In others' eyes, and most in mine.
'Sdeath! with a *page* — perchance a king
Had reconciled him to the thing;
But with a stripling of a page —
I felt — but cannot paint his rage.

IX

" 'Bring forth the horse!' — the horse was brought!
In truth, he was a noble steed,
A Tartar of the Ukraine breed,
Who looked as though the speed of thought
Were in his limbs; but he was wild,
Wild as the wild deer, and untaught,
With spur and bridle undefiled —
'Twas but a day he had been caught;
And snorting, with erected mane,
And struggling fiercely, but in vain,

In the full foam of wrath and dread
To me the desert-born was led:
They bound me on, that menial throng,
Upon his back with many a thong;
They loosed him with a sudden lash —
Away! — away! — and on we dash! —
Torrents less rapid and less rash.

X

"Away! — away! — My breath was gone,
I saw not where he hurried on:
'Twas scarcely yet the break of day,
And on he foamed — away! — away!
The last of human sounds which rose,
As I was darted from my foes,
Was the wild shout of savage laughter,
Which on the wind came roaring after
A moment from that rabble rout:
With sudden wrath I wrenched my head,
  And snapped the cord, which to the mane
  Had bound my neck in lieu of rein,
And, writhing half my form about,
Howled back my curse; but 'midst the tread,
The thunder of my courser's speed,
Perchance they did not hear nor heed:
It vexes me — for I would fain
Have paid their insult back again.
I paid it well in after days:
There is not of that castle gate,
Its drawbridge and portcullis' weight,
Stone — bar — moat — bridge — or barrier left;
Nor of its fields a blade of grass,
  Save what grows on a ridge of wall,
  Where stood the hearth-stone of the hall;
And many a time ye there might pass,
Nor dream that e'er the fortress was.
I saw its turrets in a blaze,
Their crackling battlements all cleft,
  And the hot lead pour down like rain
From off the scorched and blackening roof,
Whose thickness was not vengeance-proof.
  They little thought that day of pain,
When launched, as on the lightning's flash,
They bade me to destruction dash,
  That one day I should come again,
With twice five thousand horse, to thank

The Count for his uncourteous ride.
They played me then a bitter prank,
When, with the wild horse for my guide,
They bound me to his foaming flank:
At length I played them one as frank —
For Time at last sets all things even —
And if we do but watch the hour,
There never yet was human power
Which could evade, if unforgiven,
The patient search and vigil long
Of him who treasures up a wrong.

XI

"Away! — away! — my steed and I,
Upon the pinions of the wind!
All human dwellings left behind,
We sped like meteors through the sky,
When with its crackling sound the night
Is chequered with the Northern light.
Town — village — none were on our track,
But a wild plain of far extent,
And bounded by a forest black;
And, save the scarce seen battlement
On distant heights of some strong hold,
Against the Tartars built of old,
No trace of man. The year before
A Turkish army had marched o'er;
And where the Spahi's hoof hath trod,
The verdure flies the bloody sod:
The sky was dull, and dim, and gray,
And a low breeze crept moaning by —
I could have answered with a sigh —
But fast we fled, — away! — away! —
And I could neither sigh nor pray;
And my cold sweat-drops fell like rain
Upon the courser's bristling mane;
But, snorting still with rage and fear,
He flew upon his far career:
At times I almost thought, indeed,
He must have slackened in his speed;
But no — my bound and slender frame
Was nothing to his angry might,
And merely like a spur became:
Each motion which I made to free
My swoln limbs from their agony
Increased his fury and affright:

I tried my voice, — 'twas faint and low —
But yet he swerved as from a blow;
And, starting to each accent, sprang
As from a sudden trumpet's clang:
Meantime my cords were wet with gore,
Which, oozing through my limbs, ran o'er;
And in my tongue the thirst became
A something fierier far than flame.

XII

"We neared the wild wood — 'twas so wide,
I saw no bounds on either side:
'Twas studded with old sturdy trees,
That bent not to the roughest breeze
Which howls down from Siberia's waste,
And strips the forest in its haste, —
But these were few and far between,
Set thick with shrubs more young and green,
Luxuriant with their annual leaves,
Ere strown by those autumnal eves
That nip the forest's foliage dead,
Discoloured with a lifeless red,
Which stands thereon like stiffened gore
Upon the slain when battle's o'er;
And some long winter's night hath shed
Its frost o'er every tombless head —
So cold and stark — the raven's beak
May peck unpierced each frozen cheek:
'Twas a wild waste of underwood,
And here and there a chestnut stood,
The strong oak, and the hardy pine;
   But far apart — and well it were,
Or else a different lot were mine —
   The boughs gave way, and did not tear
My limbs; and I found strength to bear
My wounds, already scarred with cold;
My bonds forbade to loose my hold.
We rustled through the leaves like wind, —
Left shrubs, and trees, and wolves behind;
By night I heard them on the track,
Their troop came hard upon our back,
With their long gallop, which can tire
The hound's deep hate, and hunter's fire:
Where'er we flew they followed on,
Nor left us with the morning sun;
Behind I saw them, scarce a rood,

At day-break winding through the wood,
And through the night had heard their feet
Their stealing, rustling step repeat.
Oh! how I wished for spear or sword,
At least to die amidst the horde,
And perish — if it must be so —
At bay, destroying many a foe!
When first my courser's race begun,
I wished the goal already won;
But now I doubted strength and speed:
Vain doubt! his swift and savage breed
Had nerved him like the mountain-roe —
Nor faster falls the blinding snow
Which whelms the peasant near the door
Whose threshold he shall cross no more,
Bewildered with the dazzling blast,
Than through the forest-paths he passed —
Untired, untamed, and worse than wild —
All furious as a favoured child
Balked of its wish; or — fiercer still —
A woman piqued — who has her will!

XIII

"The wood was passed; 'twas more than noon,
But chill the air, although in June;
Or it might be my veins ran cold —
Prolonged endurance tames the bold;
And I was then not what I seem,
But headlong as a wintry stream,
And wore my feelings out before
I well could count their causes o'er:
And what with fury, fear, and wrath,
The tortures which beset my path —
Cold — hunger — sorrow — shame — distress —
Thus bound in Nature's nakedness;
Sprung from a race whose rising blood
When stirred beyond its calmer mood,
And trodden hard upon, is like
The rattle-snake's, in act to strike —
What marvel if this worn-out trunk
Beneath its woes a moment sunk?
The earth gave way, the skies rolled round,
I seemed to sink upon the ground;
But erred — for I was fastly bound.
My heart turned sick, my brain grew sore,
And throbbed awhile, then beat no more:

The skies spun like a mighty wheel;
I saw the trees like drunkards reel,
And a slight flash sprang o'er my eyes,
Which saw no farther. He who dies
Can die no more than then I died,
O'ertortured by that ghastly ride.
I felt the blackness come and go,
  And strove to wake; but could not make
My senses climb up from below:
I felt as on a plank at sea,
When all the waves that dash o'er thee,
At the same time upheave and whelm,
And hurl thee towards a desert realm.
My undulating life was as
The fancied lights that flitting pass
Our shut eyes in deep midnight, when
Fever begins upon the brain;
But soon it passed, with little pain,
  But a confusion worse than such:
  I own that I should deem it much,
Dying, to feel the same again;
And yet I do suppose we must
Feel far more ere we turn to dust!
No matter! I have bared my brow
Full in Death's face — before — and now.

XIV

"My thoughts came back. Where was I? Cold,
  And numb, and giddy: pulse by pulse
Life reassumed its lingering hold,
And throb by throb, — till grown a pang
  Which for a moment would convulse,
  My blood reflowed, though thick and chill;
My ear with uncouth noises rang,
  My heart began once more to thrill;
My sight returned, though dim; alas!
And thickened, as it were, with glass.
Methought the dash of waves was nigh;
There was a gleam too of the sky,
Studded with stars; — it is no dream;
The wild horse swims the wilder stream!
The bright broad river's gushing tide
Sweeps, winding onward, far and wide,
And we are half-way, struggling o'er
To yon unknown and silent shore.
The waters broke my hollow trance,

And with a temporary strength
   My stiffened limbs were rebaptized.
My courser's broad breast proudly braves,
And dashes off the ascending waves,
And onward we advance!
We reach the slippery shore at length,
   A haven I but little prized,
For all behind was dark and drear,
And all before was night and fear.
How many hours of night or day
In those suspended pangs I lay,
I could not tell; I scarcely knew
If this were human breath I drew.

XV

"With glossy skin, and dripping mane,
   And reeling limbs, and reeking flank,
The wild steed's sinewy nerves still strain
   Up the repelling bank.
We gain the top: a boundless plain
Spreads through the shadow of the night,
   And onward, onward, onward — seems,
   Like precipices in our dreams,
To stretch beyond the sight;
And here and there a speck of white,
   Or scattered spot of dusky green,
In masses broke into the light,
And rose the moon upon my right:
   But nought distinctly seen
In the dim waste would indicate
The omen of a cottage gate;
No twinkling taper from afar
Stood like a hospitable star;
Not even an ignis-fatuus rose
To make him merry with my woes:
   That very cheat had cheered me then!
Although detected, welcome still,
Reminding me, through every ill,
   Of the abodes of men.

XVI

"Onward we went — but slack and slow;
   His savage force at length o'erspent,
The drooping courser, faint and low,
   All feebly foaming went:

A sickly infant had had power
To guide him forward in that hour!
  But, useless all to me,
His new-born tameness nought availed —
My limbs were bound; my force had failed,
  Perchance, had they been free.
With feeble effort still I tried
To rend the bonds so starkly tied,
  But still it was in vain;
My limbs were only wrung the more,
And soon the idle strife gave o'er,
  Which but prolonged their pain.
The dizzy race seemed almost done,
Although no goal was nearly won:
Some streaks announced the coming sun —
  How slow, alas! he came!
Methought that mist of dawning gray
Would never dapple into day,
How heavily it rolled away!
  Before the eastern flame
Rose crimson, and deposed the stars,
And called the radiance from their cars,
And filled the earth, from his deep throne,
With lonely lustre, all his own.

XVII

"Uprose the sun; the mists were curled
Back from the solitary world
Which lay around — behind — before.
What booted it to traverse o'er
Plain — forest — river? Man nor brute,
Nor dint of hoof, nor print of foot,
Lay in the wild luxuriant soil —
No sign of travel, none of toil —
The very air was mute:
And not an insect's shrill small horn,
Nor matin bird's new voice was borne
From herb nor thicket. Many a *werst*,
Panting as if his heart would burst,
The weary brute still staggered on;
And still we were — or seemed — alone:
At length, while reeling on our way,
Methought I heard a courser neigh,
From out yon tuft of blackening firs.
Is it the wind those branches stirs?
No, no! from out the forest prance

  A trampling troop; I see them come!
In one vast squadron they advance!
  I strove to cry — my lips were dumb!
The steeds rush on in plunging pride;
But where are they the reins to guide?
A thousand horse, and none to ride!
With flowing tail, and flying mane,
Wide nostrils never stretched by pain,
Mouths bloodless to the bit or rein,
And feet that iron never shod,
And flanks unscarred by spur or rod,
A thousand horse, the wild, the free,
Like waves that follow o'er the sea,
    Came thickly thundering on,
As if our faint approach to meet!
The sight re-nerved my courser's feet,
A moment staggering, feebly fleet,
A moment, with a faint low neigh,
  He answered, and then fell!
With gasps and glazing eyes he lay,
  And reeking limbs immoveable,
    His first and last career is done!
On came the troop — they saw him stoop,
  They saw me strangely bound along
  His back with many a bloody thong.
They stop — they start — they snuff the air,
Gallop a moment here and there,
Approach, retire, wheel round and round,
Then plunging back with sudden bound,
Headed by one black mighty steed,
Who seemed the Patriarch of his breed,
  Without a single speck or hair
Of white upon his shaggy hide;
They snort — they foam — neigh — swerve aside,
And backward to the forest fly,
By instinct, from a human eye.
  They left me there to my despair,
Linked to the dead and stiffening wretch,
Whose lifeless limbs beneath me stretch,
Relieved from that unwonted weight,
From whence I could not extricate
Nor him nor me — and there we lay,
  The dying on the dead!
I little deemed another day
  Would see my houseless, helpless head.

"And there from morn to twilight bound,
I felt the heavy hours toil round,

With just enough of life to see
My last of suns go down on me,
In hopeless certainty of mind,
That makes us feel at length resigned
To that which our foreboding years
Present the worst and last of fears:
Inevitable — even a boon,
Nor more unkind for coming soon,
Yet shunned and dreaded with such care,
As if it only were a snare
  That Prudence might escape:
At times both wished for and implored,
At times sought with self-pointed sword,
Yet still a dark and hideous close
To even intolerable woes,
  And welcome in no shape.
And, strange to say, the sons of pleasure,
They who have revelled beyond measure
In beauty, wassail, wine, and treasure,
Die calm, or calmer, oft than he
Whose heritage was Misery.
For he who hath in turn run through
All that was beautiful and new,
  Hath nought to hope, and nought to leave;
And, save the future, (which is viewed
Not quite as men are base or good,
But as their nerves may be endued,)
  With nought perhaps to grieve:
The wretch still hopes his woes must end,
And Death, whom he should deem his friend,
Appears, to his distempered eyes,
Arrived to rob him of his prize,
The tree of his new Paradise.
To-morrow would have given him all,
Repaid his pangs, repaired his fall;
To-morrow would have been the first
Of days no more deplored or curst,
But bright, and long, and beckoning years,
Seen dazzling through the mist of tears,
Guerdon of many a painful hour;
To-morrow would have given him power
To rule — to shine — to smite — to save —
And must it dawn upon his grave?

XVIII

"The sun was sinking — still I lay
  Chained to the chill and stiffening steed!

I thought to mingle there our clay;
  And my dim eyes of death had need,
  No hope arose of being freed.
I cast my last looks up the sky,
  And there between me and the sun
I saw the expecting raven fly,
Who scarce would wait till both should die,
  Ere his repast begun;
He flew, and perched, then flew once more,
And each time nearer than before;
I saw his wing through twilight flit,
And once so near me he alit
  I could have smote, but lacked the strength;
But the slight motion of my hand,
And feeble scratching of the sand,
The exerted throat's faint struggling noise,
Which scarcely could be called a voice,
  Together scared him off at length.
I know no more — my latest dream
  Is something of a lovely star
  Which fixed my dull eyes from afar,
And went and came with wandering beam,
And of the cold — dull — swimming — dense
Sensation of recurring sense,
And then subsiding back to death,
And then again a little breath,
A little thrill — a short suspense,
  An icy sickness curdling o'er
My heart, and sparks that crossed my brain —
A gasp — a throb — a start of pain,
  A sigh — and nothing more.

XIX

"I woke — where was I? — Do I see
A human face look down on me?
And doth a roof above me close?
Do these limbs on a couch repose?
Is this a chamber where I lie?
And is it mortal yon bright eye,
That watches me with gentle glance?
  I closed my own again once more,
As doubtful that my former trance
  Could not as yet be o'er.
A slender girl, long-haired, and tall,
Sate watching by the cottage wall.
The sparkle of her eye I caught,
Even with my first return of thought;

For ever and anon she threw
   A prying, pitying glance on me
   With her black eyes so wild and free:
I gazed, and gazed, until I knew
   No vision it could be, —
But that I lived, and was released
From adding to the vulture's feast:
And when the Cossack maid beheld
My heavy eyes at length unsealed,
She smiled — and I essayed to speak,
   But failed — and she approached, and made
   With lip and finger signs that said,
I must not strive as yet to break
The silence, till my strength should be
Enough to leave my accents free;
And then her hand on mine she laid,
And smoothed the pillow for my head,
And stole along on tiptoe tread,
   And gently oped the door, and spake
In whispers — ne'er was voice so sweet!
Even music followed her light feet.
   But those she called were not awake,
And she went forth; but, ere she passed,
Another look on me she cast,
   Another sign she made, to say,
That I had nought to fear, that all
Were near, at my command or call,
   And she would not delay
Her due return: — while she was gone,
Methought I felt too much alone.

XX

"She came with mother and with sire —
What need of more? — I will not tire
With long recital of the rest,
Since I became the Cossack's guest.
They found me senseless on the plain,
   They bore me to the nearest hut,
They brought me into life again —
Me — one day o'er their realm to reign!
   Thus the vain fool who strove to glut
His rage, refining on my pain,
   Sent me forth to the wilderness,
Bound — naked — bleeding — and alone,
To pass the desert to a throne, —
   What mortal his own doom may guess?
   Let none despond, let none despair!

To-morrow the Borysthenes
May see our coursers graze at ease
Upon his Turkish bank, — and never
Had I such welcome for a river
  As I shall yield when safely there.
Comrades, good night!" — The Hetman threw
  His length beneath the oak-tree shade,
  With leafy couch already made —
A bed nor comfortless nor new
To him, who took his rest whene'er
The hour arrived, no matter where:
  His eyes the hastening slumbers steep.
And if ye marvel Charles forgot
To thank his tale, *he* wondered not, —
  The King had been an hour asleep!

THE PROPHECY OF DANTE

"'T is the sunset of life gives me mystical lore,
And coming events cast their shadows before."

CAMPBELL

DEDICATION

LADY! if for the cold and cloudy clime
  Where I was born, but where I would not die,
  Of the great Poet-Sire of Italy
I dare to build the imitative rhyme,
Harsh Runic copy of the South's sublime,
  THOU art the cause; and howsoever I
  Fall short of his immortal harmony,
Thy gentle heart will pardon me the crime.
Thou, in the pride of Beauty and of Youth,
  Spakest; and for thee to speak and be obeyed
Are one; but only in the sunny South
  Such sounds are uttered, and such charms displayed,
So sweet a language from so fair a mouth —
  Ah! to what effort would it not persuade?

CANTO THE FIRST

ONCE more in Man's frail world! which I had left
  So long that 'twas forgotten; and I feel

The weight of clay again, — too soon bereft
Of the Immortal Vision which could heal
My earthly sorrows, and to God's own skies
Lift me from that deep Gulf without repeal,
Where late my ears rung with the damned cries
Of Souls in hopeless bale; and from that place
Of lesser torment, whence men may arise
Pure from the fire to join the Angelic race;
Midst whom my own bright Beatricē blessed
My spirit with her light; and to the base
Of the Eternal Triad! first, last, best,
Mysterious, three, sole, infinite, great God!
Soul universal! led the mortal guest,
Unblasted by the Glory, though he trod
From star to star to reach the almighty throne.
Oh Beatricē! whose sweet limbs the sod
So long hath pressed, and the cold marble stone,
Thou sole pure Seraph of my earliest love,
Love so ineffable, and so alone,
That nought on earth could more my bosom move,
And meeting thee in Heaven was but to meet
That without which my Soul, like the arkless dove,
Had wandered still in search of, nor her feet
Relieved her wing till found; without thy light
My Paradise had still been incomplete.
Since my tenth sun gave summer to my sight
Thou wert my Life, the Essence of my thought,
Loved ere I knew the name of Love, and bright
Still in these dim old eyes, now overwrought
With the World's war, and years, and banishment,
And tears for thee, by other woes untaught;
For mine is not a nature to be bent
By tyrannous faction, and the brawling crowd,
And though the long, long conflict hath been spent
In vain, — and never more, save when the cloud
Which overhangs the Apennine my mind's eye
Pierces to fancy Florence, once so proud
Of me, can I return, though but to die,
Unto my native soil, — they have not yet
Quenched the old exile's spirit, stern and high.
But the Sun, though not overcast, must set
And the night cometh; I am old in days,
And deeds, and contemplation, and have met
Destruction face to face in all his ways.
The World hath left me, what it found me, pure,
And if I have not gathered yet its praise,
I sought it not by any baser lure;

Man wrongs, and Time avenges, and my name
May form a monument not all obscure,
Though such was not my Ambition's end or aim,
To add to the vain-glorious list of those
Who dabble in the pettiness of fame,
And make men's fickle breath the wind that blows
Their sail, and deem it glory to be classed
With conquerors, and Virtue's other foes,
In bloody chronicles of ages past.
I would have had my Florence great and free;
Oh Florence! Florence! unto me thou wast
Like that Jerusalem which the Almighty He
Wept over, "but thou wouldst not;" as the bird
Gathers its young, I would have gathered thee
Beneath a parent pinion, hadst thou heard
My voice; but as the adder, deaf and fierce,
Against the breast that cherished thee was stirred
Thy venom, and my state thou didst amerce,
And doom this body forfeit to the fire.
Alas! how bitter is his country's curse
To him who *for* that country would expire,
But did not merit to expire *by* her,
And loves her, loves her even in her ire.
The day may come when she will cease to err,
The day may come she would be proud to have
The dust she dooms to scatter, and transfer
Of him, whom she denied a home, the grave.
But this shall not be granted; let my dust
Lie where it falls; nor shall the soil which gave
Me breath, but in her sudden fury thrust
Me forth to breathe elsewhere, so reassume
My indignant bones, because her angry gust
Forsooth is over, and repealed her doom;
No, — she denied me what was mine — my roof,
And shall not have what is not hers — my tomb.
Too long her armèd wrath hath kept aloof
The breast which would have bled for her, the heart
That beat, the mind that was temptation proof,
The man who fought, toiled, travelled, and each part
Of a true citizen fulfilled, and saw
For his reward the Guelf's ascendant art
Pass his destruction even into a law.
These things are not made for forgetfulness,
Florence shall be forgotten first; too raw
The wound, too deep the wrong, and the distress
Of such endurance too prolonged to make
My pardon greater, her injustice less,

Though late repented; yet — yet for her sake
  I feel some fonder yearnings, and for thine,
  My own Beatricē, I would hardly take
Vengeance upon the land which once was mine,
  And still is hallowed by thy dust's return,
  Which would protect the murderess like a shrine,
And save ten thousand foes by thy sole urn.
  Though, like old Marius from Minturnæ's marsh
  And Carthage ruins, my lone breast may burn
At times with evil feelings hot and harsh,
  And sometimes the last pangs of a vile foe
  Writhe in a dream before me, and o'erarch
My brow with hopes of triumph, — let them go!
  Such are the last infirmities of those
  Who long have suffered more than mortal woe,
And yet being mortal still, have no repose
  But on the pillow of Revenge — Revenge,
  Who sleeps to dream of blood, and waking glows
With the oft-baffled, slakeless thirst of change,
  When we shall mount again, and they that trod
  Be trampled on, while Death and Até range
O'er humbled heads and severed necks —— Great God!
  Take these thoughts from me — to thy hands I yield
  My many wrongs, and thine Almighty rod
Will fall on those who smote me, — be my Shield!
  As thou hast been in peril, and in pain,
  In turbulent cities, and the tented field —
In toil, and many troubles borne in vain
  For Florence, — I appeal from her to Thee!
  Thee, whom I late saw in thy loftiest reign,
Even in that glorious Vision, which to see
  And live was never granted until now,
  And yet thou hast permitted this to me.
Alas! with what a weight upon my brow
  The sense of earth and earthly things come back,
  Corrosive passions, feelings dull and low,
The heart's quick throb upon the mental rack,
  Long day, and dreary night; the retrospect
  Of half a century bloody and black,
And the frail few years I may yet expect
  Hoary and hopeless, but less hard to bear,
  For I have been too long and deeply wrecked
On the lone rock of desolate Despair,
  To lift my eyes more to the passing sail
  Which shuns that reef so horrible and bare;
Nor raise my voice — for who would heed my wail?
  I am not of this people, nor this age,

And yet my harpings will unfold a tale
Which shall preserve these times when not a page
Of their perturbèd annals could attract
An eye to gaze upon their civil rage,
Did not my verse embalm full many an act
Worthless as they who wrought it: 'tis the doom
Of spirits of my order to be racked
In life, to wear their hearts out, and consume
Their days in endless strife, and die alone;
Then future thousands crowd around their tomb,
And pilgrims come from climes where they have known
The name of him — who now is but a name,
And wasting homage o'er the sullen stone,
Spread his — by him unheard, unheeded — fame;
And mine at least hath cost me dear: to die
Is nothing; but to wither thus — to tame
My mind down from its own infinity —
To live in narrow ways with little men,
A common sight to every common eye,
A wanderer, while even wolves can find a den,
Ripped from all kindred, from all home, all things
That make communion sweet, and soften pain —
To feel me in the solitude of kings
Without the power that makes them bear a crown —
To envy every dove his nest and wings
Which waft him where the Apennine looks down
On Arno, till he perches, it may be,
Within my all inexorable town,
Where yet my boys are, and that fatal She,
Their mother, the cold partner who hath brought
Destruction for a dowry — this to see
And feel, and know without repair, hath taught
A bitter lesson; but it leaves me free:
I have not vilely found, nor basely sought,
They made an Exile — not a Slave of me.

CANTO THE SECOND

THE Spirit of the fervent days of Old,
When words were things that came to pass, and Thought
Flashed o'er the future, bidding men behold
Their children's children's doom already brought
Forth from the abyss of Time which is to be,
The Chaos of events, where lie half-wrought
Shapes that must undergo mortality;
What the great Seers of Israel wore within,

That Spirit was on them, and is on me,
And if, Cassandra-like, amidst the din
Of conflict none will hear, or hearing heed
This voice from out the Wilderness, the sin
Be theirs, and my own feelings be my meed,
The only guerdon I have ever known.
Hast thou not bled? and hast thou still to bleed,
Italia? Ah! to me such things, foreshown
With dim sepulchral light, bid me forget
In thine irreparable wrongs my own;
We can have but one Country, and even yet
Thou'rt mine — my bones shall be within thy breast,
My Soul within thy language, which once set
With our old Roman sway in the wide West;
But I will make another tongue arise
As lofty and more sweet, in which expressed
The hero's ardour, or the lover's sighs,
Shall find alike such sounds for every theme
That every word, as brilliant as thy skies,
Shall realise a Poet's proudest dream,
And make thee Europe's Nightingale of Song;
So that all present speech to thine shall seem
The note of meaner birds, and every tongue
Confess its barbarism when compared with thine.
This shalt thou owe to him thou didst so wrong,
Thy Tuscan bard, the banished Ghibelline.
Woe! woe! the veil of coming centuries
Is rent, — a thousand years which yet supine
Lie like the ocean waves ere winds arise,
Heaving in dark and sullen undulation,
Float from Eternity into these eyes;
The storms yet sleep, the clouds still keep their station,
The unborn Earthquake yet is in the womb,
The bloody Chaos yet expects Creation,
But all things are disposing for thy doom;
The Elements await but for the Word,
"Let there be darkness!" and thou grow'st a tomb!
Yes! thou, so beautiful, shalt feel the sword,
Thou, Italy! so fair that Paradise,
Revived in thee, blooms forth to man restored:
Ah! must the sons of Adam lose it twice?
Thou, Italy! whose ever golden fields,
Ploughed by the sunbeams solely, would suffice
For the world's granary; thou, whose sky Heaven gilds
With brighter stars, and robes with deeper blue;
Thou, in whose pleasant places Summer builds
Her palace, in whose cradle Empire grew,

And formed the Eternal City's ornaments
From spoils of Kings whom freemen overthrew;
Birthplace of heroes, sanctuary of Saints,
Where earthly first, then heavenly glory made
Her home; thou, all which fondest Fancy paints,
And finds her prior vision but portrayed
In feeble colours, when the eye — from the Alp
Of horrid snow, and rock, and shaggy shade
Of desert-loving pine, whose emerald scalp
Nods to the storm — dilates and dotes o'er thee,
And wistfully implores, as 'twere, for help
To see thy sunny fields, my Italy,
Nearer and nearer yet, and dearer still
The more approached, and dearest were they free,
Thou — Thou must wither to each tyrant's will:
The Goth hath been, — the German, Frank, and Hun
Are yet to come, — and on the imperial hill
Ruin, already proud of the deeds done
By the old barbarians, there awaits the new,
Throned on the Palatine, while lost and won
Rome at her feet lies bleeding; and the hue
Of human sacrifice and Roman slaughter
Troubles the clotted air, of late so blue,
And deepens into red the saffron water
Of Tiber, thick with dead; the helpless priest,
And still more helpless nor less holy daughter,
Vowed to their God, have shrieking fled, and ceased
Their ministry: the nations take their prey,
Iberian, Almain, Lombard, and the beast
And bird, wolf, vulture, more humane than they
Are; these but gorge the flesh, and lap the gore
Of the departed, and then go their way;
But those, the human savages, explore
All paths of torture, and insatiate yet,
With Ugolino hunger prowl for more.
Nine moons shall rise o'er scenes like this and set;
The chiefless army of the dead, which late
Beneath the traitor Prince's banner met,
Hath left its leader's ashes at the gate;
Had but the royal Rebel lived, perchance
Thou hadst been spared, but his involved thy fate.
Oh! Rome, the Spoiler or the spoil of France,
From Brennus to the Bourbon, never, never
Shall foreign standard to thy walls advance,
But Tiber shall become a mournful river.
Oh! when the strangers pass the Alps and Po,
Crush them, ye Rocks! Floods whelm them, and for ever!
Why sleep the idle Avalanches so,

To topple on the lonely pilgrim's head?
Why doth Eridanus but overflow
The peasant's harvest from his turbid bed?
Were not each barbarous horde a nobler prey?
Over Cambyses' host the desert spread
Her sandy ocean, and the Sea-waves' sway
Rolled over Pharaoh and his thousands, — why,
Mountains and waters, do ye not as they?
And you, ye Men! Romans, who dare not die,
Sons of the conquerors who overthrew
Those who overthrew proud Xerxes, where yet lie
The dead whose tomb Oblivion never knew,
Are the Alps weaker than Thermopylæ?
Their passes more alluring to the view
Of an invader? is it they, or ye,
That to each host the mountain-gate unbar,
And leave the march in peace, the passage free?
Why, Nature's self detains the Victor's car,
And makes your land impregnable, if earth
Could be so; but alone she will not war,
Yet aids the warrior worthy of his birth
In a soil where the mothers bring forth men:
Not so with those whose souls are little worth;
For them no fortress can avail, — the den
Of the poor reptile which preserves its sting
Is more secure than walls of adamant, when
The hearts of those within are quivering.
Are ye not brave? Yes, yet the Ausonian soil
Hath hearts, and hands, and arms, and hosts to bring
Against Oppression; but how vain the toil,
While still Division sows the seeds of woe
And weakness, till the Stranger reaps the spoil.
Oh! my own beauteous land! so long laid low,
So long the grave of thy own children's hopes,
When there is but required a single blow
To break the chain, yet — yet the Avenger stops,
And Doubt and Discord step 'twixt thine and thee,
And join their strength to that which with thee copes;
What is there wanting then to set thee free,
And show thy beauty in its fullest light?
To make the Alps impassable; and we,
Her Sons, may do this with *one* deed —— Unite.

CANTO THE THIRD

FROM out the mass of never-dying ill,
The Plague, the Prince, the Stranger, and the Sword,

Vials of wrath but emptied to refill
And flow again, I cannot all record
That crowds on my prophetic eye: the Earth
And Ocean written o'er would not afford
Space for the annal, yet it shall go forth;
Yes, all, though not by human pen, is graven,
There where the farthest suns and stars have birth,
Spread like a banner at the gate of Heaven,
The bloody scroll of our millennial wrongs
Waves, and the echo of our groans is driven
Athwart the sound of archangelic songs,
And Italy, the martyred nation's gore,
Will not in vain arise to where belongs
Omnipotence and Mercy evermore:
Like to a harpstring stricken by the wind,
The sound of her lament shall, rising o'er
The Seraph voices, touch the Almighty Mind.
Meantime I, humblest of thy sons, and of
Earth's dust by immortality refined
To Sense and Suffering, though the vain may scoff,
And tyrants threat, and meeker victims bow
Before the storm because its breath is rough,
To thee, my Country! whom before, as now,
I loved and love, devote the mournful lyre
And melancholy gift high Powers allow
To read the future: and if now my fire
Is not as once it shone o'er thee, forgive!
I but foretell thy fortunes — then expire;
Think not that I would look on them and live.
A Spirit forces me to see and speak,
And for my guerdon grants *not* to survive;
My Heart shall be poured over thee and break:
Yet for a moment, ere I must resume
Thy sable web of Sorrow, let me take
Over the gleams that flash athwart thy gloom
A softer glimpse; some stars shine through thy night,
And many meteors, and above thy tomb
Leans sculptured Beauty, which Death cannot blight:
And from thine ashes boundless Spirits rise
To give thee honour, and the earth delight;
Thy soil shall still be pregnant with the wise,
The gay, the learned, the generous, and the brave,
Native to thee as Summer to thy skies,
Conquerors on foreign shores, and the far wave,
Discoverers of new worlds, which take their name;
For *thee* alone they have no arm to save,
And all thy recompense is in their fame,

A noble one to them, but not to thee —
Shall they be glorious, and thou still the same?
Oh! more than these illustrious far shall be
The Being — and even yet he may be born —
The mortal Saviour who shall set thee free,
And see thy diadem, so changed and worn
By fresh barbarians, on thy brow replaced;
And the sweet Sun replenishing thy morn,
Thy moral morn, too long with clouds defaced,
And noxious vapours from Avernus risen,
Such as all they must breathe who are debased
By Servitude, and have the mind in prison.
Yet through this centuried eclipse of woe
Some voices shall be heard, and Earth shall listen;
Poets shall follow in the path I show,
And make it broader: the same brilliant sky
Which cheers the birds to song shall bid them glow,
And raise their notes as natural and high;
Tuneful shall be their numbers; they shall sing
Many of Love, and some of Liberty,
But few shall soar upon that Eagle's wing,
And look in the Sun's face, with Eagle's gaze,
All free and fearless as the feathered King,
But fly more near the earth; how many a phrase
Sublime shall lavished be on some small prince
In all the prodigality of Praise!
And language, eloquently false, evince
The harlotry of Genius, which, like Beauty,
Too oft forgets its own self-reverence,
And looks on prostitution as a duty.
He who once enters in a Tyrant's hall
As guest is slave — his thoughts become a booty,
And the first day which sees the chain enthral
A captive, sees his half of Manhood gone —
The Soul's emasculation saddens all
His spirit; thus the Bard too near the throne
Quails from his inspiration, bound to *please*, —
How servile is the task to please alone!
To smooth the verse to suit his Sovereign's ease
And royal leisure, nor too much prolong
Aught save his eulogy, and find, and seize,
Or force, or forge fit argument of Song!
Thus trammelled, thus condemned to Flattery's trebles,
He toils through all, still trembling to be wrong:
For fear some noble thoughts, like heavenly rebels,
Should rise up in high treason to his brain,
He sings, as the Athenian spoke, with pebbles

In's mouth, lest Truth should stammer through his strain.
But out of the long file of sonneteers
There shall be some who will not sing in vain,
And he, their Prince, shall rank among my peers,
And Love shall be his torment; but his grief
Shall make an immortality of tears,
And Italy shall hail him as the Chief
Of Poet-lovers, and his higher song
Of Freedom wreathe him with as green a leaf.
But in a farther age shall rise along
The banks of Po two greater still than he;
The World which smiled on him shall do them wrong
Till they are ashes, and repose with me.
The first will make an epoch with his lyre,
And fill the earth with feats of Chivalry:
His Fancy like a rainbow, and his Fire,
Like that of Heaven, immortal, and his Thought
Borne onward with a wing that cannot tire;
Pleasure shall, like a butterfly new caught,
Flutter her lovely pinions o'er his theme,
And Art itself seem into Nature wrought
By the transparency of his bright dream.—
The second, of a tenderer, sadder mood,
Shall pour his soul out o'er Jerusalem;
He, too, shall sing of Arms, and Christian blood
Shed where Christ bled for man; and his high harp
Shall, by the willow over Jordan's flood,
Revive a song of Sion, and the sharp
Conflict, and final triumph of the brave
And pious, and the strife of Hell to wrap
Their hearts from their great purpose, until wave
The red-cross banners where the first red Cross
Was crimsoned from His veins who died to save,
Shall be his sacred argument; the loss
Of years, of favour, freedom, even of fame
Contested for a time, while the smooth gloss
Of Courts would slide o'er his forgotten name
And call Captivity a kindness — meant
To shield him from insanity or shame —
Such shall be his meek guerdon! who was sent
To be Christ's Laureate — they reward him well!
Florence dooms me but death or banishment,
Ferrara him a pittance and a cell,
Harder to bear and less deserved, for I
Had stung the factions which I strove to quell;
But this meek man who with a lover's eye
Will look on Earth and Heaven, and who will deign

To embalm with his celestial flattery,
As poor a thing as e'er was spawned to reign,
What will *he* do to merit such a doom?
Perhaps he'll *love,* — and is not Love in vain
Torture enough without a living tomb?
Yet it will be so — he and his compeer,
The Bard of Chivalry, will both consume
In penury and pain too many a year,
And, dying in despondency, bequeath
To the kind World, which scarce will yield a tear,
A heritage enriching all who breathe
With the wealth of a genuine Poet's soul,
And to their country a redoubled wreath,
Unmatched by time; not Hellas can unroll
Through her Olympiads two such names, though one
Of hers be mighty; — and is this the whole
Of such men's destiny beneath the Sun?
Must all the finer thoughts, the thrilling sense,
The electric blood with which their arteries run,
Their body's self turned soul with the intense
Feeling of that which is, and fancy of
That which should be, to such a recompense
Conduct? shall their bright plumage on the rough
Storm be still scattered? Yes, and it must be;
For, formed of far too penetrable stuff,
These birds of Paradise but long to flee
Back to their native mansion, soon they find
Earth's mist with their pure pinions not agree,
And die or are degraded; for the mind
Succumbs to long infection, and despair,
And vulture Passions flying close behind,
Await the moment to assail and tear;
And when, at length, the wingéd wanderers stoop,
Then is the Prey-birds' triumph, then they share
The spoil, o'erpowered at length by one fell swoop.
Yet some have been untouched who learned to bear,
Some whom no Power could ever force to droop,
Who could resist themselves even, hardest care!
And task most hopeless; but some such have been,
And if my name amongst the number were,
That Destiny austere, and yet serene,
Were prouder than more dazzling fame unblessed;
The Alp's snow summit nearer heaven is seen
Than the Volcano's fierce eruptive crest,
Whose splendour from the black abyss is flung,
While the scorched mountain, from whose burning breast
A temporary torturing flame is wrung,

Shines for a night of terror, then repels
Its fire back to the Hell from whence it sprung,
The Hell which in its entrails ever dwells.

CANTO THE FOURTH

MANY are Poets who have never penned
Their inspiration, and perchance the best:
They felt, and loved, and died, but would not lend
Their thoughts to meaner beings; they compressed
The God within them, and rejoined the stars
Unlaurelled upon earth, but far more blessed
Than those who are degraded by the jars
Of Passion, and their frailties linked to fame,
Conquerors of high renown, but full of scars.
Many are Poets but without the name;
For what is Poesy but to create
From overfeeling Good or Ill; and aim
At an external life beyond our fate,
And be the new Prometheus of new men,
Bestowing fire from Heaven, and then, too late,
Finding the pleasure given repaid with pain,
And vultures to the heart of the bestower,
Who, having lavished his high gift in vain,
Lies chained to his lone rock by the sea-shore?
So be it: we can bear. — But thus all they
Whose Intellect is an o'ermastering Power
Which still recoils from its encumbering clay
Or lightens it to spirit, whatsoe'er
The form which their creations may essay,
Are bards; the kindled Marble's bust may wear
More poesy upon its speaking brow
Than aught less than the Homeric page may bear;
One noble stroke with a whole life may glow,
Or deify the canvass till it shine
With beauty so surpassing all below,
That they who kneel to Idols so divine
Break no commandment, for high Heaven is there
Transfused, transfigurated: and the line
Of Poesy, which peoples but the air
With Thought and Beings of our thought reflected,
Can do no more: then let the artist share
The palm, he shares the peril, and dejected
Faints o'er the labour unapproved — Alas!
Despair and Genius are too oft connected.
Within the ages which before me pass

Art shall resume and equal even the sway
Which with Apelles and old Phidias
She held in Hellas' unforgotten day.
Ye shall be taught by Ruin to revive
The Grecian forms at least from their decay,
And Roman souls at last again shall live
In Roman works wrought by Italian hands,
And temples, loftier than the old temples, give
New wonders to the World; and while still stands
The austere Pantheon, into heaven shall soar
A Dome, its image, while the base expands
Into a fane surpassing all before,
Such as all flesh shall flock to kneel in: ne'er
Such sight hath been unfolded by a door
As this, to which all nations shall repair,
And lay their sins at this huge gate of Heaven.
And the bold Architect unto whose care
The daring charge to raise it shall be given,
Whom all Arts shall acknowledge as their Lord,
Whether into the marble chaos driven
His chisel bid the Hebrew, at whose word
Israel left Egypt, stop the waves in stone,
Or hues of Hell be by his pencil poured
Over the damned before the Judgement-throne,
Such as I saw them, such as all shall see,
Or fanes be built of grandeur yet unknown —
The Stream of his great thoughts shall spring from me
The Ghibelline, who traversed the three realms
Which form the Empire of Eternity.
Amidst the clash of swords, and clang of helms,
The age which I anticipate, no less
Shall be the Age of Beauty, and while whelms
Calamity the nations with distress,
The Genius of my Country shall arise,
A Cedar towering o'er the Wilderness,
Lovely in all its branches to all eyes,
Fragrant as fair, and recognised afar,
Wafting its native incense through the skies.
Sovereigns shall pause amidst their sport of war,
Weaned for an hour from blood, to turn and gaze
On canvass or on stone; and they who mar
All beauty upon earth, compelled to praise,
Shall feel the power of that which they destroy;
And Art's mistaken gratitude shall raise
To tyrants, who but take her for a toy,
Emblems and monuments, and prostitute
Her charms to Pontiffs proud, but who employ

The man of Genius as the meanest brute
 To bear a burthen, and to serve a need,
 To sell his labours, and his soul to boot.
Who toils for nations may be poor indeed,
 But free; who sweats for Monarchs is no more
 Than the gilt Chamberlain, who, clothed and feed,
Stands sleek and slavish, bowing at his door.
 Oh, Power that rulest and inspirest! how
 Is it that they on earth, whose earthly power
Is likest thine in heaven in outward show,
 Least like to thee in attributes divine,
 Tread on the universal necks that bow,
And then assure us that their rights are thine?
 And how is it that they, the Sons of Fame,
 Whose inspiration seems to them to shine
From high, they whom the nations oftest name,
 Must pass their days in penury or pain,
 Or step to grandeur through the paths of shame,
And wear a deeper brand and gaudier chain?
 Or if their Destiny be born aloof
 From lowliness, or tempted thence in vain,
In their own souls sustain a harder proof,
 The inner war of Passions deep and fierce?
 Florence! when thy harsh sentence razed my roof,
I loved thee; but the vengeance of my verse,
 The hate of injuries which every year
 Makes greater, and accumulates my curse,
Shall live, outliving all thou holdest dear —
 Thy pride, thy wealth, thy freedom, and even *that,*
 The most infernal of all evils here,
The sway of petty tyrants in a state;
 For such sway is not limited to Kings,
 And Demagogues yield to them but in date,
As swept off sooner; in all deadly things,
 Which make men hate themselves, and one another,
 In discord, cowardice, cruelty, all that springs
From Death the Sin-born's incest with his mother,
 In rank oppression in its rudest shape,
 The faction Chief is but the Sultan's brother,
And the worst Despot's far less human ape.
 Florence! when this lone spirit, which so long
 Yearned, as the captive toiling at escape,
To fly back to thee in despite of wrong,
 An exile, saddest of all prisoners,
 Who has the whole world for a dungeon strong,
Seas, mountains, and the horizon's verge for bars,
 Which shut him from the sole small spot of earth

Where — whatsoe'er his fate — he still were hers,
His Country's, and might die where he had birth —
Florence! when this lone Spirit shall return
To kindred Spirits, thou wilt feel my worth,
And seek to honour with an empty urn
The ashes thou shalt ne'er obtain — Alas!
"What have I done to thee, my People?" Stern
Are all thy dealings, but in this they pass
The limits of Man's common malice, for
All that a citizen could be I was —
Raised by thy will, all thine in peace or war —
And for this thou hast warred with me. — 'Tis done:
I may not overleap the eternal bar
Built up between us, and will die alone,
Beholding with the dark eye of a Seer
The evil days to gifted souls foreshown,
Foretelling them to those who will not hear;
As in the old time, till the hour be come
When Truth shall strike their eyes through many a tear,
And make them own the Prophet in his tomb.

THE VISION OF JUDGMENT

BY

QUEVEDO REDIVIVUS

SUGGESTED BY THE COMPOSITION SO ENTITLED
BY THE AUTHOR OF "WAT TYLER"

"A Daniel come to judgment! yea, a Daniel!
I thank thee, Jew, for teaching me that word."

I

SAINT PETER sat by the celestial gate:
His keys were rusty, and the lock was dull,
So little trouble had been given of late;
Not that the place by any means was full,
But since the Gallic era "eighty-eight"
The Devils had ta'en a longer, stronger pull,
And "a pull altogether," as they say
At sea — which drew most souls another way.

II

The Angels all were singing out of tune,
  And hoarse with having little else to do,
Excepting to wind up the sun and moon,
  Or curb a runaway young star or two,
Or wild colt of a comet, which too soon
  Broke out of bounds o'er the ethereal blue,
Splitting some planet with its playful tail,
As boats are sometimes by a wanton whale.

III

The Guardian Seraphs had retired on high,
  Finding their charges past all care below;
Terrestrial business filled nought in the sky
  Save the Recording Angel's black bureau;
Who found, indeed, the facts to multiply
  With such rapidity of vice and woe,
That he had stripped off both his wings in quills,
And yet was in arrear of human ills.

IV

His business so augmented of late years,
  That he was forced, against his will, no doubt,
(Just like those cherubs, earthly ministers,)
  For some resource to turn himself about,
And claim the help of his celestial peers,
  To aid him ere he should be quite worn out
By the increased demand for his remarks:
Six Angels and twelve Saints were named his clerks.

V

This was a handsome board — at least for Heaven;
  And yet they had even then enough to do,
So many Conquerors' cars were daily driven,
  So many kingdoms fitted up anew;
Each day, too, slew its thousands six or seven,
  Till at the crowning carnage, Waterloo,
They threw their pens down in divine disgust —
The page was so besmeared with blood and dust.

VI

This by the way; 'tis not mine to record
  What Angels shrink from: even the very Devil

On this occasion his own work abhorred,
  So surfeited with the infernal revel:
Though he himself had sharpened every sword,
  It almost quenched his innate thirst of evil.
(Here Satan's sole good work deserves insertion —
'Tis, that he has both Generals in reversion.)

VII

Let's skip a few short years of hollow peace,
  Which peopled earth no better, Hell as wont,
And Heaven none — they form the tyrant's lease,
  With nothing but new names subscribed upon 't;
'Twill one day finish: meantime they increase,
  "With seven heads and ten horns," and all in front,
Like Saint John's foretold beast; but ours are born
Less formidable in the head than horn.

VIII

In the first year of Freedom's second dawn
  Died George the Third; although no tyrant, one
Who shielded tyrants, till each sense withdrawn
  Left him nor mental nor external sun:
A better farmer ne'er brushed dew from lawn,
  A worse king never left a realm undone!
He died — but left his subjects still behind,
One half as mad — and t'other no less blind.

IX

He died! his death made no great stir on earth:
  His burial made some pomp; there was profusion
Of velvet — gilding — brass — and no great dearth
  Of aught but tears — save those shed by collusion:
For these things may be bought at their true worth;
  Of elegy there was the due infusion —
Bought also; and the torches, cloaks and banners,
Heralds, and relics of old Gothic manners,

X

Formed a sepulchral melodrame. Of all
  The fools who flocked to swell or see the show,
Who cared about the corpse? The funeral
  Made the attraction, and the black the woe,
There throbbed not there a thought which pierced the pall;
  And when the gorgeous coffin was laid low,

It seemed the mockery of hell to fold
The rottenness of eighty years in gold.

XI

So mix his body with the dust! It might
   Return to what it *must* far sooner, were
The natural compound left alone to fight
   Its way back into earth, and fire, and air;
But the unnatural balsams merely blight
   What Nature made him at his birth, as bare
As the mere million's base unmummied clay —
Yet all his spices but prolong decay.

XII

He's dead — and upper earth with him has done;
   He's buried; save the undertaker's bill,
Or lapidary scrawl, the world is gone
For him, unless he left a German will:
But where's the proctor who will ask his son?
   In whom his qualities are reigning still,
Except that household virtue, most uncommon,
Of constancy to a bad, ugly woman.

XIII

"God save the king!" It is a large economy
   In God to save the like; but if he will
Be saving, all the better; for not one am I
   Of those who think damnation better still:
I hardly know too if not quite alone am I
   In this small hope of bettering future ill
By circumscribing, with some slight restriction,
The eternity of Hell's hot jurisdiction.

XIV

I know this is unpopular; I know
   'Tis blasphemous; I know one may be damned
For hoping no one else may e'er be so;
   I know my catechism; I know we're crammed
With the best doctrines till we quite o'erflow;
   I know that all save England's Church have shammed,
And that the other twice two hundred churches
And synagogues have made a *damned* bad purchase.

XV

God help us all! God help me too! I am,
  God knows, as helpless as the Devil can wish,
And not a whit more difficult to damn,
  Than is to bring to land a late-hooked fish,
Or to the butcher to purvey the lamb;
  Not that I'm fit for such a noble dish,
As one day will be that immortal fry
Of almost every body born to die.

XVI

Saint Peter sat by the celestial gate,
  And nodded o'er his keys: when, lo! there came
A wondrous noise he had not heard of late —
  A rushing sound of wind, and stream, and flame;
In short, a roar of things extremely great,
  Which would have made aught save a Saint exclaim;
But he, with first a start and then a wink,
Said, "There's another star gone out, I think!"

XVII

But ere he could return to his repose,
  A Cherub flapped his right wing o'er his eyes —
At which Saint Peter yawned, and rubbed his nose:
  "Saint porter," said the angel, "prithee rise!"
Waving a goodly wing, which glowed, as glows
  An earthly peacock's tail, with heavenly dyes:
To which the saint replied, "Well, what's the matter?
"Is Lucifer come back with all this clatter?"

XVIII

"No," quoth the Cherub: "George the Third is dead."
  "And who *is* George the Third?" replied the apostle:
"*What George? what Third?*" "The King of England," said
  The angel. "Well! he won't find kings to jostle
Him on his way; but does he wear his head?
  Because the last we saw here had a tustle,
And ne'er would have got into Heaven's good graces,
Had he not flung his head in all our faces.

XIX

"He was — if I remember — King of France;
  That head of his, which could not keep a crown

On earth, yet ventured in my face to advance
   A claim to those of martyrs — like my own:
If I had my sword, as I had once
   When I cut ears off, I had cut him down;
But having but my *keys*, and not my brand,
I only knocked his head from out his hand.

XX

"And then he set up such a headless howl,
   That all the Saints came out and took him in;
And there he sits by Saint Paul, cheek by jowl;
   That fellow Paul — the parvenù! The skin
Of Saint Bartholomew, which makes his cowl
   In heaven, and upon earth redeemed his sin,
So as to make a martyr, never sped
Better than did this weak and wooden head.

XXI

"But had it come up here upon its shoulders,
   There would have been a different tale to tell:
The fellow-feeling in the Saint's beholders
   Seems to have acted on them like a spell;
And so this very foolish head Heaven solders
   Back on its trunk: it may be very well,
And seems the custom here to overthrow
Whatever has been wisely done below."

XXII

The Angel answered, "Peter! do not pout:
   The King who comes has head and all entire,
And never knew much what it was about —
   He did as doth the puppet — by its wire,
And will be judged like all the rest, no doubt:
   My business and your own is not to inquire
Into such matters, but to mind our cue —
Which is to act as we are bid to do."

XXIII

While thus they spake, the angelic caravan,
   Arriving like a rush of mighty wind,
Cleaving the fields of space, as doth the swan
   Some silver stream (say Ganges, Nile, or Inde,
Or Thames, or Tweed), and midst them an old man

With an old soul, and both extremely blind,
Halted before the gate, and, in his shroud,
Seated their fellow-traveller on a cloud.

XXIV

But bringing up the rear of this bright host
A Spirit of a different aspect waved
His wings, like thunder-clouds above some coast
Whose barren beach with frequent wrecks is paved;
His brow was like the deep when tempest-tossed;
Fierce and unfathomable thoughts engraved
Eternal wrath on his immortal face,
And *where* he gazed a gloom pervaded space.

XXV

As he drew near, he gazed upon the gate
Ne'er to be entered more by him or Sin,
With such a glance of supernatural hate,
As made Saint Peter wish himself within;
He pottered with his keys at a great rate,
And sweated through his Apostolic skin:
Of course his perspiration was but ichor,
Or some such other spiritual liquor.

XXVI

The very Cherubs huddled all together,
Like birds when soars the falcon; and they felt
A tingling to the tip of every feather,
And formed a circle like Orion's belt
Around their poor old charge; who scarce knew whither
His guards had led him, though they gently dealt
With royal Manes (for by many stories,
And true, we learn the Angels all are Tories).

XXVII

As things were in this posture, the gate flew
Asunder, and the flashing of its hinges
Flung over space an universal hue
Of many-coloured flame, until its tinges
Reached even our speck of earth, and made a new
Aurora borealis spread its fringes
O'er the North Pole; the same seen, when ice-bound,
By Captain Parry's crew, in "Melville's Sound."

XXVIII

And from the gate thrown open issued beaming
  A beautiful and mighty Thing of Light,
Radiant with glory, like a banner streaming
  Victorious from some world-o'erthrowing fight:
My poor comparisons must needs be teeming
  With earthly likenesses, for here the night
Of clay obscures our best conceptions, saving
Johanna Southcote, or Bob Southey raving.

XXIX

'Twas the Archangel Michael: all men know
  The make of Angels and Archangels, since
There's scarce a scribbler has not one to show,
  From the fiends' leader to the Angels' Prince.
There also are some altar-pieces, though
  I really can't say that they much evince
One's inner notions of immortal spirits;
But let the connoisseurs explain *their* merits.

XXX

Michael flew forth in glory and in good;
  A goodly work of him from whom all Glory
And Good arise; the portal past — he stood;
  Before him the young Cherubs and Saints hoary —
(I say *young*, begging to be understood
  By looks, not years; and should be very sorry
To state, they were not older than St. Peter,
But merely that they seemed a little sweeter).

XXXI

The Cherubs and the Saints bowed down before
  That arch-angelic Hierarch, the first
Of Essences angelical who wore
  The aspect of a god; but this ne'er nursed
Pride in his heavenly bosom, in whose core
  No thought, save for his Maker's service, durst
Intrude, however glorified and high;
He knew him but the Viceroy of the sky.

XXXII

He and the sombre, silent Spirit met —
  They knew each other both for good and ill;

Such was their power, that neither could forget
His former friend and future foe; but still
There was a high, immortal, proud regret
In either's eye, as if 'twere less their will
Than destiny to make the eternal years
Their date of war, and their "Champ Clos" the spheres.

XXXIII

But here they were in neutral space: we know
From Job, that Satan hath the power to pay
A heavenly visit thrice a-year or so;
And that the "Sons of God," like those of clay,
Must keep him company; and we might show
From the same book, in how polite a way
The dialogue is held between the Powers
Of Good and Evil — but 'twould take up hours.

XXXIV

And this is not a theologic tract,
To prove with Hebrew and with Arabic,
If Job be allegory or a fact,
But a true narrative; and thus I pick
From out the whole but such and such an act
As sets aside the slightest thought of trick.
'Tis every tittle true, beyond suspicion,
And accurate as any other vision.

XXXV

The spirits were in neutral space, before
The gate of Heaven; like eastern thresholds is
The place where Death's grand cause is argued o'er,
And souls despatched to that world or to this;
And therefore Michael and the other wore
A civil aspect: though they did not kiss,
Yet still between his Darkness and his Brightness
There passed a mutual glance of great politeness.

XXXVI

The Archangel bowed, not like a modern beau,
But with a graceful oriental bend,
Pressing one radiant arm just where below
The heart in good men is supposed to tend;
He turned as to an equal, not too low,
But kindly; Satan met his ancient friend

With more hauteur, as might an old Castilian
Poor Noble meet a mushroom rich civilian.

XXXVII

He merely bent his diabolic brow
  An instant; and then raising it, he stood
In act to assert his right or wrong, and show
  Cause why King George by no means could or should
Make out a case to be exempt from woe
  Eternal, more than other kings, endued
With better sense and hearts, whom History mentions,
Who long have "paved Hell with their good intentions."

XXXVIII

Michael began: "What wouldst thou with this man,
  Now dead, and brought before the Lord? What ill
Hath he wrought since his mortal race began,
  That thou canst claim him? Speak! and do thy will,
If it be just: if in this earthly span
  He hath been greatly failing to fulfil
His duties as a king and mortal, say,
And he is thine; if not — let him have way."

XXXIX

"Michael!" replied the Prince of Air, "even here
  Before the gate of Him thou servest, must
I claim my subject: and will make appear
  That as he was my worshipper in dust,
So shall he be in spirit, although dear
  To thee and thine, because nor wine nor lust
Were of his weaknesses; yet on the throne
He reigned o'er millions to serve me alone.

XL

"Look to *our* earth, or rather *mine;* it was,
  Once, more thy master's: but I triumph not
In this poor planet's conquest; nor alas!
  Need he thou servest envy me my lot:
With all the myriads of bright worlds which pass
  In worship round him, he may have forgot
Yon weak creation of such paltry things:
I think few worth damnation save their kings,

XLI

"And these but as a kind of quit-rent, to
 Assert my right as Lord: and even had
I such an inclination, 'twere (as you
 Well know) superfluous; they are grown so bad,
That Hell has nothing better left to do
 Than leave them to themselves: so much more mad
And evil by their own internal curse,
Heaven cannot make them better, nor I worse.

XLII

"Look to the earth, I said, and say again:
 When this old, blind, mad, helpless, weak, poor worm
Began in youth's first bloom and flush to reign,
 The world and he both wore a different form,
And much of earth and all the watery plain
 Of Ocean called him king: through many a storm
His isles had floated on the abyss of Time;
For the rough virtues chose them for their clime.

XLIII

"He came to his sceptre young; he leaves it old:
 Look to the state in which he found his realm,
And left it; and his annals too behold,
 How to a minion first he gave the helm;
How grew upon his heart a thirst for gold,
 The beggar's vice, which can but overwhelm
The meanest hearts; and for the rest, but glance
Thine eye along America and France.

XLIV

" 'Tis true, he was a tool from first to last
 (I have the workmen safe); but as a tool
So let him be consumed. From out the past
 Of ages, since mankind have known the rule
Of monarchs — from the bloody rolls amassed
 Of Sin and Slaughter — from the Cæsars' school,
Take the worst pupil; and produce a reign
More drenched with gore, more cumbered with the slain.

XLV

"He ever warred with freedom and the free:
 Nations as men, home subjects, foreign foes,

So that they uttered the word 'Liberty!'
  Found George the Third their first opponent. Whose
History was ever stained as his will be
  With national and individual woes?
I grant his household abstinence; I grant
His neutral virtues, which most monarchs want;

XLVI

"I know he was a constant consort; own
  He was a decent sire, and middling lord.
All this is much, and most upon a throne;
  As temperance, if at Apicius' board,
Is more than at an anchorite's supper shown.
  I grant him all the kindest can accord;
And this was well for him, but not for those
Millions who found him what Oppression chose.

XLVII

"The New World shook him off; the Old yet groans
  Beneath what he and his prepared, if not
Completed: he leaves heirs on many thrones
  To all his vices, without what begot
Compassion for him — his tame virtues; drones
  Who sleep, or despots who have now forgot
A lesson which shall be re-taught them, wake
Upon the thrones of earth; but let them quake!

XLVIII

"Five millions of the primitive, who hold
  The faith which makes ye great on earth, implored
A *part* of that vast *all* they held of old, —
  Freedom to worship — not alone your Lord,
Michael, but you, and you, Saint Peter! Cold
  Must be your souls, if you have not abhorred
The foe to Catholic participation
In all the license of a Christian nation.

XLIX

"True! he allowed them to pray God; but as
  A consequence of prayer, refused the law
Which would have placed them upon the same base
  With those who did not hold the Saints in awe."
But here Saint Peter started from his place

And cried, "You may the prisoner withdraw:
Ere Heaven shall ope her portals to this Guelph,
While I am guard, may I be damned myself!

L

"Sooner will I with Cerberus exchange
My office (and *his* is no sinecure)
Than see this royal Bedlam-bigot range
The azure fields of Heaven, of that be sure!"
"Saint!" replied Satan, "you do well to avenge
The wrongs he made your satellites endure;
And if to this exchange you should be given,
I'll try to coax *our* Cerberus up to Heaven!"

LI

Here Michael interposed: "Good Saint! and Devil!
Pray, not so fast; you both outrun discretion.
Saint Peter! you were wont to be more civil:
Satan! excuse this warmth of his expression,
And condescension to the vulgar's level:
Even Saints sometimes forget themselves in session.
Have you got more to say?" — "No." — "If you please,
I'll trouble you to call your witnesses."

LII

Then Satan turned and waved his swarthy hand,
Which stirred with its electric qualities
Clouds farther off than we can understand,
Although we find him sometimes in our skies;
Infernal thunder shook both sea and land
In all the planets — and Hell's batteries
Let off the artillery, which Milton mentions
As one of Satan's most sublime inventions.

LIII

This was a signal unto such damned souls
As have the privilege of their damnation
Extended far beyond the mere controls
Of worlds past, present, or to come; no station
Is theirs particularly in the rolls
Of Hell assigned; but where their inclination
Or business carries them in search of game,
They may range freely — being damned the same.

LIV

They are proud of this — as very well they may,
   It being a sort of knighthood, or gilt key
Stuck in their loins; or like to an "entré"
   Up the back stairs, or such free-masonry.
I borrow my comparisons from clay,
   Being clay myself. Let not those spirits be
Offended with such base low likenesses;
We know their posts are nobler far than these.

LV

When the great signal ran from Heaven to Hell —
   About ten million times the distance reckoned
From our sun to its earth, as we can tell
   How much time it takes up, even to a second,
For every ray that travels to dispel
   The fogs of London, through which, dimly beaconed,
The weathercocks are gilt some thrice a year,
If that the *summer* is not too severe:

LVI

I say that I can tell — 'twas half a minute;
   I know the solar beams take up more time
Ere, packed up for their journey, they begin it;
   But then their Telegraph is less sublime,
And if they ran a race, they would not win it
   'Gainst Satan's couriers bound for their own clime.
The sun takes up some years for every ray
To reach its goal — the Devil not half a day.

LVII

Upon the verge of space, about the size
   Of half-a-crown, a little speck appeared
(I've seen a something like it in the skies
   In the Ægean, ere a squall); it neared,
And, growing bigger, took another guise;
   Like an aërial ship it tacked, and steered,
Or *was* steered (I am doubtful of the grammar
Of the last phrase, which makes the stanza stammer;

LVIII

But take your choice): and then it grew a cloud;
   And so it was — a cloud of witnesses.

But such a cloud! No land ere saw a crowd
Of locusts numerous as the heavens saw these;
They shadowed with their myriads Space; their loud
And varied cries were like those of wild geese,
(If nations may be likened to a goose),
And realised the phrase of "Hell broke loose."

LIX

Here crashed a sturdy oath of stout John Bull,
Who damned away his eyes as heretofore:
There Paddy brogued "By Jasus!" — "What's your wull?"
The temperate Scot exclaimed: the French ghost swore
In certain terms I shan't translate in full,
As the first coachman will; and 'midst the war,
The voice of Jonathan was heard to express,
"*Our* President is going to war, I guess."

LX

Besides there were the Spaniard, Dutch, and Dane;
In short, an universal shoal of shades
From Otaheite's isle to Salisbury Plain,
Of all climes and professions, years and trades,
Ready to swear against the good king's reign,
Bitter as clubs in cards are against spades:
All summoned by this grand "subpœna," to
Try if kings mayn't be damned like me or you.

LXI

When Michael saw this host, he first grew pale,
As Angels can; next, like Italian twilight,
He turned all colours — as a peacock's tail,
Or sunset streaming through a Gothic skylight
In some old abbey, or a trout not stale,
Or distant lightning on the horizon *by* night,
Or a fresh rainbow, or a grand review
Of thirty regiments in red, green, and blue.

LXII

Then he addressed himself to Satan: "Why —
My good old friend, for such I deem you, though
Our different parties make us fight so shy,
I ne'er mistake you for a *personal* foe;
Our difference is *political,* and I
Trust that, whatever may occur below,

You know my great respect for you: and this
Makes me regret whate'er you do amiss —

LXIII

"Why, my dear Lucifer, would you abuse
My call for witnesses? I did not mean
That you should half of Earth and Hell produce;
'Tis even superfluous, since two honest, clean,
True testimonies are enough: we lose
Our Time, nay, our Eternity, between
The accusation and defence: if we
Hear both, 'twill stretch our immortality."

LXIV

Satan replied, "To me the matter is
Indifferent, in a personal point of view:
I can have fifty better souls than this
With far less trouble than we have gone through
Already; and I merely argued his
Late Majesty of Britain's case with you
Upon a point of form: you may dispose
Of him; I've kings enough below, God knows!"

LXV

Thus spoke the Demon (late called "multifaced"
By multo-scribbling Southey). "Then we'll call
One or two persons of the myriads placed
Around our congress, and dispense with all
The rest," quoth Michael: "Who may be so graced
As to speak first? there's choice enough — who shall
It be?" Then Satan answered, "There are many;
But you may choose Jack Wilkes as well as any."

LXVI

A merry, cock-eyed, curious-looking Sprite
Upon the instant started from the throng,
Dressed in a fashion now forgotten quite;
For all the fashions of the flesh stick long
By people in the next world; where unite
All the costumes since Adam's, right or wrong,
From Eve's fig-leaf down to the petticoat,
Almost as scanty, of days less remote.

LXVII

The Spirit looked around upon the crowds
Assembled, and exclaimed, "My friends of all
The spheres, we shall catch cold amongst these clouds;
So let's to business: why this general call?
If those are freeholders I see in shrouds,
And 'tis for an election that they bawl,
Behold a candidate with unturned coat!
Saint Peter, may I count upon your vote?"

LXVIII

"Sir," replied Michael, "you mistake; these things
Are of a former life, and what we do
Above is more august; to judge of kings
Is the tribunal met: so now you know."
"Then I presume those gentlemen with wings,"
Said Wilkes, "are Cherubs; and that soul below
Looks much like George the Third, but to my mind
A good deal older — bless me! is he blind?"

LXIX

"He is what you behold him, and his doom
Depends upon his deeds," the Angel said;
"If you have aught to arraign in him, the tomb
Gives license to the humblest beggar's head
To lift itself against the loftiest." — "Some,"
Said Wilkes, "don't wait to see them laid in lead,
For such a liberty — and I, for one,
Have told them what I thought beneath the sun."

LXX

"*Above* the sun repeat, then, what thou hast
To urge against him," said the Archangel. "Why,"
Replied the spirit, "since old scores are past,
Must I turn evidence? In faith, not I.
Besides, I beat him hollow at the last,
With all his Lords and Commons: in the sky
I don't like ripping up old stories, since
His conduct was but natural in a prince.

LXXI

"Foolish, no doubt, and wicked, to oppress
A poor unlucky devil without a shilling;

But then I blame the man himself much less
   Than Bute and Grafton, and shall be unwilling
To see him punished here for their excess,
   Since they were both damned long ago, and still in
Their place below: for me, I have forgiven,
And vote his *habeas corpus* into Heaven."

LXXII

"Wilkes," said the Devil, "I understand all this;
   You turned to half a courtier ere you died,
And seem to think it would not be amiss
   To grow a whole one on the other side
Of Charon's ferry; you forget that *his*
   Reign is concluded; whatsoe'er betide,
He won't be sovereign more: you've lost your labour,
For at the best he will but be your neighbour.

LXXIII

"However, I knew what to think of it,
   When I beheld you in your jesting way,
Flitting and whispering round about the spit
   Where Belial, upon duty for the day,
With Fox's lard was basting William Pitt,
   His pupil; I knew what to think, I say:
That fellow even in Hell breeds farther ills;
I'll have him *gagged* — 'twas one of his own Bills.

LXXIV

"Call Junius!" From the crowd a shadow stalked,
   And at the name there was a general squeeze,
So that the very ghosts no longer walked
   In comfort, at their own aërial ease,
But were all rammed, and jammed (but to be balked,
   As we shall see), and jostled hands and knees,
Like wind compressed and pent within a bladder,
Or like a human colic, which is sadder.

LXXV

The shadow came — a tall, thin, grey-haired figure,
   That looked as it had been a shade on earth;
Quick in its motions, with an air of vigour,
   But nought to mark its breeding or its birth;
Now it waxed little, then again grew bigger,

With now an air of gloom, or savage mirth;
But as you gazed upon its features, they
Changed every instant — to *what,* none could say.

LXXVI

The more intently the ghosts gazed, the less
Could they distinguish whose the features were;
The Devil himself seemed puzzled even to guess;
Thy varied like a dream — now here, now there;
And several people swore from out the press,
They knew him perfectly; and one could swear
He was his father; upon which another
Was sure he was his mother's cousin's brother:

LXXVII

Another, that he was a duke, or knight,
An orator, a lawyer, or a priest,
A nabob, a man-midwife; but the wight
Mysterious changed his countenance at least
As oft as they their minds: though in full sight
He stood, the puzzle only was increased;
The man was a phantasmagoria in
Himself — he was so volatile and thin.

LXXVIII

The moment that you had pronounced him *one,*
Presto! his face changed, and he was another;
And when that change was hardly well put on,
It varied, till I don't think his own mother
(If that he had a mother) would her son
Have known, he shifted so from one to t'other;
Till guessing from a pleasure grew a task,
At this epistolary "Iron Mask."

LXXIX

For sometimes he like Cerberus would seem —
"Three gentlemen at once" (as sagely says
Good Mrs. Malaprop); then you might deem
That he was not even *one;* now many rays
Were flashing round him; and now a thick steam
Hid him from sight — like fogs on London days:
Now Burke, now Tooke, he grew to people's fancies
And certes often like Sir Philip Francis.

LXXX

I've an hypothesis — 'tis quite my own;
  I never let it out till now, for fear
Of doing people harm about the throne,
  And injuring some minister or peer,
On whom the stigma might perhaps be blown;
  It is — my gentle public, lend thine ear!
'Tis, that what Junius we are wont to call,
Was *really* — *truly* — nobody at all.

LXXXI

I don't see wherefore letters should not be
  Written without hands, since we daily view
Them written without heads; and books, we see,
  Are filled as well without the latter too:
And really till we fix on somebody
  For certain sure to claim them as his due,
Their author, like the Niger's mouth, will bother
The world to say if *there* be mouth or author.

LXXXII

"And who and what art thou?" the Archangel said.
  "For *that* you may consult my title-page,"
Replied this mighty shadow of a shade:
  "If I have kept my secret half an age,
I scarce shall tell it now." — "Canst thou upbraid,"
  Continued Michael, "George Rex, or allege
Aught further?" Junius answered, "You had better
First ask him for *his* answer to my letter:

LXXXIII

"My charges upon record will outlast
  The brass of both his epitaph and tomb."
"Repent'st thou not," said Michael, "of some past
  Exaggeration? something which may doom
Thyself if false, as him if true? Thou wast
  Too bitter — is it not so? — in thy gloom
Of passion?" — "Passion!" cried the phantom dim,
"I loved my country, and I hated him.

LXXXIV

"What I have written, I have written: let
  The rest be on his head or mine!" So spoke

Old "*Nominis Umbra;*" and while speaking yet,
  Away he melted in celestial smoke.
Then Satan said to Michael, "Don't forget
  To call George Washington, and John Horne Tooke,
And Franklin;" — but at this time there was heard
A cry for room, though not a phantom stirred.

LXXXV

At length with jostling, elbowing, and the aid
  Of Cherubim appointed to that post,
The devil Asmodeus to the circle made
  His way, and looked as if his journey cost
Some trouble. When his burden down he laid,
  "What's this?" cried Michael; "why, 'tis not a ghost?"
"I know it," quoth the Incubus; "but he
Shall be one, if you leave the affair to me.

LXXXVI

"Confound the renegado! I have sprained
  My left wing, he's so heavy; one would think
Some of his works about his neck were chained.
  But to the point; while hovering o'er the brink
Of Skiddaw (where as usual it still rained),
  I saw a taper, far below me, wink,
And stooping, caught this fellow at a libel —
No less on History — than the Holy Bible.

LXXXVII

"The former is the Devil's scripture, and
  The latter yours, good Michael: so the affair
Belongs to all of us, you understand.
  I snatched him up just as you see him there,
And brought him off for sentence out of hand:
  I've scarcely been ten minutes in the air —
At least a quarter it can hardly be:
I dare say that his wife is still at tea."

LXXXVIII

Here Satan said, "I know this man of old,
  And have expected him for some time here;
A sillier fellow you will scarce behold,
  Or more conceited in his petty sphere:
But surely it was not worth while to fold
  Such trash below your wing, Asmodeus dear:

We had the poor wretch safe (without being bored
With carriage) coming of his own accord.

LXXXIX

"But since he's here, let's see what he has done."
"Done!" cried Asmodeus, "he anticipates
The very business you are now upon,
And scribbles as if head clerk to the Fates.
Who knows to what his ribaldry may run,
When such an ass as this, like Balaam's, prates?"
"Let's hear," quoth Michael, "what he has to say:
You know we're bound to that in every way."

XC

Now the bard, glad to get an audience, which
By no means often was his case below,
Began to cough, and hawk, and hem, and pitch
His voice into that awful note of woe
To all unhappy hearers within reach
Of poets when the tide of rhyme's in flow;
But stuck fast with his first hexameter,
Not one of all whose gouty feet would stir.

XCI

But ere the spavined dactyls could be spurred
Into recitative, in great dismay
Both Cherubim and Seraphim were heard
To murmur loudly through their long array;
And Michael rose ere he could get a word
Of all his foundered verses under way,
And cried, "For God's sake stop, my friend! 'twere best —
'*Non Di, non homines*' — you know the rest."

XCII

A general bustle spread throughout the throng,
Which seemed to hold all verse in detestation;
The Angels had of course enough of song
When upon service; and the generation
Of ghosts had heard too much in life, not long
Before, to profit by a new occasion:
The Monarch, mute till then, exclaimed, "What! what!
Pye come again? No more — no more of that!"

XCIII

The tumult grew; an universal cough
  Convulsed the skies, as during a debate,
When Castlereagh has been up long enough
  (Before he was first minister of state,
I mean — the *slaves hear now*); some cried "Off, off!"
  As at a farce; till, grown quite desperate,
The Bard Saint Peter prayed to interpose
(Himself an author) only for his prose.

XCIV

The varlet was not an ill-favoured knave;
  A good deal like a vulture in the face,
With a hook nose and a hawk's eye, which gave
  A smart and sharper-looking sort of grace
To his whole aspect, which, though rather grave,
  Was by no means so ugly as his case;
But that, indeed, was hopeless as can be,
Quite a poetic felony "*de se*."

XCV

Then Michael blew his trump, and stilled the noise
  With one still greater, as is yet the mode
On earth besides; except some grumbling voice,
  Which now and then will make a slight inroad
Upon decorous silence, few will twice
  Lift up their lungs when fairly overcrowed;
And now the Bard could plead his own bad cause,
With all the attitudes of self-applause.

XCVI

He said — (I only give the heads) — he said,
  He meant no harm in scribbling; 'twas his way
Upon all topics; 'twas, besides, his bread,
  Of which he buttered both sides; 'twould delay
Too long the assembly (he was pleased to dread),
  And take up rather more time than a day,
To name his works — he would but cite a few —
"Wat Tyler" — "Rhymes on Blenheim" — "Waterloo."

XCVII

He had written praises of a Regicide;
  He had written praises of all kings whatever;

He had written for republics far and wide,
  And then against them bitterer than ever;
For pantisocracy he once had cried
  Aloud, a scheme less moral than 'twas clever;
Then grew a hearty anti-jacobin —
Had turned his coat — and would have turned his skin.

XCVIII

He had sung against all battles, and again
  In their high praise and glory; he had called
Reviewing "the ungentle craft," and then
  Became as base a critic as e'er crawled —
Fed, paid, and pampered by the very men
  By whom his muse and morals had been mauled:
He had written much blank verse, and blanker prose,
And more of both than any body knows.

XCIX

He had written Wesley's life: — here turning round
  To Satan, "Sir, I'm ready to write yours,
In two octavo volumes, nicely bound,
  With notes and preface, all that most allures
The pious purchaser; and there's no ground
  For fear, for I can choose my own reviewers:
So let me have the proper documents,
That I may add you to my other saints."

C

Satan bowed, and was silent. "Well, if you,
  With amiable modesty, decline
My offer, what says Michael? There are few
  Whose memoirs could be rendered more divine.
Mine is a pen of all work; not so new
  As it was once, but I would make you shine
Like your own trumpet. By the way, my own
Has more of brass in it, and is as well blown.

CI

"But talking about trumpets, here's my 'Vision!'
  Now you shall judge, all people — yes — you shall
Judge with my judgment! and by my decision
  Be guided who shall enter heaven or fall.
I settle all these things by intuition,

Times present, past, to come — Heaven — Hell — and all,
Like King Alfonso. When I thus see double,
I save the Deity some worlds of trouble."

CII

He ceased, and drew forth an MS.; and no
Persuasion on the part of Devils, Saints,
Or Angels, now could stop the torrent; so
He read the first three lines of the contents;
But at the fourth, the whole spiritual show
Had vanished, with variety of scents,
Ambrosial and sulphureous, as they sprang,
Like lightning, off from his "melodious twang."

CIII

Those grand heroics acted as a spell;
The Angels stopped their ears and plied their pinions;
The Devils ran howling, deafened, down to Hell;
The ghosts fled, gibbering, for their own dominions —
(For 'tis not yet decided where they dwell,
And I leave every man to his opinions);
Michael took refuge in his trump — but, lo!
His teeth were set on edge, he could not blow!

CIV

Saint Peter, who has hitherto been known
For an impetuous saint, upraised his keys,
And at the fifth line knocked the poet down;
Who fell like Phaeton, but more at ease,
Into his lake, for there he did not drown;
A different web being by the Destinies
Woven for the Laureate's final wreath, whene'er
Reform shall happen either here or there.

CV

He first sank to the bottom — like his works,
But soon rose to the surface — like himself;
For all corrupted things are buoyed like corks,
By their own rottenness, light as an elf,
Or wisp that flits o'er a morass: he lurks,
It may be, still, like dull books on a shelf,
In his own den, to scrawl some "Life" or "Vision,"
As Welborn says — "the Devil turned precisian."

CVI

As for the rest, to come to the conclusion
   Of this true dream, the telescope is gone
Which kept my optics free from all delusion,
   And showed me what I in my turn have shown;
All I saw farther, in the last confusion,
   Was, that King George slipped into Heaven for one;
And when the tumult dwindled to a calm,
I left him practising the hundredth psalm.

STANZAS WRITTEN ON THE ROAD BETWEEN FLORENCE AND PISA

1

Oh, talk not to me of a name great in story —
The days of our Youth are the days of our glory;
And the myrtle and ivy of sweet two-and-twenty
Are worth all your laurels, though ever so plenty.

2

What are garlands and crowns to the brow that is wrinkled?
'Tis but as a dead flower with May-dew besprinkled:
Then away with all such from the head that is hoary,
What care I for the wreaths that can *only* give glory?

3

Oh Fame! — if I e'er took delight in thy praises,
'Twas less for the sake of thy high-sounding phrases,
Than to see the bright eyes of the dear One discover,
She thought that I was not unworthy to love her.

4

There chiefly I sought thee, *there* only I found thee;
Her Glance was the best of the rays that surround thee,
When it sparkled o'er aught that was bright in my story,
I knew it was Love, and I felt it was Glory.

CAIN:

A MYSTERY

"Now the Serpent was more subtil than any beast of the field which the Lord God had made."

Genesis iii.1.

DRAMATIS PERSONÆ

Men

ADAM
CAIN
ABEL

Spirits

ANGEL OF THE LORD
LUCIFER

Women

EVE
ADAH
ZILLAH

ACT I

SCENE I. — *The Land without Paradise. — Time, Sunrise.*

ADAM, EVE, CAIN, ABEL, ADAH, ZILLAH, *offering a Sacrifice.*

Adam. GOD, the Eternal! Infinite! All-wise! —
Who out of darkness on the deep didst make
Light on the waters with a word — All Hail!
Jehovah! with returning light — All Hail!
Eve. God! who didst name the day, and separate
Morning from night, till then divided never —
Who didst divide the wave from wave, and call
Part of thy work the firmament — All Hail!
Abel. God! who didst call the elements into
Earth, ocean, air and fire — and with the day
And night, and worlds which these illuminate,

Or shadow, madest beings to enjoy them,
And love both them and thee — All Hail! All Hail!
Adah. God! the Eternal parent of all things!
Who didst create these best and beauteous beings,
To be belovéd, more than all, save thee —
Let me love thee and them: — All Hail! All Hail!
Zillah. Oh, God! who loving, making, blessing all,
Yet didst permit the Serpent to creep in,
And drive my father forth from Paradise,
Keep us from further evil: — Hail! All Hail!
Adam. Son Cain! my first-born — wherefore art thou silent?
Cain. Why should I speak?
Adam. To pray.
Cain. Have ye not prayed?
Adam. We have, most fervently.
Cain. And loudly: I
Have heard you.
Adam. So will God, I trust.
Abel. Amen!
Adam. But thou my eldest born? art silent still?
Cain. 'Tis better I should be so.
Adam. Wherefore so?
Cain. I have nought to ask.
Adam. Nor aught to thank for?
Cain. No.
Adam. Dost thou not *live?*
Cain. Must I not die?
Eve. Alas!
The fruit of our forbidden tree begins
To fall.
Adam. And we must gather it again.
Oh God! why didst thou plant the tree of knowledge?
Cain. And wherefore plucked ye not the tree of life?
Ye might have then defied him.
Adam. Oh! my son,
Blaspheme not: these are Serpent's words.
Cain. Why not?
The snake spoke *truth;* it *was* the Tree of Knowledge;
It *was* the Tree of Life: knowledge is good,
And Life is good; and how can both be evil?
Eve. My boy! thou speakest as I spoke in sin,
Before thy birth: let me not see renewed
My misery in thine. I have repented.
Let me not see my offspring fall into
The snares beyond the walls of Paradise,
Which even in Paradise destroyed his parents.

Content thee with what *is.* Had we been so,
Thou now hadst been contented. — Oh, my son!
Adam. Our orisons completed, let us hence,
Each to his task of toil — not heavy, though
Needful: the earth is young, and yields us kindly
Her fruits with little labour.
Eve. Cain — my son —
Behold thy father cheerful and resigned —
And do as he doth. [*Exeunt* ADAM *and* EVE.
Zillah. Wilt thou not, my brother?
Abel. Why wilt thou wear this gloom upon thy brow,
Which can avail thee nothing, save to rouse
The Eternal anger?
Adah. My belovéd Cain
Wilt thou frown even on me?
Cain. No, Adah! no;
I fain would be alone a little while.
Abel, I'm sick at heart; but it will pass;
Precede me, brother — I will follow shortly.
And you, too, sisters, tarry not behind;
Your gentleness must not be harshly met:
I'll follow you anon.
Adah. If not, I will
Return to seek you here.
Abel. The peace of God
Be on your spirit, brother!
[*Exeunt* ABEL, ZILLAH, *and* ADAH.
Cain (*solus*). And this is
Life? — Toil! and wherefore should I toil? — because
My father could not keep his place in Eden?
What had *I* done in this? — I was unborn:
I sought not to be born; nor love the state
To which that birth has brought me. Why did he
Yield to the Serpent and the woman? or
Yielding — why suffer? What was there in this?
The tree was planted, and why not for him?
If not, why place him near it, where it grew
The fairest in the centre? They have but
One answer to all questions, " 'Twas *his* will,
And *he* is good." How know I that? Because
He is all-powerful, must all-good, too, follow?
I judge but by the fruits — and they are bitter —
Which I must feed on for a fault not mine.
Whom have we here? — A shape like to the angels
Yet of a sterner and a sadder aspect
Of spiritual essence: why do I quake?

Why should I fear him more than other spirits,
Whom I see daily wave their fiery swords
Before the gates round which I linger oft,
In Twilight's hour, to catch a glimpse of those
Gardens which are my just inheritance,
Ere the night closes o'er the inhibited walls
And the immortal trees which overtop
The Cherubim-defended battlements?
If I shrink not from these, the fire-armed angels,
Why should I quail from him who now approaches?
Yet — he seems mightier far than them, nor less
Beauteous, and yet not all as beautiful
As he hath been, and might be: sorrow seems
Half of his immortality. And is it
So? and can aught grieve save Humanity?
He cometh.

Enter LUCIFER.

Lucifer. Mortal!
Cain. Spirit, who art thou?
Lucifer. Master of spirits.
Cain. And being so, canst thou
Leave them, and walk with dust?
Lucifer. I know the thoughts
Of dust, and feel for it, and with you.
Cain. How!
You know my thoughts?
Lucifer. They are the thoughts of all
Worthy of thought; — 'tis your immortal part
Which speaks within you.
Cain. What immortal part?
This has not been revealed: the Tree of Life
Was withheld from us by my father's folly,
While that of Knowledge, by my mother's haste,
Was plucked too soon; and all the fruit is Death!
Lucifer. They have deceived thee; thou shalt live.
Cain. I live,
But live to die; and, living, see no thing
To make death hateful, save an innate clinging,
A loathsome, and yet all invincible
Instinct of life, which I abhor, as I
Despise myself, yet cannot overcome —
And so I live. Would I had never lived!
Lucifer. Thou livest — and must live for ever. Think not
The Earth, which is thine outward cov'ring, is
Existence — it will cease — and thou wilt be —

No less than thou art now.
Cain. No *less!* and why
No more?
Lucifer. It may be thou shalt be as we.
Cain. And ye?
Lucifer. Are everlasting.
Cain. Are ye happy?
Lucifer. We are mighty.
Cain. Are ye happy?
Lucifer. No: art thou?
Cain. How should I be so? Look on me!
Lucifer. Poor clay!
And thou pretendest to be wretched! Thou!
Cain. I am: — and thou, with all thy might, what art thou?
Lucifer. One who aspired to be what made thee, and
Would not have made thee what thou art.
Cain. Ah!
Thou look'st almost a god; and ——
Lucifer. I am none:
And having failed to be one, would be nought
Save what I am. He conquered; let him reign!
Cain. Who?
Lucifer. Thy Sire's maker — and the Earth's.
Cain. And Heaven's,
And all that in them is. So I have heard
His Seraphs sing; and so my father saith.
Lucifer. They say — what they must sing and say, on pain
Of being that which I am, — and thou art —
Of spirits and of men.
Cain. And what is that?
Lucifer. Souls who dare use their immortality —
Souls who dare look the Omnipotent tyrant in
His everlasting face, and tell him that
His evil is not good! If he has made,
As he saith — which I know not, nor believe —
But, if he made us — he cannot unmake:
We are immortal! — nay, he'd *have* us so,
That he may torture: — let him! He is great —
But, in his greatness, is no happier than
We in our conflict! Goodness would not make
Evil; and what else hath he made? But let him
Sit on his vast and solitary throne —
Creating worlds, to make eternity
Less burthensome to his immense existence
And unparticipated solitude;
Let him crowd orb on orb: he is alone
Indefinite, Indissoluble Tyrant;

Could he but crush himself, 'twere the best boon
He ever granted: but let him reign on!
And multiply himself in misery!
Spirits and Men, at least we sympathise —
And, suffering in concert, make our pangs
Innumerable, more endurable,
By the unbounded sympathy of all
With all! But *He!* so wretched in his height,
So restless in his wretchedness, must still
Create, and re-create — perhaps he'll make
One day a Son unto himself — as he
Gave you a father — and if he so doth,
Mark me! that Son will be a sacrifice!
Cain. Thou speak'st to me of things which long have swum
In visions through my thought: I never could
Reconcile what I saw with what I heard.
My father and my mother talk to me
Of serpents, and of fruits and trees: I see
The gates of what they call their Paradise
Guarded by fiery-sworded Cherubim,
Which shut them out — and me: I feel the weight
Of daily toil, and constant thought: I look
Around a world where I seem nothing, with
Thoughts which arise within me, as if they
Could master all things — but I thought alone
This misery was *mine*. My father is
Tamed down; my mother has forgot the mind
Which made her thirst for knowledge at the risk
Of an eternal curse; my brother is
A watching shepherd boy, who offers up
The firstlings of the flock to him who bids
The earth yield nothing to us without sweat;
My sister Zillah sings an earlier hymn
Than the birds' matins; and my Adah — my
Own and belovéd — she, too, understands not
The mind which overwhelms me: never till
Now met I aught to sympathise with me.
'Tis well — I rather would consort with spirits.
Lucifer. And hadst thou not been fit by thine own soul
For such companionship, I would not now
Have stood before thee as I am: a serpent
Had been enough to charm ye, as before.
Cain. Ah! didst *thou* tempt my mother?
Lucifer. I tempt none,
Save with the truth: was not the Tree, the Tree
Of Knowledge? and was not the Tree of Life
Still fruitful? Did *I* bid her pluck them not?

Did I plant things prohibited within
The reach of beings innocent, and curious
By their own innocence? I would have made ye
Gods; and even He who thrust ye forth, so thrust ye
Because "ye should not eat the fruits of life,
"And become gods as we." Were those his words?
Cain. They were, as I have heard from those who heard them,
In thunder.
Lucifer. Then who was the Demon? He
Who would not let ye live, or he who would
Have made ye live for ever, in the joy
And power of Knowledge?
Cain. Would they had snatched both
The fruits, or neither!
Lucifer. One is yours already,
The other may be still.
Cain. How so?
Lucifer. By being
Yourselves, in your resistance. Nothing can
Quench the mind, if the mind will be itself
And centre of surrounding things — 'tis made
To sway.
Cain. But didst thou tempt my parents?
Lucifer. I?
Poor clay — what should I tempt them for, or how?
Cain. They say the Serpent was a spirit.
Lucifer. Who
Saith that? It is not written so on high:
The proud One will not so far falsify,
Though man's vast fears and little vanity
Would make him cast upon the spiritual nature
His own low failing. The snake *was* the snake —
No more; and yet not less than those he tempted,
In nature being earth also — *more* in *wisdom,*
Since he could overcome them, and foreknew
The knowledge fatal to their narrow joys.
Think'st thou I'd take the shape of things that die?
Cain. But the thing had a demon?
Lucifer. He but woke one
In those he spake to with his forky tongue.
I tell thee that the Serpent was no more
Than a mere serpent: ask the Cherubim
Who guard the tempting tree. When thousand ages
Have rolled o'er your dead ashes, and your seed's,
The seed of the then world may thus array
Their earliest fault in fable, and attribute
To me a shape I scorn, as I scorn all

That bows to him, who made things but to bend
Before his sullen, sole eternity;
But we, who see the truth, must speak it. Thy
Fond parents listened to a creeping thing,
And fell. For what should spirits tempt them? What
Was there to envy in the narrow bounds
Of Paradise, that spirits who pervade
Space — but I speak to thee of what thou know'st not,
With all thy Tree of Knowledge.
Cain. But thou canst not
Speak aught of Knowledge which I would not know,
And do not thirst to know, and bear a mind
To know.
Lucifer. And heart to look on?
Cain. Be it proved.
Lucifer. Darest thou look on Death?
Cain. He has not yet
Been seen.
Lucifer. But must be undergone.
Cain. My father
Says he is something dreadful, and my mother
Weeps when he's named; and Abel lifts his eyes
To Heaven, and Zillah casts hers to the earth,
And sighs a prayer; and Adah looks on me,
And speaks not.
Lucifer. And thou?
Cain. Thoughts unspeakable
Crowd in my breast to burning, when I hear
Of this almighty Death, who is, it seems,
Inevitable. Could I wrestle with him?
I wrestled with the lion, when a boy,
In play, till he ran roaring from my gripe.
Lucifer. It has no shape; but will absorb all things
That bear the form of earth-born being.
Cain. Ah!
I thought it was a being: who could do
Such evil things to beings save a being?
Lucifer. Ask the Destroyer
Cain. Who?
Lucifer. The Maker — Call him
Which name thou wilt: he makes but to destroy.
Cain. I knew not that, yet thought it, since I heard
Of Death: although I know not what it is —
Yet it seems horrible. I have looked out
In the vast desolate night in search of him;
And when I saw gigantic shadows in
The umbrage of the walls of Eden, chequered

By the far-flashing of the Cherubs' swords,
I watched for what I thought his coming; for
With fear rose longing in my heart to know
What 'twas which shook us all — but nothing came.
And then I turned my weary eyes from off
Our native and forbidden Paradise,
Up to the lights above us, in the azure,
Which are so beautiful: shall they, too, die?

Lucifer. Perhaps — but long outlive both thine and thee.

Cain. I'm glad of that: I would not have them die —
They are so lovely. What is Death? I fear,
I feel, it is a dreadful thing; but what,
I cannot compass: 'tis denounced against us,
Both them who sinned and sinned not, as an ill —
What ill?

Lucifer. To be resolved into the earth.

Cain. But shall I know it?

Lucifer. As I know not death,
I cannot answer.

Cain. Were I quiet earth,
That were no evil: would I ne'er had been
Aught else but dust!

Lucifer. That is a *grovelling* wish,
Less than thy father's — for he wished to know!

Cain. But not to live — or wherefore plucked he not
The Life-tree?

Lucifer. He was hindered.

Cain. Deadly error!
Not to snatch first that fruit: — but ere he plucked
The knowledge, he was ignorant of Death.
Alas! I scarcely now know what it is,
And yet I fear it — fear I know not what!

Lucifer. And I, who know all things, fear nothing; see
What is true knowledge.

Cain. Wilt thou teach me all?

Lucifer. Aye, upon one condition.

Cain. Name it.

Lucifer. That
Thou dost fall down and worship me — thy Lord.

Cain. Thou art not the Lord my father worships.

Lucifer. No.

Cain. His equal?

Lucifer. No; — I have nought in common with him!
Nor would: I would be aught above — beneath —
Aught save a sharer or a servant of
His power. I dwell apart; but I am great: —
Many there are who worship me, and more

Who shall — be thou amongst the first.
Cain. I never
As yet have bowed unto my father's God.
Although my brother Abel oft implores
That I would join with him in sacrifice: —
Why should I bow to thee?
Lucifer. Hast thou ne'er bowed
To him?
Cain. Have I not said it? — need I say it?
Could not thy mighty knowledge teach thee that?
Lucifer. He who bows not to him has bowed to me.
Cain. But I will bend to neither.
Lucifer Ne'er the less,
Thou art my worshipper; not worshipping
Him makes thee mine the same.
Cain. And what is that?
Lucifer. Thou'lt know here — and hereafter.
Cain. Let me but
Be taught the mystery of my being.
Lucifer. Follow
Where I will lead thee.
Cain. But I must retire
To till the earth — for I had promised ——
Lucifer. What?
Cain. To cull some first-fruits.
Lucifer. Why?
Cain. To offer up
With Abel on an altar.
Lucifer. Said'st thou not
Thou ne'er hadst bent to him who made thee?
Cain. Yes —
But Abel's earnest prayer has wrought upon me;
The offering is more his than mine — and Adah ——
Lucifer. Why dost thou hesitate?
Cain. She is my sister,
Born on the same day, of the same womb; and
She wrung from me, with tears, this promise; and
Rather than see her weep, I would, methinks,
Bear all — and worship aught.
Lucifer. Then follow me!
Cain. I will.

Enter Adah.

Adah. My brother, I have come for thee;
It is our hour of rest and joy — and we

Have less without thee. Thou hast laboured not
This morn; but I have done thy task: the fruits
Are ripe, and glowing as the light which ripens:
Come away.
Cain. Seest thou not?
Adah. I see an angel;
We have seen many: will he share our hour
Of rest? — he is welcome.
Cain. But he is not like
The angels we have seen.
Adah. Are there, then, others?
But he is welcome, as they were: they deigned
To be our guests — will he?
Cain (to Lucifer). Wilt thou?
Lucifer. I ask
Thee to be mine.
Cain. I must away with him.
Adah. And leave us?
Cain. Aye.
Adah. And *me*?
Cain. Belovéd Adah!
Adah. Let me go with thee.
Lucifer. No, she must not.
Adah. Who
Art thou that steppest between heart and heart?
Cain. He is a God.
Adah. How know'st thou?
Cain. He speaks like
A God.
Adah. So did the Serpent, and it lied.
Lucifer. Thou errest, Adah! — was not the Tree that
Of Knowledge?
Adah. Aye — to our eternal sorrow.
Lucifer. And yet that grief is knowledge — so he lied not:
And if he did betray you, 'twas with Truth;
And Truth in its own essence cannot be
But good.
Adah. But all we know of it has gathered
Evil on ill; expulsion from our home,
And dread, and toil, and sweat, and heaviness;
Remorse of that which was — and hope of that
Which cometh not. Cain! walk not with this Spirit.
Bear with what we have borne, and love me — I
Love thee.
Lucifer. More than thy mother, and thy sire?
Adah. I do. Is that a sin, too?
Lucifer. No, not yet;

It one day will be in your children.
Adah. What!
Must not my daughter love her brother Enoch?
Lucifer. Not as thou lovest Cain.
Adah. Oh, my God!
Shall they not love and bring forth things that love
Out of their love? have they not drawn their milk
Out of this bosom? was not he, their father,
Born of the same sole womb, in the same hour
With me? did we not love each other? and
In multiplying our being multiply
Things which will love each other as we love
Them? — And as I love thee, my Cain! go not
Forth with this spirit; he is not of ours.
Lucifer. The sin I speak of is not of my making,
And cannot be a sin in you — whate'er
It seem in those who will replace ye in
Mortality.
Adah. What is the sin which is not
Sin in itself? Can circumstance make sin
Or virtue? — if it doth, we are the slaves
Of ——
Lucifer. Higher things than ye are slaves: and higher
Than them or ye would be so, did they not
Prefer an independency of torture
To the smooth agonies of adulation,
In hymns and harpings, and self-seeking prayers,
To that which is omnipotent, because
It is omnipotent, and not from love,
But terror and self-hope.
Adah. Omnipotence
Must be all goodness
Lucifer. Was it so in Eden?
Adah. Fiend! tempt me not with beauty; thou art fairer
Than was the Serpent, and as false.
Lucifer. As true.
Ask Eve, your mother: bears she not the knowledge
Of good and evil?
Adah. Oh, my mother! thou
Hast plucked a fruit more fatal to thine offspring
Than to thyself; thou at the least hast passed
Thy youth in Paradise, in innocent
And happy intercourse with happy spirits:
But we, thy children, ignorant of Eden,
Are girt about by demons, who assume
The words of God, and tempt us with our own
Dissatisfied and curious thoughts — as thou

Wert worked on by the snake, in thy most flushed
And heedless, harmless wantonness of bliss.
I cannot answer this immortal thing
Which stands before me; I cannot abhor him;
I look upon him with a pleasing fear,
And yet I fly not from him: in his eye
There is a fastening attraction which
Fixes my fluttering eyes on his; my heart
Beats quick; he awes me, and yet draws me near,
Nearer and nearer: — Cain — Cain — save me from him!
Cain. What dreads my Adah? This is no ill spirit.
Adah. He is not God — nor God's: I have beheld
The Cherubs and the Seraphs; he looks not
Like them.
Cain. But there are spirits loftier still —
The archangels.
Lucifer. And still loftier than the archangels.
Adah. Aye — but not blesséd.
Lucifer. If the blessedness
Consists in slavery — no.
Adah. I have heard it said,
The Seraphs *love most* — Cherubim *know most* —
And this should be a Cherub — since he loves not.
Lucifer. And if the higher knowledge quenches love,
What must *he be* you cannot love when known?
Since the all-knowing Cherubim love least,
The Seraphs' love can be but ignorance:
That they are not compatible, the doom
Of thy fond parents, for their daring, proves.
Choose betwixt Love and Knowledge — since there is
No other choice: your sire hath chosen already:
His worship is but fear.
Adah. Oh, Cain! choose Love.
Cain. For thee, my Adah, I choose not — It was
Born with me — but I love nought else.
Adah. Our parents?
Cain. Did they love us when they snatched from the Tree
That which hath driven us all from Paradise?
Adah. We were not born then — and if we had been,
Should we not love them — and our children, Cain?
Cain. My little Enoch! and his lisping sister!
Could I but deem them happy, I would half
Forget —— but it can never be forgotten
Through thrice a thousand generations! never
Shall men love the remembrance of the man
Who sowed the seed of evil and mankind
In the same hour! They plucked the tree of science

And sin — and, not content with their own sorrow,
Begot *me* — *thee* — and all the few that are,
And all the unnumbered and innumerable
Multitudes, millions, myriads, which may be,
To inherit agonies accumulated
By ages! — and *I* must be sire of such things!
Thy beauty and thy love — my love and joy,
The rapturous moment and the placid hour,
All we love in our children and each other,
But lead them and ourselves through many years
Of sin and pain — or few, but still of sorrow,
Interchecked with an instant of brief pleasure,
To Death — the unknown! Methinks the Tree of Knowledge
Hath not fulfilled its promise: — if they sinned,
At least they ought to have known all things that are
Of knowledge — and the mystery of Death.
What do they know? — that they are miserable.
What need of snakes and fruits to teach us that?
  Adah. I am not wretched, Cain, and if thou
Wert happy ——
  Cain. Be thou happy, then, alone —
I will have nought to do with happiness,
Which humbles me and mine.
  Adah. Alone I could not,
Nor *would* be happy; but with those around us
I think I could be so, despite of Death,
Which, as I know it not, I dread not, though
It seems an awful shadow — if I may
Judge from what I have heard.
  Lucifer. And thou couldst not
Alone, thou say'st, be happy?
  Adah. Alone! Oh, my God!
Who could be happy and alone, or good?
To me my solitude seems sin; unless
When I think how soon I shall see my brother,
His brother, and our children, and our parents.
  Lucifer. Yet thy God is alone; and is he happy?
Lonely, and good?
  Adah. He is not so; he hath
The angels and the mortals to make happy,
And thus becomes so in diffusing joy.
What else can joy be, but the spreading joy?
  Lucifer. Ask of your sire, the exile fresh from Eden;
Or of his first-born son: ask your own heart;
It is not tranquil.
  Adah. Alas! no! and you —
Are you of Heaven?

Lucifer. If I am not, enquire
The cause of this all-spreading happiness
(Which you proclaim) of the all-great and good
Maker of life and living things; it is
His secret, and he keeps it. *We* must bear,
And some of us resist — and both in vain,
His Seraphs say: but it is worth the trial,
Since better may not be without: there is
A wisdom in the spirit, which directs
To right, as in the dim blue air the eye
Of you, young mortals, lights at once upon
The star which watches, welcoming the morn.
Adah. It is a beautiful star; I love it for
Its beauty.
Lucifer. And why not adore?
Adah. Our father
Adores the Invisible only.
Lucifer. But the symbols
Of the Invisible are the loveliest
Of what is visible; and yon bright star
Is leader of the host of Heaven.
Adah. Our father
Saith that he has beheld the God himself
Who made him and our mother.
Lucifer Hast *thou* seen him?
Adah. Yes — in his works.
Lucifer. But in his being?
Adah. No —
Save in my father, who is God's own image;
Or in his angels, who are like to thee —
And brighter, yet less beautiful and powerful
In seeming: as the silent sunny noon,
All light, they look upon us; but thou seem'st
Like an ethereal night, where long white clouds
Streak the deep purple, and unnumbered stars
Spangle the wonderful mysterious vault
With things that look as if they would be suns;
So beautiful, unnumbered, and endearing,
Not dazzling, and yet drawing us to them,
They fill my eyes with tears, and so dost thou.
Thou seem'st unhappy: do not make us so,
And I will weep for thee.
Lucifer. Alas! those tears!
Couldst thou but know what oceans will be shed ——
Adah. By me?
Lucifer. By all.
Adah. What all?

Lucifer. The million millions —
The myriad myriads — the all-peopled earth —
The unpeopled earth — and the o'er-peopled Hell,
Of which thy bosom is the germ.
Adah. O Cain!
This spirit curseth us.
Cain. Let him say on;
Him will I follow.
Adah. Whither?
Lucifer. To a place
Whence he shall come back to thee in an hour;
But in that hour see things of many days.
Adah. How can that be?
Lucifer. Did not your Maker make
Out of old worlds this new one in few days?
And cannot I, who aided in this work,
Show in an hour what he hath made in many,
Or hath destroyed in few?
Cain. Lead on.
Adah. Will he,
In sooth, return within an hour?
Lucifer. He shall.
With us acts are exempt from time, and we
Can crowd eternity into an hour,
Or stretch an hour into eternity:
We breathe not by a mortal measurement —
But that's a mystery. Cain, come on with me.
Adah. Will he return?
Lucifer. Aye, woman! he alone
Of mortals from that place (the first and last
Who shall return, save ONE), shall come back to thee,
To make that silent and expectant world
As populous as this: at present there
Are few inhabitants.
Adah. Where dwellest thou?
Lucifer. Throughout all space. Where should I dwell? Where are
Thy God or Gods — there am I: all things are
Divided with me: Life and Death — and Time —
Eternity — and heaven and earth — and that
Which is not heaven nor earth, but peopled with
Those who once peopled or shall people both —
These are my realms! so that I do divide
His, and possess a kingdom which is not
His. If I were not that which I have said,
Could I stand here? His angels are within
Your vision.
Adah. So they were when the fair Serpent

Spoke with our mother first.
Lucifer. Cain! thou hast heard.
If thou dost long for knowledge, I can satiate
That thirst; nor ask thee to partake of fruits
Which shall deprive thee of a single good
The Conqueror has left thee. Follow me.
Cain. Spirit, I have said it.

[*Exeunt* LUCIFER *and* CAIN.

Adah (*follows exclaiming*). Cain! my brother! Cain!

ACT II

SCENE I. — *The Abyss of Space.*

Cain. I tread on air, and sink not — yet I fear
To sink.
Lucifer. Have faith in me, and thou shalt be
Borne on the air, of which I am the Prince.
Cain. Can I do so without impiety?
Lucifer. Believe — and sink not! doubt — and perish! thus
Would run the edict of the other God,
Who names me Demon to his angels; they
Echo the sound to miserable things,
Which, knowing nought beyond their shallow senses,
Worship the *word* which strikes their ear, and deem
Evil or good what is proclaimed to them
In their abasement. I will have none such:
Worship or worship not, thou shalt behold
The worlds beyond thy little world, nor be
Amerced for doubts beyond thy little life,
With torture of *my* dooming. There will come
An hour, when, tossed upon some water-drops,
A man shall say to a man, "Believe in me,
And walk the waters;" and the man shall walk
The billows and be safe. *I* will not say,
Believe in *me*, as a conditional creed
To save thee; but fly with me o'er the gulf
Of space an equal flight, and I will show
What thou dar'st not deny, — the history
Of past — and present, and of future worlds.
Cain. Oh God! or Demon! or whate'er thou art,
Is yon our earth?
Lucifer. Dost thou not recognise
The dust which formed your father?
Cain. Can it be?
Yon small blue circle, swinging in far ether,

With an inferior circlet purpler it still,
Which looks like that which lit our earthly night?
Is this our Paradise? Where are its walls,
And they who guard them?
Lucifer. Point me out the site
Of Paradise.
Cain. How should I? As we move
Like sunbeams onward, it grows small and smaller,
And as it waxes little, and then less,
Gathers a halo round it, like the light
Which shone the roundest of the stars, when I
Beheld them from the skirts of Paradise:
Methinks they both, as we recede from them,
Appear to join the innumerable stars
Which are around us; and, as we move on,
Increase their myriads.
Lucifer. And if there should be
Worlds greater than thine own — inhabited
By greater things — and they themselves far more
In number than the dust of thy dull earth,
Though multiplied to animated atoms,
All living — and all doomed to death — and wretched,
What wouldst thou think?
Cain. I should be proud of thought
Which knew such things.
Lucifer. But if that high thought were
Linked to a servile mass of matter — and,
Knowing such things, aspiring to such things,
And science still beyond them, were chained down
To the most gross and petty paltry wants,
All foul and fulsome — and the very best
Of thine enjoyments a sweet degradation,
A most enervating and filthy cheat
To lure thee on to the renewal of
Fresh souls and bodies, all foredoomed to be
As frail, and few so happy ——
Cain. Spirit! I
Know nought of Death, save as a dreadful thing
Of which I have heard my parents speak, as of
A hideous heritage I owe to them
No less than life — a heritage not happy,
If I may judge, till now. But, Spirit! if
It be as thou hast said (and I within
Feel the prophetic torture of its truth),
Here let me die: for to give birth to those
Who can but suffer many years, and die —
Methinks is merely propagating Death,

And multiplying murder.
Lucifer. Thou canst not
All die — there is what must survive.
Cain. The Other
Spake not of this unto my father, when
He shut him forth from Paradise, with death
Written upon his forehead. But at least
Let what is mortal of me perish, that
I may be in the rest as angels are.
Lucifer. I am angelic: wouldst thou be as I am?
Cain. I know not what thou art: I see thy power,
And see thou show'st me things beyond my power,
Beyond all power of my born faculties,
Although inferior still to my desires
And my conceptions.
Lucifer. What are they which dwell
So humbly in their pride, as to sojourn
With worms in clay?
Cain. And what art thou who dwellest
So haughtily in spirit, and canst range
Nature and immortality — and yet
Seem'st sorrowful?
Lucifer. I seem that which I am;
And therefore do I ask of thee, if thou
Wouldst be immortal?
Cain. Thou hast said, I must be
Immortal in despite of me. I knew not
This until lately — but since it must be,
Let me, or happy or unhappy, learn
To anticipate my immortality.
Lucifer. Thou didst before I came upon thee.
Cain. How?
Lucifer. By suffering.
Cain. And must torture be immortal?
Lucifer. We and thy sons will try. But now, behold!
Is it not glorious?
Cain. Oh thou beautiful
And unimaginable ether! and
Ye multiplying masses of increased
And still-increasing lights! what are ye? what
Is this blue wilderness of interminable
Air, where ye roll along, as I have seen
The leaves along the limpid streams of Eden?
Is your course measured for ye? Or do ye
Sweep on in your unbounded revelry
Through an aërial universe of endless
Expansion — at which my soul aches to think —

Intoxicated with eternity?
Oh God! Oh Gods! or whatsoe'er ye are!
How beautiful ye are! how beautiful
Your works, or accidents, or whatsoe'er
They may be! Let me die, as atoms die,
(If that they die), or know ye in your might
And knowledge! My thoughts are not in this hour
Unworthy what I see, though my dust is;
Spirit! let me expire, or see them nearer.
Lucifer. Art thou not nearer? look back to thine earth!
Cain. Where is it? I see nothing save a mass
Of most innumerable lights.
Lucifer. Look there!
Cain. I cannot see it.
Lucifer. Yet it sparkles still.
Cain. That! — yonder!
Lucifer. Yea.
Cain. And wilt thou tell me so?
Why, I have seen the fire-flies and fire-worms
Sprinkle the dusky groves and the green banks
In the dim twilight, brighter than yon world
Which bears them.
Lucifer. Thou hast seen both worms and worlds,
Each bright and sparkling — what dost think of them?
Cain. That they are beautiful in their own sphere,
And that the night, which makes both beautiful,
The little shining fire-fly in its flight,
And the immortal star in its great course,
Must both be guided.
Lucifer. But by whom or what?
Cain. Show me.
Lucifer. Dar'st thou behold?
Cain. How know I what
I *dare* behold? As yet, thou hast shown nought
I dare not gaze on further.
Lucifer. On, then, with me.
Wouldst thou behold things mortal or immortal?
Cain. Why, what are things?
Lucifer. *Both* partly: but what doth
Sit next thy heart?
Cain. The things I see.
Lucifer. But what
Sate nearest it?
Cain. The things I have not seen,
Nor ever shall — the mysteries of Death.
Lucifer. What, if I show to thee things which have died,
As I have shown thee much which cannot die?

Cain. Do so.
Lucifer. Away, then! on our mighty wings!
Cain. Oh! how we cleave the blue! The stars fade from us!
The earth! where is my earth? Let me look on it,
For I was made of it.
Lucifer. 'Tis now beyond thee,
Less, in the universe, than thou in it;
Yet deem not that thou canst escape it; thou
Shalt soon return to earth, and all its dust:
'Tis part of thy eternity, and mine.
Cain. Where dost thou lead me?
Lucifer. To what was before thee!
The phantasm of the world; of which thy world
Is but the wreck.
Cain. What! is it not then new?
Lucifer. No more than life is; and that was ere thou
Or *I* were, or the things which seem to us
Greater than either: many things will have
No end; and some, which would pretend to have
Had no beginning, have had one as mean
As thou; and mightier things have been extinct
To make way for much meaner than we can
Surmise; for *moments* only and the *space*
Have been and must be all *unchangeable*.
But changes make not death, except to clay;
But thou art clay — and canst but comprehend
That which was clay, and such thou shalt behold.
Cain. Clay — Spirit — what thou wilt — I can survey.
Lucifer. Away, then!
Cain. But the lights fade from me fast,
And some till now grew larger as we approached,
And wore the look of worlds.
Lucifer. And such they are.
Cain. And Edens in them?
Lucifer. It may be.
Cain. And men?
Lucifer. Yea, or things higher.
Cain. Aye! and serpents too?
Lucifer. Wouldst thou have men without them? must no reptiles
Breathe, save the erect ones?
Cain. How the lights recede!
Where fly we?
Lucifer. To the world of phantoms, which
Are beings past, and shadows still to come.
Cain. But it grows dark, and dark — the stars are gone!
Lucifer. And yet thou seest.
Cain. 'Tis a fearful light!

No sun — no moon — no lights innumerable —
The very blue of the empurpled night
Fades to a dreary twilight — yet I see
Huge dusky masses; but unlike the worlds
We were approaching, which, begirt with light,
Seemed full of life even when their atmosphere
Of light gave way, and showed them taking shapes
Unequal, of deep valleys and vast mountains;
And some emitting sparks, and some displaying
Enormous liquid plains, and some begirt
With luminous belts, and floating moons, which took,
Like them, the features of fair earth: — instead,
All here seems dark and dreadful.
Lucifer. But distinct.
Thou seekest to behold Death, and dead things?
Cain. I seek it not; but as I know there are
Such, and that my sire's sin makes him and me,
And all that we inherit, liable
To such, I would behold, at once, what I
Must one day see perforce.
Lucifer. Behold!
Cain. 'Tis darkness!
Lucifer. And so it shall be ever — but we will
Unfold its gates!
Cain. Enormous vapours roll
Apart — what's this?
Lucifer. Enter!
Cain. Can I return?
Lucifer. Return! be sure: how else should Death be peopled?
Its present realm is thin to what it will be,
Through thee and thine.
Cain. The clouds still open wide
And wider, and make widening circles round us!
Lucifer. Advance!
Cain. And thou!
Lucifer. Fear not — without me thou
Couldst not have gone beyond thy world. On! on!
[*They disappear through the clouds.*

SCENE II. — *Hades*

Enter LUCIFER *and* CAIN.

Cain. How silent and how vast are these dim worlds!
For they seem more than one, and yet more peopled
Than the huge brilliant luminous orbs which swung
So thickly in the upper air, that I

Had deemed them rather the bright populace
Of some all unimaginable Heaven,
Than things to be inhabited themselves,
But that on drawing near them I beheld
Their swelling into palpable immensity
Of matter, which seemed made for life to dwell on,
Rather than life itself. But here, all is
So shadowy, and so full of twilight, that
It speaks of a day past.

Lucifer. It is the realm
Of Death. — Wouldst have it present?

Cain. Till I know
That which it really is, I cannot answer.
But if it be as I have heard my father
Deal out in his long homilies, 'tis a thing —
Oh God! I dare not think on't! Cursèd be
He who invented Life that leads to Death!
Or the dull mass of life, that, being life,
Could not retain, but needs must forfeit it —
Even for the innocent!

Lucifer. Dost thou curse thy father?

Cain. Cursed he not me in giving me my birth?
Cursed he not me before my birth, in daring
To pluck the fruit forbidden?

Lucifer. Thou say'st well:
The curse is mutual 'twixt thy sire and thee —
But for thy sons and brother?

Cain. Let them share it
With me, their sire and brother! What else is
Bequeathed to me? I leave them my inheritance!
Oh, ye interminable gloomy realms
Of swimming shadows and enormous shapes,
Some fully shown, some indistinct, and all
Mighty and melancholy — what are ye?
Live ye, or have ye lived?

Lucifer. Somewhat of both.

Cain. Then what is Death?

Lucifer. What? Hath not he who made ye
Said 'tis another life?

Cain. Till now he hath
Said nothing, save that all shall die.

Lucifer. Perhaps
He one day will unfold that further secret.

Cain. Happy the day!

Lucifer. Yes; happy! when unfolded,
Through agonies unspeakable, and clogged
With agonies eternal, to innumerable

Yet unborn myriads of unconscious atoms,
All to be animated for this only!
Cain. What are these mighty phantoms which I see
Floating around me? — They wear not the form
Of the Intelligences I have seen
Round our regretted and unentered Eden;
Nor wear the form of man as I have viewed it
In Adam's and in Abel's, and in mine,
Nor in my sister-bride's, nor in my children's:
And yet they have an aspect, which, though not
Of men nor angels, looks like something, which,
If not the last, rose higher than the first,
Haughty, and high, and beautiful, and full
Of seeming strength, but of inexplicable
Shape; for I never saw such. They bear not
The wing of Seraph, nor the face of man,
Nor form of mightiest brute, nor aught that is
Now breathing; mighty yet and beautiful
As the most beautiful and mighty which
Live, and yet so unlike them, that I scarce
Can call them living.
Lucifer. Yet they lived.
Cain. Where?
Lucifer. Where
Thou livest.
Cain. When?
Lucifer. On what thou callest earth
They did inhabit.
Cain. Adam is the first.
Lucifer. Of thine, I grant thee — but too mean to be
The last of these.
Cain. And what are they?
Lucifer. That which
Thou shalt be.
Cain. But what *were* they?
Lucifer. Living, high,
Intelligent, good, great, and glorious things,
As much superior unto all thy sire
Adam could e'er have been in Eden, as
The sixty-thousandth generation shall be,
In its dull damp degeneracy, to
Thee and thy son; — and how weak they are, judge
By thy own flesh.
Cain. Ah me! and did *they* perish?
Lucifer. Yes, from their earth, as thou wilt fade from thine.
Cain. But was *mine* theirs?
Lucifer. It was.

Cain. But not as now.
It is too little and too lowly to
Sustain such creatures.
Lucifer. True, it was more glorious.
Cain. And wherefore did it fall?
Lucifer. Ask him who fells.
Cain. But how?
Lucifer. By a most crushing and inexorable
Destruction and disorder of the elements,
Which struck a world to chaos, as a chaos
Subsiding has struck out a world: such things,
Though rare in time, are frequent in eternity. —
Pass on, and gaze upon the past.
Cain. 'Tis awful!
Lucifer. And true. Behold these phantoms! they were once
Material as thou art.
Cain. And must I be
Like them?
Lucifer. Let He who made thee answer that.
I show thee what thy predecessors are,
And what they *were* thou feelest, in degree
Inferior as thy petty feelings and
Thy pettier portion of the immortal part
Of high intelligence and earthly strength.
What ye in common have with what they had
Is Life, and what ye *shall* have — Death: the rest
Of your poor attributes is such as suits
Reptiles engendered out of the subsiding
Slime of a mighty universe, crushed into
A scarcely-yet shaped planet, peopled with
Things whose enjoyment was to be in blindness —
A Paradise of Ignorance, from which
Knowledge was barred as poison. But behold
What these superior beings are or were;
Or, if it irk thee, turn thee back and till
The earth, thy task — I'll waft thee there in safety.
Cain. No: I'll stay here.
Lucifer. How long?
Cain. For ever! Since
I must one day return here from the earth,
I rather would remain; I am sick of all
That dust has shown me — let me dwell in shadows.
Lucifer. It cannot be: thou now beholdest as
A vision that which is reality.
To make thyself fit for this dwelling, thou
Must pass through what the things thou seest have passed —
The gates of Death.

Cain. By what gate have we entered
Even now?
Lucifer. By mine! But, plighted to return,
My spirit buoys thee up to breathe in regions
Where all is breathless save thyself. Gaze on;
But do not think to dwell here till thine hour
Is come!
Cain. And these, too — can they ne'er repass
To earth again?
Lucifer. *Their* earth is gone for ever —
So changed by its convulsion, they would not
Be conscious to a single present spot
Of its new scarcely hardened surface — 'twas —
Oh, what a beautiful world it *was!*
Cain. And is!
It is not with the earth, though I must till it,
I feel at war — but that I may not profit
By what it bears of beautiful, untoiling,
Nor gratify my thousand swelling thoughts
With knowledge, nor allay my thousand fears
Of Death and Life.
Lucifer. What thy world is, thou see'st,
But canst not comprehend the shadow of
That which it was.
Cain. And those enormous creatures,
Phantoms inferior in intelligence
(At least so seeming) to the things we have passed,
Resembling somewhat the wild habitants
Of the deep woods of earth, the hugest which
Roar nightly in the forest, but ten-fold
In magnitude and terror; taller than
The cherub-guarded walls of Eden — with
Eyes flashing like the fiery swords which fence them —
And tusks projecting like the trees stripped of
Their bark and branches — what were they?
Lucifer. That which
The Mammoth is in thy world; — but these lie
By myriads underneath its surface.
Cain. But
None on it?
Lucifer. No: for they frail race to war
With them would render the curse on it useless —
'Twould be destroyed so early.
Cain. But why *war?*
Lucifer. You have forgotten the denunciation
Which drove your race from Eden — war with all things,
And death to all things, and disease to most things,

And pangs, and bitterness; these were the fruits
Of the forbidden tree.
Cain. But animals —
Did they, too, eat of it, that they must die?
Lucifer. Your Maker told ye, *they* were made for you,
As you for him. — You would not have their doom
Superior to your own? Had Adam not
Fallen, all had stood.
Cain. Alas! the hopeless wretches!
They too must share my sire's fate, like his sons;
Like them, too, without having shared the apple;
Like them, too, without the so dear-bought *knowledge!*
It was a lying tree — for we *know* nothing.
At least it *promised knowledge* at the *price*
Of death — but *knowledge* still: but what *knows* man?
Lucifer. It may be death leads to the *highest* knowledge;
And being of all things the sole thing certain,
At least leads to the *surest* science: therefore
The Tree was true, though deadly.
Cain. These dim realms!
I see them, but I know them not.
Lucifer. Because
Thy hour is yet afar, and matter cannot
Comprehend spirit wholly — but 'tis something
To know there are such realms.
Cain. We knew already
That there was Death.
Lucifer. But not what was beyond it.
Cain. Nor know I now.
Lucifer. Thou knowest that there is
A state, and many states beyond thine own —
And this thou knewest not this morn.
Cain. But all
Seems dim and shadowy.
Lucifer. Be content; it will
Seem clearer to thine immortality.
Cain. And yon immeasurable liquid space
Of glorious azure which floats on beyond us,
Which looks like water, and which I should deem
The river which flows out of Paradise
Past my own dwelling, but that it is bankless
And boundless, and of an ethereal hue —
What is it?
Lucifer. There is still some such on earth,
Although inferior, and thy children shall
Dwell near it — 'tis the phantasm of an Ocean.
Cain. 'Tis like another world; a liquid sun —

And those inordinate creatures sporting o'er
Its shining surface?
Lucifer. Are its inhabitants,
The past Leviathans.
Cain. And yon immense
Serpent, which rears his dripping mane and vasty
Head, ten times higher than the haughtiest cedar,
Forth from the abyss, looking as he could coil
Himself around the orbs we lately looked on —
Is he not of the kind which basked beneath
The Tree in Eden?
Lucifer. Eve, thy mother, best
Can tell what shape of serpent tempted her.
Cain. This seems too terrible. No doubt the other
Had more of beauty.
Lucifer. Hast thou ne'er beheld him?
Cain. Many of the same kind (at least so called)
But never that precisely, which persuaded
The fatal fruit, nor even of the same aspect.
Lucifer. Your father saw him not?
Cain. No: 'twas my mother
Who tempted him — she tempted by the serpent.
Lucifer. Good man! whene'er thy wife, or thy sons' wives,
Tempt thee or them to aught that's new or strange,
Be sure thou seest first who hath tempted *them!*
Cain. Thy precept comes too late: there is no more
For serpents to tempt woman to.
Lucifer. But there
Are some things still which woman may tempt man to,
And man tempt woman: — let thy sons look to it!
My counsel is a kind one; for 'tis even
Given chiefly at my own expense; 'tis true,
'Twill not be followed, so there's little lost.
Cain. I understand not this.
Lucifer. The happier thou! —
Thy world and thou are still too young! Thou thinkest
Thyself most wicked and unhappy — is it
Not so?
Cain. For crime, I know not; but for pain,
I have felt much.
Lucifer. First-born of the first man!
They present state of sin — and thou art evil,
Of sorrow — and thou sufferest, are both Eden
In all its innocence compared to what
Thou shortly may'st be; and that state again,
In its redoubled wretchedness, a Paradise
To what thy sons' sons' sons, accumulating

In generations like to dust (which they
In fact but add to), shall endure and do. —
Now let us back to earth!
Cain. And wherefore didst thou
Lead me here only to inform me this?
Lucifer. Was not thy quest for knowledge?
Cain. Yes — as being
The road to happiness!
Lucifer. If truth be so,
Thou hast it.
Cain. Then my father's God did well
When he prohibited the fatal Tree.
Lucifer. But had done better in not planting it.
But ignorance of evil doth not save
From evil; it must still roll on the same,
A part of all things.
Cain. Not of all things. No —
I'll not believe it — for I thirst for good.
Lucifer. And who and what doth not? *Who* covets evil
For its own bitter sake? — *None* — nothing! 'tis
The leaven of all life, and lifelessness.
Cain. Within those glorious orbs which we behold,
Distant, and dazzling, and innumerable,
Ere we came down into this phantom realm,
Ill cannot come: they are too beautiful.
Lucifer. Thou hast seen them from afar.
Cain. And what of that?
Distance can but diminish glory — they,
When nearer, must be more ineffable.
Lucifer. Approach the things of earth most beautiful,
And judge their beauty near.
Cain. I have done this —
The loveliest thing I know is loveliest nearest.
Lucifer. Then there must be delusion. — What is that
Which being nearest to thine eyes is still
More beautiful than beauteous things remote?
Cain. My sister Adah. — All the stars of heaven,
The deep blue noon of night, lit by an orb
Which looks a spirit, or a spirit's world —
The hues of twilight — the Sun's gorgeous coming —
His setting indescribable, which fills
My eyes with pleasant tears as I behold
Him sink, and feel my heart float softly with him
Along that western paradise of clouds —
The forest shade, the green bough, the bird's voice —
The vesper bird's, which seems to sing of love,
And mingles with the song of Cherubim,

As the day closes over Eden's walls; —
All these are nothing, to my eyes and heart,
Like Adah's face: I turn from earth and heaven
To gaze on it.
   Lucifer.   'Tis fair as frail mortality,
In the first dawn and bloom of young creation,
And earliest embraces of earth's parents,
Can make its offspring; still it is delusion.
   Cain. You think so, being not her brother.
   Lucifer.   Mortal!
My brotherhood's with those who have no children.
   Cain. Then thou canst have no fellowship with us.
   Lucifer. It may be that thine own shall be for me.
But if thou dost possess a beautiful
Being beyond all beauty in thine eyes,
Why art thou wretched?
   Cain.   Why do I exist?
Why art *thou* wretched? why are all things so?
Ev'n he who made us must be, as the maker
Of things unhappy! To produce destruction
Can surely never be the task of joy,
And yet my sire says he's omnipotent:
Then why is Evil — he being Good? I asked
This question of my father; and he said,
Because this Evil only was the path
To Good. Strange Good, that must arise from out
Its deadly opposite. I lately saw
A lamb stung by a reptile: the poor suckling
Lay foaming on the earth, beneath the vain
And piteous bleating of its restless dam;
My father plucked some herbs, and laid them to
The wound; and by degrees the helpless wretch
Resumed its careless life, and rose to drain
The mother's milk, who o'er it tremulous
Stood licking its reviving limbs with joy.
Behold, my son! said Adam, how from Evil
Springs Good!
   Lucifer.   What didst thou answer?
   Cain.   Nothing; for
He is my father: but I thought, that 'twere
A better portion for the animal
Never to have been *stung at all,* than to
Purchase renewal of its little life
With agonies unutterable, though
Dispelled by antidotes.
   Lucifer.   But as thou saidst
Of all belovéd things thou lovest her

Who shared thy mother's milk, and giveth hers
Unto thy children ——
Cain. Most assuredly:
What should I be without her?
Lucifer. What am I?
Cain. Dost thou love nothing?
Lucifer. What does thy God love?
Cain. All things, my father says; but I confess
I see it not in their allotment here.
Lucifer. And, therefore, thou canst not see if *I* love
Or no — except some vast and general purpose,
To which particular things must melt like snows.
Cain. Snows! what are they?
Lucifer. Be happier in not knowing
What thy remoter offspring must encounter;
But bask beneath the clime which knows no winter.
Cain. But dost thou not love something like thyself?
Lucifer. And dost thou love *thyself?*
Cain. Yes, but love more
What makes my feelings more endurable,
And is more than myself, because I love it!
Lucifer. Thou lovest it, because 'tis beautiful,
As was the apple in thy mother's eye;
And when it ceases to be so, thy love
Will cease, like any other appetite.
Cain. Cease to be beautiful! how can that be?
Lucifer. With time.
Cain. But time has passed, and hitherto
Even Adam and my mother both are fair:
Not fair like Adah and the Seraphim —
But very fair.
Lucifer. All that must pass away
In them and her.
Cain. I'm sorry for it; but
Cannot conceive my love for her the less:
And when her beauty disappears, methinks
He who creates all beauty will lose more
Than me in seeing perish such a work.
Lucifer. I pity thee who lovest what must perish.
Cain. And I thee who lov'st nothing.
Lucifer. And thy brother —
Sits he not near thy heart?
Cain. Why should he not?
Lucifer. Thy father loves him well — so does thy God.
Cain. And so do I.
Lucifer. 'Tis well and meekly done.
Cain. Meekly!

Lucifer. He is the second born of flesh,
And is his mother's favourite.
Cain. Let him keep
Her favour, since the Serpent was the first
To win it.
Lucifer. And his father's?
Cain. What is that
To me? should I not love that which all love?
Lucifer. And the Jehovah — the indulgent Lord,
And bounteous planter of barred Paradise —
He, too, looks smilingly on Abel.
Cain. I
Ne'er saw him, and I know not if he smiles.
Lucifer. But you have seen his angels.
Cain. Rarely.
Lucifer. But
Sufficiently to see they love your brother:
His sacrifices are acceptable.
Cain. So be they! wherefore speak to me of this?
Lucifer. Because thou hast thought of this ere now.
Cain. And if
I *have* thought, why recall a thought that —— (*he pauses as agitated*)
— Spirit!
Here we are in *thy* world; speak not of *mine.*
Thou hast shown me wonders: thou hast shown me those
Mighty Pre-Adamites who walked the earth
Of which ours is the wreck: thou hast pointed out
Myriads of starry worlds, of which our own
Is the dim and remote companion, in
Infinity of life: thou hast shown me shadows
Of that existence with the dreaded name
Which my sire brought us — Death; thou hast shown me much
But not all: show me where Jehovah dwells,
In his especial Paradise — or *thine:*
Where is it?
Lucifer. *Here,* and o'er all space.
Cain. But ye
Have some allotted dwelling — as all things;
Clay has its earth, and other worlds their tenants;
All temporary breathing creatures their
Peculiar element; and things which have
Long ceased to breathe *our* breath, have theirs, thou say'st;
And the Jehovah and thyself have thine —
Ye do not dwell together?
Lucifer. No, we reign
Together; but our dwellings are asunder.
Cain. Would there were only one of ye! perchance

An unity of purpose might make union
In elements which seem now jarred in storms.
How came ye, being Spirits wise and infinite,
To separate? Are ye not as brethren in
Your essence — and your nature, and your glory?
Lucifer. Art not thou Abel's brother?
Cain. We are brethren,
And so we shall remain; but were it not so,
Is spirit like to flesh? can it fall out —
Infinity with Immortality?
Jarring and turning space to misery —
For what?
Lucifer. To reign.
Cain. Did ye not tell me that
Ye are both eternal?
Lucifer. Yea!
Cain. And what I have seen —
Yon blue immensity, is boundless?
Lucifer. Aye.
Cain. And cannot ye both *reign*, then? — is there not
Enough? — why should ye differ?
Lucifer. We *both* reign.
Cain. But one of you makes evil.
Lucifer. Which?
Cain. Thou! for
If thou canst do man good, why dost thou not?
Lucifer. And why not he who made? *I* made ye not;
Ye are *his* creatures, and not mine.
Cain. Then leave us
His creatures, as thou say'st we are, or show me
Thy dwelling, or *his* dwelling.
Lucifer. I could show thee
Both; but the time will come thou shalt see one
Of them for evermore.
Cain. And why not now?
Lucifer. Thy human mind hath scarcely grasp to gather
The little I have shown thee into calm
And clear thought: and *thou* wouldst go on aspiring
To the great double Mysteries! the *two Principles!*
And gaze upon them on their secret thrones!
Dust! limit thy ambition; for to see
Either of these would be for thee to perish!
Cain. And let me perish, so I see them!
Lucifer. There
The son of her who snatched the apple spake!
But thou wouldst only perish, and not see them;
That sight is for the other state.

Cain. Of Death?
Lucifer. That is the prelude.
Cain. Then I dread it less,
Now that I know it leads to something definite.
Lucifer. And now I will convey thee to thy world,
Where thou shalt multiply the race of Adam,
Eat, drink, toil, tremble, laugh, weep, sleep — and die!
Cain. And to what end have I beheld these things
Which thou hast shown me?
Lucifer. Didst thou not require
Knowledge? And have I not, in what I showed,
Taught thee to know thyself?
Cain. Alas! I seem
Nothing.
Lucifer. And this should be the human sum
Of knowledge, to know mortal nature's nothingness;
Bequeath that science to thy children, and
'Twill spare them many tortures.
Cain. Haughty spirit!
Thou speak'st it proudly; but thyself, though proud,
Hast a superior.
Lucifer. No! By heaven, which he
Holds, and the abyss, and the immensity
Of worlds and life, which I hold with him — No!
I have a Victor — true; but no superior.
Homage he has from all — but none from me:
I battle it against him, as I battled
In highest Heaven — through all Eternity,
And the unfathomable gulfs of Hades,
And the interminable realms of space,
And the infinity of endless ages,
All, all, will I dispute! And world by world,
And star by star, and universe by universe,
Shall tremble in the balance, till the great
Conflict shall cease, if ever it shall cease,
Which it ne'er shall, till he or I be quenched!
And what can quench our immortality,
Or mutual and irrevocable hate?
He as a conqueror will call the conquered
Evil; but what will be the *Good* he gives?
Were I the victor, *his* works would be deemed
The only evil ones. And you, ye new
And scarce-born mortals, what have been his gifts
To you already, in your little world?
Cain. But few; and some of those but bitter.
Lucifer. Back
With me, then, to thine earth, and try the rest

Of his celestial boons to you and yours.
Evil and Good are things in their own essence,
And not made good or evil by the Giver;
But if he gives you good — so call him; if
Evil springs from *him,* do not name it *mine,*
Till ye know better its true fount; and judge
Not by words, though of Spirits, but the fruits
Of your existence, such as it must be.
One good gift has the fatal apple given, —
Your *reason:* — let it not be overswayed
By tyrannous threats to force you into faith
'Gainst all external sense and inward feeling:
Think and endure, — and form an inner world
In your own bosom — where the outward fails;
So shall you nearer be the spiritual
Nature, and war triumphant with your own.

[*They disappear.*

ACT III

SCENE I. — *The Earth, near Eden, as in Act I.*

Enter CAIN *and* ADAH.

Adah. Hush! tread softly, Cain!
Cain. I will — but wherefore?
Adah. Our little Enoch sleeps upon yon bed
Of leaves, beneath the cypress.
Cain. Cypress! 'tis
A gloomy tree, which looks as if it mourned
O'er what it shadows; wherefore didst thou choose it
For our child's canopy?
Adah. Because its branches
Shut out the sun like night, and therefore seemed
Fitting to shadow slumber.
Cain. Aye, the last —
And longest; but no matter — lead me to him.

[*They go up to the child.*

How lovely he appears! his little cheeks,
In their pure incarnation, vying with
The rose leaves strewn beneath them.
Adah. And his lips, too,
How beautifully parted! No; you shall not
Kiss him, at least not now: he will awake soon —
His hour of mid-day rest is nearly over;

But it were pity to disturb him till
'Tis closed.
Cain. You have said well; I will contain
My heart till then. He smiles, and sleeps! — sleep on,
And smile, thou little, young inheritor
Of a world scarce less young: sleep on, and smile!
Thine are the hours and days when both are cheering
And innocent! *thou* hast not plucked the fruit —
Thou know'st not thou art naked! Must the time
Come thou shalt be amerced for sins unknown,
Which were not thine nor mine? But now sleep on!
His cheeks are reddening into deeper smiles,
And shining lids are trembling o'er his long
Lashes, dark as the cypress which waves o'er them;
Half open, from beneath them the clear blue
Laughs out, although in slumber. He must dream —
Of what? Of Paradise! — Aye! dream of it,
My disinherited boy! 'Tis but a dream;
For never more thyself, thy sons, nor fathers,
Shall walk in that forbidden place of joy!
Adah. Dear Cain! Nay, do not whisper o'er our son
Such melancholy yearnings o'er the past:
Why wilt thou always mourn for Paradise?
Can we not make another?
Cain. Where?
Adah. Here, or
Where'er thou wilt: where'er thou art, I feel not
The want of this so much regretted Eden.
Have I not thee — our boy — our sire, and brother,
And Zillah — our sweet sister, and our Eve,
To whom we owe so much besides our birth?
Cain. Yes — Death, too, is amongst the debts we owe her.
Adah. Cain! that proud Spirit, who withdrew thee hence,
Hath saddened thine still deeper. I had hoped
The promised wonders which thou hast beheld,
Visions, thou say'st, of past and present worlds,
Would have composed thy mind into the calm
Of a contented knowledge; but I see
Thy guide hath done thee evil: still I thank him,
And can forgive him all, that he so soon
Hath given thee back to us.
Cain. So soon?
Adah. 'Tis scarcely
Two hours since ye departed: two *long* hours
To *me*, but only *hours* upon the sun.
Cain. And yet I have approached that sun, and seen
Worlds which he once shone on, and never more

Shall light; and worlds he never lit: methought
Years had rolled o'er my absence.
Adah. Hardly hours.
Cain. The mind then hath capacity of time,
And measures it by that which it beholds,
Pleasing or painful; little or almighty.
I had beheld the immemorial works
Of endless beings; skirred extinguished worlds;
And, gazing on eternity, methought
I had borrowed more by a few drops of ages
From its immensity: but now I feel
My littleness again. Well said the Spirit,
That I was nothing!
Adah. Wherefore said he so?
Jehovah said not that.
Cain. No: *he* contents him
With making us the *nothing* which we are;
And after flattering dust with glimpses of
Eden and Immortality, resolves
It back to dust again — for what?
Adah. Thou know'st —
Even for our parents' error.
Cain. What is that
To us? they sinned, then *let them* die!
Adah. Thou hast not spoken well, nor is that thought
Thy own, but of the Spirit who was with thee.
Would *I* could die for them, so *they* might live!
Cain. Why, so say I — provided that one victim
Might satiate the Insatiable of life,
And that our little rosy sleeper there
Might never taste of death nor human sorrow,
Nor hand it down to those who spring from him.
Adah. How know we that some such atonement one day
May not redeem our race?
Cain. By sacrificing
The harmless for the guilty? what atonement
Were there? why, *we* are innocent: what have we
Done, that we must be victims for a deed
Before our birth, or need have victims to
Atone for this mysterious, nameless sin —
If it be such a sin to seek for knowledge?
Adah. Alas! thou sinnest now, my Cain: thy words
Sound impious in mine ears.
Cain. Then leave me!
Adah. Never,
Though thy God left thee.
Cain. Say, what have we here?

Adah. Two altars, which our brother Abel made
During thine absence, whereupon to offer
A sacrifice to God on thy return.
Cain. And how knew *he*, that *I* would be so ready
With the burnt offerings, which he daily brings
With a meek brow, whose base humility
Shows more of fear than worship — as a bribe
To the Creator?
Adah. Surely, 'tis well done.
Cain. One altar may suffice; *I* have no offering.
Adah. The fruits of the earth, the early, beautiful,
Blossom and bud — and bloom of flowers and fruits —
These are a goodly offering to the Lord,
Given with a gentle and a contrite spirit.
Cain. I have toiled, and tilled, and sweaten in the sun,
According to the curse: — must I do more?
For what should I be gentle? for a war
With all the elements ere they will yield
The bread we eat? For what must I be grateful?
For being dust, and grovelling in the dust,
Till I return to dust? If I am nothing —
For nothing shall I be an hypocrite,
And seem well-pleased with pain? For what should I
Be contrite? for my father's sin, already
Expiate with what we all have undergone,
And to be more than expiated by
The ages prophesied, upon our seed.
Little deems our young blooming sleeper, there,
The germs of an eternal misery
To myriads is within him! better 'twere
I snatched him in his sleep, and dashed him 'gainst
The rocks, than let him live to ——
Adah. Oh, my God!
Touch not the child — my child! *thy* child! Oh, Cain!
Cain. Fear not! for all the stars, and all the power
Which sways them, I would not accost yon infant
With ruder greeting than a father's kiss.
Adah. Then, why so awful in thy speech?
Cain. I said,
'Twere better that he ceased to live, than give
Life to so much of sorrow as he must
Endure, and, harder still, bequeath; but since
That saying jars you, let us only say —
'Twere better that he never had been born.
Adah. Oh, do not say so! Where were then the joys,
The mother's joys of watching, nourishing,
And loving him? Soft! he awakes. Sweet Enoch!
[*She goes to the child.*

Oh, Cain! look on him; see how full of life,
Of strength, of bloom, of beauty, and of joy —
How like to me — how like to thee, when gentle —
For *then* we are *all* alike; is't not so, Cain?
Mother, and sire, and son, our features are
Reflected in each other; as they are
In the clear waters, when *they* are *gentle*, and
When *thou* art *gentle*. Love us, then, my Cain!
And love thyself for our sakes, for we love thee.
Look! how he laughs and stretches out his arms,
And opens wide his blue eyes upon thine,
To hail his father; while his little form
Flutters as winged with joy. Talk not of pain!
The childless cherubs well might envy thee
The pleasures of a parent! Bless him, Cain!
As yet he hath no words to thank thee, but
His heart will, and thine own too.
Cain. Bless thee, boy!
If that a mortal blessing may avail thee,
To save thee from the Serpent's curse!
Adah. It shall.
Surely a father's blessing may avert
A reptile's subtlety.
Cain. Of that I doubt;
But bless him ne'er the less.
Adah. Our brother comes.
Cain. Thy brother Abel.

Enter ABEL.

Abel. Welcome, Cain! My brother,
The peace of God be on thee!
Cain. Abel, hail!
Abel. Our sister tells me that thou hast been wandering,
In high communion with a Spirit, far
Beyond our wonted range. Was he of those
We have seen and spoken with, like to our father?
Cain. No.
Abel. Why then commune with him? he may be
A foe to the Most High.
Cain. And friend to man.
Has the Most High been so — if so you term him?
Abel. *Term him!* your words are strange to-day, my brother.
My sister Adah, leave us for awhile —
We mean to sacrifice.
Adah. Farewell, my Cain;
But first embrace thy son. May his soft spirit,
And Abel's pious ministry, recall thee

To peace and holiness!

[*Exit* Adah, *with her child.*

Abel. Where hast thou been?
Cain. I know not.
Abel. Nor what thou hast seen?
Cain. The dead —
The Immortal — the Unbounded — the Omnipotent —
The overpowering mysteries of space —
The innumerable worlds that were and are —
A whirlwind of such overwhelming things,
Suns, moons, and earths, upon their loud-voiced spheres
Singing in thunder round me, as have made me
Unfit for mortal converse: leave me, Abel.
Abel. Thine eyes are flashing with unnatural light —
Thy cheek is flushed with an unnatural hue —
Thy words are fraught with an unnatural sound —
What may this mean?
Cain. It means — I pray thee, leave me.
Abel. Not till we have prayed and sacrificed together.
Cain. Abel, I pray thee, sacrifice alone —
Jehovah loves thee well.
Abel. *Both* well, I hope.
Cain. But thee the better: I care not for that;
Thou art fitter for his worship than I am;
Revere him, then — but let it be alone —
At least, without me.
Abel. Brother, I should ill
Deserve the name of our great father's son,
If, as my elder, I revered thee not,
And in the worship of our God, called not
On thee to join me, and precede me in
Our priesthood — 'tis thy place.
Cain. But I have ne'er
Asserted it.
Abel. The more my grief; I pray thee
To do so now: thy soul seems labouring in
Some strong delusion; it will calm thee.
Cain. No;
Nothing can calm me more. *Calm!* say I? Never
Knew I what calm was in the soul, although
I have seen the elements stilled. My Abel, leave me!
Or let me leave thee to thy pious purpose.
Abel. Neither; we must perform our task together.
Spurn me not.
Cain. If it must be so —— well, then,
What shall I do?
Abel. Choose one of those two altars.

Cain. Choose for me: they to me are so much turf
And stone.
Abel. Choose thou!
Cain. I have chosen.
Abel. 'Tis the highest,
And suits thee, as the elder. Now prepare
Thine offerings.
Cain. Where are thine?
Abel. Behold them here —
The firstlings of the flock, and fat thereof —
A shepherd's humble offering.
Cain. I have no flocks;
I am a tiller of the ground, and must
Yield what it yieldeth to my toil — its fruit:
[*He gathers fruits.*
Behold them in their various bloom and ripeness.
[*They dress their altars, and kindle a flame upon them.*
Abel. My brother, as the elder, offer first
Thy prayer and thanksgiving with sacrifice.
Cain. No — I am new to this; lead thou the way,
And I will follow — as I may.
Abel (kneeling). Oh, God!
Who made us, and who breathed the breath of life
Within our nostrils, who hath blessed us,
And spared, despite our father's sin, to make
His children all lost, as they might have been,
Had not thy justice been so tempered with
The mercy which is thy delight, as to
Accord a pardon like a Paradise,
Compared with our great crimes: — Sole Lord of light!
Of good, and glory, and eternity!
Without whom all were evil, and with whom
Nothing can err, except to some good end
Of thine omnipotent benevolence!
Inscrutable, but still to be fulfilled!
Accept from out thy humble first of shepherds'
First of the first-born flocks — an offering,
In itself nothing — as what offering can be
Aught unto thee? — but yet accept it for
The thanksgiving of him who spreads it in
The face of thy high heaven — bowing his own
Even to the dust, of which he is — in honour
Of thee, and of thy name, for evermore!
Cain (standing erect during this speech). Spirit whate'er
or whosoe'er thou art,
Omnipotent, it may be — and, if good,
Shown in the exemption of thy deeds from evil;

Jehovah upon earth! and God in heaven!
And it may be with other names, because
Thine attributes seem many, as thy works: —
If thou must be propitiated with prayers,
Take them! If thou must be induced with altars,
And softened with a sacrifice, receive them;
Two beings here erect them unto thee.
If thou lov'st blood, the shepherd's shrine, which smokes
On my right hand, hath shed it for thy service
In the first of his flock, whose limbs now reek
In sanguinary incense to thy skies;
Or, if the sweet and blooming fruits of earth,
And milder seasons, which the unstained turf
I spread them on now offers in the face
Of the broad sun which ripened them, may seem
Good to thee — inasmuch as they have not
Suffered in limb or life — and rather form
A sample of thy works, than supplication
To look on ours! If a shrine without victim,
And altar without gore, may win thy favour,
Look on it! and for him who dresseth it,
He is — such as thou mad'st him; and seeks nothing
Which must be won by kneeling: if he's evil,
Strike him! thou art omnipotent, and may'st —
For what can he oppose? If he be good,
Strike him, or spare him, as thou wilt! since all
Rests upon thee; and Good and Evil seem
To have no power themselves, save in thy will —
And whether that be good or ill I know not,
Not being omnipotent, nor fit to judge
Omnipotence — but merely to endure
Its mandate; which thus far I have endured.

[*The fire upon the altar of* ABEL *kindles into a column of the brightest flame, and ascends to heaven; while a whirlwind throws down the altar of* CAIN, *and scatters the fruits abroad upon the earth.*

Abel (*kneeling*). Oh, brother, pray! Jehovah's wroth with thee.
Cain. Why so?
Abel. Thy fruits are scattered on the earth.
Cain. From earth they came, to earth let them return;
Their seed will bear fresh fruit there ere the summer:
Thy burnt flesh-offering prospers better; see
How Heaven licks up the flames, when thick with blood!
Abel. Think not upon my offering's acceptance,
But make another of thine own — before
It is too late.
Cain. I will build no more altars,

Nor suffer any ——
Abel (*rising*). Cain! what meanest thou?
Cain. To cast down yon vile flatterer of the clouds,
The smoky harbinger of thy dull prayers —
Thine altar, with its blood of lambs and kids,
Which fed on milk, to be destroyed in blood.
Abel (*opposing him*). Thou shalt not: — add not impious works to impious
Words! let that altar stand — 'tis hallowed now
By the immortal pleasure of Jehovah,
In his acceptance of the victims.
Cain. *His!*
His pleasure! what was his high pleasure in
The fumes of scorching flesh and smoking blood,
To the pain of the bleating mothers, which
Still yearn for their dead offspring? or the pangs
Of the sad ignorant victims underneath
Thy pious knife? Give way! this bloody record
Shall not stand in the sun, to shame creation!
Abel. Brother, give back! thou shalt not touch my altar
With violence: if that thou wilt adopt it,
To try another sacrifice, 'tis thine.
Cain. Another sacrifice! Give way, or else
That sacrifice may be ——
Abel. What mean'st thou?
Cain. Give —
Give way! — thy God loves blood! — then look to it: —
Give way, ere he hath *more!*
Abel. In *his* great name,
I stand between thee and the shrine which hath
Had his acceptance.
Cain. If thou lov'st thyself,
Stand back till I have strewed this turf along
Its native soil: — else ——
Abel (*opposing him*). I love God far more
Than life.
Cain (*striking him with a brand, on the temples, which he snatches from the altar*). Then take thy life unto thy God,
Since he loves lives.
Abel (*falls*). What hast thou done — my brother?
Cain. Brother!
Abel. Oh, God! receive thy servant! and
Forgive his slayer, for he knew not what
He did — Cain, give me — give me thy hand; and tell
Poor Zillah —
Cain (*after a moment's stupefaction*). My hand! 'tis all red, and with ——

What? [*A long pause. — Looking slowly round.*
Where am I? alone! Where's Abel? where
Cain? Can it be that I am he? My brother,
Awake! — why liest thou so long on the green earth?
'Tis not the hour of slumber: — why so pale?
What hast thou! — thou wert full of life this morn!
Abel! I pray thee, mock me not! I smote
Too fiercely, but not fatally. Ah, why
Wouldst thou oppose me? This is mockery;
And only done to daunt me: — 'twas a blow —
And but a blow. Stir — stir — nay, only stir!
Why, so — that's well! — thou breathest! breathe upon me!
Oh God! Oh God!

Abel (*very faintly*). What's he who speaks of God?

Cain. Thy murderer.

Abel. Then may God forgive him! Cain,
Comfort poor Zillah: — she has but one brother
Now. [ABEL *dies.*

Cain. And I none! — Who makes me brotherless?
His eyes are open! then he is not dead!
Death is like sleep; and sleep shuts down our lids.
His lips, too, are apart; why then he breathes;
And yet I feel it not. — His heart! — his heart! —
Let me see, doth it beat? methinks —— No! — no!
This is a vision, else I am become
The native of another and worse world.
The earth swims round me: — what is this? — 'tis wet;
[*Puts his hand to his brow, and then looks at it.*
And yet there are no dews! 'Tis blood — my blood —
My brother's and my own! and shed by me!
Then what have I further to do with life,
Since I have taken life from my own flesh?
But he can not be dead! — Is silence death?
No; he will wake; then let me watch by him.
Life cannot be so slight, as to be quenched
Thus quickly! — he hath spoken to me since —
What shall I say to him? — My brother! — No:
He will not answer to that name; for brethren
Smite not each other. Yet — yet — speak to me.
Oh! for a word more of that gentle voice,
That I may bear to hear my own again!

Enter ZILLAH.

Zillah. I heard a heavy sound; what can it be?
'Tis Cain; and watching by my husband. What
Dost thou there, brother? Doth he sleep? Oh, Heaven!

What means this paleness, and yon stream? — No, no!
It is not blood; for who would shed his blood?
Abel! what's this? — who hath done this? He moves not;
He breathes not: and his hands drop down from mine
With stony lifelessness! Ah! cruel Cain!
Why camest thou not in time to save him from
This violence? Whatever hath assailed him,
Thou wert the stronger, and shouldst have stepped in
Between him and aggression! Father! — Eve! —
Adah! — come hither! Death is in the world!
[*Exit* ZILLAH, *calling on her Parents, etc.*

Cain (*solus*). And who hath brought him there? — I — who abhor
The name of Death so deeply, that the thought
Empoisoned all my life, before I knew
His aspect — I have led him here, and given
My brother to his cold and still embrace,
As if he would not have asserted his
Inexorable claim without my aid.
I am awake at last — a dreary dream
Had maddened me; — but *he* shall ne'er awake!

Enter ADAM, EVE, ADAH, *and* ZILLAH.

Adam. A voice of woe from Zillah brings me here —
What do I see? — 'Tis true! — My son! — my son!
Woman, behold the Serpent's work, and thine! [*To* EVE.

Eve. Oh! speak not of it now: the Serpent's fangs
Are in my heart! My best beloved, Abel!
Jehovah! this is punishment beyond
A mother's sin, to take *him* from me!

Adam. Who,
Or what hath done this deed? — speak, Cain, since thou
Wert present; was it some more hostile angel,
Who walks not with Jehovah? or some wild
Brute of the forest?

Eve. Ah! a livid light
Breaks through, as from a thunder-cloud! yon brand
Massy and bloody! snatched from off the altar,
And black with smoke, and red with ——

Adam. Speak, my son!
Speak, and assure us, wretched as we are,
That we are not more miserable still.

Adah. Speak, Cain! and say it was not *thou!*

Eve. It was!
I see it now — he hangs his guilty head,
And covers his ferocious eye with hands
Incarnadine!

Adah. Mother, thou dost him wrong —
Cain! clear thee from this horrible accusal,
Which grief wrings from our parent.
Eve. Hear, Jehovah!
May the eternal Serpent's curse be on him!
For he was fitter for his seed than ours.
May all his days be desolate! May ——
Adah. Hold!
Curse him not, mother, for he is thy son —
Curse him not, mother, for he is my brother,
And my betrothed.
Eve. He hath left thee no brother —
Zillah no husband — me *no son!* for thus
I curse him from my sight for evermore!
All bonds I break between us, as he broke
That of his nature, *in yon* — Oh Death! Death!
Why didst thou not take *me,* who first incurred thee?
Why dost thou not so now?
Adam. Eve! let not this,
Thy natural grief, lead to impiety!
A heavy doom was long forespoken to us;
And now that it begins, let it be borne
In such sort as may show our God, that we
Are faithful servants to his holy will.
Eve (pointing to Cain). His will! the will of yon Incarnate Spirit
Of Death, whom I have brought upon the earth
To strew it with the dead. May all the curses
Of life be on him! and his agonies
Drive him forth o'er the wilderness, like us
From Eden, till his children do by him
As he did by his brother! May the swords
And wings of fiery Cherubim pursue him
By day and night — snakes spring up in his path —
Earth's fruits be ashes in his mouth — the leaves
On which he lays his head to sleep be strewed
With scorpions! May his dreams be of his victim!
His waking a continual dread of Death!
May the clear rivers turn to blood as he
Stoops down to stain them with his raging lip!
May every element shun or change to him!
May he live in the pangs which others die with!
And Death itself wax something worse than Death
To him who first acquainted him with man!
Hence, fratricide! henceforth that word is *Cain,*
Through all the coming myriads of mankind,
Who shall abhor thee, though thou wert their sire!
May the grass wither from thy feet! the woods

Deny thee shelter! earth a home! the dust
A grave! the sun his light! and heaven her God!

[*Exit* EVE.

Adam. Cain! get thee forth: we dwell no more together.
Depart! and leave the dead to me — I am
Henceforth alone — we never must meet more.
Adah. Oh, part not with him thus, my father: do not
Add thy deep curse to Eve's upon his head!
Adam. I curse him not: his spirit be his curse.
Come, Zillah!
Zillah. I must watch my husband's corse.
Adam. We will return again, when he is gone
Who hath provided for us this dread office.
Come, Zillah!
Zillah. Yet one kiss on yon pale clay,
And those lips once so warm — my heart! my heart!

[*Exeunt* ADAM *and* ZILLAH *weeping.*

Adah. Cain! thou hast heard, we must go forth. I am ready,
So shall our children be. I will bear Enoch,
And you his sister. Ere the sun declines
Let us depart, nor walk the wilderness
Under the cloud of night. — Nay, speak to me.
To *me* — *thine own.*
Cain. Leave me!
Adah. Why, all have left thee.
Cain. And wherefore lingerest thou? Dost thou not fear
To dwell with one who hath done this?
Adah. I fear
Nothing except to leave thee, much as I
Shrink from the deed which leaves thee brotherless.
I must not speak of this — it is between thee
And the great God.
A Voice from within exclaims. Cain! Cain!
Adah. Hear'st thou that voice?
The Voice within. Cain! Cain!
Adah. It soundeth like an angel's tone.

Enter the ANGEL *of the Lord.*

Angel. Where is thy brother Abel?
Cain. Am I then
My brother's keeper?
Angel. Cain! what hast thou done?
The voice of thy slain brother's blood cries out,
Even from the ground, unto the Lord! — Now art thou
Cursed from the earth, which opened late her mouth
To drink thy brother's blood from thy rash hand.

Henceforth, when thou shalt till the ground, it shall not
Yield thee her strength; a fugitive shalt thou
Be from this day, and vagabond on earth!
Adah. This punishment is more than he can bear.
Behold thou drivest him from the face of earth,
And from the face of God shall he be hid.
A fugitive and vagabond on earth,
'Twill come to pass, that whoso findeth him
Shall slay him.
Cain. Would they could! but who are they
Shall slay me? Where are these on the lone earth
As yet unpeopled?
Angel. Thou hast slain thy brother,
And who shall warrant thee against thy son?
Adah. Angel of Light! be merciful, nor say
That this poor aching breast now nourishes
A murderer in my boy, and of his father.
Angel. Then he would but be what his father is.
Did not the milk of Eve give nutriment
To him thou now seest so besmeared with blood?
The fratricide might well engender parricides. —
But it shall not be so — the Lord thy God
And mine commandeth me to set his seal
On Cain, so that he may go forth in safety.
Who slayeth Cain, a sevenfold vengeance shall
Be taken on his head. Come hither!
Cain. What
Wouldst thou with me?
Angel. To mark upon thy brow
Exemption from such deeds as thou hast done.
Cain. No, let me die!
Angel. It must not be.
[THE ANGEL *sets the mark on* CAIN's *brow.*
Cain. It burns
My brow, but nought to that which is within it!
Is there more? let me meet it as I may.
Angel. Stern hast thou been and stubborn from the womb,
As the ground thou must henceforth till; but he
Thou slew'st was gentle as the flocks he tended.
Cain. After the fall too soon was I begotten;
Ere yet my mother's mind subsided from
The Serpent, and my sire still mourned for Eden.
That which I am, I am; I did not seek
For life, nor did I make myself; but could I
With my own death redeem him from the dust —
And why not so? let him return to day,
And I lie ghastly! so shall be restored

By God the life to him he loved; and taken
From me a being I ne'er loved to bear.
Angel. Who shall heal murder? what is done, is done;
Go forth! fulfil thy days! and be thy deeds
Unlike the last! [*The* ANGEL *disappears.*
Adah. He's gone, let us go forth;
I hear our little Enoch cry within
Our bower.
Cain. Ah! little knows he what he weeps for!
And I who have shed blood cannot shed tears!
But the four rivers would not cleanse my soul.
Think'st thou my boy will bear to look on me?
Adah. If I thought that he would not, I would ——
Cain (*interrupting her*). No,
No more of threats: we have had too many of them:
Go to our children — I will follow thee.
Adah. I will not leave thee lonely with the dead —
Let us depart together.
Cain. Oh! thou dead
And everlasting witness! whose unsinking
Blood darkens earth and heaven! what thou *now* art
I know not! but if *thou* seest what *I* am,
I think thou wilt forgive him, whom his God
Can ne'er forgive, nor his own soul. — Farewell!
I must not, dare not touch what I have made thee.
I, who sprung from the same womb with thee, drained
The same breast, clasped thee often to my own,
In fondness brotherly and boyish, I
Can never meet thee more, nor even dare
To do that for thee, which thou shouldst have done
For me — compose thy limbs into their grave —
The first grave yet dug for mortality.
But who hath dug that grave? Oh, earth! Oh, earth!
For all the fruits thou hast rendered to me, I
Give thee back this. — Now for the wilderness!
[ADAH *stoops down and kisses the body of* ABEL.
Adah. A dreary, and an early doom, my brother,
Has been thy lot! Of all who mourn for thee,
I alone must not weep. My office is
Henceforth to dry up tears, and not to shed them;
But yet of all who mourn, none mourn like me,
Not only for thyself, but him who slew thee.
Now, Cain! I will divide thy burden with thee.
Cain. Eastward from Eden will we take our way;
'Tis the most desolate, and suits my steps.
Adah. Lead! thou shalt be my guide, and may our God
Be thine! Now let us carry forth our children.

Cain. And *he* who lieth there was childless! I
Have dried the fountain of a gentle race,
Which might have graced his recent marriage couch,
And might have tempered this stern blood of mine,
Uniting with our children Abel's offspring!
O Abel!
Adah. Peace be with him!
Cain. But with *me!* ——

[*Exeunt.*

HEAVEN AND EARTH;

A MYSTERY

Founded on the Following Passage in Genesis, Chap. vi.

"And it came to pass . . . that the sons of God saw the daughters of men that they were fair; and they took them wives of all which they chose."

"And woman wailing for her demon lover." — Coleridge.

Dramatis Personæ

Angels

Samiasa
Azaziel
Raphael, the Archangel

Men

Noah and his Sons
Irad
Japhet

Women

Anah
Aholibamah

Chorus of Spirits of the Earth. — Chorus of Mortals.

PART I

Scene I. — *A woody and mountainous district near Mount Ararat. — Time, midnight.*

Enter Anah *and* Aholibamah.

Anah. Our father sleeps: it is the hour when they
Who love us are accustomed to descend
Through the deep clouds o'er rocky Ararat: —
How my heart beats!
Aholibamah. Let us proceed upon
Our invocation.
Anah. But the stars are hidden.
I tremble.

Aholibamah. So do I, but not with fear
Of aught save their delay.
Anah. My sister, though
I love Azaziel more than —— oh, too much!
What was I going to say? my heart grows impious.
Aholibamah. And where is the impiety of loving
Celestial natures?
Anah. But, Aholibamah,
I love our God less since his angel loved me:
This cannot be of good; and though I know not
That I do wrong, I feel a thousand fears
Which are not ominous of right.
Aholibamah. Then wed thee
Unto some son of clay, and toil and spin!
There's Japhet loves thee well, hath loved thee long:
Marry, and bring forth dust!
Anah. I should have loved
Azaziel not less were he mortal; yet
I am glad he is not. I cannot outlive him.
And when I think that his immortal wings
Will one day hover o'er the sepulchre
Of the poor child of clay which so adored him,
As he adores the Highest, death becomes
Less terrible; but yet I pity him:
His grief will be of ages, or at least
Mine would be such for him, were I the Seraph,
And he the perishable.
Aholibamah. Rather say,
That he will single forth some other daughter
Of earth, and love her as he once loved Anah.
Anah. And if it should be so, and she loved him,
Better thus than that he should weep for me.
Aholibamah. If I thought thus of Samiasa's love,
All Seraph as he is, I'd spurn him from me.
But to our invocation! — 'Tis the hour.
Anah. Seraph!
From thy sphere!
Whatever star contain thy glory;
In the eternal depths of heaven
Albeit thou watchest with "the seven,"
Though through space infinite and hoary
Before thy bright wings worlds be driven,
Yet hear!
Oh! think of her who holds thee dear!
And though she nothing is to thee,
Yet think that thou art all to her.
Thou canst not tell, — and never be

Such pangs decreed to aught save me, —
The bitterness of tears.
Eternity is in thine years,
Unborn, undying beauty in thine eyes;
With me thou canst not sympathise,
Except in love, and there thou must
Acknowledge that more loving dust
Ne'er wept beneath the skies.
Thou walk'st thy many worlds, thou see'st
The face of him who made thee great,
As he hath made me of the least
Of those cast out from Eden's gate:
Yet, Seraph dear!
Oh hear!
For thou hast loved me, and I would not die
Until I know what I must die in knowing,
That thou forget'st in thine eternity
Her whose heart Death could not keep from o'er-flowing
For thee, immortal essence as thou art!
Great is their love who love in sin and fear;
And such, I feel, are waging in my heart
A war unworthy: to an Adamite
Forgive, my Seraph! that such thoughts appear,
For sorrow is our element;
Delight
An Eden kept afar from sight,
Though sometimes with our visions blent.
The hour is near
Which tells me we are not abandoned quite. —
Appear! Appear!
Seraph!
My own Azaziel! be but here,
And leave the stars to their own light!
Aholibamah. Samiasa!
Wheresoe'er
Thou rulest in the upper air —
Or warring with the spirits who may dare
Dispute with him
Who made all empires, empire; or recalling
Some wandering star, which shoots through the abyss,
Whose tenants dying, while their world is falling,
Share the dim destiny of clay in this;
Or joining with the inferior cherubim,
Thou deignest to partake their hymn —
Samiasa!
I call thee, I await thee, and I love thee.
Many may worship thee, that will I not:

If that thy spirit down to mine may move thee,
Descend and share my lot!
Though I be formed of clay,
And thou of beams
More bright than those of day
On Eden's streams,
Thine immortality can not repay
With love more warm than mine
My love. There is a ray
In me, which, though forbidden yet to shine,
I feel was lighted at thy God's and thine.
It may be hidden long: death and decay
Our mother Eve bequeathed us — but my heart
Defies it:though this life must pass away,
Is *that* a cause for thee and me to part?
Thou art immortal — so am I: I feel —
I feel my immortality o'ersweep
All pains, all tears, all fears, and peal,
Like the eternal thunders of the deep,
Into my ears this truth — "Thou liv'st for ever!"
But if it be in joy
I know not, nor would know;
That secret rests with the Almighty giver,
Who folds in clouds the fonts of bliss and woe.
But thee and me he never can destroy;
Change us he may, but not o'erwhelm; we are
Of as eternal essence, and must war
With him if he will war with us; with *thee*
I can share all things, even immortal sorrow;
For thou hast ventured to share life with *me*,
And shall *I* shrink from thine eternity?
No! though the serpent's sting should pierce me thorough,
And thou thyself wert like the serpent, coil
Around me still! and I will smile,
And curse thee not; but hold
Thee in as warm a fold
As —— but descend, and prove
A mortal's love
For an immortal. If the skies contain
More joy than thou canst give and take, remain!

Anah. Sister! sister! I view them winging
Their bright way through the parted night.

Aholibamah. The clouds from off their pinions flinging,
As though they bore to-morrow's light.

Anah. But if our father see the sight!

Aholibamah. He would but deem it was the moon
Rising unto some sorcerer's tune

An hour too soon.
Anah. They come! *he* comes! — Azaziel!
Aholibamah. Haste
To meet them! Oh! for wings to bear
My spirit, while they hover there,
To Samiasa's breast!
Anah. Lo! they have kindled all the west,
Like a returning sunset; — lo!
On Ararat's late secret crest
A mild and many-coloured bow,
The remnant of their flashing path,
Now shines! and now, behold! it hath
Returned to night, as rippling foam,
Which the Leviathan hath lashed
From his unfathomable home,
When sporting on the face of the calm deep,
Subsides soon after he again hath dashed
Down, down, to where the Ocean's fountains sleep.
Aholibamah. They have touched earth! Samiasa!
Anah. My Azaziel!
[*Exeunt.*

SCENE II. — *Enter* IRAD *and* JAPHET.

Irad. Despond not: wherefore wilt thou wander thus
To add thy silence to the silent night,
And lift thy tearful eye unto the stars?
They cannot aid thee.
Japhet. But they soothe me — now
Perhaps she looks upon them as I look.
Methinks a being that is beautiful
Becometh more so as it looks on beauty,
The eternal beauty of undying things.
Oh, Anah!
Irad. But she loves thee not.
Japhet. Alas!
Irad. And proud Aholibamah spurns me also.
Japhet. I feel for thee too.
Irad. Let her keep her pride,
Mine hath enabled me to bear her scorn:
It may be, time too will avenge it.
Japhet. Canst thou
Find joy in such a thought?
Irad. Nor joy nor sorrow.
I loved her well; I would have loved her better,
Had love been met with love: as 'tis, I leave her
To brighten destinies, if so she deems them.

Japhet. What destinies?
Irad. I have some cause to think
She loves another.
Japhet. Anah!
Irad. No; her sister.
Japhet. What other?
Irad. That I know not; but her air,
If not her words, tells me she loves another.
Japhet. Aye, but not Anah: she but loves her God.
Irad. Whate'er she loveth, so she loves thee not,
What can it profit thee?
Japhet. True, nothing; but
I love.
Irad. And so did I.
Japhet. And now thou lov'st not,
Or think'st thou lov'st not, art thou happier?
Irad. Yes.
Japhet. I pity thee.
Irad. Me! why?
Japhet. For being happy,
Deprived of that which makes my misery.
Irad. I take thy taunt as part of thy distemper,
And would not feel as thou dost for more shekels
Than all our father's herds would bring, if weighed
Against the metal of the sons of Cain —
The yellow dust they try to barter with us,
As if such useless and discoloured trash,
The refuse of the earth, could be received
For milk, and wool, and flesh, and fruits, and all
Our flocks and wilderness afford. — Go, Japhet,
Sigh to the stars, as wolves howl to the moon —
I must back to my rest.
Japhet. And so would I
If I could rest.
Irad. Thou wilt not to our tents then?
Japhet. No, Irad; I will to the cavern, whose
Mouth they say opens from the internal world,
To let the inner spirits of the earth
Forth when they walk its surface.
Irad. Wherefore so?
What wouldst thou there?
Japhet. Soothe further my sad spirit
With gloom as sad: it is a hopeless spot,
And I am hopeless.
Irad. But 'tis dangerous;
Strange sounds and sights have peopled it with terrors.
I must go with thee.

Japhet. Irad, no; believe me
I feel no evil thought, and fear no evil.
Irad. But evil things will be thy foe the more
As not being of them: turn thy steps aside,
Or let mine be with thine.
Japhet. No, neither, Irad;
I must proceed alone.
Irad. Then peace be with thee!
[*Exit* IRAD.

Japhet (solus). Peace! I have sought it where it should be found,
In love — with love, too, which perhaps deserved it;
And, in its stead, a heaviness of heart,
A weakness of the spirit, listless days,
And nights inexorable to sweet sleep
Have come upon me. Peace! what peace? the calm
Of desolation, and the stillness of
The untrodden forest, only broken by
The sweeping tempest through its groaning boughs;
Such is the sullen or the fitful state
Of my mind overworn. The Earth's grown wicked,
And many signs and portents have proclaimed
A change at hand, and an o'erwhelming doom
To perishable beings. Oh, my Anah!
When the dread hour denounced shall open wide
The fountains of the deep, how mightest thou
Have lain within this bosom, folded from
The elements; this bosom, which in vain
Hath beat for thee, and then will beat more vainly,
While thine — Oh, God! at least remit to her
Thy wrath! for she is pure amidst the failing
As a star in the clouds, which cannot quench,
Although they obscure it for an hour. My Anah!
How would I have adored thee, but thou wouldst not;
And still would I redeem thee — see thee live
When Ocean is earth's grave, and, unopposed
By rock or shallow, the Leviathan,
Lord of the shoreless sea and watery world,
Shall wonder at his boundlessness of realm. [*Exit* JAPHET.

Enter NOAH *and* SHEM.

Noah. Where is thy brother Japhet?
Shem. He went forth,
According to his wont, to meet with Irad,
He said; but, as I fear, to bend his steps
Towards Anah's tents, round which he hovers nightly,
Like a dove round and round its pillaged nest;

Or else he walks the wild up to the cavern
Which opens to the heart of Ararat.
Noah. What doth he there? It is an evil spot
Upon an earth all evil; for things worse
Than even wicked men resort there: he
Still loves this daughter of a fated race,
Although he could not wed her if she loved him,
And that she doth not. Oh, the unhappy hearts
Of men! that one of my blood, knowing well
The destiny and evil of these days,
And that the hour approacheth, should indulge
In such forbidden yearnings! Lead the way;
He must be sought for!
Shem. Go not forward, father:
I will seek Japhet.
Noah. Do not fear for me:
All evil things are powerless on the man
Selected by Jehovah. — Let us on.
Shem. To the tents of the father of the sisters?
Noah. No; to the cavern of the Caucasus.
[*Exeunt* NOAH *and* SHEM.

SCENE III. — *The mountains. — A cavern, and the rocks of Caucasus.*

Japhet (*solus*). Ye wilds, that look eternal; and thou cave,
Which seem'st unfathomable; and ye mountains,
So varied and so terrible in beauty;
Here, in your rugged majesty of rocks
And toppling trees that twine their roots with stone
In perpendicular places, where the foot
Of man would tremble, could he reach them — yes,
Ye look eternal! Yet, in a few days,
Perhaps even hours, ye will be changed, rent, hurled
Before the mass of waters; and yon cave,
Which seems to lead into a lower world,
Shall have its depths searched by the sweeping wave,
And dolphins gambol in the lion's den!
And man —— Oh, men! my fellow-beings! Who
Shall weep above your universal grave,
Save I? Who shall be left to weep? My kinsmen,
Alas! what am I better than ye are,
That I must live beyond ye? Where shall be
The pleasant places where I thought of Anah
While I had hope? or the more savage haunts,
Scarce less beloved, where I despaired for her?
And can it be! — Shall yon exulting peak,

Whose glittering top is like a distant star,
Lie low beneath the boiling of the deep?
No more to have the morning sun break forth,
And scatter back the mists in floating folds
From its tremendous brow? no more to have
Day's broad orb drop behind its head at even,
Leaving it with a crown of many hues?
No more to be the beacon of the world,
For angels to alight on, as the spot
Nearest the stars? And can those words *"no more"*
Be meant for thee, for all things, save for us,
And the predestined creeping things reserved
By my sire to Jehovah's bidding? May
He preserve *them,* and I *not* have the power
To snatch the loveliest of earth's daughters from
A doom which even some serpent, with his mate,
Shall 'scape to save his kind to be prolonged,
To hiss and sting through some emerging world,
Reeking and dank from out the slime, whose ooze
Shall slumber o'er the wreck of this, until
The salt morass subside into a sphere
Beneath the sun, and be the monument,
The sole and undistinguished sepulchre,
Of yet quick myriads of all life? How much
Breath will be stilled at once! All beauteous world!
So young, so marked out for destruction, I
With a cleft heart look on thee day by day,
And night by night, thy numbered days and nights.
I cannot save thee, cannot save even her
Whose love had made me love thee more; but as
A portion of thy dust, I cannot think
Upon thy coming doom without a feeling
Such as — Oh God! and canst thou — [*He pauses.*

[*A rushing sound from the cavern is heard, and shouts of laughter — afterwards a Spirit passes.*

Japhet. In the name
Of the Most High, what art thou?
Spirit (laughs). Ha! ha! ha!
Japhet. By all that earth holds holiest, speak!
Spirit (laughs). Ha! ha!
Japhet. By the approaching deluge! by the earth
Which will be strangled by the ocean! by
The deep which will lay open all her fountains!
The heaven which will convert her clouds to seas,
And the Omnipotent who makes and crushes!
Thou unknown, terrible, and indistinct,
Yet awful Thing of Shadows, speak to me!

Why dost thou laugh that horrid laugh?
Spirit. Why weep'st thou?
Japhet. For earth and all her children.
Spirit. Ha! ha! ha!
[*Spirit vanishes.*
Japhet. How the fiend mocks the tortures of a world,
The coming desolation of an orb,
On which the sun shall rise and warm no life!
How the earth sleeps! and all that in it is
Sleep too upon the very eve of death!
Why should they wake to meet it? What are here,
Which look like death in life, and speak like things
Born ere this dying world? They come like clouds!
[*Various Spirits pass from the cavern.*
Spirit. Rejoice!
The abhorréd race
Which could not keep in Eden their high place,
But listened to the voice
Of Knowledge without power,
Are nigh the hour,
Of Death!
Not slow, not single, not by sword, nor sorrow,
Nor years, nor heart-break, nor Time's sapping motion,
Shall they drop off. Behold their last to-morrow!
Earth shall be Ocean!
And no breath,
Save of the winds, be on the unbounded wave!
Angels shall tire their wings, but find no spot:
Not even a rock from out the liquid grave
Shall lift its point to save,
Or show the place where strong Despair hath died,
After long looking o'er the ocean wide
For the expected ebb which cometh not:
All shall be void,
Destroyed!
Another element shall be the lord
Of life, and the abhorred
Children of dust be quenched; and of each hue
Of earth nought left but the unbroken blue;
And of the variegated mountain
Shall nought remain
Unchanged, or of the level plain;
Cedar and pine shall lift their tops in vain:
All merged within the universal fountain,
Man, earth, and fire, shall die,
And sea and sky
Look vast and lifeless in the eternal eye.

Upon the foam
Who shall erect a home?
Japhet (coming forward). My sire!
Earth's seed shall not expire;
Only the evil shall be put away
From day.
Avaunt! ye exulting demons of the waste!
Who howl your hideous joy
When God destroys whom you dare not destroy:
Hence! haste!
Back to your inner caves!
Until the waves
Shall search you in your secret place,
And drive your sullen race
Forth, to be rolled upon the tossing winds,
In restless wretchedness along all space!
Spirit. Son of the saved!
When thou and thine have braved
The wide and warring element;
When the great barrier of the deep is rent,
Shall thou and thine be good or happy? — No!
Thy new world and new race shall be of woe —
Less goodly in their aspect, in their years
Less than the glorious giants, who
Yet walk the world in pride,
The Sons of Heaven by many a mortal bride
Thine shall be nothing of the past, save tears!
And art thou not ashamed
Thus to survive,
And eat, and drink, and wive?
With a base heart so far subdued and tamed,
As even to hear this wide destruction named,
Without such grief and courage, as should rather
Bid thee await the world-dissolving wave,
Than seek a shelter with thy favoured father,
And build thy city o'er the drowned earth's grave?
Who would outlive their kind,
Except the base and blind?
Mine
Hateth thine
As of a different order in the sphere,
But not our own.
There is not one who hath not left a throne
Vacant in heaven to dwell in darkness here,
Rather than see his mates endure alone.
Go, wretch! and give
A life like thine to other wretches — live!

And when the annihilating waters roar
Above what they have done,
Envy the giant patriarchs then no more,
And scorn thy sire as the surviving one!
Thyself for being his son!

Chorus of Spirits issuing from the cavern.

Rejoice!
No more the human voice
Shall vex our joys in middle air
With prayer;
No more
Shall they adore;
And we, who ne'er for ages have adored
The prayer-exacting Lord,
To whom the omission of a sacrifice
Is vice;
We, we shall view the deep's salt sources poured
Until one element shall do the work
Of all in chaos; until they,
The creatures proud of their poor clay,
Shall perish, and their bleached bones shall lurk
In caves, in dens, in clefts of mountains, where
The deep shall follow to their latest lair;
Where even the brutes, in their despair,
Shall cease to prey on man and on each other,
And the striped tiger shall lie down to die
Beside the lamb, as though he were his brother;
Till all things shall be as they were,
Silent and uncreated, save the sky:
While a brief truce
Is made with Death, who shall forbear
The little remnant of the past creation,
To generate new nations for his use;
This remnant, floating o'er the undulation
Of the subsiding deluge, from its slime,
When the hot sun hath baked the reeking soil
Into a world, shall give again to Time
New beings — years, diseases, sorrow, crime —
With all companionship of hate and toil,
Until ——

Japhet (*interrupting them*). The eternal Will
Shall deign to expound this dream
Of good and evil; and redeem
Unto himself all times, all things;
And, gathered under his almighty wings,

Abolish Hell!
And to the expiated Earth
Restore the beauty of her birth,
Her Eden in an endless paradise,
Where man no more can fall as once he fell,
And even the very demons shall do well!

Spirits. And when shall take effect this wondrous spell?

Japhet. When the Redeemer cometh; first in pain,
And then in glory.

Spirit. Meantime still struggle in the mortal chain,
Till Earth wax hoary;
War with yourselves, and Hell, and Heaven, in vain,
Until the clouds look gory
With the blood reeking from each battle-plain;
New times, new climes, new arts, new men; but still,
The same old tears, old crimes, and oldest ill,
Shall be amongst your race in different forms;
But the same moral storms
Shall oversweep the future, as the waves
In a few hours the glorious giants' graves.

Chorus of Spirits.

Brethren, rejoice!
Mortal, farewell!
Hark! hark! already we can hear the voice
Of growing Ocean's gloomy swell;
The winds, too, plume their piercing wings;
The clouds have nearly filled their springs;
The fountains of the great deep shall be broken,
And heaven set wide her windows; while mankind
View, unacknowledged, each tremendous token —
Still, as they were from the beginning, blind.
We hear the sound they cannot hear,
The mustering thunders of the threatening sphere;
Yet a few hours their coming is delayed;
Their flashing banners, folded still on high,
Yet undisplayed,
Save to the Spirit's all-pervading eye.
Howl! howl! oh Earth!
Thy death is nearer than thy recent birth;
Tremble, ye mountains, soon to shrink below
The Ocean's overflow!
The wave shall break upon your cliffs; and shells,
The little shells, of ocean's least things be
Deposed where now the eagle's offspring dwells —
How shall he shriek o'er the remorseless sea!

And call his nestlings up with fruitless yell,
Unanswered, save by the encroaching swell; —
While man shall long in vain for his broad wings,
  The wings which could not save: —
Where could he rest them, while the whole space brings
  Nought to his eye beyond the deep, his grave?
          Brethren, rejoice!
  And loudly lift each superhuman voice —
            All die,
  Save the slight remnant of Seth's seed —
           The seed of Seth,
  Exempt for future sorrow's sake from death.
         But of the sons of Cain
          None shall remain;
      And all his goodly daughters
  Must lie beneath the desolating waters;
  Or, floating upward, with their long hair laid
  Along the wave, the cruel heaven upbraid,
          Which would not spare
         Beings even in death so fair.
           It is decreed,
            All die!
    And to the universal human cry
  The universal silence shall succeed!
          Fly, brethren, fly!
          But still rejoice!
            We fell!
          They fall!
           So perish all
These petty foes of Heaven who shrink from Hell!
                [*The Spirits disappear, soaring upwards.*

Japhet (*solus*). God hath proclaimed the destiny of earth;
My father's ark of safety hath announced it;
The very demons shriek it from their caves;
The scroll of Enoch prophesied it long
In silent books, which, in their silence, say
More to the mind than thunder to the ear:
And yet men listened not, nor listen; but
Walk darkling to their doom: which, though so nigh,
Shakes them no more in their dim disbelief,
Than their last cries shall shake the Almighty purpose,
Or deaf obedient Ocean, which fulfils it.
No sign yet hangs its banner in the air;
The clouds are few, and of their wonted texture;
The Sun will rise upon the Earth's last day
As on the fourth day of creation, when
God said unto him, "Shine!" and he broke forth
Into the dawn, which lighted not the yet

Unformed forefather of mankind — but roused
Before the human orison the earlier
Made and far sweeter voices of the birds,
Which in the open firmament of heaven
Have wings like angels, and like them salute
Heaven first each day before the Adamites:
Their matins now draw nigh — the east is kindling —
And they will sing! and day will break! Both near,
So near the awful close! For these must drop
Their outworn pinions on the deep; and day,
After the bright course of a few brief morrows, —
Aye, day will rise; but upon what? — a chaos,
Which was ere day; and which, renewed, makes Time
Nothing! for, without life, what are the hours?
No more to dust than is Eternity
Unto Jehovah, who created both.
Without him, even Eternity would be
A void: without man, Time, as made for man,
Dies with man, and is swallowed in that deep
Which has no fountain; as his race will be
Devoured by that which drowns his infant world. —
What have we here? Shapes of both earth and air?
No — *all* of heaven, they are so beautiful.
I cannot trace their features; but their forms,
How lovelily they move along the side
Of the grey mountain, scattering its mist!
And after the swart savage spirits, whose
Infernal immortality poured forth
Their impious hymn of triumph, they shall be
Welcome as Eden. It may be they come
To tell me the reprieve of our young world,
For which I have so often prayed. — They come!
Anah! oh, God! and with her ——

Enter Samiasa, Azaziel, Anah, *and* Aholibamah.

Anah. Japhet!
Samiasa. Lo!
A son of Adam!
Azaziel. What doth the earth-born here,
While all his race are slumbering?
Japhet Angel! what
Dost thou on earth when thou should'st be on high?
Azaziel. Know'st thou not, or forget'st thou, that a part
Of our great function is to guard thine earth?
Japhet. But all good angels have forsaken earth,
Which is condemned; nay, even the evil fly
The approaching chaos. Anah! Anah! my

In vain, and long, and still to be, beloved!
Why walk'st thou with this Spirit, in those hours
When no good Spirit longer lights below?
Anah. Japhet, I cannot answer thee; yet, yet
Forgive me ——
Japhet. May the Heaven, which soon no more
Will pardon, do so! for thou art greatly tempted.
Aholibamah. Back to thy tents, insulting son of Noah!
We know thee not.
Japhet. The hour may come when thou
May'st know me better; and thy sister know
Me still the same which I have ever been.
Samiasa. Son of the patriarch, who hath ever been
Upright before his God, whate'er thy gifts,
And thy words seem of sorrow, mixed with wrath,
How have Azaziel, or myself, brought on thee
Wrong?
Japhet. Wrong! the greatest of all wrongs! but, thou
Say'st well, though she be dust — I did not, could not,
Deserve her. Farewell, Anah! I have said
That word so often! but now say it, ne'er
To be repeated. Angel! or whate'er
Thou art, or must be soon, hast thou the power
To save this beautiful — *these* beautiful
Children of Cain?
Azaziel. From what?
Japhet. And is it so,
That ye too know not? Angels! angels! ye
Have shared man's sin, and, it may be, now must
Partake his punishment; or, at the least,
My sorrow.
Samiasa. Sorrow! I ne'er thought till now
To hear an Adamite speak riddles to me.
Japhet. And hath not the Most High expounded them?
Then ye are lost as they are lost.
Aholibamah. So be it!
If they love as they are loved, they will not shrink
More to be mortal, than I would to dare
An immortality of agonies
With Samiasa!
Anah. Sister! sister! speak not
Thus.
Azaziel. Fearest thou, my Anah?
Anah. Yes, for thee:
I would resign the greater remnant of
This little life of mine, before one hour
Of thine eternity should know a pang.
Japhet. It is for *him,* then! for the Seraph thou

Hast left me! That is nothing, if thou hast not
Left thy God too! for unions like to these,
Between a mortal and an immortal, cannot
Be happy or be hallowed. We are sent
Upon the earth to toil and die; and they
Are made to minister on high unto
The Highest: but if he can *save* thee, soon
The hour will come in which celestial aid
Alone can do so.

Anah. Ah! he speaks of Death.

Samiasa. Of death to *us!* and those who are with us!
But that the man seems full of sorrow, I
Could smile.

Japhet. I grieve not for myself, nor fear.
I am safe, not for my own deserts, but those
Of a well-doing sire, who hath been found
Righteous enough to save his children. Would
His power was greater of redemption! or
That by exchanging my own life for hers,
Who could alone have made mine happy, she,
The last and loveliest of Cain's race, could share
The ark which shall receive a remnant of
The seed of Seth!

Aholibamah. And dost thou think that we,
With Cain's, the eldest born of Adam's, blood
Warm in our veins, — strong Cain! who was begotten
In Paradise, — would mingle with Seth's children?
Seth, the last offspring of old Adam's dotage?
No, not to save all Earth, were Earth in peril!
Our race hath always dwelt apart from thine
From the beginning, and shall do so ever.

Japhet. I did not speak to thee, Aholibamah!
Too much of the forefather whom thou vauntest
Has come down in that haughty blood which springs
From him who shed the first, and that a brother's!
But thou, my Anah! let me call thee mine,
Albeit thou art not; 'tis a word I cannot
Part with, although I must from thee. My Anah!
Thou who dost rather make me dream that Abel
Had left a daughter, whose pure pious race
Survived in thee, so much unlike thou art
The rest of the stern Cainites, save in beauty,
For all of them are fairest in their favour ——

Aholibamah (interrupting him). And would'st thou have her like our father's foe
In mind, in soul? If *I* partook thy thought,
And dreamed that aught of *Abel* was in *her!* —
Get thee hence, son of Noah; thou makest strife.

Japhet. Offspring of Cain, thy father did so!
Aholibamah. But
He slew not Seth: and what hast thou to do
With other deeds between his God and him?
Japhet. Thou speakest well: his God hath judged him, and
I had not named his deed, but that thyself
Didst seem to glory in him, nor to shrink
From what he had done.
Aholibamah. He was our father's father;
The eldest born of man, the strongest, bravest,
And most enduring: — Shall I blush for him
From whom we had our being? Look upon
Our race; behold their stature and their beauty,
Their courage, strength, and length of days ——
Japhet. They are numbered.
Aholibamah. Be it so! but while yet their hours endure,
I glory in my brethren and our fathers.
Japhet. My sire and race but glory in their God,
Anah! and thou? ——
Anah. Whate'er our God decrees,
The God of Seth as Cain, I must obey,
And will endeavour patiently to obey.
But could I dare to pray in his dread hour
Of universal vengeance (if such should be),
It would not be to live, alone exempt
Of all my house. My sister! oh, my sister!
What were the world, or other worlds, or all
The brightest future, without the sweet past —
Thy love, my father's, all the life, and all
The things which sprang up with me, like the stars,
Making my dim existence radiant with
Soft lights which were not mine? Aholibamah!
Oh! if there should be mercy — seek it, find it:
I abhor Death, because that thou must die.
Aholibamah. What, hath this dreamer, with his father's ark,
The bugbear he hath built to scare the world,
Shaken *my* sister? Are *we* not the loved
Of Seraphs? and if we were not, must we
Cling to a son of Noah for our lives?
Rather than thus —— But the enthusiast dreams
The worst of dreams, the fantasies engendered
By hopeless love and heated vigils. Who
Shall shake these solid mountains, this firm earth,
And bid those clouds and waters take a shape
Distinct from that which we and all our sires
Have seen them wear on their eternal way?
Who shall do this?

Japhet. He whose one word produced them.
Aholibamah. Who *heard* that word?
Japhet. The universe, which leaped
To life before it. Ah! smilest thou still in scorn?
Turn to thy Seraphs: if they attest it not,
They are none.
Samiasa. Aholibamah, own thy God!
Aholibamah. I have ever hailed our Maker, Samiasa,
As thine, and mine: a God of Love, not Sorrow.
Japhet. Alas! what else is Love but Sorrow? Even
He who made earth in love had soon to grieve
Above its first and best inhabitants.
Aholibamah. 'Tis said so.
Japhet. It is even so.

Enter NOAH *and* SHEM.

Noah. Japhet! What
Dost thou here with these children of the wicked?
Dread'st thou not to partake their coming doom?
Japhet. Father, it cannot be a sin to seek
To save an earth-born being; and behold,
These are not of the sinful, since they have
The fellowship of angels.
Noah. These are they, then,
Who leave the throne of God, to take them wives
From out the race of Cain; the sons of Heaven,
Who seek Earth's daughters for their beauty?
Azaziel. Patriarch!
Thou hast said it.
Noah. Woe, woe, woe to such communion!
Has not God made a barrier between Earth
And Heaven, and limited each, kind to kind?
Samiasa. Was not man made in high Jehovah's image?
Did God not love what he had made? And what
Do we but imitate and emulate
His love unto created love?
Noah. I am
But man, and was not made to judge mankind,
Far less the sons of God; but as our God
Has deigned to commune with me, and reveal
His judgments, I reply, that the descent
Of Seraphs from their everlasting seat
Unto a perishable and perishing,
Even on the very *eve* of *perishing*, world,
Cannot be good.

Azaziel. What! though it were to save?
Noah. Not ye in all your glory can redeem
What he who made you glorious hath condemned.
Were your immortal mission safety, 'twould
Be general, not for two, though beautiful;
And beautiful they are, but not the less
Condemned.
Japhet. Oh, father! say it not.
Noah. Son! son!
If that thou wouldst avoid their doom, forget
That they exist: they soon shall cease to be,
While thou shalt be the sire of a new world,
And better.
Japhet. Let me die with *this,* and *them!*
Noah. Thou *shouldst* for such a thought, but shalt not: he
Who *can,* redeems thee.
Samiasa. And why him and thee,
More than what he, thy son, prefers to both?
Noah. Ask him who made thee greater than myself
And mine, but not less subject to his own
Almightiness. And lo! his mildest and
Least to be tempted messenger appears!

Enter RAPHAEL *the Archangel.*

Raphael. Spirits!
Whose seat is near the throne,
What do ye here?
Is thus a Seraph's duty to be shown,
Now that the hour is near
When Earth must be alone?
Return!
Adore and burn,
In glorious homage with the elected "Seven."
Your place is Heaven.
Samiasa. Raphael!
The first and fairest of the sons of God,
How long hath this been law,
That Earth by angels must be left untrod?
Earth! which oft saw
Jehovah's footsteps not disdain her sod!
The world he loved, and made
For love; and oft have we obeyed
His frequent mission with delighted pinions:
Adoring him in his least works displayed;
Watching this youngest star of his dominions;
And, as the latest birth of his great word,

Eager to keep it worthy of our Lord.
Why is thy brow severe?
And wherefore speak'st thou of destruction near?
Raphael. Had Samiasa and Azaziel been
In their true place, with the angelic choir,
Written in fire
They would have seen
Jehovah's late decree,
And not enquired their Maker's breath of me:
But ignorance must ever be
A part of sin;
And even the Spirits' knowledge shall grow less
As they wax proud within;
For Blindness is the first-born of Excess.
When all good angels left the world, ye stayed,
Stung with strange passions, and debased
By mortal feelings for a mortal maid:
But ye are pardoned thus far, and replaced
With your pure equals. Hence! away! away!
Or stay,
And lose Eternity by that delay!
Azaziel. And thou! if Earth be thus forbidden
In the decree
To us until this moment hidden,
Dost thou not err as we
In being here?
Raphael. I came to call ye back to your fit sphere,
In the great name and at the word of God,
Dear, dearest in themselves, and scarce less dear —
That which I came to do: till now we trod
Together the eternal space; together
Let us still walk the stars. True, Earth must die!
Her race, returned into her womb, must wither,
And much which she inherits: but oh! why
Cannot this Earth be made, or be destroyed,
Without involving ever some vast void
In the immortal ranks? immortal still
In their immeasurable forfeiture.
Our brother Satan fell; his burning will
Rather than longer worship dared endure!
But ye who still are pure!
Seraphs! less mighty than the mightiest one, —
Think how he was undone!
And think if tempting man can compensate
For Heaven desired too late?
Long have I warred,
Long must I war

With him who deemed it hard
To be created, and to acknowledge him
Who midst the cherubim
Made him as suns to a dependent star,
Leaving the archangels at his right hand dim.
I loved him — beautiful he was: oh, Heaven!
Save *his* who made, what beauty and what power
Was ever like to Satan's! Would the hour
In which he fell could ever be forgiven!
The wish is impious: but, oh ye!
Yet undestroyed, be warned! Eternity
With him, or with his God, is in your choice:
He hath not tempted you; he cannot tempt
The angels, from his further snares exempt:
But man hath listened to his voice,
And ye to woman's — beautiful she is,
The serpent's voice less subtle than her kiss.
The snake but vanquished dust; but she will draw
A second host from heaven, to break Heaven's law.
Yet, yet, oh fly!
Ye cannot die;
But they
Shall pass away,
While ye shall fill with shrieks the upper sky
For perishable clay,
Whose memory in your immortality
Shall long outlast the Sun which gave them day.
Think how your essence differeth from theirs
In all but suffering! why partake
The agony to which they must be heirs —
Born to be ploughed with years, and sown with cares,
And reaped by Death, lord of the human soil?
Even had their days been left to toil their path
Through time to dust, unshortened by God's wrath,
Still they are Evil's prey, and Sorrow's spoil.
Aholibamah. Let them fly!
I hear the voice which says that all must die,
Sooner than our white-bearded patriarchs died;
And that on high
An ocean is prepared,
While from below
The deep shall rise to meet Heaven's overflow —
Few shall be spared,
It seems; and, of that few, the race of Cain
Must lift their eyes to Adam's God in vain.
Sister! since it is so,
And the eternal Lord

In vain would be implored
For the remission of one hour of woe,
Let us resign even what we have adored,
And meet the wave, as we would meet the sword,
If not unmoved, yet undismayed,
And wailing less for us than those who shall
Survive in mortal or immortal thrall,
And, when the fatal waters are allayed,
Weep for the myriads who can weep no more.
Fly, Seraphs! to your own eternal shore,
Where winds nor howl, nor waters roar.
Our portion is to die,
And yours to live for ever:
But which is best, a dead Eternity,
Or living, is but known to the great Giver.
Obey him, as we shall obey;
I would not keep this life of mine in clay
An hour beyond his will;
Nor see ye lose a portion of his grace,
For all the mercy which Seth's race
Find still.
Fly!
And as your pinions bear ye back to Heaven,
Think that my love still mounts with thee on high,
Samiasa!
And if I look up with a tearless eye,
'Tis that an angel's bride disdains to weep, —
Farewell! Now rise, inexorable deep!
Anah. And must we die?
And must I lose thee too,
Azaziel?
Oh, my heart! my heart!
Thy prophecies were true!
And yet thou wert so happy too!
The blow, though not unlooked for, falls as new:
But yet depart!
Ah! why?
Yet let me not retain thee — fly!
My pangs can be but brief; but thine would be
Eternal, if repulsed from Heaven for me.
Too much already hast thou deigned
To one of Adam's race!
Our doom is sorrow: not to us alone,
But to the Spirits who have not disdained
To love us, cometh anguish with disgrace.
The first who taught us knowledge hath been hurled
From his once archangelic throne

Into some unknown world:
And thou, Azaziel! No —
Thou shalt not suffer woe
For me. Away! nor weep!
Thou canst not weep; but yet
May'st suffer more, not weeping: then forget
Her, whom the surges of the all-strangling deep
Can bring no pang like this. Fly! fly!
Being gone, 'twill be less difficult to die.
Japhet. Oh say not so!
Father! and thou, archangel, thou!
Surely celestial mercy lurks below
That pure severe serenity of brow:
Let them not meet this sea without a shore,
Save in our ark, or let me be no more!
Noah. Peace, child of passion, peace!
If not within thy heart, yet with thy tongue
Do God no wrong!
Live as he wills it — die, when he ordains,
A righteous death, unlike the seed of Cain's.
Cease, or be sorrowful in silence; cease
To weary Heaven's ear with thy selfish plaint.
Wouldst thou have God commit a sin for thee?
Such would it be
To alter his intent
For a mere mortal sorrow. Be a man!
And bear what Adam's race must bear, and can.
Japhet. Aye, father! but when they are gone,
And we are all alone,
Floating upon the azure desert, and
The depth beneath us hides our own dear land,
And dearer, silent friends and brethren, all
Buried in its immeasurable breast,
Who, who, our tears, our shrieks, shall then command?
Can we in Desolation's peace have rest?
Oh God! be thou a God, and spare
Yet while 'tis time!
Renew not Adam's fall:
Mankind were then but twain,
But they are numerous now as are the waves
And the tremendous rain,
Whose drops shall be less thick than would their graves,
Were graves permitted to the seed of Cain.
Noah. Silence, vain boy! each word of thine 's a crime.
Angel! forgive this stripling's fond despair.
Raphael. Seraphs! these mortals speak in passion: Ye!
Who are, or should be, passionless and pure,

May now return with me.
Samiasa. It may not be:
We have chosen, and will endure.
Raphael. Say'st thou?
Azaziel. He hath said it, and I say, Amen!
Raphael. Again!
Then from this hour,
Shorn as ye are of all celestial power,
And aliens from your God,
Farewell!
Japhet. Alas! where shall they dwell?
Hark, hark! Deep sounds, and deeper still,
Are howling from the mountain's bosom:
There's not a breath of wind upon the hill,
Yet quivers every leaf, and drops each blossom:
Earth groans as if beneath a heavy load.
Noah. Hark, hark! the sea-birds cry!
In clouds they overspread the lurid sky,
And hover round the mountain, where before
Never a white wing, wetted by the wave,
Yet dared to soar,
Even when the waters waxed too fierce to brave.
Soon it shall be their only shore,
And then, no more!
Japhet. The sun! the sun!
He riseth, but his better light is gone;
And a black circle, bound
His glaring disk around,
Proclaims Earth's last of summer days hath shone!
The clouds return into the hues of night,
Save where their brazen-coloured edges streak
The verge where brighter morns were wont to break.
Noah. And lo! yon flash of light,
The distant thunder's harbinger, appears!
It cometh! hence, away!
Leave to the elements their evil prey!
Hence to where our all-hallowed ark uprears
Its safe and wreckless sides!
Japhet. Oh, father, stay!
Leave not my Anah to the swallowing tides!
Noah. Must we not leave all life to such? Begone!
Japhet. Not I.
Noah. Then die
With them!
How darest thou look on that prophetic sky,
And seek to save what all things now condemn,
In overwhelming unison

With just Jehovah's wrath!
Japhet. Can rage and justice join in the same path?
Noah. Blasphemer! darest thou murmur even now!
Raphael. Patriarch, be still a father! smooth thy brow:
Thy son, despite his folly, shall not sink:
He knows not what he says, yet shall not drink
With sobs the salt foam of the swelling waters;
But be, when passion passeth, good as thou,
Nor perish like Heaven's children with man's daughters.
Aholibamah. The tempest cometh; heaven and earth unite
For the annihilation of all life.
Unequal is the strife
Between our strength and the Eternal Might!
Samiasa. But ours is with thee; we will bear ye far
To some untroubled star,
Where thou, and Anah, shalt partake our lot:
And if thou dost not weep for thy lost earth,
Our forfeit Heaven shall also be forgot.
Anah. Oh! my dear father's tents, my place of birth,
And mountains, land, and woods! when ye are not,
Who shall dry up my tears?
Azaziel. Thy spirit-lord.
Fear not; though we are shut from Heaven,
Yet much is ours, whence we can not be driven.
Raphael. Rebel! thy words are wicked, as thy deeds
Shall henceforth be but weak: the flaming sword,
Which chased the first-born out of Paradise,
Still flashes in the angelic hands.
Azaziel. It cannot slay us: threaten dust with death,
And talk of weapons unto that which bleeds.
What are thy swords in our immortal eyes?
Raphael. The moment cometh to approve thy strength;
And learn at length
How vain to war with what thy God commands:
Thy former force was in thy faith.

Enter Mortals, flying for refuge.

Chorus of Mortals.

The heavens and earth are mingling — God! oh God!
What have we done? Yet spare!
Hark! even the forest beasts howl forth their prayer!
The dragon crawls from out his den,
To herd, in terror, innocent with men;
And the birds scream their agony through air.
Yet, yet, Jehovah! yet withdraw thy rod

Of wrath, and pity thine own world's despair!
Hear not man only but all nature plead!
Raphael. Farewell, thou earth! ye wretched sons of clay,
I cannot, must not, aid you. 'Tis decreed!
[*Exit* RAPHAEL.
Japhet. Some clouds sweep on as vultures for their prey,
While others, fixed as rocks, await the word
At which their wrathful vials shall be poured.
No azure more shall robe the firmament,
Nor spangled stars be glorious: Death hath risen:
In the Sun's place a pale and ghastly glare
Hath wound itself around the dying air.
Azaziel. Come, Anah! quit this chaos-founded prison,
To which the elements again repair,
To turn it into what it was: beneath
The shelter of these wings thou shalt be safe,
As was the eagle's nestling once within
Its mother's. — Let the coming chaos chafe
With all its elements! Heed not their din!
A brighter world than this, where thou shalt breathe
Ethereal life, will we explore:
These darkened clouds are not the only skies.
[AZAZIEL *and* SAMIASA *fly off, and disappear with* ANAH *and* AHOLIBAMAH.
Japhet. They are gone! They have disappeared amidst the roar
Of the forsaken world; and never more,
Whether they live, or die with all Earth's life,
Now near its last, can aught restore
Anah unto these eyes.

Chorus of Mortals.

Oh son of Noah! mercy on thy kind!
What! wilt thou leave us all — all — *all* behind?
While safe amidst the elemental strife,
Thou sitt'st within thy guarded ark?
A Mother (*offering her infant to* JAPHET). Oh, let this child embark!
I brought him forth in woe,
But thought it joy
To see him to my bosom clinging so.
Why was he born?
What hath he done —
My unweaned son —
To move Jehovah's wrath or scorn?
What is there in this milk of mine, that Death
Should stir all Heaven and Earth up to destroy
My boy,

And roll the waters o'er his placid breath?
Save him, thou seed of Seth!
Or curséd be — with him who made
Thee and thy race, for which we are betrayed!
Japhet. Peace! 'tis no hour for curses, but for prayer!

Chorus of Mortals.

For prayer! ! !
And where
Shall prayer ascend,
When the swoln clouds unto the mountains bend
And burst,
And gushing oceans every barrier rend,
Until the very deserts know no thirst?
Accursed
Be he who made thee and thy sire!
We deem our curses vain; we must expire;
But as we know the worst,
Why should our hymns be raised, our knees be bent
Before the implacable Omnipotent,
Since we must fall the same?
If he hath made Earth, let it be his shame,
To make a world for torture. — Lo! they come,
The loathsome waters, in their rage!
And with their roar make wholesome nature dumb!
The forest's trees (coeval with the hour
When Paradise upsprung,
Ere Eve gave Adam knowledge for her dower,
Or Adam his first hymn of slavery sung),
So massy, vast, yet green in their old age,
Are overtopped,
Their summer blossoms by the surges lopped,
Which rise, and rise, and rise.
Vainly we look up to the lowering skies —
They meet the seas,
And shut out God from our beseeching eyes.
Fly, son of Noah, fly! and take thine ease,
In thine allotted ocean-tent;
And view, all floating o'er the element,
The corpses of the world of thy young days:
Then to Jehovah raise
Thy song of praise!
A Mortal. Blesséd are the dead
Who die in the Lord!
And though the waters be o'er earth outspread,
Yet, as *his* word,
Be the decree adored!

He gave me life — he taketh but
The breath which is his own:
And though these eyes should be for ever shut,
Nor longer this weak voice before his throne
Be heard in supplicating tone,
Still blesséd be the Lord,
For what is past,
For that which is:
For all are his,
From first to last —
Time — Space — Eternity — Life — Death —
The vast known and immeasurable unknown.
He made, and can unmake;
And shall *I*, for a little gasp of breath,
Blaspheme and groan?
No; let me die, as I have lived, in faith,
Nor quiver, though the Universe may quake!

Chorus of Mortals.

Where shall we fly?
Not to the mountains high;
For now their torrents rush, with double roar,
To meet the Ocean, which, advancing still,
Already grasps each drowning hill,
Nor leaves an unsearched cave.

Enter a Woman.

Woman. Oh, save me, save!
Our valley is no more:
My father and my father's tent,
My brethren and my brethren's herds,
The pleasant trees that o'er our noonday bent,
And sent forth evening songs from sweetest birds,
The little rivulet which freshened all

Our pastures green,
No more are to be seen.
When to the mountain cliff I climbed this morn,
I turned to bless the spot,
And not a leaf appeared about to fall; —
And now they are not! —
Why was I born?
Japhet. To die! in youth to die!
And happier in that doom,
Than to behold the universal tomb,
Which I

Am thus condemned to weep above in vain.
Why, when all perish, why must I remain?

[*The waters rise; Men fly in every direction; many are overtaken by the waves: the Chorus of Mortals disperses in search of safety up the mountains:* JAPHET *remains upon a rock, while the Ark floats towards him in the distance.*

ON THIS DAY I COMPLETE MY THIRTY-SIXTH YEAR

1

'T IS time this heart should be unmoved,
Since others it hath ceased to move:
Yet, though I cannot be beloved,
Still let me love!

2

My days are in the yellow leaf;
The flowers and fruits of Love are gone;
The worm, the canker, and the grief
Are mine alone!

3

The fire that on my bosom preys
Is lone as some Volcanic isle;
No torch is kindled at its blaze —
A funeral pile.

4

The hope, the fear, the jealous care,
The exalted portion of the pain
And power of love, I cannot share,
But wear the chain.

5

But 't is not *thus* — and 't is not *here* —
Such thoughts should shake my soul, nor *now*
Where Glory decks the hero's bier,
Or binds his brow.

6

The Sword, the Banner, and the Field,
  Glory and Greece, around me see!
The Spartan, borne upon his shield,
    Was not more free.

7

Awake! (not Greece — she *is* awake!)
  Awake, my spirit! Think through *whom*
Thy life-blood tracks its parent lake,
    And then strike home!

8

Tread those reviving passions down,
  Unworthy manhood! — unto thee
Indifferent should the smile or frown
    Of Beauty be.

9

If thou regret'st thy youth, *why live?*
  The land of honourable death
Is here: — up to the Field, and give
    Away thy breath!

10

Seek out — less often sought than found —
  A soldier's grave, for thee the best;
Then look around, and choose thy ground,
    And take thy Rest.

LETTERS

TO MRS. CHRISTOPHER PARKER[1]

Newstead Abbey, Nov. 8th, 1798.

DEAR MADAM,

My Mamma being unable to write herself desires I will let you know that the potatoes are now ready and you are welcome to them whenever you please.

She begs you will ask Mrs. Parkyns if she would wish the poney to go round by Nottingham or to go home the nearest way as it is now quite well but too small to carry me.

I have sent a young Rabbit which I beg Miss Frances will accept off and which I promised to send before. My Mamma desires her best compliments to you all in which I join.

I am, Dear Aunt, yours sincerely,
BYRON.

I hope you will excuse all blunders as it is the first letter I ever wrote.

[1] Charlotte Augusta Byron, daughter of Admiral John Byron, therefore sister of the Poet's father, married Christopher Parker (1761–1804), who became Vice-Admiral in 1804.

TO AUGUSTA BYRON

Harrow-on-the-Hill, Novr., Saturday, 17th, 1804.

I am glad to hear, My dear Sister, that you like Castle Howard so well, I have no doubt what you say is true and that Lord C. is much more amiable than he has been represented to me. Never having been much with him and always hearing him reviled, it was hardly possible I should have conceived a very *great friendship* for his L^{d}.ship.[1] My mother, you inform me, commends my *amiable disposition* and *good understanding;* if she does this to you, it is a great deal more than I ever hear myself, for the one or the other is always found fault with, and I am told to copy the *excellent pattern* which I see before me in *herself*. You have got an invitation too, you may accept it if you please, but if you value your own comfort, and like a pleasant situa-

[1] Frederick Howard, fifth Earl of Carlisle (1748–1825), related to the Byron family, became Byron's guardian in 1799; his subsequent relations with Mrs. Byron were hardly pleasant.

tion, I advise you to avoid Southwell. — I thank you, My dear Augusta, for your readiness to assist me, and will in some manner avail myself of it; I do not however wish to be separated from *her* entirely, but not to be so much with her as I hitherto have been, for I do believe she likes me; she manifests that in many instances, particularly with regard to money, which I never want, and have as much as I desire. But her conduct is so strange, her caprices so impossible to be complied with, her passions so outrageous, that the evil quite overbalances her *agreeable qualities*. Amongst other things I forgot to mention a most *ungovernable appetite* for Scandal, which she never can govern, and employs most of her time abroad, in displaying the faults, and censuring the foibles, of her acquaintance; therefore I do not wonder, that my precious Aunt, comes in for her share of encomiums; This however is nothing to what happens when my conduct admits of animadversion; "then comes the tug of war." My whole family from the conquest are upbraided! myself abused, and I am told that what little accomplishments I possess either in mind or body are derived from her and *her alone*.

When I leave Harrow I know not; that depends on her nod; I like it very well. The master Dr. Drury, is the most amiable *clergyman* I ever knew; he unites the Gentleman with the Scholar, without affectation or pedantry, what little I have learnt I owe to him alone, nor is it his fault that it was not more. I shall always remember his instructions with Gratitude, and cherish a hope that it may one day be in my power to repay the numerous obligations, I am under; to him or some of his family.[2]

Our holidays come on in about a fortnight. I however have not mentioned that to my mother, nor do I intend it; but if I can, I shall contrive to evade going to Southwell. Depend upon it I will not approach her for some time to come if It is in my power to avoid it, but she must not know, that it is my wish to be absent. I hope you will excuse my sending so short a letter, but the Bell has just rung to summon us together. Write Soon, and believe me,

Ever your affectionate Brother,

BYRON.

I am afraid you will have some difficulty in decyphering my epistles, but *that* I know you will excuse. Adieu. Remember me to L[d] Carlisle.

[2] Joseph Drury, D. D. (1750–1834), was Headmaster of Harrow from 1784 to 1805.

TO JOHN HANSON

Trin. Coll. Cambridge, Novr. 23, 1805.

DEAR SIR,

Your Advice was good but I have not determined whether I shall follow it; this Place is the *Devil* or at least his principal residence. They call it the University, but any other Appellation would have suited it much better, for Study is the last pursuit of the Society; the Master eats, drinks, and sleeps, the Fellows *Drink, dispute and pun;* the Employment of the Under graduates you will probably conjecture without my description. I sit down to write with a Head confused with Dissipation which, tho' I hate, I cannot avoid.

I have only supped at Home 3 times since my Arrival, and my table is constantly covered with invitations, after all I am the most *steady* Man in College, nor have I got into many Scrapes, and none of consequence. Whenever you appoint a day my Servant shall come up for "Oateater," and as the Time of paying my Bills now approaches, the remaining £50 will be very *agreeable*. You need not make any deductions as I shall want most of it; I will settle with you for the Saddle and Accoutrements *next* quarter. The Upholsterer's Bill will not be sent in yet as my rooms are to be papered and painted at Xmas when I will procure them. No Furniture has been got except what was absolutely necessary including some Decanters and Wine Glasses.

Your Cook certainly deceived you, as I know my Servant was in Town 5 days, and she stated 4. I have yet had no reason to distrust him, but we will examine the affair when I come to Town when I intend lodging at Mrs. Massingbird's. My Mother and I have quarrelled, which I bear with the *patience* of a Philosopher; custom reconciles me to everything.

In the Hope that Mrs. H. and the *Battalion* are in good Health.

I remain, Sir, etc., etc.,

BYRON.

TO ROBERT CHARLES DALLAS[1]

Dorant's, January 21, 1808.

SIR,

Whenever leisure and inclination permit me the pleasure of a visit, I shall feel truly gratified in a personal acquaintance with one whose mind has been long known to me in his writings.

You are so far correct in your conjecture, that I am a member of the University of Cambridge, where I shall take my degree of A.M. this term; but were reasoning, eloquence, or virtue, the objects of my search, Granta is not their metropolis, nor is the place of her situation an "El Dorado," far less an Utopia. The intellects of her children are as stagnant as her Cam, and their pursuits limited to the church — not of Christ, but of the nearest benefice.

As to my reading, I believe I may aver, without hyperbole, it has been tolerably extensive in the historical department; so that few nations exist, or have existed, with whose records I am not in some degree acquainted, from Herodotus down to Gibbon. Of the classics, I know about as much as most school-boys after a discipline of thirteen years; of the law of the land as much as enables me to keep "within the statute" — to use the poacher's vocabulary. I did study the "Spirit of Laws" and the Law of Nations; but when I saw the latter violated every month, I gave up my attempts at so useless an accomplishment: — of geography, I have seen more land on maps than I should wish to traverse on foot; — of mathematics, enough to give me the headach without clearing the part affected; — of philosophy, astronomy, and metaphysics, more than I can comprehend; and of common sense so little, that I mean to leave a Byronian prize at each of our "Almæ Matres" for the first discovery, — though I rather fear that of the longitude will precede it.

I once thought myself a philosopher, and talked nonsense with great decorum: I defied pain, and preached up equanimity. For some time this did very well, for no one was in *pain* for me but my friends, and none lost their patience but my hearers. At last, a fall from my horse convinced me bodily suffering was an evil; and the worst of an argu-

[1] Robert Charles Dallas (1754–1824), related by marriage to Byron, introduced himself to the young man in a letter of early January 1808. Well-intentioned though self-righteous, Dallas set himself up, between 1808 and 1814, as Byron's moral and literary adviser, directing many of the affairs relating to the publication of *English Bards and Scotch Reviewers,* the first two cantos of *Childe Harold's Pilgrimage,* and *The Corsair.*

ment overset my maxims and my temper at the same moment: so I quitted Zeno for Aristippus, and conceive that pleasure constitutes the *το καλον*.[2]

In morality, I prefer Confucius to the Ten Commandments, and Socrates to St. Paul (though the two latter agree in their opinion of marriage). In religion, I favour the Catholic emancipation, but do not acknowledge the Pope; and I have refused to take the sacrament, because I do not think eating bread or drinking wine from the hand of an earthly vicar will make me an inheritor of heaven. I hold virtue, in general, or the virtues severally, to be only in the disposition, each a *feeling*, not a principle. I believe truth the prime attribute of the Deity, and death an eternal sleep, at least of the body. You have here a brief compendium of the sentiments of the *wicked* George, Lord Byron; and, till I get a new suit, you will perceive I am badly cloathed.

I remain yours, etc.,
BYRON.

2 The Beautiful.

TO MRS. BYRON

Gibraltar, August 11th, 1809.

DEAR MOTHER,

I have been so much occupied since my departure from England, that till I could address you at length I have forborne writing altogether. As I have now passed through Portugal, and a considerable part of Spain, and have leisure at this place, I shall endeavour to give you a short detail of my movements.

We sailed from Falmouth on the 2nd of July, reached Lisbon after a very favourable passage of four days and a half, and took up our abode in that city. It has been often described without being worthy of description; for, except the view from the Tagus, which is beautiful, and some fine churches and convents, it contains little but filthy streets, and more filthy inhabitants. To make amends for this, the village of Cintra, about fifteen miles from the capital, is, perhaps in every respect, the most delightful in Europe; it contains beauties of every description, natural and artificial. Palaces and gardens rising in the midst of rocks, cataracts, and precipices; convents on stupendous heights — a distant view of the sea and the Tagus; and, besides (though that is a secondary consideration), is remarkable as the scene of Sir Hew

Dalrymple's Convention.[1] It unites in itself all the wildness of the western highlands, with the verdure of the south of France. Near this place, about ten miles to the right, is the palace of Mafra, the boast of Portugal, as it might be of any other country, in point of magnificence without elegance. There is a convent annexed; the monks, who possess large revenues, are courteous enough, and understand Latin, so that we had a long conversation: they have a large library, and asked me if the *English* had *any books* in their country?

I sent my baggage, and part of the servants, by sea to Gibraltar, and travelled on horseback from Aldea Galbega (the first stage from Lisbon, which is only accessible by water) to Seville (one of the most famous cities in Spain), where the Government called the Junta is now held. The distance to Seville is nearly four hundred miles, and to Cadiz almost ninety farther towards the coast. I had orders from the governments, and every possible accommodation on the road, as an English nobleman, in an English uniform, is a very respectable personage in Spain at present. The horses are remarkably good, and the roads (I assure you upon my honour, for you will hardly believe it) very far superior to the best English roads, without the smallest toll or turnpike. You will suppose this when I rode post to Seville, in four days, through this parching country in the midst of summer, without fatigue or annoyance.

Seville is a beautiful town; though the streets are narrow, they are clean. We lodged in the house of two Spanish unmarried ladies, who possess *six* houses in Seville, and gave me a curious specimen of Spanish manners. They are women of character, and the eldest a fine woman, the youngest pretty, but not so good a figure as Donna Josepha. The freedom of manner, which is general here, astonished me not a little; and in the course of further observation, I find that reserve is not the characteristic of the Spanish belles, who are, in general, very handsome, with large black eyes, and very fine forms. The eldest honoured your *unworthy* son with very particular attention, embracing him with great tenderness at parting (I was there but three days), after cutting off a lock of his hair, and presenting him with one of her own, about three feet in length, which I send, and beg you will retain till my return. Her last words were, *Adios, tu hermoso! me gusto mucho* — "Adieu, you pretty fellow! you please me much." She offered me a share of her apartment, which my *virtue* induced me to decline; she laughed, and said I had some English *amante* (lover),

[1] The Convention of Cintra, signed 31 August 1808 by Sir Hew Dalrymple (1750–1830) as commander of the British forces during this phase of the Peninsular War.

and added that she was going to be married to an officer in the Spanish army.

I left Seville, and rode on to Cadiz, through a beautiful country. At *Xeres,* where the sherry we drink is made, I met a great merchant — a Mr. Gordon of Scotland — who was extremely polite, and favoured me with the inspection of his vaults and cellars, so that I quaffed at the fountain head.

Cadiz, sweet Cadiz, is the most delightful town I ever beheld, very different from our English cities in every respect except cleanliness (and it is as clean as London), but still beautiful, and full of the finest women in Spain, the Cadiz belles being the Lancashire witches of their land. Just as I was introduced and began to like the grandees, I was forced to leave it for this cursed place; but before I return to England I will visit it again. The night before I left it, I sat in the box at the opera with Admiral Cordova's family; he is the commander whom Lord St. Vincent defeated in 1797, and has an aged wife and a fine daughter, Sennorita Cordova. The girl is very pretty, in the Spanish style; in my opinion, by no means inferior to the English in charms, and certainly superior in fascination. Long black hair, dark languishing eyes, *clear* olive complexions, and forms more graceful in motion than can be conceived by an Englishman used to the drowsy, listless air of his countrywomen, added to the most becoming dress, and, at the same time, the most decent in the world, render a Spanish beauty irresistible.

I beg leave to observe that intrigue here is the business of life; when a woman marries she throws off all restraint, but I believe their conduct is chaste enough before. If you make a proposal, which in England will bring a box on the ear from the meekest of virgins, to a Spanish girl, she thanks you for the honour you intend her, and replies, "Wait till I am married, and I shall be too happy." This is literally and strictly true.

Miss Cordova and her little brother understood a little French, and, after regretting my ignorance of the Spanish, she proposed to become my preceptress in that language. I could only reply by a low bow, and express my regret that I quitted Cadiz too soon to permit me to make the progress which would doubtless attend my studies under so charming a directress. I was standing at the back of the box, which resembles our Opera boxes, (the theatre is large and finely decorated, the music admirable,) in the manner which Englishmen generally adopt, for fear of incommoding the ladies in front, when this fair Spaniard dispossessed an old woman (an aunt or a duenna) of her chair, and commanded me to be seated next herself, at a tolerable distance from her mamma. At the close of the performance I withdrew, and was lounging with a party of men in the passage, when, *en passant,* the lady turned round and called me, and I had the honour of attending her to the admiral's mansion. I have an invitation on my return to Cadiz, which I shall accept if I repass through the country on my return from Asia.

I have met Sir John Carr, Knight Errant, at Seville and Cadiz. He is a pleasant man. I like the Spaniards much. You have heard of the battle near Madrid, and in England they would call it a victory — a pretty victory! Two hundred officers and five thousand men killed, all English, and the French in as great force as ever.[2] I should have joined the army, but we have no time to lose before we get up the Mediterranean and Archipelago. I am going over to Africa tomorrow; it is only six miles from this fortress. My next stage is Cagliari in Sardinia, where I shall be presented to His Majesty. I have a most superb uniform as a court dress, indispensable in travelling.

August 13. — I have not yet been to Africa — the wind is contrary — but I dined yesterday at Algesiras, with Lady Westmorland, where I met General Castanos, the celebrated Spanish leader in the late and present war. To-day I dine with him. He has offered me letters to Tetuan in Barbary, for the principal Moors, and I am to have the house for a few days of one of the great men, which was intended for Lady W., whose health will not permit her to cross the Straits.

August 15. — I could not dine with Castanos yesterday, but this afternoon I had that honour. He is pleasant and, for aught I know to the contrary, clever. I cannot go to Barbary. The Malta packet sails to-morrow, and myself in it. Admiral Purvis, with whom I dined at Cadiz, gave me a passage in a frigate to Gibraltar, but we have no ship of war destined for Malta at present. The packets sail fast, and have good accommodation. You shall hear from me on our route.

Joe Murray delivers this; I have sent him and the boy back.[3] Pray show the lad kindness, as he is my great favourite; I would have taken him on. And say this to his father, who may otherwise think he has behaved ill.

I hope this will find you well. Believe me,

Yours ever sincerely,
BYRON.

2 The Battle of Talavera, 27 and 28 July 1809, of which the report sent to the Spanish government stressed the size of British losses.

3 Robert Rushton, son of a neighboring farmer, who accompanied Byron as far as Gibraltar, where, because of his homesickness and supposed dangers ahead, he was sent home in the care of Joe Murray, an ancient servant at Newstead Abbey.

P.S. — So Lord G——[4] is married to a rustic. Well done! If I wed, I will bring home a Sultana, with half a dozen cities for a dowry, and reconcile you to an Ottoman daughter-in-law, with a bushel of pearls not larger than ostrich eggs, or smaller than walnuts.

[4] The twentieth Lord Grey de Ruthyn (1780–1810), who leased Newstead Abbey for a five-year period during Byron's minority, from 1803 to 1808.

TO FRANCIS HODGSON[1]

Newstead Abbey. Oct[r]. 10th. *1811*

MY DEAR HODGSON,

I have returned from Lancashire, where I went on *business*, but unluckily receiving an Invitation to a pleasant country seat near Rochdale[2] full of the fair & fashionable sex, I left my affairs to my agent (who however managed better without me) never went within ken of a coalpit, & am returned with six new acquaintances but little topographical knowledge. — However the concern is more valuable than I expected, but playing troublesome, it has been surveyed &c. &c. & will no doubt benefit my heirs. ——— Yours arrived this Even. — Your lines are some of the best you have ever written in that department, & as far as regards myself, extremely apropos, for I am just about to be connected with a very lucrative old Lady for the love of money. — So you & Drury[3] may drink my "Hymeneals" in good earnest, *anybody* may marry a young woman. *I* kindly take to the elderly for the sake of Humour. I shall have such pleasure in showing her to my friends, & then we shall be so happy in my house here, — *one* in each *Wing*. — Prithee, set folks right about the title of my bokie [*Scottish dialect:* a small book], a pize upon Murray's man![4] I want you to see the thing, Murray *would* shew it to M[r]. Gifford[5] without my knowledge, before he undertook it, & the *Great*-man, (unless much belied) gave an "Im-

[1] Francis Hodgson (1781–1852), at this time resident tutor at King's College, Cambridge, was Byron's friend from 1807. In 1812 Hodgson took orders, and in 1816 he was given a living at Bakewell; he became Archdeacon of Derby in 1836 and Provost of Eton in 1840. Through much of their genial correspondence, Byron and Hodgson argued matters of religion.

[2] The coal mines on the Rochdale estate, illegally leased by the fifth Lord Byron, were the subject of litigation during much of the life of his successor.

[3] Henry Joseph Drury (1778–1841), eldest child of the Headmaster of Harrow, became an assistant master at Harrow. He and Hodgson married sisters.

[4] Two days before, Hodgson had written Byron that one of John Murray's shopmen referred to Byron's forthcoming volume as "Child of Harrow's Pilgrimage."

[5] William Gifford (1756–1826), Editor of *The Quarterly Review* from 1809 to 1824 and one of Murray's principal advisers, reacted favorably to the poem.

primatur." ——— Cawthorn must keep back the "Hints" as we want the other out first,[6] — but dont let him into that secret lest he be savage; Hobhouse is anangered with him, so he writes from Enniscorthy, *his* Quarto with *cuts* from drawings *liberally* furnished by me, will be forth also.[7] — I must send Drury some Game, — is Bland[8] returned? what will become of his Dutch Parishioners! — Write unto me[.] I don't know that I shan't soon be in London, but don't expect me. — Every thing about & concerning me bears a gloomy aspect, still I keep up my spirit, it may be broken but it shall never be bent. — I heard of a death the other day that shocked me more than any of the preceding, of one whom I once loved more than I ever loved a living thing, & one who I believe loved me to the last,[9] yet I had not a tear left for an event which five years ago would have bowed me to the dust; still it sits heavy on my heart & calls back what I wish to forget, in many a feverish dream. —— Y^rs^ ever

B.

[6] Dallas had persuaded Byron that in publication *Childe Harold's Pilgrimage* should precede *Hints from Horace,* of which the publisher, James Cawthorn, had already prepared a proof. Indefinitely suppressed by Byron somewhat later, *Hints from Horace* did not appear in full text until 1831.

[7] Not until 1813 did Cawthorn publish the elaborately illustrated book by Hobhouse to which Byron refers, *A Journey through Albania and Other Provinces of Turkey in Europe and Asia to Constantinople during the Years 1809 and 1810.*

[8] The Reverend Robert Bland (1780–1825), assistant master at Harrow while Byron was there, returned in 1811 from Amsterdam, where he had served as Chaplain.

[9] John Edleston, whom Byron had known at Cambridge. Within several months Byron had also lost his mother, his Cambridge friend Charles Skinner Matthews, and his Harrow schoolfellow John Wingfield.

TO JOHN CAM HOBHOUSE

8, St. James' Street, *December 9th,* 1811.

MY DEAR HOBHOUSE,

At length I am your rival in good fortune. I, this night, saw *Robert Coates* perform Lothario at the Haymarket,[1] the house crammed, but bribery (a bank token) procured an excellent place near the stage.

Before the curtain drew up, a performer (all gemmen) came forward and thus addressed the house, Ladies, &c., "A melancholy accident has happened to the gentleman who undertook the part of Altamont —— (here a dead stop — then —) this accident has happened to

[1] Robert Coates (1790–1869), who played Lothario in Nicholas Rowe's *The Fair Penitent.*

his brother, who fell this afternoon through a *loop-hole* into the *London Dock,* and was taken up dead, Altamont has just entered the house, distractedly, is — now dressing! ! ! and will appear in five minutes"! ! ! Such were verbatim the words of the apologist; they were followed by a roar of laughter, and Altamont himself, who did not fall short of Coates in absurdity. Damn me, if I ever saw such a scene in my life; the play was closed in 3rd act; after Bob's demise, nobody would hear a syllable, he was interrupted several times before, and made speeches, every soul was in hysterics, and all the actors on his own model. You can't conceive how I longed for *you*; your taste for the ridiculous would have been gratified to surfeit.

A farce followed in dumb-show, after Bob had been hooted from the stage, for a bawdy address he attempted to deliver between play and farce.

"Love à la mode" was damned, Coates was damned, everything was damned, and damnable.

His enacting I need not describe, you have seen him at Bath. But never did you see the *others,* never did you hear the *apology,* never did you behold the "distracted" survivor of a "brother neck-broken through a *loop-hole* in y^e^ *London Docks.*"

Like George Faulkner these fellows defied burlesque. Oh, Captain! eye hath not seen, ear hath not heard, nor can the heart of man conceive to-night's performance.

Baron Geramb was in the stage box, and Coates in his address *nailed* the *Baron* to the infinite amusement of the audience, and the discomfiture of *Geramb,* who grew very wroth indeed.[2]

I meant to write on other topics, but I must postpone. I can think, and talk, and dream only of these buffoons.

" 'Tis done, 'tis numbered with the things that were, would, would it were to come" and you by my side to see it.

Heigh ho! Good-night.

Yours ever,
B.

2 Baron Geramb, a flamboyant German, who, becoming obnoxious to the British government in pressing certain claims against it, was deported in 1812 under the Aliens Act.

TO LORD HOLLAND[1]

8, St. James's Street, February 25, 1812.

MY LORD,

With my best thanks, I have the honour to return the Notts. letter to your Lordship. I have read it with attention, but do not think I shall venture to avail myself of its contents, as my view of the question differs in some measure from Mr. Coldham's. I hope I do not wrong him, but *his* objections to the bill appear to me to be founded on certain apprehensions that he and his coadjutors might be mistaken for the "*original advisers*" (to quote him) of the measure.[2] For my own part, I consider the manufacturers as a much injured body of men, sacrificed to the views of certain individuals who have enriched themselves by those practices which have deprived the frame-workers of employment. For instance; — by the adoption of a certain kind of frame, one man performs the work of seven — six are thus thrown out of business. But it is to be observed that the work thus done is far inferior in quality, hardly marketable at home, and hurried over with a view to exportation. Surely, my Lord, however we may rejoice in any improvement in the arts which may be beneficial to mankind, we must not allow mankind to be sacrificed to improvements in mechanism. The maintenance and well-doing of the industrious poor is an object of greater consequence to the community than the enrichment of a few monopolists by any improvement in the implements of trade, which deprives the workman of his bread, and renders the labourer "unworthy of his hire."

My own motive for opposing the bill is founded on its palpable injustice, and its certain inefficacy. I have seen the state of these miserable men, and it is a disgrace to a civilized country. Their excesses may be condemned, but cannot be subject of wonder. The effect of the present bill would be to drive them into actual rebellion. The few words I shall venture to offer on Thursday will be founded

[1] Henry Richard Vassall Fox, third Lord Holland (1773–1840), who did more than any other English statesman to hold the Whigs together during the long years of their exclusion.

[2] As a result of riots by stocking-weavers of Nottingham and their destruction of equipment between November 1811 and January 1812, a bill establishing the death penalty for frame-breaking passed its third reading in the House of Commons on 20 February 1812 and in the House of Lords on 5 March. On the second reading in the House of Lords, on 27 February, Byron made his first speech in the House, opposing the bill.

upon these opinions formed from my own observations on the spot. By previous inquiry, I am convinced these men would have been restored to employment, and the county to tranquillity. It is, perhaps, not yet too late, and is surely worth the trial. It can never be too late to employ force in such circumstances. I believe your Lordship does not coincide with me entirely on this subject, and most cheerfully and sincerely shall I submit to your superior judgment and experience, and take some other line of argument against the bill, or be silent altogether, should you deem it more advisable. Condemning, as every one must condemn, the conduct of these wretches, I believe in the existence of grievances which call rather for pity than punishment. I have the honour to be, with great respect, my Lord, your Lordship's

Most obedient and obliged servant,

BYRON.

P.S. — I am a little apprehensive that your Lordship will think me too lenient towards these men, and half a *frame-breaker myself.*

TO WALTER SCOTT

St. James's Street, July 6, 1812.

SIR,

I have just been honoured with your letter. — I feel sorry that you should have thought it worth while to notice the "evil works of my nonage," as the thing is suppressed *voluntarily,* and your explanation is too kind not to give me pain. The Satire was written when I was very young and very angry, and fully bent on displaying my wrath and my wit, and now I am haunted by the ghosts of my wholesale assertions.[1] I cannot sufficiently thank you for your praise; and now, waving myself, let me talk to you of the Prince Regent. He ordered me to be presented to him at a ball; and after some sayings peculiarly pleasing from royal lips, as to my own attempts, he talked to me of you and your immortalities: he preferred you to every bard past and present, and asked which of your works pleased me most. It was a difficult question. I answered, I thought the *Lay.* He said his own opinion was nearly similar. In speaking of the others, I told him that I thought you more particularly the poet of *Princes,* as *they* never appeared more fascinating than in *Marmion* and the *Lady of the Lake.* He was pleased to coincide, and to dwell on the description of your

1 *English Bards and Scotch Reviewers* contained an attack on Scott (lines 171–74), which he understandably resented; by this time, however, Byron had suppressed the poem, as a fifth edition was in process.

Jameses as no less royal than poetical. He spoke alternately of Homer and yourself, and seemed well acquainted with both; so that (with the exception of the Turks[2] and your humble servant) you were in very good company. I defy Murray to have exaggerated his Royal Highness's opinion of your powers, nor can I pretend to enumerate all he said on the subject; but it may give you pleasure to hear that it was conveyed in language which would only suffer by my attempting to transcribe it, and with a tone and taste which gave me a very high idea of his abilities and accomplishments, which I had hitherto considered as confined to *manners,* certainly superior to those of any living *gentleman.*

This interview was accidental. I never went to the levee; for having seen the courts of Mussulman and Catholic sovereigns, my curiosity was sufficiently allayed; and my politics being as perverse as my rhymes, I had, in fact, "no business there." To be thus praised by your Sovereign must be gratifying to you; and if that gratification is not alloyed by the communication being made through me, the bearer of it will consider himself very fortunately and sincerely,

Your obliged and obedient servant,

BYRON.

P.S. — Excuse this scrawl, scratched in a great hurry, and just after a journey.

2 At a private party during the last week of June, the Prince Regent asked to have Byron presented to him, and they conversed for half an hour. Byron's reference is to the Turkish Ambassador and his retinue, who were also present.

TO LADY CAROLINE LAMB

4, Bennet St., *April 29th,* 1813.

If you still persist in your intention of meeting me in opposition to the wishes of your own friends and of mine, it must even be so. I regret it and acquiesce with reluctance. I am not ignorant of the very extraordinary language you have held not only to me but others, and your avowal of your determination to obtain what you are pleased to call "revenge"; nor have I now to learn that an incensed woman is a dangerous enemy.

Undoubtedly, those against whom we can make no defence, whatever they say or do, must be formidable. Your words and actions have lately been tolerably portentous, and might justify me in avoiding the demanded interview, more especially as I believe you to be fully capable of performing all your menaces, but as I once hazarded everything *for* you, I will not shrink *from* you. Perhaps I deserve punishment, if so, you are quite as proper a person to inflict it as any other. You say you will "*ruin* me." I thank you, but I have done that for myself already; you say you will "destroy me," perhaps you will only save me the trouble. It is useless to reason with you — to repeat what you already know, that I have in reality saved you from utter and impending destruction. Everyone who knows you knows this also, but they do not know — as yet — what you may and I will tell them as I now tell you, that it is in a great measure owing to this persecution; to the accursed things you have said; to the extravagances you have committed, that I again adopt the resolution of quitting this country. In your assertions you have either belied or betrayed me — take your choice; in your actions you have hurt only yourself — but is that nothing to one who wished you well? I have only one request to make, which is, not to attempt to see Lady O.: on her you have no claim.[1] You will settle as you please the arrangement of this conference. I do not leave England till June, but the sooner it is over the better, I once wished, for your own sake, Lady M.[2] to be present — but if you are to fulfil any of your threats in word or deed we had better be alone.

Yours,
B.

1 Lady Oxford, to whom Byron was attached in 1812.

2 Lady Melbourne, the mother of William Lamb and therefore Lady Caroline's mother-in-law.

TO LADY MELBOURNE

October 13*th*, 1813.

MY DEAR L^y^ M.,

You must pardon the quantity of my letters, and much of the *quality* also, but I have really no other *confidential* correspondent on earth, and much to say which may call forth the advice which has so often been to me of essential service. Anything, you will allow, is better than the *last*; and I cannot exist without some object of attachment. You will laugh at my perpetual *changes,* but recollect, the circumstances which have broken off the last and don't exactly attribute their conclusion to caprice. I think you will at least admit, whatever C. may assert, that I did not use her ill, though I find *her own* story, even in this part of the world, to be the *genuine* narrative; as to L^y^ O., that I did to please you, and luckily, finding it pleasant to myself also, and very useful to C., it might have lasted longer, but for the voyage. I spare you the third.

I am so spoilt by intellectual *drams* that I begin to believe that *danger* and *difficulty* render these things more piquant to my taste. As far as the *former* goes, C. might have suited me very well, but though we may admire *drams,* nobody is particularly fond of *aqua fortis*; at least, I should have liked it a *little diluted,* the liquid I believe which is now slowly mingling in my cup.

In the meantime, let us laugh while we can, for I see no reason why you should be tormented with sentimental or solid sorrows of your acquaintance.

I think you will allow that I have as little of that affectation as any person of similar pursuits.

I mentioned to you yesterday a laughable occurrence at dinner. This morning *he* burst forth with a homily upon the subject to the *two* and myself, instead of taking us separately (like the last of the *Horatii* with the *Curiatii*). You will easily suppose with such odds he had the worst of it, and the satisfaction of being laughed at into the bargain.

Serious as I am, I really cannot frequently keep my countenance: yesterday, *before my face,* they disputed about their apartments at N[ewstead], *she* insisting that her sister should share her room, and he very properly, but heinously out of place, maintaining, and proving to his own satisfaction, that none but husbands have any legal claim to divide their spouse's pillow.[1] You may suppose, notwithstanding the ludicrous effect of the scene, I felt and looked a little uncomfortable; this she must have seen — for, of course, I said not a word — and turning round at the close of the dialogue, she whispered, "N'importe, this is all nothing," an ambiguous sentence which I am puzzled to translate; but, as it was meant to console me, I was very glad to hear it, though quite unintelligible.

As far as I can pretend to judge of her disposition and character — I will say, of course, I am partial — she is, you know, very handsome, and very gentle, though sometimes decisive; fearfully romantic, and singularly warm in her *affections*; but I should think of a *cold* temperament, yet I have my doubts on that point, too; accomplished (as all decently educated women are), and clever, though her style a little too *German*; no dashing nor desperate talker, but never — and I have watched in *mixed* conversation — saying a silly thing (*duet dialogues*

[1] James Wedderburn Webster (1789–1840) and his wife, the former Lady Frances Caroline Annesley, visited Byron at Newstead from 10 October 1813, where, as Byron carried on a flirtation with Lady Frances, Webster negotiated a loan of £1000 from Byron. Lady Frances' sister was Lady Catherine Annesley.

in course between young and Platonic people must be varied with a little chequered absurdity); good tempered (always excepting L^y^ O[xford], which was, outwardly, the *best* I ever beheld), and jealous as *myself* — the *ne plus ultra* of green-eyed monstrosity; seldom abusing other people, but listening to it with great patience. These qualifications, with an unassuming and sweet voice, and very soft manner, constitute the *bust* (all I can yet pretend to model) of my present idol.

You, who know me and my weakness so well, will not be surprised when I say that I am totally absorbed in this passion — that I am even ready to take a *flight* if necessary, and as she says, "We cannot part," it is no impossible *dénouement* — though as yet *one* of us at least does not think of it. W. will probably want to cut my throat, which would not be a difficult task, for I trust I should not return the fire of a man I had injured, though I could not refuse him the pleasure of trying me as a target. But I am not sure I shall not have more work in that way. There is a friend in the house who looks a little suspicious; he can only conjecture, but if he *Iagonizes*, or finds, or makes mischief, let him look to it. To W[ebster] I am decidedly wrong, yet he almost provoked me into it — *he* loves other women; at least he follows them; *she* evidently did not love him, even before.

I came here with no plan, no intention of the kind as my former letters will prove to *you* (the only person to whom I care about proving it) and have not yet been here *ten* days — a week yesterday, on recollection: you cannot be more astonished than I am how, and why all this has happened.

All my correspondences, and every other business, are at a standstill; I have not answered A., no, nor B., nor C.,[2] nor any *initial* except your own, you will wish me to be less troublesome to *that* one, and I shall now begin to draw at longer dates upon y^r^ patience.

Ever yours,

B.

P.S. — *always P.S.* I begged you to pacify C., who is pettish about what she calls a *cold* letter; it was not so, but she evidently has been too long quiet; she threatens me with growing very bad, and says that if so, "I am the sole cause." This I should regret, but she is in no danger; no one in his senses will run the risk, till her late exploits are forgotten. Her last I shall not answer; it was very silly in me to write at all; but I did it with the best intention, like the Wiseacre in "The

2 In Byron's letters to Lady Melbourne, Augusta Leigh was consistently indicated by "A," Caroline Lamb by "C"; quite likely the "B" stood for "Belle" (Anne Isabella Milbanke, Lady Melbourne's niece, whom Byron later married).

Rovers," — "Let us by a song conceal our purposes," you remember in the "Anti-Jacobin."[3] I have gone through a catechism about her, without abusing or betraying her; this is not exactly the way to recommend myself; I have generally found that the *successor* likes to hear both of the last *regnante*. But I really did not, notwithstanding the temptation.

[3] In the periodical *The Anti-Jacobin* (1797–98), "The Rovers" was a burlesque of contemporary German drama.

TO JOHN MURRAY

Newstead Abbey, February 4, 1814.

DEAR SIR,

I need not say that your obliging letter[1] was very welcome, and not the less so for being unexpected. At the same time I received a very kind one from Mr. D'Israeli, which I shall acknowledge and thank him for to-morrow.[2]

It doubtless gratifies me much that our *Finale* has pleased, and that the Curtain drops gracefully. *You* deserve it should, for your promptitude and good nature in arranging immediately with Mr. D[alla]s; and I can assure you that I esteem your entering so warmly into the subject, and writing to me so soon upon it, as a personal obligation. We shall now part, I hope, satisfied with each other. I *was* and *am* quite in earnest in my prefatory promise not to intrude any more; and this not from any affectation, but a thorough conviction that it is the best policy, and is at least respectful to my readers, as it shows that I would not willingly run the risk of forfeiting their favour in future.[3] Besides, I have other views and objects, and think that I shall keep *this* resolution; for, since I left London, though shut up, *snow*-bound, *thaw*-bound, and tempted with all kinds of paper, the dirtiest of ink, and the bluntest of pens, I have not even been haunted by a wish to put them to their combined uses, except in letters of business — my rhyming propensity is quite gone, and I feel much as I did at Patras on recovering from my fever — weak, but in health, and only afraid of a relapse. I do most fervently hope I never shall.

[1] Murray wrote on 3 February to announce that he had sold ten thousand copies of *The Corsair* on the day of publication — "a thing perfectly unprecedented."

[2] Isaac D'Israeli (1766–1848), author of *Curiosities of Literature* (1791 and after) and *The Literary Character* (1795), was one of Murray's authors. He had spoken highly of *The Corsair*.

[3] Byron had announced that *The Corsair* would be his last work for many years.

I see by the *Morning Chronicle* there hath been discussion in the *Courier;* and I read in the *Morning Post* a wrathful letter about Mr. Moore, in which some Protestant Reader has made a sad confusion about *India* and Ireland.[4]

You are to do as you please about the smaller poems; but I think removing them *now* from *The Corsair* looks like *fear;* and if so, you must allow me not to be pleased. I should also suppose that, after the *fuss* of these Newspaper Esquires, they would materially assist the circulation of *The Corsair;* an object I should imagine at *present* of more importance to *yourself* than *Childe Harold*'s 7th appearance. Do as you like; but don't allow the withdrawing that *poem* to draw any imputation of *dismay* upon me. I care about as much for the *Courier* as I do for the Prince, or all princes whatsoever, except Kozlovsky.[5]

Pray make my respects to Mr. Ward, whose praise I value most highly, as you well know; it is in the approbation of such men that fame becomes worth having. To Mr. G. I am always grateful, and surely not less so now than ever.[6] And so Good Night to my Authorship.

I have been sauntering and dozing here very quietly, and not unhappily. You will be happy to hear that I have completely established my title-deeds as *marketable,* and that the Purchaser has succumbed to the terms, and fulfils them, or is to fulfil them forthwith — he is now here, and we go on very amicably together, — one in each *wing* of the Abbey. We set off on Sunday — I for town, he for Cheshire.[7]

Mrs. Leigh is with me — much pleased with the place, and less so with me for parting with it, to which not even the price can reconcile her. Your parcel has not yet arrived — at least the *Mags.* etc.; but I have received *Childe Harold* and the *Corsair.*

I believe both are very correctly printed, which is a great satisfaction.

I thank you for wishing me in town; but I think one's success is

[4] Two letters signed "Hibernicus" and supposedly written by a native of Ireland appeared in the Tory *Morning Post* on 3 and 4 February, denying that Thomas Moore was Ireland's *first* poet or that Ireland's wrongs were comparable to India's.

[5] *The Courier* was staunchly Tory. Prince Kozlovsky was Russian Minister at Turin; Byron's intention in this reference has remained obscure.

[6] The Honorable John William Ward, a literary critic, and William Gifford.

[7] Nearly eighteen months earlier, Thomas Claughton had offered Byron £140,000 for Newstead Abbey, but on the pretense that Byron's title was not clear he had continually delayed making payments that were due; finally, in August 1814, he forfeited to Byron £25,000 of the money already paid and relinquished all further claim to the Abbey.

most felt at a distance, and I enjoy my solitary self-importance in an agreeable sulky way of my own — upon the strength of your letter for which I once more thank you, and am,

Very truly yours,

B.

P.S. — Don't you think Bonaparte's next *publication* will be rather expensive to the Allies? Perry's Paris letter of yesterday looks very reviving.[8] What a Hydra and Briareus it is! I wish they would pacify: there is no end to this campaigning.

[8] Written by James Perry, Editor of *The Morning Chronicle,* this column appeared on 2 February, detailing the great activity in the French capital that would encourage those who, like Byron, ambivalently supported Napoleon.

TO ANNE ISABELLA MILBANKE

Novr. 23*rd* 1814.

MY LOVE,

While I write this letter I have desired my very old & kind friend Mr. Hodgson to send you a note, which I will enclose, as it contains a piece of information that will come better from him than me — and yet not give you less pleasure. I think of setting off for London tomorrow — where I will write again. I am quite confused and bewildered here with the voting and the fuss & the crowd — to say nothing of yesterday's dinner & meeting all one's old acquaintances, the consequence of which is that infallible next-day's headache ever attendant upon sincere Friendship. Here are Hobhouse and our cousin George Lamb[1] — who called on me; & we have all voted the same way, but they say nevertheless our man won't win — but have many votes howbeit. Today I dine with Clarke the traveller — one of the best and most goodnatured of souls — and uniformly kind to me.[2] When we meet I think and hope I shall make you laugh at the scene I went through — or rather which went through me; for I was quite unprepared, & am not at the best of times sufficiently master of "the family shyness" to acquit myself otherwise than awkwardly on such an occasion.

Well but — sweet Heart — do write & love me — and regard me as thine

ever & most

[1] George Lamb (1784–1834), the fourth son of Lady Melbourne.

[2] Edward Daniel Clarke (1769–1822), whose six-volume *Travels in Various Countries of Europe, Asia, and Africa* was published between 1810 and 1823, was Professor of Minerology at Cambridge.

P.S. — Love to parents. I have not and am not to see H's note, so I hope it is all very correct.[3]

[3] Byron's reference is either to John Hanson, his solicitor and therefore representative in the marriage settlements, or to John Cam Hobhouse, who was to be his best man.

TO SAMUEL TAYLOR COLERIDGE

Piccadilly, March 31, 1815.

DEAR SIR,

It will give me great pleasure to comply with your request, though I hope there is still taste enough left amongst us to render it almost unnecessary, sordid and interested as, it must be admitted, many of "the trade" are, where circumstances give them an advantage.[1] I trust you do not permit yourself to be depressed by the temporary partiality of what is called "the public" for the favourites of the moment; all experience is against the permanency of such impressions. You must have lived to see many of these pass away, and will survive many more — I mean personally, for *poetically*, I would not insult you by a comparison.

If I may be permitted, I would suggest that there never was such an opening for tragedy. In Kean, there is an actor worthy of expressing the thoughts of the characters which you have every power of embodying; and I cannot but regret that the part of Ordonio was disposed of before his appearance at Drury Lane. We have had nothing to be mentioned in the same breath with *Remorse* for very many years;[2] and I should think that the reception of that play was sufficient to encourage the highest hopes of author and audience. It is to be hoped that you are proceeding in a career which could not but be successful. With my best respects to Mr. Bowles,[3] I have the honour to be,

Your obliged and very obedient servant,
BYRON.

[1] In a recent letter Coleridge had asked Byron to intercede for him with a publisher for the publication of a collection of his mature poems written between 1795 and the present. Probably as a result of Byron's activities, Murray published a single volume of Coleridge's poems in 1816 and *Zapolya, a Christmas Tale* in 1817.

[2] Through Byron's intercession with the Drury Lane Theatre, Coleridge's tragedy *Remorse* had been successfully produced in January 1813.

[3] The Reverend William Lisle Bowles (1762–1850), Vicar of Bremhill, near Calne, where Coleridge was now staying. In 1821 Byron was to engage with Bowles in a controversy of pamphlets over the literary merits of Alexander Pope.

P.S. — You mention my "Satire," lampoon, or whatever you or others please to call it. I can only say that it was written when I was very young and very angry, and has been a thorn in my side ever since; more particularly as almost all the persons animadverted upon became subsequently my acquaintances, and some of them my friends, which is "heaping fire upon an enemy's head," and forgiving me too readily to permit me to forgive myself. The part applied to you is pert, and petulant, and shallow enough;[4] but, although I have long done every thing in my power to suppress the circulation of the whole thing, I shall always regret the wantonness or generality of many of its attempted attacks.

[4] *English Bards and Scotch Reviewers,* lines 255–64, 918.

TO LEIGH HUNT

January 29th, 1816.

DEAR HUNT,

I return your extract with thanks for the perusal and hope you are by this time on the verge of publication. My pencil-marks on the margin of your former MSS. I never thought worth the trouble of deciphering, but I had no such meaning as you imagine for their being withheld from Murray, from whom I differ entirely as to the *terms* of your agreement; nor do I think you asked a piastre too much for the Poem.[1] However, I doubt not he will deal fairly by you on the whole; he is really a very good fellow, and his faults are merely the leaven of his "trade" — "the trade!" the slave-trade of many an unlucky writer.

The said Murray and I are just at present in no good humour with each other; but he is not the worse for that. I feel sure that he will give your work as fair or a fairer chance in every way than your late publishers; and what he can't do for it, it will do for itself.

Continual business and occasional indisposition have been the causes of my negligence (for I deny neglect) in not writing to you immediately. These are excuses; I wish they may be more satisfactory to you than they are to me. I opened my eyes yesterday morning on your compliment of Sunday.[2] If you knew what a hopeless and

[1] Byron had brought Hunt and John Murray together to negotiate for the publication of Hunt's *The Story of Rimini.* Published by Murray later in 1816, this poem was dedicated to Byron.

[2] In an article "Men of Talent in Parliament," appearing in *The Examiner* of 28 January 1816, Hunt had praised Byron.

lethargic den of dulness and drawling our hospital is during a debate, and what a mass of corruption in its patients, you would wonder, not that I very seldom speak, but that I ever attempted it, feeling as I trust I do, independently. However, when a proper spirit is manifested "without doors," I will endeavour not to be idle within. Do you think such a time is coming? Methinks there are gleams of it. My forefathers were of the other side of the question in Charles' days, and the fruit of it was a title and the loss of an enormous property.[3]

If the old struggle comes on, I may lose the one, and shall never regain the other; but no matter: there are things, even in this world, better than either.

Very truly, ever yours,
B.

[3] Sir John Byron, a supporter of Charles I, was created Baron Byron of Rochdale on 24 October 1643, but during the Civil War the family lost most of its property.

TO LADY BYRON

[Easter] Sunday April [14] 1816

"More last words" — not many — and such as you will attend to — answer I do not expect — nor does it import — but you will hear me. — — I have just parted from Augusta — almost the last being you had left me to part with — & the only unshattered tie of my existence — wherever I may go — & I am going far — you & I can never meet again in this world — nor in the next — Let this content or atone. —— If any accident occurs to me — be kind to *her*, — — if she is then nothing — to her children; — —

Some time ago — I informed you that with the knowledge that any child of ours was already provided for by other & better means — I had made my will in favor of her & her children — as prior to my marriage: — this was not done in prejudice ["anger" is effaced] to you for we had not then differed — & even this is useless during your life by the settlements — I say therefore — be kind to her & hers — for never has she acted or spoken otherwise towards you — she has ever been your friend — this may seem valueless to one who has now so many: — — be kind to her — however — & recollect that though it may be advantage to you to have lost your husband — it is sorrow to her to have the waters now — or the earth hereafter — between her & her brother. —

She is gone — I need hardly add that of this request she knows nothing — your late compliances have not been so extensive — as to render this an encroachment: — I repeat it — (for deep resentments have but *half* recollections) that you once did promise me thus much — do not forget it — nor deem it cancelled it was not a vow. — — —

Mr Wharton[1] has sent me a letter with one question & two pieces of intelligence — to the question I answer that the carriage is yours — & as it has only carried us to Halnaby — & London — & you to Kirkby — I hope it will take you many a more propitious journey. —

The receipts can remain — unless troublesome, if so — they can be sent to Augusta— & through her I would also hear of my little daughter — my address will be left for Mrs Leigh. — The ring is of no lapidary value — but it contains the hair of a king and an ancestor — which I should wish to preserve to Miss Byron. —

To a subsequent letter of Mr Wharton's I have to reply that it is the "law's delay" not mine, — & that when he & M^r^ H have adjusted the tenor of the bond — I am ready to sign

Y^rs^ Ever
very truly
BYRON

[1] Gerard Blisson Wharton, attorney to Sir Ralph Milbanke, Lady Byron's father.

TO JOHN HANSON

Dover, April 24th, 1816.

DEAR SIR,

Denan[1] has distrained on the effects left at the house in Piccadilly terrace for the half year's rent; — I know not if this be lawful *without* a *previous action*. This *you* know best. If it be, there is one trunk of wood, with papers, letters, etc., also some *shoes,* and another thing or two, which I could wish redeemed from the wreck.

They have seized all the *servants' things,* Fletcher's and his wife's, etc. I hope you will see to these poor creatures having *their* property secured; as for *mine,* it must be sold. I wish Mr. Hobhouse to confer with you upon it.

Many thanks for your good wishes. I sail tonight for Ostend.[2] My

[1] An auctioneer, called "Dever" by Hobhouse, who seized Byron's property for the rent due the Duchess of Devonshire, owner of the house at 13 Piccadilly Terrace.

[2] Byron actually sailed the next day, 25 April.

address had best be (for the present) A — Milord Byron — Poste Restante — *à Genève.*

I hope that you will not forget to seize an early opportunity of bringing Rochdale and Newstead to the hammer, or private contract. I wish you for yourself and family every possible good and beg my remembrances to all, particularly to Lady P[ortsmouth] and Charles.[3] I am, with great sincerity,

Yours very affectionately,

BYRON.

P.S. — Send me some news of my *child* every now and then. I beg as a favour not to hear a word of that branch of the family. Of course I do not mean *my own* immediate relatives.

[3] Lady Portsmouth was Mary Anne Hanson, the solicitor's daughter, and Charles was his son.

TO JOHN CAM HOBHOUSE

Carlsruhe, *May 16th,* 1816.

ME DEAR HOBHOUSE,

We are thus far by the Rhenish route on our way to Switzerland, where I shall wait to hear of your intentions as to junction, before I go to Italy.

We were obliged to diverge from Anvers and Mechlin to Brussels, for some wheel repairs, and in course seized the opportunity to visit Mont St Jean, &c., where I had a gallop over the field on a Cossac horse (left by some of the Don gentlemen at Brussels), and after a tolerably minute investigation returned by Soignies, having purchased a quantity of helmets, sabres, &c., all of which are consigned to Mr. Gordon[1] at Brussels (an old acquaintance) who was desired to forward them to Mr. Murray, in whose keeping I hope to find them safe, some day or other.

Our route by the Rhine has been beautiful, and much surpassing my expectation; though much answering in its outlines to my previous conception.

The plain at Waterloo is a fine one — but not much after Marathon and Troy, Cheronæa and Platæa.

Perhaps there is something of prejudice in this, but I detest the cause, &c., the victors and the victory, including Blucher and the Bourbons.

[1] Pryce Lockhart Gordon, then living in Brussels, had known Byron in 1802; he was to recall Byron in his book *Personal Memoirs* (1830).

From Bonn to Coblentz, and Coblentz again to Bingen and Mayence, nothing can exceed the prospects at every point; not even any of our old scenes; though this is in a different style. What it most reminded me of were parts of Cintra, and the valley which leads from Delimachi — by Limochabo and Argyrocastro (on the opposite mountains) to Tepalini — the last resemblance struck even the learned Fletcher, who seems to thrive upon his present expedition; and is full of comparisons and preferences of the present to the last, particularly in the articles of provision and caravanseras.

Poor Polidori[2] is devilish ill — I do not know with what, nor does he — but he seems to have a slight constitution, and is seriously laid up; if he does not get well soon, he will be totally unfit for travelling; his complaints are headaches and feverishness: — all the rest are well for the present, nor has he had any patients except a Belgian blacksmith (at Lo-Kristy, a village where our wheels stuck) and himself.

We have seen all the sights, churches, and so forth, and at Coblentz crossed the Rhine, and scrambled up the fortress of Ehrenbreitstein — now a ruin. We also saw the road to the sepulchres, and monuments of Generals Marceau and Hoche, and went up to examine them. They are simple and striking, but now much neglected, not to say defaced by the change of times, and this cursed after-crop of rectilignes and legitimacy.

At Mannheim we crossed the river, and keep on this side to avoid the French segment of territory at Strasburg, as we have not French passports, and no desire to view a degraded country and oppressed people.

This town (a very pretty one) is the seat of the Court of the Grand Duke of Baden: — to-morrow I mean to proceed (if Polidori is well enough) on our journey.

At Geneva I expect to hear from you. Tell me of Scrope and his intentions,[3] and of all or any things or persons, saving and except one subject, which I particularly beg never to have mentioned again, unless as far as regards my *child* and *my child only.*

If Scrope comes out, tell him there are some "light wines," which will bring to his recollection "the day of Pentecost" and other branches of his vinous thirty-nine articles.

I have solaced myself moderately with such "flaggons of Rhenish" as have fallen in my way; but without our Yorick they are nothing.

[2] John William Polidori (1795–1821) accompanied Byron as his physician, but after nearly continual disagreement, they parted, in September 1816.

[3] Scrope Berdmore Davies (1783–1852), Fellow at King's College, Cambridge, until 1816, was a popular member of society, known for his wit and his daring as a gambler.

I hope your book of letters is not slack in sale,[4] and I can't see why Ridgway should not pay "a few *paounds*" for the 2nd Edition, unless it be that I did not pay him his bill, and that he thinks therefore *you* should.

I trust that you will give *Spooney*[5] a jog, as to selling and so forth; and tell my *Potestas*[6] to come the committee over him. I suppose poor K. will be devilishly bothered with his Drury Lane speech this year — how does Maturin's play go on — or rather go off — of course the prologue has fallen to your lot, and the Comedy — eh?[7]

I hope you executed the thousand petty commissions I saddled you withal. Pray remember me to all the remembering, and not less to the superb Murray, who is now enjoying inglorious ease at his green table, and wishing for somebody to keep him in hot water.

Wishing you all prosperity, I am ever

Yrs. most truly,
BYRON.

[4] *The Substance of Some Letters, written by an Englishman Resident at Paris during the Last Reign of the Emperor Napoleon* was published in London in 1816.

[5] Hanson.

[6] Douglas Kinnaird (1788–1830), Byron's banker and close personal friend, was a member of the committee managing the Drury Lane Theatre.

[7] Charles Robert Maturin's tragedy *Bertram* was successfully produced at the Drury Lane in May 1816.

TO AUGUSTA LEIGH

Venice, Decr. 19th. 1816.

MY DEAREST AUGUSTA,

I wrote to you a few days ago. Your letter of the 1st is arrived, and you have "a *hope*" for me, it seems: what "*hope*," child? my dearest Sis. I remember a methodist preacher who, on perceiving a profane grin on the faces of part of his congregation, exclaimed "no *hopes* for them as *laughs*." And thus it is with us: we laugh too much for hopes, and so even let them go. I am sick of sorrow, and must even content myself as well as I can: so here goes — I won't be woeful again if I can help it.

My letter to my moral Clytemnestra[1] required no answer, and I would rather have none. I was wretched enough when I wrote it, and had been so for many a long day and month: at present I am less so, for reasons explained in my late letter (a few days ago); and as I

[1] Lady Byron.

never pretend to be what I am not, you may tell her if you please that I am recovering, and the reason also if you like it.

I do not agree with you about Ada: there was *equivocation* in the answer, and it shall be settled one way or the other. I wrote to Hanson to take proper steps to prevent such a removal of my daughter, and even the probability of it.[2]

I have heard of Murray's squabble with one of his brethren, who is an impudent impostor, and should be trounced.

You do not say whether the *true po's* are out: I hope you like them.

You are right in saying that I like Venice: it is very much what you would imagine it, but I have no time just now for description. The Carnival is to begin in a week, and with it the mummery of masking.

I have not been out a great deal, but quite as much as I like. I am going out this evening in my *cloak* and *Gondola* — there are two nice Mrs. Radcliffe words for you. And then there is the place of St. Mark, and conversaziones, and various fooleries, besides many *nau:* indeed, every body is *nau*,[3] so much so, that a lady with only *one lover* is not reckoned to have overstepped the modesty of marriage — that being a regular thing. Some have two, three, and so on to twenty, beyond which they don't account; but they generally begin by one. The husbands of course belong to any body's wives — but their own.

The music here is famous, and there will be a whole tribe of singers and dancers during the Carnival, besides the usual theatres.

The Society here is something like our own, except that the women sit in a semicircle at one end of the room, and the men stand at the other.

I pass my mornings at the Armenian convent studying Armenian, — my evenings here and there. To-night I am going to the Countess Albrizzi's, one of the *noblesse*.[4] I have also been at the Governor's, who is an Austrian, and whose wife, the Countess Goetz, appears to me in the little I have seen of her a very amiable and pleasing woman, with remarkably good manners, as many of the German women have.

There are no English here, except birds of passage, who stay a day and then go on to Florence or Rome.

I mean to remain here till Spring. When you write address *directly* here, as in your present letter.

Ever, dearest, yours,

B.

2 Byron was concerned over a rumor he had heard that Lady Byron intended to pass the winter abroad; he did not want Ada removed from England.

3 Naughty.

4 Isabella Teotochi, Countess Albrizzi, whose *conversazione* drew together many of the literary and social figures of Venice.

TO JOHN CAM HOBHOUSE[1]

Venice, June, 1818.

SIR,

With great grief I inform you of the death of my late dear Master, my Lord, who died this morning at ten of the Clock of a rapid decline and slow fever, caused by anxiety, sea-bathing, women, and riding in the Sun against my advice.

He is a dreadful loss to every body, mostly to me, who have lost a master and a place — also, I hope you, Sir, will give me a charakter.

I saved in his service as you know several hundred pounds. God knows how, for I don't, nor my late master neither; and if my wage was not always paid to the day, still it was or is to be paid sometime and somehow. You, Sir, who are his executioner won't see a poor Servant wronged of his little all.

My dear Master had several phisicians and a Priest: he died a Papish, but is to be buried among the Jews in the Jewish burying ground; for my part I don't see why — he could not abide them when living nor any other people, hating whores who asked him for money.

He suffered his illness with great patience, except that when in extremity he twice damned his friends and said they were selfish rascals — you, Sir, particularly and Mr. Kinnaird, who had never answered his letters nor complied with his repeated requests. He also said he hoped that your new tragedy would be damned — God forgive him — I hope that my master won't be damned like the tragedy.

His nine whores are already provided for, and the other servants; but what is to become of me? I have got his Cloathes and Carriages, and Cash, and everything; but the Consul quite against law has clapt his seal and taken an invent*a*ry and swears that *he* must account to my Lord's heirs — who they are, I don't know — but they ought to consider poor Servants and above all his Vally de Sham.

My Lord never grudged me perquisites — my wage was the least I got by him; and if I did keep the Countess (she is, or ought to be, a Countess, although she is upon the town) Marietta Monetta Piretta, after passing my word to you and my Lord that I would not never no more — still he was an indulgent master, and only said I was a damned fool, and swore and forgot it again. What could I do? she said as how she should die, or kill herself if I did not go with her, and

[1] Byron is writing in the role of his valet, William Fletcher, reporting the Poet's death.

so I did — and kept her out of my Lord's washing and ironing — and nobody can deny that, although the charge was high, the linen was well got up.

Hope you are well, Sir — am, with tears in my eyes,

Yours faithfoolly to command,
W^m. FLETCHER.

P.S. — If you know any Gentleman in want of a Wally — hope for a charakter. I saw your late Swiss Servant in the Galleys at Leghorn for robbing an Inn — he produced your recommendation at his trial.

TO JOHN MURRAY

Venice, June 16, 1818.

DEAR SIR,

Your last letter was dated the 28th of April. Consequently a much longer period has elapsed than usual without my hearing from you (or indeed from any one else), and, considering all things and the time you have chosen for this cessation, methinks it is not well done. If you have anything uncomfortable to say, recollect it must come out at last, and had better be said at once than retained to terminate a disagreeable suspense.

I have written repeatedly to Mr. Hobhouse and Mr. Kinnaird without the smallest effect, and am fortunate in such friends and correspondents. Most of my letters to them and you required an answer. The only thing Mr. H. has done has been to advise me to go to Geneva, which would have been the cause of much useless expense and trouble to no purpose, as the Hanson Messenger is not yet arrived, if even set out.

Tell Hobhouse that I trust his tragedy will be damned, and that the Chevalier de Brême[1] has written to me a long letter, attacking *him* (Hobhouse) for abusing the Italian *Romantici* in his notes.[2] Mr. H. will answer for himself. I never read the notes.

Yours very truly,
B.

P.S. — Mr. H. and Kid. will have something to say to you from me; at least if they give themselves the trouble to comply with my request.

[1] Luigi di Breme (1781–1820), second son of the Marchese di Breme (1754–1828), who had served as Ministre de l'Intérieur under Eugène Beauharnais.

[2] An essay on Italian literature, published as part of Hobhouse's *Historical Illustrations of the Fourth Canto of Childe Harold*, was actually written by the exiled Italian patriot Ugo Foscolo.

TO LADY BYRON

Venice, Novr 18th 1818.

Sir Samuel Romilly has cut his throat for the loss of his wife.[1] It is now nearly three years since he became, in the face of his compact (by a retainer — previous, and, I believe, general), the advocate of the measures and the Approver of the proceedings, which deprived me of mine.[2] I would not exactly, like Mr. Thwackum, when Philosopher Square bit his own tongue — "saddle him with a Judgement;"[3] but

> "This even-handed Justice
> Commends the ingredients of our poisoned Chalice
> To our own lips."[4]

This Man little thought, when he was lacerating my heart according to law, while he was poisoning my life at it's sources, aiding and abetting in the blighting, branding, and exile that was to be the result of his counsels in their indirect effects, that in less than thirty-six moons — in the pride of his triumph as the highest candidate for the representation of the Sister-City of the mightiest of Capitals — in the fullness of his professional career — in the greenness of a healthy old age — in the radiance of fame, and the complacency of self-earned riches — that a domestic affliction would lay him in the earth, with the meanest of malefactors, in a cross-road with the stake in his body, if the verdict of insanity did not redeem his ashes from the sentence of the laws he had lived upon by interpreting or misinterpreting, and died in violating.

This man had eight children, lately deprived of their mother: could he not live? Perhaps, previous to his annihilation, he felt a portion of what he contributed his legal mite to make me feel; but I have lived — lived to see him a Sexagenary Suicide.

It was not in vain that I invoked Nemesis in the midnight of Rome from the awfullest of her ruins.

Fare you well. B.

[1] Sir Samuel Romilly (1757–1818), attorney and reformer, was so affected by the death of his wife in late October 1818 that he committed suicide soon thereafter.

[2] Byron's hatred for Sir Samuel derived from a misunderstanding at the time of the separation; not realizing that he had a general retainer for Byron, Sir Samuel counselled Lady Byron's mother when she came to him with a recital of her daughter's wrongs at the hands of the Poet.

[3] *Tom Jones,* Book V, Chapter II. Byron misquotes.

[4] *Macbeth,* I, vii.

TO DOUGLAS KINNAIRD

Venice, *October 26th,* 1819.

MY DEAR DOUGLAS,

My late expenditure has arisen from living at a distance from Venice, and being obliged to keep up two establishments, from frequent journeys, and buying some furniture and books as well as a horse or two; and not from any renewal of the EPICUREAN system as you suspect.

I have been faithful to my honest liaison with Countess Guiccioli, and I can assure you that *She* has never cost me, directly or indirectly, a sixpence. Indeed the circumstances of herself and family render this no merit.

I never offered her but one present — a broach of brilliants — and she sent it back to me with her *own hair* in it, and a note to say that she was not in the habit of receiving presents of that value, but hoped that I would not consider her sending it back as an affront, nor the value diminished by the enclosure.

Damn your delicacy. It is a low commercial quality, and very unworthy a man who prefixes "honourable" to his nomenclature. If you say that I must sign the bonds, I suppose that I must, but it is very iniquitous to make me pay my debts; you have no idea of the pain it gives one.

Pray do three things. Get my property out of the *funds,* get me some more information from Perry about *South America,* and thirdly ask Lady Noel not to live so very long.[1]

As to "Don Juan" confess, confess, you dog, and be candid, that it is the sublime of *that there* sort of writing. I have written about a hundred stanzas of a Third Canto, but it is damned modest; the outcry has frightened me.[2] I had such projects for the Don, but the benefit of my experiences must now be lost to despairing posterity.

After all, what stuff this outcry is. Lalla Rookh and Little are more dangerous than any burlesque poem can be.

Moore has been here; we got tipsy together, and were very amicable. He is gone on to Rome. I put my life (in MS.) into his hands

1 Lady Noel, Lady Byron's mother, lived for two more years, until 28 January 1822. By the terms of the separation settlement, after the death of his mother-in-law Byron would receive a significant share of a large income. Furthermore, Byron blamed Lady Noel for the major part in bringing about the separation.

2 Murray published the first two cantos of *Don Juan,* with the printer's name but not his own as publisher on the title page, on 15 July 1819.

(*not* for publication). You, or anybody else, may see it at his return. It only comes up to 1816.

He is a noble fellow, and looks quite fresh and poetical, nine years (the age of a poem's education) my senior. He looks younger — this comes of marriage, and being settled in the country.

I want to go to South America. I have written to Hobhouse all about it.

I wrote to my wife three months ago, under care to Murray. Has she got the letter, or is the letter got into "Blackwood's Magazine"?

You ask after my Christmas pye. Remit it anyhow, *Circulars* are the best. You are right about *income*. I must have it all. How the devil do I know that I may live a year, or a month?

I wish I knew, that I might regulate my spending in more ways than one. As it is, one always thinks that there is but a span. A man may as well break, or be damned for a large sum as a small one. I should be loth to pay the devil, or any other creditor more than sixpence in the pound.

Yours,
B.

TO JOHN MURRAY

Ravenna, February 21, 1820.

DEAR MURRAY,

The Bulldogs will be very agreeable: I have only those of this country, who, though good, and ready to fly at any thing, yet have not the tenacity of tooth and Stoicism in endurance of my canine fellow-citizens: then pray send them by the readiest conveyance — perhaps best by Sea. Mr. Kinnaird will disburse for them, and deduct from the amount on your application or on that of Captain Fyler.

I see the good old King[1] is gone to his place: one can't help being sorry, though blindness, and age, and insanity, are supposed to be drawbacks on human felicity; but I am not at all sure that the latter, at least, might not render him happier than any of his subjects.

I have no thoughts of coming to the Coronation, though I should like to see it, and though I have a right to be a puppet in it; but my division with Lady Byron, which has drawn an equinoctial line between me and mine in all other things, will operate in this also to prevent my being in the same procession.

[1] George III died 29 January 1820.

By Saturday's post I sent you four packets, containing Cantos third and fourth of *D*[*on*] *J*[*uan*]; recollect that these two cantos reckon only as *one* with you and me, being, in fact, the third Canto cut into two, because I found it too long. Remember this, and don't imagine that there could be any other motive. The whole is about 225 Stanzas, more or less, and a lyric of 96 lines, so that they are no longer than the first *single* cantos: but the truth is, that I made the first too long, and should have cut those down also had I thought better. Instead of saying in future for so many cantos, say so many *Stanzas* or pages: it was Jacob Tonson's way,[2] and certainly the best: it prevents mistakes. I might have sent you a dozen cantos of 40 Stanzas each, — those of *the Minstrel* (Beattie's) are no longer, — and ruined you at once, if you don't suffer as it is; but recollect you are not *pinned down* to anything you say in a letter, and that, calculating even these two cantos as *one* only (which they were and are to be reckoned), you are not bound by your offer: act as may seem fair to all parties.

I have finished my translation of the first Canto of the "*Morgante Maggiore*" of Pulci, which I will transcribe and send: it is the parent, not only of *Whistlecraft*,[3] but of all jocose Italian poetry. You must print it side by side with the original Italian, because I wish the reader to judge of the fidelity: it is stanza for stanza, and often line for line, if not word for word.

You ask me for a volume of manners, etc., on Italy: perhaps I am in the case to know more of them than most Englishmen, because I have lived among the natives, and in parts of the country where Englishmen never resided before (I speak of Romagna and this place particularly); but there are many reasons why I do not choose to touch in print on such a subject. I have lived in their houses and in the heart of their families, sometimes merely as "*amico di casa*," and sometimes as "*Amico di cuore*" of the *Dama*, and in neither case do I feel myself authorized in making a book of them. Their moral is not your moral; their life is not your life; you would not understand it: it is not English, nor French, nor German, which you would all understand. The Conventual education, the Cavalier Servitude, the habits of thought and living are so entirely different, and the difference becomes so much more striking the more you live intimately with them,

[2] Jacob Tonson (1656–1736), purchaser of the copyright of *Paradise Lost* and publisher of the works of Dryden and others.

[3] Byron's translation of the first canto of Luigi Pulci's *Il Morgante Maggiore* was published not by Murray but by John Hunt, in the fourth number of *The Liberal*, on 30 July 1823. Modelled upon Pulci's work, John Hookham Frere's mock-heroic poem *Prospectus and Specimen of an Intended National Work, by William and Robert Whistlecraft* (1817–18) became in turn Byron's immediate model for *Beppo* and *Don Juan*.

that I know not how to make you comprehend a people, who are at once temperate and profligate, serious in their character and buffoons in their amusements, capable of impressions and passions, which are at once *sudden* and *durable* (what you find in no other nation), and who actually have *no society* (what we would call so), as you may see by their Comedies: they have no real comedy, not even in Goldoni; and that is because they have no Society to draw it from.

Their Conversazioni are not Society at all. They go to the theatre to talk, and into company to hold their tongues. The *women* sit in a circle, and the men gather into groupes, or they play at dreary *Faro* or "*Lotto reale*," for small sums. Their Academie are Concerts like our own, with better music and more form. Their best things are the Carnival balls and masquerades, when every body runs mad for six weeks. After their dinners and suppers, they make extempore verses and buffoon one another; but it is in a humour which you would not enter into, ye of the North.

In their houses it is better. I should know something of the matter, having had a pretty general experience among their women, from the fisherman's wife up to the *Nobil' Donna*, whom I serve. Their system has its rules, and its fitnesses, and decorums, so as to be reduced to a kind of discipline or game at hearts, which admits few deviations, unless you wish to lose it. They are extremely tenacious, and jealous as furies; not permitting their lovers even to marry if they can help it, and keeping them always close to them in public as in private whenever they can. In short, they transfer marriage to adultery, and strike the *not* out of that commandment. The reason is, that they marry for their parents, and love for themselves. They exact fidelity from a lover as a debt of honour, while they pay the husband as a tradesman, that is, not at all. You hear a person's character, male or female, canvassed, not as depending on their conduct to their husbands or wives, but to their mistress or lover. And — and — that's all. If I wrote a quarto, I don't know that I could do more than amplify what I have here noted. It is to be observed that while they do all this, the greatest outward respect is to be paid to the husbands, not only by the ladies, but by their *Serventi* — particularly if the husband serves no one himself (which is not often the case, however): so that you would often suppose them relations — the *Servente* making the figure of one adopted into the family. Sometimes the ladies run a little restive and elope, or divide, or make a scene; but this is at starting, generally, when they know no better, or when they fall in love with a foreigner, or some such anomaly, — and is always reckoned unnecessary and extravagant.

You enquire after "Dante's prophecy:"[4] I have not done more than six hundred lines, but will vaticinate at leisure.

Of the bust I know nothing. No Cameos or Seals are to be cut here or elsewhere that I know of, in any good style. Hobhouse should write himself to Thorwalsen: the bust was made and paid for three years ago.

Pray tell Mrs. Leigh to request Lady Byron to urge forward the transfer from the funds, which Hanson is opposing, because he has views of investment for some Client of his own, which I can't consent to. I wrote to Lady B. on business this post, addressed to the care of Mr. D. Kinnaird.

Somebody has sent me some American abuse of *Mazeppa* and "the Ode:" in future I will compliment nothing but Canada, and desert to the English.

By the king's death Mr. H[obhouse], I hear, will stand for Westminster:[5] I shall be glad to hear of his standing any where except in the pillory, which, from the company he must have lately kept (I always except Burdett, and Douglas K., and the genteel part of the reformers), was perhaps to be apprehended. I was really glad to hear it was for libel instead of larceny; for, though impossible in his own person, he might have been taken up by mistake for another at a meeting. All reflections on his present case and place are so *Nugatory,* that it would be useless to pursue the subject further. I am out of all patience to see my friends sacrifice themselves for a pack of blackguards, who disgust one with their Cause, although I have always been a friend to and a Voter for reform. If Hunt[6] had addressed the language to me which he did to Mr. H. last election, I would not have descended to call out such a miscreant who won't fight; but have passed my sword-stick through his body, like a dog's, and then thrown myself on my Peers, who would, I hope, have weighed the provocation: at any rate, it would have been as public a Service as Walworth's chastisement of Wat. Tyler.[7] If we must have a tyrant, let him at least be a gentleman who has been bred to the business, and let us fall by the axe and not by the butcher's cleaver.

[4] Murray published *The Prophecy of Dante* with *Marino Faliero* on 21 April 1821.

[5] In 1819 Hobhouse had unsuccessfully opposed George Lamb for the seat from Westminster. With the dissolution of Parliament following the death of George III, Hobhouse again stood for Westminster, this time successfully. He represented Westminster until 1833.

[6] Henry ("Orator") Hunt (1773–1835), radical politician, who had been active in the opposition to Hobhouse in 1819 and later that year presided over the meeting that became the Peterloo Massacre.

[7] In 1381, Sir William Walworth, Lord Mayor of London, in the presence of Richard II, killed Wat Tyler, leader of the Peasants' Revolt.

No one can be more sick of, or indifferent to, politics than I am, if they let me alone; but if the time comes when a part must be taken one way or the other, I shall pause before I lend myself to the views of such ruffians, although I cannot but approve of a Constitutional amelioration of long abuses.

Lord George Gordon, and Wilkes, and Burdett, and Horne Tooke, were all men of education and courteous deportment: so is Hobhouse; but as for these others, I am convinced that Robespierre was a Child, and Marat a Quaker in comparison of what they would be, could they throttle their way to power.

Yours ever,
B.

TO THOMAS MOORE

Ravenna, Dec. 9, 1820.

I open my letter to tell you a fact, which will show the state of this country better than I can. The commandant of the troops is *now* lying *dead* in my house.[1] He was shot at a little past eight o'clock, about two hundred paces from my door. I was putting on my great-coat to visit Madame la Contessa G. when I heard the shot. On coming into the hall, I found all my servants on the balcony, exclaiming that a man was murdered. I immediately ran down, calling on Tita[2] (the bravest of them) to follow me. The rest wanted to hinder us from going, as it is the custom for every body here, it seems, to run away from "the stricken deer."

However, down we ran, and found him lying on his back, almost, if not quite, dead, with five wounds; one in the heart, two in the stomach, one in the finger, and the other in the arm. Some soldiers cocked their guns, and wanted to hinder me from passing. However, we passed, and I found Diego, the adjutant, crying over him like a child — a surgeon, who said nothing of his profession — a priest, sobbing a frightened prayer — and the commandant, all this time, on his back, on the hard, cold pavement, without light or assistance, or any thing around him but confusion and dismay.

As nobody could, or would, do any thing but howl and pray, and as no one would stir a finger to move him, for fear of consequences, I

[1] The commandant's name was Luigi Dal Pinto. Some weeks later, on 22 January 1821, Cardinal Antonio Rusconi issued an edict offering a reward of 1000 scudi for information leading to the conviction of Dal Pinto's assassin.

[2] Giovanni Battista Falcieri, Byron's gondolier.

lost my patience — made my servant and a couple of the mob take up the body — sent off two soldiers to the guard — despatched Diego to the Cardinal with the news, and had the commandant carried upstairs into my own quarter. But it was too late, he was gone — not at all disfigured — bled inwardly — not above an ounce or two came out.

I had him partly stripped — made the surgeon examine him, and examined him myself. He had been shot by cut balls or slugs. I felt one of the slugs, which had gone through him, all but the skin. Everybody conjectures why he was killed, but no one knows how. The gun was found close by him — an old gun, half filed down.

He only said, *O Dio!* and *Gesu!* two or three times, and appeared to have suffered very little. Poor fellow! he was a brave officer, but had made himself much disliked by the people. I knew him personally, and had met with him often at conversazioni and elsewhere. My house is full of soldiers, dragoons, doctors, priests, and all kinds of persons, — though I have now cleared it, and clapt sentinels at the doors. To-morrow the body is to be moved. The town is in the greatest confusion, as you may suppose.

You are to know that, if I had not had the body moved, they would have left him there till morning in the street, for fear of consequences. I would not choose to let even a dog die in such a manner, without succour: — and, as for consequences, I care for none in a duty.

Yours, etc.

P.S. — The lieutenant on duty by the body is smoking his pipe with great composure. — A queer people this.

TO ELIZABETH, DUCHESS OF DEVONSHIRE[1]

Ravenna, February 15, 1821.

MADAM,

I am about to request a favor of your Grace without the smallest personal pretensions to obtain it. It is not however for myself, and yet I err — for surely what we solicit for our friends is, or ought to be, nearest to ourselves. If I fail in this application, my intrusion will be its own reward; if I succeed, your Grace's reward will consist in having done a good action, and mine in your pardon for my pre-

[1] Lady Elizabeth Foster (1759–1824), a widow, married the fifth Duke of Devonshire in 1809; after his death, in 1811, she lived abroad.

sumption. My reason for appealing to you is this — your Grace has been long in Rome, and could not be long any where without the influence and the inclination to do good.

Among the list of exiles on account of the late suspicions — and the intrigues of the Austrian Government (the most infamous in history) there are many of my acquaintances in Romagna and some of my friends; of these more particularly are the two Counts Gamba (father and son) of a noble and respected family in this city.[2] In common with thirty or more of all ranks they have been hurried from their home without process — without hearing — without accusation. The father is universally respected and liked, his family is numerous and mostly young — and these are now left without protection: the son is a very fine young man, with very little of the vices of his age or climate; he has I believe the honor of an acquaintance with your Grace — having been presented by Madame Martinetti. He is but one and twenty and lately returned from his studies at Rome. Could your Grace, or would you — ask the repeal of both, or at least of *one* of these from those in power in the holy City? They are not aware of my solicitation in their behalfs — but I will take it upon me to say that they shall neither dishonour your goodness nor my request. If only one can be obtained — let it be the father on account of his family. I can assure your Grace and the very pious Government in question that there can be no danger in this act of — *clemency* shall I call it? It would be but justice with us — but here! let them call it what they will. . . . I cannot express the obligation which I should *feel* — I say *feel* only — because I do not see how I could repay it to your Grace — I have not the slightest claim upon you, unless perhaps through the memory of our late friend, Lady Melbourne — I say friend only — for my relationship with her family has not been fortunate for them, nor for me.[3] If therefore you should be disposed to grant my request I shall set it down to your tenderness for her who is gone, and who was to me the best and kindest of friends. The persons for whom I solicit will (in case of success) neither be in ignorance of their protectress, nor indisposed to acknowledge their sense of her kindness by a strict observance of such conduct as may justify her interference. If my acquaintance with your Grace's character were even slighter than it is through the medium of some of our English

[2] The Counts Ruggero and Pietro Gamba, father and brother of the Countess Teresa Guiccioli.

[3] Lady Melbourne died on 6 April 1818, at sixty-eight years of age. Byron refers to the fact that she was Lady Caroline Lamb's mother-in-law and Lady Byron's aunt.

friends, I had only to turn to the letters of Gibbon (now on my table) for a full testimony to its high and amiable qualities.[4]

I have the honor to be, with great respect,
Your Grace's most obedient very humble Servant,
BYRON.

P.S. — Pray excuse my scrawl which perhaps you may be enabled to decypher from a long acquaintance with the handwriting of Lady Bessborough.[5] I omitted to mention that the measures taken here have been as *blind* as impolitic — this I happen to *know*. Out of the list in Ravenna — there are at least *ten* not only innocent, but even opposite in principles to the liberals. It has been the work of some blundering Austrian spy or angry priest to gratify his private hatreds. Once more your pardon.

4 Edward Gibbon abundantly praised Lady Elizabeth Foster in his letters, and in 1787 he proposed marriage to her.
5 Lady Bessborough, mother of Lady Caroline Lamb.

TO PERCY BYSSHE SHELLEY

Ravenna, April 26, 1821.

The child continues doing well, and the accounts are regular and favourable. It is gratifying to me that you and Mrs. Shelley do not disapprove of the step which I have taken, which is merely temporary.[1]

I am very sorry to hear what you say of Keats[2] — is it *actually* true? I did not think criticism had been so killing. Though I differ from you essentially in your estimate of his performances, I so much abhor all unnecessary pain, that I would rather he had been seated on the highest peak of Parnassus than have perished in such a manner. Poor fellow! though with such inordinate self-love he would probably have not been very happy. I read the review of *Endymion* in the *Quarterly*.[3] It was severe, — but surely not so severe as many reviews in that and other journals upon others.

I recollect the effect on me of the *Edinburgh* on my first poem; it

1 On 1 March 1821 Byron placed Allegra in the convent school of San Giovanni Battista in Bagnacavallo, between Ravenna and Bologna. The child of Byron and Claire Clairmont, Mary Shelley's stepsister, Allegra was born 12 January 1817. Her custody and education were a point of conflict between her parents and a source of tension between Byron and Shelley, who served in these matters as Claire's representative with Byron. Allegra died in the convent on 20 April 1822.
2 John Keats died at Rome on 23 February 1821.
3 *The Quarterly Review*, XIX (1818), 204–08. Dated April, the number containing the review did not appear until September.

was rage, and resistance, and redress — but not despondency nor despair. I grant that those are not amiable feelings; but, in this world of bustle and broil, and especially in the career of writing, a man should calculate upon his powers of *resistance* before he goes into the arena.

> "Expect not life from pain nor danger free,
> Nor deem the doom of man reversed for thee."[4]

You know my opinion of *that second-hand* school of poetry. You also know my high opinion of your own poetry, — because it is of *no* school. I read *Cenci*[5] — but, besides that I think the *subject* essentially *un*dramatic, I am not an admirer of our old dramatists as *models.* I deny that the English have hitherto had a drama at all. Your *Cenci,* however, was a work of power, and poetry. As to *my* drama, pray revenge yourself upon it, by being as free as I have been with yours.[6]

I have not yet got your *Prometheus,*[7] which I long to see. I have heard nothing of mine, and do not know that it is yet published. I have published a pamphlet on the Pope controversy, which you will not like.[8] Had I known that Keats was dead — or that he was alive and so sensitive — I should have omitted some remarks upon his poetry, to which I was provoked by his *attack* upon *Pope,*[9] and my disapprobation of *his own* style of writing.

You want me to undertake a great poem — I have not the inclination nor the power. As I grow older, the indifference — *not* to life, for we love it by instinct — but to the stimuli of life, increases. Besides, this late failure of the Italians has latterly disappointed me for many reasons, — some public, some personal. My respects to Mrs. S.

Yours ever,

B.

P.S. — Could not you and I contrive to meet this summer? Could not you take a run here *alone?*

[4] A misquotation of Samuel Johnson's "The Vanity of Human Wishes," lines 153–54.

[5] Shelley's tragedy *The Cenci* was published in the early spring of 1820.

[6] Murray had recently announced publication of *Marino Faliero,* completed by Byron during the preceding summer.

[7] *Prometheus Unbound* was published in the summer of 1820.

[8] Byron's pamphlet *Letter to* **** ****** [John Murray], *Esqre, on the Rev. W. L. Bowles's Strictures on the Life and Writings of Pope* was published in March 1821.

[9] Keats attacked Pope in "Sleep and Poetry," lines 193–206. Byron's remarks were not in the pamphlet published in 1821 but in its successor, *A Second Letter to John Murray, Esq.,* which was not published until 1835, and then with the passage about Keats suppressed.

TO JOHN MURRAY

Pisa, December 10, 1821.

DEAR SIR,

This day and this hour, (one, on the clock,) my daughter is six years old. I wonder when I shall see her again, or if ever I shall see her at all.

I have remarked a curious coincidence, which almost looks like a fatality.

My *mother,* my *wife,* my *daughter,* my *half-sister,* my *sister's mother,* my natural daughter (as far at least as *I* am concerned), and *myself,* are all *only children.*

My father, by his first marriage with Lady Conyers (an only child), had only my sister; and by his second marriage with another only child, an only child again. Lady Byron, as you know, was one also, and so is my daughter, etc.

Is not this rather odd — such a complication of only children? By the way, send me my daughter Ada's miniature. I have only the print, which gives little or no idea of her complexion.

I heard the other day from an English voyager, that her temper is said to be extremely violent. Is it so? It is not unlikely considering her parentage. My temper is what it is — as you may perhaps divine, — and my Lady's was a nice little sullen nucleus of concentrated Savageness to mould my daughter upon, — to say nothing of her two Grandmothers, both of whom, to my knowledge, were as pretty specimens of female Spirit as you might wish to see on a Summer's day.

I have answered your letters, etc., either to you in person, or through Mr. D. Kd

The broken Seal and *Edinburgh R[eview]*, etc., arrived safely. The others are I presume upon their way.

Yours, etc.,
N. B.[1]

1 By the terms of Lady Noel's will, Byron, who was to share in the income from her estate, was to take the Noel arms and might sign himself "Noel Byron" —for which, he pointed out, the initials were the same as those of Napoleon. The interesting fact of Byron's use of the signature here, as in a letter of 17 November 1821 addressed but never sent to Lady Byron, is that it anticipates the death of his mother-in-law, which did not actually occur until 28 January 1822.

TO THOMAS MOORE

Pisa, August 27, 1822.

It is boring to trouble you with "such small gear;"[1] but it must be owned that I should be glad if you would enquire whether my Irish subscription ever reached the committee in Paris from Leghorn. My reasons, like Vellum's, "are threefold:"[2] — First, I doubt the accuracy of all almoners, or remitters of benevolent cash; second, I do suspect that the said Committee, having in part served its time to time-serving, may have kept back the acknowledgment of an obnoxious politician's name in their lists; and third, I feel pretty sure that I shall one day be twitted by the government scribes for having been a professor of love for Ireland, and not coming forward with the others in her distresses.

It is not, as you may opine, that I am ambitious of having my name in the papers, as I can have that any day in the week gratis. All I want is to know if the Reverend Thomas Hall[3] did or did not remit my subscription (200 scudi of Tuscany, or about a thousand francs, more or less,) to the Committee at Paris.

The other day at Viareggio, I thought proper to swim off to my schooner (the Bolivar) in the offing, and thence to shore again — about three miles, or better, in all.[4] As it was at mid-day, under a broiling sun, the consequence has been a feverish attack, and my whole skin's coming off, after going through the process of one large continuous blister, raised by the sun and sea together. I have suffered much pain; not being able to lie on my back, or even side; for my shoulders and arms were equally St. Bartholomewed. But it is over, — and I have got a new skin, and am as glossy as a snake in its new suit.

We have been burning the bodies of Shelley and Williams on the sea-shore, to render them fit for removal and regular interment. You can have no idea what an extraordinary effect such a funeral pile has, on a desolate shore, with mountains in the back-ground and the sea

1 Perhaps a misquotation of a phrase from *King Lear* (III, iv): "But mice and rats, and such small deer,/ Have been Tom's food for seven long year."

2 Vellum, a character in Joseph Addison's play *The Drummer,* habitually enumerates his reasons for any action.

3 The English Chaplain at Leghorn.

4 Byron does not make clear in this instance that he swam out to the *Bolivar* on the day of Shelley's cremation, 16 August 1822. Edward Ellerker Williams, Shelley's companion, had been cremated the preceding day.

before, and the singular appearance the salt and frankincense gave to the flame. All of Shelley was consumed, except his *heart*, which would not take the flame, and is now preserved in spirits of wine.

Your old acquaintance Londonderry has quietly died at North Cray![5] and the virtuous De Witt was torn in pieces by the populace! What a lucky * * the Irishman has been in his life and end. In him your Irish Franklin *est mort!*

Leigh Hunt is sweating articles for his new Journal; and both he and I think it somewhat shabby in *you* not to contribute.[6] Will you become one of the *properrioters?* "Do, and we go snacks."[7] I recommend you to think twice before you respond in the negative.

I have nearly (*quite three*) four new cantos of *Don Juan* ready. I obtained permission from the female Censor Morum of *my* morals to continue it, provided it were immaculate;[8] so I have been as decent as need be. There is a deal of war — a siege, and all that, in the style, graphical and technical, of the shipwreck in Canto Second, which "took," as they say in the Row.

Yours, etc.

P.S. — That * * * Galignani has about ten lies in one paragraph. It was not a Bible that was found in Shelley's pocket, but John Keats's poems.[9] However, it would not have been strange, for he was a great admirer of Scripture as a composition. *I* did not send my bust to the academy of New York; but I sat for my picture to young West,[10] an American artist, at the request of some members of that Academy to *him* that he would take my portrait, — for the Academy, I believe.

I had, and still have, thoughts of South America, but am fluctuating between it and Greece. I should have gone, long ago, to one of them, but for my liaison with the Countess G[i].; for love, in these days, is little compatible with glory. *She* would be delighted to go too; but I do not choose to expose her to a long voyage, and a residence in an unsettled country, where I shall probably take a part of some sort.

[5] Robert Stewart, second Marquis of Londonderry and Viscount Castlereagh (1769–1822), British Foreign Secretary, became a suicide on 12 August 1822.

[6] *The Liberal*, toward which Moore was unsympathetic.

[7] From Pope's "Epistle to Dr. Arbuthnot," line 66.

[8] The Countess Teresa Guiccioli had extracted from Byron a promise not to continue *Don Juan*, which she regarded as an improper poem.

[9] Byron may be referring to the obituary of Shelley in Galignani's *Paris Monthly Review*, II (August 1822), 392. If this is the case, however, he is confused, for the *Review* did not suggest that a Bible was found in Shelley's pocket.

[10] William Edward West (1788–1857), who painted a portrait of Byron and was commissioned by him to do a portrait of Teresa Guiccioli.

TO JOHN HUNT

Genoa, Jy. 8th, 1823.

SIR,

I have written more than once to Mr. Kinnaird, to sanction his employment of the best counsel in your defence, and I forwarded a note to the same gentleman (to the same purport) to your brother.[1] This he was to enclose to you in his own letter, and you were to have the goodness to deliver it in person. I understand but little of the jargon, but you have every thing to apprehend from the abuse of these factions. I offered to your brother to stand the trial instead, and to go over to England for that purpose, but he tells me that this would be of no use to you, nor would probably be permitted by the gang. With regard to the arrangements for the publication of the *D. J.*, Mr. Kinnaird is my trustee in all matters of business.[2] I am not very sanguine on the subject, and would not have *you* be so, for you must be aware how violent public opinion is at this moment against myself, and others — besides the combination against you which you may expect from "the trade," as it is called. I sent a 12th canto to Mr. K., on the 14th of December, 1822. The whole series would form two vols. of the same size as former ones, and I expect to have the proofs soon, that they may be correct, or at least corrected. With regard to *The Liberal*,[3] perhaps towards the middle of the year you might collect any pieces of mine from the past numbers, and republish them in a volume correspondent to my other works. How far such a plan may be useful I know not at present, but I trust that no time will be lost. Mr. K. is providing you with the best counsel, and seeing the question at least *fairly* tried — it is an important one in a general point of view, or there is an end of history.[4] *Southey's* "Vision" ought to be cited in your defence, and also it ought to be *stated how* the obnoxious passages (at least some of them) came to

[1] In December 1822 John Hunt was indicted, as publisher of "The Vision of Judgment" in the first number of *The Liberal*, for libel against the memory of George III.

[2] Murray published the first five cantos of *Don Juan*, but John Hunt brought forth the sixth through sixteenth (1823–24).

[3] *The Liberal* appeared four times, on 15 October 1822, 1 January, 25 April, and 30 July 1823.

[4] John Hunt's defense was to be based in large measure upon the proposition that to convict him of libel was to negate the right of the historian to pass judgment upon national leaders who had died.

remain in the published text.[5] But all this is for your counsel's consideration. — Let them lose no time.[6] I have the honour to be very truly,

Yours, ever, etc., etc.,
N. B.

P.S. — The principal object for you in *The Liberal* is to employ good writers and to pay them handsomely. I have no personal objections to any gentleman you may wish to engage, nor, if I had, would I allow such to weigh with me a moment when it can be of service to you.

[5] John Murray, running a proof of "The Vision of Judgment" though hesitating to publish it, later failed to give John Hunt the corrected proof and a preface, as Byron instructed him to do.

[6] Despite a well-founded and articulate defense, John Hunt was convicted in January 1824; five months later, on 19 June 1824, he was sentenced to pay a fine of £100.

TO EDWARD BLAQUIERE[1]

Albaro, April 5, 1823.

DEAR SIR,

I shall be delighted to see you and your Greek friend, and the sooner the better. I have been expecting you for some time, — you will find me at home. I cannot express to you how much I feel interested in the cause, and nothing but the hopes I entertained of witnessing the liberation of Italy itself prevented me long ago from returning to do what little I could, as an individual, in that land which it is an honour even to have visited.

Ever yours truly,
NOEL BYRON.

[1] This letter represents Byron's first significant commitment to the Greek cause. Blaquiere, a representative of the Greek Committee newly formed in London, was on his way from England to the Morea, where he arrived on 3 May 1823.

TO EDWARD JOHN TRELAWNY[1]

June 15, 1823.

MY DEAR T.,

You must have heard that I am going to Greece. Why do you not come to me? I want your aid, and am exceedingly anxious to see you.

[1] Edward John Trelawny (1792–1881), an adventurer and in later years an author, was a member of the Pisan Circle. He did indeed join Byron in the

Pray come, for I am at last determined to go to Greece; it is the only place I was ever contented in. I am serious, and did not write before, as I might have given you a journey for nothing; they all say I can be of use in Greece. I do not know how, nor do they; but at all events let us go.

Yours, etc., truly,
N. BYRON.

TO THOMAS MOORE

Cephalonia, December 27, 1823.

I received a letter from you some time ago. I have been too much employed latterly to write as I could wish, and even now must write in haste.

I embark for Missolonghi to join Mavrocordato[1] in four-and-twenty hours. The state of parties (but it were a long story) has kept me here till *now;* but now that Mavrocordato (their Washington, or their Kosciusko) is employed again, I can act with a *safe conscience.* I carry money to pay the squadron, etc., and I have influence with the Suliotes,[2] *supposed* sufficient to keep them in harmony with some of the dissentients; — for there are plenty of differences, but trifling.

It is imagined that we shall attempt either Patras or the castles on the Straits; and it seems, by most accounts, that the Greeks, at any rate the Suliotes, who are in affinity with me of "bread and salt," — expect that I should march with them, and — be it even so! If any thing in the way of fever, fatigue, famine, or otherwise, should cut short the middle age of a brother warbler, — like Garcilasso de la Vega, Kleist, Korner, Joukoffsky (a Russian nightingale — see Bowring's *Anthology*), or Thersander,[3] or, — or somebody else — but never

---

Greek expedition but soon left him in Cephalonia to become one of the followers of Odysseus, the leader of the insurgents, then at Athens. In later years Trelawny wrote of his experiences with the two poets, showing increasing bias toward Shelley and against Byron.

1 Prince Alexander Mavrocordatos (1791–1865), regarded by Byron as the most enlightened and reliable of the rival Greek leaders, had been elected President of the first National Assembly, in 1822. Forced from power by his rivals early the next year, he was at length able to establish himself in western Greece.

2 One of Byron's major difficulties in Greece was with the large number of Suliotes among the Greek forces, who were often unruly and demanding.

3 Byron's reference is to other poets turned soldier, most fatally: Garcilaso de la Vega (1503–36), Ewald Christian von Kleist (1715–59), Karl Theodor Körner (1781–1813), Vasili Andreevich Zhukovski (1783–1852), and the mythic Thersander, accompanying Agamemnon against Troy.

mind — I pray you to remember me in your "smiles and wine."[4]

I have hopes that the cause will triumph; but whether it does or no, still "honour must be minded as strictly as milk diet." I trust to observe both.

Ever, etc.

[4] A reference to Moore's poem "The Legacy": "When in death I shall calmly recline,/ O bear my heart to my mistress dear,/ Tell her it liv'd upon smiles and wine/ Of the brightest hue, while it lingered here."

TO DOUGLAS KINNAIRD

Messalonghi, *March 13th,* 1824.

DEAR DOUGLAS,

I write without much certainty that the letter will reach you, for the plague has broken out this morning in the town, and of course precautions will be taken in the islands, and elsewhere.

It has been supposed to be communicated from the Morea. Be that as it may a man from thence has just died of it, as my physician says, whom I have just seen, as well as the Prince Mavrocordato. What the event may be cannot of course be foreseen.

To resume. It would be advantageous, nay even necessary, for me or for my heirs, that you should sell out of the 3 per cent. consols now, while they are so high. It might make a difference of ten thousand pounds in our favour on the original sum invested. Surely Bland would consent to this, and wait for the occurrence of a mortgage at 4 per cent., or take one on fair security. I wish much to impress this upon your mind.

I hope that you have arranged the Rochdale business as well as you could, and completely according to your wishes.[1] I hear that Hunt has been found libellous; we must pay the expenses of his fine.[2] If he had consented to my coming over as I requested, this would not have fallen upon *him*; but to this he frequently objected, declaring that they would not prosecute the author, but the publisher.

I shall be the more anxious to hear from you as the communication will probably be interrupted for some time to come. Whatever may [happen] to me, believe me that I ever am, and was, and will be (as long as I am at all),

Ever yours very faithfully and affectionately,

NOEL BYRON.

[1] On 2 November 1823 Kinnaird wrote that Rochdale, now clear of litigation, had been purchased by Mr. James Dearden for £11,225, but on 20 February 1824 he reported that the money had not yet been paid. At the time of Byron's death, Dearden's son was on his way to Greece, with the deeds of conveyance for Byron's signature.

[2] John Hunt's costs and fine were paid by Byron's estate.

TO CHARLES F. BARRY[1]

April 9th 1824.

DEAR BARRY,

The Account up to 11th July was 40,541, etc., Genoese livres in my favour: since then I have had a letter of Credit of Messrs. Webb for 60,000 Genoese livres, for which I have drawn; but how the account stands *exactly,* you do not state. The balance will of course be replaced by my London Correspondent, referring more particularly to the Honble Douglas Kinnaird, who is also my Agent and trustee, as well as banker, and a friend besides since we were at College together — which is favourable to business, as it gives confidence, or ought to do so.

I had hoped that you had obtained the price of the Schooner from Ld Blessington:[2] you must really tell him that I must make the affair public, and take other steps which will be agreeable to neither, unless he speedily pays the money, so long due, and contracted by his own headstrong wish to purchase. You *know* how fairly I treated him in the whole affair.

Every thing except the best (*i.e.* the Green travelling Chariot) may be disposed of, and that speedily, as it will assist to balance our accompt. As the Greeks have gotten their loan, they may as well repay mine, which they no longer require: and I request you to forward a copy of the agreement to Mr. Kinnaird, and direct him from me to claim the money from the Deputies. They were welcome to it in their difficulties, and also for good and all, supposing that they had not got out of them; but, as it is, they can afford repayment, and I assure you that, besides *this,* they have had many "a strong and "long pull" at my purse, which has been (and still is) disbursing pretty freely in their cause: besides, I shall have a *re-expend* the same monies, having some hundred men under orders, at my own expense, for the Gk. Government and National service.

Of all their proceedings here, health, politics, plans, acts, and deeds, etc. — good or otherwise, Gamba or others will tell you — truly or not truly, according to their habits.

Yours ever,
N. BN

1 Perhaps the last letter that Byron wrote, this was directed to his banker at Genoa, a member of Webb and Company. That same day he returned from his ride soaked by rain and perspiration, probably initiating the illness that brought death on 19 April.

2 The Earl of Blessington agreed to purchase the *Bolivar* for four hundred guineas.

SELECT BIBLIOGRAPHY

BIBLIOGRAPHIES

Chew, Samuel C. "Byron." *The English Romantic Poets: A Review of Research,* ed. Thomas M. Raysor. Revised edition, New York, 1956.

———. *Byron in England: His Fame and After-Fame.* London, 1924; reprinted New York, 1965.

Coleridge, Ernest Hartley. "A Bibliography of the Successive Editions and Translations of Lord Byron's *Poetical Works." The Works of Lord Byron: Poetry,* ed. Ernest Hartley Coleridge. 7 vols. London, 1898–1904. See VII, 89–348.

Escarpit, Robert. "Bibliographie." *Lord Byron: Un Tempérament Littéraire.* 2 vols. Paris, 1957. See II, 269–324.

Fogle, Richard Harter. *Romantic Poets and Prose Writers.* New York, 1967.

Wise, Thomas James. *A Bibliography of the Writings in Verse and Prose of George Gordon Noel, Baron Byron.* 2 vols. London, 1932–33.

See the appropriate section in the annual bibliographies: *Publications of the Modern Language Association,* XXXVII *et seq.* (1922 —); "The Romantic Movement: A Selective and Critical Bibliography," *ELH: A Journal of English Literary History,* IV–XVI (1937–49), *Philological Quarterly,* XXIX–XLIII (1950–64), *English Language Notes,* III *et seq.* (1965 —); "Current Bibliography," *Keats-Shelley Journal,* I *et seq.* (1952 —).

EDITIONS: POEMS, PROSE, LETTERS

Byron: A Self-Portrait, ed. Peter Quennell. 2 vols. London, 1950.

Byron's Don Juan: A Variorum Edition, ed. Truman Guy Steffan and Willis W. Pratt. 4 vols. Austin, 1957.

The Complete Poetical Works of Byron, ed. Paul Elmer More. Cambridge, Massachusetts, 1905; reissue 1952.

Don Juan, ed. Leslie A. Marchand. Boston, 1958.

Lord Byron's Correspondence, Chiefly with Lady Melbourne, Mr. Hobhouse, The Hon. Douglas Kinnaird, and P. B. Shelley, ed. John Murray. 2 vols. London, 1922.

The Works of Lord Byron: Letters and Journals, ed. Rowland E. Prothero. 6 vols. London, 1898–1901.

The Works of Lord Byron: Poetry, ed. Ernest Hartley Coleridge. 7 vols. London, 1898–1904.

RECOLLECTIONS BY CONTEMPORARIES

Blessington, Marguerite, Countess of. *A Journal of Conversations with Lord Byron.* London, 1834. Edited, Ernest J. Lovell, Jr. Austin, 1968.

Dallas, R. C. *Recollections of the Life of Lord Byron, from the Year 1808 to the End of 1814.* London, 1824.

Gamba, Pietro. *A Narrative of Lord Byron's Last Journey to Greece.* London, 1825.

Hobhouse, John Cam, Lord Broughton. *Recollections of a Long Life,* ed. Lady Dorchester. 6 vols. London, 1909–11.

Hunt, Leigh. *Lord Byron and Some of His Contemporaries.* London, 1828.

Kennedy, James. *Conversation on Religion with Lord Byron and Others, Held in Cephalonia, A Short Time Previous to His Lordship's Death.* London, 1830.

Medwin, Thomas. *Journal of the Conversations of Lord Byron: Noted during a Residence with His Lordship at Pisa, in the Years 1821 and 1822.* London, 1824. Edited, Ernest J. Lovell, Jr. Princeton, 1966.

Parry, William. *The Last Days of Lord Byron.* London, 1825.

Trelawny, Edward John. *Recollections of the Last Days of Shelley and Byron.* London, 1858.

BIOGRAPHIES

Borst, William A. *Lord Byron's First Pilgrimage.* New Haven, 1948.

Cline, C. L. *Byron, Shelley, and Their Pisan Circle.* Cambridge, Massachusetts, 1952.

Drinkwater, John. *The Pilgrim of Eternity: Byron — A Conflict.* New York, 1925.

Lovell, Ernest J., Jr., ed. *His Very Self and Voice: Collected Conversations of Lord Byron.* New York, 1954.

Marchand, Leslie A. *Byron: A Biography.* 3 vols. New York, 1957.

Marshall, William H. *Byron, Shelley, Hunt, and* The Liberal. Philadelphia, 1960.

Maurois, André. *Byron,* trans. Hamish Miles. London, 1930.

Mayne, Ethel Colburn. *Byron.* 2 vols. London, 1912. Revised, 1 vol. 1924.

Moore, Thomas. *Letters and Journals of Lord Byron: with Notices of His Life.* 2 vols. London, 1830.

Nicolson, Harold. *Byron. The Last Journey: April 1823–April 1824.* London, 1924. New edition, 1948.

Origo, Iris. *The Last Attachment: The Story of Byron and Teresa Guiccioli.* London, 1949.

Pratt, Willis W. *Byron at Southwell: The Making of a Poet.* Austin, 1948.

Quennell, Peter. *Byron in Italy.* London, 1941.

———. *Byron: The Years of Fame.* London, 1935.

Vulliamy, C. E. *Byron.* London, 1948.

WORKS OF BIOGRAPHICAL SIGNIFICANCE

The Letters of Mary W. Shelley, ed. Frederick L. Jones. 2 vols. Norman, Oklahoma, 1944.

The Letters of Percy Bysshe Shelley, ed. Frederick L. Jones. 2 vols. Oxford, 1964.

The Letters of Thomas Moore, ed. Wilfred S. Dowden. 2 vols. Oxford, 1964.

Mary Shelley's Journal, ed. Frederick L. Jones. Norman, Oklahoma, 1947.

Elwin, Malcolm. *Lord Byron's Wife*. London, 1962.

Fox, Sir John. *The Byron Mystery*. London, 1924.

Joyce, Michael. *My Friend H: John Cam Hobhouse*. London, 1948.

Mayne, Ethel Colburn. *The Life and Letters of Anne Isabella, Lady Noel Byron*. London, 1929.

Moore, Doris Langley. *The Late Lord Byron*. London, 1961.

CRITICISM

Arnold, Matthew. "Byron." *Essays in Criticism*, Second Series. London, 1888.

Blackstone, Bernard. "Guilt and Retribution in Byron's Sea Poems," *Review of English Literature*, II (1961), 58–69.

Bloom, Harold. "George Gordon, Lord Byron." *The Visionary Company: A Reading of English Romantic Poetry*. New York, 1961.

Bostetter, Edward E. "Byron." *The Romantic Ventriloquists*. Seattle, 1963.

Butler, E. M. *Byron and Goethe: Analysis of a Passion*. London, 1956.

Calvert, William J. *Byron: Romantic Paradox*. Chapel Hill, 1935.

Chew, Samuel C. *The Dramas of Lord Byron: A Critical Study*. Baltimore, 1915; reprinted New York, 1964.

Cooke, Michael G. *The Blind Man Traces the Circle: On the Patterns and Philosophy of Byron's Poetry*. Princeton, 1968.

Eliot, T. S. "Byron." *On Poetry and Poets*. London, 1937.

Elledge, W. Paul. *Byron and the Dynamics of Metaphor*. Nashville, 1968.

Elliott, G. R. "Byron and the Comic Spirit," *Publications of the Modern Language Association*, XXXIX (1924), 897–909.

Fuess, Claude M. *Lord Byron as a Satirist in Verse*. New York, 1912; reprinted 1964.

Gleckner, Robert F. *Byron and the Ruins of Paradise*. Baltimore, 1967.

Goode, Clement Tyson. *Byron as Critic*. Weimar, 1923.

Hudson, A. P. "Byron and the Ballad," *Studies in Philology*, XLII (1945), 594–608.

Joseph, M. K. *Byron the Poet*. London, 1964.

Lefevre, Carl. "Byron's Fiery Convert of Revenge," *Studies in Philology*, XLIX (1952), 468–87.

Lovell, Ernest J., Jr. *Byron: The Record of a Quest. Studies in a Poet's Concept and Treatment of Nature*. Austin, 1949; reprinted Hamden, Connecticut, 1966.

Marchand, Leslie A. *Byron's Poetry: A Critical Introduction.* Boston, 1965.

Marjarum, Edward Wayne. *Byron as Skeptic and Believer.* Princeton, 1938; reprinted New York, 1962.

Marshall, William H. *The Structure of Byron's Major Poems.* Philadelphia, 1962.

Read, Herbert. *Byron.* London, 1955.

Russell, Bertrand. "Byron and the Modern World," *Journal of the History of Ideas,* I (1940), 24–37. See "Byron." *A History of Western Philosophy.* New York, 1945.

Rutherford, Andrew. *Byron: A Critical Study.* Edinburgh, 1961.

Steffan, T. G. *Lord Byron's Cain: Twelve Essays and a Text with Variants and Annotations.* Austin, 1968.

Thorslev, Peter L., Jr. *The Byronic Hero: Types and Prototypes.* Minneapolis, 1962.

West, Paul. *Byron and the Spoiler's Art.* London, 1960.

NOTES TO THE POEMS

Lachin y Gair *Page 3*

Written probably in 1806; published in 1807 in *Hours of Idleness.* "Near Lachin y Gair I spent some of the early part of my life, the recollection of which has given birth to the following stanzas," Byron wrote in a passage prefixed to the poem. Two years earlier, in a letter to his Harrow friend Charles O. Gordon dated 14 August 1805, he wrote:

> I suppose you will soon have a view of the eternal snows that summit the top of Lachin y Gair, which towers so magnificently above the rest of our *Northern Alps.* I still remember with pleasure the admiration which filled my mind, when I first beheld it, and further on the dark frowning mountains which rise near Invercauld, together with the romantic rocks that overshadow Mar Lodge, a seat of Lord Fife's, and the cataract of the Dee, which dashes down the declivity with impetuous violence in the grounds adjoining to the House.

8 Loch na Garr: Byron pointed to this as the Erse pronunciation of Lachin y Gair. **25–26 "Ill-starr'd . . . cause?":** Byron was here referring to his maternal ancestors, the Gordons, from whom came a number of the supporters of Prince Charles, the Pretender. **27 Culloden:** The battle took place 16 April 1746. **30 Braemar:** Highland tracts. **31 Pibroch:** In *Hours of Idleness* Byron glossed this word as "bagpipe," but it actually refers to the air played upon the bagpipe.

Lines Inscribed upon a Cup Formed from a Skull *Page 4*

Written in late 1808; published in 1814 in the seventh edition of *Childe Harold's Pilgrimage.* Medwin recorded Byron's recollections of the skull: "There had been found by the gardener, in digging, a skull that had probably belonged to some jolly friar or monk of the Abbey about the time it was dis-monasteried. . . . Observing it to be of giant size, and in a perfect state of preservation, a strange fancy seized me of having it set and mounted as a drinking-cup. I accordingly sent it to town, and it returned with a very high polish, and of a mottled colour like tortoise-shell" (*Journal of the Conversations of Lord Byron: Noted during a Residence with His Lordship at Pisa, in the Years 1821 and 1822* [1824], p. 64).

Well! Thou Art Happy *Page 5*

Written on 2 November 1808; published in 1809, in John Cam Hobhouse's *Imitations and Translations.* Shortly before Byron wrote the poem, he and Hobhouse had visited Mrs. Chaworth-Musters, the former Mary Anne Chaworth, at Annesley Hall. The object of Byron's intense affections in the summer of 1803, the grand-niece of the Mr. Chaworth killed by Byron's great uncle and predecessor, the fifth Lord Byron, Mary Anne had married John Musters in 1805; their daughter, referred to in the poem, was born in 1806. Mrs. Musters died in 1832.

English Bards and Scotch Reviewers; A Satire *Page 7*

Written, with continual revision, in 1808 and early 1809, as an expansion of a poem originally composed in 1807 and entitled *British Bards;* published anonymously in March 1809. In its extended form, *English Bards and Scotch Reviewers* was Byron's reply, calculated to be in the tradition of Pope's *Dunciad,* to the review of *Hours of Idleness,* written by Henry Brougham and published anonymously in the *Edinburgh Review* (XI, 285–89), in January 1808. The second edition of the poem, which appeared in October 1809, while Byron was travelling on the Continent, bore the author's name. "My Satire, it seems, is in a fourth edition," he wrote on 28 June 1811, during his return voyage, to his literary adviser, R. C. Dallas. "At this period, when I can think and act more coolly, I regret that I have written it, though I shall probably find it forgotten by all except those whom it has offended." It is not surprising that, though he prepared and printed a fifth edition, Byron soon thereafter suppressed the poem in this edition, ordering that all copies be burned. Of those few which escaped destruction, one became the basis for the text of the poem in John Murray's six-volume edition *The Complete Works of Lord Byron* (1831), and thus the basis for subsequent reliable texts. Byron did not again alter his view of *English Bards and Scotch Reviewers,* writing in Switzerland in 1816: "The greater part of this satire I most sincerely wish had never been written — not only on account of the injustice of much of the critical, and some of the personal part of it — but the tone and temper are such as I cannot approve." For the moment he was right in believing that those offended would not forget. His close association with Thomas Moore began when the Irish poet challenged Byron to a duel for his remarks about Moore's abortive duel with Francis Jeffrey, and there was at least one other near-challenge, that of Colonel Greville, founder of the Argyle Institution. In time, however, Byron came to friendship, or at least mutual respect, with a majority of the truly important literary and political figures mentioned in the satire, such as Walter Scott, Francis Jeffrey, "Monk" Lewis, Lord Holland, and perhaps even Coleridge; he remained at enmity, or at least at odds, with a few, like Robert Southey, to the end of his life.

It would have been unfortunate had Byron not written *English Bards and Scotch Reviewers.* Of its kind it is a worthy example, weakened only by the fact that, though admiring the *genre* and able to imitate Pope's technique and much of his idiom, Byron did not really share Pope's world view and was unable therefore to imply, by his attack on the failure of contemporary poets, the nature of the poetic ideal; the poem, as a result, though frequently brilliant, lacks cohesiveness.

For further critical discussion of *English Bards and Scotch Reviewers,* see the appropriate chapters or sections in the following: Claude M. Fuess, *Lord Byron as a Satirist in Verse* (1912; 1964); Clement Tyson Goode, *Byron as Critic* (1923); William J. Calvert, *Byron: Romantic Paradox* (1935); William H. Marshall, *The Structure of Byron's Major Poems* (1962); Leslie A. Marchand, *Byron's Poetry: A Critical Introduction* (1965).

Epigraphs: *Henry IV, Part I,* III, i, 129–30; *An Essay on Criticism,* III, 51–52.

1: William Thomas Fitzgerald (1759–1829), who wrote verses on national occasions, such as *Nelson's Triumph* (1798) and *Nelson's Tomb* (1806), was termed by William Cobbett the "Small Beer Poet." **21:** Cid Hamet, the chronicler in *Don Quixote,* offers a farewell address to his pen at the end of his narrative. **49–50 A schoolboy freak . . . older children do the same:** Byron described himself on the title page of *Hours of Idleness* as "A Minor" — a fact which was not neglected by the reviewer in the *Edinburgh Review.* **55–58:** George Lamb (1784–1834), third son of Lord and Lady Melbourne, wrote farces (such as *Whistle for It,* performed at the Covent Garden Theatre in 1807) and more recently anonymous articles in the *Edinburgh Review.* **59–62:** Francis Jeffrey (1773–1850), one of the principal founders of the *Edinburgh Review* in 1802, served as Editor from 1803 to 1829; he is implicitly compared here to Judge George Jeffreys (1648–89) of the Bloody Assizes (1685). **65:** Joseph or Josias ("Joe") Miller (1684–1738), an English Comedian, whose name was unwarrantably used by John Mottley (1692–1750) after his death in *Joe Miller's Jest-book* (1739). **94:** Alexander Pope (1688–1744) was always Byron's poetic ideal, and satire was Pope's principal form. William Gifford (1756–1826), poet, critic, first Editor of the *Quarterly Review* (1809–24), had attacked a number of minor contemporary writers in *The Baviad* (1794) and *The Maeviad* (1795); Byron consistently esteemed his literary judgments though he differed from him politically. **100–02:** Henry James Pye (1745–1813), who was Poet Laureate from 1790 until his death, after Thomas Warton and before Robert Southey, wrote incredibly bad verse and was on frequent occasions an object of ridicule, as here and in "The Vision of Judgment," stanza xcii. **109 ff:** With limited success, Byron is probably punning on the word *Pope,* comparing former days of literary authority with those of religious authority. **113:** John Dryden (1631–1700). **115:** William Congreve (1670–1729), Thomas Otway (1652–85). **127:** Robert Southey (1774–1843). **128:** The early poems of Thomas Moore (1779–1852) were published in duodecimo as *The Poetical Works of the Late Thomas Little, Esq.* (1801). **129–30:**

Cf. *Ecclesiastes,* i:9. **132 The Cow-pox, Tractors, Galvanism, and Gas:** The references are to vaccination, which was still opposed in some quarters; metallic "tractors" as a highly advertised quack remedy for various (and unrelated) disorders; the work of Luigi Galvani (1737–98) with electricity; and the gases used by Thomas Beddoes (1760–1808) for the treatment of diseases. **142:** Robert Stott, a writer for the *Morning Post.* **148 Tales of Terror:** Although subsequent bibliographers and literary historians erroneously attributed a work entitled *Tales of Terror* to Matthew Gregory Lewis (1775–1818), Byron refers to such works as Scott's *An Apology for Tales of Terror* (1799), Lewis' *Tales of Wonder* (1801), an anonymous *Tales of Terror; with an Introductory Dialogue* (1801), as well as generally to the Gothic novels that were popular at the turn of the century. See Louis F. Peck, *A Life of Matthew G. Lewis* (1961), pp. 119, 132–33, 311. **153–64:** Walter Scott's metrical romance *The Lay of the Last Minstrel* (1805) was based upon the border legend of Gilpin Horner. **165–84:** Scott's *Marmion* (1808) was purchased by the Scottish publisher Archibald Constable, who then sold one fourth of the copyright to each of his two colleagues in London, John Murray and William Miller, creating thereby a situation which opened Scott to Byron's charge of prostituting his genius. The words "Good night to Marmion" are spoken by Henry Blount, on the death of Marmion (*Marmion,* Canto VI, 869). **205–10:** Southey's *Joan of Arc* was written in 1793 and published in 1796. **211–20:** In Southey's *Thalaba the Destroyer* (1801), the protagonist sacrifices his life in destroying a race of evil magicians inhabiting Domdaniel, a submarine palace. Here he is compared, with appropriate irony, to the hero of Henry Fielding's farce *The Tragedy of Tragedies; or, the Life and Death of Tom Thumb the Great* (1730). **221–24:** The setting of Southey's *Madoc* (1805) is in both Mexico and Wales, where Madoc is, respectively, a kind of chief (he founds a colony) and a prince. Sir John Mandeville (d. 1372) was the presumed author of a book of travels, written originally in French and appearing between 1357 and 1371. **231–32:** In Southey's ballad "The Old Woman of Berkeley," an aged lady is carried away by the Devil on the third night after her death. **234:** "The last line, 'God help thee,' is an evident plagiarism from the *Anti-Jacobin* to Mr. Southey, on his Dactylics: — 'God help thee, silly one!' *Poetry of the Anti-Jacobin,* p. 23" (Byron's note). *The Anti-Jacobin; or, Weekly Examiner,* edited by William Gifford, appeared in thirty-six numbers between 20 November 1797 and 9 July 1798, in brilliant support of the Government. In 1799 J. Wright of London published *Poetry of the Anti-Jacobin.* By George Canning, J. H. Frere, G. Ellis, and Others, a book which had reached its fourth edition by 1801. The verse to which Byron refers in his note, entitled "Dactylics" and appearing in the sixth number of *The Anti-Jacobin,* on 18 December 1797, concludes with the lines, presumably addressed to Southey: "Dactylics, call'st thou em? 'God help thee, silly one!' " See *Parodies and Other Burlesque Pieces by George Canning, George Ellis and John Hookham Frere with the Whole Poetry of the Anti-Jacobin,* ed. Henry Morley (1890), pp. 174–75. **239–40:** Cf. Wordsworth's poem "The Tables Turned" (1798):

"Up! up! my Friend, and quit your books; / Or surely you'll grow double: / Up! up! my Friend, and clear your looks; / Why all this toil and trouble?" **241–42:** "By the foregoing quotation it has been shown that the language of Prose may yet be well adapted to Poetry; and it was previously asserted, that a large portion of the language of every good poem can in no respect differ from that of good Prose. We will go further. It may be safely affirmed, that there neither is, nor can be, any *essential* difference between the language of prose and metrical composition" (Wordsworth, Preface to the Second Edition . . . of *Lyrical Ballads* [1800]). **247–54:** Wordsworth's poem "The Idiot Boy" (published in *Lyrical Ballads,* 1798) concludes with Johnny's answer to the question of his mother, Betty Foy, about his adventures during the night of his misguided journey: " 'The cocks did crow to-whoo, to-whoo, / And the sun did shine so cold!' / — Thus answered Johnny in his glory, / And that was all his travel's story." **259–64:** Coleridge's poems "Songs of the Pixies" (written in 1793, published in 1796) and "To A Young Ass" (1794) would particularly offend Byron's inbred classical tastes. **265–82:** Matthew Gregory Lewis' *Ambrosio, or The Monk* (1795) was the most popular and sensational of the novels of terror; Lewis' play *The Castle Spectre* was performed at the Drury Lane Theatre, 14 December 1797. Between 1796 and 1802 Lewis was a Member of Parliament from the pocket borough of Hindon in Wiltshire. St. Luke, supposedly a physician, is the patron saint of physicians; the sense of the passage is that only by supernatural means might Lewis' afflictions be cured. **287 LITTLE:** Thomas Moore, who as writer and singer of lyrics had by this time attained great popularity among the socially elite of London. **294:** Significantly, the Muse is here made to echo Jesus' words to the woman taken in adultery, after her accusers had vanished: "Neither do I condemn thee: go, and sin no more" (*St. John,* viii:11). **295–308:** Percy Clinton Sydney Smythe, sixth Viscount Strangford (1780–1855), in a note to his *Translations from the Portuguese by Luis de Camoens* (1803), comments somewhat inappropriately on his own blue eyes and auburn hair. **309–18:** William Hayley (1745–1820) wrote *The Triumphs of Temper* (1781) and *The Triumphs of Music* (1804) as well as biographies of Milton (1796) and Cowper (1803–04); he also produced various plays. See line 923, below. **319–26:** James Grahame (1765–1811) wrote *The Sabbath* (1804) and *Biblical Pictures* (1807). **331–84:** The Reverend William Lisle Bowles (1762–1850) published his *Fourteen Sonnets* in 1789, a work hailed for its naturalness and simplicity. The fall of various ancient empires is a significant theme in Bowles' long poem *The Spirit of Discovery by Sea* (1805), and among his shorter poems are "The Withered Leaf," "Oxford Revisited" (which opens with references to the bells of Oxford), and "The Bells, Ostend." Byron quotes the opening line of *The Spirit of Discovery* ("Awake a louder and a loftier strain"), a poem assuming the form of a dream-vision, in which Noah foresees some of the major maritime discoveries of history, concluding with those of James Cook (1728–1779). In the fourth book of this poem Bowles recounted the episode of the flight of the lovers Robert à

Machin and Anna d'Arfet: "A kiss / Stole on the listening silence; ne'er till now / Here heard; they trembled, ev'n as if the Power / That made the world, that planted the first pair / In Paradise, amid the garden walked" (346–50); in his note to his own lines Byron revealed that he had read the lines to mean that the woods of Madeira rather than the lovers "trembled," an error which he later recognized. Bowles' edition of Pope's *Works* (10 vols., 1807) infuriated Byron and eventually involved him in the pamphlet controversy of 1821, though here it was sufficient for him to attack Bowles in Popean terms: "Lord Fanny" was the name by which Pope attacked Lord Hervey (1696–1743); Edmund Curll (1675–1747) was the bookseller made one of the heroes of the *Dunciad;* Henry St. John, first Viscount Bolingbroke (1678–1751), closely associated with Pope during the poet's life but, angered by Pope's failure to destroy one of Bolingbroke's suppressed works, hired David Mallet (1705–65) to traduce Pope after his death; the critic John Dennis (1657–1734) and the minor writer James Ralph (1695–1762) were satirized by Pope. **387–410 Bœotian Cottle:** In his own note to *English Bards,* Byron wrote of the brothers Cottle, Bristol booksellers: "Mr. Cottle, Amos, Joseph, I don't know which, but one or both, once sellers of books they did not write, and now writers of books they do not sell, have published a pair of Epics . . . *Alfred* and the Fall of *Cambria.*" Byron indeed confused them, for Amos, upon whom he settled in *English Bards,* had died in 1800, and Joseph (1770–1853) was the author of *Alfred* (1801) and *The Fall of Cambria* (1807). **411–17:** The Reverend Thomas Maurice (1754–1824) was the author of, *inter alia,* a poem *Richmond Hill* (1807) **424 Sheffield:** James Montgomery (1771–1854), called by Byron in his note to *English Bards* "the Bard of Sheffield," author of *The Wanderer of Switzerland* (1806), was attacked by the *Edinburgh Review* in 1807. **429 Northern Wolves:** The Scotch Reviewers. **437 Arthur's Seat:** a hill overhanging Edinburgh. **439 almost the same:** The comparison between Francis Jeffrey and Judge Jeffreys of the Bloody Assizes, implicit in lines 60–62, is made explicit here; they were nearly identical in function and in name. **446 Bred in the Courts betimes:** Francis Jeffrey had been called to the Scottish bar in 1794. **466 Little's leadless pistol met his eye:** After Jeffrey's remarks in the *Edinburgh Review* of July 1806 (VIII, 456–65) about Thomas Moore's *Epistles, Odes, and Other Poems,* Moore challenged Jeffrey to a duel; they met at Chalk Farm in August but were interrupted by the police, who, on examining the pistols, discovered that Jeffrey's was without a bullet; Moore, with the help of Jeffrey's second, satisfied the police that both pistols had been charged at the time of the meeting, so that the condition of Jeffrey's pistol could be attributed only to accident. To this effect Moore published a statement in the *Morning Post* on 18 August 1806. Byron, like many of his contemporaries, was confused about the identity of the "leadless pistol," a fact that is hardly surprising, since the affair received much attention from the press and the gossips. In the note to this passage appearing in the first four editions of *English Bards,* Byron remarked, "the balls of the pistols, like the courage of the combatants, were found to have evaporated." When Moore learned that Byron was the author of the poem, he directed a challenge to him (1 January 1810), but since Byron was on the Continent at the time, he did not receive the letter (though he knew of it) until his return, by which time Moore's anger was sufficiently cooled that he might accept Byron's explanation and apology. See *The Letters of Thomas Moore,* ed. Wilfred S. Dowden (1964), I, 102–07, 135. **469 Dunedin:** Edinburgh. **472–73 Tweed ruffled . . . career:** "The Tweed here behaved with proper decorum; it would have been highly reprehensible in the English half of the river to have shown the smallest symptom of apprehension" (Byron's note). **475 Tolbooth:** The prison in Edinburgh. **485 Canongate:** The lower part of a principal street in Edinburgh. **509 Athenian Aberdeen:** George Hamilton Gordon, fourth Earl of Aberdeen (1784–1860), known for his travels, was a member of the Athenian Society. **510:** William Herbert (1778–1847), an early contributor to the *Edinburgh Review,* published the translation "The Song of Thyrm, or The Recovery of the Hammer" in 1803. **512:** The Reverend Sydney Smith (1771–1845) was a founder and, briefly, the Editor of the *Edinburgh Review.* **513:** Henry Hallam (1777–1859), the historian. **515:** James Pillans (1778–1864), Professor of Humanity in the University, Edinburgh. **516–17:** George Lamb's farce *Whistle for It* had received an unfavorable reception. **519–21:** Henry Richard Vassall Fox, third Baron Holland (1773–1840), whose London house was the center of social and political activities of the Whigs. **523 of Saffron and of Blue:** The colors of the covers of the *Edinburgh Review,* sometimes called "buff and blue." **524:** Henry Peter Brougham, later Baron Brougham and Vaux (1778–1868), Scottish jurist and statesman, was one of the founders of the *Edinburgh Review.* **542:** Henry Petty (1780–1863), who was to become third Marquis of Lansdowne in 1809, was a very active Whig, closely associated with his kinsman Lord Holland. **551:** "Lord Holland has translated some specimens of Lope de Vega, inserted in his life of the author. Both are bepraised by his *disinterested* guests" (Byron's note). Lord Holland's *Life of Lope de Vega* was published in 1806. **554–59:** Of Lady Holland Byron wrote in his note to this passage: "Certain it is, her ladyship is suspected of having displayed her matchless wit in the *Edinburgh Review.* However that may be, we know from good authority, that the manuscripts are submitted to her perusal — no doubt, for correction." **562:** "In the melo-drama of *Tekeli,* that heroic prince is clapt into a barrel on the stage" (Byron's note). *Tekeli* was produced in 1806 by Theodore Hook (1788–1841). **563:** The actor Thomas John Dibdin (1771–1841). **564 the Roscomania's o'er:** This refers to the excitement attending the stage debut in 1804 of William Henry West Betty (1791–1874), known as "the Young Roscius." **568–69:** Frederick Reynolds (1764–1841), producer of many plays. **570–71:** James Kenney (1780–1849). **572–73:** Thomas Sheridan (1775–1817), adapted Beaumont and Fletcher's *Bonduca,* for a performance at Covent Garden on 3 May 1808, stripping the tragedy of its dialogue and exhibiting "the scenes as the spectacle of *Caractacus*"

(Byron's note). **578:** The playwrights George Colman, the younger (1762–1836) and Richard Cumberland (1732–1811). **582–83:** Sheridan's translation of *Pizarro* by August Friedrich Ferdinand von Kotzebue (1761–1819) was produced at the Drury Lane Theatre in 1799. **587:** David Garrick (1717–79) was triumphant on the London stage from 1741 until his retirement in 1776, and Mrs. Sarah Siddons (1755–1831) was not to retire until 1812. **591:** The actor Andrew Cherry (1762–1812), the playwright Lumley St. George Skeffington (1771–1850), and Dibdin's pantomime *Mother Goose,* successfully produced at Covent Garden in 1807. **601:** "Mr. Greenwood is, we believe, scene-painter to Drury Lane theatre — as such, Mr. Skeffington is much indebted to him" (Byron's note. **602:** Skeffington's play *The Sleeping Beauty.* **612–15:** The operatic performers Guiseppe Naldi (1770–1820) and Angelica Catalani (1780?–1849). **618 Ausonia:** Italy. Presumably, Byron wrote this twenty-line section one night after returning from the opera and sent it to the printer the next morning. **622:** Deshayes, for some years the *ballet* master at the King's Theatre, London, was perhaps a member of the family of Prosper-Didier Deshayes, *ballet* master of the Théâtre Français, who was to die between 1815 and 1820. **624–31:** Gayton, Presle, Angiolini, and Collini were female performers at the King's Theatre. **632:** The Society for the Suppression of Vice. **639 Greville and Argyle:** The Argyle Institution, founded by Colonel Greville, which Byron severely criticized in a note to this passage. **674 Nick:** Score. The reference is presumably to dice. **678–86 Powell's pistol . . . Falkland fall:** Charles John Carey, ninth Viscount Falkland, died, probably on 2 March, from a wound received two days earlier in a duel with Mr. A. Powell, which arose over a supposed insult by Falkland at Steven's Coffee House, in Bond Street. "I knew the late Lord Falkland well," Byron recalled in his note to this passage. "On Sunday night I beheld him presiding at his own table, in all the honest pride of hospitality; on Wednesday morning [1 March], at three o'clock, I saw stretched before me all that remained of courage, feeling, and a host of passions." Byron immediately wrote and dispatched these lines to the printer. Clodius intrigued with Pompeia, Caesar's wife. **708:** Shams ud-din Mohammed Hafiz, a fourteenth-century Persian Poet. **713 Ton:** Fashion. **716 Sir T:** Any fashionable man. **717:** Miles Peter Andrews (d. 1824), industrialist and M. P., was credited with the authorship of a play, *Better Late Than Never,* produced at the Drury Lane Theatre, 17 October 1790. **723:** Wentworth Dillon, fourth Earl of Roscommon (1633–85), author of a translation in blank verse of Horace's *Ars Poetica* (1680). John Sheffield, third Earl of Mulgrave and later first Duke of Buckingham (1648–1721), author of *Essay upon Poetry* (1682). **726:** Frederick Howard, fifth Earl of Carlisle (1748–1825), was Byron's first cousin once removed, who, in 1799, became guardian of the young Lord in order to facilitate litigation for the recovery of the Rochdale estate, illegally leased by the fifth Lord Byron. Although Byron came to regret his attack on Carlisle, he never held his guardian in high esteem. **732 pamphleteer:** In 1808 Carlisle published a pamphlet concerned with theatrical conditions. **734–36 His scenes alone . . . the tragic stuff:** Carlisle was author of two tragedies, *The Father's Revenge* (1783) and *The Stepmother* (1800). **743–44 GIFFORD's heavy hand:** *The Baviad* (1794) and *The Mæviad* (1795). **745 "All the Talents":** A work by William Henry Ireland (1777–1835), *All the Blocks, or an Antidote to "All the Talents,"* by Flagellum (1807). **748:** " 'MELVILLE's Mantle,' a parody on *Elijah's Mantle,* a poem" (Byron's note). James Sayers, *Elijah's Mantle, being verses occasioned by the death of that illustrious statesman, the Right Hon. W. Pitt* (1807). Anonymous, *Melville's Mantle, being a Parody on the poem entitled "Elijah's Mantle"* (1807). **756:** Rosa King, the daughter of a London money-lender, presumably a minor writer. **759–64:** The Della Cruscans, a school of pretentious minor verse-writers, who took their names from the Della Cruscan Academy at Florence, to which their leader, Robert Merry (1755–98), actually belonged. John Bell (1745–1831), who published the poetical correspondence of the group in *The British Album* (1789), was a proprietor of the *Morning Post.* Charlotte Dacre, wife of the Editor of the *Morning Post,* used the pseudonym "Rosa Matilda," and Robert Stott, a writer for that newspaper, used the name "Hafiz." Of "O. P. Q.," Byron wrote in his note: "These are the signatures of various worthies who figure in the poetical departments of the newspapers." Gifford attacked the Della Cruscans in *The Baviad* and *The Mæviad.* **765–70:** Byron later noted that this passage was meant to refer to Joseph Blacket (1786–1810), a cobbler turned poet. St. Crispin is the patron of shoemakers. **774–77:** Capel Lofft (1751–1824), a jurist and poet, patronized Robert Bloomfield (1766–1823), another cobbler turned poet. Robert Burns was a farmer. **778:** William Gifford was at one time the apprentice of a shoemaker. **782:** Nathaniel Bloomfield, less successful as a poet, was by trade a tailor. **795 Moorland weavers:** Thomas Bakewell, *The Moorland Bard; or Poetical Recollections of a Weaver, in the Moorlands of Staffordshire* (1807). **801–04:** "It would be superfluous to recall to the mind of the reader the authors of *The Pleasures of Memory* and *The Pleasures of Hope,* the most beautiful didactic poems in our language, if we except Pope's *Essay on Man*" (Byron's note). Thomas Campbell (1777–1844) was author of *The Pleasures of Hope* (1799), and Samuel Rogers (1763–1855) *The Pleasures of Memory* (1792). Although Byron was to alter his views of the literary attainments of many of those with whom he dealt in *English Bards,* he esteemed Campbell and Rogers throughout his life. **810–12:** The poet William Cowper lived from 1731 to 1800 and Robert Burns from 1759 to 1796. **818:** William Sotheby (1757–1833), translator and poet. Hector Macneill (1746–1818), a Scottish poet. **831–48:** Henry Kirke White (1785–1806), a young poet of Cambridge, author of *Clifton Grove, A Sketch in Verse, with Other Poems* (1803). In his note Byron attributed White's death to "too much exertion in the pursuit of studies that would have matured a mind which disease and poverty could not impair, and which Death itself destroyed rather than subdued." **857:** George Crabbe (1754–1832), author of *The Village* (1783), *The Parish Register*

(1807), and *The Borough* (1810). **859–66:** Sir Martin Arthur Shee (1770–1850), who wrote *Rhymes on Art* (1805), and *Elements of Art* (1809), was President of the Royal Academy from 1830 to 1845. **877–80:** Waller (Walter) Rodwell Wright (d. 1826) wrote *Horæ Ionicæ, a Poem, Descriptive of the Ionian Islands, and Part of the Adjacent Coast of Greece* (1809), which, in his note, Byron described as "a very beautiful poem, just published." **881 associate Bards:** "The translators of the Anthology have since published separate poems, which evince genius that only requires opportunity to attain eminence" (Byron's note). *Translations chiefly from the Greek Anthology, with Tales and Miscellaneous Poems* (1806) was by Byron's old Harrow schoolmaster and friend, the Reverend Robert Bland (1780–1825), with the assistance of perhaps several others, certainly of John Herman Merivale (1779–1844). **893–902:** Erasmus Darwin (1731–1802), author of the poem *The Botanic Garden* (1789–92), about which Byron commented in his note to this passage: "The neglect of *The Botanic Garden* is some proof of returning taste. The scenery is its sole recommendation." **906:** Charles Lamb (1775–1834) and Charles Lloyd (1775–1839), whom Byron described in his note to this line as "the most ignoble followers of Southey and Co." Lloyd's publications include *Poems on the Death of Priscilla Farmer* (1796), a novel *Edmund Oliver* (1798), and, written in collaboration with Lamb, *Poems in Blank Verse* (1798). **917 childish verse:** A particular reference to "We Are Seven," published in *Lyrical Ballads* (1798), and a general reference to many Wordsworthian poems. **918 Coleridge lull the babe at nurse:** A reference to "Frost at Midnight" (1798). **931 Thou:** Walter Scott. **961 Granta:** The river Cam and, by extension, Cambridge. **964–66 Seaton's prize . . . Hoare . . . Hoyle:** The Seatonian Prize at Cambridge was won in 1807 by Charles James Hoare (1781–1865), with the poem "The Shipwreck of St. Paul," as it once had been by Edmund Hoyle (1672–1769), the writer on card games and the author of the epic *Exodus*. **972 Helicon:** Byron was here confusing the mountain *Helicon*, supposed residence of Apollo and the Muses, with the fountain *Hippocrene*, which is located on the mountain and from the waters of which supposedly comes poetic inspiration. He made the same mistake in line 391 but corrected it in the fifth edition of *English Bards*. **973–80:** Hewson Clarke (1787–1832), a prolific writer, left Cambridge without his degree and became, among other things, a frequent contributor to *The Satirist* (1808–14). **981 a Vandal race:** "'Into Cambridgeshire the Emperor Probus transported a considerable body of Vandals.' — Gibbon's *Decline and Fall*, ii, 83. There is no reason to doubt the truth of this assertion; the breed is still in high perfection" (Byron's note). **983:** Francis Hodgson (1781–1852), Byron's close friend. **984:** Hewson Clarke. **989:** The Reverend George Richards (1769–1835), of Oriel College, Cambridge, author of the prize poem *The Aboriginal Britons* (published in 1792), which, in his note, Byron described as "an excellent poem." **1015:** George Canning (1770–1827), who was at this time (1807–10) Foreign Secretary. **1016 old dame Portland:** "A friend of mine being asked, why his Grace of Portland was likened to an old woman? replied, 'he supposed it was because he was past bearing'" (Byron's note). William Henry Cavendish, third Duke of Portland (1738–1809), was Prime Minister from 1807 until shortly before his death, in October 1809. **1019 Calpe:** Gibraltar. **1020 Stamboul's:** Constantinople's. **1021 Beauty's native clime:** "Georgia" (Byron's note). **1022 Kaff:** "Mount Caucasus" (Byron's note). **1026:** Sir John Carr (1772–1832), author of various books of travel, who unsuccessfully sued the publishers of parodies of his books. **1027–34:** The fourth Earl of Aberdeen published in the *Edinburgh Review* of July 1805 an adverse criticism of *The Topography of Troy and Its Vicinity* (1804) by Sir William Gell (1777–1836). Thomas Bruce, seventh Earl of Elgin (1766–1841), arranged for the transfer of numerous major artifacts, including the Parthenon frieze, from the Acropolis to the British Museum, during the years 1803 to 1812. Byron satirized the undertaking in *The Curse of Minerva,* a poem which he wrote in 1811 and privately circulated in 1812. **1057 so changed since youth:** A reference to the words "A Minor" after the author's name on the title page of *Hours of Idleness.*

Childe Harold's Pilgrimage *Page 31*

The composition and publication of this poem divide themselves into three phases (Cantos I and II, Canto III, Canto IV), thereby supporting the doubt of the unity of the poem already existing on critical grounds. Byron began the first canto at Jannina on 31 October 1809 and concluded the second canto at Smyrna on 28 March 1810. After his return to England, in July 1811, he gave the manuscript to R. C. Dallas, his adviser in the publication of *English Bards,* who placed it in the hands of John Murray, beginning one of the richest associations between author and publisher in English literary history. The first two cantos of *Childe Harold's Pilgrimage* were published as a quarto volume on 10 March 1812, and within several days a second edition was demanded; before Byron took up his pen to continue the poem, Murray had published ten editions of the first two cantos. In early May 1816, less than two weeks after Byron left England, he was writing verses about his impressions of his travels which were to become part of the third canto of *Childe Harold's Pilgrimage;* by 27 June he had finished the new poem, which was published by John Murray on 18 November 1816. In late June 1817 Byron began the fourth canto, which by 20 July he considered complete at 126 stanzas. However, he continued to expand the poem, in each instance announcing that he had concluded it, until 8 January 1818, when John Cam Hobhouse, ending a visit with Byron in Venice, carried the manuscript back to John Murray, who published the poem on 28 April 1818. To the first three cantos Byron had appended rather abundant explanatory notes, but for the fourth canto, though Byron himself offered an occasional comment, these were provided by John Cam Hobhouse. Presumably accepting Byron's frequently repeated assertion that the fourth was the "ultimate Canto," John Murray published the collected cantos as one poem in 1819.

An artificial "Romaunt" written in the Spenserian stanza and containing archaisms occasionally too self-consciously contrived, *Childe Harold's Pilgrimage* is a most uneven piece of work. Harold, the nominal protagonist, "a fictitious character . . . introduced for the sake of giving some connection to the piece" (Preface to the first and second cantos), emerges uncertainly in the first two cantos from his background of darkness and guilt, and in the third canto he disappears entirely from the narrative, giving way to the more compelling personality of the narrator himself. Supposedly likened to the Romance hero, the "Childe" has been not so much seeking a holy object as fleeing his own unholy sense of sin and isolation, and in this respect the first two cantos of *Childe Harold's Pilgrimage* constitute a strikingly modern poem. Otherwise, this first installment is characteristic of a type of descriptive-contemplative poem, expressing an admiration for nature and containing melancholy intimations, which appeared with some frequency toward the end of the eighteenth century. If its uneven quality can be attributed to any single cause, it might be to the fact to which Byron pointed in his Preface, that the "poem was written, for the most part, amidst the scenes which it attempts to describe"; there was not, perhaps, sufficient "recollection in tranquillity" (to use Wordsworth's phrase) between the experience and the attempt to record a distillation of that experience. Each of the last two cantos was written in a somewhat similar fashion, and though the fourth, expressing Byron's love and hope for Italy and her people, is, in kind, a poem similar to the first two cantos, it avoids the dangers of personal preoccupation apparent in the earlier cantos, and it more frequently sustains itself by the natural descriptions and the emotional intensity for which all the cantos are justly esteemed. The third canto alone attains dramatic unity; here the speaker attempts, by the creation in Harold of a poetic figment or an alter-ego, to divest himself of the burden of his own grief and isolation, but he fails to sustain the image of Harold, and in the end he turns once more in sorrow to the daughter whom he addressed in the beginning. In the speaker's dramatic failure to find absolution from pain lies the poet's own remarkable achievement.

Most usefully concerned with the biographical background of *Childe Harold's Pilgrimage* are William A. Borst, *Lord Byron's First Pilgrimage* (1948), and Leslie A. Marchand, *Byron. A Biography* (3 vols. 1957). For further critical discussion of the poem, see the appropriate chapters or sections in the following: William J. Calvert, *Byron: Romantic Paradox* (1935); Ernest J. Lovell, Jr., *Byron: The Record of a Quest* (1949); Andrew Rutherford, *Byron: A Critical Study* (1961); William H. Marshall, *The Structure of Byron's Major Poems* (1962); Leslie A. Marchand, *Byron's Poetry: A Critical Introduction* (1965).

Epigraph: "The universe is a type of book, of which one has read only the first page when he has seen only his own country. I have passed over a rather large number of pages, which I have found equally bad. This survey has not been to me unfruitful. I hated my native land. All the impertinences of the various peoples among whom I have lived have reconciled me with her. While I have not drawn any other benefit from my travels than that, I have regretted neither the expenses nor the hardships."

To Ianthe: Lady Charlotte Mary Harley, second daughter of Edward, fifth Earl of Oxford and Mortimer, was eleven years old when Byron met her during his visit to her parents, at Eywood House, in Herefordshire, in the autumn of 1812; she married Captain Anthony Bacon (d. 1864) in 1823, and she died in 1880. The dedication was published for the first time in the seventh edition of *Childe Harold*, in 1814. **13 Love's . . . without his wing:** Cf. the French proverb "L'amitie est l'amour sans ailes." **20:** In 1814, Byron was twenty-six, and "Ianthe" was in her thirteenth year.

Canto I. 4 sacred Hill: Helicon. **7 that feeble fountain:** Hippocrene. **18 flaunting wassailers:** Taken by most critics as a reference to Byron and his friends in their visits to Newstead Abbey during the Cambridge years. **19 hight:** The passive cf the preterite, meaning "was called," so that Byron's use of "was" is actually redundant. **23 losel:** In 1765, William, the fifth Lord Byron, killed in a duel his neighbor and kinsman William Chaworth, for which he was convicted by the House of Lords of manslaughter. **39–45 though he loved but one, . . . to taste:** Mary Anne Chaworth, for whom Byron had felt intense love in 1803, married John Musters in 1805, a man whom Byron and others regarded as coarse and unconcerned with her happiness; the marriage was not successful. **55 his father's hall:** Newstead Abbey. **77 lemans:** An archaism, meaning in the singular "sweetheart," "lover," and, in later usage, "mistress." **79:** " 'Feere,' a consort or mate" (Byron's note.) **84 A sister whom he loved:** Augusta Byron (1783–1851), the daughter of Byron's father by his first marriage, to the Marchioness of Carmarthen, Baroness Conyers. Augusta married her first cousin Colonel George Leigh, in 1807. **134 my little page:** Robert Rushton, the son of a local farmer, entered Byron's employ and accompanied him from England in 1809, only to be sent back from Gibraltar after he had become homesick. **158 my staunch yeoman:** William Fletcher, who was to serve as valet until Byron's death. **202 Cintra's mountain:** Located to the northwest of Lisbon. **204 golden tribute:** Small particles of gold have supposedly been found in the Tagus River, flowing westward through Spain and Portugal. **216 Lisboa:** Portuguese, "Lisbon." Many of Byron's impressions of this phase of his journey are recorded in his letter to his mother dated 11 August 1809, reprinted in this edition. **255:** The convent of Nossa Señora de Peña, which by the second edition of the first two cantos of *Childe Harold*, Byron had come to translate as "Our Lady of the Rock." **259:** St. Honorius (d. 159) supposedly dug his own den, over which an epitaph was later placed. **275 Vathek:** William Beckford (1759–1844), the enormously wealthy author of *Vathek* (1786), passed two years (1794–96) in retirement near Cintra. **288:** By the Convention of Cintra (30 August 1808),

Napoleon's forces, though defeated, were permitted safe passage out of Portugal; understandably, the agreement was unpopular in England. Byron believed that the Convention had been signed in the palace of the Marchese Marialva. **324–25:** Arriving in Lisbon on 7 July, Byron and Hobhouse visited Cintra and Mafra on 12 July and left Lisbon for Seville on 21 July. See Borst's "Byron in Portugal and Spain: A Revised Itinerary" (*Lord Byron's First Pilgrimage,* pp. 156–57). **333:** In his note Byron emphasized the magnificance of Mafra, with its "palace, convent, and most superb church" — products of the early eighteenth century. **334 the Lusians' luckless queen:** Maria I (1734–1816), who became insane in her later years, during much of which (1799–1816) her son (to become John VI) ruled as Regent. **368 rocks:** The Pyrenees. **369 silver streamlet:** The Caia. **388 that standard which Pelagio bore:** The cross, supposed to have falled from heaven, before the Gothic chieftain Pelayo (d. 737) defeated the Moslems at Covadonga, in 718, to begin the Christian reconquest of Spain. **389 Cava's traitor sire:** Traditionally, Count Julian, a lieutenant of Roderick the Goth, went over to the side of the Moors when Roderick violated Julian's daughter Cava. **393:** In 1492, during the reign of Ferdinand and Isabella, the Moors were driven from Granada. **423 Gian:** Mars, or the personification of War. **430 three potent nations:** The British and Spanish fought against the French in the battle of Talavera, concluded after two days, on 28 July, with an Allied victory. **432 a splendid sight to see:** Byron himself did not see any part of the battle, which took place at the small town in central Spain; he reached Seville on 25 July and left for Cadiz on 28 July. **459:** The British defeated the French at Albuera on 16 May 1811, in what soon appeared to have been an extremely costly victory. **509:** Manuel de Godoy (1767–1851), as Prime Minister (1792–97) was defeated by the French and made the Treaty of Basel (1795), which granted enormous concessions to France. **510:** Charles IV (1748–1819), who was forced to abdicate in 1808, after the French invasion of Spain, in favor of his son, Ferdinand VII (1784–1833). **511:** Maria Louisa of Parma (1751–1819), wife of Charles and mother of Ferdinand, was Queen of Spain from 1788 to 1808. **513–21:** The Sierra Morena, which had been the scene of fighting in 1808. **523 badge of crimson hue:** "The red cockade, with 'Fernando Septimo' in the centre" (Byron's note). **560 Anlace:** A short two-edged dagger. **584:** The allusion is to the presumed feat of the Maid of Saragossa, who, finding the gunners dead at a battery near the gate, took over the large cannon herself and stayed with them until the retreat of the French. **607 Houries:** Women of perpetual beauty supposed to inhabit the Mohammedan paradise. **612 Parnassus:** The speaker's abrupt shift from Spain to Greece, to the mountain that is the seat of the Muses, is a form of invocation, which is to be recollected in lines 639–41. **675:** Cf. *Paradise Lost,* I, 742–44: "from Morn/ To noon he fell, from Noon to dewy Eve,/ A Summers day." **679 kibes:** Byron's misuse, for the word means "chilblain" rather than "heel." **693 seventh day:** The Christian Sabbath, in London and elsewhere, is of course on the first day, Sunday.

707 the solemn Horn: A social ritual, "swearing on the horns" at Highgate, by which one swears before horns fixed upon poles that he will pursue the pleasurable things in life. **776 brast:** An archaism, "burst." **778 Matadores:** Byron was confused, for in each bullfight there is but one matador. **802 Centinel:** Sentinel. **To Inez:** Written on 25 January 1810, this poem was not initially intended to be part of *Childe Harold.* "Inez" might well have been Theresa Macri (1797–1875), the eldest of three daughters of the widow of an English vice-consul, in whose house Byron and Hobhouse stayed in Athens; Theresa was the addressee of the poem "Maid of Athens." **854 fabled Hebrew Wanderer:** The so-called Wandering Jew, often called "Ahasuerus," who, according to legend, refused to aid Christ on his way to Calvary and for this was condemned to live and wander, without the comfort of home or of death, until Christ's Second Coming. Like Cain, the Wandering Jew appealed to the Romantic mind as the mythic representative of post-Enlightenment man in his alienation. **873:** Byron left Cadiz on 3 August 1809. **876:** Cadiz had been the first city freed from the Moors and was the last subdued by the French. **879 A Traitor only:** The Marquis of Solano, commander-in-chief of the forces at Cadiz, suffered death at the hands of the populace in May 1808, after he had refused the order of the Supreme Junta at Seville to attack the French fleet, at anchor off Cadiz. **884 A Kingless people:** In May 1808 both the former King, Charles IV, and his son and successor, Ferdinand VII, renounced all claim to the throne in favor of Napoleon. **890:** " 'War to the knife.' Palafox's answer to the French general at the siege of Saragoza" (Byron's note). When José de Palafox y Melzi (1775–1847), commander of the forces at Saragossa, was asked by the French to surrender, he is supposed to have replied, "Guerra al cuchillo." **916 Quito:** The capital of Ecuador, bearing the name of the place of which Atahualpa (executed by the Pizarros in 1533), the Inca, was king. During the Peninsular War, Spain's American colonies saw the opportunity to rebel; there was an uprising in Quito in August 1810. **919:** The battle of Barossa took place on 5 March 1811. **926:** An allusion to the custom developing during the American and French Revolutions of planting a tree to symbolize freedom. **927 And thou, my friend:** John Wingfield, Byron's friend at Harrow, who joined the Coldstream Guards, died of a fever, at Coimbra, on 14 May 1811. **945 fytte:** A division of a poem, in this case a canto.

Canto II. 1 blue-eyed Maid of Heaven: Athena. **4:** "Part of the Acropolis was destroyed by the explosion of a magazine during the Venetian siege [1687]" (Byron's note). **55 Athena's wisest son:** Socrates. **61 Acheron:** The River of Woe, a river in Hades, thus the place of death. **64 Yet if, as holiest men have deemed:** This is not an affirmation on the part of the speaker, but it is a tentative reversal of the philosophic direction of the preceding stanza. **73:** Stanza IX is a late addition to the poem, sent forth in October 1811; Byron was careful not to reveal the intended identity of the "Thou" addressed. **84:** The Temple of Zeus

Olympius, on the southeastern side of the Acropolis, of which in 1810 sixteen of the original 104 columns remained. **91:** Thomas Bruce, seventh Earl of Elgin (1766–1841), a Scot, arranged the transfer of various early Greek artifacts from the Acropolis to the British Museum. **99 the long-reluctant brine:** One of Elgin's ships was wrecked in 1803, and only two years later were its treasures fully recovered. **100:** An allusion to a deep cutting made in the plaster wall of one of the ruins: "Quod non fecerunt Goti,/ Hoc fecerunt Scoti." **117 Eld:** An archaism, "age" or "time." **118–19:** Alaric, the Visigoth King, occupied Athens in A.D. 395 and removed portable treasures from the city; the tradition exists that he was frightened away by Minerva and Achilles. **120 Peleus' son:** Achilles. **144 the land of War and Crimes:** Spain. **155 the netted canopy:** "To prevent blocks or splinters from falling on deck during action" (Byron's note). **174–75:** The reference is to a convoy, in which the last of the ships escorted must pass ahead of the flagship. On 19 August 1809, Byron left Gibraltar for Malta on the *Townshend Packet,* and on 19 September he sailed for Greece on the *Spider,* which, under the command of a Captain Oliver, was attached to a full convoy; the second phase of Byron's voyage from Spain to Greece became the basis for his description of Harold's journey in these lines. **194:** The moon is in the southern skies. **258 him:** Odysseus. **266 Sweet Florence:** The allusion is to Mrs. Constance Spencer Smith (born 1785), wife of the British Minister at Stuttgart, who was, in 1806, made a prisoner of Napoleon's forces and daringly rescued by the Marquis de Salvo; Byron met her at Malta and became suddenly and intensely infatuated, at one point planning an elopement, though his passion cooled with his departure from Malta. **277 the Boy:** Cupid. **322 ared:** Counselled. **334 Iskander:** Alexander, whose mother came from Epirus. **343–44 the barren spot . . . wave:** Ithaca. **353 Leucadia's cape:** Cape Ducato, where Sappho supposedly threw herself from a rock. **356:** The reference is to three sea battles — at Actium in 31 B.C., where Octavius Caesar defeated Antony and Cleopatra; at Lepanto in 1571, where the Spanish were victorious over the Turks; and at Trafalgar in 1805, where the British defeated the French and Spanish. **371 Suli's rocks:** The district in southern Epirus, which as a republic at the end of the eighteenth century resisted Ali Pasha. From this district came the troops who were to constitute much of Byron's command during his final journey to Greece. **397–98:** Actium is at the entrance to the Ambracian Gulf. **400:** "It is said, that on the day previous to the battle of Actium, Antony had thirteen kings at his levee" (Byron's note). **402:** Augustus built Nicopolis to commemorate the victory. **416:** Prevesa. **418 Albania's Chief:** Ali Pasha (1741–1822), whom Byron and Hobhouse visited in the town of Tepelene, in October 1809. **421–23:** Although Ali prevailed in most things political and military, a small army of Suliotes, well entrenched in their castle and the hills, successfully resisted his large Albanian forces from 1788 to 1803, when they were betrayed by their bribed leaders. **438 caloyer:** "The Greek monks are so called" (Byron's note). Actually, Byron and Hobhouse visited the monastery at Zitza on their way from Ali's temporary location at Tepelene to his capital city, Jannina. **453 Chimæra's Alps:** Ceraunian Alps. **456:** "Now called Kalamis" (Byron's note). **469 Dodona:** The seat of a famous oracle of Zeus, in Epirus. **481 yclad:** Clad, in this form a past participle rather than, as Byron's use would indicate, a preterite. **502 santons:** In Moslem life, dervishes, regarded as saintly. **532 Ramazani's feast:** The Ramadan or holy season of the Mohammedans, falling in the ninth month of the year; since the Mohammedans reckon by lunar time, each year it occurs eleven days earlier than in the year before. **534–35:** During the Ramadan one must fast during the day but can feast at night. **562 the Teian:** Anacreon. **632:** "The Albanian Mussulmans do not abstain from wine, and, indeed, very few of the others" (Byron's note). **637:** "Palikar . . . a general name for a soldier amongst the Greeks and Albanese, who speak Romaic: it means, properly, 'a lad' " (Byron's note). **649 Tambourgi:** Drummer. Of the war song included here, Byron in his note remarked: "These stanzas are partly taken from different Albanese songs, as far as I was able to make them out by the exposition of the Albanese in Romaic and Italian." **654 camese:** A white kilt worn by some Albanians at the time. **677:** Taken from the Venetians by the French in 1797, Prevesa fell to Ali, acting for the Sultan, in 1798. **685:** Mukhtar, the son of Ali, had been sent against the Russians, who had invaded the Ottomon provinces on the other side of the Danube. **686 Giaours:** Infidels, in this instance the Russians. The horse-tail was the Pasha's insignia. **687 Delhis:** Literally, madmen, coming to be a term of honor applied to Turkish warriors because of their fierceness. **689 Selictar:** Sword-bearer. **702–03:** "Phyle, which commands a beautiful view of Athens, has still considerable remains: it was seized by Thrasybulus, previous to the expulsion of the Thirty [in 404 B.C.]" (Byron's note). **733–35:** "Mecca and Medina were taken some time ago by the Wahabees, a sect yearly increasing" (Byron's note). From central Arabia, the Wahabees arose in the eighteenth century as a reformed Mohammedan sect seeking to return to the pure teachings of the Koran and rebelling against the Sultan; in 1803–04 they attacked Mecca and Medina. **748 Stamboul:** Byron visited Constantinople from mid-May to mid-July 1810. **765 Caique:** Skiff. **776 searment:** A plaster or binding of a wound. **812 Tritonia's:** Athena's. **822 Hymettus:** A mountain near Athens, known for its honey. **836–54:** On 25 January 1810, Byron and Hobhouse visited the site of the battle of Marathon (490 B.C.).

Canto III. Epigraph: After Jean le Rond d'Alembert (1717–83), the French mathematician and philosopher, lost a close personal friend, Frederick II proposed that he apply himself to a problem most difficult to solve, "in order that this application might force you to think of something else; indeed, as a remedy there are only that and time" (*Œuvres de Frédéric II, Roi de Prusse* [1790]). The remark relates to Byron's situation in 1816 as well, for having lost custody of his daughter and deciding to leave England as a result of his separation from Lady Byron, he applied himself to the poem, which, with time, might be his only remedy for sorrow. **2 sole daughter of my house and heart:** Augusta Ada Byron (1815–52) married in 1835 William King Noel (1805–93), eighth Baron King, who was created Lord Lovelace in 1838. Ada's father last saw her on 15 January 1816, when Lady Byron took the infant from 13 Piccadilly Terrace, in the move preliminary to the separation. **7–9:** On 21 April Byron signed the deed of separation from Lady Byron, and on 25 April he embarked from Dover. **19 One:** Childe Harold, of the first two cantos. **87–90:** Harold's present search and that which Manfred has completed by the opening of the play are comparable. **145:** The Napoleonic Empire. **153 Thou first and last of Fields:** Waterloo, where the Duke of Wellington (1769–1852) and Marshal Gebhard von Blucher (1742–1819) defeated Napoleon on 18 June 1815. Byron visited the battlefield on 4 May 1816. **158:** " 'Pride of place' is a term of falconry, and means the highest pitch of flight" (Byron's note). **179 myrtle wreathes a Sword:** In one of its traditions, the myrtle stands for Love, Mirth, and Joy — the attributes of peace. **180 Harmodius:** An Athenian youth, one of the two assassins of the tyrant Hipparchus, in 514 B.C. **181–89:** On 15 June 1815, the Duchess of Richmond gave a ball for the Allied officers at Brussels; during the evening, the story circulated that the armies were to march the following day. Like Byron, William Makepeace Thackeray (1811–1863) was to use the famed ball for literary purposes, as a scene in the twenty-ninth chapter of *Vanity Fair*. **199–207:** Frederick William, Duke of Brunswick (1771–1815), nephew to King George III, was killed in an early phase of the battle; his father, Charles William Ferdinand (1735–1806), had been killed at the battle of Auerstädt, in October 1806. **234:** Sir Evan Cameron (1629–1719) fought against Cromwell and later for James II, at Killiecrankie (1689); his grandson, Donald Cameron (1695–1748), was wounded at Culloden (1746); his great-grandson, John Cameron (1771–1815) was killed at Waterloo. **235:** Revealing some confusion Byron wrote in his note, "The wood of Soignies is supposed to be a remnant of the forest of Ardennes, famous in Bojardo's *Orlando*, and immortal in Shakespeare's *As You Like It*." **256–61 I did his Sire some wrong . . . gallant Howard:** Major Frederick Howard (1785–1815), third son of Byron's guardian, Frederick, fifth Earl of Carlisle (1748–1825), was killed on 18 June. Byron refers to his attack upon his guardian in *English Bards and Scotch Reviewers* (lines 725–40). **303 the Dead Sea's shore:** "The (fabled) apples on the brink of the lake Asphaltites were said to be fair without, and, within, ashes" (Byron's note). **307–10:** The "threescore years and ten" foretold by the Psalmist (xc: 10), though in themselves a "fleeting span," are "more than enough" when compared to the short lives of those killed at Waterloo. **316:** Napoleon, whom Byron always regarded with ambivalence. **323:** Even in exile, on St. Helena, Napoleon demanded, but from the British did not receive, imperial honors. **366 Philip's son:** Alexander the Great. **410:** Harold, reflecting Byron in 1816, has crossed Belgium into Prussia and travels up the Rhine to Switzerland. **420 battles:** An archaism, "battalions." **474–77:** Probably an allusion to Byron's sister, Augusta Leigh. **493 peril, dreaded most in female eyes:** Scandal. This has been taken by some as an allusion to the accusations made about Byron and his sister at the time of the separation, but others regard it merely as a reference to the fact that when her brother was ostracized, Mrs. Leigh stood by him. **496:** Located on the summit of one of the Siebengebirge (seven volcanic hills on the right bank of the Rhine between Remagen and Bonn), the Castle of Drachenfels is not, as Byron asserted in his note, on the highest of these. In a manuscript note, Byron indicated that he wrote this interpolated song on 11 May 1816. **541:** General François Sévérin Marceau (1769–96), of the army of the French Republic, killed in battle on the Rhine. **554 Ehrenbreitstein:** described by Byron in his note as "one of the strongest fortresses in Europe," held out against Marceau in 1795 and 1796, capitulating to the French only in 1799. **599–607:** The battle of Morat, at which, in 1476, the Swiss defeated the Burgundians, killing perhaps as many as twenty thousand; the dead were thrown into a pit, and, though on various occasions through the centuries the bones were covered and monuments were built over them, they were continually exposed anew to public view, even in Byron's time. **608–09:** Like the battle of Marathon, at which the Greeks defeated the invading Persians, Morat was fought in a meaningful and honorable cause, whereas Waterloo represented purposeless slaughter, like the battle of Cannæ, in which, in 216 B.C., during the Second Punic War, Hannibal defeated the Romans. **625:** "Aventicum, near Morat, was the Roman capital of Helvetia, where Avenches now stands" (Byron's note). **626–34:** The lines refer to Julia, legendary daughter of one Julius Alpinus, a Helvetian condemned to die by the Romans for leading a rebellion against the Romans; the daughter is supposed to have made a vain effort to save her father and then to have died herself. **642 like yonder Alpine snow:** Byron was here writing as himself, as he observed Mont Blanc and Mont Argentière, in June and July 1816. **648 There is too much of Man here:** At Geneva, Byron was besieged by the curious British tourists. **669 wanderers o'er Eternity:** This phrase became the basis for Shelley's imaging of Byron, as one of the mourners for Adonais (John Keats): "The Pilgrim of Eternity, whose fame/ Over his living head like Heaven is bent,/ An early but enduring monument,/ Came, veiling all the lightnings of his son/ In sorrow" (*Adonais* [1821], xxx). **673:** "The colour of the Rhone at Geneva is blue, to a depth of tint which I have never seen equalled in water, salt or fresh, except in the Mediterranean and Archipelago" (Byron's note). **674 its nursing Lake:** Geneva. **725:** Jean Jacques Rousseau (1712–78) was born at Geneva. **743:** *Julie, ou la Nouvelle Héloise* was published in 1761. **745–51:** "This refers to the account, in his *Confessions*, of his passion for the Comtesse d'Houdetot [1730–1813] (the mistress of St. Lambert), and his long walk every morning, for the sake of the single kiss which was the common salutation of French acquaintance" (Byron's note). **761–69:** Much of the *rationale* for the French Revolution was supposedly drawn from Rousseau's writings. **900 knoll:** An archaism and dialect form, "knell." **923 Clarens:** Setting of *La Nou-*

velle Héloise. **977–78:** Edward Gibbon (1737–94) finished *The Decline and Fall of the Roman Empire* at Lausanne, in 1788. François Marie Arouet de Voltaire (1694–1778) lived at Ferney from 1759 to 1777. **986 The one:** Voltaire. **995 The other:** Gibbon. **999 a solemn creed:** Christianity. **1022:** Italy is the object of the speaker's pilgrimage, as it has been of others' ambitions. Byron reached Italy on 10 October 1816. **1085–88:** One of Byron's dominant fears was that Ada would be taught to hate him, or — perhaps worse — taught nothing of him, by her mother and her grandmother, Lady Noel.

Canto IV. Epigraph: "I have seen Tuscany, Lombardy, Romagna,/ That mountain which divides, and that which will be/ Italy, both one sea and the other which washes her." The source is the fourth *Satire* of Ariosto (lines 58–60) rather than, as was indicated on the title page of the first edition of Canto IV, the third *Satire.* Italy's divided condition in 1817 might lead Byron to find an element of prophecy in the use of "serra" (will be) in the second line. **1 "Bridge of Sighs":** This connects the ducal palace and the prison of Venice. Byron lived in Venice from late 1816 to 1819. **10 Cybele:** Originally the nature goddess of Anatolia, she was identified by the Greeks as a mother of gods and goddesses and represented as crowned; here, Venice is associated with her as wearing a crown of "proud towers" and rising triumphant from the sea. It is also significant that in her earliest form, Cybele was a preserver of cities and nations. **19–20:** An allusion to the practice of gondoliers in past times of singing alternate stanzas of Torquato Tasso's *Gerusalemme Liberata.* **33–34:** In addition to Shakespeare's *The Merchant of Venice* and *Othello,* Byron alludes to the less familiar work of Thomas Otway, *Venice Preserved; or, A Plot Discovered* (1682), in which Pierre is a principal character. **37 Beings of the Mind:** The creations of the poet or of the playwright. **46–47:** Cf. "In youth I wrote, because my mind was full,/ And now because I feel it growing dull" (*Don Juan,* XIV, x). **86:** The mother of Brasidas, the Lacedæmonian general, replied in this way, according to tradition, to those praising the memory of her son. **91–94:** The *Bucentaur* was the barge from which on Ascension Day the Doge of Venice, by dropping a ring into the sea, customarily "wed" the Adriatic. In 1797, the barge was broken by the French. **95 Lion:** The four bronze horses of the Church of St. Mark's, brought to Venice by the Doge Enrico Dandolo (1108–1205) after the fall of Constantinople (1204), had been removed to Paris in 1797 but were restored to Venice by the Austrians in 1815. **97–101:** An allusion to the public humiliation of Frederick Barbarossa before Pope Alexander III at Venice, in 1177. **106 Lauwine:** Avalanche. Byron used the word as a plural. **107–08:** "The reader will recollect the exclamation of the Highlanders, *'Oh, for one hour of Dundee!'* Henry Dandolo, when elected Doge, in 1192, was eighty-five years of age. When he commanded the Venetians at the taking of Constantinople, he was consequently ninety-seven years old" (Hobhouse's note). **111:** Pietro Doria, a Genoese Admiral who, according to tradition, refused to grant peace terms to the Venetians after the battle of Pola, in 1379, until the Genoese had put reins upon the bronze horses of St. Mark's; the Venetians would not surrender, and eventually they triumphed over the Genoese, after the death of Doria. **120:** "That is, the Lion of St. Mark, the standard of the republic, which is the origin of the word Pantaloon — Piantaleone, Pantaleon, Pantaloon" (Byron's note). Byron's etymology is unnecessarily ingenious: the Venetians were called "Pantaloni" and the character in their comedy assumed the name "pantalone" after St. Pantaleon (d. 305), patron of Venice. **124:** Candia, like Troy, was besieged for many years, falling to the Turks in 1669. **133 Thin streets:** By 1816 the Venetian population had dropped to little more than half of what it had been a century and a quarter before. **148:** Torquato Tasso (1544–95). **151–52 the Ocean queen . . . Ocean's children:** By the Treaty of Paris (3 May 1814), in which Great Britain participated, Venice had been returned to Austria. **158:** "Venice Preserved; Mysteries of Udolpho; The Ghost-Seer, or Armenian; The Merchant of Venice; Othello" (Byron's note). **172 Tannen:** Fir trees. **238 Friuli's mountains:** The Julian Alps, to the northeast of Venice, on the border of what today is Yugoslavia. **250:** The Brenta, a river of one hundred miles in length, flows into the lagoons of Venice. **271 he:** Francesco Petrarch (1304–74). **307–15:** The Este family came to power in Ferrara during the late twelfth century. The tragic second marriage of Duke Nicolo III is the subject of Byron's poem *Parisina* (1816). **316:** Tasso was patronized by Alfonso II, Duke of Ferrara, but he was also confined by the Duke to the madhouse of Sant' Anna from 1579 to 1586 — unjustly, it was long and erroneously believed. **339–40:** His *Gerusalemme Liberata* (1575) was attacked by both Nicolas Boileau-Despréaux (1636–1711) and the Cruscan Academy of Florence (founded 1582). **355:** Dante began his *Divina Commedia* about 1307, five years after his banishment from Florence. **357 the southern Scott:** Lodovico Ariosto (1474–1533). **361–62:** "Before the remains of Ariosto were removed from the Benedictine church to the library of Ferrara, his bust, which surmounted the tomb, was struck by lightning, and a crown of iron laurels melted away" (Hobhouse's note). **388 him:** Servius Sulpicius, writing to Cicero on the death of his daughter, recalls his course of travel, which is here described by Byron. **411 storm:** Austrian power overwhelming Italy. **431:** The power and the nobility of Florence rested upon her mercantile success. **433:** The Venus de'Medici. **450 prize:** The golden apple which Paris gave to Aphrodite. **478:** Santa Croce, which Byron once called "the Westminster Abbey of Italy," was built in the late thirteenth century. **484–88:** Michelangelo Buonarroti (1475–1564), Vittorio Alfieri (1749–1803), Galileo Galilei (1564–1642), Niccolò Machiavelli (1469–1527). **495:** The sculptor Antonio Canova (1757–1822). **498–99 The Bard of Prose . . . the Hundred Tales of Love:** Giovanni Boccaccio (1313–75) and the *Decameron* (1353). **505:** Dante died and was buried at Ravenna. **506:** According to one tradition, Scipio was buried at Liternum. **513 though rifled:** In 1630, supposedly by a group of Venetians. **514–15:** The tombstone of Boccaccio, buried in the Church of St. Michael and St. James, at Certaldo, was removed by local authorities in the late eighteenth century. **523–26:** Referring to the pageant ordered by the Emperor Tiberius, Byron recalled that at the funeral of Junia, the sister of Brutus (A.D. 22), the bust of Julius Cæsar's assassin was barred. But by its absence it was more remarkable. **532 Pyramid of precious stones:** The Medici Chapel, in the church of San Lorenzo. **551–52:** In 217 B.C., at Lake Trasimene, near Perugia, the Carthaginians lured the Romans into a trap and overwhelmingly defeated them. **563:** Some historians reported that an earthquake occurring at the same time was obscured by the fury of the battle. **586, 595:** The temple near the spring from which rises the river Clitumnus, in Umbria, converted in later times into a Christian church. **590:** An allusion to the belief that the rivers of certain streams can make white the cattle drinking their waters. **600:** Trout. **604: Genius of the place:** The river was personified as a god, hence the reason for the temple. **612 disgust:** The inability to enjoy nature. **613–39:** The falls of the Velino (Cascate delle Marmore), near Terni. **665:** Soracte is a mountain in the province of Rome. **707:** In 1780, the contents of the sarcophagus of the great-grandfather of Scipio Africanus were removed. **711:** An allusion to the various recorded occasions of flooding of the Tiber. **712:** Those groups, forces, and elements which have, in their various ways, besieged Rome. **740:** Lucius Cornelius Sulla (138–78 B.C.). **765:** Oliver Cromwell died in 1658, on 3 September, the same date on which he had defeated the Scots at Dunbar (1650) and forces of Charles II at Worcester (1651). **775 dread Statue:** Supposedly the same statue of Pompey at the base of which Cæsar fell. **785: She-wolf:** The bronze statue called the "Wolf of the Capitol." **796 things:** The men of earlier Rome, whom the men of the later Roman nations had once feared and now imitated with their blood-letting pursuit of glory. **800 one vain Man:** Napoleon. **856–57:** Though tyranny seems to beget tyranny, Freedom appears to find no continuity through "Champion" and "Child." **871 the base pageant:** The series of meetings and treaties, beginning with the Congress of Vienna (September 1815), by which the pre-Revolution tyranny was reestablished. **883 stern round tower:** The tomb of Cecilia Metella, wife of Marcus Licinius Crassus (115–53 B.C.), one of Rome's wealthiest men and the financial backer of the First Triumvirate. **927 his love or pride:** The two possible motivations for Crassus to erect the tomb. **963:** "The Palatine is one mass of ruins, particularly on the side towards the Circus Maximus. The very soil is formed of crumbled brickwork" (Byron's note). **981 golden roofs:** Of Nero's *Domus Aurea,* in the Palatine. **983 nameless column:** By the time Byron wrote this the identity of the column had been established by the uncovering of its base; it had been built in A.D. 608 in honor of Phocas, Emperor of the Eastern Empire (602–10). **989:** On the column of Trajan is a statue of St. Peter, and on that of Aurelius is the statue of St. Paul. **1000 the rock of Triumph:** The Temple of Jupiter Optimus Maximus, of which the precise location was not known. **1022:** Niccolo Gabrini Rienzi (1313–54). **1026**

Numa: Legendary king of Rome (seventh and eighth centuries B.C.). **1027:** The fountain nymph, after whom the Roman grotto was named; also, supposedly an adviser to King Numa. **1129 Upas:** A poisonous tree. **1144 Arches on arches:** The Colosseum. **1163:** Time adorns the ruin with foliage. **1180 ff:** In his appeal to Nemesis, to right the wrongs that he has suffered, the speaker is now fully identifiable with Byron contemplating the ruin of his marriage and his ostracism. **1222 to lie with silence:** The party of Lady Byron in the negotiations for the separation would not state its charges against Byron, thereby leaving the public mind open to conjecture. **1252 the Gladiator:** The statue "The Dying Gaul," in the Museum of the Capitol. **1275 the playthings of a crowd:** "When one gladiator wounded another, . . the wounded combatant dropped his weapon, and advancing to the edge of the arena, supplicated the spectators. If he had fought well, the people saved him; if otherwise, or as they happened to be inclined, they turned down their thumbs, and he was slain" (Hobhouse's note). **1297–99:** Attributed by Edward Gibbon to Anglo-Saxon pilgrims who came to Rome in the seventh or eighth century. **1324 ff:** These lines relate to the Roman legend of the daughter who kept her imprisoned father alive by giving him the milk of her breast. **1351:** Juno rejected the infant Hercules when he was placed at her breast, and the drops of milk that fell into space became the stars of the Milky Way. **1360 the Mole:** The Castle of San Angelo. **1369 the Dome:** St. Peter's. **1372 the Ephesian's miracle:** The ruins of the second Temple of Artemis, which Byron believed he had seen, were not uncovered until many years later. **1433 Laocöon's torture:** The statue in the Vatican here mentioned was in the palace of Titus and described by Pliny. **1441–42:** The Apollo Belvedere. **1468 the Pilgrim of my Song:** Harold, actually abandoned in the third canto. **1495–1503:** Princess Charlotte Augusta, the only daughter of the Prince Regent, died in childbirth, 6 November 1817. **1521 The husband of a year:** On 8 April 1795, the Prince of Wales had married Princess Caroline of Brunswick, but they were separated a year later. **1549–57:** Nemi is a village not far from Albano, whose lake is made from the crater of a presumably extinct volcano; hence Byron compared it with a coiled snake. **1574 Calpe's rock:** Gibraltar. **1575 Euxine:** Black Sea. **1576 Symplegades:** Two island rocks, one on either side of the strait where the Bosphorous joins the Black Sea. **1588 her:** Byron's sister, Mrs. Augusta Leigh. **1620 lay:** A solecism, "lie."

Maid of Athens, Ere We Part *Page 164*

Written in 1810; published as "Song" in the first edition of the first two cantos of *Childe Harold,* 1812. Theresa Macri (1797–1875) was the eldest of the three daughters of Theodora Macri, widow of an English vice-consul, in whose house Byron and Hobhouse lived during their visit to Athens from 25 December 1809 to 4 March 1810. See C. G. Brouzas, "Theresa Macri, the 'Maid of Athens,' 1797–1875," *West Virginia University Bulletin:*

Philological Papers, V (1947), 1–31; "Byron's Maid of Athens, Her Family and Surroundings," *Ibid.,* VII (1949), 1–65.

6: "Romaic expression of tenderness. If I translate it, I shall affront the gentlemen, as it may seem that I supposed they could not; and if I do not, I may affront the ladies. For fear of any misconstruction on the part of the latter, I shall do so, begging pardon of the learned. It means, 'My life, I love you!' which sounds very prettily in all languages, and is as much in fashion in Greece at this day as, Juvenal tells us, the two first words were amongst the Roman ladies, whose erotic expressions were all Hellenised" (Byron's note).

Lines to a Lady Weeping *Page 164*

Written and published in 1812, anonymously in the *Morning Chronicle* in March, then republished under Byron's name in the second edition of *The Corsair* (1814). At Carlton House on 22 February 1812, the Prince Regent expressed great agitation when he learned of the Whig leaders' reaction to his renunciation of their cause; aware of the intensity of her father's irritation, the Princess Charlotte suddenly began weeping. Expectedly, the incident filled the public press.

The Bride of Abydos. A Turkish Tale *Page 165*

Written in November and published in early December 1813. Only after publication, on 6 December, did Byron write in his journal that the title was somewhat inappropriate: "*She* is not a *bride,* only about to be one." The poem, nevertheless, remains one of the more striking examples, perhaps the most widely read, of Byron's early tales. The narrative itself, almost entirely concerned with action, develops from a viewpoint generally detached from those of the characters, who move on one plane of existence, in simple response to stimuli. The motifs in the poem, in terms of which the conflict sustaining the narrative might be conceived, are of Love and Death, with Zuleika representing the one and Giaffir the other, while Selim responds appropriately to each.

For further critical discussion of *The Bride of Abydos* and of Byron's early narratives, see the appropriate chapters or sections in the following: Karl Kroeber, *Romantic Narrative Art* (1960); Andrew Rutherford, *Byron: A Critical Study* (1961); William H. Marshall, *The Structure of Byron's Major Poems* (1962); Peter L. Thorslev, Jr., *The Byronic Hero: Types and Prototypes* (1962); Leslie A. Marchand, *Byron's Poetry: A Critical Introduction* (1965).

Epigraph: *Ae Fond Kiss,* 13–16.

Canto I. 8 Gúl: The rose. **144 Arab:** "The Turks abhor the Arabs (who return the compliment a hundredfold) even more than they hate the Christians" (Byron's note). **147 Houris' hymn:** The song of the nymphs of the Mohammedan paradise, who were supposedly endowed with everlasting beauty. **151 Peri:** In this sense, a beautiful being. **201–04:** "Carasman Oglou, or Kara Osman Oglou, is the principal landholder in Turkey; he governs Magnesia: those who, by a kind of feudal tenure, possess land on condition of service, are called Timariots: they serve as Spahis, according to the extent of territory, and bring a certain number into the field, generally cavalry" (Byron's note). **206 Bey Oglou:** A high-ranking chief. **211–14:** "When a Pacha is sufficiently strong to resist, the single messenger, who is always the first bearer of the order for his death, is strangled instead, and sometimes five or six, one after the other, on the same errand, by command of the refactory patient" (Byron's note). **235 Maugrabee:** "Moorish mercenaries" (Byron's note). **236 Delis:** "Bravos who form the forlorn hope of the cavalry, and always begin the action" (Byron's note). **239 Kislar:** In this sense, the head of the eunuchs guarding the harem. **248:** "A twisted fold of *felt* is used for scimitar practice by the Turks" (Byron's note). **251 Ollahs:** A Turkish battle cry. **270:** " 'Atar-gul,' ottar of roses. The Persian is the finest" (Byron's note). **288 Bulbul:** A Persian songbird, thus, metaphorically, any singer of sweet songs. **323 Azrael:** The angel of death. **358 Istakar:** "The treasures of the Pre-Adamite Sultans" (Byron's note). **374 Musselim:** "A governor, the next in rank after a Pacha" (Byron's note). **375 Egripo:** In his note Byron cited a proverbial belief that the Turks of Egripo were the worst of their race. **449:** " 'Tchocador' — one of the attendants who precedes a man of authority" (Byron's note).

Canto II. 483–501: The allusion in these lines is to the mythical lovers, Hero of Sestos and her lover Leander of Abydos; each night he swam the Hellespont to be with her, until he was drowned; thereafter, she cast herself into the sea. **509:** Homer. **527:** Achilles, killed by Paris. **529:** Ammon is an epithet for Zeus as worshipped in Egypt. **548:** Byron had in mind the production of a slight odor by the rubbing of amber. **551:** "The belief in amulets engraved on gems, or enclosed in gold boxes, containing scraps from the Koran, worn round the neck, wrist, or arm, is still universal in the East. The Koorsee (throne) verse in the second cap. of the Koran ["The Chapter of the Heifer," verse 257] describes the attributes of the Most High, and is engraved in this manner, and worn by the pious, as the most esteemed and sublime of all sentences" (Byron's note). **554:** The comboloio, which Byron described in his note as "a Turkish rosary," consists of ninety-eight beads. **563:** Shiraz, capital of the province of Fars in Persia, a celebrated source for the attar of roses. **588–89:** Apparently Byron himself did not believe that the Koran made to women no promise of salvation; in a note to the poem *The Giaour,* he called such a belief "vulgar error." **632 Galiongée:** "A Turkish sailor" (Byron's note). **671–72:** "The characters of all Turkish scimitars contain sometimes the name of the place of their manufacture, but more generally a text from the Koran, in letters of gold" (Byron's note). **679–80:** That Selim and Zuleika are made to be first cousins rather than half-siblings removed for the British public of 1813 any question of incest.

702: "Paswan Oglou [1758–1807], the rebel of Widdin; who, for the last years of his life, set the whole power of the Porte at defiance" (Byron's note). **714:** " 'Horse-tail' — the standard of a Pacha" (Byron's note). **839:** "The Turkish notions of almost all islands are confined to the Archipelago, the sea alluded to" (Byron's note). **862:** "Lambro Canzani [Lambros Katzones], a Greek famous for his efforts, in 1789–90, for the independence of his country. Abandoned by the Russians, he became a pirate, and the Archipelago was the scene of his enterprises" (Byron's note). Holding the rank of Major in the service of the Empress, Katzones commanded twelve vessels before his defeat, in May 1790, off the coast of the Morea; thereafter, he continued to sail under the Russian flag until war with Turkey was concluded by the Treaty of Jassy, on 9 January 1792. **866 Rayahs:** Those who pay the capitation tax levelled on the non-believing male population, thus for the Turks, Infidels. **871:** The Tartar was a wanderer. **873 Serais:** Inns. **891 Aden:** Mohammedan Paradise, Eden. **1100:** "A turban is carved in stone above the graves of *men* only" (Byron's note). **1109 Wul-wulleh:** "The death-song of the Turkish women. The 'silent slaves' are the men, whose notions of decorum forbid complaint in *public*" (Byron's note).

Ode to Napoleon Buonaparte *Page 194*

Written on 10 April and published anonymously on 16 April 1814. Rumors were rife, but it was not until the day after Byron composed the poem, 11 April 1814, that by the Treaty of Fontainebleau Napoleon abdicated and was banished to Elba. The poem illustrates Byron's ambivalence toward Napoleon, which remained to the end of his life.

Epigraphs: Juvenal, Liber IV, Satire X, lines 147–48: "Weigh [the ashes of] Hannibal: — how many pounds do you find in the greatest leader?" Gibbon, Chapter XXXVI. Julius Nepos, next to the last of the Roman Emperors of the West (474–75), fled from revolt into Dalmatia and lived at Salona until he was assassinated in 480.

46–47 He who . . . rebound: Milo of Crotona, the Greek athlete of perhaps the sixth century B.C., whose death, according to tradition, resulted from his attempt to rend a partially split tree, which, dropping the wedge that was in it, closed on Milo's hand and held him while the wolves devoured him. **55 The Roman:** Lucius Cornelius Sulla (138–78 B.C.), Roman general and dictator. **64 The Spaniard:** Charles V (1500–58), Holy Roman Emperor, who abdicated two years before his death and retired to a monastery in western Spain. **109–10 And she . . . bride:** The Empress Marie Louise (1791–1847), Napoleon's second wife, who, upon his abdication, took their son to Vienna. **118 thy sullen Isle:** Elba, where Napoleon remained until February 1815, landing in Cannes on 1 March. **125 Corinth's pedagogue:** Dionysius the Younger (fourth century B.C.), on his second banishment from Syracuse, fled to Corinth, where he opened a school. **127 Thou Timour:** An allusion to the traditional account of Tamerlane's confining the Sultan Bajazet I in a cage, where he might be viewed by all: here, Napoleon, once the Tamerlane of his own age, is now confined to a cage. **131 he of Babylon:** A solecism referring to Nebuchadrezzar II, who suffered from lycanthropy for a period. **132:** Rumors were prevalent, of which Byron was aware, that Napoleon had lost his faculties. **136 the thief of fire:** Prometheus. **150:** On 14 June 1800, Napoleon resoundingly defeated the Austrians at Marengo, a village in northern Italy.

She Walks in Beauty *Page 199*

Written in June 1814; published in *Hebrew Melodies,* in April 1815. Though supposedly conceived by Byron's friend Douglas Kinnaird, the volume called *Hebrew Melodies* — which is but partially made up of poems actually composed after Kinnaird's suggestion and far more secular than the title indicates — may reveal one of the temporary effects of Byron's engagement to the somewhat less worldly Anne Isabella Milbanke, in September 1814. In keeping with the original scheme, the poems were published with musical accompaniments by John Braham (1774–1856) and Isaac Nathan (1792–1864). See Joseph Slater, "Byron's *Hebrew Melodies,*" *Studies in Philology,* XLIX (1952), 75–94.

Attending a social affair on 11 June 1814, Byron saw for the first time his beautiful second cousin by marriage, Mrs. Robert John Wilmot, then in mourning, about whom he composed this poem the following day.

Oh! Snatched Away in Beauty's Bloom *Page 199*

Written probably in 1814; published in *Hebrew Melodies,* 1815.

5: In the West the cypress symbolizes death and mourning.

By the Rivers of Babylon We Sat Down and Wept *Page 200*

Written January 1813; published in *Hebrew Melodies,* 1815. The source is clearly *Psalm* cxxxvii, pointedly descriptive of the Babylonian Captivity, beginning: "By the rivers of Babylon, there we sat down, yea, we wept when we remembered Zion."

The Destruction of Sennacherib *Page 201*

Written in January 1815; published in *Hebrew Melodies,* 1815. Sennacherib was king of the Assyrians in the eighth and seventh centuries B.C. The source for the poem is *Isaiah,* xxxvii: 36, "Then the angel of the Lord went forth, and smote in the camp of the Assyrians a hundred and fourscore and five thousand: and when they arose early in the morning, behold, they *were* all dead corpses."

Stanzas for Music *Page 202*

Written in 1814; published in 1830. Byron sent the poem to Thomas Moore on 4 May 1814, but Moore held it until his own *Letters and Journals of Lord Byron: With Notices of His Life* (1830). Although Moore and Byron's later editor, Ernest Hartley Coleridge, seem to have been unaware of the fact, most recent biographers and critics believe that the person addressed in the poem was Augusta Leigh.

When We Two Parted *Page 202*

Written and published in 1816. Byron enclosed this poem in a letter to John Murray dated 16 February 1816, in which he thanked Murray for advising him of the successful libel suit of James Wedderburn Webster against the editor of the *Morning Chronicle,* who had linked the names of Lady Frances Webster and the Duke of Wellington. Byron had spent much time with the Websters in 1813, and he had been attracted to Lady Frances, especially since he felt a degree of contempt for her husband. But the picture in this poem and the emotion evoked are somewhat idealized, a fact that may assume new dimensions when it is recalled that Byron wrote the poem during the period between his wife's departure from 13 Piccadilly Terrace and the signing of the separation.

Fare Thee Well *Page 203*

Written 18 March and published 4 April 1816. These stanzas, addressed to Lady Byron in the period after her departure from their London home, were composed, so Byron claimed and Moore in his book recorded, with "the tears . . . falling fast over the paper as he wrote them." That this was a gesture of unparalleled histrionics, as is suggested by the fact that on the recovered first draft there are no tear-stains, will long be disputed, but the poem, hovering at the edge of pathos, has become an essential part of the Byron legend, a prelude to what Matthew Arnold was to call "the pageant of his bleeding heart" ("Stanzas from the Grande Chartreuse").

34: Augusta Ada Byron (1815–52).

The Prisoner of Chillon *Page 204*

Written in late June and published in December 1816. As Byron conceived of the poem and particularly as he made clear in the prefatory sonnet and in a note written somewhat after the poem, the speaker as a champion of human liberty was to be identified with François Bonivard (1496–1570), the Savoyard religious leader imprisoned by Duke Charles III of Savoy in a subterranean dungeon of the Castle of Chillon (1530–36). In reality, Bonivard was far less committed to principle than Byron believed him to be, though he was probably somewhat more than the amoral opportunist caught between the forces of Catholicism and the Reformation described by some historians. The poem itself, a dramatic monologue, transcends the limits of particular historical association, and, in fact, the speaker, while voicing Renaissance and modern man's aspiration for freedom, becomes a striking instance of the alienation and reorientation characteristic of the Romantic mind, here portrayed with significant psychological realism.

For further critical discussion of *The Prisoner of Chillon,* see my book *The Structure of Byron's Major Poems* (1962), pp. 82–96.

17: Actually, Bonivard was one of three brothers. **168:** That Bonivard's father was "martyred" is of uncertain authority. **230 a selfish death:** Suicide. **236–38 Among the stones . . . shrubless crags within the mist:** In the fashion of some Renaissance thinkers, the speaker expresses himself in terms of an essentially Medieval construct, the concept of the Chain of Being, emphasizing that in his desolation he has sunk from the human through the animal and vegetable levels to that of mere extension, thereby losing all sense — spatial, temporal, and ultimately moral. The quality of his alienation is characteristic of the Romantic mind and is reflected in a number of major literary works, such as Samuel Taylor Coleridge's *Rime of the Ancient Mariner* (1798) and Alfred Tennyson's *In Memoriam* (1850). **339 the white-walled distant town:** Villeneuve. **341–50:** "Between the entrances of the Rhone and Villeneuve, not far from Chillon, is a very small island; the only one I could perceive in my voyage round and over the lake, within its circumference. It contains a few trees (I think not above three), and from its singleness and diminutive size has a peculiar effect upon the view" (Byron's note). **370:** Bonivard was liberated by the Bernese, in 1536.

The Dream *Page 214*

Written and published in 1816. A concise and somewhat idealized history of Byron's emotional development, this poem emphasizes his recollections of Mary Ann Chaworth, his distant cousin and neighbor, with whom he was in love in 1803–04. Two years later, in August 1805, Mary married John Musters.

46 The Boy had fewer summers: Byron was Mary's junior by two years. The date of this first scene is presumably 1803, when Byron was fifteen. **64 Even as a brother:** Thomas Medwin recorded Byron's recollection: "I now began to fancy myself a man, and to make love in earnest. . . . But the ardour was all on my side. I was serious: she was volatile. She liked me as a younger brother, and treated and laughed at me as a boy" (*Journal of the Conversations of Lord Byron: Noted during a Residence with His Lordship at Pisa, in the Years 1821 and 1822* [1824], pp. 59–60). **67–68 Herself . . . time-honoured race:** In 1661, William, third Lord Byron, married Elizabeth, a daughter of John, Viscount Chaworth, of Ireland. A century later, in 1765, William, the fifth Lord, killed in a duel his cousin and neighbor William Chaworth, of Annesley Hall, from whom Mary was descended. Mary Chaworth's father died during her chidhood, but as heiress she continued to live at Annesley Hall, with her mother and, later, her stepfather, a Mr. Clarke. **76 ancient mansion:** Annesley Hall. Byron's parting from Mary took place in August 1804. **104:** Actually, Byron visited Mary and her husband in early November 1808. See the poem "Well! Thou Art Happy." **105–25:** During Byron's travels in the East, the recollected scene of a caravan halted at noon, near a fountain. **126–43:** In actuality, Mary's cause for grief was the faithlessness of her husband, John Musters, from whom she separated in 1814, though they were subsequently reconciled. In late 1813, Mary wrote Byron, asking him to visit her, and in the following year she sent him many more letters, but he preferred the sentimental recollection to what he suspected was the reality, and he managed to avoid Mary Chaworth-Musters during his remaining two years in England. **148 The Starlight of his Boyhood:** At the time of his infatuation with Mary, Byron supposedly called her his "bright morning star of Annesley." **153–58:** The distracted appearance of the bridegroom described here is not unlike what John Cam Hobhouse, Byron's best man, recorded of Byron's behavior immediately before and during his wedding (2 January 1815). **167–76:** In the autumn of 1814, Mary suffered a mental breakdown, though she recovered within a few months. Byron, to whom she had written before her collapse, heard of her illness, expressed concern, but made no attempt to visit her. **191:** Mithridates VI (ca. 163–32 B.C.), King of Pontus, who, fearing treachery, is supposed to have raised his own tolerance for poison by administering to himself gradually increasing doses; later, when he wished to commit suicide by poison, he was unable to do so.

Darkness *Page 219*

Written and published in 1816. Byron used the theme of earth's sole human survivor, which had an obvious appeal to the Romantic imagination, in a far more devastating way than did Thomas Campbell in his poem "The Last Man" (1823) or Mary Shelley in her novel *The Last Man* (1826). In the one occurs an affirmation of faith, and in the other the protagonist wanders in solitude through a pestilence-ridden world, but in Byron's poem the universe itself is disintegrating, without discernible purpose or meaning.

50 clung: Now dialectical, the past tense of "shrivel."

Prometheus *Page 221*

Written and published in 1816.

Monody on the Death of the Right Hon. R. B. Sheridan *Page 223*

Written and published in 1816. Byron met Richard Brinsley Sheridan in the spring of 1813, and during his remaining years in England he was often in Sheridan's company. Born 30 October 1751, Sheridan died, supposedly in squalor, on 7 July 1816. Byron, immediately asked to write a poem on the occasion, completed the "Monody" by 18 July and dispatched it to Douglas Kinnaird two days later. The poem was spoken at the Drury Lane Theatre in September 1816.

41–46: Elected to Parliament in 1780, Sheridan attained fame as one of its major orators. His most memorable speech, lasting more than five hours, and engendering such excitement that the House had to be adjourned, was that of 7 February 1787, in which he supported the charges made against Warren Hastings (1732–1818) for his handling of Indian affairs. **47 And here, oh! here:** The Drury Lane Theatre, where some of Sheridan's plays first appeared. **63–64:** Here Byron was making an indirect defense of Sheridan against the accusations that had become almost legend. **80:** There was extensive disagreement among Sheridan's friends and biographers concerning the degree of poverty in which he died. **103 the wondrous *Three*:** "Fox — Pitt — Burke" (Byron's note).

Stanzas to Augusta *Page 225*

Written and published in 1816. On 28 August 1816 — at the time that Byron gave Shelley the manuscripts of the third canto of *Childe Harold, The Prisoner of Chillon,* and other poems, to be delivered to John Murray in London — he wrote the publisher: "There is in the volume — an epistle to Mrs. Leigh — on which I should wish her to have her opinion consulted — before the publication; if she objects, of course *omit* it." Murray visited Augusta, who, after some hesitation, allowed the poem to be published. It appeared in *The Prisoner of Chillon, and Other Poems* (and thereafter until 1830) as "Stanzas to — ." In *The Works of Lord Byron* (6 vols. Murray, 1831), the poem for the first time carried its present title.

Manfred: A Dramatic Poem *Page 227*

Written during the latter part of 1816 and in early 1817; published in June 1817. In some of the contemporary reviews and in subsequent criticism, the question of the antecedent to *Manfred* has loomed large. Byron denied that he had read Christopher Marlowe's *Doctor Faustus,* and he claimed that his only contact with Goethe's *Faust* had been in the late summer of 1816, when Matthew Gregory Lewis, visiting Byron at Diodati, orally translated some of the scenes from the play. But the situation which Byron explored in *Manfred* had far more persistent significance for the advanced minds of his own time than propositions about literary influence suggest: Manfred has passed to the ends of knowledge, to the point at which the basis for all earlier belief and hope has been dissolved, but in the wake of such disorientation has come neither wisdom nor new faith. His situation is cast in the images of guilt, but the guilt can be taken as a violation of the limits of his own nature. He can embrace neither the good nor the evil, neither the Witch of the Alps nor Arimanes, and at the moment of crisis, as he faces the recalled but insubstantial spirit of Astarte, he finds neither forgiveness nor condemnation by which he might give dimension to his life and reincorporate himself in mankind's moral tradition. At the end of the work, as Manfred dies, he is sublime in his alienation, a figure significantly foretelling the protagonist of the twentieth century.

For further discussion of *Manfred,* see the following: Samuel C. Chew, *The Dramas of Lord Byron: A Critical Study* (1915; 1964); Bertrand Evans, "Manfred's Remorse and Dramatic Tradition," *Publications of the Modern Language Association,* LXII (1947), 752–73; Maurice J. Quinlan, "Byron's *Manfred* and Zoroastrianism," *Journal of English and Germanic Philology,* LVII (1958), 726–38; Andrew Rutherford, *Byron: A Critical Study* (1961); William H. Marshall, *The Structure of Byron's Major Poems* (1962); Ward Pafford, "Byron and the Mind of Man: *Childe Harold III–IV* and *Manfred,*" *Studies in Romanticism,* I (1962), 105–27; Peter J. Thorslev, Jr., *The Byronic Hero: Types and Prototypes* (1962); Leslie A. Marchand, *Byron's Poetry: A Critical Introduction* (1965).

Epigraph. "There are . . . your philosophy": *Hamlet,* I, v, 166–67.

Act I, Scene I. 147: If the Spirits are projections of Manfred's own mind rather than supernatural beings invoked, as some have believed (offering an explanation in terms of psychology rather than of magic), then they cannot do for him what he is unable to do for himself, since their nature is limited by whatever may be the dimensions of his mind. If, on the other hand, the Spirits are drawn from a realm of being outside earthly existence, their inability to aid Manfred merely emphasizes how he is representative of the human dilemma: through reason and imagination man can aspire, but the limitations imposed upon him prevent him from attaining the object of his aspiration. **251 Thyself to be thy proper Hell:** Cf. Act III, Scene 1, 69–78. Also, cf. Mephistophilis' speech in Christopher Marlowe's *Doctor Faustus,* v, 124–26: "Hell hath no limits, nor is circumscribed / In one self place, for where we are is hell, / And where hell is there must we ever be"; *Paradise Lost,* IV, 20–23: "The Hell within him, for within him Hell / He brings, and round about him, nor from Hell / One step no more then from himself can fly / By change of place."

Act I, Scene II. 40 Half dust, half deity: Manfred's summation of the causes for the human dilemma. **99:** On 2 September 1806 the slide of the Rossberg occurred, covering three villages and part of a fourth and killing more than four hundred persons. **111 guilty blood:** A suicide necessarily dies outside the state of grace, according to Christian belief.

Act II, Scene I. 24–27: The first of the allusions to incest in the play, these lines drew the censure of critics in Byron's day and at least the attention of biographers in our own. See also Act II, Scene II, 105–17; Act II, Scene IV, 117–23; Act III, Scene III, 42–47. **51–52:** The Chamois Hunter measures time, like other aspects of being, in absolute and spatial terms, whereas Manfred, who can of course comprehend such traditional measurement, ultimately conceives of reality in internal or psychological terms.

Act II, Scene II. 6–7: *Revelations,* vi: 8. **92–93:** "The philosopher Jamblicus. The story of the raising of Eros and Anteros may be found in his life by Eunapius" (Byron's note). **158 ff:** The point of these lines is that Manfred, having pursued analytic knowledge to the point that he has destroyed his faith in all realities outside of himself without finding a significant substitute for that faith, is unable to swear fealty to any other being; if he were able to do so, he would thereby not be in need of the very help which he seeks from the other being. The Witch of the Alps and Arimanes, both of whom demand but do not receive Manfred's obeisance, represent different aspects of being, through commitment to which man might hope to escape the human dilemma. **181–91:** Consulting the Witch of Endor before the battle of Gilboa, in which he was killed, Saul received from the spirit of Samuel a prophecy of his own death. Pausanias, the King of Sparta, asking forgiveness of the spirit of his would-be mistress, Cleonice, for his accidental killing of her, received from her not pardon but a prevision of his own death. In the case of Manfred, it is not to be the spirits of the lower world but Astarte who, offering him neither forgiveness nor condemnation, releases him from all motivation, either hope or guilt, thereby making the death that she foretells psychologically feasible for him.

Act II, Scene IV. Arimanes: Analogous to Ahriman, who, in Zoroastrianism, is the principle of evil, in perpetual conflict with Ormazd, the principle of good. As the one who evokes the spirit of Astarte he is not so much the principle of evil as the lord of the lower world, or Hades, the realm of the dead, thus comparable to Pluto. **83 Astarte:** The name is derived from Astaroth, the Phoenician goddess of fertility and sexual love, identifiable with Aphrodite.

Act III, Scene I. 13 "Kalon": Beauty. **19:** The Abbey of St. Maurice, near Villeneuve, in Switzerland, was founded in the fourth century. **47 I come to save, and not destroy:** The role of the Abbot may clearly recall that of the Chamois Hunter, in attempting to save Manfred from himself. It is structurally significant in the play that Manfred encounters the Hunter early in the action and the Abbot later, with the appearance of Astarte intervening, for, though both adhere to the same cosmological position, the Abbot is far more sophisticated than the Hunter in his use of argument and brings to his words the authority of the Church and the Western philosophic tradition, thereby posing to Manfred an intellectual challenge for which, by contemplation and experience, he must be made ready. **88 Rome's sixth Emperor:** Nero, who was declared a public enemy by the Senate. **128 Simoom:** A dry, violent desert wind, filled with dust and dangerous to life.

Act III, Scene IV. 92–94: The Abbot refuses to recognize the spirits of evil for entirely orthodox reasons, the doctrine that evil has no existence but appears to be and to exercise its function only in the absence of good. Manfred refuses them recognition because of his moral alienation: he is unable to affirm the reality of any values, either good or evil.

So We'll Go No More A-Roving *Page 262*

Written in 1817; published in 1830. These lines were first part of a letter dated 28 February 1817 which Byron wrote to Thomas Moore, who published the poem many years later in his *Letters and Journals of Lord Byron: With Notices of His Life.* "At present, I am on the invalid regimen myself," Byron wrote Moore, in a paragraph prefatory to the poem. "The Carnival — that is, the latter part of it, and sitting up late o' nights, had knocked me up a little. But it is over, — and it is now Lent, with all its abstinence and sacred music." Ash Wednesday was on 19 February and Easter on 6 April 1817. Byron's poem echoed, consciously or otherwise, a Scottish air ("And we'll gang nae mair a roving / Sae late into the nicht") published in Herd's *Ancient and Modern Scots Songs* in 1776 (see James A. S. McPeek, "A Note on 'So We'll Go No More a-Roving,'" *Modern Language Notes,* XLVI [1931], 118–19).

The Lament of Tasso *Page 262*

Written in April and published in July 1817. Passing through Ferrara on his way to Rome, Byron visited the Hospital of Sant' Anna, where Torquato Tasso (1544–95) had been confined from 1579 to 1586, and almost at once he began writing this poem. "As misfortune has a greater interest for posterity, and little or none for the contemporary, the cell where Tasso was confined . . . attracts a more fixed attention than the residence or the monument of Ariosto [which he also visited] — at least it had this effect on me," Byron wrote in the Advertisement to his poem. Accepting the tradition that the Duke Alfonso II (1533–97) of Ferrara had Tasso confined to the madhouse because of the poet's infatuation with Leonora d'Este, the Duke's sister, Byron conceived of Tasso as the sensitive being persecuted by his own unfeeling society. Subsequent research has revealed that Tasso's political intrigues and emotional outbursts, rather than the Duke's schemes, brought about his confinement, but an altered historical view should not adversely affect an estimate of the poem, which is cast as an interior monologue and sustained by the ironic interplay between the speaker's point of view and the situation in which he has been placed. Tasso's reactions and judgments, with their inconsistencies and subtleties, become the measure of all things in a world that is removed emotionally as well as physically from the larger world of ordinary men.

21–26: Tasso's *Gerusalemme Liberata,* finished in 1575 and published in 1580, is an epic concerning the capture of Jerusalem during the Crusades.
69–73 There be some . . . the lust of doing ill: The guards, driven by cruelty, subservience to the Duke and his orders, or simple officiousness.

To Thomas Moore *Page 268*

Written in April 1816 and July 1817; published in 1821. The poem constitutes part of a letter which, at Venice, Byron wrote to Moore on 10 July

1817. "This should have been written fifteen months ago — the first stanza was," he remarked, recalling the time of the separation from Lady Byron and his departure from England, when Moore was among the few who had stood by him.

Beppo *Page 269*

Written in September and October 1817; published in February 1818. The model for this work was the mock-heroic poem of John Hookham Frere (1769–1846) entitled *Prospectus and Specimen of an Intended National Work, by William and Robert Whistlecraft* (1817), itself based upon an Italian verse form and type of satiric poem most clearly identified with Luigi Pulci (1432–84). The *ottava rima* (with its rhyme scheme: a, b, a, b, a, b, c, c) was to be used in *Don Juan* and *The Vision of Judgment,* which, with *Beppo,* represent Byron's supreme achievement as an ironist. The rhymes themselves are frequently contrived, or even forced (as in lines 39–40, 43–45, 63–64, 223–24), displaying an ironic sense that undercuts the speaker's pretended purpose in telling his story; puns are frequent, and the *double entendre,* especially that based on the language of the street, abounds. The story itself, ultimately with little meaning or cohesiveness, is essentially an amusing device for sustaining continuity during the speaker's digressions. The protagonist is without seriousness or substance, an amusing fellow given his identity primarily because of the exigencies of rhyme ("Aleppo" and "Beppo"), whose experiences occur in a world that seems to be without firm moral order. He is a kind of forerunner to the so-called "anti-hero" of the twentieth century, though he has been conceived and developed with a sense of irony and a warmth not always present in the works of more recent times.

The history of the composition of the poem, based upon a study of the manuscript revisions, appears in Truman Guy Steffan, "The Devil a Bit of Our *Beppo,*" *Philological Quarterly,* XXXII (1953), 154–71. For critical consideration of the poem, see the appropriate chapters in Claude M. Fuess, *Byron as a Satirist in Verse* (1912; 1964); Andrew Rutherford, *Byron: A Critical Study* (1961); William H. Marshall, *The Structure of Byron's Major Poems* (1962); Leslie A. Marchand, *Byron's Poetry: A Critical Introduction* (1965).

Epigraph: The "Annotation" cited by Byron is from Samuel Ayscough, *The Dramatic Works of William Shakespeare, with Explanatory Notes* (1807), p. 242. In the original the word "licentiousness" occurs where Byron used "dissoluteness."

30 Phlegethon: The mythical river of Hades composed of fire rather than water. **35 in Monmouth-street, or in Rag Fair:** Known before Byron's time as centers for the sale of second-hand clothes. **42 "farewell to flesh":** Italian, "Carnevale." **95–96 his Son, and Wife, And self:**

Actually, Georgio Barbarelli, or "Georgione" (1478–1511), was not married. **112 the lost Pleiad seen no more below:** The seven daughters of Atlas, who were changed into stars. **117:** Carlo Goldoni (1707–93), Italian comic dramatist. **136 "Cavalier Servente":** Among the Italian aritocracy in Byron's era, the socially accepted lover of a married woman. **154:** In reality, the Rialto is an island in Venice, not the bridge (*Il ponte di Rialto*), with which, by an abbreviation, the English have tended to identify it. **195 pratique:** Clearance given a ship after quarantine or the receipt of a clean bill of health. **200 Beppo:** The nickname (Joe) for Giuseppe (Joseph). **246 sock and buskin:** Comedy and tragedy. **248 "seccatura":** Tiresomeness or thing, a word from one or more in the audience indicating disapproval. **318 His is no sinecure:** In a letter to Richard Belgrave Hoppner (1786–1872), English Consul at Venice, dated 31 January 1820, Byron commented upon his own duties as *Cavalier Servente* to the Countess Guiccioli: "I am drilling very hard to learn how to double a shawl, and should succeed to admiration if I did not always double it the wrong side out; and then I sometimes confuse and bring away two, so as to put all the *Serventi* out, besides keeping their *Servite* in the cold till every body can get back their property." **337 becaficas:** Plural variant of "beccafico," a songbird, especially the garden warbler, which feeds on fruit (literally, "figpecker") and, especially when it is well fed in the autumn, is esteemed by the Italians as a delicacy. **363:** Raphael (1483–1520) died of overwork and of malaria. **368:** Antonio Canova (1757–1822), Italian sculptor. **369:** William Cowper, *The Task,* II, 206. **411–12 And take for rhyme . . . Walker's Lexicon unravels:** Of the two major works of John Walker (1732–1807), it is likely that Byron here refers to the *Rhyming Dictionary* (1775) rather than the even more successful *Critical Pronouncing Dictionary* (1791). **445 Mrs. Boehm's masquerade:** Occurring on 16 June 1817, at Mrs. Boehm's residence, in St. James's Square, and reported the following day in the *Morning Chronicle.* If Byron did not know the hostess, he did know some of the guests listed. **457 Ridotto:** A public entertainment, with music and dancing and perhaps masquerade, originating in Italy. **461 Vauxhall:** A public pleasure resort in London, which existed from 1661 to 1859. **527–28:** *Macbeth,* IV, i, 112–18. **543:** William Wilberforce (1759–1833) and Sir Samuel Romilly (1757–1818), British reformers. **575 *Botherby*:** A reference to William Sotheby (1757–1833), author of the epic *Saul* (1807). Byron had made negative reference to him in *English Bards and Scotch Reviewers,* line 818. **603:** Walter Scott (1771–1832), Samuel Rogers (1763–1855), and Thomas Moore (1779–1852). **624:** A presumed allusion to Lady Byron's interest in mathematics. **685 Bow-street gem'men:** The Bow Street Runners, the precursors to Scotland Yard, were appointed in 1805 and attached to the Bow Street Court. **759 polacca:** A three-masted merchant vessel, which was once abundant in the eastern Mediterranean. **768 Cape Bonn:** The northern point of Tunisia.

Mazeppa *Page 292*

Written in late 1818; published in June 1819. Ivan Stepanovich Mazepa-Koledinsky (1644?–1709), a leader or hetman of the Cossacks, who, with King Charles XII of Sweden, fled after the battle of Pultowa (8 July 1709) and escaped to Turkey, was the subject of Byron's poem. But Byron knew little more of Mazeppa than the legend of his mad ride recorded by Voltaire in his *Histoire de Charles XII* (1730), from which Byron quoted in his Advertisement in the first edition: "An intrigue which he had in his youth with the wife of a Polish gentleman having been discovered, the husband forced him to lie totally naked on a ferocious horse and sent him forth in that state. The horse, which was from the Ukrainian countryside, carried Mazeppa there, half dead from fatigue and hunger. Some peasants rescued him; he remained a long time among them" (my translation). But Byron's achievement in the poem transcends the question of the fullness of his knowledge, for the old Mazeppa — telling his King the story of his own survival of a time of horror in his youth, that he might show reason to hope for their survival of the present ordeal as the enemy troops search through the night for them — attains a human quality that is at once noble and pathetic. The ultimate irony of Mazeppa's attempt, perhaps as representative of the human situation, becomes apparent only in the final line of the poem.

For further discussion of the historical background of the poem, see Lydia Holubnychy, "Mazepa in Byron's Poem and in History," *Ukrainian Quarterly,* XV (1959), 336–45; and for some further critical comments, see my own article "A Reading of Byron's *Mazeppa,*" *Modern Language Notes,* LXXVI (1961), 120–24 (largely republished in *The Structure of Byron's Major Poems* [1962]).

1: At the Battle of Pultowa, in the northern Ukraine, on 8 July 1709, the Russians, under the Emperor Peter the Great, defeated the Swedes, under Charles XII. **9:** The time of Napoleon's invasion of Russia, in 1812. **16 The wounded Charles:** The Swedish monarch had sustained a wound in the foot. **23 Gieta:** A colonel in the Swedish army, who, according to Voltaire (*Histoire de Charles XII*), when the King's horse was killed beneath him, though "wounded and losing all of his own blood, he gave him his own." **101–04:** Bucephalus was the war horse of Alexander the Great, hence by generalization, any war horse. **116 Borysthenes:** The Dniéper River. **128–29:** John II Casimir (1609–72), King of Poland from 1648 until 1668; a Jesuit and a Cardinal, he was absolved from his vows when he became King, though after he gave up the throne he went to France as Abbé de Saint-Germain. **155 a certain Palatine:** A Lord Falbowski. **157:** Salt mines constitute a major form of Poland's wealth. **664 *werst:*** A Russian measure, equalling 1.0668 kilometres or 3510 feet. **859:** The King and Mazeppa, after a perilous flight, received asylum in Turkey.

The Prophecy of Dante *Page 312*

Written in June 1819; published with the drama *Marino Faliero,* in April 1821. In an adaptation of the *terza rima* of Dante's *Commedia* (with the rhyme scheme: aba, bcb, cdc, ded), the poem offers hope for eventual Italian unity and liberty, voiced by the exiled Florentine poet, with whom, for personal as well as literary reasons, Byron was deeply sympathetic. "The reader is requested to suppose that Dante addresses him in the interval between the conclusion of the *Divina Commedia* and his death, and shortly before the latter event," Byron wrote in his Preface. Here he also foretold that if his four cantos were approved, he would "continue the poem in various other cantos to its natural conclusion in the present age." The poem was approved, but Byron did not continue, sacrificing nothing, for in its present form it is meaningful and integrated, moving to an intellectual conclusion and an emotional climax in the fourth canto.

Epigraph: Thomas Campbell, *Lochiel's Warning,* 55–56.

Dedication. 1 Lady: The Countess Teresa Guiccioli, whom Byron visited in Ravenna in June 1819 and at whose suggestion he wrote the poem. **5 Runic:** Northern. **9 of Beauty and of Youth:** Teresa's year of birth was probably 1800.

Canto I. 1–2 Once more . . . forgotten: Dante alludes to his imaginary journey in the *Commedia.* **8–9 that place/Of lesser torment:** Purgatory. **11:** "The reader is requested to adopt the Italian pronunciation of Beatricē, sounding all the syllables" (Byron's note). **28–30:** In *La Vita Nuova,* Dante recorded seeing Beatricē for the first time during his tenth year. **68 forfeit to the fire:** The Florentines condemned Dante, on 27 January 1302, to a fine of 8000 lire and banishment for two years, but on 11 March they decreed that if he were to fall into their hands he would be burned. **76:** Dante is buried at Ravenna. **90:** Dante was a Guelph partisan but was banished as a result of factional strife among the Florentine Guelphs. **104–05:** During the Civil War in Rome, Gaius Marius (155?–86 B.C.), first defeated by Sulla, fled by plunging into the marsh of Minturnae and was later barred from Carthage. For Dante, Marius is a happy choice for comparison: he later returned to Rome in triumph over his enemies. **172 that fatal She:** Gemma Donati, Dante's wife, who bore him seven children. There is no authority for the belief in Dante's unhappy marriage, but the possibility would have obvious appeal to Byron.

Canto II. 34 the banished Ghibelline: In their exile the "White" Guelphs made an alliance with the Ghibellines. This act, in effect, seemed to bear out the charge which had been made by the "Black" faction of the Florentine Guelphs, that the "Whites" were Ghibelline enemies of the state. **90:** The Count Ugolino della Gherardesca (1220?–89), celebrated in the *Divina Commedia* (*Inferno,* XXXIII), a Guelph leader imprisoned in Pisa in 1288 and allowed to starve. **93 the traitor Prince's banner:** Charles IV, Constable of Bourbon and Count of Montpensier (1490–1527), leader of Spanish and German mercenaries, was killed when his troops entered Rome, on 6 May 1527; Rome was then sacked and the Pope, Clement VII, captured. **98 Brennus:** Supposed Gallic chieftain of the fourth century B.C., who attacked and burned Rome. **108 Cambyses' host:** Sent against the Ammonians by Cambyses II of Persia, this army perished in the desert. **114 Those who overthrew proud Xerxes:** The Greeks.

Canto III. 47 Discoverers . . . their name: Christopher Columbus (1451–1506) and Amerigo Vespucci (1451–1512). **59 Avernus:** A deep lake in Campania, Italy, from which the rising vapors were supposedly lethal to the birds flying above. **100 he, their Prince:** Francesco Petrarch (1304–74). **110 The first:** Lodovico Ariosto (1474–1533). **119 The second:** Torquato Tasso (1544–95). **139:** Tasso was confined as a madman to the Hospital of Sant' Anna, in Ferrara, from 1579 to 1586. **145:** Duke Alfonso II (1533–97) of Ferrara, Tasso's patron, who later ordered his confinement. **149–50 his compeer, The Bard of Chivalry:** Ariosto.

Canto IV. 33 transfigurated: Now a rare form for "transfigure." **42:** Apelles was a Greek painter of the fourth century B.C., Phidias a sculptor of the fifth century B.C. **50–51 into heaven shall soar A Dome:** The dome of St. Peter's was completed in 1590. **57 the bold Architect:** Michelangelo Buonarroti (1475–1564). **61 the Hebrew:** Michelangelo's statue of Moses, in the Church of St. Pietro-in-Vincoli. **64:** Michelangelo's painting "The Last Judgment," in the Sistine Chapel. **68–69:** The *Divina Commedia* is divided into three parts, reflecting the three phases of the poet's journey: the *Inferno,* the *Purgatorio,* the *Paradiso.* **75:** The cedar traditionally represents nobility and incorruptibility. **85–90 who but take her for a toy . . . his labours, and his soul to boot:** "See the treatment of Michel Angelo by Julius II, and his neglect by Leo X" (Byron's note). **124:** The tradition that particular evils were born of the woman Sin raped by her own son Death, reflected in Milton's *Paradise Lost,* II, 777–802, dramatizes Dante's assertion that evil begets evil and survives in endless particulars. **141 "What . . . People?":** A translation of the opening of one of Dante's letters to the people of Florence.

The Vision of Judgment *Page 327*

Written between May and October 1821; published 1822. Culminating a feud of some years' standing between Robert Southey and himself, Byron wrote this poem as a travesty of Southey's official composition as Poet Laureate on the death of George III on 29 January 1820. Southey's *A Vision of Judgment,* published 11 April 1821, records as a dream-vision the presumed apotheosis of the late King, carrying him past his silent accusers (such as John Wilkes) and his earthly opponents now turned absolvers (such as George Washington) to the throne of Grace. In reality, it is a work displaying far less taste and restraint than Byron's travesty, though John Murray, to whom Byron sent his own poem in October 1821, hesitated to publish the later poem, fearing legal repercussions. Murray had *The Vision of Judgment* set in type, and Byron corrected proofs, but by the summer of 1822, after Leigh Hunt had come to Italy to edit a literary journal in which Byron and Shelley and he were to publish their works, the travesty of Southey remained unpublished. Byron directed Murray to turn over to John Hunt, Leigh's brother who was to print the new journal in London, the corrected proofs and the Preface to the poem, which Byron had written to make clear that Southey and not George III was the object of his irony. Murray gave Hunt either the manuscript or a copy, so that *The Vision of Judgment* appeared in the first number of *The Liberal,* on 15 October 1822, without the supposedly mitigating Preface and corrections. In December, John Hunt as publisher of Byron's poem was indicted for libel against the memory of George III, and thirteen months later, on 15 January 1824, he was convicted. The fact that the fine, imposed the following June and paid out of Byron's estate, was merely £100 has been taken as evidence of a major step toward British freedom of the press. Whatever the historical implications of the situation might be, it is clear that Byron, substituting the *ottava rima* of the Italian satiric tradition for Southey's hexameters and apparently missing none of the opportunities with which Southey had provided him, wrote the poem in whose shadow Southey's official utterance has maintained a dubious fame.

For a fuller treatment of the history of the composition and publication of *The Vision of Judgment,* see my book *Byron, Shelley, Hunt, and* The Liberal (1960). For critical discussion of the poem, see the appropriate chapters in Claude M. Fuess, *Lord Byron as a Satirist in Verse* (1912; 1964), and Andrew Rutherford, *Byron: A Critical Study* (1961).

Title. Quevedo: Francisco Gomez de Quevedo y Villegas (1580–1645), Spanish prose satirist. **THE AUTHOR OF "WAT TYLER":** Southey, who wrote this radical drama in 1794; it was published without his permission in 1817.

Epigraph: *The Merchant of Venice,* IV, i, 223, 341. The first line is spoken by Shylock, the second by Gratiano.

5: France at the beginning of the Revolution. **48 both Generals:** Napoleon and Arthur Wellesley, first Duke of Wellington (1769–1852). **57–58:** King George III died on 29 January 1820. **60 nor mental nor external sun:** In the last years of his life, George was deranged and blind. By the Regency Act of 1811, his son the Prince of Wales (to become George IV) was created Regent and ruled in his father's place. **92 German will:** The will of George I, the first Hanoverian King, was hidden by his son, George II, on his ascension in 1727. **94–96:** George III married, in 1761, and was faithful to the Princess Charlotte Sophia of Mecklenburg-Stretlitz; in 1795 his son married the Princess Caroline of Brunswick, but he separated from her soon thereafter. **142 the last we**

saw here: Louis XVI of France, guillotined 21 January 1793. **148 A claim . . . my own:** According to tradition, St. Peter was martyred at Rome in A.D. 67, during the reign of Nero. **156–60:** By tradition, St. Bartholomew was first flayed, then crucified. **216:** An allusion to the record of the voyage made by Sir William Edward Parry (1790–1855) in search of the Northwest Passage. See his *Voyages in 1819–20* (1821), p. 135. **224:** Joanna Southcott (1750–1814), author of the prophetic *Book of Wonders* (1814), declared that on 19 October 1814 she would give birth to a second messiah. Instead, she died two months later of brain disease. The word "conceptions" in the preceding line may therefore be an intended pun. **256 "Champ Clos":** Tourney-ground. **257–64:** An allusion to the first two chapters of *Job.* **265–72:** In *The Book of Job* (1812), John Mason Good (1764–1827), using citations from the Hebrew and Arabic versions, argued for the historical and biographical validity of *Job.* **274 like eastern thresholds:** Traditionally, in the East, the city gates were used for deliberation and the administration of justice. **296:** A proverbial idea, expressed by Samuel Johnson, "Sir, Hell is paved with good intentions" (James Boswell, *The Life of Samuel Johnson*). **337:** George III ascended the throne in 1760, when he was twenty-two years old. **340 a minion:** John Stuart, Earl of Bute, Prime Minister (1762–63). **364:** Marcus Gavius Apicius, a Roman epicure of the first century A.D. **377–84:** George III had consistently opposed Catholic Emancipation. **391:** The Hanoverians were the modern representatives of the Guelphs. **393:** In Greek mythology, Cerberus is the guardian of the lower regions, hence of what in the Christian tradition would be hell. **415–16:** *Paradise Lost,* VI, 469–536. **426 gilt key:** An insignia of office of certain court officials. **444:** Sir Francis Ronalds (1788–1873) invented an electric telegraph in 1816. **464:** *Paradise Lost,* IV, 918. **471–72:** "Brother Jonathan," a figure representing the United States, from the name of the American statesman Jonathan Trumbull (1710–85). **475 Otaheite's isle:** Tahiti. **478:** In ombre, in which the ace of clubs ranks below the ace of spades. **513 "multifaced":** See Southey's *A Vision of Judgment,* V, 70. **520:** John Wilkes (1727–97), founder of the *North Briton,* in which, in 1763, he attacked George III for falsehood. A Member of Parliament, he was expelled from the House in 1764, then several times re-elected and re-expelled, until 1774, when he was seated and served sixteen years. He was Lord Mayor of London in 1774 and Chamberlain of the City of London from 1779 until 1797. **564:** Augustus Henry Fitzroy, third Duke of Grafton (1735–1811), Prime Minister (1768–70). **581:** Charles James Fox (1749–1806), leader of the Whig opposition; William Pitt the Younger (1759–1806), Prime Minister (1783–1801, 1804–06). **584:** The repressive "Treason" and "Sedition" Bills, introduced in November 1795. **585:** *The Letters of Junius,* attacking members of the Ministry and even the King, appeared anonymously in the *Public Advertiser* (1769–72); their author's identity has never been fully established. **624:** The "Man in the Iron Mask," a mysterious prisoner in the Bastille (1698–1703), now believed to have been Count Ercole Antonio Mattioli (1640–

1703), an Italian diplomat and statesman. **626–27:** See Richard Brinsley Sheridan's *The Rivals,* IV, ii. **631–32:** Edmund Burke (1729–97) and John Horne Tooke (1736–1812) have been advanced as possibly responsible for the Junius letters, but Sir Philip Francis (1740–1818), a political writer, has seemed the more likely candidate. **650 title-page:** *Letters of Junius, Stat Nominis Umbra.* **675 Asmodeus:** A traditional demon figure. **681 renegado:** Southey in his youth had opposed the Tories. **685 Skiddaw:** A mountain of about three thousand feet in Cumberland, near Southey's home. **687–88 libel . . . Bible:** An allusion to Southey's own poem *A Vision of Judgment.* **728 *'Non Di, non homines':*** From Horace, *Ars Poetica:* "Neither gods nor men will tolerate mediocre poets." **736:** Henry James Pye (1745–1813) was appointed Poet Laureate in 1790. His bad verse made him a frequent object of ridicule, as in *English Bards and Scotch Reviewers:* "Better to err with Pope, than shine with Pye" (line 102). **739:** Robert Stewart, Viscount Castlereagh (1769–1822), Foreign Secretary and leader in the House of Commons (1812–22). **768:** Southey's *Wat Tyler,* "The Battle of Blenheim" (the *Annual Anthology* of 1800), *The Poet's Pilgrimage to Waterloo* (1816). **769 Regicide:** An allusion to a poem which Southey wrote in his youth about Henry Martin the Regicide. **773 pantisocracy:** The scheme for an ideal community, to be established in America, which Southey and Coleridge shared in 1794. **785:** *The Life of Wesley: and the Rise and Progress of Methodism* (2 vols. 1820). **807:** "King Alfonso [X, of Castille (1226?–84)], speaking of the Ptolomean system, said, that 'had he been consulted at the creation of the world, he would have spared the Maker some absurdities'" (Byron's note). **840:** Wellborn is a character in Philip Massinger's comedy *A New Way to Pay Old Debts* (1633). **848 the hundredth psalm:** The ironic significance in this context of the second and fourth verses is especially apparent: "Serve the Lord with gladness: come before his presence with singing. . . . Enter into his gates with thanksgiving, and into his courts with praise: be thankful unto him, and bless his name."

Stanzas Written on the Road between Florence and Pisa *Page 352*

Written in the autumn of 1821; published in Moore's *Letters and Journals of Lord Byron,* in 1830.

Cain: A Mystery *Page 353*

Written in the summer and published in December of 1821. As early as 18 January, Byron was contemplating a drama on "a metaphysical subject, something in the style of Manfred." The resulting work concerned the dualism by which man exists and the established argument for the justification of evil in a universe presumably conceived with purpose and meaning. Though Cain is the protagonist, it easily becomes apparent that the determining viewpoint is Lucifer's rather than Adam's. "With regard to the language of Lucifer, it was difficult for me to make him talk like a clergyman upon the same subjects," Byron wrote in his Preface. "But I have done what I could to restrain him within the bounds of spiritual politeness." Byron's protest was not entirely persuasive, for after the publication of the play there was strong reaction against it in the press and the pulpit, and when John Murray applied to the courts for an injunction against those publishing pirated editions, he was met with a long delay and with the implication of other legal difficulties that might follow. Nevertheless, the play survived the attempts of those who would suppress it, and today it is regarded as one of Byron's most important achievements.

For further discussion of *Cain,* see the following: Samuel C. Chew, *The Dramas of Lord Byron: A Critical Study* (1915; 1964). Stopford Brooke, "Byron's *Cain,*" *Hibbert Journal,* XVIII (1919), 74–94; R. W. Babcock, "The Inception and Reception of Byron's *Cain,*" *South Atlantic Quarterly,* XXVI (1927), 178–88; Edward Wayne Marjarum, *Byron as Skeptic and Believer* (1938; 1962); Paul Siegel, "'A Paradise within Thee' in Milton, Byron, and Shelley," *Modern Language Notes,* LVI (1941), 615–17; Edward E. Bostetter, "Byron and the Politics of Paradise," *Publications of the Modern Language Association,* LXXV (1960), 571–76; William H. Marshall, *The Structure of Byron's Major Poems* (1962); Peter L. Thorslev, Jr., *The Byronic Hero: Types and Prototypes* (1962); Leslie A. Marchand, *Byron's Poetry: A Critical Introduction* (1965).

Act I. 102–04, 305–10, 546–55: Lucifer's position is Manichean, asserting that two irreconcilable principles, the intellectual and the material, divide the rule of the universe. Lucifer himself represents the former, whereas the Creator of physical existence represents the latter. The orthodox association of the devil and the flesh is thereby reversed. Good and evil are not really aspects of the division, except when they are conceived from the point of view of one or the other of the two principles. Thus, from the Creator's viewpoint, to which Adam and his family (except Cain) subscribe, Lucifer is evil, a corrupting force, one working against the order produced by creation; from Lucifer's point of view, however, the creation and containment of man in a physical state, from which he cannot freely and fully enter the world of ideas, is evil. The question concerns Lucifer's credibility. The readers of 1821 were of course disposed, by all their training and the traditions of the world in which they lived, not to believe Lucifer, but they encountered difficulty arising from the fact that as a dramatic character Lucifer derives a degree of reality that goes far in demonstrating the very conflict between the two principles that he describes to Cain. Thus, had Byron chosen a form other than the dramatic, his work might have been less disturbing to those readers who felt within themselves an unidentifiable and unresolvable struggle between two different kinds of faith. **163–66:** Lucifer's allusions to the Redemption, here and elsewhere (I, i, 541–42; II, i, 16–20), seem to violate Byron's self-imposed restriction asserted in his Preface: "It is to be recollected that my present subject has nothing to do with the *New Testament,* to which no reference can be here made without anachronism." In defense of Byron's practice, however, it can be argued that Lucifer, representing the intellectual principle, would possess a knowledge of the activities of the material or creative principle although he is unable to participate in these. **183 shepherd boy:** The name "Abel" may derive from a word meaning "herdsman." **223–27:** "The reader will recollect that the book of Genesis does not state that Eve was tempted by a demon, but by 'the Serpent;' and that only because he was 'the most subtil of all the beasts of the field' " (Byron, Preface to *Cain*). **284 Death:** A central point of difference between the intellectual and the material principles concerns the nature of death: in terms of the one it is a release from physical bondage, but in terms of the other it means passage to non-being.

Act II, Scene I. 3: Cf. *Ephesians,* ii:2. **16–20:** *St. Matthew,* xiv:25–31. **151–53:** The belief in pre-Adamite existences is particularly suited to Lucifer's argument, since it implies repeated attempts and failures on the part of the physical principle to create the perfect world.

Act II, Scene II. 44–62: In a letter to Thomas Moore (19 September 1821) Byron identified the beings that Cain sees as "the *rational* Pre-adamites, beings endowed with a higher intelligence than man, but totally unlike him in form, and with much greater strength of mind and person." The fact that in man there is less of the intellectual and more of the physical than in this predecessor implies something of the way in which the Creator has "conquered" (see I, i, 130). **88 Let He:** A solecism. **108–09:** The measure of Cain's intellectual change is in his view of death; here he regards it as the freedom for fulfillment which life inhibits, though earlier (II, ii, 18–19) he has seen it as the non-existence to which life leads. In each instance he repudiates life and, by implication, the creation that made life possible. **132–44:** "I have gone upon the notion of Cuvier, that the world has been destroyed three or four times, and was inhabited by mammoths, behemoths, and what not; but *not* by man till the Mosaic period, as, indeed, is proved by the strata of bones found; — those of all unknown animals, and known, being dug out, but none of mankind" (Letter to Moore, 19 September 1821). **282–305:** Adam's theology rests upon acceptance of *felix culpa,* the proposition that evil or guilt is justified as the means by which good will be fulfilled. Thus, in his own case the Fall would be, paradoxically, fortunate, making possible the Redemption. Cain's repudiation of this paradox rests upon empirical grounds. **420–21:** Of the effect of Cain's relation to Lucifer, Byron wrote to John Murray, on 3 November 1821: "the object of the Demon is to *depress* him still further in his own estimation . . . by showing him infinite things and his own abasement, till he falls into the frame of mind that leads to the Catastrophe, from mere *internal* irritation, *not* premeditation, or envy of *Abel* . . . but from the rage and fury against the inadequacy of his state to his conceptions."

Act III, Scene I. 213–335: See *Genesis,* iv:2–8. Abel's words some moments before his death (lines 318–30) recall Jesus' words as reported in *St. Luke* (xxiii:34), but Byron's allusion is in no sense an anachronism, since it places both Abel and Jesus in the same tradition, in keeping with either the Adamic or the Luciferian theology. **468–500:** See *Genesis,* iv:9–15, in which the Lord, rather than the Angel of the Lord, imposes the sentence and places the mark upon Cain. **522:** "And a river went out of Eden to water the garden; and from thence it was parted, and became into four heads" (*Genesis,* ii:10). As subsequently named, the four rivers of Eden were Pison, Gihon, Hiddekel, and Euphrates. **552–53:** "And Cain went out from the presence of the Lord, and dwelt in the land of Nod, on the east of Eden" (*Genesis,* iv:16).

Heaven and Earth; A Mystery *Page 403*

Written in October 1821; published in the second number of *The Liberal,* 1 January 1823. Taking his subject from *Genesis* (vi:1–2), Byron interpreted "the sons of God" to mean angels and "the daughters of men" to be the female descendants of Cain, who were condemned to destruction in the Flood. As the action closes, the lovers have fled, and Japhet, the elect but disconsolate son of Noah, waits for the arrival of the Ark as the waters rise about him. Byron told Thomas Medwin of a plan for the second part of the drama (in which the fallen angels are brought to punishment and the daughters of Cain are destroyed in the Flood), but he seems not to have regarded it with great seriousness. As it stands, the play is a distinct unit, in which Byron questioned, particularly through the troubled thoughts of Japhet and the image of undeserved sorrow in Anah, the doctrine of predestination — of the election of some and the damnation of others — which had disturbed him since he was a child. As in *Cain,* the question that is posed offers no solution; Japhet in his final solitude can bring no emotional affirmation to what he knows he must accept.

Heaven and Earth was extensively reviewed, frequently as a work distinct from *The Liberal* itself and often in comparison with Thomas Moore's somewhat similar but more orthodox poem *The Loves of the Angels,* published about a week earlier. Goethe esteemed *Heaven and Earth* more than Byron's other serious work, and though more recent critics have not placed it so high as this, the Mystery has come to be regarded as a deeply significant, if somewhat unusual, piece of poetry.

The two principal discussions of the drama are to be found in Samuel C. Chew's *The Dramas of Lord Byron* (1915; 1964) and my own book *The Structure of Byron's Major Poems* (1962).

Epigraphs: *Genesis,* vi:1–2; *Kubla Khan,* 16 (the original has "By" where Byron uses "And.").

Part I, Scene I. 40: "The archangels, said to be seven in number" (Byron's note). **140–42:** Sorcerers have been regarded in various ways as capable of controlling the moon. Aholibamah, whose theology is a mixture of rationalism and a belief in the power of love, is thus attributing superstition to her father.

Part I, Scene II. 32: Tubalcain, seven generations descended from Cain, is described as "an instructor of every artificer in brass and iron" (*Genesis,* iv:22).

Part I, Scene III. 217 the glorious giants' graves: "There were giants in the earth in those days; and also after that, when the sons of God came in unto the daughters of men, and they bare children to them, the same became mighty men which were of old, men of renown" (*Genesis,* vi:4). **224–25:** "The same day were all the fountains of the great deep broken up, and the windows of heaven were opened" (*Genesis,* vii:11). **238–40:** An allusion to a popular belief that marine fossils found above the level of the sea were deposited during the Flood. **275:** "The Book of Enoch, preserved by the Ethiopians, is said by them to be anterior to the flood" (Byron's note). **390–91 Cain! who was begotten in Paradise:** Such is not according to the record of events in *Genesis,* iii:23–iv:1.

On This Day I Complete My Thirty-Sixth Year

Page 432

Written on 22 January and published on 29 October 1824.

INDEX TO TITLES OF POEMS

[Page numbers in italic type refer to notes to the poems.]